States of Childhood

States of Childhood

From the Junior Republic to the American Republic, 1895–1945

Jennifer S. Light

The MIT Press
Cambridge, Massachusetts
London, England

© 2020 Massachusetts Institute of Technology

This work is subject to a Creative Commons CC-BY-NC-ND license. Subject to such license, all rights are reserved.

The open access edition of this book was made possible by generous funding from Arcadia—a charitable fund of Lisbet Rausing and Peter Baldwin.

This book was set in Stone Serif by Westchester Publishing Services.

Library of Congress Cataloging-in-Publication Data

Names: Light, Jennifer S., 1971– author.
Title: States of childhood : from the junior republic to the American republic, 1895–1945 / Jennifer S. Light.
Description: Cambridge, Massachusetts : The MIT Press, [2020] | Includes bibliographical references and index.
Identifiers: LCCN 2019039482 | ISBN 9780262539012 (paperback)
Subjects: LCSH: George, William R. (William Reuben), 1866–1936. | George Junior Republic (Freeville, N.Y.) | Junior republics—History. | Child welfare—United States—History. | Youth—United States—Social conditions—History. | Youth—Political activity—United States—History. | Youth—Employment—United States—History.
Classification: LCC HV876 .L54 2020 | DDC 362.73/2--dc23
LC record available at https://lccn.loc.gov/2019039482

153493941

To Felix and Anja

It seems as though boys live a sort of double life, not only the practical, real life of to-day, but the life of the fancy. I remember once I was going away to give a little talk, and as I came downstairs and stepped into my wife's room, I noticed a very funny odor, as though something were burning. I came into the chamber, and I saw a company of little people grouped over a gas stove…I didn't know what they were doing, but I thought I could discern a smell of smoked halibut. I was told I was mistaken, it was venison; I had come across a hunting party, under their mother's leadership, camping on the prairies of Wyoming.
—William Byron Forbush, 1914

A Junior Republic is a Community, the citizens of which are boys and girls…in other respects it is just the same in all essentials as any community in the United States of America…the whole point of the Junior Republic is to develop the inhabitants of an institution or community under conditions approximating as closely as possible the actual conditions which they must face in real life…to develop the character of each individual simultaneously with the development of the social consciousness of the whole group.
—Lyman Beecher Stowe, 1914

Contents

Acknowledgments ix

    Introduction: Child Protection or Child Labor? 1

I Performing Adulthood

    1 The Smallest Republic in the World 21
    2 Stages of Childhood 51

II The Rhetoric and Reality of Child Protection

    3 Constructing Youth, Constructing Youth-Serving Institutions 89
    4 The Drama of the Street 127

III From Models and Dramatizations to Education and Recreation

    5 Serving Community and Nation 165
    6 Expanding and Erasing the Republic Idea 201
    Conclusion: The Legacies of William R. George 239
    Epilogue: What Happened to Junior Republics? 253

Notes 257
Index 453

Acknowledgments

Many individuals and institutions made this sprawling project possible, and I am grateful for their assistance.

Fifteen years at Northwestern's School of Communication offered an informal education in media and performance studies, and I am grateful to my colleagues there. Undergraduates and graduate students at the Northwestern University School of Communication, including Alan Clark, Hannah Dawe, Maggie Donnelly, Brian Keegan, and Angela Xiao Wu, tracked down obscure articles and visual materials to get the research off the ground. Librarians and archivists at the American Jewish Historical Society, Martin Luther King Jr. Library in San Jose, Cornell University Archives, National Archives and Records Administration, San Francisco History Center, and Western Reserve Historical Society helped to locate a range of unpublished materials from junior republics across the United States. Ronald B. Saunders shared memories of his father's work on Pittsburgh's Hill City.

A fellowship year at the Institute for Advanced Study, in particular conversations with Danielle Allen, transformed the project beyond the straightforward history of the republic movement I had originally planned. At MIT, colleagues and students in the Program in Science, Technology, and Society; the History, Theory, and Criticism of Architecture and Art program; and the Design and Computation Group in the Department of Architecture provided feedback as the arguments took shape. At the Dartmouth Department of Geography; Harvard Working Group on the History of Modern Sciences; Radcliffe Seminar on Data, Design and Decisions; School of Social Science at the Institute for Advanced Study; University of Colorado Department of Information Science; Columbia University Buell Center for the Study of American Architecture; NYU School of Engineering; Tufts STS Program; University of Pennsylvania Department of History and Sociology of Science; York University Department of Science and Technology Studies; University of Toronto Institute for the History and Philosophy of Science; Max-Planck-Institut für Gesellschaftsforschung; and Rome Science Festival, faculty, students, and other listeners offered valuable comments and constructive criticisms. Three anonymous referees' detailed feedback on a much longer version of the manuscript was invaluable. Katie Helke has been judicious and wise in her editorial assistance. Lunaea Weatherstone's careful editing streamlined the prose. Sherry Gerstein was a delight to work with throughout the production process.

Without getting excessively philosophical about mind/body matters, thanks are also due to Trevor Kafka and Marisa Frank.

Introduction: Child Protection or Child Labor?

Travelers should be sure to visit the curious community in Freeville, New York, where boys and girls were in charge, wrote Baedeker's turn-of-the-twentieth-century guide to the United States. This "miniature republic modelled on the government of the United States" was well worth a detour to observe the "legislature, court-house, jail, school, church and public library" staffed by citizens aged fourteen to twenty-one, most of them immigrants or impoverished youth. Of course, these young Americans were not actual members of the civil service—the republic's legal status was "similar to that of a state reformatory"—but their adultlike activities were exceedingly realistic nonetheless. They "elect their rulers, make and enforce laws, and carry on business just as adults do in the greater world," author James Muirhead marveled. "This interesting experiment seems to work well, and a visit to Freeville rivals in sociological interest that to Ellis Island."[1]

The brainchild of philanthropist William R. George, Freeville's juvenile society was the period's most famous junior republic, but it was hardly alone. In the late nineteenth and early twentieth centuries, a motley crew of reformers helped scores of American youth to construct thousands of cities, states, and nations around the country "on a similar plan" as later editions of Baedeker's explained. In these child societies, boys and girls of all races and ethnicities and from across the economic spectrum were the officials and citizens. They made laws, sat for civil service exams, and paid taxes. They constructed buildings and swimming pools, ran hotels and restaurants, and printed newspapers and currency. They opened juvenile libraries and museums, tended vegetable gardens and zoos, organized cooperative stores and charities, staffed banks and post offices, performed in theaters and on radio broadcasts, and administered hospitals and schools of law. During an era of vigorous campaigns against young people's presence in the nation's labor force and on its streets, junior republics supplied opportunities for youth to play adultlike roles in age-restricted worlds. Some, like George's later "junior municipalities," expanded their activities beyond campuses and clubhouses into the surrounding communities, incorporating public spaces into these civic dramatizations.[2]

Each of these environments was a "village like any other" as George frequently observed of Freeville. He insisted that the junior republic's simultaneous resemblance to and separation from the "big republic"—in his words, "no one can tell where the big Republic leaves off and the Junior Republic begins"—enabled young people to learn valuable life skills and called for building still more such similar juvenile societies across the nation. News media and travel guides shared his enthusiasm and his interpretive framework. They reported regularly on elections and publicized the latest accomplishments of the inhabitants, some as young as five, whose daily lives were "passed in experiences and obligations of mature citizens," while reassuring visitors and readers that the adultlike experiences that improved kids' character "without taking away their independence" were merely "miniature" and "model" versions of their elders' activities: work-like educational and recreational experiences rather than work itself. Later, they reported stories of lives transformed upon graduation into adult society, thanks to the training these youth-only settings supplied, particularly for immigrant, working class, and minority youth. From Chicago judge Sidney Marovitz (Boys Brotherhood Republic) to Milwaukee mayor Carl Zeidler (Newsboy Republic), from US surgeon general Julius Richmond (Allendale) to University of Michigan labor economist William Haber (Newsboy Republic), from Philadelphia superintendent of schools Constance Clayton (Youth City) to Motown songwriter Alfred Cleveland (Hill City), from Pulitzer Prize–winning journalists William Dapping (George Junior Republic) and Theodore White (George Junior Republic) to actors Steve McQueen (California Boys Republic) and Jerry Stiller (Boys Brotherhood Republic), distinguished and lesser-known alumni credited their republic experiences with offering them practice in the personal and professional skills critical to their successes in later life.[3]

The massive movement that mobilized about these curious communities in the late nineteenth and early twentieth century United States drew in psychologists and educators, ministers and police, juvenile judges and businesspeople, playground advocates and the American Legion, efficiency experts and good government activists, the federal Bureau of Indian Affairs, and the National Youth Administration. Jacob Riis, Jane Addams, G. Stanley Hall, Ben Lindsey, Cyrus McCormick, Andrew Carnegie, Eliot Ness, and J. Edgar Hoover offered vocal backing. International curiosity brought numerous visitors to the republics and inspired adaptations abroad.[4]

Impressive for the scope of support it generated, the junior republic movement was on the leading edge of an even broader trend. In an era when public opinion increasingly favored segregating young people from the world of adults, the Freeville republic and its many descendants allowed young people to simultaneously inhabit both a rural village and a miniature United States, to simultaneously be kids from the tenements of New York City on summer vacation and US senators debating matters of national importance—in short, to live what American Institute of Child Life director William Forbush called a "double life." Similar opportunities lay at the center of the era's broader efforts to fashion a new identity for the nation's youth. Educators and youth workers like Forbush soon discovered that as young people playing adult roles

GENERAL VIEW OF GEORGE JUNIOR REPUBLIC, Freeville, N. Y.
(All of the buildings shown in picture are Republic Buildings—and four others, which, because of location, could not be included.)

Figure 0.1
George Junior Republic at Freeville.
Source: William R. George, *Nothing Without Labor* (Freeville, NY: George Junior Republic, 1902).

seemed to enjoy adjusting themselves to the era's new social expectations, these virtual adults were also helping to build and operate the institutions that sheltered them as they learned and played. In schools and settlements, YMCAs and Boys and Girls Clubs, churches and summer camps, orphanages and reformatories, the many institutions devoted to serving young people embraced the component activities of these child societies. Vocational education and home economics enabled kids to construct their housing and prepare their meals. Youth congresses and junior sanitation squads helped them to maintain order in their institutions and neighborhoods. The result was that the dual experience of protected childhood and of virtual adulthood that characterized participants' lives inside junior republics became a defining feature of modern youth.[5]

The lack of a sustained and unified national junior republic movement—William R. George's ultimate ambition—marked not George's failure but rather the popularity and broad diffusion of his republic's core principles. The Freeville republic indeed became a village like any other well beyond George's original intent, not merely a microcosm of adult society but a microcosm of the American youth experience itself. Whether playing alone or under adult supervision, whether inside age-restricted environments or moving through their communities, the generation that came of age in this period found this juxtaposition at the center of how the nation understood its youth as a biological and social category distinct from adults. In short, the "sheltered childhood" that historians agree became a reality by World War II depended in large part on the proliferation, over several decades, of these role-plays of adulthood and the broader embrace of the idea of a double life for modern youth. How the history of the junior republic movement makes visible the overarching importance of these everyday performances in the emergence of the sheltered childhood as a disciplinary category and a set of supporting institutions is the subject of this book. The decline of role-playing adulthood as a constitutive practice of the modern American youth experience and the lasting legacies of the republic movement will also be addressed.[6]

The Double Lives of Modern Youth

Conceptions of youth in America have varied over time. Paintings from early in the nation's history depict young people as pint-size adults, an understanding embedded in laws about their eligibility to work, make contracts, marry, accept criminal responsibility, and testify in court. In the twenty-first century, by contrast, discussions of the "no-risk childhood" and "helicopter parenting," with scientific and legal support from neurochemical studies of teenage decision-making and criminal prosecutions of parents for allowing their children to play in public, point to how much assumptions about youth capacities have changed.[7]

An especially dramatic shift in prevailing assumptions about young people's place in American society occurred between the late nineteenth and mid-twentieth centuries. The population of the increasingly industrial and urban nation began to question some long-held beliefs—for example, that work experience was preferable to school attendance, that kids should be responsible for crimes committed, and that leisure activities such as smoking, moviegoing, driving, and wandering the streets at night should be permissible at any age. Scholars agree that over this extended period associated with the arrival of modernity many young people were excluded from the arenas and activities that came to be thought of as adult society. Pushed out of the labor force and public life and into extended education and recreation, their youth-directed activities were replaced by adult-supervised alternatives that sought to build character and teach values for future citizenship, previously supplied by work and other modes of public engagement. The youth who remained in adult society faced diminishing autonomy, such as requiring adult escorts in public at night or parental consent to enter legal contracts.[8]

Economic history features prominently in accounts of the broad transformation in social expectations about youth. The turn of the twentieth century was a time of significant transition as a wage economy located in factories and firms replaced the prior family economy in which men, women, and children worked together at home. Social roles diverged as new cultural scripts directed men to go off to earn for their families, women to tend to domestic concerns, and kids to attend school and participate in organized play. The separation and gendering of home and work, the creation of a family wage for men, the introduction of laborsaving machines at work and at home, and the proliferation of mass-produced goods and entertainments—including specialized markets for children—are all part of this story of the construction and maintenance of a new identity category that has been called the "sheltered" or protected childhood. So too are the host of individuals and institutions that helped young people adjust to the new order so as to avoid the perils of "precocity"—that is, premature access to adult experience. These included developmental psychologists and university child study programs; educators and public schools; justices, probation officers, and the juvenile court system; youth workers and playgrounds; boys clubs and Scout troops. Contrasting this era's programs with an earlier generation that exploited kids, scholars describe how individual philanthropists, religious charities, and female volunteers sustained them until, in many cases, the state assumed responsibility for the child welfare programs and services that private institutions pioneered.[9]

Existing histories recognize that this modern youth experience came unevenly to different populations based on class, race, region, religion, and nationality, and they qualify claims of young people's total separation by pointing to exceptions such as continued involvement in farm labor and the preparatory nature of activities that youth workers and youth-serving institutions supplied. Yet they say little about the mechanisms that persuaded young people to accept these new social norms before the widespread enforcement of child labor and compulsory schooling laws. Such accounts raise critical concerns about schools and youth-serving institutions—for example, how vocational education reinforced class divisions and gendered identities rather than providing occupational mobility or how juvenile courts restricted the legal rights of youth people in the name of child protection. Yet these histories typically accept the self-depictions of schools and youth-serving institutions as havens or islands from the labor force and public life in a modern world.[10]

This book documents how in junior republics and beyond role-plays of adulthood were well suited to making the transition to the new identity for youth that scholars already have described. Since, by definition, a dramatization of an experience is not the thing in itself, yet is like that thing in itself, by performing adult roles young people vicariously experienced this life stage while defining themselves in opposition to it. Of course, young people have long played at being adults, and most of the component activities of George's Freeville republic predate the period under discussion. Critical connections to turn-of-the-century popular culture and scientific thought help to explain why these specific activities gained mass popularity and why the practice more generally held special significance for the generations who came of age between the late nineteenth century and World War II.[11]

In an era of public fascination with a range of model environments and vicarious experiences from wax museums to stereoscopes, a period when leading scientists believed imitation and impersonation were central processes in youth development, the virtual adulthoods at Freeville and elsewhere enabled young people to enjoy being disciplined to their reduced status while educators and youth workers congratulated themselves on designing child-saving programs on scientific grounds. Long before the theoretical and empirical investigations of Victor Turner, Erving Goffman, Michel Foucault, or Judith Butler, this body of theory and practice about young people's "dramatic instinct" articulated how, through performance, a new social category could take shape. The construction of youth was a result of what kids did as much as who they were, and it involved virtually experiencing adulthood on equal grounds with removal to age-restricted sheltered space. These role-playing programs were wildly popular—many sustained active alumni associations—and young people's voluntary participation in their ever-expanding uses proved key to the disciplining and behavior modification that resulted. The spread of republics and their component activities beyond marginal youth to the mainstream and later into American institutions serving adult populations (including factories, prisons, and internment camps) reworks our understanding of the uneven arrival of the sheltered childhood and highlights the widespread confidence in the uses of role-plays as behavior management tools. In turn, it points to a rich history of children and performance beyond the school pageants, children's educational theater, and working child actors that have been the focus of prior inquiries. These everyday performances make clear how age—like gender and race—may be performed, and that the impact of such performances on youth, on sponsoring institutions, and on state building, have gone unrecognized to date.[12]

As this rich array of activities made encounters with "adulthood" a routine feature of the American youth experience, the associations with vicarious experience that helped to popularize such behavior management techniques masked the value young people brought to schools, youth-serving institutions, and the state. The role-plays that tapped young people's predilections for performance inside campuses and clubhouses, and their "migratory instincts" throughout the community, were not merely developmentally productive—they were economically productive as well. Like the artisans-turned-factory-workers who found their craft knowledge reorganized out of their hands by a new managerial class, so too in this period young Americans found their preferred playtime activities becoming the lifeblood of adult-sponsored programs, with the further indignity that the most basic fact of their productive energies went largely unseen.

Young people role-played a range of adulthoods—caring for playgrounds, cleaning streets, conducting school health inspections, chasing truants, adjudicating cases of juvenile delinquency, policing neighborhoods, taking local censuses, collecting fingerprints, manufacturing military goods, and advertising government programs. In so doing, they built the institutions that were to shelter them from adult society: helping resource-poor schools and youth-serving institutions get off the ground, improving the communities they were ostensibly to be protected from, and expanding services supplied by the state. As educators, youth workers, and public officials took on the role of parens patriae, then, a novel variation on the family economy appeared. Activities publically characterized as merely representational had real impacts, and the parental institutions that scholars associate with young people's removal from the labor force and public life were in fact economically dependent on "sheltered" children's education and play.[13]

If they shared with factory workers the experience of being deskilled by the reorganization of knowledge, American youth shared with the era's women a common experience of being divorced from the economy in ways that were as much rhetorical as real. Historians have described women's experience of the disintegration of the family economy and its replacement with the wage economy and how an ideology of separate spheres redefined female domestic activities as "unproductive" despite alternative measures of the value they produced. This book proposes that, in constructing and operating the institutions that sheltered them, young people faced a similar fate and that age, like gender, played a critical role in the definition of work. For young people, the framework applied to diminishing their economic contributions was one that focused on the "double life" rather than the "separate sphere" of sheltered childhood, which tells us about only one of the lives that these populations led. In their attention to the developmental possibilities of playing adult roles in supervised settings, theorists of education and recreation—and the schools and youth-serving institutions that applied their ideas—divorced youth from the economy by articulating a distinction between the copy and the real thing. As educational philosopher and Chicago Laboratory School director John Dewey put it, "Cooking, sewing, manual training...in the school...represent, as types, fundamental forms of social activity...it is possible and desirable that the child's introduction into the more formal subjects of the curriculum be through the medium of these activities." Edward Devine, of the New York School of Philanthropy and the New York Charity Organization Society, concurred: "Work which we deny...in the factory, for profit, may be demanded in school...for education and training." Neither mentioned the fact that such child-centered "media," to use Dewey's term for these activities, helped their institutions' bottom lines.[14]

Identifying in the theory and practice of developmental psychology, education, and youth work a vibrant conversation about mediated experiences and child development suggests the recent revival of interest in the educational and socialization potentials of role-playing that has accompanied new technologies—from video games and virtual worlds to augmented realities and live-action role-playing—is merely a variation on discussions held by earlier generations. These conversations gave attention to harnessing kids' leisure-time interests to gamify learning as a response to the failures of prior modes of instruction. Educators were confident that mediated experiences could teach the requisite skills for the era's new economy and offer tryouts of future careers. Their experiments with the performance of alternative selves with real and yet "not real" consequences, and their ambition to simultaneously build simulated worlds that resembled reality and to make reality into simulation, provide a rich body of evidence about past theory and practice in the science and technology of role-playing as a resource for guiding future talk and action in the field. In an era of increasing algorithmic regulation in politics and society, when user-generated content is a staple of the digital economy, the awareness of how earlier generations' models of political and social life obscured as much as they revealed and how an older discourse of virtuality and play diminished young people's economic contributions invites critical engagements with both the reality and the rhetoric of this generation's latest tools. Recovering this set of older understandings reveals how a multiplicity of concepts associated with twenty-first century computing and information technology—including virtuality, gamification, and labors of fun—have deep roots in American life as well as consequences that seem to have been overlooked. These materials invite new kinds of questions for present-day reflection, for example, about the real-world status of virtual activities, the models of citizenship that participatory simulations embed, the implications of the discourses that accompany new technologies, and the shifting border between the meanings of *reality* and *virtuality* as virtual activities become increasingly routine.[15]

Over the nearly half-century that is the focus of this story, the adult experiences that young people vicariously encountered changed. Activities inside schools and youth-serving institutions expanded into public settings, with ever-growing engagements with industrial machines—for example, in junior traffic patrols and school film and radio production. Yet the belief endured that educational and recreational variations on adult occupations and the environments associated with childhood stood outside the market. Adult-organized youth activities thus did ultimately spawn a "sheltered childhood"—just not in the ways scholars have previously presumed.

William R. "Daddy" George: Father of National Trends

Junior republics, as total simulated societies for youth, illustrate the claims of this book in the clearest terms. Drawing on new sources and looking with fresh eyes at familiar subjects finds that the youth societies previously regarded as fringe phenomena were in fact part of a larger grouping of institutions and programs with expansive reach across the United States. Many offered training for staff and citizens, ensuring that republic affiliates went on to careers in education and youth work and, in so doing, spread the movement's basic ideas.[16]

Each republic, a world in itself, could be the subject of an extended study. This book details the histories of those that illustrate the movement's evolution as well as broader efforts to engage young people in the constant performance of adult roles as a means to promote the double life they embraced. Its focus is the adults in the story, but, where possible, it excavates the views of youthful participants. At the center of this story is William R. "Daddy" George, a businessman and good government reformer whose junior republics and later junior municipalities aimed to set national standards.

Compared by contemporaries to figures such as Charles Darwin, Thomas Edison, Samuel Morse, Alexander Graham Bell, Jacob Riis, and Booker T. Washington, George is all but forgotten today. The six chapters of this book recount the story of how George, unable to control the runaway popularity of his ideas, found the institutions he had organized outnumbered by the school republics, Boy Cities, playground democracies, junior towns, garden cities, child commonwealths, Boys Towns, Junior States, and

Figure 0.2
William R. George.
Source: William R. George Family Papers, box 122, folder 10–27, envelope 16, "Activities and Group Pictures." Courtesy Division of Rare and Manuscript Collections, Cornell University Library.

youth cities that sprang up across the nation. Yet as these diverse juvenile democracies escaped George's oversight, they further fueled public confidence that environments providing young people with access to vicarious experiences of adulthood—whether in total youth societies or through their component activities—would benefit individual Americans and American society more generally in the short and longer term.[17]

Chapter 1 recounts how, during the summer of 1895 in rural Freeville, New York, George invented the first junior republic, an agrarian democracy populated by immigrant youth from New York City's slums. Anxious about the future of the increasingly multiracial nation, he hoped this civic dramatization might integrate new Americans into the body politic by familiarizing them with the democratic values and practices he and other white, middle-class elites preferred. Like many inventors, past and present, George borrowed liberally from the work of his contemporaries already engaged in scattered efforts to teach city children to farm and administer youth governments and courts. His genius was to combine these activities into a whole that was more than the sum of its parts: a total environment that removed young people from participation in labor, politics, the military, and other public engagements and substituted an adult-supervised simulation instead. The camp was an immediate hit with participants, who surprised even George with their enthusiasm and their competency at playing adult roles.

This first chapter situates George's work within the context of the broad cultural fascination with simulated environments and vicarious experiences as well as extant practices at the period's youth-serving institutions. The travel guides that pointed visitors to Freeville were equally besotted with a variety of other educational amusements that dotted the nation—for example, Palestine Park, "a copy in miniature of the famous Holy Land," in Chautauqua, New York. A shared vocabulary of "miniature" and "model" linked junior republics and their components in the public mind to these opportunities for surrogate encounters with alternative times, places, and identities, engaging visitors' sense of simultaneous distance from and immersion in a second reality. The immersive experiences of panoramas, world's fairs, and wax museums sped up and slowed down time, enlarged and condensed space, and, subsequently became symbols of broader cultural transformation. These associations suggest why the George Junior Republic was an international tourist destination and why republic building blocks such as vocational education and youth congresses gained support for mass diffusion thanks to these new interpretations. Equally they suggest why, compared to other reform-oriented institutions, the George Junior Republic was so beloved by participating youth.[18]

Chapter 2 describes how the enthusiastic reception of the Freeville experiment prompted George to replicate his work in new settings and how other reformers—impatient to spread the junior republic idea—soon eclipsed his efforts with their own variations on his work. Engineer and fellow good government reformer Wilson Gill, who organized juvenile republics and cities inside urban public schools from 1897, established that the locations for such child democracies mattered less than their internal structures. The discovery that environments offering realistic roles to play were more important than realistic environments for role-playing, and that republics could be organized inside existing institutions, hastened the spread of these youth democracies and the lessons they supplied.

The new field of developmental psychology, led by G. Stanley Hall, rooted these alternative environmental theories of behavior in an interpretation of youth biology that, like the human science tradition it drew on, resonated with the culture's fascination with the copy—most notably in its attention to young people's instincts for imitating past and present adult roles and by extension living double lives as they played. The era's popular recapitulation theory suggested that young people reenacted the history of the human race as they matured, and the broader concept of "playworlds" enabled them to simultaneously inhabit two different times and places. Observations of young people discovered that role-plays of adulthood dominated their activities at all stages of development, from young children's recreations of Eskimo villages and reenactments of the settlement of Plymouth Rock to older children's more general enthusiasm for dramatic "play-adultism." These findings offered still more evidence about how young people naturally lived one life in the here-and-now and another life removed in time and space—and how adults could guide biological instincts for impersonating adults toward pedagogical ends in the junior republics, schools, and youth-serving institutions that "carried still further" these ideas.[19]

Synergies between Gill's plans to establish mirror societies inside schools and the work of educators including Hall's student John Dewey to fashion schools as miniature societies where young people's play instincts were guided to pedagogical ends point to the growing consensus around a curriculum that paired sheltered childhood and simulated adulthood in the era's campaigns for the "new education." Indeed, Dewey would later join the advisory board of Gill's organization. In his calls to vitalize education by bringing it into contact with "life," and his practical experiments with learning-by-doing through a "culture epoch" curriculum in which children progressed through earlier eras of civilization, Dewey's widely influential plans for an ideal school prioritized the reproduction of adult occupations past and present inside a society in miniature where students were "freed from economic stress." The writings and laboratory school that became models for many educators thus pressed to expand pupils' opportunities to live simultaneously as virtual adults and real kids. As scientists and educators increasingly agreed that vicarious experiences had important pedagogical possibilities—whether or not they took place inside environments that duplicated someplace else—the building blocks of the Freeville republic such as youth congresses and model kitchens became mass educational activities.[20]

Chapter 3 documents an explosive surge of copycat youth societies during the first decade of the twentieth century, thanks to support from prominent developmental psychologists and educators and the growing recognition that republics could be integrated into the programming at existing public and private institutions. A renewed effort from George to reassert jurisdiction with a National Association of Junior Republics proved powerless to stop this trend. At schools, reformatories, orphanages, settlements, YMCAs, boys clubs, and playgrounds—institutions that already had embraced building blocks of the junior republic idea—juvenile democracies opened their doors to thousands of mostly needy kids, diversifying the range of role-plays available and setting the movement on a new, largely urban course.

Junior republics did not bypass America's small town, rural, and middle-class populations, however. Optimistic about such youth societies' preventive potentials, juvenile judge Willis Brown set out to organize a national network of Boy Cities for these populations and a competitor organization to George's and Gill's republic variations that would link year-round republics at schools and youth-serving institutions with a centralized summer camp. The introduction of two Boy Cities into the Gary, Indiana, public schools—a system lauded and imitated across the nation for its "social efficiency" as well as its "new education"—showcases how even individuals and institutions at odds on curricular questions (most notably Teachers College colleagues John Dewey and David Snedden) placed vicarious access to adult experience front and center in their educational plans. Equally, it underscores their shared belief that these activities' economic benefits—including making school lunches and furniture, organizing school records, repairing facilities, and reducing strain on the juvenile court system by diverting cases to student juries—constituted not child labor but a campaign against it instead. Sharing with advocates of dramatic education such as Minnie Herts Heiniger the view that "the fact acted out is the fact remembered," Brown and his colleagues were unable to grasp the full impact of these everyday performances. Gary's educators, leading the charge for school measurement, failed to measure the economic value of the goods and services they did not see.[21]

The invisible productivity of youth in Gary underscores how the interpretive framework linking junior republics and components to educational entertainments—which suggests reasons for mass popularity during this period—equally explains why activities at junior republics and other youth-serving institutions could be read as reducing rather than expanding the child labor pool. This influential set of beliefs about mediated experience concealed how many of the institutions scholars link to the construction of the sheltered childhood—most notably schools and playgrounds—were built in part by kids. Duplications of adult occupations that were realistic but not real, even the activities within the Gary schools' work-study-play system that were labeled "work," were exempt on account of their educational ambitions, an interpretation the US Children's Bureau spread in its praise for these educational methods.[22]

Chapter 4 describes how, in the 1910s, junior republic organizers, recognizing the impossibility of reaching all youth with programs confined to age-restricted campuses and clubhouses, designed new kinds of juvenile democracies to improve the environments young people were to be protected from and reshape youth behavior in public spaces. William George played a leading role in these efforts as he once again aimed to recapture his influential position on the national stage, this time with a program of "junior municipalities" that expanded junior citizens' activities into public settings. Other reformers were similarly inspired, organizing community-based role-plays such as newsboy republics, juvenile health inspectors, and Boy Scouts. The schools and settlements, orphanages and churches, camps and YMCAs, playgrounds and boys clubs that had welcomed junior republics and the component activities of these complete societies to their campuses and clubhouses embraced these developments, now in partnership with local officials who recognized that, when faced with shortages of municipal workers, they could rely on children to play these roles.[23]

From Boston to Birmingham, young people impersonated sanitation workers and police officers, explorers and queens, expressing their dramatic instincts in public and bringing to communities the behavioral improvements and cost savings already seen at junior republics, schools, and youth-serving institutions as they patrolled parks, enforced street trades laws, beautified their communities, and adjudicated delinquency cases involving other youth. Lacking direct adult supervision, these new activities were exceedingly popular. Yet if these vicarious experiences of adulthood at first appeared to offer young people greater autonomy, in fact they signaled youths' increased self-monitoring and the state's growing recognition of the disciplinary power and economic benefits of everyday performance as well. Chicago's Boys Brotherhood Republic (BBR), a vocal advocate on youth issues, showcases how the republic movement's institutionalization and its growing conservatism were linked. As the nation's republics were increasingly found inside schools and youth-serving institutions, political expression and economic innovation gave way to institutional maintenance and adjusting youth to new social expectations. BBR's departures from republics' business-as-usual equally highlight how claims about the realism of civic dramatizations obscured the narrow vision of democratic participation they taught. In an era marked by controversies about the adult institutions young people were modeling—including the inhumanity of the industrial system and the need for more unions, the economic status and individualized nature of housework, and the meaning of citizenship in a democracy—most organizers carefully directed youth attention to accept the status quo.[24]

Shifting participants' attention from making republics more like the real world to making the real world more like republics, these proliferating "clubs based on imaginative play...in which every activity is made a part of a play-world, in which the members live during and, to some extent, between, the sessions of the club" as Forbush described them, transformed communities into simulations, into stages, into institutions without walls as young people cleaned neighborhoods, controlled crime, and expanded state surveillance—helping to "save the city" like the women whose labor was explained away as "municipal housekeeping" during this period. Local officials' growing participation in youth work during this decade, widely covered in professional journals such as *American City* and *Municipal Journal*, thus reflected not merely their increasing commitment to child protection; their support for activities that gamified public service directly addressed cities' and towns' ever-present financial concerns. The early twentieth century appearance of "mayor for a day" programs, in which municipalities turned over the reins of government to local youth, obscures these populations' everyday contributions to their communities and how many local government operations depended on a hidden force of kids.[25]

Chapter 5 tracks the republic movement into World War I, as federal officials followed local authorities into the education and youth work fields. William George's decision to install a workshop inside the republic for making military uniforms and to dispatch citizens for government work in Syracuse captured the ambiguities that characterized how educators, youth workers, and government authorities "protected" young people from the war. Eschewing old-fashioned methods of military preparedness instruction in favor of the vocational and physical training embraced by progressive educators, federal agencies facing the national security crisis helped to make democratic occupational role-plays even more widely used educational and recreational pursuits. This was nowhere more evident than inside the nation's schools. At the same time government authorities encouraged young people to continue their educations, they remade these educational institutions into economic engines for the wartime nation. As young people manufactured military goods in vocational education classes and home economics courses, print shops and art studios, they contributed "surgical dressings, hospital supplies, hospital garments, refugee garments, articles for soldiers and miscellaneous items totaling 15,722,073 in number and valued at $10,152,461.96, or ten percent of the entire Red Cross production during the war." Junior civic leagues, Knights of King Arthur, Camp Fire Girls, and Scouts reoriented their service activities around national needs: gathering scrap metals, canning vegetables, hawking war bonds, and distributing government information. Opportunities for military role-playing expanded during the conflict but never rivaled the already popular virtual adulthoods that were such effective ideological maintenance, institution building, and community improvement tools.[26]

Developments during the 1920s at junior republics, schools, and youth-serving institutions expanded on prewar trends to meet new postwar challenges. Pupil traffic patrols helped municipalities address a shortage of police by stationing students in the streets to protect their classmates. Girl Scout cookie sales raised money for program activities and recruited new troop leaders, while the Boy Scouts helped US armed forces make the transition to a national wireless emergency communications system. Favoring a language of "education" and "recreation" to describe activities that their predecessors had proposed were expressions of young people's natural inclination to impersonate their elders, educators, youth workers, and public officials offered new rationales for the child protection and segregation from the labor market such programs supplied.

Taking the focus off the referent to some adult activity—for example, the talk of safety education that drowned out earlier discussions of pupil squads "organized just like real cops"—made young people's economic contributions even more difficult to see.[27]

A new generation of research across psychology and the social sciences backed this altered explanatory framework, accounting for environmental alongside biological factors in the evolution of self and society, with special interest in the influences of groups. Moving talk of imitation and impersonation to the analysis of symbolic communication and mass media, this research now assigned the successes of junior republics, junior police, Scouts, and other popular programs to their peer orientations. The earlier view that such activities provided young people with opportunities to live double lives by inhabiting multiple times, places, or identities through role-playing was superseded by attention to participants' roles as individuals within social groups. Academic questions about peer influences on community organization and public opinion took on national significance during the Depression as economic and political conditions prompted widespread youth activism against the status quo.

Chapter 6 follows the republic movement into the 1930s, to its renewal in the face of new anxieties about the present and future of American youth as this biological and social category expanded to include African Americans and postadolescents. In a period when increasing numbers of young people, chafing against the economic and political conditions of the Depression as well as adult efforts to restrict their behaviors, were coming to demand new rights and even questioning the democratic foundations of the American republic, the opportunities that junior republics supplied to address the nation's "youth problem" appealed to adults and youth alike. In light of William George's death in 1936 and the proliferation of school cities and boystowns as points of access to the republic's core principles, links to the original Freeville experiment were largely forgotten. Yet George's vision of how such programs could simultaneously serve as tools for personal and professional development and for the maintenance of law and order persisted—now with new stakeholder support as America's crises of community disorganization and public opinion, the larger framework for the "youth problem," came to be seen as national security concerns. The academics, educators, youth workers, and public officials who documented how effectively young people disciplined one another identified potential solutions in peers' positive influences on peers.[28]

Keeping tabs on youth movements in other nations, the federal government was the most enthusiastic of these stakeholders. The US National Youth Administration, making use of republics' building blocks from its debut, created nearly six hundred self-contained communities to get young people off the streets and redirect their energies toward public works activities from building infrastructure to building morale. Local governments, led by police departments, similarly embraced juvenile democracies and their component activities in ways that guided youth toward the creation of new, less tangible kinds of value for the state. Turning participants' attention to newspaper publishing, radio broadcasting, filmmaking, and public relations alongside now-common youth programming, adult authorities in these settings (together with colleagues at schools and other youth-serving institutions) discovered that as young people persuaded themselves and their peers about the value of the American system, they sold a range of youth programs to adults in their communities as well. Once again, activities undertaken to be developmentally beneficial for youth were equally economically beneficial for their adult sponsors, revealing how a more complete understanding of the intertwined histories of youth reform and government reform in the United States requires attending not only to what the state did for youth but also what youth did for the state.[29]

The state-led expansion of the republic movement during the 1930s marked the disappearance of the double life as a guiding principle for educators and youth workers, as the sheltered childhood was achieved for a majority of youth. Vocational education, home economics, student government, and Scouting—once seen as surrogate encounters with the lives of adult factory workers, homemakers, US senators, and pioneer explorers—shed their associations with mirroring adult reality and instead came to be reconceived as authentic youth-training tools. As a language of "education" and "recreation" replaced an older vocabulary of "model" and "miniature," organizers of these and other youth activities departed from their predecessors' long-standing ambitions to copy specific antecedents in the "real" or adult world. Student senates and congresses gave way to student councils; disciplinary boards and pupil patrols replaced junior juvenile courts and junior police; Scouts no longer explicitly aspired to duplicate the heroism of earlier generations. Preparation for later life remained a transcendent ambition for youth activities, but role-plays of adulthood declined in urgency when a majority of young people now accepted their diminished social roles. The experiences of American youth during World War II, which scaled back but did not eliminate young people's economic contributions, underscore the social transformation that had taken place while simultaneously reminding us that, within educational and recreational contexts, activities with hidden value never entirely disappeared.[30]

These six chapters thus establish the broad historical significance of a set of children's communities previously understood as merely fringe tools for juvenile reform. They expand the evidence about the sheer numbers of lives that junior republics touched and reveal the broader societal embrace of virtual adulthood as a means of easing the transition to the sheltered childhood and, in turn, constructing youth-serving institutions and the modern American state. Taken together, the evidence presented here adds up to a new understanding of the common life experiences of youth in the United States, how their experiences resonated with the broader technological and cultural transformations of modernity, and the route by which the construction of the sheltered childhood as a cultural category was ultimately achieved. The "double life" that William Forbush identified more accurately captures the period's dominant ideology than scholars' previous focus on the "separate spheres" of sheltered childhood alone. And the growth of state interest in child protection was inseparable from the people power youthful populations supplied to local, state, and federal governments.

Tracing the rise and fall of the junior republic movement calls attention to the nation's vibrant conversations about models and dramatizations in education and recreation, revealing how deep engagement with cultural questions about mediation in this era was even more pervasive than previously presumed. Alongside the mimetic comedy, sham battles, and living villages that scholars have described, participatory performances of adult experience were among the most common subjects for representation. Cataloguing the diverse roles that young people performed on a massive scale—for example, as truant officers, health inspectors, and traffic police—identifies their previously hidden contributions to American political development as they learned and played. With the normalization of the sheltered childhood, the importance of role-playing adulthood receded, but its deep influences on American cultural and economic history remain. A conclusion traces the junior republic movement's legacies beyond the continued operations of a few scattered institutions.

I Performing Adulthood

1 The Smallest Republic in the World

At an 1897 address to the American Social Science Association, Cornell University political economist Jeremiah Jenks reported on his recent investigations of William George's Junior Republic in nearby Freeville. "Mr. George's plan is to put the children, so far as possible, into the conditions of real adult life, by throwing upon them individually the entire responsibility of earning their own living and governing themselves," he explained. George's program, which removed youth from that society only to immerse them in a model of it, seemed a rather curious approach to child saving in an era when public opinion increasingly favored separating young people from regular contact with adult society. Yet Jenks saw something compelling in the unusual activities there. "The children learn their lessons by experience; and, as in life, they find out that they must take the consequences of their acts," he reported. "The child learns to see things as they are in actual life far more easily and clearly than he can see them in the society of adults." The republic was "one of the most helpful means of training and reclaiming children whose lives have been started on the downward path," he concluded, and eagerly volunteered for service on its board of trustees.[1]

Why did Jenks, like so many social scientists, journalists, tourists, and others flock to this child society at the close of the nineteenth century when its approach to child saving seemed to run counter to common wisdom of the day? This chapter describes the founding of the George Junior Republic and its evolution from a summer program into a year-round operation hailed across the United States and around the world. To date, scholarship on William George's work has been limited, significantly out of proportion to its public stature in the late nineteenth and early twentieth centuries. Historians typically mention the Freeville republic in passing alongside schools and reformatories, two institutions for educating and improving the lives of the era's youth with more lasting footprints in both contemporary American society and the historiography of youth.[2]

Yet the enthusiastic media attention to this curious community during its heyday, participants' obvious enjoyment of their experiences there, and the language that adults and youth employed in their descriptions of life in Freeville suggest affinities with another set of institutions as well. From exhibition halls and panoramas to arcades and scale models, from galleries and department stores to photography and film, from planetariums and living villages to wax museums and miniature railways, Americans of the period "thrived on a traffic in reproductions and replications of every possible sort," as Miles Orvell has put it, many of which offered access to experiences and events formerly distant in time and space. Simulated environments and vicarious experiences—copies, miniatures, the real and yet not-quite-real—had become mainstays of modern life. The early years of George's Junior Republic illustrate why copies and miniatures of adult activities soon came to serve a special function in the lives of the nation's youngest populations: how, in an era when common wisdom stressed the need to shelter young people from adult society, a growing community of reformers arrived at the consensus that the best way to do so was to immerse them in carefully designed models of that society instead.[3]

Steps Toward Youth Reform

William George first grew interested in working with young people as a businessman in New York City, where the combined forces of immigration, urbanization, and industrialization, together with an economic depression, had produced an increasingly visible cesspool of social problems, including poverty, crime, and unrest. American identity had long been associated with the nation's agrarian roots and cities presented growing contrasts to the pastoral ideal. Anxieties about the flood of new populations regarded as distinct racial groups prompted public discussions about the possibilities of assimilation to white, middle-class ideals. Like many of the genteel American elites worried about the nation's long-term stability in light of these economic, social, and cultural transformations, George was sympathetic to the children who represented the future of the United States and hopeful that he might rescue them from their parents' fate. Initially working as a Sunday school teacher with the Christian Endeavor movement, from the late 1880s George began to reach out to boys on the city's streets. He made contact with the Graveyard Gang on Manhattan's lower east side. Barely older than the gang members, George's abilities as a boxer won the boys' respect, and soon he found himself in a brotherly role providing charity and running an informal club in the hopes of channeling the boys' energies in more constructive directions.[4]

Social and business contacts soon enmeshed George with reformers in the city's good government movement (the "Goo Goos"), who had also recently turned their attention to youth. The Goo Goo's agenda was improving public administration, particularly in the nation's cities. Like many self-styled progressives, Goo Goos placed their confidence in scientific methods and technological tools as the primary routes to achieve their ambitions for making government operations more rational and efficient and implementing policies above politics. Historians have traced these reformers' successful introduction of municipal research bureaus for urban data gathering across the nation and their role in regularizing civil service exams ensuring that government workers possessed "scientific" expertise.[5]

Less well known are the civic education projects the Goo Goos initiated to complement these top-down strategies for municipal reform. Frustrated that the immigrants whose needs were reasonably well served by political machines seemed to like the quasi-monarchical style of government that George and others judged to be corrupt and inefficient, and increasingly cognizant that native-born middle classes had grown too apathetic to prevent boss rule, the Goo Goos identified citizens alongside governments as targets for change. At the center of their strategy was information sharing based on the belief that citizens who understood the workings of government would recognize there was a "right" way to govern. Pilot projects with worker clubs disappointed, however, leading many Goo Goos to wonder if kids might be more willing audiences. Youthful gangs, for example, were already regular participants in New York City politics—not for the good of the system in George's and others' estimation given that early gang participation and later political corruption were linked.[6]

It was in this context that George, still working with local youth and by then a police deputy, offered the Graveyard Gang's services to the neighborhood's police department. He proposed the boys help keep order in the neighborhood. The gang's inner circle, called the "Sons of Arrest" because it was comprised of boys previously rounded up for lawbreaking, would patrol for violations. Later, George infiltrated Harlem's Duffyville gang and subsequently enlisted both groups as monitors for the city's 1894 election. The boys' efforts to root out double voting convinced city police commissioner and fellow Goo Goo Theodore Roosevelt to delegate to them the authority to arrest other youthful delinquents. Soon the boys chose new names for their informal organizations: the Parkhurst Cops (named for clergyman and Goo Goo Charles Parkhurst) and the Law and Order Gang.[7]

Despite these small victories, George believed there were limits to the reforms that could be achieved when young people remained in neighborhoods whose conditions were so overwhelmingly detrimental to their physical and moral health. As the agrarian ideal at the heart of American identity stirred elites' anxieties about the nation's changing conditions, it inspired programs to bring less-advantaged adults and youth closer to nature, from urban parks to orphan trains. As early as summer 1890, guided by the era's common wisdom about the value of time spent in nature, George set out to create a "fresh air camp" for an even greater number of kids, including girls. Together with several adult volunteers, most connected to local churches and the larger "social gospel" movement that linked religion and reform, and with sponsorship from the *New-York Tribune*, they headed to rural Freeville, New York. George's family owned property there, and he was eager to give immigrant children the experience of country life. Equally influenced by the period's popular association between military education and order, the camp was organized "on a semi-military basis," with George as commander-in-chief. (A member of the 22nd regiment, he had occasionally drilled with boy gangs.)[8]

Unfortunately, George's assumptions that a change in environment would alter the campers' behavior and that military discipline would keep the children in line were called into question from the start. The boys and girls seemed more interested in receiving charity than in self-improvement. One-tenth of the kids, he estimated, came to have fun terrorizing the countryside, while the other nine-tenths came for the food and clothing that locals had donated. Syracuse economics professor John Commons, among George's close associates, reported how, "From arrival to departure their constant clamour was, 'What are dese farmers goin' to give us to take back?'" As one camper put it, "The woman I was by last year gave me two dresses, and sent us three barrels of potatoes in the winter. What are youse going to give me?" Although George continued his camp in subsequent summers, he grew increasingly frustrated at its "degrading effects" and concluded that his program might be doing more harm than good.[9]

George's work with youth gangs in New York City prompted him to change course in summer 1894. Taking the view that the recipients of charity might fare better if they took active roles in their own salvation and disciplining, he instituted a work requirement and subsequently a child court. Participating youth would pay for their food and lodging by participating in projects around the camp. And they would adjudicate all disciplinary matters by sitting in judgment of their peers.[10]

These changes to the camp's operations transformed the summer experience. Children increasingly came to appreciate the goods they received, having earned them with their own efforts. And campers' zest for lawbreaking rapidly declined. The new arrangements were not entirely successful—indeed, a wave of crime followed the initial reduction of misbehaviors. But George was pleased with the overwhelming improvements: "Human beings can't be good all the time," he later explained.[11]

As the summer went on, George continued to experiment with the system of youth responsibilities. For example, when the adult volunteer who supervised the young people sentenced by their peers to hard labor fell ill, George put a camper and former gang member named Banjo in charge. (Banjo was a member of the Park gang.) To his delight, after Banjo's installation there were no new violators for several days. "Banjo got much better and harder work out of the boys than did the adult, for they could not deceive him," Commons observed, and "Banjo himself became the most self-respecting upholder of law and order in the entire community." George assigned Banjo to the post for the remainder of the summer.[12]

By the close of the 1894 season, George was speculating about delegating to the campers even greater responsibilities for its operations in future years. The assistance rendered by gang members in the city's fall elections bolstered his confidence in this idea. The following summer, as a group numbering nearly 150 drawn from missions, settlements, and boys clubs departed by train from New York City, he presented them with an even more ambitious plan. With a constitution he had written as the guiding document, that summer's camp would be known as the George Junior Republic, a youth commonwealth modeled on the laws of the United States and New York State.[13]

George invited the children to envision themselves as pioneers settling a new land. He explained that he would initially serve as president of the rudimentary society, and other participating adults would hold the major political positions. This arrangement was to be temporary, however. Once the republic was up and running he expected the campers to play all of the political roles. These included an elected president, senators and representatives, and appointed officials for police and health departments and a court and jail. Eligibility for many of these positions would require passage of "civil service exams" that George had prepared, following recently established precedent in New York. A civil society would thus replace the prior summer's military government, although a boys' militia would be retained as the republic's standing army. The economic system of the previous summer similarly would be enhanced to include a bank, a legal tender (initially made of cardboard and later of tin), and a set of gendered occupations, including gardeners, carpenters, seamstresses, and cooks, paid at different rates. Here too, he explained, adults would initially supervise but later turn over greater control to participating youth.[14]

George hoped that, through their experiences as officials and as citizens, farming their food and building their furniture, making clothing and keeping house, campers would leave the summer program personally transformed. By holding elections at frequent intervals as well as welcoming young people's entrepreneurship, he hoped to expose them to a diversity of political and economic activities that could be found in the adult world. Participating youth would learn the mechanics of government as well as the norms of civic behavior that Goo Goos aimed to spread. They would gain marketable skills for an urbanizing economy, appreciate the value of labor, and learn the importance of thrift as well. In short, by compressing time and space, a life lived responsibly in the George Junior Republic would "fit them for years of acceptable service in our larger Republic." Over its first three years George, his wife, two dozen adult volunteers, and the young participants transformed the republic from an experimental community run by adults to an established self-governing juvenile society that was known around the world.[15]

Late nineteenth-century youth programs operated with limited oversight. Controversies about earlier examples of child exploitation had prompted the organization of some state charity boards. Yet, by and large, adult organizers continued to have great discretion to organize programs as they saw fit—and this included the discretion to delegate decision-making to youth. In summer 1895, then, George mixed adult control with youth responsibility. He installed himself as president, with a veto on all laws. His adult assistants served as chief justice of the supreme court, civil and criminal court judges, chief of police, civil service examiners, board of health, postmaster, and bank president. Boys and girls filled the remainder of the positions from police officers and lawyers to senators and representatives. (A bar exam was introduced as a condition for membership in the republic's bar association.) Members of the congress were drawn from each of the industrial classes, which included gardening, landscaping, and carpentry for boys, and millinery, cooking, and sewing for girls. This guaranteed a mixed gender slate. The militia, comprised of all the boys in the camp, drilled twice each day.[16]

The adult volunteers similarly controlled the economic system, overseeing "contracts" (actually classes in industrial skills), which participants were paid to attend. George set the daily wages for each job based on three skill levels: 50 cents for unskilled, 70 cents for semiskilled, and 90 cents for skilled. The expectation was that campers' earnings would cover the costs of their food and lodging, as well as a civic tax.[17]

The first summer in the newly settled colony was devoted to making the campus more habitable and passing a suite of basic laws. Upon their arrival at the forty-eight-acre site, which held a farm, a two-story house, a shed, and several dilapidated barns, the junior citizens faced the challenge of constructing buildings, streets, furniture, and other facilities. They designated one barn as the main government building with courthouse, bank, jail, and sleeping quarters for the adults. A shed housed the industries. As in previous summers, the campers lived in tents.

Once the wheels of government were set in motion, the camp was animated by all manner of legislative debates. Female suffrage was an early hot-button issue. Having modeled the junior republic on the United States, girls were taxpaying citizens without the same suffrage rights as boys. Frustrated by their second-class status and aware of ongoing agitation for female suffrage in the "big Republic" outside—which had already been partially achieved in some state and local elections—several girls pressed to place all the campers on equal footing. With careful lobbying and "white dresses to make a good impression," they were successful in obtaining the vote. A girl senator was elected that summer.[18]

The question of whether welfare benefits should be provided by the state was another source of lively conversation. Annoyed that the republic's civic tax initially sponsored meals for campers who refused to join the industrial classes, the juvenile legislators swiftly passed a law to end this practice. One day, "the members of the House of Representatives of the republic introduced a bill to stop the pauper evil," explained an observer. "He was the son of parents in New York City who lived almost entirely on charity. In his speech he said, with bluntness, 'A feller what won't work hadn't orter be fed by us fellers what do work.' The bill provided that none of the tax money be used for the support of paupers, and it passed unanimously." The consequences were immediate. "The next meal the chronic paupers presented themselves as usual at the dining tent, but the little uniformed police man said, 'Move on.' The last two weeks there were no paupers."[19]

Over the course of summer 1895, the children introduced approximately two hundred bills, nearly sixty of which became law. "They were real laws, too," reported *Harper's*,

Figure 1.1
George Junior Republic legislature in session.
Source: "The George Junior Republic," *Harper's Weekly*, May 23, 1896.

"and the debates on them had a serious side such as no amateur debating society ever knew." True to his long-term ambitions, George rarely exercised his veto powers. For example, he told the *New York Times* that he was not sure if he favored female suffrage "in reality," but he supported the efforts by participating girls to practice it at the camp. Although political and economic life now dominated the summer experience, George retained the recreational aspects of his original fresh air camp. After a half day engaged in industrial classes and political business, campers enjoyed outdoor activities that included sports, singing, and theatricals.[20]

The summer program's new direction did not eradicate all misbehavior. There were cases of bribery, robbery, and voter fraud. But overall, George was pleased. In winter 1895–1896, he doubled down with the goal of making total youth self-government a reality for the following summer. Five boys who begged George to let them continue the republic during the winter months accelerated these plans. Moving into the adults' housing to weather the harsh conditions over the coming months, they continued to build out the physical plant and offered George further organizational suggestions for the next summer's experience. Freed from pressure to keep adults in charge as he had during the summer season, George started to assign political positions to the boys, who eventually numbered about fifteen. In December, he appointed as judge Jacob "Jakey" Smith, "the son of parents who are chronic paupers."[21]

When the republic's population swelled once again in summer 1896, George was emboldened to appoint campers to nearly every political office, reserving the presidency for himself. He offered them increasing control over the republic's economic affairs as well. Now George auctioned off contracts to run businesses on the republic grounds in exchange for a licensing fee or a percentage of profits. This included the industrial classes from the previous year, a decreasing proportion of the republic's economic system as the junior citizens' entrepreneurial activities blossomed. In the first few summers, campers established a barber shop, shoe shop, tailor shop, hotels, and restaurants. The hotels included the Waldorf, Ithaca, and Dryden for boys and the Elmira for girls. The restaurants were Delmonico's and Sherry's. All of these businesses bore the names of actual New York institutions. The children could also hire one another informally for odd jobs such as pressing clothes or polishing shoes.[22]

Swarthmore social scientist William Hull, who visited the republic, was fascinated by these developments:

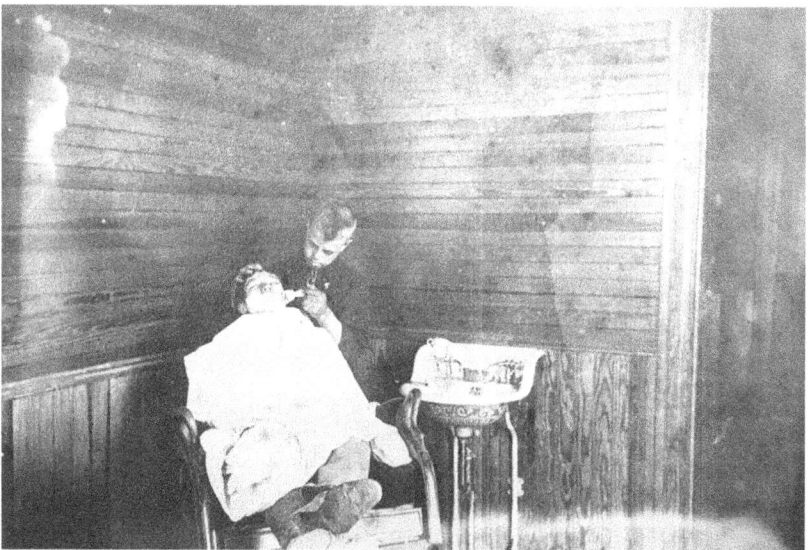

Figure 1.2
George Junior Republic barber shop.
Source: William R. George Family Papers, box 121, folder 1–62, envelope 20, "Early days." Courtesy Division of Rare and Manuscript Collections, Cornell University Library.

Figure 1.3
George Junior Republic, Hotel Waldorf dining room.
Source: "The George Junior Republic," *Harper's Weekly*, May 23, 1896.

"One boy has purchased the privilege of giving to the boy citizens their weekly bath, the taking of which is enforced by fine and imprisonment; another boy has purchased the privilege of conducting a barber shop; several have the contract of providing lodgings for the citizens and of furnishing their meals.... Each hotel keeper had to keep order, hire servants and keep things clean. An inspector employed by the government inspected the properties."

As political and economic activities multiplied—for example, citizens-for-hire prepared maps, surveys, and mathematical calculations for various businesses—the boys and girls created procedures and paperwork to match the bureaucracy that increasingly characterized employment, banking, and arrests in the adult world. In the spirit of government transparency, weekly budgets, government bulletins, regular censuses, and a police blotter were publicly posted for all citizens to review. (Later they were published in the community newspaper, the *Junior Citizen*, in press from 1898.)[23]

The transfer of political authority went relatively smoothly, and the young officials and citizens took up new issues from smoking and cruelty to animals to visitors' policy in their legislative session. Discussions about the minimum wage were especially intense. Junior citizens' increasing autonomy in the economic arena, by contrast, created such sharp divisions between "capitalists" and "laborers" that George ultimately intervened at the children's request. The initial pay distinctions among skilled, semi-skilled, and unskilled labor had spawned clear classes of citizens as well as new businesses catering to these different economic groups. There were three grades of hotel, for example, "from the Hotel Waldorf, on the second floor of the main building, where the millionaires sleep, and pay twenty-five cents per night for the privilege of having a tastily furnished room to themselves, to the lowest class of lodgings in the attic, where the unsuccessful business men or the idlers must take up their quarters, at ten cents a night," as William Hull observed. Children unable to pay for lodging slept in the station house, got arrested, and were fined. "This arrangement is rather undemocratic, to be sure," he explained, "but it is relied upon, and with good reason, as a means of cultivating the ways of polite society."[24]

Given the opportunity to start new enterprises, savvy citizens realized they could increase profits in several ways. Some bought goods in the nearby village store, paid the republic's "import tariff," and then resold them at high prices to fellow citizens. Mary Gay Humphreys recounted the exploits of one boy, Dover, for whom "speculation was the chief source" of wealth. "He brought up United States money, floating dimes and nickels, from the little boys." He used this to purchase caramels and gumdrops from the village store. "After paying the tariff levied on all goods from outside countries, these candies were sold to the same small and greedy little boys at five cents apiece. The profit was enormous." More children followed Dover's example, "and speculation filled the air." Others lent money at high interest rates. Most controversial were those who bid for the republic's contracts and then hired other kids to labor at low wage rates.[25]

George was eager to let the kids work out a solution. Yet the junior citizens frustrated by the growing class segmentation, inflation, depression, and other financial developments begged "Daddy" George, now seen as a parental rather than brotherly figure, to intervene. He eventually acceded to their request to return to the older economic system in which he set pay rates and awarded contracts, giving him discretion to limit the growth of millionaires. George's faith in the campers' abilities to administer their age-restricted society remained undiminished, however, and in winter 1896–1897 total youth representation in the republic's political system was finally achieved. Thanks to George's recent marriage to Esther Brewster (aka "Mrs. Daddy"), this winter's citizens included girls as well as boys, although only a total of thirty-two children, a small fraction of all who had hoped to remain. The group elected a slate of officials, including their first youth president, sixteen-year-old Jakey Smith. The secretary of the treasury was a girl. With the transfer of authority to a junior citizen, George retreated to a position as superintendent.[26]

George viewed the junior republic, like the greater republic, as a work in progress. Ever in need of financial support, he initially tapped his social connections in New York City and the region—figures such as Washington Gladden, Josiah Strong, Charles Parkhurst, Lyman Abbott, William Howe Tolman, Theodore Roosevelt, R. Montgomery Schell, Richard Welling, Jacob Riis, Albert Shaw, Charles Eliot, and Thomas Osborne—in the same circles of Christian charity and urban reform that supplied his adult volunteers and gave him ideas about structuring political activities. (Notably the republic was explicitly nonsectarian, despite its close ties to religious reformers.) They created and incorporated a George Junior Republic Association, helping to raise money to improve the physical plant by remodeling buildings, adding new facilities, and supplying equipment for the print shop, laundry, and other industries. And they hired a teacher, Willard "Uncle Hotchy" Hotchkiss, to supplement a "publishing house" scheme in which kids were contracted to complete arithmetic, spelling, and writing exercises for pay.[27]

To complement these efforts, George gave frequent lectures in New York City and beyond, bringing junior officials along to speak to audiences even before full self-government had been achieved. (He did not take any with him on his 1896 honeymoon, although he did stop in Chicago to address a convention of sociologists.) A number of entrepreneurial youth had given stereopticon lectures at the republic as a money-making scheme. Jakey Smith became a frequent guest on the lecture circuit, explaining the republic's operations, noting bills under consideration, and describing the accomplishments of individual children, such as twelve-year-old "little Arthur" who had singlehandedly replaced an eight-person police force. Overflow crowds were dazzled by their public performances. "A lad just out of knickerbockers" was a speaker at the YMCA Harlem branch, the *New York Times* reported on one of Jakey's public presentations, "and talked so intelligently of tariffs, currency rations, and legislative problems that his hearers were subdued with astonishment."[28]

George also encouraged visitors to come to see the youth democracy in operation for themselves. From its first summer, journalists, scholars, religious authorities, local police, and other curious parties swarmed Freeville to observe the unusual self-governing child society, marveling at the lack of gates, the rarity of inmates seeking to escape, and the ways in which immigrant youth were modeling the kinds of civic behavior the Goo Goos hoped to see from adults. "Not a day goes by but that the camp is visited by more or less interested persons," wrote the *New York Times*, "many driving miles to see it or coming by train." The police court session "is the event of the day," another visitor explained.

> The procedure is modeled after the police courts in New York City.... It is held at nine o'clock, and to be there in time, carryalls and wheels are seen coming over the road from Freeville, Dryden, Elmira, and the surrounding towns, and visiting professors in sociology from the colleges beg to stay over night that they may be present...when the policeman posted at the bar calls "Hats off," the citizens square themselves around into orderly rows, and even the visitors,

disposed to regard the affair as a bit of play-acting, drop their voices to a whisper, and finally cease trying to communicate at all.

The children assigned a bus driver to shuttle visitors from the railway station to the republic and installed a visitors' box at the courthouse to accommodate the growing hordes. They did not, however, charge admission—despite the constant need for funds.[29]

Visitors frequently described the landscape and customs of "the smallest republic in the world" in travelogue style, as if it were a new state of the union whose history recapitulated the development of the larger US with its "group of colonists" and "Indian and cow-boy days." Their accounts of life in Freeville all differed from George's and from one another on account of the rapidity with which George and the children were making alterations to their residential community. "Just as the United States has been the theme for many a varied account from Mrs. Trollope and Charles Dickens down to Sir Lepel Griffin and Mr. Bryce," explained Thomas Osborne, a businessman in nearby Auburn who would head the George Junior Republic Association, "so the little republic has had chroniclers of many minds and differing conclusions." Variations in these details aside, ample coverage in the news media enthusiastically recounted tales of the young citizens' vicarious experiences of adulthood inside this realistic yet age-restricted society—their sham battles, their political debates, their entrepreneurship—and celebrated the social inventiveness of William George. In the eyes of both its organizers and outside observers, the republic was a near-exact copy of the US, a "complete though simple form of society," a place where "the conditions, social, civic and economic are made to conform as near as possible to those of the great republic" such that "everything is conducted upon the identical plan which rules life at large."[30]

If such statements ignored how the republic had deliberately transplanted kids from an urban context where George saw democracy in crisis to a rural environment where he believed democracy naturally thrived, the possibility of democracy's multiple manifestations went unremarked. Instead, as the comparison to the great republic and to life at large suggested, they focused their attention on correspondences between adult life in the larger United States and the junior citizens' activities on the republic's smaller scale. This "plain matter-of-fact United States on a small scale," was a "miniature state," or a "Lilliputian commonwealth" when compared to the big republic beyond. Participating children left their "real life" behind to form "a real community of their own." In this *imperium in imperio*," they learned "by actual experience," Osborne explained. "These children are being prepared for the world by gaining a knowledge of law, of order, of society, in the only way that such children can be made to learn it; not by reasoning from the abstract to the concrete...but by living in the midst of concrete examples." Recognizing the debates about issues from female suffrage and pauperism to import-export tariffs and the minimum wage, he and others approvingly described how the questions the children weighed in on were the same questions that are being discussed in the great republic. Indeed, as one observer put it, "One could easily multiply parallels between the life of the Junior Republic and of society at large."[31]

A Marvel of the Century

Such early descriptions of republic life, which emphasized its resemblances to "real life" rather than focus on the particular reform agenda being taught, set the tone for public perceptions of this curious community in the longer term. By the turn of the century, numerous journalistic and scholarly accounts—many of them widely reprinted—had publicized the astounding story of how the republic's "system of emulation," as George put it, helped children help themselves. "The reports of the work done read more like a novel than a picture of real life," wrote one observer. For the junior citizens "of a sort which would have argued to the uninitiated mind a brief and disastrous career for the new nation" had instead proven themselves to be capable citizens who treated political and economic life with greater seriousness than many adults.[32]

In the political arena, for example, boys and girls enforced the laws they made with zeal: "These young minions of the law understand the laws of their little republic as thoroughly as, perhaps in some cases more thoroughly than, the regularly accredited officers of some large cities, and more, too, they keep their eyes open for violations of the law and make arrests with a promptness that is sometimes surprising," wrote the *New York Times* of the child police, and recounted the story of a police official dismissed when he failed to arrest a citizen who had been smoking. "The police magistrate is a boy fifteen years of age, who has been with Mr. George several years. His parents are drunkards. The efficiency and modesty with which he deals with the varied cases that come before him is amazing." Another observed how "Naturally the highest ambition of each boy is to become a policeman," and wear the uniform and badge. Yet "civil service examinations are so thorough in this department that only the very best and most efficient boys can pass them. When they do they almost invariably make good officers of the law, exhibiting a zeal, tempered with fairness, which is said to be very remarkable." The superintendent of police in nearby Cortland, New York, paid a visit to see what he might learn.[33]

The courts, like the police, similarly impressed. "In the open court, over which a judge of sixteen was presiding with impressive seriousness and dignity...you often see with surprise a courtliness toward one another as well as to the adults, and listen to a purity and choice of language not to have been anticipated from children of their antecedents," reported James Price. "What especially impressed me was their court room," agreed another visitor, noting how "the young judge is as careful in rendering his decisions as the most serious judge in a genuine tribunal, and the order as dignified as in any court of the land." The republic "has had many Daniel Websters and Patrick Henrys in embryo."[34]

Children's professionalism in politics and law enforcement was matched in their business dealings, norms that surprised observers who expected less from urban youth. "I saw two boys go without breakfast because on the day before they loafed, and so failed to earn cash for a day's meals and lodging," reported US education commissioner William T. Harris on a visit to Freeville. "Mr. George himself escapes the odium of enforcing this harsh penalty, for it is enforced by the boy proprietor of the hotel, to whom it is a matter of business." This "indirect coercion" was a valuable "educational device." Sometimes the expression of business acumen was to comic effect. "The proprietor of the girls' hotel, a little Irish lass of thirteen years, was piqued because she was not invited to a party given by a dozen of the best girls to a few of the best boys," recounted one journalist. "She startled the ice cream eaters by rushing in, only for a moment, to say in tones the reader must imagine: 'Youse'll pay fifteen centers fer yer beds tonight.'"[35]

Upstate New York at the turn of the twentieth century was home to utopian communities such as the Oneida Community, Skaneateles Community, and Sodus Bay Phalanx. Each of these experiments, by removing populations from their regular environments, aimed to demonstrate variations on a more perfect society for potential adoption at larger scale. In this context George felt the need to be explicit that his ambition was not to create a perfect society. From smoking to swearing to setting fires, crime and bad behavior were routine parts of republic life. So too were legislative choices he considered ill-advised. Yet in an immersive environment where kids could see the consequences of their choices play out, George was unfazed by these missteps. Indeed, the possibility of making mistakes and subsequently recovering from them was central to the republic's learning objectives, so long as the children were given free rein to make them and sort things out for themselves. "When such problems arise it is Mr. George's policy to leave to the boys" and girls "the solution of them," William Hull confirmed, "his aim being to fix upon the citizens themselves the responsibility for their own acts, and to permit them to learn by experience." Freeville affiliate Frederic Almy contrasted the republic's dramatic and democratic approach with the military-style discipline found in other institutions, optimistically predicting that its lessons were more likely to stick:

> Where the germ of pauperism or of vice cannot be killed, may there not be a treatment by antitoxin, as at the George Republic, by deliberately helping the poison to run its course in a mild form in order to prevent future attacks? It may be well to let a boy be idle and lazy for a time and suffer all the consequences of hunger and cold; to let him be violent, and as a penalty be duly and severely punished by his peers; in fact, to give him a brief rehearsal of life under natural conditions which will be very profitable when life arrives in grim earnest. These lessons are taught in a reformatory of the military type, but the more voluntary and natural the lesson is, and the more the child can be made to feel that he has chosen his own course and experienced its natural result, the deeper will be the impress on his life.[36]

Reports from numerous visitors carried George's ideas beyond Freeville as they described how participation in this juvenile society developed "character" alongside the lessons in politics and business it taught. Such language was code for politeness, orderliness, and devotion to educational improvement and hard work—and typically associated with native-born, middle-class whites. The immigrants and first-generation Americans who were a source of fear in urban contexts, associated with racialized criminality and potential threats to the American way of life, here appeared open to new behavioral norms. "There is a vast amount of enthusiasm for everything American in this miniature Republic," Hull explained, "and it is sought to direct this into channels of patriotism and love for the big Republic by elaborate ceremonies when raising and lowering the 'Stars and Stripes,' by singing patriotic songs and declaiming patriotic addresses." Children saw both the immorality and the financial costs of crime—how "it costs more to be bad dan good," in the words of one boy. "Youse has to work harder an' get no pay, sleep in a cell an' get bread, water and soup, and be followed wid a gun, an' hev all de blokes in de Republic down on yourself if yer bad," this junior citizen reported to George. "If youse is good, youse only hev to work es hard es in de prison an' git de biggest money in de camp, and wid dat youse ken sleep in de best room in de botel, and eat de finest feed, an' de girls an' fellers don't git down on youse like dey do if youse is a prisoner. I figgered dat all out one night in de cell, an' I made up me mind dat I can't afford to be bad, an' I'm goin' to try now to go to de top." (That boy eventually became speaker of Freeville's house of representatives.)[37]

Participating youth also revised their attitudes toward education. This was not only because, as Thomas Osborne explained, kids were paid for schoolwork in republic currency "much as if they were working in a factory." With civil service and bar exams determining eligibility for popular positions, including police, attorney, and the slate of presidentially appointed posts, the relationship between knowledge and career advancement became abundantly clear. Seeing how "the boys who had been 'contemptible grinds'" swiftly occupied the positions of authority to which they aspired, "boys with truancy earmarks" could be seen "wrestling over textbooks" to prepare for civil service exams and "boys who in New York are dodging the police" were "here in the corners studying the statutes of New York, codes of procedure, or Reed's parliamentary rules." As Washington Gladden recounted of his encounter with one boy, "One youngster, who had risen, hopelessly plucked, from this examination, explained: 'I don't play hooky this winter, you bet! I'll come back here next year and git to be a cop." Another child, Foxy, told a journalist, "Ain't but one thing riles me, that's me mudder didn't lick me and make me go ter school so's I could pass the civil service examination fer the police force. A copper's all I want 'er be in dat republic, an' you's kin bet all yer blooming shiners' dat I'll be one, too, next year."[38]

The young citizens' altered attitudes toward charity attracted ample commentary because these departed so substantially from expectations about impoverished youth. One boy discovered that items given away for free rarely attracted the appreciation of

Figure 1.4
George Junior Republic, prisoner sentenced to hard labor.
Source: "The George Junior Republic," *Harper's Weekly*, May 23, 1896.

those with a financial cost. Having previously "collected animals, plants, and stones from the neighborhood," and "vainly tried to interest his fellow-citizens in this branch of inquiry," he decided to open a dime museum and charge admission for viewings. "At the hour appointed a line of two hundred citizens, each with his dime, was waiting at the door. They marched through the museum, examined the very specimens they had spurned, and voted the show a success." Another told Mr. George that his father typically spent his weekly wage early in the week, so that he and his siblings went hungry "unless the 'mission folks'" offered aid. "'An' I was t'inkin' just now, when you come up, dat if dis fixin' up camp money worked for me all right, I could tell me parents, an' mebby we could make it work wid pop's money.'" He underscored this point to

Figure 1.5
George Junior Republic prison.
Source: William George, *The Junior Republic: Its History and Ideals* (New York: Appleton, 1910).

George at summer's end: "I hev learned how to save money, and how to work for my money.... At first I was paupper caus I did not no how to save money but I no how to save money now and I am not paupper any more."[39]

As the children separated the "deserving" from the "undeserving" recipients of charity, they established a Society for the Prevention of Cruelty to Children within the republic. This organization ensured that the older youth who served as guardians to younger kids treated them well and organized ad hoc collections to help out friends in need. Journalist Adele Fielde reported on how "These waifs are often very generous to each other," giving the example of "E., who is only sixteen years old, and who was poverty-stricken and most cruelly treated at home" and who "had never seen F. till the two met here in the Junior Republic." F. was "a lazy, thievish child of ten" who E. took "under his care in a spirit that would do credit to an angel. He has paid F.'s debts, amounting to twenty-one dollars, of his own hard-earned money; has defended him when others reviled him, and then privately expostulated with him, and has encouraged him with the devotion and patience of a true older brother." Journalist Mary Humphreys recounted the story of a girl who, after spending all her money on caramels, was unable to pay for her bed at the Hotel Elmira and how friends sponsored her so that she could sleep well for a week.[40]

Most unexpected among the republic's many accomplishments was how many of the participating youth relished life in the environment in which these lessons were learned. George was an avid record-keeper, consistent with the Goo Goo agenda. Inviting the kids to report on their summer experiences, he printed the choicest testimonials in the republic's annual report. "I have learned a great deal," one boy wrote at summer's end. "I didn't know what the Legislature was when I came here, but I know what it is good for now. I have saved $45 since I am here. I have worked for every cent I got. I think I am a good citizen now. I know how to vote and I am proud of it." Even those who spent time in the republic's jail had something positive to report. "The prison taught me a good lesson. You bet I won't get in there any more," another insisted.[41]

Of course, George, constantly in search of financial assistance, typically publicized the statements of enthusiastic participants. Yet he catalogued the resisters as well. Some ran away in protest of the idea that they would be controlled by other kids. Four departing children wrote back to "'Tell Mr. George we liked der place, but didn't want ter be arrested by kid cops.'" Others were unable to manage the daily expectation of work. "I don't like sinc im here for we starf an i wish i wars home caus i dont had to work," said one boy. Another complained at being teased because he was poor. Still others appeared to be beyond reform, such as Citizen 121, described as "unpromising" on entry and "devil" on departure.[42]

Taken together, the evidence overwhelmingly backs George's view that the majority of youth in residence at his republic were energetically participating in their own reform, making expulsion the highest order disciplinary tool and a punishment they sought to avoid. George's contemporaries were highly impressed. Adopting a hagiographic tone that placed him in the company of other genius inventors, they celebrated his "experiment," calling it a "workshop" and "machinery" for democratic citizenship (and, later, a "laboratory" and "factory" as well). "Benjamin Franklin said that he would like to come back to our country after one hundred years," wrote minister Theodore Cuyler, "and if 'Poor Richard' had been with us yesterday, he would have jumped for joy." In an era John Kasson and others have characterized as manic about invention, including the invention of "social technologies," George and his republic were widely hailed as a "marvel of the century."[43]

As they reflected on the genius of George's "invention" (which George himself later described as resulting from a flash of inspiration from God), many concluded the republic offered young people access to a new life. Some, following Jean-Jacques Rousseau's famous claim in *Emile, or On Education*, that all individuals were born twice—once into the world and once into adulthood—or the more common religious formulation of an afterlife, emphasized the sequencing of these events to describe a life in the tenements followed by a new life in the republic, or a life in the republic followed by a "second life" back in New York City. "In this Republic a boy takes up a new life, with the old life left behind and forgotten," explained one writer in the *New York Evangelist*. "A fellow that has been through a Junior Republic has a chance to live his life over again. He knows what he can do because he did it on a small scale there. He knows, too, what he can't do, because he tried that, too, in the Republic and found it failed," wrote a later observer in the *Young Woman's Journal*. The junior citizens used similar language themselves. As one boy wrote to George in a letter after summer's end, "It's like as if they have two lifetimes to live through. The first is the time they spend in the Republic in which they gain experience, and the second when they get back to New York.'"[44]

In the eyes of other observers, however, the republic enabled these multiple lifetimes to be simultaneously lived. As Thomas Osborne observed how "the children form, in fact, a real community of their own, an *imperium in imperio*," he also noted that "being in reality children and not men and women" they had to attend school. Journalists celebrated the enthusiastic participation of youth in the governance and labor that maintaining the republic required, as one put it, "the republic is the children's affair entirely." Yet in reminding readers that adults were ultimately in charge ("of course there are resident citizens at Freeville to assist.... in the capacities of teachers and advisers"), these observers proposed the republic instead supplied opportunities to live two lives at once: the protected life of a real young person and the dramatized life of a virtual adult.[45]

Figure 1.6
George Junior Republic, street sweepers.
Source: Abigail Powers, "The George Junior Republic," *The Puritan* 9 (1901).

World's Fair, Wax Museum, Junior Republic

In their descriptions of the republic as a copy, a miniature, and an environment at the border of real life and the not-quite-real, and in their attention to how participating youth had reenacted the settlement and development of the agrarian democracy that was the "great republic," these accounts' style and content followed established conventions not for describing youth-serving institutions but instead for discussing the period's proliferating simulated environments and vicarious experiences. Historians have documented public fascination during the latter half of the nineteenth century with cultural products that claimed to reproduce reality and linked them to the transformation of perceptual experience in the modern era. Taxidermy, historical reenactments, sham battles, living villages, world's fairs, panoramas, spectrographs, Hale's Tours, stereoscopes, photographs, miniature railways, films, daguerreotypes, planetariums, greenhouses and winter gardens, wax museums, national parks, "genuine reproduction" furniture, shopping arcades, mimetic comedy, lantern slide lectures, morgues, phonographs, spectacle plays, dioramas, and archaeological sites analyzed separately and together add weight to these accounts. Of course there is a longer history to such representations of reality, and many of the cultural products that became popular among Americans were European in origin. Yet scholars recognize a particular proliferation in the turn-of-the-century United States made possible by new modes of production and distribution. Some of the large-scale forces that historians of American childhood attach to the emergence of a new youth ideal—such as mass production and the rise of a consumer market for artifacts and experiences—are, in these accounts, sources of cultural change and the emergence of a distinctly modern subjectivity.[46]

Whether they make reference to a "spectacular reality," an "enframing," a "museum effect," a "theme space," or a "double position," these studies take note of how such varied representations, many blending entertainment and education, offered simultaneous immersion in and distance from the subjects they presented, oftentimes virtually transporting audiences to experience a different time, place, or identity. Americans were thrilled by the possibility that they might travel over the Alps from Paris to Rome by panorama, assured that "many gentlemen who have made the tour in very deed have certified to the accuracy of the representation." They were equally enthused by the Biblical scenes from the distant past brought to life in panoramas "second in interest only to an actual tour of Palestine"—as well as in stereoscopic views, in large-scale reenactments such as those of Imrie Kiralfy, and in attractions such as Palestine Park. Accounts of the proliferation of simulated environments and vicarious experiences argue for their significance as merely the most visible signs of larger cultural transformations in which entire societies were being reconstituted around representation. Such shifting perceptual norms and the public conversations about the meaning of reality in an era of proliferating reproductions are recognized as critical foundations for a later mass-mediated world. According to this view, long before Jean Baudrillard proposed that "Disneyland is presented as imaginary in order to make us believe that the rest is real, when in fact all of Los Angeles and the America surrounding it are no longer real, but of the order of the hyperreal and of simulation," these virtual experiences were redefining American life.[47]

World's fairs modeled on European expositions were the central sites for concentrating such cultural products in a single location. The Chicago World's Fair of 1893, which took cues from the 1889 Paris Exposition, assembled a multiplicity of educational amusements, simulated environments, and vicarious experiences spanning diverse times and places inside a "world in miniature." These included a "real African village," a Cairo street "representing faithfully the population of the old City of Egypt in its unimpaired splendor of the days before much modern civilization invaded it," a Native American encampment that was "the most realistic reproduction on the Midway," and an authentic Irish town that was an "exact reproduction (on a scale of two-thirds) of the stronghold of the old McCarthys" including "real Irish sod." Visitors to these and other living villages could examine "real and typical representatives of nearly all the races of the earth, living in their natural methods, practicing their home arts, and presenting their so-called native amusements," as attorney and senator Chauncey Depew put it.[48]

Notably, one could even travel virtually to the exposition itself. "A stereoscopic visit to an exhibition is not at all fatiguing," one journalist reported. "You miss all the worry and expense of travel and get the very choicest views of the fair."[49]

A central message across such displays was the hierarchy of civilizations in which racialized performances lay on a spectrum of societal development. Such exhibits "made America seem anywhere but near," Depew explained, giving observers "an opportunity to investigate these barbarous and semi-civilized civilizations without the unpleasant accompaniments of travel through their countries and contact with their peoples." Indeed, college anthropology students undertook world's fair study tours in lieu of fieldwork in distant climes. They offered a stark contrast to "the progress of our [US] civilization," he concluded, progress that was itself on display as industrial machinery, model prisons, and other exhibits fleshed out the narrative about the superiority of American industrial society.[50]

Despite William George's showmanship and the "living exhibits" on the value of white modernity that the junior citizens supplied to thousands of tourists, neither the George Junior Republic nor youth activities more generally have previously figured in studies of the cultural underpinnings of the modern media age. Yet the thematic and rhetorical continuities across these proliferating educational entertainments and the public talk about mediation they inspired—especially the living villages that were so popular at world's fairs and as traveling exhibitions—make clear that George's contemporaries recognized the resemblances they shared. Young people were routinely part of these attractions, from the babies born to parents who worked in the model

Figure 1.7
Street in Cairo, reproduced for the 1893 Chicago World's Fair.
Source: James W. Shepp and Daniel B. Shepp, *Shepp's World's Fair Photographed* (Chicago: Globe Bible Publishing, 1893).

villages, to the Egyptian youths at school in "Cairo," to the three dozen Native American pupils demonstrating "educational work among the Indians." Public responses to these cultural products typically vacillated between hope and anxiety as hope for new ways to see the world was accompanied by anxieties about the potential loss of authentic experience they represented. Reactions to the George Junior Republic, by contrast, were largely one-sided. George's idea that a "mimic" adult society could serve as a tool for social reform generated great hopes and few concerns, concerns that were largely limited to the details of the dramatization rather than questions about the value of role-playing adulthood itself.[51]

A rare exception appeared in the *Rochester Herald* in summer 1897. A journalist's report on the dirty facilities, hazardous work environment, "improper" mixing of the sexes, and harsh jail punishments was much less flattering than typical republic coverage, prompting the New York State Board of Charities to advise George to reorganize the republic so it resembled a more recognizable institution. Supporters pushed back immediately, insisting the newspaper and the board had missed the point of the entire operation. "Some so-called evils are no evils at all, simply appearances made necessary by the method," they explained. The republic's conditions were designed to replicate the early days of a new colony, so the lack of facilities and the participants' need to make improvements was part of the plan. The recent visitors from Rochester overlooked what other visitors had understood from the republic's inception: "There is the appearance, and also the reality, of great poverty about the camp," journalist Adele Fielde had written. "Everything is cheap, rough and hard, except the spirit that is in it all." So too the miniature prison environment was an essential feature of the republic's unique system, they insisted, one that reduced the likelihood the children would find their way to state prisons for longer sentences in later years. "I don't like this prison part, of course," George admitted, "but there are several hundred other things in the world at large which we do not like, but which seem to be essential. We could have made the prison part milder... but then they would have formed a very wrong impression of the actual State Prison, and we do not wish them to glean the impression that a penal institution is a kind of picnic ground." In any case it was "better to give a boy a few months in prison at the Junior Republic under good influences than two or three years of it at the expense of the state."[52]

The republic's trustees appointed a committee to respond to the charities board and further publicize the republic's unusual approach to child saving, including Professor Jeremiah Jenks and Professor Benjamin Ide Wheeler of Cornell, Professor William Blackman of Yale, Professor John Commons of Syracuse, Thomas Osborne and F. W. Richardson of Auburn, and Frederic Almy of the Charity Organization Society of Buffalo. "We agree, of course, with your committee that there is, in many cases, lack of system, of order, of cleanliness," the committee explained. "But, on the other hand, it must be kept in mind that in many instances, if the plan of reform of the republic is to be carried out, this could not be otherwise." Emphasizing how the republic succeeded because children were "led gradually to adopt these new habits of their own free choice," they noted, "It is a fact that there is found a decided improvement in these particulars among the citizens who have been the longest residents." Their point-by-point counter-report, which laid out the republic's many benefits and suggested George was fully within his rights to delegate such responsibilities to his charges, prompted the agency to back down. Subsequent surveys by the Bureau of Labor and Charities and the Society for the Prevention of Cruelty to Children also rebutted earlier complaints.[53]

Although public portrayals were overwhelmingly positive, the republic was not immune from further criticisms as supporters eagerly suggested how it might be improved. Focusing their attention on how "Some social questions receive a peculiar illustration there," as Jenks put it—the ways in which specific practices in the youth society deviated from their real-world counterparts—they expressed concerns that revisions were required lest George's charges leave with the wrong lessons. "So many of the essential conditions of real life are necessarily wanting at this Junior republic that any attempt to illustrate such vital matters...would probably result in more harm than good," one anonymous author explained in *Gunton's Magazine*, pointing to the lack of opportunity for kids to organize trade unions and strike for better wages, or even to improve production processes by machine. "The vital points necessary to an accurate understanding of the capitalist and wages question are absent in the conditions at the George Junior Republic," he concluded,

> and hence it is far better that no attempt be made to illustrate the workings of this matter than that the boys should be allowed to carry away the wrong-headed ideas which an experiment with such absurdly incomplete conditions would give.... like endeavoring to explain the solar system with the sun left out. The matter is too seriously important to be handled in such as way as to spread misinformation and false, ill-digested ideas among the boys who will eventually have to decide the public policy of the nation in regard to this class of problems.

Others criticized the addition of town meetings to an otherwise national government, full female suffrage, that jobs were always available, and that George owned all of the land. Washington Gladden had other concerns. "Some limit should be placed upon the admission of visitors," he grumbled, because in their presence "the time of the officers is absorbed and the business of the community impeded."[54]

George took these suggestions under advisement as potential future revisions to the republic plan. Yet he stood firm on more than a few of the departures from reality that, in his mind, made the overall experience a more effective tool for teaching the specific lessons he hoped to instill. The town meeting, for example, ensured that more voices could be heard. Work was always available, including the dreaded stone pile, so that kids could learn the value of employment, money, and thrift. Like his contemporaries who organized the living villages at world's fairs—where Native American participants wore anachronistic clothing, sported wigs to hide their modern haircuts, and reenacted rituals long ago discarded in actual Native communities, and where the Cairo street was "not a reproduction of an actual section of Cairo, but a general combination" of typical features to illustrate the premodern city—he too believed that some artifice would ensure more "realism" and hence greater learning. Exhibit organizers, aware of at least some of these irregularities, typically approved them in the service of teaching larger truths. This was a common strategy in other "realistic" media, such as the staged subjects of documentary photographs and films or the panoramas and other thrill rides that eliminated the boring aspects of the travel experience they aimed to duplicate. It was particularly necessary for the republic, wrote Jacob Riis, given that this living village had been "developed not as an amusement but to meet the most fundamental practical problem of sociology—the education of personal character for both individual and social responsibilities." Friend to the republic from its debut, Riis routinely used this strategy himself, staging boy gangs in his famous photographic works on account of the possibility of presenting larger truths about poverty and urban youth.[55]

Next Steps for Freeville

Summer 1897 would prove to be decisive in the institutional history of this anti-institution, in part because of legislation the winter citizens passed. The thirty-two boys and girls had adopted a new constitution that imposed limits on eligibility for elected office by age and length of citizenship. The presidency was reserved for citizens above fifteen, the senate and house for those above thirteen and twelve, respectively. Junior citizens now had to live in the republic for one month before they could stand for election, which all but closed off office-holding opportunities to summer-only youth.[56]

When the customary "tide of immigration" swelled the ranks of the republic's population that summer, these regulations not surprisingly created tensions between the (few) year-round and (more numerous) seasonal citizens, prompting George to contemplate constructing two separate camps. Under the leadership of President Smith, elected during the winter months and by this time a Sunday school teacher headed to Cornell to study law and sociology, the tension between summer and year-round residents gave the populations of largely immigrant youth a sense of how native-born Americans felt about the newcomers in their midst. Guided by William Dapping, the criminal court focused its activities on the summer citizens. But the year-round citizens' conviction that length of term in the republic was closely associated with mastery of the lessons in civics and character education that were the juvenile democracy's raison d'être led George instead to make the republic a year-round only operation.[57]

Although in its initial years the Freeville republic was a temporary community, it eventually established itself on a permanent basis. The young citizens further extended the probationary period for office-holding to three months. And they collaborated with George, who now envisioned a more substantial campus of cottages, each "accommodating ten or fifteen citizens, instead of the existing large barracks and tents," to further develop the republic's physical plant. Fifty-three stayed on in winter 1897–1898 to make the transition. Many more wished to but could not secure adequate funds.[58]

The decision to become a year-round institution gave George greater control over participating youth as parents signed over their children for indeterminate sentences. It simultaneously presented him with a new funding challenge. His wife, frustrated that "much of the money expended during summer by business manager could have been saved," suggested there would be significant cost reductions if money "that was spent on men's work" was allocated to other expenses while formerly men's tasks were assigned to the youth. "Several large boys, who are extremely useful... have more than paid their way by work they have done, which men would have had to be hired for if they had not been here," she explained, noting for example that among their accomplishments "over 700 ft of ditch has been done by Mr. George and the boys, water pipes and sewer and drainage pipes laid accordingly."[59]

These savings aside, greater resources were needed to expand republic programming. George's efforts to publicize its good works went into overdrive with help from colleagues at the association. A growing network of supporters beyond the social gospel and good government movements offered money and publicity for the Freeville institution. Prominent businessmen, including John Rockefeller and Andrew Carnegie, who feared labor unrest, rallied behind the republic's instruction in capitalism, offering assistance via board service and financial contributions. Social scientists, working in a period when description and prescription were deeply entangled, expressed great interest in how the republic might help them devise better theory and practice alike. Women's clubs, a relatively new form of voluntary organization, organized an auxiliary association. The Daughters of the American Revolution were great enthusiasts; so too were advocates for female suffrage. Complete strangers sent George donations in the mail as well. Despite ongoing financial concerns, the republic did not accept every offer of assistance. In 1896, William Randolph Hearst's *New York Journal* attempted to organize a campaign to raise money for the republic to compete with the *Tribune*'s Fresh Air Fund. The republic board rejected his help.[60]

With growing support came still more publicity, and then an ever-longer waiting list. As George and the republic's young district attorney told one audience in 1899, there were four hundred eager applicants for only fifty-five spots. Other reform institutions such as orphanages and reform schools were being roundly criticized for failing to adequately prepare inmates to participate in the real world. "The longer he is in the Asylum, the less likely he is to do well in outside life," Children's Aid Society founder Charles Loring Brace put it, observing how dysfunctional institutional cultures were poor instructors for future success and that even model inmates could become lost when introduced into social conditions of real life beyond their institutions. By

Figure 1.8
George Junior Republic, contractors digging a ditch.
Source: William George, *The Junior Republic: Its History and Ideals* (New York: Appleton, 1910).

contrast, the George Junior Republic's simultaneous resemblance to and yet separation from "real life" dazzled the public and the reform community. So too did the affection participants held for its approach to self-improvement; they created an alumni association in 1898 and an annual town meeting day for former citizens to return.[61]

These widening circles of discussion opened a conversation about duplicating the republic and the dramatizations of adult life it supplied that transformed George's experiment from a unique curiosity to the motive force for a movement. A prophecy on New Year's Eve as 1899 gave way to 1900 suggested to George that one hundred years in the future there would be junior states across America, all members of a larger junior nation. These programs' success would upend Americans' approach to juvenile reform such that there would be "no reform schools, no Homes with a capital H," and boarding schools would routinely embrace such methods as well. The nation itself would be improved, as graduates served honorably in congress and industry, and communities stocked with populations with republic experience would "be remarkable for their local government." This prophecy would prove highly influential, guiding George's work for the rest of his life.[62]

As talk of a possible republic movement continued, one of this conversation's central assumptions—that the simultaneous immersion in and distance from experiences that so fascinated adult patrons of wax museums, panoramas, and other modern entertainments held special benefits for the nation's youth—soon inflected discussions about the republic's component activities as well. For lost in much of the early excitement about George's work was the fact that, like many other "recombinant" inventors, he had not ignored the era's existing youth activities in his work. As George had tapped into the cultural fascination with representation, he had repackaged a scattered suite of approaches to handling young people as components of a total youth society that removed them from the political and economic worlds of adults and substituted a supervised simulation instead. Like living villages and stereoscopes, these too had old-world origins, but in George's hands they became part of a uniquely American institution.[63]

How aware George was of precedents at the outset of the republic remains an open question; only later in his career did he devote attention to finding out. John Commons, whose Syracuse University class did an independent study of the republic, was one of the first to publically recognize how it "carries to a consistent extreme" ideas that theorists and practitioners in "charity, penology, and pedagogy" had been urging for more than a decade—if not that what the youth congress, token economy, manual training, children's gardens, youth court, boy militia, model kitchens, and juvenile publishing shared went beyond anecdotal evidence about their effects on civics and character education. Each of these components of the total republic experience, already tried at reformatories, schools, boys clubs, girls clubs, settlements, young men's voluntary associations, camps, and asylums, now gave young people simultaneous access to a protected childhood and a virtual adulthood—a double life that introduced them to modern subjectivity as well. As much as the founding of the republic, this new way of thinking about its component activities as role-plays of adulthood would be a lasting legacy of George's work. How the effort to grow the republic movement became part of a larger conversation among developmental psychologists and educators about young people's natural penchant for living double lives, and how a new emphasis on realistic roles versus realistic environments expanded the significance of such component activities in sculpting these instincts to positive ends, are the subjects of chapter 2.[64]

2 Stages of Childhood

In a 1902 lecture to the Harvard Teachers Union, Clark University president and psychology professor G. Stanley Hall praised the George Junior Republic for placing pedagogy on scientific grounds. "Children are imitative to a degree that neither they nor teachers have until lately dreamed of," he told the assembled crowd. Their play "mirrors and epitomizes life.... The play world reproduces in rudimentary form the serious business of both primitive and modern man." Observing how curricular innovations such as home economics, nature study, and student government channeled young people's imitative instincts toward pedagogical ends, he lamented that only reformatories and industrial schools for "negroes and Indians" routinely provided such programming in "knowing by doing." His former student John Dewey's laboratory school was now pilot-testing role-plays of past eras' adult activities to teach history, although the results "from this most fascinating experiment" had yet to be seen. The George Junior Republic, the Hampton Institute, and the Carlisle Indian School, by contrast, already had demonstrated how the "natural stimulus of education" could be "such a power in the world."[1]

Why, at the turn of the century, would Hall vest greater confidence in the Freeville republic than in John Dewey's laboratory school, calling it a model boarding school and suggesting it was organized around principles of child development, when William George was not trained in psychology and was adamant that the republic was not, in fact, a school? And why did Hall see affinities between the republic and so many other educational institutions given its fringe status in histories of the period? This chapter describes early efforts to copy George's republic and how these proliferating youth societies became part of a larger conversation among psychologists and educators about the developmental and pedagogical functions of role-playing adulthood in the modern age. During a period when schools already were experimenting with a variety of curricular innovations to bring new populations into the educational system and keep them engaged, junior republics fit well to supplement or even coordinate these programs. As George worked to transform his republic from a summer camp to a year-round operation, his friend Wilson Gill demonstrated how such juvenile societies could be introduced into schools and the comparatively greater importance of realistic vicarious experiences over realistic simulated environments in teaching their lessons.[2]

Histories of the shift from family economy to sheltered childhood have noted turn-of-the-century ties between developmental psychology and the school modernization movement known as the "new education." They highlight the important work from G. Stanley Hall and John Dewey to identify young people's natural play instincts as the bases for a child-centered curriculum that directed pupils' energy and attention and expanded in-school populations. Neither the George Junior Republic nor the dramatizations of adult life at the center of its curriculum figure in these accounts.

Yet in an era when anthropologists and sociologists viewed cultural transmission as imitation in "primitive" and "modern" societies, and psychologists proposed that the "double consciousness" previously associated with pathological states was a normal feature of identity, the human sciences offered biological rationales for the appeal of educational entertainments that offered vicarious access to alternative times, places, and selves—and the modern subjectivity that resulted. In their theories of playworlds and recapitulation in which young people reproduced past and present adult occupations, and their philosophy of learning by doing in which students were simultaneously virtual adults at work and young people at play, psychologists and educators including Hall and Dewey attest to how the era's common wisdom about mediated experience and the making of modern youth as a biological and social category were linked. The equal attention, across these professions, to vicarious experiences of adulthood alongside sheltered childhood suggests why Hall, like so many contemporaries, saw the Freeville republic typifying a modern approach to education.[3]

More Republics Needed

Word spread quickly about the junior republic's novel approach and with it interest in duplicating George's work. The question on many minds was whether Freeville's success depended on Daddy George's charisma or if there might be generalizable principles for replicating the republic's results. George initially had little to offer on this question. Flooded by requests to establish new republics, he hesitated, believing Freeville "a very crude and imperfect embodiment" of his ideas. He focused instead on local improvements: expanding the physical plant, setting up a school, and replacing tents and barracks with cottage housing. (The school's existence gave George further ammunition for his argument that the republic was not a school.) The junior citizens took responsibility for many of these tasks. Peterboro Avenue, for example, was "the most popular rendezvous on the grounds—the broad piazza nearly surrounding the Republic Building," reported the *Junior Citizen*, noting that "Daddy and the citizens love [it] best because from nail to paint it was made almost wholly by the boys." Financial needs were a continuing concern. As George confessed, "There has never been a time in its history when there was enough money in its treasury to carry it beyond the current month, and frequently not even that." Board members, friends, and citizens helped with publicity and fundraising, as when ten-year-old republic mail carrier Billy Zavenski joined Thomas Osborne on the stereopticon lecture circuit.[4]

As George demurred, impatient admirers set out to discover the mechanism that made the republic work. Many of them, noting its origins in a fresh air camp and the environmental theories of behavior that inspired it, believed the republic worked because it removed children from slum environments to a pastoral setting. "They were not all of the highest type of childhood that the mind can imagine," wrote one observer, but two months in the country "enjoying the fresh air and beauty of the trees and flowers...brought them nearer to it than they would have come if they had been obliged to endure the stifling air and shabby streets of the poorer parts of the metropolis." Situating poverty and juvenile delinquency in social environments rather than individual biologies, these admirers were hopeful about the possibilities for changing lives. As journalist Adele Fielde put it, "A thing that is being proven in the experience of the Junior Republic is the truth that it is not heredity so much as environment that makes a child good or bad." Many of the children "had been punished as criminals before they were snatched away from the corrupting influences of the slums," concurred the *New York Evangelist*. "In the Republic are children whose heredity is as bad as it well can be and who two years ago were living out their inborn characteristics as vagabonds and actually criminals who now are law abiding, hard-working, honest child-citizens. All they needed...was a favorable environment" for their metamorphoses to begin.[5]

The earliest efforts to duplicate the republic followed this line of thinking. In summer 1896, former boys club manager and Boys Brigade leader Edward Bradley, having learned of George's work from colleagues at Chicago's Hull House, accompanied approximately a dozen orphan boys, aged twelve to sixteen, into the Illinois countryside to found a juvenile democracy. The children, removed from the dangers of life in Chicago, became citizens of a "Chicago on a small scale" on the prairie, much like the actual city in its earliest days. They called the miniature municipality Allendale after Cicero Allen, first owner of the land on which they settled. Facilities were spare: a single cottage served as city headquarters and dining hall. To fund the summer program the boys let out the other cottages on the site to vacationers and slept in tents. Outdoor recreational activities such as boating, swimming, and outdoor games fleshed out the summer experience.[6]

"Cap" Bradley initially placed himself in the key political positions, serving as mayor and judge with the boys in other posts. The campers established a bank and local currency and got to work cooking, farming, housekeeping, and selling farm goods to vacationers to earn their room and board. Bradley encouraged entrepreneurship, and the boys responded with enthusiasm. "Nearly everything necessary for the maintenance of the farm is done by the citizens under contract," one early visitor described. "Wood carrying, garbage removal, and half a dozen other things are advertised and bid for." Gardening was a particularly lucrative business. Boys could rent one of six garden plots and grow produce for "the public dining hall in the 'Auditorium Hotel,' as the main cottage is called [after a Chicago hotel], and to the 'resorters' in the various cottages." Each citizen "was allowed every freedom to exercise his money-making talent, if he had any." Thus while "one had a bootblack stand, some were painters, and some were carpenters," others took more creative approaches, including lending money at higher interest rates than the republic bank and paying youths low wages for contract work.

> Not long ago one of these capitalists had a contract to dig a ditch of some size on the property. His bid of $2.50 was far enough under all other estimates to assure him the work. He then engaged a number of laborers at 20 cents an hour, the highest rate paid, and sat on the grass and watched them work. Labor cost him $1.25, and he made a like amount on the deal...under the laws of the republic, it is impossible to force the contractor to do any work himself.[7]

Allendale soon encountered the economic problems that had faced Freeville: "Capitalists a Problem" the *Chicago Daily Tribune* declared. Yet Bradley's enthusiasm that a simulated society provided an ideal environment for youth reform was undiminished. The boys' equal enthusiasm persuaded him to continue Allendale after summer's end. Bradley took up residency in Chicago's recently opened Kirkland Settlement and reestablished the miniature municipality there. Returning to the city was less than ideal: settlement facilities could not accommodate a residential component and stifled possibilities for a robust economic system. He worried about the boys' fate in a potentially corrosive urban setting.[8]

Bradley made the most of the situation, running Allendale as an evening program for a larger population. Seventy-five boys aged twelve to seventeen (some in school, some working, and some simply roaming the streets) participated, holding elections at six-week intervals to cycle youth through the diverse posts. Civil service exams made the system more selective. With several boys having stayed on, Bradley turned over to them the mayoral office while continuing as president himself. Winter citizens were freed from the expense of room and board, so Bradley abandoned the economic system. Instead, he arranged industrial classes in pressed iron work, whittling, carpentry, and electricity at a nearby two-flat to familiarize the boys with a range of adult occupations.[9]

The observers who characterized the wintertime "city within a city" in language that echoed depictions of its summertime setting did not sway Bradley from his preference for a rural location. "Getting the boys away from their [urban] environment" and "molding their lives upon entirely different lines," was essential so that they might have "a chance to get away from their bad habits." As the weather improved, he moved Allendale to rural Lake Villa, Illinois, making it into a full-time operation from summer 1897 with financial help from industrialist Cyrus McCormick and a women's auxiliary.[10]

The importance of pastoral settings for improving the physical and moral health of urban youth, particularly immigrants, was a common theme in other early republic-building efforts. Public talk about "farm republics" modeled on agrarian villages inspired modifications of the farm school idea, as in the Industrial Colony Association's nearby experiment on the "county plan." Boston area pastor William Forbush created the "USA" for boys in his Christian Endeavor summer camp. Observers surveying the landscape of youth-oriented programs suggested that other "duplicates" predated the Freeville settlement. At Baltimore's McDunough Farm School and Boston's Farm School, for example, boy-run societies had emerged on students' own initiative years before William George was a household name.[11]

Cottage Row appeared in 1888 on the playground at Boston's Farm School, one of the first US educational institutions to offer agricultural and industrial training. By 1897, when George's republic became a year-round operation, Boston boys already had built a village of cottages, a city hall and library, and a "zoological museum" to house the school's pets. Virtual property ownership was central to the playground economy, with the result that "knowledge of deeds, mortgages, certificates of stock and the transference of property" was part of its informal curriculum. Journalist Max Bennett Thrasher recounted,

> One winter while I was there when property was low, two boys who were both good carpenters bought a small run-down cottage as a speculation. When it came spring, they repaired it thoroughly and painted it. Then they advertised it to be sold at auction, held the sale, though neither of them had ever been at an auction in his life, and cleared $2.50 by the deal.

Figure 2.1
Cottage Row and some of its property owners.
Source: H. Bruce Addington, "A Vocational School a Hundred Years Old," *Outlook*, July 28, 1915.

The Beacon, the students' newspaper, featured regular reports on such property transfers and how enterprising boys created businesses as architects and builders to contract work for peers. Hundreds of visitors came annually to see the playground city in operation. Hearing talk of its similarities to George's republic, headmaster Charles Bradley visited Freeville in 1896.[12]

Meanwhile, George, who now recognized the difficulty of stopping determined imitators, devised a scheme for settling new republics, a testimonial to his confidence in young people's capabilities and his frustrations that most adults took a different view. "The task of securing suitable men as superintendants or head workers, men who realized that the great art of running the Republic was not to run it at all" was difficult, he later observed, so instead he deputized experienced junior citizens as "pioneers" for the new communities, giving them "the same practical training that would be given to a colony about to migrate to a new country." In 1897, they founded the Carter Junior Republic in rural Redington, Pennsylvania. Citizens 21, 35, 45, and 61 made themselves "useful therein...rendering valuable service in organizing that new Republic, along the lines of our Commonwealth." Others settled a National Junior Republic in Annapolis, Maryland, which opened in 1899.[13]

Establishing new institutions was a slow process, however, and admirers were eager to create republics at a faster pace. Although Edward Bradley did not enjoy Allendale's temporary Chicago setting, another man, aware of the difficulties George had encountered with his initial fresh air camp, thought that the growing array of institutions that already tended urban youth might offer the movement fresh possibilities. This was George's friend Wilson Gill, who had visited Freeville and had an alternative explanation for the republic's success. In Gill's view it was the opportunity for young people to replicate adult roles at a distance from the worlds of adults, rather than the pastoral, village-like location where they did so, that mattered most to the outcomes so many praised. One of the era's emerging breed of technocratic reformers who challenged the primacy of social gospel methods, Gill determined that schools would be the ideal place to test his hypothesis about the possibility of piggybacking junior republics on the programming at institutions that already engaged immigrant and indigent youth.

From Junior Republics to School Cities

Gill, a businessman and engineer, began his reform career as a participant in the good government movement, with special interest in municipal improvement. This was his point of contact with William George. Disappointed by his own voter education efforts in the 1880s, Gill was among the Goo Goos who turned their attention to civic education for youth. After a brief collaboration with the Daughters and Sons of the American Revolution, he established the Patriotic League in 1891 to improve civics instruction in schools. Around this time he also led the charge to construct a children's building at the 1893 World's Columbian Exposition in Chicago to bring the latest in scientific knowledge about child-rearing to mass audiences.[14]

Chapter 1 described how world's fairs exemplified the environments and experiences whose proliferation made visible the emergence of a distinctly modern subjectivity. Scholars of media and modernity have argued that, in gathering together educational entertainments from living villages to industrial machinery, events such as Chicago's 1893 World's Columbian Exposition exposed audiences to a packaged and "spectacularized" reality that soon defined the broader experience of moving through the modern world. For historians of youth, the Chicago fair is significant as the launch pad for the mother study clubs which translated developmental psychology into guidance for women who increasingly took seriously the profession of raising kids.[15]

Missing from these accounts are connections between modern subjectivity and the exposition's youth-focused programs, connections that contextualize the popularity of the junior republic idea. If the young people attending school in the fair's living villages help to explain why the miniature United States run by kids in Freeville became a tourist attraction, the opportunities for young people to play house, practice military maneuvers, and learn manual skills at the fair's children's building attest to the era's growing interest in educational activities that enabled young people to vicariously experience adult occupations within a distinctly children's space. Gill's view that "Childhood is the real life, as much as manhood or womanhood," and yet simultaneously that "Every little girl is a little woman, every little boy a little man," and the fair's opportunities for kids to explore building-block activities of the soon-to-be established George Junior Republic, suggests that his thinking was moving in a parallel direction even before George's republic debuted.[16]

Gill's chance to pilot school republics came in February 1897. As he worked with the Patriotic League "to lay out a course of instruction in citizenship sufficiently simple for young schoolchildren," Bernard Cronson, a New York City educator and league chapter president, solicited his advice about a situation at the West Farms School. Students were out of control. Administrators had stationed a police officer in the playground to address the worsening situation, to no avail. Gill suggested to Cronson that the school modify George's junior republic plan. The pupils elected a president and officials, including truant officers and health inspectors. With the responsibility for discipline placed in the hands of the most unruly pupils, order was swiftly restored. The transformation at West Farms underscored how republics need not be confined to countryside settings, inspiring Gill to press for more republics inside New York City schools.[17]

He approached fellow Goo Goo and Patriotic League board member R. Fulton Cutting. Cutting headed the New York Association for Improving the Conditions of the Poor, which administered the city's summer vacation schools. Reporting on the West Farms experiment, Gill hypothesized that "school republics" could reach the same populations that George's republic had targeted but at much lower cost because there were neither facilities to build nor staff to hire. Cutting offered Gill the Norfolk Street vacation school, where about 1,200 immigrant children ages five to fifteen spent the summer months, mostly "Russian, Polish, or Hungarian Jews, unpromising material, it might have seemed, for educational experiments." Gill organized the students as a city government based on the soon-to-be-consolidated Greater New York. He called this plan the School City and later the School Republic. Each class became an election district, with groups of classrooms forming boroughs. Boys and girls were eligible to vote, a decision taken not on account of girls' activism, but rather Goo Goos' belief in the possibilities for "purification" that female suffrage represented. The pupils chose a mayor and common council and a range of other elected and appointed officials as well, including health inspectors, police, judges, and a court clerk. Teachers and administrators granted the city's charter, and served as appeals court judges and as representatives to the board of health (alongside the student mayor and police commissioner).[18]

With the Norfolk Street's curriculum already prioritizing manual training, the school republic's major business was government itself. Norfolk's juvenile citizens greeted the experiment with enthusiasm and got to work passing legislation. Many reflected the Goo Goo agenda, which prioritized cleanliness and administrative rationality. Ordinances targeted students who littered or came to school untidy, assigning them to pick up waste around the school. Repeat violators and students who defaced school property faced expulsion. Teachers gave students a wide berth to design this legal system as well as opportunities to revise their laws.[19]

Although the school grounds comprised these young officials' primary jurisdiction, pupils occasionally brought their role-plays into the surrounding community. Student police, for example, arrested truants outside school bounds. The health department printed leaflets for community distribution, "not the serious and scientific leaflets of the larger [NYC health] department, but bright and popular pamphlets suited to the neighborhood," reflecting the Patriotic League's secondary goal to reach parents through their kids.[20]

Compressing space and time, Gill's school-based republic thus refocused attention away from the realism of the juvenile democracy's environment to the realism of the roles the junior citizens played. Well connected to New York City officials thanks to his municipal reform work, Gill asked colleagues who occupied the offices the children were mimicking for guidance. Police and sanitation department heads Theodore Roosevelt and George Waring, both of whom already had close relationships with William George, were especially eager to help, offering official assistance to the pupils. Mayor William Strong also visited the school.[21]

Colonel Waring went the furthest in building ties between the two New York cities on account of how Gill's methods resonated with administrative changes he was making at the city's street cleaning department, as well as his ongoing efforts to advise Freeville's street cleaning brigade. Waring had recently implemented an early form of industrial democracy, creating an elected board of members to hear disciplinary cases and grievances. He also had recently launched a juvenile street cleaning league to enlist young New Yorkers in patrolling neighborhood streets. Waring sent staff from his office to help the pupils organize their street cleaning corps, encouraging them to remain in the role off campus, policing their neighborhoods and instructing their parents about local ordinances and the importance of clean streets.[22]

As journalistic coverage and visitors from near and far spread word of this low-cost republic adaptation, other New York educators proposed introducing school republics more widely that academic year. And so, in fall 1897, as George was transforming the Freeville republic from a summer program to a year-round operation and training youth to settle new George Junior Republics, Gill worked along a parallel path. Envisioning primary, grammar, and high schools across the city participating, first as independent school cities and subsequently as collaborative state and national school governments, he rallied his local government contacts to help flesh out the details of his plan. Describing Gill's intention "that the pupils shall get a good idea of the actual work and purpose of the real city department whose name it bears," a journalist for *The Sun* reported how "In order to bring this about nearly every city department has been asked to aid in preparing the rules for the mimic city government."[23]

At the core of the team's proposals was maximizing the numbers exposed to vicarious municipal work. New York City schools served nearly 1,500 students on average. The plan was to add officials so that up to 200 kids could simultaneously participate in governing schools. Monthly elections ensured that kids experienced a variety of civic occupations. In Alfred Beebe's proposal for the board of health, for example, a president, a commissioner, the president of the police board, a secretary, a sanitary superintendent, five assistant sanitary superintendents, ten food inspectors, fifteen sanitary inspectors, five hygiene inspectors, and several medical inspectors, together with a squad of ten sanitary policemen commanded by a sergeant were charged with health matters:

> The food inspectors," says the sanitary code, "shall inspect all articles of food and drink brought into the city for consumption within its limits. They shall give information to citizens regarding properly preparing food for consumption and for removal of the decayed parts of fruit, etc. The hygiene inspectors shall examine the citizens with reference to cleanliness of face and hands, condition of hair, condition of clothes in respect to cleanliness, neatness, repair, etc. The sanitary inspectors shall inspect the condition of desks, school books, clothes, closets, toilets, etc., as to neatness and cleanliness, They shall prevent spitting on the floors, staircases, etc., and shall warn citizens against spitting on sidewalks or elsewhere, except into proper receptacles, and then only when absolutely necessary. The medical inspectors shall examine the citizens daily, immediately after they enter the city, and shall report to the assistant sanitary superintendant the names of any who do not feel well. The sanitary police are to enforce the regulations, and reports are to be made. Verbal reports on the part of each assistant

sanitary superintendent to the proper teachers each morning in regard to those citizens who do not feel well, and warnings and complaints are to be issued.[24]

Gill lacked George's hesitations about spreading the gospel of youth self-government. Informal support from many principals convinced him to eschew official channels for curricular reforms in favor of promoting school cities' voluntary adoption. Unfortunately, his colleagues failed to complete the promised plans. As the school year got underway in 1897, civil service commissioners were still preparing examination questions, police had not completed a security program, and the charities commissioner had barely begun his work. (Even Waring was delinquent drafting an expanded street cleaning organization.) School administrators thus took on the organizational burden. Gill prepared a model charter to share with school boards and administrations in support of these efforts. Philadelphia school board president Simon Gratz was among the first to use it in 1898, reworking the charter to match local laws. After a pilot project at the Hollingsworth elementary school, the board endorsed school cities for all two dozen area institutions. Elsewhere—for example, in Omaha, Nebraska—school cities appeared on a case-by-case basis.[25]

The following year, Gill prepared "An Outline of American Government for Use in City and Country Schools in Connection with the Gill School City and Other Organizations for Self Government" (1899) together with fellow Goo Goo Delos Wilcox, a

Figure 2.2
Counting the votes, Kellom School, Omaha.
Source: Albert Shaw, "The School City—A Method of Pupil Self Government," *Review of Reviews* 20 (1899).

handbook pairing civics instruction with advice on starting a school city. The school city was a natural fit to a civics curriculum that aimed to stamp out bossism and assimilate immigrants, they explained, contrasting the democratic educational methods of school republics with the monarchical systems of immigrants' countries of origin as well as the autocratic methods so typical of American schools. A simplified New York City government supplied a template for adaptation to local settings. The authors encouraged schools to begin with government on a small scale such as the ward or even the city and then, through institutional partnerships, to scale up to school states and eventually nations. And they addressed educators beyond urban districts, suggesting school villages or school towns for rural and smaller communities. This expanded focus reflected Gill's conviction that the structure of republics mattered more than their location and that middle-class native-born students could profit from vicarious civic learning as much as immigrant and indigent youth. William George shared this view; the Freeville republic had recently begun accepting better-off junior citizens to defray costs for those without means.[26]

Thanks to Gill's handbook and his occasional hands-on assistance, school-based republics proliferated across the US. They did so with one major departure from his well-documented plans, however. Gill had speculated in 1899 that, thanks to close collaboration with local officials, the school city would be "not a moot or play city, but, when undertaken with the right spirit and authority," would be "a branch of the government of the State." School cities, in short, were an indirect route to the broader governmental reform the Goo Goos sought. Yet as the difficulties Gill had faced securing local officials' commitment to design the program proved to be a common obstacle, school administrators around the country followed their New York City colleagues and abandoned such collaborations.[27]

The Enthusiasm Builds

Even before the turn of the century, then, a diversity of junior republics were operating: rural and urban, residential and nonresidential, single sex and coed, part-time and year-round, some modeled on the federal government and others on municipalities, some with an economic system and others oriented around the business of politics alone. Despite these differences their effects followed those of the original George Junior Republic. Junior police and juvenile courts, and youth-made laws, transformed institutional discipline. At New York City's PS 125, for example, where police chief Rocco Montemora wasn't "much over three feet high," truants no longer went missing. "He only gets the cases pronounced incorrigible by the school attendance officer, a man of middle age and experience, but he is sure to find the truant if he is still within the district." Court rulings there were "obeyed without question, though the prisoners are often great hulking bullies and the judges are only three winsome little girls." Pupils

Figure 2.3
Truancy squad, PS 125, New York City.
Source: Bernard Cronson, *Pupil Self-Government: Its Theory and Practice* (New York: Macmillan, 1907).

clearly possessed "a knowledge of the Italian small boy" among others, "that would be of advantage to many a judge in the Children's Court."[28]

In republics with economic systems young people saw firsthand the results of hard work, thrift, and entrepreneurship. At Allendale, for example, one savvy boy contractor profited from his fellow citizens' ditch-digging work. Another boy had "worked up a considerable reputation as an attorney," and was said to be "as sharp to take advantage" of any situation "as the most experienced lawyer." Still another, seeking to capitalize on the boys' frustration with the high cost of board at the Auditorium, opened Blanchard's Cafeteria. "His charges are reasonable," one journalist recounted, "but it is not often that a boarder stays long with him, for the fare consists wholly and invariably of beans."[29]

School cities and republics lacking economic systems taught similar lessons, many observers proposed. "If you could have seen the actual work done in these conventions, common council meetings, court trials, etc., you would be surprised—at least I was—at the business methods employed most earnestly by the children," Milwaukee principal R. J. O'Hanlan confirmed. "Perfect decorum in their relations to each other and yet freedom enough to make interesting sessions with very ordinary routine work of legislation, election, trials, etc.," he noted. "I cannot begin to tell you of the great amount

Figure 2.4
Elections, 21st District School, Milwaukee.
Source: Albert Shaw, "The School City—A Method of Pupil Self Government," *Review of Reviews* 20 (1899).

of interest taken in practical affairs by those pupils who had the initial training in the School City." Some, such as Cronson's West Farms school, added school banks to teach financial lessons in the absence of paid occupations.[30]

Republics thus turned individual and community values upside down as the worst-behaved children became schools' best civic leaders and the youth who previously received charity became charitable donors. Marie Parola, the "terror of Grammar School No. 1, New York City," was elected councilman in fall 1897, to her teacher's dismay. The principal advised Marie's instructor "to wait until the following morning," when the children would "find out how men get rid of the wrong man when he's elected." These anxieties turned out to be unwarranted: "Marie appeared punctually, the first time in weeks. She was tidily dressed, and amiable in affection to her fellow-pupils and deference to her teacher." Two years later, "she was still a model, and to-day she is a young woman of many charms, all due to her election as alderman from her school room." At Allendale, one boy "capitalist" gave all his money to start "a hospital fund for 'indigent boys'" before leaving for a foster placement.[31]

Across these juvenile democracies, participating youth appeared to be having fun as such transformations took place. "Wherever the School City is tried the periodical election of officers awakens more intense interest than the most exciting ball game," journalist Albert Shaw explained." Ten years of Cottage Row "shows that this is not only the most fascinating play which the boys can have," but "they become more thoroughly versed in the practical duties of citizenship than many adult voters ever become." The USA, reported Forbush, was "received with delight by the boys." Like the children who left Freeville and subsequently wrote to George of their homesickness for republic life, boys brought to Allendale and other youthful republics rejected opportunities to return home and considered expulsion the greatest possible punishment.[32]

To be clear, these miniature democracies were no more utopian than Freeville. Replicating adult life meant that corrupt practices could be found. In one Philadelphia school city, "boys were administering their particular school city government just as the men were administering their government in the city of Philadelphia" such that "'pull' and a certain amount of graft prevailed," and the police were "lax for a certain number of peanuts, or for so much candy or a top, or something else." Nor could every child be reformed. At the National Republic, the jail was "the most popular part of the institution."[33]

Given time to play out the consequences of such corrupt practices, however, the vast majority appeared to improve, leading observers to encourage adults to follow the example set by these youth. "When they take their places as real citizens in the United States" Freeville youth would "be more intelligent than nine-tenths of those who cast their ballot." There was "more real self-government in these school cities than in most of our larger cities," social reformer and vocational guidance advocate Frank Parsons concluded, "for there is no apathy in the school city, no stay-at-home vote, no political machine or boss." Ballots marked by eleven- to fifteen-year-olds "were remarkably free from mistakes, both as to marks and folding," praised a California journalist. "There is not a single precinct in Alameda that could have done so well." Goo Goo and New York City minister Thomas Slicer suggested to the National Municipal League that city charters follow the streamlined model that Gill and Wilcox prepared, "uninvaded by the details which have been the cause of confusion and misunderstanding and contradiction in so many charters of American cities."[34]

These outcomes settled the argument as to how republics worked. Countryside settings were "picturesque in the extreme." But more important, the proliferating media coverage now suggested, was for each republic to supply opportunities to learn by experience, to enable young people to perform realistic adult roles in a youth society that maintained some sort of separation from adults. These adultlike roles could be ones such as police detective, hotel maid, soldier, or farmer—jobs formerly held by youth. Or they could be roles such as mayor, judge, or assessor, positions long restricted to adults. Whatever the role, its status as an experience that was simultaneously real and not real, both a protected childhood and virtual adulthood, was key. "The scheme has the fascination of a play for the children and appeals to their love of imitation and 'make-believe,' yet it is not a mock government," a contributor to *Congregationalist* explained. Although participating youth were not actual government officials, inside these child administered societies they governed their peers.

> There are always numerous candidates for appointment on the school police force; and this is owing doubtless to the normal instinct that impels children to play at being policemen, firemen, or other familiar functionaries. But the larger interest in the matter doubtless grows out of the fact that the school policemen make real arrests for real offenses. The trials of the arrested offenders involve the enforcement of real rules and regulations that the school community has adopted for its own well-being. The sentences that are pronounced by the court mean real punishment of some kind that is no more a part of a children's game than are the punishments meted out under the municipal government to disorderly persons arraigned before the police magistrates.

Thus, while their actions were "shielded from more serious and lasting consequences which would follow him into the world," simultaneously "a child learns and feels the consequences of his acts." Like so many other marvels of the modern age, then, the magic of republics lay in how they enabled young people to inhabit multiple realities at once.[35]

Bringing Developmental Psychology to the Republic Conversation

By calling attention to the comparatively greater significance of realistic roles versus realistic environments in supplying young people access to a "double life," Gill shifted the terms of the conversation away from what republics looked like to the adultlike experiences they supplied. In so doing he suggested affinities to the era's educational entertainments. Equally, he brought conversations about republics closer to ongoing discussions about young people's natural affinity for playing at adulthood and the possible applications for this knowledge taking place within developmental psychology, a field whose stature soared after the 1893 World's Fair.[36]

Turn-of-the-century child studies are closely associated with G. Stanley Hall. Trained in Europe, Hall was a pioneer in American psychology and education, founding the leading journals in both fields, the *American Journal of Psychology* and the *Pedagogical Seminary*. Motivated by a desire to identify the general principles that organized development from birth to adulthood, and particularly interested in adolescents' "rebirth," Hall and his students studied young people in their everyday worlds. Their systematic investigations of youth at play grew from the belief that in an era of increasingly supervised youth activities, play expressed children's natural biological instincts. They tabulated information on boys' and girls' play at different ages and analyzed the implications for mental, moral, social, and physical growth. What these scientists saw and how they interpreted it reflected trends across the era's human sciences, which placed imitation at the center of societal and individual development and posited the existence of multiple simultaneous realities in the self and in the world.[37]

Anthropologists and sociologists, with ambitions to understand patterns of cultural transmission and societal evolution, had recently determined that imitation lay at the heart of these interpersonal processes and indeed social reality itself. The process of imitation, Gabriel Tarde explained, was like a "quasi-photographic reproduction of a cerebral image upon the sensitive plate of another brain," suggesting analogy between humans and machines. Although he subscribed to common views about evolutionary hierarchies separating past and present cultures, Tarde contended that such reproductions were found across industrial and pre-industrial societies, monarchies and democracies alike. "Civilized peoples flatter themselves with thinking that they have escaped from this dogmatic slumber," he noted, finding similarities between these imitations and hypnotic states, also referred to as somnambulism. "Society is imitation and imitation is a kind of somnambulism," Tarde famously declared, inspiring empirical studies that elaborated how the "primitive" and "civilized" societies that shared mimetic instincts expressed them in decidedly different ways (for example, using effigies versus advertising), how the body was a medium that filtered information, and why despite the dominance of imitation in social relations everyone was not exactly the same. Imitative action, in short, was a valuable concept for explaining much of human experience, concluded US education commissioner William T. Harris.

> [It] explains the mode in which the individual man unites with his fellow men to form a social whole. It introduces us to the formation of institutions, the family, civil community, the state, the church—those greater selves which reinforce the little selves of isolated individuals. For the study of imitation leads to the discovery of the modes by which the individual man repeats for himself the thinking and doing and feeling of his fellows, and thus enriches his own life by adding to it the lives of others. Thus his own life becomes vicarious for others, and he participates vicariously in the life of the society.[38]

Colleagues in psychology were inspired by this work as they turned their attention to identity development. James Mark Baldwin employed biological theories about heredity as repetition and the brain as a repeating organism to propose individual biological substrates that mapped onto Tarde's social claims. "The self is realized," he explained, "by taking in 'copies' from the world." People were "mechanical ... copying machines," social psychologist Charles Ellwood agreed, quoting Tarde's view that

> there is not a word you say which is not the reproduction, now unconscious but formerly conscious and voluntary, of verbal articulation reaching back to the most distant past, with some special accent due to your immediate surroundings—even your very originality itself is made up of accumulated commonplaces, and aspired to become commonplace in turn.

This social orientation to understanding personality, which increasingly suggested that reality and representation existed as much within the observer as in the external world, organized the new field of social psychology.[39]

Sharing with anthropologists and sociologists the conviction that imitation was a critical force in human society, psychologists similarly came to believe that hypnotic states and the "double consciousness" they supplied were far more common than previously presumed. (This is to be distinguished from the double consciousness of African Americans that W. E. B. Du Bois describes in *The Souls of Black Folk* (1903), although the concept is similarly about experiential perception.) Inquiries into behaviors under hypnotic trance—more specifically how individuals used their "alters" as vicarious experiences to express socially unacceptable thoughts and behaviors—laid the foundation for these scientists' belief in the existence of a nonunitary self. Like the anthropologists who now linked "primitive" and "modern" cultures through theories of imitation, their inquiries soon linked pathological and normal personality through ideas about the universality of a double consciousness in human identity formation. According to this view, the development of the self was like a medium in more ways than one; each person was not only like a copying machine, she or he was like the human mediums who vicariously experienced other personae on a regular basis. From Freud's work on the unconscious to William James's elaboration of the four selves within each person—the material self, the spiritual self, the pure ego, and the social self (which could itself be multiple)—prominent figures supported this new understanding. "A man has as many social selves as there are individuals who recognize him and carry an image of him in their mind," James explained. These findings resonated with explanatory frameworks from physical and natural scientists that posited the existence of multiple simultaneous realities beyond the self, from Einstein's studies of relativity to biologists' investigations of animals' outer-, inner- and counter-worlds.[40]

Hall and his colleagues soon imported these ideas into the new field of scientific child research. This work proposed that the patterns of imitation and double consciousness that their colleagues identified among adults were particularly meaningful in the context of child development. As human scientists' findings suggested that the access to multiple identities and realities—such as the double position of modern subjectivity—supplied by panoramas, photography, taxidermy, film, and wax museums merely made visible the world's everyday state of affairs, then, developmental psychologists articulated how, even without exposure to a junior republic or its component activities, vicarious experience of adulthood already was a defining feature in the lives of modern youth.[41]

Histories of developmental psychology, elaborating on the evolutionary framework that dominated turn-of-the-century thought, have focused on scientists' efforts to establish a sequence of life stages for understanding universal maturation patterns. Missing from these accounts is an equally important unifying theme. Like the anthropologists who saw imitation across primitive and modern societies, and the psychologists who saw double consciousness in both pathological and normal personalities, Hall and his colleagues agreed that, across the lifespan of childhood and its many play genres, young people had instincts for dramatization, and their preferred genre was impersonating adults. Surveys, photographs, and phonographic recordings of youth at play found particular interest in performing adult occupations: farmer, teacher, parent, mechanic, electric light men, ragman, and Salvation Army officers. Dress-up and props were common, but more important were young people's imaginations. In these early performance studies, psychologists described how young people experienced multiple realities that were close cousins of hypnotic states as they imagined themselves in other times and places—soldiers on the battlefield, cowboys and Indians on the plains, knights in the castle courtyard, firefighters in the city.[42]

To be sure, children's behaviors varied by age and by sex. Yet performing adulthood was near universal. Recreation, in short, was characterized by the experience of re-creation. Play was a "vicarious" experience and at its center lay the imitation of "adult ancestral or present day occupations" that "set the goal and prescribe the ideals to be obtained during the period of youth," as Hall's one-time colleague and later Ohio University professor of psychology and pedagogy Arthur Allin explained. "Play, as an activity of youth, is an initiation into society.... Throughout all play runs the great principle of vicarious stimuli... certain activities and habits of reaction... later may be attached to the so-called serious ideals or stimuli of the more earnest storm and stress of life."[43]

These findings verified earlier speculations that young people were even more susceptible to the biological and social forces that influenced adults. Tarde, for example,

Figure 2.5
Children playing Indian, c. 1905.
Source: State Archives of Florida, *Florida Memory*, https://floridamemory.com/items/show/138541.

proposed that children were more imitative than their elders—in his words "a child is, unquestioningly, a true somnambulist." Baldwin observed that kids got impressions "of a model as a photographic plate receives an image." Double consciousness particularly appealed to this age group, suggested William James, on account of the "peculiar sense of power in stretching one's personality, so as to include that of a strange person" that "the dramatic impulse, the tendency to pretend one is someone else" contained. "In young children this instinct often knows no bounds. For a few months in one of my children's third year, he literally hardly ever appeared in his own person." His colleague Josiah Royce concurred. Although the "process of acquiring one's selfhood vicariously" did not "cease with childhood," childhood was the time of its greatest expression: "Children are imitative...to be a horse, or a coachman, or a soldier, or the hero of a favorite story, or a fairy, that is to be somebody, for that sort of self one first witnesses from without, or finds portrayed in the fascinating tale, and then imitatively assimilates, so that one thereupon conceives the new self from within." Suggesting that such behaviors expressed a dramatic instinct and were vital outlets for balancing youthful energy, their theories of playworlds and recapitulation fleshed out how such forces served young people's developmental needs—articulating how childhood was characterized by stages in both meanings of the term.[44]

Playworlds, Recapitulation, and Double Lives

The concept of the playworld, a term only rarely used by Hall himself, did not originate with his research group. An umbrella concept that spanned children's imaginative universes, it was already in use among followers of Friedrich Froebel, the German educational theorist whose kindergarten brought ideas about a play-based curriculum to broad audiences in the United States. "In the play world, as in the actual world, there are parents and children, nurses and babies, teachers and pupils," kindergarten advocate Susan Blow explained in 1894.

> There is social life, with its interchange of visits, its entertainments, and its gossip; there are weddings, baptisms, and funerals. Again, the play world has its trades and professions, its varied round of work, its circle of pleasures. Here the miniature Barnum exhibits his menagerie of wild beasts; yonder is a theater on whose boards a coquettish Cinderella tries on her diminutive slipper, or the Sleeping Beauty is awakened by the Fairy Prince. Now we come to a church from whose pulpit some infant Boanerges thunders wrath upon the doers of evil, and anon we enter a hospital where grave child-doctors are examining pulses and taking temperatures with buttonhooks, while little white-capped nurses vibrate between the enormities of Sairey Gamp and the devotion of Sister Dora.

In short, she concluded, "As it becomes social," play was "clearly revealed in its double nature—as, on the one hand, the expression of indwelling force, and, on the other, the mirror held up to life."[45]

T. Benjamin Atkins, writing *Out of the Cradle and Into the World or, Self-Education Through Play* (1895), offered a nearly identical account of the close relations between children's play and adults' work. Although Hall himself was a Froebel devotee, a review of Atkins's study in Hall's journal *Pedagogical Seminary* criticized the lack of scientific basis for its claims. Hall's research group soon confirmed playworlds' significance using the "genetic method." Arthur Allin summarized the scientific consensus:

> Play is a serious occupation with the child and adolescent. There are moments, it is true, occurring with greater frequency the nearer the adult stage is reached, in which there is a consciousness of the simulation of adult activities; yet, on the whole, play is taken in an objective and business-like way. It is not so much a pretense or a preparation for life to them as it is life itself. The objects of the play-world are as important to them as are our business aims. They also live in a business world. If it were not so there would be no place for them in the so-called serious world of their later adult life. Shielded as they are from the incidence of natural selection, they are nevertheless subject to a natural selection of their own, typical of a struggle yet to come. Mistakes in this preparatory school may be made, and yet a place be still left them for repentance.[46]

One specific genre of playworld that attracted outsized attention among these scientific observers was those in which recapitulation—where play "rehearsing racial history"—occurred. Recapitulation was not Hall's concept but rather attested to the era's embrace of theories of evolutionary development across scientific fields, the same theory organizing world's fair displays. In the human sciences it suggested that both individual organisms and human societies passed through stages resembling the evolution of their remote ancestors as they matured. According to this view, children, "savages," and animals had much in common, and distinctions between the cultures of preindustrial and industrial societies could be explained with reference to the childhood versus the adulthood of the human race.[47]

Historians of youth typically discuss recapitulation theory as the backbone of efforts to devise stage theories of development. According to this view, Hall's contribution to the theory of how young people recapitulate "lower stages of civilization" before becoming modern adults begat his efforts to associate specific developmental stages with specific historical epochs. In *Adolescence* (1904), for example, he wrote,

> Imitation plays a very important role, and girls take far more kindly than boys to societies organized by adults for their benefit. They are also more governed by adult and altruistic motives in forming their organizations, while boys are nearer to primitive man. Before ten comes the period of free spontaneous imitation of every form of adult institution. The child reproduces sympathetically miniature copies of the life around him. On a farm, his play is raking, threshing, building barns, or on the seashore he makes ships and harbors. In general, he plays family, store, church, and chooses officers simply because adults do.... From ten to fourteen, however, associations assume a new character; boys especially cease to imitate adult organizations and tend to form social units characteristic of lower stages of human evolution—pirates, robbers, soldiers, lodges, and other savage reversionary combinations, where the strongest and boldest

is the leader. They build huts, wear feathers and tomahawks as badges, carry knives and toy-pistols, make raids and sell the loot.[48]

Understood within the context of scientists' interest in how imitation and vicarious experience explained the development of human societies and selves, recapitulation also can be understood as a performance-oriented theory of child development which articulated the changing role-plays of adult life that young people typically desired as they aged. Equally, it normalized young people's experience of dual realities in the adulthood of a past racial stage and the childhood of the present day. "The boy is the father of the man in a new sense, in that his qualities are indefinitely older and existed well compacted, untold ages before distinctly human attributes were developed," Hall observed.[49]

Although their accounts of playworlds and recapitulation emphasized young people's affinities for reproducing adult society, developmental psychologists did not believe such role-plays had to duplicate reality precisely to be beneficial. There were cases, Hall discovered, when copies of adult life that were too realistic lost their playful appeal. In a widely reprinted 1887 study of a "Lilliputian" community that evolved from a pioneer settlement to a complex government on a Boston-area sandlot he explained. "The institution is in general very real" to the children, he observed. Yet, "the more

Figure 2.6
The Sand Pile.
Source: G. Stanley Hall, *The Story of a Sand Pile* (New York: Kellogg, 1897).

finished and like reality the objects became the less interest the boys have in them," he observed. By contrast, the play was more real than reality—giving the example of "two little girls who were sisters were overheard saying, 'let's play we are sisters,' almost as if the play made the relation more real than the fact."[50]

The new research tradition offered more nuanced interpretations of subjects previously seen in black and white. It suggested that activities formerly regarded as pathological might have some positive features. Children's lies, for example, expressed imitative instincts necessary to the maturation process. Gang participation, which expressed social instincts, frequently taught cooperation and leadership skills. Hypnotic trance, too, was a catalyst for youth development as the vicarious experiences these altered states supplied were close cousins of imitative play. Reflecting on an encounter with a young woman who had managed a difficult upbringing by "evolving an inner world that more than made up for all that she missed from the outer reality, from which she had effectively taken flight," Hall noted that this altered state, by "widening experience," gave her access to behaviors for which in regular life she would be shamed:

> She can blurt out things which ordinarily maidenly modesty would never permit her to say or hear. Such tender and delicate girls often feel themselves possessed by some rugged, potent, and often uncouth male spirit, and delight to swagger in diction and manner, to be bluntly slangy, to uncork and vent elements of consult and psychic action—types for which nothing in normal experience give such opportunity or such inventive. The girl is thus using new powers and in some sense may be better for it.

Like children's playworlds, filled with activities for which they'd be criticized in "real life," the girl's hypnotic state functioned similarly, offering her vicarious access to alternative times, places, and selves. She "evidently loved" these episodes much as other children loved their dramatic play.[51]

Hall and his colleagues also arrived at a conclusion at odds with previous common wisdom about work versus play. In this formulation, work and play were not opposites—one generative and the other idle—but rather related activities on parallel planes. "The antithesis between play and work is generally wrongly conceived," Hall explained, "for the difference is essentially in the degree of the psycho-physical motivations. The young often do their hardest work in play." According to this view, early work was an undesirable sign of precocity—to be avoided where possible—but work-like play in a sheltered context, by contrast, was useful, an essential feature of a healthy maturation process that transformed play instincts into work instincts in the longer term.[52]

Toward the New Education: Growing Appetites for Educational Role-Playing

Alongside Wilson Gill's empirical analyses, then, psychologists' inquiries into the developmental significance of children's role-plays of adult life and everyday experience of multiple identities confirmed that junior republics' power lay in the vicarious experience they offered. Taking Froebel's view that "the child creates himself by reproducing his environment within himself," this work supplied biological rationales for why these environments produced the desired effects. And it solved the mystery of children's enthusiastic participation in their own reform: because unsupervised children also played at adult occupations and evolved self-governing societies. As Max Bennett Thrasher put it following his visit to the Boston Farm School, "There is no instinct stronger in the minds of children than that of imitation, and no amusement more universal and enduring than that of 'playing house.'" Although "baseball and football, King Philip, tag, quoits, bows and marbles and a dozen other games came and went, the one interest which never flagged was that in 'Cottage Row,' the city of playhouses which the boys have built, care for, own and govern."[53]

These findings identified a middle ground in continuing debates about nature versus nurture. Psychology applied to pedagogy offered hope for the nation's future, US education commissioner Harris declared, explaining how George's republic productively married the two. By orienting life around children's natural activities and guiding them by gentle suggestions rather than more monarchical modes of supervision, George taught lessons that the children enjoyed. Such methods were particularly valuable as assimilation tools. "While the boys make their own laws, Mr. George controls them actually by suggestion rather than dictation," the committee responding to Rochester found. "I believe that the young boys who come from the slums of our cities can be beneficially treated by this powerful hypnotic influence," the nation's foremost educator remarked. "I therefore believe in the George Junior Republic." With these observations Harris backed the view that role-plays of adulthood, guided by adults' gentle suggestion, should serve as more widespread educational techniques.[54]

Having identified the secrets of junior republics, supporters redoubled their efforts to bring the republic experience to youth in greater numbers. At the turn of the century they were joined by a community of educators who saw synergies between republics and the reform movement known as the "new education." These synergies lay in educators' growing commitment to activities in which vicarious experiences of adulthood within a protected environment were central to directing students' energies and attention to positive ends.

Public schools figure prominently in accounts of the emergence of the modern youth ideal. Historians observe how reformers opposing child labor who encountered legal obstacles restricting young people's work opportunities promoted compulsory schooling to expand the nation's protected environments for children and replace the character education formerly supplied by work. Making the case that schools could serve as substitute parents in an era when families were ill-equipped to train their offspring for industrial era employment, they were particularly eager to engage youth outside the mainstream. From immigrants to orphans, marginal populations lacked acquaintance with middle-class manners, and reformers believed that schools training pupils for the industrial economy could assist in their socialization. Standard curricula were ill-suited to meet these goals, however, neither focused on industrial careers nor engaging for children who found greater satisfaction at work.[55]

Drawing on European educational theory and practice, late nineteenth-century US public schools undertook scattershot efforts to address these concerns. Experiential learning in laboratory science, object lessons, manual training, educational games, school pageants, and museums replaced lectures, textbooks, and rote memorization. Visual education and picture learning with stereoscopes, lantern slides, and photographs adapted new entertainment technologies to pedagogical ends. Activities including youth congresses, field trips, school banks, student courts, school farms and gardens, and team sports and military drills supplemented these efforts. Teachers modified their instructional approaches—for example, reconceptualizing themselves as substitute parents—to test if alternative methods of delivering lessons and discipline might succeed. In short, a shared goal across these endeavors was to bring new audiences into the protective enclosures of schools while expanding pupils' opportunities for vicarious contact with the larger world.[56]

Developmental psychology would be instrumental in transforming such uncoordinated efforts into common practices, providing new rationales for these curricular choices and a motivation to systematically expand them under the rubric of scientific pedagogy for the industrial age. From his first faculty appointment at Johns Hopkins, G. Stanley Hall bridged departments of psychology and education, with ambitions to become a leading voice in discussions about school reform. Critical of American educational institutions not merely for their archaic goals but equally for their unscientific pedagogical methods, he was confident the science of youth development was the key to curricular reorganization. In his sandlot study, for example, Hall had observed how, as this "ideal little republic" evolved from frontier to industrial society, the children developed increasingly complex economic and political systems. He was struck by the civic and industrial training this recapitulation in action supplied, "about as much yearly educational value to the boys as the eight months of school." This "may perhaps be called one illustration of the education, according to nature we so often hear and speak of...boys are quickened by the imagination to realize their conceptions of adult life." A later essay on "The Ideal School as Based on Child Study" (1901) argued for a curriculum of active learning organized around children's natural inclinations, coordinated with their developmental stages, and focused on exploring compelling problems through multidisciplinary inquiry.[57]

In making these proposals, Hall implicitly urged expanding the applications of Froebel's kindergarten methods. "The tendency to imitate in children should be most carefully cultivated," Froebel had written, encouraging parents and teachers to model good behavior as an efficient route to desired results. "Such culture will lighten by one-half, the work of education." Gentle suggestion, rather than dictatorship, would further channel young people's natural instincts for "imitative personification" toward pedagogical ends, Susan Blow elaborated, on account of how "the condition of the young child presents many analogies to that of the hypnotic patient, and that as the latter responds to the suggestions of the operator, so the former responds to the suggestions of his environment." Although not central to histories of the kindergarten movement, an emphasis on expanding opportunities for vicariously experiencing adulthood while creating a protected childhood—directed role-play, not just directed play—was a key aspect of its appeal. Following Froebel's proposal that adults "live with the children," US kindergarten educators such as Katherine Beebe called for her colleagues to "go a considerable distance into the play-world" since "meeting them there on their own ground, playing with them in a real play-spirit," would be the source of "influence over them" to be turned "to the most practical account." To do otherwise would lose their attention, she cautioned:

> [Children] have lived most of the hours of their few years in a playworld. There is no doubt in the mind of one who thoughtfully watches a playing child that he is "all there," that the whole child plays, while it is a common experience of first grade teachers to have in the class or seat work only the bodily presence of the child, his mind and soul roaming far afield into his familiar world of play.[58]

Thus, in this context of consensus "that imitation is the true point of departure, both for educational psychology and from the wise 'nurture of childhood,'" the primary task for educators was "to protect the child from bad models, and to supply him with good ones" to copy. Tarde had earlier mused about how education was "one of the forms by which imitation spreads"—that kids were "true somnambulists," who when they attended school experienced "a piling up of slumbers," as they reoriented away from imitating parents to teachers and classmates. Now, from kindergartens to high schools, teachers soon embraced such activities as vocational education, youth congresses, and children's gardens using this rationale. Schools for "negroes" and "Indians" and other populations perceived as least suited to traditional book learning were on the front lines of these developments, as Hall's 1902 remarks indicated, but they slowly spread to the middle classes as well. Backed by science, then, the component activities of the Freeville republic with scattered precedents became mass educational phenomena at the same time that school cities and junior republics helped the republic movement itself to spread. Conversations about these school-based activities came to share with conversations about republics and so many of the period's other educational entertainments the language of "miniature" and "reproduction," revealing how the institutions most closely associated with sheltering young people equally embraced a variety of vicarious adulthoods. As a result, the double life that characterized life inside junior republics became a defining feature in the educational experiences of the nation's youth.[59]

Such developments had some critics. Charles Ellwood argued the imitation theory "is impractical," and that "the practical worker, the legislator, the social reformer and the philanthropist" would find it "little help in their work." William James was skeptical that adults could meet children in their playworlds. Arthur Allin, more optimistic that adults could enter children's imaginary worlds, saw mixed results from these interventions: "Undue influence and interference from the adult-world in this serious playworld," he observed, "may often throw an air of unreality over it, causing the players to live in a world of simulation and engendering confusion and disorder in the growing habits very detrimental in after life."[60]

These criticisms aside, by and large most saw the possibility, like Tarde, "to assimilate...through the contagion of imitation" as lower-status individuals (children) duplicated the models set by "higher" types (adults). Popular support for activities such as the "mimic congresses and councils" brought to Chicago's public schools alongside good government and improvement clubs—the "Miniature city councils upon which the public searchlight may be turned at any time; miniature legislatures minus the shadow of the octopus; and near-real congresses in which the national policy will be molded without regard to party prejudices [that] are to be organized in the Chicago Public Schools"—exemplified how even in schools without junior republics educators seeking to modernize instructional practices found value in role-plays of adult life. "The Junior American Republic, composed of the pupils of the public schools, is a thing of life," one journalist reported on a youth congress inside several city schools. "Not still life, but gingery, boiling, effervescent life that betokens a vigorous and useful future." John Dewey's nearby Laboratory School soon made famous this educational approach, and how new education proponents envisioned instructors following the teachers, doctors, psychiatrists, and criminologists who employed suggestion in their work.[61]

John Dewey's Laboratory School

As Hall's remarks to teachers at Harvard attest, the school his former student John Dewey organized in Chicago in 1896 and typically cited as the vanguard of pedagogical methods in fact was merely a particularly influential example of the era's broader educational trends. Dewey's Laboratory School never organized a school city or school republic. (Instructor Harry Gillette did spend some time at the George Junior Republic during the summers.) But there is ample evidence in Dewey's writings that he conceived of the activities his institution offered—for example, cooking, shopwork, gardening, weaving, even building a small city—as deriving value from how they enabled young people to be sheltered while simultaneously gaining vicarious access to past and present adult roles. Dewey was well known for his vision of school as "an embryonic community," his call for child-centered education, and his pedagogical philosophies of learning by doing and "bringing school close to life." A closer look at the lab school curriculum and the language Dewey used to describe it finds he was also one of the most prominent advocates for role-playing as a pedagogical tool.[62]

Figure 2.7
Building a clubhouse at the University of Chicago Laboratory School, c. 1899.
Source: Katherine Camp Mayhew Papers, box 17, folder 9, "Parents and Children."
Courtesy Division of Rare and Manuscript Collections, Cornell University Library.

Dewey elaborated on these ideas in *My Pedagogical Creed* (1897) and *The School and Society* (1899). "The school has been so set apart, so isolated from the ordinary conditions and motives of life," he wrote, that it sheltered pupils from the "experience" that should be at the heart of the curriculum. Education, he declared, must come through "forms of life" that were "as real and vital to the child as that which he carries on in home, in the neighborhood, or on the play ground." Such forms were not the same as the "genuine reality" of "existing social life" itself, but rather simplified and vicarious versions in a sheltered space. In agreement with Hall that "outside of school children's plays are simply more or less miniature and haphazard attempts at reproducing social occupations," and the nuanced relationship of play and work (as he wrote a decade and a half later, "play and industry are by no means so antithetical to one another as is often assumed, any sharp contrast being due to undesirable social conditions"), when Dewey sketched an ideal school in an 1899 book he envisioned "an embryonic community" that would be "active with types of occupations that reflect the larger society." This was learning by doing so long as the doing was at some remove from the thing itself. For by occupation he meant "a mode of activity...that reproduces, or runs parallel to, some form of work" but was "freed from all economic stress"—in other words, simulations of adult work undertaken in the work-free context of the school. "The absence of economic pressure in schools supplies an opportunity for reproducing industrial situations of mature life under conditions where the occupation can be carried out for its own sake," Dewey explained, while noting that occasional payment could heighten the learning experience. "If in some cases, pecuniary recognition is also a result of an action, though not the chief motive for it," Dewey noted, "that fact may well increase the significance of the occupation."[63]

In this setting, the educator's first task was to devise a curriculum that simplified real life. Although Hall had observed in his sandlot study how youth lost interest as the community's realism increased, Dewey argued that realistic reproductions (he liked the phrase "sense of reality") were essential to motivating youth: "Children want to 'help'; they are anxious to engage in the pursuits of adults which effect external changes: setting the table, washing dishes, helping care for animals, etc. In their plays, they like to construct their own toys and appliances." As a result, "activity which does not give back results of tangible and visible achievement loses its interest.... When make-believe is recognized to be make-believe, the device of making objects in fancy alone is too easy to stimulate intense action."[64]

The educator's second task was to guide young people's play instincts toward pedagogical ends. Like Hall, Dewey had studied hypnosis earlier in his career and viewed suggestion as one technique to achieve this aim. Recognizing that it was "through imitation, suggestion, direct instruction, and even more indirect unconscious tuition, that the child learns," he encouraged a child-centered educational process in which "the suggestion must *fit in* with the dominant mode of growth in the child" so as "to help him carry out his own wishes and ideas." The upshot for instruction was clear: "Let the child first express his impulse, and then through criticism, question, and suggestion bring him to consciousness of what he has done, and what he needs to do." William Clark, whose University of Chicago doctoral thesis-turned-book (*Suggestion in Education*) held up Dewey's lab school as a model for educational practice, summarized the approach.

> Just as in the theological world man has suffered untold miseries from regarding the present life as a mere "probationary state," preparation for a "heaven" after death, so in the educational world the school life is vitiated by "preparing to live" in the "real life" of the business and social world.... All life prepares for life, and there is no preparation for life but life itself.... Pedagogical suggestion, it must be insisted, is a normal life process...suggestion in hypnosis is essentially the same as suggestion in the normal state.[65]

Like Gill's school cities and school republics, where students governed one another while being removed from actual public life and where teachers aimed to lead in democratic rather than autocratic fashion, in Dewey's educational environment students recreated past and present work practices at a remove from the world of work, guided by instructors but not directly led. Such activities vivified traditional subjects as well. The history curriculum invited kids to "recapitulate the industrial history of man by cooking, spinning, weaving, dyeing, drawing, and so forth...reproducing ancient stages of man's development"—for example, role-playing Phoenician traders. Introduced across subjects, role-playing transformed activities such as cooking, sewing, and manual training into media for teaching larger lessons and transformed play instincts into work instincts in the longer term. "I believe that the only way to make the child conscious of his social heritage is to enable him to perform those fundamental types of activity which make civilization what it is," Dewey elaborated.

> I believe that this gives the standard for the place of cooking, sewing, manual training, etc., in the school. I believe that they are not special studies which are to be introduced over and above a lot of others in the way of relaxation or relief, or as additional accomplishments. I believe rather that they represent, as types, fundamental forms of social activity; and that it is possible and desirable that the child's introduction into the more formal subjects of the curriculum be through the medium of these activities.

In short, the separation of such activities from their typical environments, which made possible a sheltered childhood, heightened their educational potentials as well.[66]

The conception of schools as miniature communities was an idea with roots in the early nineteenth century. What distinguished Dewey's vision from these antecedents was the new cultural currency of the reproductions of adult society that his school, like so many others, now supplied. In the early twentieth century, as educational entertainments focused around virtual environments and experiences proliferated, and as scientific consensus about societal and individual development made imitation a central theme, discussions about play-based education became a central site for ongoing conversations about the educational and socialization potentials of role-playing in the lives of the nation's youth. These theoretical and empirical developments, which help to explain why Hall would juxtapose the George Junior Republic with Dewey's famous school in his 1902 address, sparked educators' continuing interest in the junior republic idea despite William George's protestations that the republic was not a school.[67]

By the first decade of the twentieth century, then, new knowledge from developmental psychology and new evidence from inside schools favored junior republics and the double lives of virtual adulthood and sheltered childhood they embraced. With Dewey's well-regarded work underscoring Wilson Gill's discovery that vicarious experience mattered most for producing positive results—and that republics' component activities, even when divorced from any realistic looking environment, could nevertheless have valuable pedagogical effects—school-based republics swiftly spread. Educators found in Johann Pestalozzi, Maria Montessori, and other European figures still more backing for William George and his imitators' interest in dramatization as a method for child guidance. "Froebel with his kindergarten, Johnson with his playschool and Tsanoff with his playground have shown conclusively that play is one of the most important factors in fastening the attention and fixing impressions upon the mind," wrote James White. Gill's school cities were "largely founded upon this principle," he explained,

> for it is one round of play, while at the same time it is actual self-government, and by frequent change of office provides a continual change of scheme. It supplies an unending amusement, because each child is both actor and spectator on a miniature stage, which counterparts the serious business of his elders. In a word, it provides unlimited opportunity for the play of the imitative and imaginative faculties, while it encourages and exercises self-respect, self-confidence, [etc.].... It is so simple and effective that educators are led to say, "Why didn't I think of this?"

School cities' installation at teacher training institutions such as the New Paltz Normal School amplified the diffusion as graduates fanned out to schools across the country.[68]

By 1901, school city boosters estimated that over 50,000 pupils had experienced the pedagogical philosophy that, through performing adult citizens' roles, "they actually experience" the political life of a city, state, or nation. Like George's republic, Gill's idea traveled to other nations. And it inspired creative modifications such as the Ray Plan in Chicago (modeled on ancient Rome) and Collegeville in New York City (focused around property ownership in a fictitious state). Yet in the early 1900s the school city remained the gold standard for introducing the republic experience into educational institutions. Following the lead of public figures such as Roosevelt and Waring, some of the social scientists who had worked with William George to promote the Freeville republic now joined Gill to assist in his work. John Commons, for example, became an instructor for the Patriotic League and contributed a chapter to Gill's 1901 book.[69]

Media coverage of life in Freeville continued, but it was school cities that actually served youth in the greatest numbers. Daddy George's visions of a nation of junior republics remained in the realm of dreams while Gill was showing on-the-ground results. For this reason, after the Spanish-American War it was Gill whom General Leonard Wood invited to Cuba to teach children about the American democratic system.

There had been earlier talk of a Cuban George Junior Republic: "The George Junior Republic furnishes on a small scale a very good illustration of the principles which should actuate, and, in a certain sense, of the methods which should be pursued by, the American Nation in dealing with its new dependencies," wrote one supporter. "Mr. George does not put the waifs and strays that he had gathered from New York together in an inclosure like Indians on a reservation and leave them to manage their problems by themselves; neither does he think of controlling them by authority from without." Yet Gill's methods could reach more children. Seeking to integrate Cuban pupils into the American empire as was already being accomplished for mainland immigrant youth, Wood named Gill Supervisor of Moral and Civic Training and asked him to organize school cities in 3,500 Cuban schoolrooms.[70]

Back on the mainland, school republics continued to proliferate, spreading westward. Gill's subsequent writings invoked developmental psychology, noting for example how

Figure 2.8
Police court, school city, Havana.
Source: Wilson Gill, "The School City," *Journal of the Franklin Institute* (July 1903).

"the rough and tumble democracy which the children get amongst themselves" prevented them from "all grow[ing] up little serfs" and how his school city perfected their knowledge of true democracy. Students "are natural imitators," he elaborated. "A child hates to be driven but loves to be led." Supporters echoed the new rationale for the "organic" educational method. "The reason why it works with young children is that they are very suggestible," observed New York Montgomery School principal Charles Drum. "The power of imitation is at its maximum in young children. They delight to play that they are 'Big Folks'…The educator who fails to use the laws of suggestion and imitation fails to use the most powerful levers for good." The American Municipal Association, American Political Science Association, and Daughters of the American Revolution subsequently endorsed school republics. Gill's publicity efforts were further assisted by the School Citizens Committee, founded by Goo Goo Richard Welling in 1904 to promote the broader youth self-government idea. A close friend of George and later president of the George Junior Republic Association, Welling (like Commons) was nonideological in promoting the spread of basic republic principles. A bridge between the municipal reform and education communities, Welling later recruited John Dewey to the organization's advisory board.[71]

Of course, school cities had their critics. The language of realism was not entirely accurate, some educators maintained. "Girl-mayors and girl-policemen are probably not 'learning by doing' any of the duties which twentieth century civilization has in store for them," one school superintendent complained. Initially there were some misunderstandings about excessive child control; Gill and his collaborators issued press releases to clear up the confusion. Still others suggested younger kids were merely playing parts they could not understand. US education commissioner Harris was among them, despite his earlier praise for George: "Dramatically adopting the supposed manner and reproducing the situation," he worried, "is not a process of cultivating the true individuality of the child but of cultivating only the ability to imitate and to play a role for the sake of producing an appearance rather than the reality of earnestness and wisdom." Even some students did not want their classmates to be in charge. These critical voices went largely unheard, however, as the new education that backed the incorporation of school cities and school republics into public schools and framed junior republics' component activities in similar terms soon awakened administrators at other youth-serving institutions to junior republics' potential applicability to their needs.[72]

Bringing Boy Republics West

The appeal of scientific pedagogy was not limited to the period's public educators. Youth-serving institutions including settlements, boys clubs, YMCAs, and orphanages increasingly sought theoretical rationales for their work to complement activities in the nation's schools as they supplied adult-supervised programming after-school, on weekends, and during school vacations. At the turn of the century, a few made attempts to incorporate junior republics into their programming.[73]

Although these leisure-time institutions offered programs of informal education for both sexes, boys were of greatest concern as the shift to an industrial economy sparked a crisis in gender roles. Anxieties about their excess energies and future public roles gave rise to "boys work" specialists among the burgeoning youth work field, a place for men in the otherwise feminized child-saving arena. As Gill saw it, men were better suited than women "who have had no practice or knowledge of citizenship" to acquaint students with school cities, and he was not alone in this view.[74]

In these budding professionals' aspirations to build an applied science of "boyology" to improve on the forms of guidance previously supplied by home and work, research from G. Stanley Hall and colleagues had much to contribute. Findings about sexual differentiation in play and development fit well with their plans for sex-segregated activities. Boys workers appreciated these scientists' view that there was more good in gangs than the mass media portrayed. As a "natural" phenomenon linked to recapitulation, gangs could not be stopped, but gang members' "social instincts" could be adapted toward positive ends. "Natural leaders" among youth "can be utilized as radiators of moral and social influence in innumerable ways," Hall explained in 1902. Student Edgar

James Swift echoed his appreciation for peer influence, noting how, inside topsy-turvy settings like George's republic, "the most hopeful cases are the leaders of the gangs of toughs, the despair of the city police."[75]

As word of eastern and midwestern republics reached the West Coast, boys workers in three San Francisco institutions piloted summer republics to complement their school-year educational programming for immigrant and working boys eight and up in drama, vocational education, and other activities. The State of Columbia, founded in 1902 by Columbia Park Boys Club worker James Rogers and later led by John Brewer; Boytown, organized in 1903 by South Park Settlement worker Arthur Todd (a participant at the initial State of Columbia); and the City of Telhi, opened in 1904 by James Rogers on his move to the Telegraph Hill Neighborhood Association, all established tent-based juvenile societies in the northern California countryside. Older boys filled most elected positions, while appointed posts were open to younger citizens. Distinct work classes organized daily tasks: "There were the camp-cooks...camp-waiters, the launderers, the dish-washers, a health department, classes in rustic basket-making, in collecting of natural objects and the preservation of them; bead belt and Indian basket-making, in keeping the camp clean, gathering wood for the fire." Recreational activities such as swimming, baseball, sham battles, theatricals, and visiting storytellers rounded out the programming. In the absence of major benefactors, funding was an ongoing concern, with the result that the boys picked fruit, made baskets, and gave performances to raise funds for self-support. Tourists flocked to see the kids in action.[76]

Although Rogers lavished praise on the bucolic setting, he chiefly located the camps' value in the double lives the children lived. As the summer escape sheltered boys from being "put to work" or left to "idle away the time on the dirty and crowded streets," it provided opportunities for "living the life for a month of a true citizen" as they "built a colony with streets and public buildings, elected their officers, legislated and enforced laws." His account of the founding of the mythical State of Columbia "in the very heart of the beautiful Santa Cruz Mountains" struck a similar tone. "The site was an open piece of unshaded land, about four acres, in extent, covered completely with underbrush which had to be cleared with poor tools, under an unrelenting summer's heat." The camp's "very isolation helped in its development as a small state....They built streets, fences, rustic seats, tables, a swimming hole—built them generally from trees felled by their own axes....The republic assumed the true dignity and tone of a law-making and law-enforcing community."[77]

Responding to critics who suggested some of these juvenile democracies offered only play acting, Rogers emphasized the realistic vicarious experience his republics supplied. Observing how, "Isolated from human life, because of its separation from town and people," Rogers insisted, "This experiment was not a matter of playing or practicing the part, but instead that of living the life for a month of a true citizen." The republic "was neither a farce, a mere burlesque of the real; nor was it a mere fancy or idea of the mind, but a successful reality proven by a set of determined and loyal boys." Popular media accounts echoed this interpretation, simultaneously emphasizing the realism of the boys' adultlike activities and their location in children-only spaces.[78]

As the San Francisco boys clubs and other youth-serving institutions added junior republics to their year-round programming, George continued his efforts to spread the republic idea, sending junior citizens from the growing list of George Junior Republics on fundraising missions and, in 1904, sending a delegation to Litchfield, Connecticut to start a republic for younger boys. He also advised several schools on adaptations of the republic plan. Although media coverage continued and prominent supporters advocated on George's behalf (now including President William McKinley, who invited several juvenile officials to make a "state visit" to the White House), the slow pace of establishing total institutions meant George found himself upstaged by Wilson Gill. Even as young people clamored for admission to Freeville, with "Parents & guardians—Judges & pastors close behind" as Thomas Osborne reported, school republics were increasingly described as an equivalent "movement" in the popular press. Gill fueled the flames of friendly competition, pointing out how his approach took the financial pressure off junior republics to be self-supporting and could reach young people in greater numbers.[79]

And so it was Gill, rather than George, to whom Philadelphia's Franklin Institute awarded its 1904 Elliott Cresson medal. Fellow honorands that year included the inventor of a coal storage system, the creator of a steam generator, and a pioneer of aluminothermics, further underscoring the association of republic technique with scientific social engineering. Even as the republic's popularity had prompted the recognition of the historical genealogy of similar ideas, and Gill himself acknowledged his debt to George—"I am not the originator of the idea by any means," he declared—nonetheless his scheme for republics that could be introduced into existing institutions continued to be greeted as innovative work.[80]

George received his own gold medal that same year at the St. Louis World's Fair. Alongside the sham battles, Hales Tours, living villages, machines of industry, and other attractions, the New York State Museum's Department of Social Economy exhibited photographs and artifacts from Freeville, including samples of its currency and bureaucratic forms. This was not, in fact, the first time his republic had been put on display. Thomas Osborne had traveled to the 1900 Paris Exposition to deliver a stereopticon lecture, enabling fairgoers to "see more of the varied life of the place than they could do by an active visit." These copies of a republic that itself copied the United States's political and economic systems highlight the complex relations between reality and representation in the modern age.[81]

The coming years witnessed a further expansion of interest in republics and their guiding principles as schools and youth-serving institutions piloted a range of novel programs organized around vicarious experiences of adulthood inside youth-only spaces. Directing their charges to play roles such as carpenter, housekeeper, and police officer, the educators and youth workers at schools, settlements, playgrounds, and boys clubs soon discovered that these programs' developmental benefits for youth were joined by economic benefits for their organizations. How ties to the proliferating cultural products that spectacularized reality help to explain both the popularization of junior republics and their component activities, and the interpretation of young people's everyday performances as reducing rather than expanding child labor, are the subjects of chapter 3.

II The Rhetoric and Reality of Child Protection

3 Constructing Youth, Constructing Youth-Serving Institutions

"Breathes there a man with soul so dead that he cannot remember those joyous days when he played at 'grown up'?" journalist Nina Carter Marbourg inquired in 1904. "There is a period of air-castle building in almost every boy's life...a season of wonderful colored paper trades and purchases, a time for the accumulation of tops and marbles. The art of bargain and exchange is all so seriously regarded...that the boy is really working at his play and carrying out in his childish way just the transactions his father is perfecting with dollars and cents." This instinct was being directed in particularly compelling ways at the George Junior Republic. Describing the "system of labor and currency" in which child carpenters "built nearly all the buildings in the republic grounds, besides making the furniture...there is the bakery and laundry, there are three hundred acres of land given over to farming and there is work in the improvement of the streets," Parker identified great value in this work-like play. "They are learning the ins and outs of the business world...training their minds to appreciate all the value that the necessity of an article lends to it. They are passing through their colored paper, tops and marble period of life with all the responsibility of a small world on their shoulders."[1]

As she reported on junior citizens constructing buildings, cultivating farmland, and improving streets, why did Marbourg emphasize developmental benefits to youth over economic benefits to the republic? And how might her account of Freeville offer insights into the broader significance of vicarious experiences of adulthood in the political economy of the era's schools and youth-serving institutions? This chapter traces the spread of republics and their component activities across schools and youth-serving institutions, from rural to urban locations and from marginal to middle-class youth. It focuses on the occupations that were staples of the programming inside these sheltered spaces, work-like activities "freed from all economic stress." Although associations with other educational entertainments and the scientific guidance of young people's play instincts help to explain these activities' widespread adoption, their cost-efficiency held equal appeal.[2]

Histories of childhood place the decline of children's labor force participation at the center of the dissolution of the family economy and its replacement with the sheltered childhood. Scholars recognize some inconsistencies in the new norm—for example, how farm work was considered beneficial rather than exploitative, how labor for marginal youth was considered to create a more "deserving" poor, and how many statutes were only minimally enforced. Classic accounts generally agree on how schools and youth-serving institutions figure in this story, however: as age-restricted spaces where young people could engage in developmentally productive training and leisure activities rather than labor or harmful amusements, sites to learn the values lost as work was being removed from kids' lives.[3]

That bucolic Freeville was not perceived as a site for child labor despite its guiding motto "Nothing without Labor" and even as junior citizens enabled the financially troubled institution to stay afloat makes sense in the context these previous accounts have sketched. Yet as republics and component activities from vocational education to home economics took root in urban institutions struggling to make ends meet, diversified their clientele to include middle-class youth, and expanded opportunities for occupational role-playing, such interpretations persisted. From schools and playgrounds to settlements and boys clubs, the parental institutions created in response to criticisms that earlier child-saving programs exploited youth created new kinds of family economies that, by drawing distinctions between reality and representation, could be seen as contracting rather than expanding the child labor pool.[4]

Activities with dual status as real and not real not only helped to construct youth, then, equally they enabled young people to produce the institutions that sheltered them while suggesting their activities were merely representations of adult jobs. Linking the reduction of child labor to the spread of modern subjectivity described in earlier chapters confirms that adult-supervised youth activities were integral to the rise of the sheltered childhood—albeit in ways that previous studies overlooked. These techniques' subsequent circulation to factories and prisons underscored their successes in disciplining the nation's youngest citizens to accept a loss of autonomy and social status and acquiesce to a more restrictive behavioral regime.

Youth-Serving Institutions Embrace the Republic Idea

By the early 1900s, a vibrant republic movement was in full swing. A few early republics folded on account of lack of administrative or financial support (among them, Milwaukee's school cities and the City of Telhi). Others backed away from youth self-government (Allendale). With enthusiasts adamant that such disappointments resulted from poor implementation, these developments did little to undermine popular enthusiasm for the republic idea. Republics' ostensibly scientific approach to education and socialization and ease of introduction into existing institutions continued to inspire educators and youth workers in the coming years.[5]

The Progressive Era witnessed the rapid rise of a variety of youth-serving (also called child-saving) institutions, many with European roots. Operating on shoestring budgets and staffed largely by volunteers, their pseudoparental programs figure prominently in accounts of the history of the American youth experience. These organizations expanded access to sheltered childhoods by offering a clientele of chiefly "needy" city boys and girls lively programs of adult-supervised activities in youth-only spaces, alternatives to labor force participation and unchaperoned play. In a continuing quest for professionalism youth workers undertook community surveys of local children's leisure activities, to identify negative influences and gather ideas for future child-centered programming. Finding growing interest in mass entertainment, Jane Addams and others called to cultivate further opportunities inside youth-serving institutions for more wholesome, educational play (the flip side of schools' emphasis on play-like education) to direct young people's attentions and energies toward positive ends. From debate and vocational education to model kitchens and children's farms, from military drill and drama to penny savings banks and newspapers, many of the programming choices already spreading across the nation's schools soon became standard fare.[6]

Youth workers subsequently added junior republics to these building blocks as independent activities or, in some cases, a means to coordination. Hired to centrally administer Louisville, Kentucky's new playground system in 1904, for example, Arthur Leland organized an inter-playground youth athletic league to offer the lessons in civics and character development associated with organized sports. A Playground Athletic Union with two representatives from each playground scheduled games and assessed player eligibility. The children were so interested in the elections that Leland introduced playground republics to expand youth involvement in playground governance. Each playground, "organized into a miniature city...elects its mayor, who appoints all of the minor officers, and aids the director in enforcing playground laws." The child citizens also selected a police judge, a board of aldermen (girls), and a council (boys), which elected their own officers and met twice a week to discuss legislative matters. Soon, in each playground, a board of public works oversaw classes in basketry, whittling, and raffia work; a board of public safety kept watch over athletic equipment; a board of health inspected children's hands and faces; and a board of park commissioners kept facilities clean and local plant life in good repair. Leland reconceived the original Playground Athletic Union as a state government, appointing the playground supervisor as judge of its supreme court of appeals.[7]

At New York City's Hebrew Sheltering Guardian Society Orphan Asylum, superintendent Ludwig Bernstein established a Boys City modeled on New York in 1906 and a similar but separate Girls City the following year. Bernstein viewed inmate self-government as the next step for institutional changes already under way. The asylum, which served more than 1,000 children ages six to sixteen, had recently expanded its extracurricular activities to include clubs run by elected officers and parliamentary procedures. It had also committed to doing away with the militaristic "monitorial" disciplinary system. Aware of republics from his work as an assistant principal and

Figure 3.1
Board of Health, Playground City, Louisville.
Source: Arthur Leland, "Playground Self-Government," *Charities* 12 (June 4, 1904).

because Richard Welling served on the asylum's board, Bernstein could barely contain his excitement about this new direction in "educational theory and practice." It was more exciting "than even improved text books" in the view of asylum vice president Samuel Levy, on account of the possibilities for inmates "to work out on a miniature scale all those problems which at some time in their future lives they will undoubtedly have to face." Although the republics lacked economic systems, the children soon administered the asylum bank, a cooperative store, and a charity for inmates without relatives or friends."[8]

At Cleveland's Hiram House settlement, a miniature Cleveland established on the playground called Progress City became the focus of a summer camp for neighborhood youth from 1906. Like Wilson Gill, settlement director George Bellamy had initially worked with adults but found kids much more amenable to his ideas. Seeking "some of the more vital methods of educating the children of our great industrial neighborhoods," as Bellamy put it, the summertime miniature municipality endorsed a "laboratory" method giving children opportunities to experiment without the full-fledged consequences of "real life." Progress City carries on "city activities in miniature" that were "as nearly like" activities in the surrounding city "as they can be made." Progress City administrator Frank Koos, who agreed with William George that, "to be a good citizen every individual must be able to make his living," organized the program to offer vocational training in gendered occupations including basket making, sewing,

Figure 3.2
Constitutional committee, Girls City, Hebrew Sheltering Guardian Society Orphan Asylum.
Source: *Annual Report of the Hebrew Sheltering Guardian Society* (New York: *Hebrew Sheltering Guardian Society*, 1907/1909).

cooking, printing, sports, carpentry, brass hammering, hammock making, gardening, street cleaning, and sign painting, with each class constituting a ward of the city.[9]

Participants were paid in a token currency that could be deposited or spent at the Progress City bank or store. Entrepreneurial youth set up other services such as a weather bureau and museum. The "model juvenile city" also served as a training ground for a new generation of youth workers: They lived at the settlement, attended evening lectures on developmental psychology and play supervision, and received course credit for participation.[10]

At the Worcester Social Settlement, not far from G. Stanley Hall's Clark University, superintendent Rev. R. J. Floody organized a Garden City in 1907 in still another variation on the republic idea. Distinct from Ebenezer Howard's urban plans of the same name, this child society took root at a community garden on the city's former Dead Cat Dump. Floody enlisted youth to clear the five-acre site, plant a garden, and tend to the animals there. Giving voting rights to the garden proprietors, they soon elected a mayor, seven councilmen, a garden commissioner, street commissioner, tool commissioner, water commissioner, animal commissioner, flower commissioner, and forty police officers to administer the juvenile town. Children in other neighborhoods clamored for

Figure 3.3
Vegetable gardeners, Progress City.
Source: *A Historical Report of the Sixteen Years' Work at Hiram House* (Cleveland: Hiram House, 1912).

similar opportunities, and soon four Garden Cities were operating around Worcester, with expanded programming including a zoo and a band. "This is truly a melting pot of the many nationalities we had in the gardens," Floody enthused. "Not only is it a melting pot but it is a Health Sanitorium, an Anti-lazy Institute, an Anti-pauper Shop, a Political Mill, a Moral Generator, and a Good Citizen's Factory all combined in one." A few years later, another Garden City debuted in Cambridge, Massachusetts, sponsored by Harvard president Charles Eliot and his colleague Professor F. W. Harris, and led by Eileen Marshal, whose brother had worked in Freeville with William George.[11]

Arthur Leland's plans for Louisville playgrounds, Ludwig Bernstein's vision for one New York orphan asylum, George Bellamy's youth programming at the Hiram House settlement, and Rev. Floody's lesser-known Garden Cities offer merely four examples of youth workers' creative modifications of the republic idea. These new stakeholders in the movement accepted educators' now-common wisdom about the value of performing adult roles in youth-only spaces. Sharing John Dewey's enthusiasm for learning by doing and bringing school closer to life, Koos explained: "The best way to mould and teach, the best way to learn to be good citizens, the best way to develop right ways of living, is by living and doing the things which are to be learned and taught. These are the methods which Progress City, a laboratory of good citizenship, has attempted to use."[12]

The framework that youth workers applied to interpreting republics soon framed their thinking on other institutional activities, such as the home economics training at Hiram House's Model Cottage. Although youth workers typically shared with educators the belief that realistic roles were more critical than realistic environments, such model environments nevertheless remained popular training tools. A publicity brochure reported the girls' response: "Is this whole house to be just for us, sitting room, dining room, kitchen and bedroom? Why, it is a regular little house," said one of the girls as she entered the cottage for the first time. "Of course a cottage is the best place to learn homemaking," read the accompanying photo captions, which emphasized the realism of the small-scale house. Implicit in this account, however, was that despite the close resemblances the cottage was not an actual home. For as the brochure elsewhere made clear, settlement programming delayed the work of these "embryo housekeepers'" in actual homes by enrolling them in educational dramatizations instead.[13]

In their programming choices and commentaries thereupon, then, youth workers who embraced the republic movement eagerly offered young people not only sheltered childhoods but also opportunities to vicariously experience adult life. Similar trends

Figure 3.4
Model cottage, Hiram House.
Source: *A Historical Report of the Sixteen Years' Work at Hiram House* (Cleveland: Hiram House, 1912).

soon inflected other youth-serving institutions where only republics' component activities were found. Mabel Kittredge's Association of Practical Housekeeping Centers, which taught domestic skills at settlements and schools, illustrates how an educational philosophy narrowly associated with Dewey's lab school was broadly influential in this period.

From Kindergarten to Kitchen Garden

At the turn of the twentieth century, as mother study clubs embraced scientific childrearing, "girls workers" revised housekeeping education in complementary ways. Promoting domestic skills development to delay girls' workforce participation, many argued that parents—rich and poor alike—were ill-equipped to school their children for the industrial age. Tutelage in "domestic science" and "household management" under scientifically trained teachers was Mabel Kittredge's ambition for the housekeeping centers she established in New York City from 1902. Recognizing how girls were "born with the controlling desire to copy" and that such instinct could be directed to pedagogical ends, Kittredge's "model flats" were

> ordinary tenement flats which find their motive power and are successful by means of the universal love in every little girl to play at keeping house, and the universal desire in every one to copy that which is just above her. A girl wants her kitchen messes, her dishes, her make-believe baby and her tiny bed or broom just as every boy wants his bat and ball. A housekeeping center takes these natural desires and cultivates them. It is furnished as a home should be furnished, and such questions are answered there as: What shall be done with the floors to insure health and save labor; what with the walls? What curtains are the best to admit light, give beauty to the room and wash easily? What proportion of the sum laid aside for furnishing should go into the buying of pots and pans, what part into mattresses, and is there any reason to spend money for ruffles? What are the proper and necessary tools to work with?[14]

Full classes and waitlists underscored the popularity of Kittredge's role-play approach to finding joy in domestic duties. "The man regards his business as a pleasure. He plays it as he plays a game, and he plays to win. And so housekeeping has become a 'game, not a duty'.... In a natural, enjoyable way our girls should be taught to play the game of household administration."[15]

Kittredge was not the first to "gamify" domestic activities. Less well known than the kindergarten movement, its contemporary the kitchen garden movement similarly rooted household training in play. Pioneered by Emily Huntington at the Wilson Industrial School for Girls during the 1870s, and spreading after 1880 thanks to Grace Dodge's New York Kitchen Garden Association, kitchen garden consisted in a substitution of household utensils in miniature for the toys, blocks, squares, and spheres of the kindergarten." Huntington initially proposed training the impoverished children who were likely future domestic service workers, but her methods proved popular with broader populations. Local Kitchen Garden Associations sprang up across the US, and the method was displayed at the World's Columbian Exposition children's building. Instructors soon replaced small-scale utensils with actual equipment and applied the language of developmental psychology to their work. Columbia University's Teachers College grew out of New York City's Kitchen Garden Association in 1892 (*Teachers College Record* was originally published as *Household Arts*), tackling a far broader range of subjects while staying committed to turning housekeeping into a game.[16]

These examples make clear how youth workers embraced learning by doing so long as the doing happened at some remove from the real world of work. Their enthusiasm for educational play rooted in developmental psychology in fact outstripped that of their educator colleagues in light of the fact that their programs required voluntary participation from kids. Organizing youth programming around activities that spectacularized reality and adopting a lexicon from developmental psychology thus heightened these activities' popular appeal and broadened the audience for their use.[17]

Bringing Junior Republics to the Middle Classes: Willis Brown's Boy Cities

Although, during the movement's first decade, George's Freeville republic served as an information clearinghouse, conversations among the growing community of republic organizers were fractured across conferences on recreation and charity, meetings on home economics and vocational education, and even on the Chautauqua circuit. Willis Brown, a charismatic Salt Lake City juvenile court judge, hoped to change this state of affairs. With ambitions for a national network of "Boy Cities" he aimed to mobilize educators and youth workers at schools, YMCAs, boys clubs, summer camps, churches and Chautauquas to pool their expertise and bring the republic experience to a new audience of middle-class boys. Ultimately unsuccessful, Brown's efforts nonetheless showcase the expanding appeal of republics and their component activities: how they traveled beyond rural landscapes and urban centers to small towns and suburban communities, beyond needy populations to mainstream populations, and how, over time, vicarious experiences of adult occupations became an increasingly familiar activity in the lives of American youth.[18]

Brown, a businessman, had no formal training in boys work or law. He first worked with youth when he made boys a target of his antismoking efforts with the Anti-Cigarette League. He discovered a gift connecting with kids and soon published *Pluck: A Paper for Earnest Boys and Girls Who Wish to Become Useful Men and Women*. Later a persuasive advocate for Utah's juvenile justice system, he became its first judge in 1905. Brown's methods were unorthodox. To understand how Salt Lake City youth spent their leisure time, he routinely trailed them around town. "A great proportion of the work of the juvenile court has been accomplished out of court," one journalist described. "A judge 'learned in the law and versed in the rules of procedure' would think it far beneath his dignity to spend his evening hours visiting pool rooms and saloons, cheap theatres, skating rinks, dance halls, homes blighted with poverty and sin in search of children in need of moral and material aid…That has not been the Brown way." Inside the courtroom Brown aimed "to rob his court of the sort of terror that, to the youthful mind, usually surround a court of justice" by making "every effort to become friendly with the boys and the girls who appear before him in chambers and in open court." Reductions in the number of children brought into court demonstrated the value of Brown's "most irregular" methods.[19]

Despite these accomplishments, Brown believed his court could do more, especially for destitute boys. For these youth he envisioned a "new life" in a Boy City, where they could learn agricultural and vocational skills and govern themselves. With assistance from private donors, Boy City debuted at Canyon Crest Ranch in 1906. "The boys themselves have a government of their own, with a mayor and other officials whose authority is unquestioned except by newcomers, and not long by them," described one journalist. Transplanted to the Utah countryside, urban youth took "pride in showing their chickens and cows, their horses, their orchard and the equipment of the place." Their physical and moral condition was transformed: "Clear-eyed, bright-faced, manly and healthy, they face the world with the courage of the lad who has discovered that everyone is anxious to help him when he is trying to help himself," he observed, noting "the wholesome atmosphere of the whole establishment."[20]

Historians have documented the juvenile court's centrality to the emergence of the sheltered childhood. Originating in 1899 in Chicago, this separate judicial system for youth was also a critical component of the "new penology," which prioritized rehabilitation rather than punishment. Convinced that placing juvenile delinquents with adults created more criminals and that young offenders should have opportunities for re-education, advocates aspired to make juvenile courts family-like educational institutions. Samuel Barrows of the International Penal and Prison Commission explained, "The true function of the court is educational." Jurists' self-styling as modern educators directed them to developmental psychology and to the view expressed by Denver's Ben Lindsey, the nation's most eminent juvenile jurist, that gangs have "many good qualities," such as "rules and laws…founded generally on really ennobling instincts" that "should be wisely controlled and directed rather than suppressed." This outlook fueled their interest in youth programs, including athletics, boys clubs, summer camps, and junior republics.[21]

Like their teacher colleagues, juvenile judges and probation officers were particularly concerned about immigrant youth on account of associations between criminality and race. And like the playground staff and settlement workers who viewed republics as natural follow-ons to extant programming, they too saw merit in these age-restricted worlds where making and enforcing laws and experiencing their consequences offered a preview of adult life. Even before Boy City's debut, juvenile judges already had begun to sentence youth to time in republics, and they joined these institutions' boards of trustees. Lindsey, on the advisory boards of George's republic and Gill's Patriotic League, was an especially vocal advocate: "My dream and hope is to see such a Republic established in every state in this Union," he declared in 1909, perhaps even in "every large city." New York City judge Max Griffenhagen became an affiliate of the Hebrew Sheltering Guardian Society, advising the boys and girls republics. California's Juvenile Court Association, led by Judge Curtis Wilbur, advocated for a California George Junior Republic and later for self-government inside the Los Angeles Parental School. Probation officers occasionally volunteered for staff positions. San Francisco's Arthur Todd, for example, participated in Boytown. Omaha's chief probation officer Harriet Hicox Heller supervised that city's playground republic. And Washington, D.C. juvenile court staff hired Progress City organizers to organize a youth democracy on their playground. These were merely early examples; republics with close ties to the juvenile justice system soon proliferated from Detroit's Ford Republic to Georgia Juvenile State.[22]

Brown had several ambitions for Boy City: expanding vocational training, building cottages, and taking more boys. His attention was soon diverted when leaders of the Chautauqua at Indiana's Winona Assembly and Summer School invited him to reorganize their boys' camp into a juvenile democracy populated not "by a citizenship of street arabs and urchins," but rather by middle-class Indiana youth. The timing was ideal. A consummate self-promoter, Brown's abrasive personal style forced him off the Utah bench in 1907. In his hands Boy City would exceed its sponsors' ambitions, further publicity for the idea that republics held value for youth from diverse backgrounds.[23]

Recruiting thousands to an untested juvenile municipality was vastly different from personally selecting, with the authority of the juvenile justice system, the handful of children who populated Canyon Crest Ranch. Assisted by "men who take a keen interest in boys" including "John M. Studebaker of South Bend, Thomas Kane of Chicago, Everett Sisson, editor of the *Interior*, J. F. Beyer and W. D. Fraxer of Warsaw, and Sol C. Dickey of Indianapolis," Brown got to work. As he sent out letters (ostensibly to every city and town in Indiana) to publicize the camp, and gave lectures across the state to rally interest, "inquiries for detailed information" began "pouring in...the 'fever' is spreading among the small boys of Indiana like a prairie fire." The program soon attracted participants from six other states.[24]

Following past practice at Freeville and Allendale, Brown planned for boys to arrive in groups as military "companies" under temporary adult command before transferring authority to a youth-run civil system. To build interest among the men he favored to serve as program staff, he planned on-site continuing education—a school for officers of the "YMCA Sunday schools, public schools, juvenile court, judges" and other "students of the boy problem." This fit well at Chautauqua, a key source of educational entertainment for the nation's rural populations. While Boy City supervisors at Canyon Crest were farmers, then, Winona Boy City was staffed by a new generation of rural youth workers, including the religious youth leaders who increasingly turned to science in their efforts to connect with kids.[25]

Brown's plans appealed to rural and small-town boys clubs, YMCAs, churches, and schools, some of which already had embraced junior republics' component activities. With Boys Brigades popular among Christian youth groups, the company model was a familiar idea. As groups signed on, Brown parceled out their summer assignments. "The boys who come from Marion have been given the privilege of publishing a daily paper, and every one of them will be a reporter, editor, copy reader or carrier," one journalist explained. Boys from Huntington "secured the banking rights of the camp and on the opening day will establish the 'Winona Rational (not National) Bank.' Several of the youngsters who are to count the money and keep the books in this institution are now receiving training in the banks at Huntington." Even before their arrivals, excited boys geared up their political campaigns.[26]

The companies erected their city of tents in July 1907. Goshen's Frank Abbott, a talented athlete and "son of a rich lumberman," who was "well known over northern Indiana," was elected mayor, and on the fourth day the boys municipality transitioned from military to civilian control. Although vocational training opportunities were scaled back from early plans in which "a grocery, a notion and candy store, a soda water fountain, a restaurant, a photographic supply shop, etc." were all "to be owned and operated by stock companies of boys," a bank, a newspaper, a restaurant, and a paving company were created by and for the youth.[27]

Alongside athletic competitions and dramatic performances, including a mock juvenile court proceeding led by Brown and starring the boys, the summer season's highlight was a circus. Judge Brown was the high diver and University of Wisconsin professor J. C. Elson the ringmaster. Madison pastor F. T. Galpin supervised the animal performance, while Portland, Indiana, Judge S. W. Haynes ran the sideshows. The boys sang, paraded, played music, and clowned. This "boy Chautauqua" became a major attraction at the assembly as Winona's adult visitors eagerly attended the performances put on by youth. Continuing education for supervisors—for example, lectures from judges from Cleveland and Indianapolis—proved so popular that Brown stayed on for ten days after the camp's closure, giving "talks to all interested in work among boys."[28]

Boy City operated for several summers at Winona and, later, for two years in Charlevoix, Michigan. "Dickey of Winona, Indiana, who first took up Brown and his Boy City, told me last summer than Brown was so dishonest that he had to get rid of him," Lindsey wrote to George, suggesting that Brown relocated the program for the same reasons he left the Utah bench. Initially supportive of Brown, Lindsey, George and their associates later turned on the Boy City movement leader when he failed to credit George. Despite their direct encounters on the Chautauqua circuit and the National Conference on Charities and Corrections, Brown insisted that Boy City was the first of its kind in the US. "Our friend Willis Brown...seems to have decided to swipe your

George Junior Republic," Lindsey wrote to George. "Brown is certainly our evil genius," George replied. "I think you and I would vote him the medal for consummate cheek." Brown's character notwithstanding, Boy City was widely hailed, expanding facilities to include a lighting plant, water works, hospital, and church, and ultimately attracting participants from two dozen states. Many kids returned for multiple seasons.[29]

Even as he frustrated Lindsey and George, Brown advanced the junior republic movement by bringing in scores of middle-class, small-town youth. As important as the summer program in ensuring their participation was the work Brown did after season's end. Recognizing that companies of boys organized before the summer helped to get the program off to a good start, he transformed Boy City into a year-round operation. Staying on for several months in Indianapolis, he worked with S. W. Haynes of Portland, Indiana, a lawyer and member of the county board of charities and corrections, and Charles Hahn (aka "Uncle Heinie"), the former chief probation officer of the Salt Lake City juvenile court, to develop satellite Boy City clubs (also called Boyvilles) in schools and youth-serving institutions in cities and towns across Indiana and further afield. Betterment for youth who were already "good" and cultivating greater professionalism in the boys work community would be at the heart of these plans.[30]

Largest among them was the 300-strong Boyville colony at Anderson, Indiana, under Hahn's direction, referred to as the Anderson Boy Movement there. With close ties to the local Christian Templars, the group met at a neighborhood church and in the town's public library. The boys organized a municipal government with mayor, city clerk, treasurer, and board of public works. They published a monthly magazine (*Club Boy*), and ran a bank, post office, and recreational activities such as athletics and parades. Although participants lacked opportunities to try out other occupations, local business leaders frequently addressed them on vocational subjects. The club was thus a miniature version of the summer operation—a copy of a Boy City that itself aimed to copy cities in the adult world.[31]

William George and Wilson Gill Press On

As Brown's efforts continued, William George grew increasingly anxious to reassert control over the republic idea. He had been working to improve Freeville—expanding industrial training for participating youth, exploring vocational opportunities at local firms, transferring cottage control to adult houseparents, and enrolling greater numbers of middle-class youth. He had opened another new republic in 1907, the California Junior Republic, in Chino, California, with assistance from enthusiastic citizens. "There was no dearth of volunteers...it seemed as though every boy and girl at Freeville was struck with the California fever." Nat Bedford, a former citizen, served as its first superintendent. He continued to correspond with a range of parties interested in organizing republics in their communities.[32]

The following year George established a National Association of Junior Republics, stepping back from Freeville's daily management with hopes of exerting greater influence on republics' spread. Initially restricting membership to republics he started, George later enrolled Illinois's Allendale, Michigan's Ford Republic, and Georgia's Juvenile State. These institutions were not carbon copies. For example, at the Ford Republic, adults could be tried in the youth-administered court and kids could appeal its decisions to a Detroit juvenile judge. Director Homer Lane decided against creating a jail to prevent what he called the "glaring defects" of the current US justice system from being replicated by participating youth. George and his associates viewed them as Freeville's closest cousins, however, "the real ones" among his imitators—especially Juvenile State, formed with his counsel. "All of us who are engaged in Junior Republic and self-government work, should bury our minor differences of opinion, and stand together shoulder to shoulder against the reactionaries and the autocrats in factor of institutionalism and militarism," wrote republic association secretary Lyman Beecher Stowe to Ford Republic administrators. Aware of efforts by Gill and Brown to mobilize their own national movements, he and other association affiliates did not always look kindly on competitors, although Gill, who credited George, escaped the harshest criticism.[33]

New George Junior Republics in Grove City, Pennsylvania (1909), Strawbridge, and Flemington Junction, New Jersey (1911) suggested George had found a way to expedite duplication. To further consolidate control, he increasingly tapped students from nearby Cornell as volunteers, training them in republic methods. And he published two books on the republic movement, *The Junior Republic: Its History and Ideals* (1910) and *Citizens Made and Remade* (1912, with Stowe, a fellow Goo Goo and secretary and vice chair of New York's Public Service Commission). Cognizant of the fashion for scientific methods in education and youth work, George revised his founding narrative to suggest that children's instincts for impersonation, "the old inclination which dwells in every boy to play court and jail and school, to govern his companions and to be governed by them in turn," had guided him from the start. A preface by Thomas Osborne, now George Junior Republic Association president, to the 1910 book emphasized similar themes. "Just as in the newer methods of teaching it has been found that in many cases the best way to learn a thing is by doing it, so one can really learn how to be a citizen only by being a citizen, can learn to bear responsibility only by bearing responsibility."[34]

Yet if George hoped to capitalize on psychologists' and educators' enthusiasm for his civic dramatization, he was unable to restrict their attention to the membership of the George Junior Republic Association. G. Stanley Hall had opened Boy City's second season with a public speech and in subsequent writings added to his praise for George kind words about Willis Brown and James Rogers. Richard Welling organized a course on pupil self-government at New York University with numerous guest speakers, making clear the growing canon even as he included George and Hall. Officially sanctioned republics were outnumbered as school cities and Boyvilles were installed in boys clubs, settlements, orphanages, and Sunday schools. They began to appear outside the US as well.[35]

After 1904, Wilson Gill turned his attention to rural districts alongside urban areas, bringing school republics to Indian reservations and Alaskan territory. Native American pupils' interest in his methods, and public recognition that school republics could help achieve "the goal of all Indian legislation...complete absorption of the Indian population into the body politic with the rights, privileges, duties and responsibilities of American citizens," got Gill appointed federal supervisor of Indian schools in 1911, with a mandate to install republics in every institution his department oversaw. At residential reservation-based "model cities," boys and girls built small cottages, raised chickens, tended gardens, constructed and maintained playground equipment, and policed the grounds. Native American adults could not vote in US elections, but their children were seen to benefit from the lessons these republics supplied.[36]

Gill too capitalized on the scientific theories that others associated with his work. Emboldened by the Cresson Medal, he declared his School City a "laboratory method," proposing that its experimental approach modernized civics much as lab science had altered chemistry curricula. Gill's collaborator Delos Wilcox followed, citing Dewey and others to explain how school-based republics helped youth to transition from "the play-world of childhood" to "the work-world of manhood and womanhood." The expanded advisory board to Gill's organization, including George Junior Republic

Figure 3.5
Taking the oath of office, Carlisle Indian School.
Source: Wilson Gill, *A New Citizenship* (Philadelphia: Patriotic League, 1913).

affiliates like Josiah Strong, Ben Lindsey, Lyman Beecher Stowe, and Jacob Riis, attested to growing nondenominational support for the republic idea.[37]

As Gill's career was expanding from urban to rural populations, Brown's took the opposite trajectory. In 1910, Gary, Indiana, school superintendent William Wirt recruited Brown to take up residence as assistant superintendent of moral and civic training and judge of the local parental court with a mandate to install a boy city in local schools. Brown's work in Gary highlights how practical as much as pedagogical concerns made role-plays of adult life so appealing to educators and youth workers alike. As schools and youth-serving institutions struggled to make ends meet, they discovered these developmentally productive activities were also economically productive. These financial factors suggest why the freestanding junior republics George endorsed were rapidly outnumbered by institution-based alternatives. And they reveal how the parental institutions that sheltered youth simultaneously sustained a variation on the family economy that reaped the rewards of children's energies while distancing these activities from child labor. That Gary, Indiana—a company town whose schools applied methods of factory efficiency—stopped short of full accounting of how young people manufactured the institutions that sheltered them points to how the associations that linked republics and their component activities to educational entertainments that were realistic but not real not only popularized them; equally it shaped the interpretation of their cost-saving effects. Emphasizing the distance between reality and representation, work and work-like activities, obscured how young people's role-plays of adult occupations assisted the family economies of individual parental institutions and in turn produced the sheltered childhood itself.[38]

Playing at Work and Working at Play in Gary, Indiana

Developments in Gary typified transformations to work in the industrial age. Scholars have described economic, social, and cultural dislocations associated with a second industrial revolution that reorganized labor processes and introduced new machines. Skilled artisans who previously produced entire products in family or neighborhood workshops now found lower-skilled laborers employed in factories or firms to be capable of doing their jobs at a faster pace. Work was said to be becoming more machine-like, and workers becoming more like machines: "animate machines," as Goo Goo William Tolman described, or "living machinery" and "human equipment" in Meadville Theological School professor N. P. Gilman's terms.[39]

As the new managerial classes engaged in conversations about maximizing production, they discovered that organized leisure refueled employees' energies, conserving human resources and increasing efficiency. Tolman, who served on the George Junior Republic's advisory board, explained: While "the essential characteristic of the industrial conditions of to-day is the substitution of mechanical for muscular power," it had been "slowly dawning upon the mind of the employer that his human machine—his hands as he sometimes calls them—needs attention, needs rest, needs the best environment for the production of the best results."[40]

Such discoveries sparked an "industrial betterment" movement organizing welfare programs toward efficiency goals. Factories and other firms planned continuing education in cooking and English, choruses, baseball teams, employee magazines, thrift savings plans, and group outings. Industrial campuses added gardens, sports fields, and other amenities. Some even established settlements or YMCAs onsite to assist with program coordination. Such efforts at worker "uplift," which were sometimes called "welfare work," aimed not to lift workers out of the existing social structure so much as adjust them to their new status and enhance their value to employers. In a context of managers' fears about interference in the new ways of doing business (whether from unionizing or striking workers or government labor regulations), these programs also publicized business leaders' "care" for employees.[41]

Although most programs targeted adults, children were the occasional beneficiaries of employer-sponsored kindergartens and schools. National Civic Federation welfare secretary and former settlement worker Gertrude Beeks, investigating such programs in several southern mills, suggested these workplaces were child-saving institutions for workers' families and child laborers: "The cotton mills are industrial training schools as well as refuges for the unfortunate," she wrote in 1906. "Too much praise cannot be given to the mill owners...giving food and shelter and an industrial training to the illiterate descendants of the first inhabitants of the colonies, but, through their Welfare Work, are a great civilizing influence and are steadily raising the standard of citizenship." Echoing an older language describing factories as schools of citizenship, now the workplaces that were the focus for anti-child-labor campaigns became citizenship schools. Gilman saw South Carolina's factories in similar terms. According to this view, child labor in settings with opportunities for education and recreation were preferable to the criminality of street life in communities lacking compulsory schooling.[42]

Such workforce trends were present in Gary, Indiana, where schools for workers' families represented one of US Steel's earliest public investments. Gary's schools paired two visions of curricular innovation for the industrial age. Superintendent Wirt, who had studied with John Dewey, prioritized play-based learning by doing, and bridging school and life. Simultaneously, Wirt applied US Steel's scientific management to education toward "social efficiency"—matching each student to the career that best suited him or her—and toward the efficient operation of the school "plant." Even before the publication of *Principles of Scientific Management* (1911), educators wondered what they could learn from Frederick Winslow Taylor's factory efficiency work. Although the two philosophies were regarded as largely incompatible, Wirt recognized that when students performed adult occupations, they could achieve educational goals while reducing institutional costs.[43]

The Emerson School, established in 1909, illustrates. On a campus rich in facilities—playground, zoo, conservatory, gardens, science labs, workshops, and pools—pupils rotated through book-based classes, play-based activities, and work training to maximize the facilities' use. Vocational education courses made playground equipment and school furniture and repaired the facilities. Home economics classes prepared meal budgets and made lunch for fellow students. Laboratory science classes assisted the city chemist "testing city water and milk supplies; his children are practically deputy food inspectors, visiting dairies, bakeries, and food-shops." Other classes kept accounts for the school office and undertook community surveys. Many teachers were working experts rather than conventionally trained instructors, bringing aspects of the apprentice system inside schools. Wirt explained:

> There is no reason why the school furniture and much of the equipment cannot be made in school cabinet shops under the direction of a cabinet-maker selected for his teaching ability as well as his mechanical skill. There is no reason why the school painting, stage scenery, plumbing, electrical work, carpentry, printing and bookbinding, forging, foundry and machine work cannot be done in the same way.... There is no reason why some of the nature-study teachers should not be selected because of their practical knowledge and skill as well as for their college degrees. A practical landscape gardener can take complete charge of the school garden, lawns, shrubbery, and trees, and the children will be delighted to assist him.

Such close relationships to the city's business community encouraged youth who otherwise might choose work to attend school instead, rewarding Emerson with low truancy rates and rewarding graduates with easy access to employment.[44]

This was the context for Boyville and Boytown, the boy cities organized by Brown. (Although Gary's schools were coed, like some classes the boy cities were single sex.) Boyville, with government of mayor, council, clerk, and police, bank, court, newspaper (*The Boyville News*), cooperative store, band, and athletic league, brought a satellite Boy City to a new audience of urban youth. Boytown, with smaller population but larger campus, more closely resembled the scheme at Canyon Crest Ranch. Located on the school's farm outside the city, it was populated by pupils who had broken school rules. They lived in cottages, attended classes, made bricks for school facilities, and cultivated the farm for wages from which they paid room and board. "In Gary we have two communities," Brown described. "One of them is a community of men and women and the other a community of boys and girls." These parallel worlds were separate but not dissimilar, went the now-familiar story.

> As all these boys are to be citizens of the adult community, and vote and obey or disobey law, what better plan than to instill in them, in their formative period, the responsibilities of citizenship...Boyville, patterned after the regular city and the city institutions, both public and private, involving social and business life places boys in a position to exercise their judgment in making their own laws, in conducting their own affairs, in devising standards of judgment and in measuring citizenship in the boy community.

Boytown was a similarly "real community" where "the boys are as much responsible individuals" as the citizens of Gary, other observers agreed. "In it all," Brown concluded, "the one requirement for citizenship is, 'Play the game square.'"[45]

Despite such familiar descriptions, the new republics departed from precedent in important ways. As the head of the new parental court, Brown added a judiciary lacking in earlier Boy Cities whose councils were responsible for discipline: a youth court with authority to sentence peers to join Boytown and "to settle all cases involving the conduct of the boys at school whether these occur in school or out." Following this precedent he invited citizens to extend other activities beyond school boundaries. Boyville ordinances discouraged littering and cutting over vacant lots, and sent child detectives to suss out businesses selling cigarettes to underage youth. "It was only a brief while before the most eager 'cigarette fiend' could not buy a cigarette from the most greedy dealer," a journalist reported. "Too many had been reported by the boy detectives." A storekeeper concurred, "There's nothing in selling to minors now. A regular policeman you can afford to smile at. But these darned little mosquitoes of our Boyville never miss seeing everything." As Brown publically campaigned to make children immune from arrest by adult authorities, then, he was optimistic about the benefits of peers adjudicating their misdeeds.[46]

Brought to life in a context where the new education and social efficiency were equal priorities, these republics' significance lies as much in their contributions to the operation of the school system and the city of Gary as in the learning by doing and bridging school and life they supplied—and, in turn, in how these economic impacts could be categorized as contributions to reducing child labor. Boyville's bankers managed savings and loans; its shopkeepers ran a store doing "real business" with "real money." The young detectives eradicated smoking more effectively than adult police; the "understanding with the city authorities" was that only delinquency cases that could not be settled by the Boyville court were seen in "the regular courts." Junior citizens built and maintained school facilities—in particular at Boytown, where the boys were paid for their activities and in turn paid for their room and board (and, indeed, could leave with the cash they earned as was the case in the Freeville republic). Yet all of these activities were conceived of as rehearsing for adult life, a "game of citizenship," that was realistic but never the real thing in itself. The Boyville bank and store, for example, were "only suggestive of things which may be done in connection with the organization of the *life* of the school to bring the various academic courses of the school into closer relation to *actual life*," noted Illinois teacher Horace Hollister. The Boy Cities' primary present-day value was not economic, then, but rather educational and recreational, constructively channeling young people's natural instincts for impersonating adults. Observers instead stressed how benefits would accrue to the boys and the community in the longer term: "The fact of the business is that in five years' time the kids of Boyville and the Emerson School will be running that town of Gary and running it right."[47]

From Gary Republics to Gary Schools

Such assessments typified discussions of the economic implications of the many component activities of junior republics that were staples of the Gary school system. This point has particular significance because the system served as model for more than 200 other communities in the short term and over 1,000 by 1929. Indeed, Gary's schools attracted so many visitors that administrators set aside open days to minimize disruptions.[48]

Proponents of the new education approvingly described Gary's schools as miniature communities. "Clearly the Gary school is organized as a community, self-supporting industrially and varied as is the larger community." They praised its curriculum for following children's natural interests. "Can you see how a school conducted on these lines will naturally hold its pupils? ... The children in the Gary schools do exactly what they would do if left to themselves." Echoing Dewey's preferences for real rather than make-believe activities, Wirt viewed "One week of two hours a day on a real job with a real workman" as "worth more from the standpoint of vocational guidance than two or three hours a day every day in the year in an artificial shop working on artificial work and under artificial conditions." Performing these adult roles bridged school and life, he asserted: "We try to give the children not a playground, not a shop, not a study room, but a life," laying the groundwork "to transform the play impulse into the work impulse" for the longer term and "to make citizens of the children." Gary's schools thus realized educators' long-standing ambitions. "It is this very thing which our best philosophers of education have had in mind for centuries," Hollister wrote, citing Froebel, Pestalozzi, and Herbart. Dewey concurred, calling in *Schools of Tomorrow* (1915) for the extension of similar programs to other schools.[49]

Proponents of social efficiency were equal fans of Gary's system for its creative applications of scientific management inside schools. "The Gary public schools are operated on the same principles of scientific management that animate the ten miles of steel works on the lake front," journalist Rheta Child Dorr explained. *McClure's* writer Burton Hendrick pushed the school-factory analogy further, noting how Gary was getting "the largest possible returns out of its raw material"—in this case "not steel and iron, but boys and girls." This outcome was welcome in a city whose community amenities were strained. Gary's population quintupled between 1906 and 1909 and, as the city's first annual report elaborated, "There was not anything with which to start. The funds for the support of the schools for the first year had to be borrowed, and thus the limited funds for the following year had to be mortgaged in order to make a start besides, every desk, map, globe, chart, reference book.... every single thing needed to be purchased at once." Following the municipal authorities who earned Gary its nickname "Economy, Indiana" and building on Goo Goos' efforts to make school administration more efficient, then, Wirt's schools exemplified municipal efficiency at the curricular level: rotating student groups to maximize use of the school plant and reducing costs by matching school needs and children's education according to laboratory methods. Hendrick elaborated, "Everything the boys and girls do has a definite end. Each shop connected with the school is a real one. A master-mechanic, in every case a trade-union man, presides over it. The boys and this mechanic, working together, produce objects of real utility which are used in the school equipment" including desks, lockers, and bookcases. And they repaired broken plumbing, electrical, and other systems. This approach had

> one remarkable result, in addition to giving these boys the needed training. These several departments cost the city of Gary practically nothing. An accurate account of all the work done is kept, and is charged up against each separate department on the basis of regular union wages. At the end of the year, it is found that the boys have earned enough—that is, saved enough for the school system—to pay the entire cost of conducting the school departments, including the salaries of the instructors.

In the girls' classes, "the same situation prevails. The lunch-room, which the girls in the cooking class daily supply with food, sells lunches enough to pay the cost of maintenance, including the salary of a woman housekeeper."[50]

Educational historians typically characterize the new education and social efficiency as being at odds on visions of education reform for democratic citizenship. According to this view, new education adherents like John Dewey favored liberal education

Figure 3.6
Vocational education classes making school furniture, Gary, Indiana.
Source: Rheta Childe Dorr, "Keeping the Children in School," *Hampton's Magazine* 27, no. 1 (July 1911).

Figure 3.7
Cooking classes making school lunch, Gary, Indiana.
Source: Henry Holmes, "The Gary System Explained," *Review of Reviews* 59 (June 1919).

whereas social efficiency types like Massachusetts education commissioner David Snedden preferred curricula stressing practical skills. The Gary experience showcases how both shared ambitions to pair a protected childhood with opportunities to vicariously experience adulthood as the centerpiece of school reform. Thus, Snedden's call for vocational schools to "reproduce practical processes" to give pupils "many hours of each working day in actual practical work" echoed Dewey's insistence that educators follow young people's basic instincts for imitating adult occupations. In the "primitive wilderness, the boy followed his father in hunting and fishing and, in time, by processes of imitation and suggestion, coupled with the learning which comes from trial and error, he became himself a fairly efficient hunter or fisherman," Snedden elaborated. "At the same time, the girl was at work with her mother, acquiring the simple arts of preparing food, dressing skins, and tilling the soil, which were the woman's contributions to the necessary work of the time." To motivate contemporary youth, he argued, "The vocational school should divest itself as completely as possible of the academic atmosphere, and should reproduce as fully as possible the atmosphere of economic endeavor in the field for which it trains"—in short, to get "near to reality" such that "shop standard, not school standards, must prevail." Although Snedden typically argued in favor of separating vocational schools from more academic institutions, he was impressed by how Gary combined the two.[51]

Across these ideological divides, cooking, making furniture, gardening, and related activities, when performed by young people as work for pay in the wider world, were understood to be increasingly culturally undesirable activities. Yet the same activities carried out as role-plays under the auspices of youth-serving institutions were the sources of civic and character education. As Edward Devine, editor of *Charities*, put it in 1908, "work which we deny...in the factory, for profit, may be demanded in school...for education and training." Cost savings accrued from this approach. But such activities were not child labor; they were dramatizations of adult labor. Although, like Devine, Gary's educators spoke of work within the tripartite division of the curriculum's "work-play-study," and appointed as workshop supervisors individuals who might have trained apprentices offsite, they classified such activities among the era's myriad ways to experience the world via representation: "It is not child labor," Wirt explained to any who might doubt this interpretation, but a "preventive agency," because "there is a wholesome environment and the children are being instructed." Even Gary's critics, such as those who argued it "turned kids into [future] factory hands" by training them for low-skill rather than complex jobs, overlooked its present-day economic implications. The popular language of schools and youth-serving institutions as "factories of citizenship" and factories as "schools of citizenship" only went so far in revealing the institutions' similarities. Such hidden economic effects are a previously unrecognized aspect of the influential Gary plan.[52]

Anti-child-labor advocates endorsed the Gary system. That "only union workmen are employed for the industrial work in connection with which pupils get vocational training" benefited both parties, observed US Bureau of Education staff. "Pupils who work with them get no pay, their services being given in exchange for the instruction which they received" and union workers found new markets for their skills. "Nearly all of these lines of work are self-supporting," and "some of them, indeed, are a source of income to the schools, to say nothing of the value of them as an educational opportunity." National Child Labor Committee staff had rejected Gertrude Beeks's claims that southern mills sheltered their child workers, but assessed Gary's schools with a different eye. Acknowledging imperfections in the system—for example, that the pupils' spelling and math errors in record keeping went uncriticized—they nonetheless praised Gary's leadership for enabling students to "practice democratic theory in school conduct and discipline" and for creating opportunities for children to "obtain educational values not only through books but through genuine life activities. ... Here at last education has been made vital and absorbing to the child," giving students "a richer, more educative life in school than any plan as yet put into execution."[53]

Beyond the Gary Plan

Close scrutiny of republics beyond Gary finds a similar story. Freeville citizens contracted projects with local businesses, joined George and board members on their fundraising trips, and settled new republics. San Francisco republic citizens picked fruit and performed minstrel shows to fund the summer communities they constructed from the ground up. Allendale and Garden City farmers and gardeners sold their produce to vacationers. School republics enlisted pupils to serve as health inspectors and truant officers, and to build baseball diamonds, playground equipment, and dormitories. Progress City street cleaners kept the playground clean and repaired the Hiram House fence. Newark's playground republic police and Hebrew Sheltering Guardian Society Orphan Asylum republic librarians reduced the need to hire supervisory staff. Boy City, Winona, citizens built a gym, paved streets, and raised money through circus performances.[54]

Children performing adult roles thus made substantial economic contributions to the institutions that sheltered them. One school administrator reported, "The time formerly spent in duties outside of their rooms saved to my teachers amounts in one day to five hours and twenty minutes, in one week twenty-six hours and four minutes, in one year 214 school days. If the teachers are using that time in preparation of lesson work, at the present salary rate, the value to my school in one year is $642." As a result, "321 days are gained, amounting to $963 per annum." Playground workers recognized similar benefits. "If the Park Board could appropriate a certain sum monthly to the juvenile city and they in return take the contract for cutting the grass, watering, assisting in cleaning the grounds, etc.," Arthur Leland proposed on his move to St. Paul, Minnesota, "a very practical method of teaching municipal methods of handling money and work could be evolved and at the same time a great deal of the work of the care of the grounds could be done more cheaply than it is at present." As social efficiency proponents increasingly cheered republics, George, Gill, and others responded with greater public talk of efficiency.[55]

Similarly, at schools and youth-serving institutions without republics, skill training and character building schemes celebrated for their future payoffs yielded more immediate benefits. Students built housing and recreational facilities at residential schools for Native Americans and African Americans. Public school pupils took attendance, managed finances, constructed libraries and gyms, prepared lunches, and printed newspapers. Even Dewey's pupils produced the lab school's "necessary articles." Summer program participants set up camp, made meals, and ran numerous activities. Youth built model kitchens and practice cottages at settlements and beyond. Mrs. Daddy's proposal that "The money that was spent on men's work" could be saved by assigning tasks to youth thus represented yet another generalizable feature of the junior republic experience. So too was Thomas Osborne's praise for Freeville as a "manufactory of citizens, men and women"—which lost sight of the extent to which participating youth manufactured the experience themselves.[56]

The possibility that such activities constituted child labor thus was nearly unthinkable. When Progress City citizens repaired the settlement's fence, sewed bloomers for gym class, and did the settlement's printing, they were pursuing educational recreation—learning by doing and "playing at citizenship." Orphans of the Hebrew Sheltering Guardian Society republic who ran the institution's library, organized clubs, administered a bank and charity enjoyed "a source of boyish fun." The Worcester children who, Rev. R. J. Floody reported, "transformed this whole district of five acres of dump into beautiful gardens...enhanced the value of land in and around the gardens about $350,000...beautified the community, filled up holes reeking with malaria and mosquitoes, raising the health rate according to the state health inspector, 72 per cent, in three years" and sold some of the produce they cultivated, were merely gaining future-oriented work training. "This kind of education teaches the boy to work, to produce something, to assume responsibility," he explained. When Newark youth transformed a junkyard into a playground which they subsequently supervised at "a savings of several hundred dollars to the city," the site by definition was for play, not work, a space where "imitation in a youngster" can "bring out all that is best" in him or her. "Your playgrounds may lack funds for equipment and salaries for a large staff of helpers," Newark playground director William McKiernan counseled other play leaders, "but if you have playground organization you will be surprised to find how many willing hands and hearts there will be at your service." Textbooks for play leaders reiterated McKiernan's suggestion, explaining how "the purpose of the use of [youth] leadership is development of the individual child along social and character-building lines rather than a solution of an administrative problem." The simultaneous realism and nonrealism of these activities—like Boy City, "so real" that "it will be as though it was an actual city"—enabled educators and youth workers to reassure themselves, their young

Figure 3.8
Progress City carpenters repairing the Hiram House fence.
Source: Charles Bushnell, "Progress City," *The World Today* 12 (1907).

charges, and the broader public that republics and their component activities supplied play-based, educational "reproductions," "miniatures," and "models" rather than the actual activities themselves.[57]

Similar interpretations framed component activities at schools and youth-serving institutions. These included the model kitchens whose girls played housekeeping games and prepared lunchroom meals for sale, and vocational education, with output of obvious economic value that Snedden encouraged "be disposed of, partly to the profit of the school, and partly to the profit of the individual worker." When students were paid for their participation, such as the girls staffing Chicago's public school cafeterias, their remuneration was instead described as financial aid enabling them to remain in school, since learning was "the business of the child's life, just as earning a living or caring for a family is to be the business of a child's adult life," as Gill explained.[58]

Although such activities now were justified in the language of efficiency and sometimes even labeled as work, although they took place in a context marked by criticisms of reformatories' contract labor and occasional debates about the economic status of schoolwork, although psychologists and educators saw play and work on a continuum, although schools and factories shared advisers as play experts counseled factories on industrial betterment and efficiency experts advised schools, and although there was some awareness that reformers occasionally exploited children in pursuit of their agendas, popular consensus was that the new curriculum removed youth from the world of actual work and substituted a vicarious experience instead. Unions had protested contract labor in reformatories and prisons as sources of unfair and underpriced competition. They raised few similar concerns about schools and youth-serving institutions suggesting they, too, did not regard these activities as child labor. Historians of youth, who have identified the exemption of farm work from classifications of child labor in this period, have not similarly registered how schools and youth-serving institutions were similarly exempt, how activities undertaken to be developmentally beneficial for youth were economically beneficial for their adult sponsors, and, in turn, how the dual realities that helped to engage youth enabled the classification of these productive activities in nonwork terms.[59]

Participating youth similarly distinguished between activities carried out within age-restricted spaces and the same activities carried out for pay in the wider world. "Just when one thinks that the citizens are working hardest," Progress City trainee Ethel Rogers reported, "he finds that they view the matter in a very different light. One young Jewish lad had mentioned working at home on a Saturday on a hammock that he was making. 'But you are not allowed to work on the Sabbath, are you?'" Rogers asked him. "Aw, dis ain't work, it's play," he explained, one of the many boys who "do not begrudge hours spent weeding under the hot July sun or pounding at brass work till hands ache and ears tingle." Instead they were more likely to plead with supervisors, "Ain't you just let me finish dis one piece?" Participants in the State of Columbia and

City of Telhi, which James Rogers, "saddened by tales of stunted, overworked children" billed as a solution to "the great social problem—child labor" so enjoyed the work he praised for its "educational value as a manual training occupation" that they rejected peers' proposals to limit their hours.[60]

Certainly, not every role-playing activity provided immediate economic benefits nor did those with value cover all costs. George, for example, took on many children at a loss. In other cases, associations with fun dulled but did not erase the awareness of children's labor. *Boys' Life* reported on the Waukesha, Wisconsin, pupils who "started a regular factory in the manual training room of their high school building" one summer, paying rent to the school board and "making money through the sale of their products." The boys "don't feel that they are 'working'—they are having a jolly, good time earning what is considerably more than pin money." Yet the new approaches' popularity meant that educational outputs with market value were common features of youth programming. Gertrude Beeks thus had been on to something in her assessments: factories, mills, schools, and youth-serving institutions were more alike than educators and youth workers cared to admit.[61]

Women's Separate Spheres and Children's Double Lives

That young people's labor at schools and youth-serving institutions was broadly overlooked paralleled the experience of women at home during this period of change in the location and meaning of work. The rise of an industrial wage economy increasingly assigned value only to money-generating activities in designated worksites. Previously the site of most productive labor, domestic spaces and the activities within them acquired new identities as unproductive.[62]

Women's exclusion from the economy took several forms. Some industries replacing home production were closed to women. Others forced them out by restricting family wages to men. Yet it was rhetorical shifts, more than changes to household activities' realities, that lay at the root of how domestic tasks previously considered productive home work were refigured as unproductive homemaking and tied to women's "natural" care instincts. Despite calls to assign economic value to household activities, efforts to industrialize household labor through scientific management and laborsaving machines, and servants' wages for the same activities, the ideology of separate spheres prevailed. This made it difficult to see how women's labor sustained households and the industrial economy.[63]

Understanding how ideas about children's unproductivity developed alongside these discourses about women calls attention to the significance of public talk about young people's activities inside sheltered spaces and to how age, like gender, played a role in defining work. Certainly, American youth experienced real reductions in child labor, as histories of childhood have already described. Yet examples from Gary and beyond make clear that the disappearance of child labor had essential rhetorical dimensions. Theoretical and practical contributions from psychologists, educators, and youth workers offered rationales for young people in schools and youth-serving institutions to engage in activities for which they would be criticized in other settings. Payments for services rendered were deemed subsidiary to the learning experience and necessary incentives for keeping these populations in school. The power to explain away young people's productivity thus lay not only in the separate spheres of the sheltered childhoods provided in schools and youth-serving institutions but also in the double lives of the simulated adulthoods they simultaneously enabled these populations to lead. Attending to the significance of such occupational simulations in the lives of modern youth reveals how child savers held more ambiguous positions on the child labor question than previously presumed. Treating the activities of young restaurateurs, newspaper publishers, and police like living villages and wax museums—as vicarious experiences that had a reality that departed from the real thing—they shaped the definitions of what counted or did not count as child labor, shaping the history of capitalism as well.[64]

Expanding Support, Debating Supervision

Support for junior republics and their component activities widened still further in the ensuing years. State and local officials such as Akron mayor William Sawyer, Scranton mayor Benjamin Dimmick, Cleveland sanitary police chief Mildred Chadsey, Ohio governor Judson Harmon, and New York parks supervisor John Neilsen now followed public educators and juvenile judges in interacting with youth through field trips and speaking engagements. Nationally recognized politicians, including Theodore Roosevelt, William Taft, Charles Fairbanks, William Jennings Bryan, and James Garfield, expressed their enthusiasm from further afield.[65]

Certainly, pockets of skepticism persisted. Most focused attention on the departures from reality in the experiences of adulthood that republics supplied, for example Boy Cities' "land" and "water" parties, Hamilton Fish Playground City's cabinet department of sports equipment, or the absence of police at the Hebrew Sheltering Guardian Society republics. Such commentaries offered evidence of broad enthusiasm for guiding young people's access "to live another life" even as they disagreed on the details. Repeating early criticisms of Freeville, some complained that as inexact replicas these juvenile democracies could not accurately teach the lessons they sought to instill. Writer Randolph Bourne accused Gary's Boyville of being "an unreality...a parody of municipal functions," even as he praised how the Gary schools' "intensive cultivation of resources produces that 'embryonic community life' which is Professor Dewey's ideal."[66]

Critics increasingly directed attention to the limits of self-government in adult-supervised settings. Visiting Freeville for two months in 1897, Hall student T. R. Crosswell had noted that, although otherwise ideal, it was "impossible to disguise the fact that at times there was a power over" the citizens "which did not originate among themselves and which at times cause many to feel that all was a sham." Later observers had noted the "mock machinery" and "pretended management of matters" there. "These laws are sometimes said to be made by the children themselves, and a part of them undoubtedly are," wrote Boston Normal School psychology department head Colin Scott, "but the original constitution was given to them by Mr. George, and other measures have also been introduced by him." According to this view, the republic was "a play which is educative in a certain sense; that is, the children get a dramatized presentation, in which they are themselves the actors, of the way in which governments are run." Yet "Mr. George, and the authority vested in him by the adult state," was "the real force back of all the children's laws.... The same thing is true, at the bottom, of the industrial and economic features." Philadelphia school superintendent Oliver Cornman similarly assessed school cities, proposing they inadvertently replicated boss rule: "Just as the modern animal trainer can teach his four-footed pupils the most marvelous tricks, the children can be made to play the game more or less well."[67]

The ambition shared by George, Gill, and Brown to encourage young people to supervise themselves had been a source of early misunderstanding, exacerbated by media reports that overstated children's authority. Now critics suggested children's agency was a sham—confusion compounded by the contradictory meanings of self-government in circulation. The term "self-government" was increasingly popular, explained Oberlin theology professor George Walter Fiske in 1912. "But it is so elastic it seems to mean various things...from mere parliamentary gymnastics under rigid adult oversight, to the other extreme...where small boys have obtained the premature dignity of doing what they please." Youth workers who approved some necessary fictions in these model communities took a harder line on questions of real power for participating youth, seeking a middle ground between Fiske's two extremes. What critics failed to realize, Gill explained, was that balancing youth agency with adult oversight mirrored the American political system:

> Some, no doubt, believe that the power of a student democracy to administer government is not real, because the principal and faculty retain their authority over the school. This is a mistaken idea. The power delegated by the principal and faculty to the School City and State is no less real than the power delegated to the county or town by New York State. The higher authority in either case retains, as it should, the right to demand that the delegated power be used wisely and justly. Thus while we do not have supreme power, we do have real power and, consequently, real responsibility.[68]

In short, successful republics demanded an approach to supervision that ensured, as Freeville board members had articulated in response to the New York state charity board's investigation, that young citizens remained engaged in life in the juvenile democracy and be "led gradually to adopt these new habits of their own free choice."

Administrators across a variety of child societies found in educators' discussions of suggestion a way forward for their work. McKiernan explained: "To make your self-government plans effective you must exercise constant supervision," he explained, "but it must be of the invisible, intangible kind. Suggestion to the juvenile officers is better than dictation, and example is more impressive than commands" because using too heavy a hand would lead participants to abandon the scheme. (Seeing McKiernan as a kindred spirit George offered him the position of superintendent at Flemington Junction. McKiernan declined due to its low salary.)[69]

Updating earlier discussions of educational suggestion, these youth workers largely dropped references to hypnosis, despite its destigmatization. Yet the basic belief in young people's natural imitativeness and suggestibility remained. Following psychologist Josiah Royce's assessment that "not only commercial panics, and mobs, and 'fads,' but also great reform movements...all illustrate...the potency of imitative tendencies," they saw an actionable theory at hand. A youth leader "can rule more by *suggestion* and by example than he can by domineering," Hall student and Lyman School principal J. Adams Puffer explained. This was precisely the kind of leadership shown by William George. "The leader must learn, like Wm. R. George, to be a member of the gang and to a certain extent to subordinate himself to the group," he elaborated, describing how George had modeled behavior as an employee for child contractors, confirming how the instincts behind antisocial behavior could be channeled toward positive ends.[70]

Departing from earlier conceptions of youth-serving institutions as surrogate families in which militaristic family discipline prevailed, "the deepest kind of trust" lay "at the heart of the republic idea," observed Freeville instructor Agnes Boyle O'Reilly Hocking, who subsequently established Shady Hill School in Cambridge, Massachusetts. George's institution treated children

> with the utmost civility and kindness....Thus they live, becoming so infatuated and delighted with their lives and daily work, that their stay goes by with the swiftness and sweetness of a May day, making them reluctant to leave upon reaching the age limit, and doing so invariably with a desire and determination to take the same part in the larger, or real republic which they have done in the junior.

Such "judicious supervision exercised along the lines of friendly control without dictation" did not turn the children into "mere puppets," Gill explained. Rather it "serves the two-fold purpose of fostering initiative and preventing the children from attempting too much."[71]

This new approach to youth work required more from supervising adults to do less. Spokane Parental School superintendent William Gute, one of many Freeville graduates who went on to youth work careers, confided to George that he "had to get rid of several of the old helpers who thought all their authority had been taken away because I gave the boys so much liberty." Hebrew Sheltering Guardian Society staff were initially hesitant to modify their administrative procedures, fearing "that anarchy would follow" and feeling "their dignity was very considerably shaken," Bernstein recounted. But once the management and supervisors "cast aside completely all officialdom" to be "considered as the children's friends, and not as their task-masters," the generations "were working harmoniously and energetically towards one end."[72]

Confronted by skeptics who viewed self-government under adult control as a fiction, educators and youth workers with firsthand republic experience thus vigorously disagreed. Edgar Robinson, who organized the City of Tuxis at the Brooklyn YMCA's Bedford branch, explained how such manipulations would be counterproductive:

> One of the most vicious and common mistakes in connection with well-meaning attempts at self-government with groups of boys has been that of giving the boys the impression that they had self-government, while in reality they were being manipulated from behind the scenes. They would gain the form but not the substance, and would soon awake to the realization that they had been duped. To play the game of municipal politics as a game is one thing. To lead the boy to think that he is really doing the thing and then for him to find out that you have only been playing with him is disastrous.[73]

Of course, some adult guidance was imperative, McKiernan counseled: "You cannot expect juveniles to conduct governmental affairs successfully unless you give a guiding hand and are ready with suggestions." Yet he cautioned "against the other extreme—that is, of going through the form of having an election, dictating the officers to be nominated, and afterward playing an arbitrary part in the government's affairs. Failure will be yours if you do that." Republic defenders had long linked failure to improper implementation; now many suggested that young people's disempowerment was a faulty application of the self-government idea. Saying "The pupils have lost interest," Gill explained, was merely another way of saying "The teacher has lost interest and has fallen back into his old ways." Old-fashioned schoolmasters were unlikely to "make a happy transition to a system of pupil government," David Snedden and Samuel Dutton observed. "They must first establish the right relations between the pupils and themselves.... They can then introduce the school city or any other mechanical agency with some hope of success." Otherwise, "It is like putting new wine into old bottles—the strain is too great."[74]

Junior Republics, Factories, and Prisons

By the first decade of the twentieth century, educators and youth workers had amassed evidence that environments offering access to vicarious experiences with real-world implications, guided by suggestion, were effective routes to behavior management. "The effect of social suggestion and imitation in reforming boys is shown in the George Junior Republic," as Edward James Swift put it. They had demonstrated democracy's efficacy as a disciplinary tool: "Judge Willis Brown...believes that the civic, rather than the military, idea of discipline should prevail in teaching boys," and that adults should be "instructors and not commanders," journalists in Washington and Indiana explained. And they had shown how, when disciplinary responsibility was taken up by the community rather than vested in designated authorities, more stringent standards prevailed. Theodore Roosevelt observed of George's republic in 1912, "An offense committed by one of their number is thought to be an offense, not against some outsider or outside body with whom or with which they have no special connection, but against themselves."[75]

Junior republics remained imperfect places—for example, reports of pretzels and apples as graft persisted. Yet the new strategies produced desirable results, engaged youth while doing so, and proved cost effective. Proposals to broaden their applications were increasingly found. "I found that, for many of the problems of our great Republic, I could gain light by studying the little republic," Thomas Osborne wrote, calling to "apply the Democratic principle to our factories and solve the labor problem.... to our prisons and reform our ignorant brethren who have failed to adapt themselves to society." David Snedden agreed: "A more strict, earnest, and heartily responsive discipline may be maintained in every school, shop and Army and Navy organization by means of democracy in the ranks than by the authority alone of teachers, foremen and officers," encouraging self-government "at West Point, Annapolis, Newport, in all Indian and other Government schools, in all public and private schools, in all reform schools and prisons, and among the enlisted men in the Army and Navy." From prisons to factories, democracy as discipline would be found more widely in the coming years.[76]

Michel Foucault's work on the transformation of discipline in Western society uses prisons to make broader arguments about cultural and social change, finding similarities across prisons, factories, and schools as they turned away from bodily focused discipline toward psychological internalization and self-regulation. Significantly, Foucault observes that methods applied to marginal populations expanded over time into the mainstream. Although scholars have questioned the extent to which theory and practice met, ample evidence from the growing communities of experts associated with the new penology and industrial betterment finds that, at the turn of the twentieth century, the preferred modes of maintaining order in prisons and factories shared with schools and youth-serving institutions a turn away from militarism toward "friendly," "neighborly" and "family-like" relations and suggestion rather than commands.[77]

Not far from Freeville, for example, the Elmira Reformatory, built by its inmates, offered vocational education, military drills, and recreation; a newspaper circulated from 1884. Under Zebulon Brockaway's leadership, the inmates implemented a limited self-government plan and a token economy, became monitors and workshop instructors—points of commonality that raise questions as to whether prisons were unacknowledged sources of inspiration for George even as he was adamant his institution was not primarily for delinquent youth. At Auburn Prison and later Sing Sing (also George's neighbors), Mutual Welfare Leagues would become the basis for self-government programs that included prisoners' courts, token economies, sports, newspapers, and a bank. Such modern penal methods were sources of pride on par with the automatic gates, electric chair, and other devices displayed at international expositions, attracting visitors to see them firsthand.[78]

Business leaders were similarly eager for workers to add responsibility for self-disciplining to their job descriptions. Self-government in industry, commonly called "industrial democracy" after World War I, was organized in the form of "workmen's councils" as an alternative to labor unions. The National Civic Federation's Conference on Welfare Work took up the matter of how suggestion could help direct these and other self-governing employee organizations. It was "an important duty of the Welfare Manager to direct recreation while appearing in the matter as seldom as may be... every effort should be made to train the workers themselves to lead and also to manage the various clubs entirely, otherwise their failure, sooner or later, is assured."[79]

These reforms were widely celebrated for reducing rioting and recidivism among prison populations, increasing worker productivity and decreasing turnover in industry, and improving the likelihood that subordinates might share the views their superiors held. "The responsibility of the prisoner becomes in part social as well as individual," Maurice Parmelee's *Criminology* textbook declared. Teaching workers that they were responsible for the community's success made "every employee an inspector" as a review of practices at New Jersey's Weston Electrical Instrument Co. explained. Although "complete self-government" could "never be attained" in either setting, such arrangements offered "an admirable training in self-control and social responsibility" relevant to "life in society at large."[80]

Parallels among behavior management strategies at institutions serving adults and those serving youth were not coincidental. Under the charge of paternalistic factory owners and prison wardens, adults were often described as children whose energies required channeling toward positive ends. Earlier speculations about the potentially broad applicability of republics and their component activities—especially their service as "substitute for spanking"—now were accompanied by more direct exchanges of ideas. Recreation consultants, including Joseph Lee and Arthur Todd, who had previously worked with youth, offered advice on planning leisure to help achieve work goals. The American Institute of Social Service, whose head Josiah Strong was affiliated with George's republic and Richard Welling's School Citizens Committee, assisted companies in developing such programs. Soon they and colleagues at the Playground Association of America were aiding prisons as well. Welling and the Self Government Committee (the School Citizens Committee's successor) went on to advise factories and other businesses on implementing programs of self-government while calling for prisons to follow suit. Adolf Lewisohn from the Hebrew Sheltering Guarding Society and Osborne from the George Junior Republic both joined the New York State Prison Commission. In fact, it was Osborne who brought self-government and token economies to Auburn and Sing Sing prisons at the same time he promoted these strategies as an advisor to the Boys Club Federation of America. (Oscar Lewis, general secretary of the Prison Association of New York, corresponded with George for guidance on the token currency to use.) Calvin Derrick, former Freeville superintendent and later head of the California State Reformatory at Ione, assisted Osborne with implementation at Sing Sing.[81]

Osborne was a quirky character, known for his love of masquerade. He had dressed up as an applicant for positions in his own factory and later as an organ grinder to visit Freeville. The role-plays central to George's program captivated his attention and his recognition that democratic rather than militaristic techniques yielded beneficial disciplinary outcomes there got him thinking about prison self-government as early as 1904, when he served as mayor in Auburn, New York. A decade later he went undercover as an inmate at that city's prison to investigate conditions there, persuading peers to adopt self-government by suggesting it was their idea.[82]

That behavior management techniques for youth might find new application to adult convicts made sense at a time when prison labor, like child labor, was coming under fire despite its long history of association with personal redemption. Rebecca McClennan has described the controversies between unions and prison workshops regarding the production of goods for private enterprise and subsequently for public sector buyers. Activities from vocational education to self-government replaced labor as the centerpiece of prison discipline, serving as outlets for prisoners' surplus energies. Like the factory supervisors who saw their role as one of educating the working classes for life beyond the factory, prison directors increasingly envisioned the prison as a training school, a preparatory community for life outside. (Elmira, for example, was described as a "great technological training school" and "prison university." The Mutual Welfare League's motto stressed "model citizens" rather than "model inmates.") In this context, prison activities such as vocational education and institutional maintenance came to be viewed as work-like but not work itself—described by Erving Goffman as "removal activities" for enabling prisoners to mentally escape their confinement and by McClennan as simulated occupations.[83]

If it remains a mystery how much prison tactics influenced George's republic, it is clear than prison reformers explicitly used Freeville as a model for their work. When the International Prison Conference took a New York field trip in 1910 to study approaches to the new penology, participants visited Elmira, Auburn, and Freeville—duplicating the tour John Commons had taken more than a decade earlier. George routinely welcomed penologists to Freeville and they installed junior republics increasingly far afield—for example, the Philippines's Iwahig Penal Colony.[84]

If the closest parallels between youth and prisoners centered on questions about channeling energies previously directed to labor toward character-building, work-like activities, the clearest points of commonality between factory workers and youth related to the reorganization of knowledge and diminution of autonomy these populations experienced: a "deskilling" in the sense that a generation lost opportunities to use its expertise, and subsequent generations were not encouraged to develop similar abilities. Like the well-known story of changing labor relations in factories and other industrial settings, in which worker knowledge moved into the hands of managers, an equivalent phenomenon can be seen in the relationships between young people and adults. Finding in young people the instinct for vicarious experiences of adulthood, educators and youth workers argued that this natural process required management, choosing tactics to adjust their charges to an expanding set of structures that confined them to the social category "youth." Making it illegal, for example, for kids to organize sports not only in school but equally on weekends left them unable to independently practice their administrative skills. Going beyond the observation from educational historians that schools taught factory discipline, this evidence finds that child savers shared much in common with the factory supervisors from whom they sought to protect their charges—with the additional indignity that, inside schools and youth-serving institutions, the full extent of young people's productive energies went unseen.[85]

There were, of course, critical differences when prisons and factories rather than schools and youth-serving institutions embraced self-government and vocational education. Adult prisoners engaged in vocational education were simulating occupations rather than adulthood. Factory self-government lacked urgency to mirror existing governmental systems, more concerned about applying general democratic theories than imitating specific roles. Yet such roughly analogous practices—as well as evidence about the George Junior Republic as a source of inspiration—confirms Michel Foucault's analysis and points to the particular significance of both suggestion and vicarious experience in achieving the self-disciplining associated with the modern age.

Perhaps the most amazing finding was how such disciplinary processes were sources of fun for youth. "Whoever heard of a boy after he has left a reform school going back to visit it?" asked one journalist. "The George Junior Republic, organized in July, 1895, has graduates who go back to it with joy in their hearts, as to a fostering mother—graduates who are making names for themselves in Harvard University, in Cornell, in Yale, and in the larger college of practical life." Letters from ex-citizens fill the George Junior Republic archives, trails of affectionate correspondence that continued decades after graduation. The republic organized an alumni association to facilitate reunions and for current citizens to consult their predecessors on administrative matters. Republics such as Allendale and Ford had active associations of graduates as well.[86]

Accounts of participants' enjoyment, which further diverted attention from the economic value participants produced, were a continuous thread in reports of republic life. In school cities, pupils "find great enjoyment in it, and that therein is its great value." As one principal put it, "They play, they learn, they develop, they prepare... What more can one ask of an educational device than that it molds character effectively and joyfully?" Boytown in Gary was "no play place, but the fact remains that the boys have a good time." Indeed, kids at the earlier Boytown outside San Francisco had complained they "were not allowed to work as hard as they wished, since the object has never been to make money." A "happier, cheerier, and more amazingly efficient set of youngsters would be hard to find anywhere," a journalist reported of Cottage Row as it stood in 1915. "They are contented because they are 'learning by doing' and are guided by men and women who know how to keep them perpetually interested." The many playground republics were by definition spaces for play rather than work.[87]

This appeal helped expand applications of such disciplinary strategies from marginal to mainstream populations, following Hall's 1902 remarks to the Harvard Teachers' Union that schools "for negroes and Indians" were on the cutting edge of curricular advancement, and David Snedden's appeal to bring the educational programming at juvenile reformatories to wider populations. Jane Addams espoused a similar view. "Many of the things that we have been accustomed to use only as cures after the child has become a truant or incorrigible, are quite as effective as preventive measures and as positive forces in the development of the normal boy or girl," reported a listener to a speech that Addams gave. "Such, for instance is the sense of responsibility in actually playing a part in community life, to which W. R. George, founder of the George Junior Republic directed attention. Such, again is the proper investigation of physical defects and the system of medical inspection—not merely for the patently abnormal child, the aggravated case, but for all school children." In a reversal of classic accounts of the sheltered childhood's advancing frontier from the mainstream to the margins, this suggests Foucault's observations about the spread of disciplinary tactics characterized the double lives of modern youth. Invitations to George for speaking engagements at elite private schools such as Exeter reflected broadening views as to the applicability of his work.[88]

Regulating Life Beyond the Institution

In Michel Foucault's reading, the prison is a microcosm of Western society whose changing disciplinary practices characterize both modern institutions and the regulation of life in noninstitutional settings. According to this view, society itself became prison-like as modes of self-disciplining seeped beyond prison walls. Historians of penology and business have built on this theoretical base to detail efforts to regulate adults' public behaviors, from prisoner parole and probation to factory sociology departments' home visits and programs of supervised leisure, and their varying levels of success expanding surveillance and self-disciplining. Scholars of youth, by contrast, have paid less attention to the regulation of young people's public behavior on account of the interest in protected, supervised settings that dominate studies of the sheltered childhood.[89]

Yet developments inside schools and youth-serving institutions constituted merely one front in educators' and youth workers' assault on young people's older ways of being in the world. For as much as kids enjoyed republic life, most did not spend time exclusively in age-restricted environments. It was the rare total institution like Freeville or Boytown where "lessons go on twenty-four hours a day." More common were school- and summer-based programs like Progress City or Boyville, which had children for only a few hours a day, during summer vacations, or afternoon and evening activities, whose time with kids was even more constrained. Cognizant of these realities and eager to control youth behavior in contexts they could not adequately supervise, child-saving professionals simultaneously set out to regulate youth activities beyond institution walls. They found in role-plays of adulthood a versatile tool.[90]

Boy Scouts are the best-chronicled example of this genre of youth activity, oriented around community-based role-playing, although Scouting's original commitment to impersonating explorers has not been central in childhood studies to date. Yet Scouting was merely a single example in a much larger field. From junior police to juvenile civic leagues, even in an era marked by the expansion of schools and youth-serving institutions, many youth activities were being introduced in the public settings from which children were otherwise being removed. How, as educators and youth workers endeavored to make junior republics, schools, and youth-serving institutions more like the real world these reformers simultaneously worked to make the real world more like a junior republic, and how as young people's public performances of adulthood helped to cement the new category "youth" they simultaneously assisted in state-building, are the subjects of chapter 4.

4   The Drama of the Street

In a 1914 letter to University of Pennsylvania sociologist Carl Kelsey, William George described his latest efforts to spread the junior republic idea. Republic principles "could be used to advantage by young people below the age of twenty-one residing in a city," he explained. George had been working toward these ends in the "junior municipalities" he had organized in Ithaca, Cortland, and further afield, each a "duplication of the senior government" in which participants received lessons in citizenship through training in "real life" affairs. Junior officials had tracked down truants, inspected street lights, monitored water filtration plants and stood in for mayors at public events—each taking "the responsibilities of his position as real with nothing of the make-believe about them."[1]

Why, when George had persuaded local governments to try his program by noting how "every adult official" would gain "a boy or girl understudy" at no expense, did he and other observers emphasize the acting over the actions of participating youth? And what does their interpretation of "the boys and girls ready to help govern the city" as being engaged in in public performances reveal about educators' and youth workers' ambitions for role-plays of adult life and young people's contributions to building the American state? This chapter traces the republic movement's evolution in the 1910s and the expanding national conversation about simulations in child development as schools and youth-serving institutions took their activities into the street. Building close relations with underresourced local authorities, community-based republics together with organizations including junior police and junior civic leagues, Boy Scouts and Knights of King Arthur added new weight to George's claim that Freeville and its descendants were each a "village like any other." At the same time that junior citizens from Freeville to Grove City constructed their republics' sewer systems, repaired buildings, and policed their peers, these young people engaged in parallel efforts to "serve real and not fictitious needs." As public officials took on new identities as youth workers and as the youth they supervised pledged to play their roles beyond adults' watchful eyes, the disciplinary and economic benefits of activities previously focused inside campuses and clubhouses now helped to improve communities from which young people were ostensibly being removed.[2]

Histories of the shift from family economy to sheltered childhood have focused on the islanding of childhood, the exclusion of young people from the labor force and public life, and the parental educators and youth workers who assisted the transition—in other words, the management of youth in supervised, age-restricted spaces. Yet child savers were equally eager to modernize the curriculum young people encountered on the streets that Gary school superintendent William Wirt called "a real school working at maximum efficiency educating children in the wrong direction." Challenged to provide supervision in the absence of supervisors, they extended republics and their component activities' geographic reach. Thus, if the first junior republics were total institutions, and subsequently proliferated in classrooms and clubhouses, later educators and youth workers hoped to remake their communities into republic-like role-playing games. The mass popularization of these institutions without walls argues for stories of peer- and self-supervision to complement narratives of the adult takeover of youth activities, and supplies further examples of performance as a disciplinary tool.[3]

As these public programs transformed young people's relationships to their communities and the communities themselves, they were regarded not as child labor but as contributions to child protection. Interpretive frameworks for such activities inside age-restricted environments carried over to conceal a full accounting, prompting contemporaries and later historians to overlook young people's contributions to American state building and to how efficiency in local government depended on the hidden labors of youth. Like the women who used a maternalist rhetoric of "municipal housekeeping" to defend their public contributions as extensions of their domestic activities, child savers' accounts of these "playworlds" reassured the public that young people were at play rather than at work.

Continued Momentum for the Republic Idea

As the junior republic movement continued in the 1910s, a number of programs failed to thrive. George's Flemington Junction republic faced financial and administrative difficulties; the trustees closed it down and moved its citizens to Freeville. Reports from Chemawa's Indian School made no mention of the republic a few years after its debut, suggesting it too had lapsed. Gary's Boyville and Boytown collapsed when Willis Brown was accused of being a con artist and run out of town.[4]

Yet these failures did not detract from the appeal of the junior republic idea. For example, in Gary, Boyville was superseded by a student council. Its bank became the Emerson School bank, while the local YMCA adopted its band. (Boytown was sold off, however, because boys preferred industrial training and there were too few delinquent youth to maintain it.) The Chicago Boys Club, which had sponsored a Boyville satellite, took over Winona Boy City's operations, restricting participation to Chicago youth. Other satellites continued at YMCAs, boys clubs, and Chautauquas, loosely coordinated by Charles Hahn, Brown's former right-hand man. The Chautauqua movement soon developed its own summer program of "junior towns."[5]

Brown was undeterred by this turn of events. Building on his West Coast connections, he teamed with Sidney Peixotto at the Columbia Park Boys' Club to plan a National Boy City as one of the living villages for San Francisco's Panama-Pacific International Exposition. The club's annual State of Columbia was still operating, and Peixotto liked Brown's variation on the republic plan. Their "model city," to be populated by companies of boys from across the US, would take the first step toward an International Boy City representing many nations, much like Gill's dreams of a Children's International State.[6]

Brown's tenaciousness typified many educators' and youth workers' unwavering commitment to the republic idea. In the coming years, they established more republics at schools and youth-serving institutions. Others expanded and evolved. When the Hebrew Sheltering Guardian Society moved to a rural campus with cottages and expanded vocational training, for example, its youth democracy shifted from a municipal to a federal self-government system. The California Junior Republic added industrial activities to its previously agriculturally focused curriculum. Component activities including youth councils, student courts, school stores, penny banks, and vocational training also proliferated in the 1910s.[7]

With sufficient time having passed to record the longer-term effects of these diverse youth programs, new empirical evidence provided fodder for future-oriented interpretations that stressed developmental payoffs over immediate economic effects. Tracking Freeville's junior citizens into the "big Republic," for example, gave many observers further confidence that good lives lived inside juvenile democracies bore fruit in the "real" lives that graduates lived. "Many [George Junior] Republic boys have entered Cornell, Harvard, Columbia, University of Pennsylvania and other colleges, where they make a particularly good showing in logic and economics," reported Jeanne Robert, looking back on the republic's first twenty years. Similar reports from other schools and youth-serving institutions fleshed out the story, diverting attention from how, long before graduation, young people continued to make value for their institutions in the present day. Hebrew Sheltering Guardian Society orphans were charged with housework and cooking, and Washington Irving High's "Business Laboratory" students served as bank tellers, bookkeepers, cashiers, and clerks. California Junior Republic citizens made more than one million bricks for new campus buildings, and Cottage Row had a veritable army of boy inspectors: bird inspectors, tree inspectors, fly inspectors, mosquito inspectors, rat inspectors, and buildings and grounds inspectors.[8]

Confident as they were about such activities' longer-term promise, reformers remained anxious about many children's continued exposures to the drama of public streets. Whether in addition to or as an alternative to playgrounds, street play had not lost its appeal, an expression of the "migratory instinct." Studies of unsupervised children in public amassed evidence about how, alone or in gangs, their activities frequently veered into lawless territory. Some young people chose street-based work as well. Legally distinct from their peers in factories, mills, and mines, street traders were considered independent "merchants" rather than "employees"—not covered by child labor laws. Many attended school, working part-time, but their rates of truancy and delinquency were higher than among nonworking peers. During widespread strikes in 1899, newsboys became the most visible of these working youth.[9]

Concerned about children's exposures to moral hazards in public settings, child savers had initially concentrated on creating age-restricted environments such as schools and youth-serving institutions and finding ways to force and entice children to spend time in these settings, each a "substitute for the lawlessness of the street which would have been the life of the children," in the words of one police officer. Facing up to the actual numbers of children still playing and working on the nation's streets, their thought processes began to shift. Chicago Boys Club director of research and programs Walter Stone explained the new consensus that youth workers "decentralize their efforts" and meet young people where they were. "The time seems past when an agency can sit snugly in a central building and expect boys to come in." The reality of course was that even if every educator and youth worker turned his or her attention to surveilling and supervising children in public it would never be enough.[10]

In fact, it was the impossibility of this surveillance and supervision that prompted another proposal to expand applications of the republic idea. Self-government programs at underresourced schools and youth-serving institutions had established that kids could learn to govern themselves and their peers beyond their supervisors' watchful eyes, reducing the necessary numbers of adult staff and making even the superintendent "dispensable as opposed to indispensable" as Scranton's Boys Industrial Association Duane Dills put it. Individual troublemakers and gangs had been domesticated as they internalized new behavioral norms—and seemed to enjoy the experience. This suggested that if children's playworlds could be extended into public settings, supervision without supervisors might be a realistic proposition in these environments as well. In the 1910s, the community of child savers diversified its strategies toward these ends by bringing club life to the street. William George's junior municipalities emblematized the new republic genre that extended participants' role-playing into their communities, redefining streets as stages for civic dramatizations and introducing both sheltered childhood and virtual adulthood into public space.[11]

Opening Republics to the Community

George's junior municipality project was well-timed. His national association had failed to gain control over the proliferation of republic offspring, and his obsessive efforts to make Freeville more "republicky," for example, by shifting to the gold standard and insisting the children not refer to it as a "camp," had distracted him from practical matters. The mother republic was nearly bankrupt. More ambitious as philosopher than manager, George asked his associates to address the money problem so he could explore new applications for the republic idea. Two visions for the movement's possible future, each prioritizing the business of politics over other occupations, reflect how after 1912 the directions taken by the imitators he once criticized increasingly influenced his work. In one, he envisioned the National Association of Junior Republics shifting its attention to cities and establishing residential urban republics closer to target populations. In the other, local governments would partner with youth to form junior municipalities, shadow governments whose young officials would gain practical civic knowledge as they extended their role-playing into community space.[12]

Recognizing the comparative difficulty of establishing new, residential organizations and preferring physical environments that appeared comparatively real, George decided to devote himself to the latter, a variation that stripped the republic idea to its barest essentials—children playing roles as political officials—and required only a commitment from public authorities to supervise local youth. Publicity for his ideas in spring 1913 fueled talk of a nationwide movement (sometimes called George Junior Municipalities) and the possibility of scaling up to form junior county, state, and national governments even before the first junior municipality got under way. Mayor John Reamer in nearby Ithaca (and his successor, Thomas Tree) gave George an opportunity to pilot the new program with help from the Freeville citizens and staff.[13]

A constitutional convention in summer 1913 attracted both students and working youth. Ithaca's coed junior government, inaugurated in December by Reamer and George, began meeting in the city council chambers, the courthouse, and the YMCA. The adults whose roles they duplicated selected the service projects for the young officials to pursue. They assisted the public works department with time-consuming inspections, monitored the water plant, supervised the waste system, studied and proposed revisions to the city's tax plan, set water rates, inspected streets, supervised playgrounds, provided crowd control at large events, and adjudicated youth crimes to relieve the city courts of "trivial" cases, with a Cornell law student presiding in the city courtroom.[14]

Thanks to widespread media coverage, officials from Houston, Texas, to Portland, Oregon, along with many nearby New York State towns, soon contacted George for advice on how they might start junior municipalities in their communities. He offered some assistance to interested parties (most enthusiastically to nearby Cortland, New York, which became his second site for experimentation) and sent junior mayor J. Bert Wilson on the road to promote a future junior municipalities league. George's chief preoccupation, however, was to first perfect Ithaca's youth government—for example, negotiating with local authorities to give participants legal powers for arrest and adjudication. He also explored the possibility of organizing a year-round citizen training school.[15]

Although the new program was the focus of George's attention in the early 1910s, he did not abandon his commitment to republics during this period. Publicity was very much on his mind. Together with his colleagues he had showcased the republic idea at world's fairs through photographs, documents, and illustrated lectures. Three Freeville buildings had been reproduced for an industrial exposition in New York City, where "New Yorkers who have never before had an opportunity to visit this self-governing community of young people" gained "a chance to see precisely what it is like and what work it accomplishes." Extending his prior public relations efforts, he established a summer officer training school for republic graduates and college students to learn to start new republics and bring self-government to other settings. He informally advised others seeking to develop republic variations in their communities, for example, on playgrounds. And he expanded association membership to include Dorset, England's Little Commonwealth—organized by Homer Lane, following a scandalous departure from the Ford Republic.[16]

This decision proved prescient, for George's plans were soon interrupted by his own scandal. Accused of improper relations with a female junior citizen and alleged to have hypnotized his charges in an exploitative, rather than educational, fashion, George was removed as republic head. The state charity board launched an investigation, recommending the republic exclude girls and dismantle self-government for the boys who remained. These troubles halted fundraising efforts, forcing the republic to close.[17]

Although general enthusiasm for the republic idea was undiminished during George's "time of troubles" (for example, Pennsylvania officials contemplated organizing all state-run child-saving institutions as republics), Freeville's local situation had to be addressed. Reprising their response to criticisms from the same regulatory body nearly three decades earlier, advocates such as Ben Lindsey suggested the problem was a misunderstanding by board observers rather than any actions George had taken. Junior citizens from Freeville and Ithaca added their voices in "Daddy's" defense. A judge absolved him of wrongdoing and the republic reopened, but it had to recruit an entire population. As George reached out to entice former citizens to return to Freeville, he continued his junior municipality work.[18]

Thanks to George's public acclaim as an inventor—he had been compared to Franklin, Morse, and Bell—junior municipalities were the best-known example of the republic movement's new direction. Yet they were neither the first youth democracies to extend participants' role-playing into their communities nor the first to enlist public officials to guide the youth who impersonated them. The Freeville republic had never closed its borders and the absence of gates received frequent public comment. Juvenile police captured young citizens out of bounds; republic businesses imported goods for sale and sold others in the "greater republic." Early school cities had similarly encouraged pupils to remain in role off-campus—tracking down truants from NYC's PS 125 and Alameda's Longfellow School, inspecting streets near Newark's 13th Avenue school for violations of city ordinances, and keeping the island of Cuba clean. Youth in Gary's Boyville set out to reduce underage cigarette sales. Relationships with local authorities were a hallmark of Gill's first school-based republic; Gill's first manual for educators had urged "the active co-operation of the children with the public authorities for many purposes, such as keeping the streets tidy and improving the health conditions of the homes." Many municipal playground directors delegated governance to participating youth. And numerous republic organizers invited local officials to speak and took field trips for junior officials to see their adult counterparts in action in the name of vitalizing civic education.[19]

The expansion of republic activities into communities in cooperation with local officials that was a hallmark of George's new project in fact already was a feature of the newsboy republics operating in several cities, many of which were extensions of the school city idea. In these year-round programs, which licensed youth as street traders in exchange for republic participation, public authorities guided thousands to participate in playworlds in public space. From Toledo to Boston, newsboy associations became newsboy republics (or in Toledo's case, Boyville). Toledo's was an independent organization, whereas Boston's organization was affiliated with the city's schools as the board of education "assumed control of all licensed minors" so as to extend into the streets

Figure 4.1
Trial board, Boston Newsboys' Republic.
Source: Philip Davis, *Street-land: Its Little People and Big Problems* (Boston: Small, Maynard, 1915).

the activities "in pupil governed schools." Largest among them was Milwaukee's newsboy republic, the sixth largest US boys club, with more than 4,000 members in the 1910s.[20]

Milwaukee had been an early adopter of school cities. These early experiments had sputtered, however, on account of fears about child control in schools. The city's YMCA had a boys republic operating in 1910. By the 1910s, wider public familiarity with student self-government and the appointment of John Commons to run the city's Bureau of Economy and Efficiency created conditions for experimentation with an alternative youth government program. Commons, who had worked closely with both George and Gill, had become aware of Boston's recent efforts to address fears about street traders' informal education on urban streets by "extending the influence of the schools" into the community in a newsboy republic. "Since it is the almost savage environment which makes many city children little savages," Boston Newsboys' Republic director Philip Davis explained, "our chief task is to civilize the environment."[21]

Commons enlisted street trades commissioner P. O. "Pop" Powell to run the experiment. From 1912, Milwaukee's newsboys, most aged twelve to sixteen, filled elected and appointed political positions in a miniature United States. Pop initially reserved several roles for their adult collaborators, who included newspaper men, educators, and representatives from the juvenile court system. Later, he turned over these roles to the youth, remaining as supreme court justice. Public officials lent their support, with Mayor Gerhard Bading, judges, police, and even Wisconsin governor Francis McGovern participating in republic events.[22]

With participants all engaged in a single trade, Milwaukee's newsboy republic followed the school city template, eschewing the broad vocational training and economic system that the Freeville republic supplied. Instead, Pop encouraged the junior citizens to improve their professionalism as street traders, make the most of their educational experiences, and think ahead to future career opportunities. Articles on these topics in *Newsboys World*, the boys' own newsmagazine, stressed the value of education for long-term economic success. "The street trades problem is an educational one and a burden for the public school system to assume," Powell explained. His office became part of the school system's extension department, and organized school-based newsboys clubs to support the scheme. This arrangement provided meeting spaces for the citizens to host debates and athletic contests, run a drama club and charity program, organize entertainment, and print *Newsboys World*. It offered opportunities for adult supervision as well. Parochial schools and a few social centers soon sponsored newsboy clubs.[23]

As important as the supervised activities in schools, social centers, and municipal buildings were, some club activities took place beyond adults' watchful eyes. For an equally critical component of this republic's programming was the requirement that participants enforce the street trades laws regulating who could sell newspapers, where, when, and how. This enforcement occurred throughout Milwaukee's streets—which, in the augmented reality of their role-playing game, were simultaneously the territory of a miniature United States. At once Milwaukee newsboys and US congressmen, the boys took on a third role as junior inspectors for the city's street trades department, arresting violators and bringing them to court. Young judges who comprised a trial board adjudicated these cases. With authority delegated by the city, only the newsboys the board judged guilty were turned over to the state industrial commission for prosecution. Although preceded by newsboy republics in Toledo and Boston, Milwaukee's was the largest and most deeply integrated into local infrastructure—in Pop's words, a "social agency of the city." Practices there soon provided guidance for Birmingham, Alabama, and Portland, Oregon.[24]

Public Role-Plays in Practice and Theory

The republic movement's turn to community-based role-plays that engaged public officials in youth work characterized a broad range of recreational programs in this period. State and local officials had occasionally interacted with republics based at playgrounds, clubs, and settlements to offer child citizens guidance on their civic dramatizations. Joining them now were a variety of public authorities as police departments, health and sanitation agencies, and juvenile courts—independently and in collaboration with schools and youth-serving institutions—guided children to direct their attention to community spaces. Having seen the benefits of juvenile police forces, health and street cleaning departments, and courts in school cities, playground republics, and beyond, they now piloted a range of single agency occupational simulations: junior police, junior sanitary inspectors, and junior juvenile courts.

A few such service-oriented programs had predated the junior republic movement. For example, Freeville's first police squad was comprised of boys in the Law and Order gang whom William George had enlisted as New York City poll watchers and juvenile police with the blessing of police commissioner Teddy Roosevelt. In 1895, New York City street cleaning director George Waring established a juvenile street cleaning brigade, which patrolled in uniforms and badges, reported violations of sanitary ordinances, and launched cleanup campaigns. A prominent Goo Goo, Waring's approach to municipal sanitation practices attracted national and international attention; cities such as Chicago and Boston swiftly copied the program.[25]

The rapid expansion of such programs occurred chiefly after 1910, however, thanks to the confidence gained from the republic experience and in dialogue with the new applied science of directed role-play. Efforts to redirect children's migratory and gang instincts to the imitation of positive models, their ambitions were individual and group transformation. Costumes, badges, and pledges heightened the reality of the role-play experience and encouraged participants to internalize the agency-promoted norms. Small group patrols and squads shared responsibility for keeping order in assigned areas. The limited need for additional facilities helped to nurture these programs' rapid spread,

Figure 4.2
The gang instinct: a club house in the woods.
Source: J. Adams Puffer, *The Boy and His Gang* (Boston: Houghton Mifflin, 1912).

revealing how the drama of the streets the nation's youngest citizens encountered was more closely tied to the transformation of childhood than previously presumed.

Junior police programs, some of which took over squads organized by youth themselves and others replacing street gangs, were the most common, a facet of police departments' broader efforts to modernize their relations with youth in the period. From New York to Berkeley, small groups of boys (and occasionally girls) could be found in uniforms and badges patrolling assigned zones. In some schemes, physical exams or continuing education on local ordinances were required for participation. In New York City alone, multiple agencies, including the police and parks departments, operated similar programs.[26]

Privately organized variations yielded similar public benefits. In New York City's Hamilton Fish Park, which, while having disbanded its playground government, now hosted the East Side Protective Association's juvenile inspectors—10,000 boys and 2,000 girls whose "'cigarette squads,' 'saloon squads,' 'movie squads' and squads that will deal specially with stores, 'crap' games, garbage cans, dirty homes, blocked fire escapes, collections of inflammable material and pretty well everything wrong…'dance hall squads' and their 'movie squads'" brought offenders to the park where a magistrate held court.

Figure 4.3
The boy cop.
Source: Clarice Baright, "Citizens in the Making: The 'Boy and Girl Cop,'" *National Magazine* 42 (1915).

Figure 4.4
Girls auxiliary to a junior police squad.
Source: Clarice Baright, "Citizens in the Making: The 'Boy and Girl Cop,'" *National Magazine* 42 (1915).

Privately organized squads in Council Bluffs, Iowa, directed their attention to enforcing a slate of new laws related to fireworks safety that were going unenforced. Thus, while police recognized that, as one Cleveland police officer cheered Progress City in 1907, "when they're in here it's less work for me in the street, that's sure," and comparing it to the work of ten policemen, training kids to improve their public behavior was an equal priority.[27]

Junior sanitary programs also surged during this decade. Waring's program lapsed after encountering the same obstacle that had thwarted Gill's initial school republic proposal: local officials did not prioritize youth work duties in this earlier period. Waring had stood for election in Freeville as state engineer and subsequently assisted Gill in Cuba, but fell ill from yellow fever and died in 1898. His program was revived in 1903 as the Juvenile City League, a private effort from the Woman's Municipal League of New York whose ambition was "enlarging the scope of the work" to include the board of health, the departments of tenement houses, water, and charities, as well as the department of street cleaning. Organizers tapped experts of the departments concerned to prepare written guidance on sanitation and other topics to local youth. The city ultimately lent support to a new public program under the leadership of R. H. Simons in 1909, as an application of the latest in civic science, which grew to more than 2,500 members by 1922.[28]

Junior street cleaning leagues and junior sanitary inspectors followed in other cities, with public officials taking the lead on organization as frequent coverage in professional journals such as *American City* and *Municipal Record* attests. In the mid-1910s, San Diego's health department organized the Junior Deputy Sanitary Inspectors, to use "the bubbling energy of enthusiastic young America" to keep themselves and their environments clean and educate adults as well. Starting with a fly-prevention campaign, the badge-wearing youth were so enthusiastic that they soon were "branching out into other phases of sanitation," attending lectures, making surveys, and reporting their findings to city officials.[29]

Junior juvenile courts became features of the juvenile court system in several cities. In a period when many in the juvenile justice system conceived of themselves as

Figure 4.5
Junior deputy sanitary inspectors, San Diego.
Source: William Seymour, "Junior Deputy Sanitary Inspectors," *American City* 15 (1916).

educators and youth workers and admired the republic idea, cities such as St. Louis, Cincinnati, and Baltimore established courts in which youth judges or juries, in collaboration with adults, adjudicated crimes involving minors—with some calling on assistance from young probation officers as well. Going beyond the sentencing of youth in small numbers to time in republics, this new approach offered similar messages to youth in greater numbers. The widely recognized discretion of juvenile courts that scholars have described was even wider than previously presumed.[30]

By the 1910s, then, public officials were increasingly on board with the idea that youth programs organized around role-playing could advance their agencies' missions. Wilson Gill had recognized this long ago—encouraging local authorities to take active roles in the republic movement such that School Cities might become "a branch of the government of the State." Yet it was only after such benefits had been seen in the microcosm of junior republics based at schools and youth-serving institutions that public figures committed to working directly with youth.[31]

Community-oriented role-playing and occasional collaborations with public officials also characterized other youth programs in the period. From Boy Scouts to Knights of King Arthur, a range of organizations that directed young people to role-plays of historical personae rather than contemporary civic occupations, hosted by schools and youth-serving institutions, highlight educators' and youth workers' expansive vision of what guided dramatizations of adult life could be directed to achieve. These too sought to provide models to improve individual and group behavior: chivalrous explorers and knights. Wearing costumes and taking pledges, and organized as self-governing troops and castles, these programs shared with each other and with civic occupational simulations ambitions for children to develop character and citizenship by impersonating someone else.

An early edition of the *Scoutmasters Handbook* described the American adaptation of the British Scouting organization and the role-play that was its central principle:

> We trace the development of our conceptions of chivalric principles back through the vistas of European history, but we Americans have examples of greater worth and more profound impression in the tribal civilizations and of the Indians of our Continent and in the lives of our pioneer forefathers. The lives of each of these types of earlier Americans furnish us with numberless concrete examples of the practice of chivalric principles, the esteem for truth and loyalty, and the worth of right living.

Reviewing the science of child development, it was clear that "reproduction," "imitation," and "impersonation" defined a successful Scouting experience or, as one headline put it: "Boy Scouts Must Be Like Daring Men."[32]

Self-supervision and community service were at the heart of Scouting in the daily good turn. The "real test" in Scouting was the "assimilation of Scout principles," as the *Scoutmaster Handbook* (1913) described. Could a boy "furnish satisfactory evidence that he has put into practice in his daily life the principles of the Scout oath and law?" In a practical sense, the good turn did not have to be a very big thing, the *Handbook for Boys* (1911) explained—for example, a boy might "help an old lady across the street; remove a banana skin from the pavement so that people may not fall; remove from streets or roads broken glass, dangerous to automobile or bicycle tires; give water to a thirsty horse; or deeds similar to these." A badge reversed or a necktie's position were proposed mnemonic devices to encourage such actions in the absence of a uniform, fellow troops, or a supervising adult. Beyond such individual acts troops could show strength in numbers. During the 1910s, "The phases of the Scout cooperation in community activities" underwent rapid expansion. "They participate in the city cleanup, 'walk-rite,' and anti-fly campaigns, work with the police and fire departments, with health officers, park commissioners, and forest and game wardens," summarized an entry in the *New International Year Book*. "In fact they stand ready to give their services freely and efficiently to whatever good cause can use their organization for service."[33]

Scouting was only one of the proliferating role-play organizations like Sons of Boone, Brotherhood of David, Woodcraft Indians, and Camp Fire Girls that attracted children's attention in this period. Even more popular for a time was the Knights of King Arthur (established 1893) and its sister organization, the Queens of Avalon (established 1902). The former was a church-based youth program in which boys imagined themselves members of King Arthur's court. Members took the names of the great figures of Arthur's court or of other heroes known for their knightly deeds and were called by those names in castle (club) meetings. By adopting these second identities, participants "reproduce the ideals and virtues of Christian knighthood...as far as boys can imitate them." The Queens of Avalon similarly supplied a "revival," a "reliving," an "imitation," and an "emulation" of the royal ladies who lived on the island of Avalon, a "Kingdom of Ideal Womanhood" and a service orientation.[34]

The brother and sister organizations were the brainchildren of William Forbush during his career as a Detroit pastor. Around this time Forbush was experimenting with several different approaches to religious education, all of which offered vicarious access to a different time, place, or identity. The USA camp he organized in the late 1890s tried a junior republic, assigning boys roles in a civic simulation. Simultaneously, he worked to develop stereoscopic media for religious education, collaborating with Underwood on immersive biblical stories to enable "the imaginative youth, or adult even, to enter so vividly into foreign experiences as to constitute if, but briefly, actual experiences of travel."[35]

Knights of King Arthur and Queens of Avalon were initially inwardly focused, like the USA camps. After further postgraduate study with G. Stanley Hall, Forbush refined program activities, adding athletics and newspapers to sustain and expand youth engagement, and turning the focus to community service: participating in cleanup campaigns, cooking meals for police, donating food to the poor, raising funds for missionary work, visiting the sick, reading to the blind, making quilts for hospitals, and running church nurseries. Costumed for rituals organized by their castles or moving

Figure 4.6
Knights of King Arthur, Castle Glamis, Spring Forge, Pennsylvania.
Source: William Byron Forbush and Frank Lincoln Masseck, *The Boys' Round Table* (Detroit: Knights of King Arthur, 1908).

through their communities, participants pledged to follow the ideals of Christian manly and womanly behavior in which they "live out virtue together." This looked much like the Scouts' "good turn." In one castle, for example, "Every night each member of the Castle put his pin inside the lapel of his coat and was not allowed to wear it on the outside until he had done some kindly act." In his later writings, Forbush leaned on developmental psychology to articulate the value of such vicarious experiences, typifying a broader shift among religious educators to scientific methods of character education and to service activities with benefits to local communities as well as the church. "Through this 'play-society,'" he explained, "they will have a good time always, but deeper than that we desire to have them live a new sort of life, a moral life transformed by romance."[36]

Symbols of monarchy aside, Forbush's programs prioritized castle self-government—a value shared by Scouts, Woodcraft Indians, Sons of Boone (Boy Pioneers), and other youth groups. The invitation by the Boy Scouts' national board for Forbush to join their organization, as well as references in Scouting handbooks to affinities with the Knights of King Arthur indicate these programs' common democratic principles. Thus, when participants in the Milwaukee newsboy republic called themselves Knights of the Canvas Bag, when William George suggested that junior municipalities followed from Scouting, and when Wilson Gill described how Scouts and Camp Fire Girls were "in the same spirit as the School Republic," they articulated the affinities across activities that emphasized role-playing and civic training, whether in age-restricted facilities or community spaces.[37]

The scientific consensus that helped popularize the first generation of role-play activities for youth provided theoretical backing for their applications in public, expanding the national conversation about these aids to child development and expanding the kinds of "constructive self-activity in real life situations" in which American youth engaged. Sponsored by the same schools and youth-serving institutions seeking to provide young people with a double life in classrooms, clubhouses, and campuses, together with a new generation of public officials who now recognized their agencies' interest could be directly advanced by these schemes, activities with scattered precedent became mass phenomena after 1910. The limited need for additional facilities helped to nurture these programs' rapid spread. A small industry soon grew up around them, selling the Native American paraphernalia advertised in *How to Play Indian* (1903), the pennants and jewels described in *Queens of Avalon* (1915), and other costumes, uniforms, and badges. G. Stanley Hall and others had proposed reading tales of chivalry and heroism as models for imitation, and related books and magazines proliferated as well.[38]

Particularly noteworthy alongside these activities' advancing geographical frontier was the confidence that program organizers expressed in the possibilities of children's self-supervision. Rural youth who wanted to participate in the Knights of King Arthur but lacked local castles were encouraged to join the national castle, participating vicariously in organization life as much as in the medieval court. "Even the solitary boy who cannot form a castle may be one of the order and in his own play and work and study take, as the others have, some knightly name as his own and try to be the finest thing on earth—a Gentle Man." The Lone Scout organization, a rural variant of Scouting that eventually merged with the Boy Scouts communicated similar messages. "Tribal papers" for regional groups and the *Lone Scout Magazine* for national circulation created community among boys who did not gather face to face. Although concerns about delinquent behavior were less extreme in rural than in urban areas, these nonetheless took the explicit view that chivalrous behavior did not require adult guides.[39]

Certainly, not every youth program in public settings or run by local authorities followed the same script. Some ad hoc efforts to enlist young people in public service eliminated role-play, from the settlements that rallied urban youth in neighborhood cleanup campaigns to the schools whose pupils helped municipal authorities on projects like survey research, birdhouse making, and tree planting but not as understudies. During his time of troubles, for example, William George convinced school administrators in nearby West Dryden to let students to take the agricultural census. Junior civic leagues became popular in public schools—partnerships between pupils and local women's groups around advancing civic beautification. Organizations with names like Junior Civic and Industrial League and Leagues of Good Citizenship also proliferated without duplicating municipal occupations. One example is Ben Lindsey's Little Citizens League, whose boys "did more to stop the use of tobacco and liquor among boys in that neighborhood than the police department or civil authorities had done in the history of the town." A few private firms organized similar efforts, such as the Health and Happiness League for the children of Metropolitan Life Insurance policy holders.[40]

These exceptions notwithstanding, programs organized around youth impersonating adults dominated community-based efforts to manage young people's public

Figure 4.7
League of Good Citizenship.
Source: Mrs. George Zimmerman, "Children's Leagues of Good Citizenship," *American City* 7, no. 5 (November 1912).

behaviors. In this context, several formerly "closed" junior republics were inspired to turn junior citizens' attention to activities beyond their campuses and clubhouses and collaborate with public authorities on matters of local concern. Activities at Cleveland's Hiram House show how even youth who did not join junior republics found their lives shaped by the movement's guiding principles.

This book has described the settlement's Progress City and how its orientation to vicarious, play-based education extended to the onsite Model Cottage. A look at the institution's other youth activities highlights how the growth of community-based republics and allied programs inspired new uses for role-playing there. In its early years, Cleveland's Progress City had enlisted youth in scattered efforts at neighborhood cleanup "somewhat to the bewilderment of some of the neighbors." From the 1910s these streets and the backyards of some houses became part of the juvenile street cleaners' regular mandate. Supervisors stepped up efforts to cultivate contacts with local officials through field trips and speaking invitations and these too expanded its programs' geographical reach. Cleveland sanitary police chief Mildred Chadsey, for example, organized a new health club which conducted a flyswatting campaign on and off campus; citizens exchanged dead flies for Progress City cash. Hiram House added a Boy Scout troop around this time as well. The settlement was a model for programs throughout the city—Progress City already had been duplicated in municipal playgrounds, and director George Bellamy later became citywide recreation department head. Kids from across Cleveland soon flooded the city's actual health department with dead flies, apparently inspired by Progress City youth.[41]

The settlement also created a junior juvenile court, which replaced the Progress City court and expanded to adjudicate delinquency cases throughout the neighborhood that surrounded Hiram House. Three adult lawyers served as judges, together with

Figure 4.8
Probation officers, junior juvenile court, Cleveland.
Source: Ellwood Street, "Going the Juvenile Court One Better," *Survey* 33 (October 24, 1914).

fourteen "probation officers," who were boys aged ten to fifteen. Judges had long supported Progress City; now they expanded its juvenile justice work. The boys turned in written complaints which generated summonses for kids to appear before the group. Those who ignored them had to face the actual juvenile court. Progress City police soon assisted the probation officers. Although the new arrangement reduced Progress City jurists' autonomy to adjudicate cases by including adults in the decision making, it communicated to neighborhood youth beyond Progress City the common message about the value of taking their role-playing into public space.[42]

Amid the proliferation of community-based role-play activities, educators and youth occasionally argued about the merits of different approaches to vicariously experiencing adulthood. In programs with recapitulation as the organizing principle, it was essential for young people to play knights, Indians, and scouts because these identities mapped onto developmental stages through which youth ordinarily progressed. Since "children in their progressive development reproduce in a general way the race life," Forbush and Frank Masseck explained in *The Boys' Round Table* (1910), age-graded activities and ladders of participation within programs such as the Scouts who outfitted themselves in "the traditional dress of the frontiersman" and the Boy Pioneers who envisioned themselves to be Davy Crockett and Johnny Appleseed, under adult guidance, would channel this natural development in the most productive ways.[43]

Others, however, echoing John Dewey's critique of pedagogy that trafficked in too much make-believe, took the view that modern occupations should be a focus for young people's impersonations. (Dewey did embrace recapitulation as an approach to teaching history, however.) Willis Brown agreed:

> Senseless manufacturing of fictitious games in which a boy will never enter as he grows older seems to me so ridiculous. To be a citizen of Boyville seems to me far more attractive than to be a "Knight of the Round Table" or a "Daniel Boone Scout." The game is more interesting. The boy will never grow into a real knight and sit with Boone companions in dress uniforms around the King's table, nor will he spend his manhood dressed in uniform scouting through the land. He will be a citizen of some man city here, and by and by of some God city in the greater citizenship, and Boyville starts him in the game aright.[44]

Luther Gulick, who helped organize the American Boy Scouts and went on to help create the Camp Fire Girls, used similar arguments to promote his new organization's efforts to prepare girls for appropriately feminine future roles. Identifying as its goal the "effort to make real things interesting," rather than "glorifying artificialities," he explained how "The spirit of adventure may be made to pervade the other tasks of everyday sweeping, dusting, putting furniture in place, washing dishes, caring in the fall for summer clothing and in the spring for winter garments, washing, ironing and what not." With this outlook, "Every sort of service, rightly managed, becomes adventurous and therefore fascinating. The whole plan of the Camp Fire Girls is to restore the spirit of adventure to the ordinary things of life." The New York City police commissioner went a step further in his call for realism, insisting that public officials rather than private citizens supervise junior civic activities.[45]

These efforts to differentiate historical from contemporary, public from private, and realistic from unrealistic simulations were frequently flawed, however, because such distinctions were imprecise. For example, Boy Scouts routinely engaged in police activities and cleanup campaigns. In some cities, such as Ann Arbor, the junior police were Scouts, their service activities supervised by Scoutmasters, local educators, and police. In Milwaukee, where newsboys joined the health department's flyswatting campaign, Boy Scouts were "assisting the health department in street sanitation work." In Cortland, Scouts and citizens of the junior municipality collaborated on local cleanup efforts. Indeed, there were numerous such public-private collaborations such as the junior civic leagues organized by women's clubs in many public schools. Wisconsin pupils cleared space for a skating rink, cleaned a riverbank, planted and landscaped their communities; Georgia students beautified parks and neighborhoods. Even parties who rejected republics did so on grounds that other youth organizations accomplished same thing—for example, Auburn's mayor, who dismissed proposals for a junior municipality as area Scouts clamored for the new organization. And when juvenile societies—from the McDunough Farm School to the Boston area sandpile made famous by Hall to the George Junior Republic and its offspring—were considered across time, evolving from frontier-like settlements to more highly developed societies, they supplied examples that spanned both historical and contemporary simulation.[46]

Such claims were equally flawed on account of how even the activities to which organizers and observers ascribed realism edited the reality they represented. Like contemporaneous modes of reproduction such as panoramas, wax museums, and taxidermy, the civic dramatizations at junior republics and beyond supplied a medium for modeling the world whose capacities for diverse expression were rarely used. Chicago's idiosyncratic Boys Brotherhood Republic (BBR) makes clear how the "reality" of so many role-plays was highly restrictive, enabling democracy to serve as a disciplinary force and constrain any uplift for participants within the social category of youth. The rhetoric of "miniature," "model," "realism," and "genuine reproduction" obscured how educators and youth workers were less interested in accuracy than in serving specific ideological ends.

Democracy and Discipline

The Boys Brotherhood Republic was established in 1914 when Jack Robbins, a tobacco salesman, encountered seven boys in Chicago's juvenile court and persuaded a judge to release them to his care. Talk of the George Junior Republic was everywhere, and it soon supplied the model for his "brotherhood," to use the term common to religious clubs. (Robbins did pay a visit to Freeville but not until 1918.) BBR grew quickly, becoming the largest independent boys club in the US by 1921. Although it never joined George's national association, George admired and endorsed Robbins's work.[47]

Like other republics, BBR modeled itself on its host city, offering recreational programming for working and nonworking boys in sports, drama, a newspaper (*Boys World*, from 1918), and a camp alongside its civic activities. The boys largely managed the club; when the population swelled to 1,000 boys, there were only three adult staff. Initially adding satellite clubhouses, BBR eventually consolidated in a central city hall. While not a conventionally trained youth worker, Robbins was a committed administrator—giving up his marriage to focus on the boys. He sought advice from Richard Welling, who by this time had worked with George's Freeville republic, school cities, the Hebrew Sheltering Guardian Society, and junior municipalities, inviting him to join the BBR advisory board. An active alumni association provided additional help.[48]

BBR also extended its activities beyond clubhouse walls. The junior citizens cultivated close relationships with public officials, particularly juvenile judges and police, encouraging them to parole to the club boys sentenced to reform school or jail. In short, BBR shared many features with other republics, and public descriptions largely followed a familiar script. The club "prepares boys for citizenship by educating them in citizenship," philanthropist Mrs. Frank Gordon described, "not by taking them out of their homes or away from their jobs, but by teaching them to live in the world as they find it, and in so doing to live right."[49]

It is BBR's departures from republic precedent, however, that are most revealing on account of the commonalities they highlight across civic education at the period's republics and youth activities. For as the boys of the BBR ran their club and partnered with local authorities, these junior citizens also advocated on matters of concern to boys beyond the club's membership. The investigating committee made "an average of three calls a week in homes where there are boys in trouble," met those discharged from orphan homes, communicated with those in institutions, investigated cases of children's mistreatment, and ran a free boys' dormitory at the city hall. The board of health found ways to convert vacant lots into playgrounds, sent needy boys camping, forced "improvement in dirty factories where boys are employed," and secured "medical attention for those in need of care." The board of education helped boys to attend night school, purchased books for those without means, and conducted lectures, classes, and debates. The social committee provided entertainment and furnished "music instruction to boys who are musically inclined."[50]

Even as they played roles as mayors, aldermen, police, and judges and worked in partnership with adults whose jobs they copied, these junior citizens simultaneously concerned themselves with a broader range of social, political, and economic issues of interest to the nation's youth. Occasional public protests and other acts of civil disobedience revealed the boys' impatience with business as usual and an effort to change the status quo. As a result, during the club's first few years members compelled the city of Chicago to stop fingerprinting all children on arrest, persuaded Chicago's Saddle and Cycle Club to open its private beach to public bathing, lobbied New York governor Charles Whitman to parole a fourteen-year-old boy sentenced to death, and hosted an annual jobs day from 1916—when they found employment for more than 500 boys. A few years later, the boys indicted the city of Chicago for causing boy crime and later aimed to disbar a juvenile court judge for his lack of kindness. They subsequently raised money to pay off Judge Ben Lindsey's $500 fine for refusing to reveal a boy's confidences. Hearing of these activities and the club's mission "to aid all boys in securing proper housing, clothing, education, and to help them become self-sustaining," entire gangs routinely appeared at city hall asking to join. In regular contact with city and state officials to locate missing boys, report on "pool-room proprietors who admit minors to play pool and gamble...junk dealers who buy stolen goods from boys...aid the enforcement of the child labor law, factory, legislature, and street ordinance," and encourage reformation through club participation, these relationships were more equitable than the uneven power dynamics of "friendly" relations in other settings.[51]

A few other republics had advocated on behalf of other youth. For example, the discovery that Ithaca's government no longer had sufficient funds to pay for police protection at the cross streets near the Buffalo Hill East neighborhood playground—suggesting closure was the only option—prompted the junior municipality to assign junior police to cross children at the intersection. Yet these actions, and political engagement more generally, were rare, even in republics with a community orientation. More common was a vision of democratic participation approximating the "coercive voluntarism" that Christopher Capozolla has described: public authorities' interest in youth assistance was contingent on contributions that disciplined them to the current system rather than identify new issues of concern.[52]

Thus, if in its early years George's republic had offered citizens opportunities for political and economic innovation, the movement's expansion and institutionalization in schools and youth-serving institutions brought with it greater conservatism. Although journalists occasionally highlighted "radical" aspects of the republic idea such as their preemption of female suffrage in the real world, in fact, debates on political and economic issues increasingly gave way to administrative maintenance and law and order concerns. The extension of youth activities into public settings, in which kids lacked adults' legal agency and adults typically determined their agendas, cemented the new, reduced status for youth, largely limiting their creative outlets to event planning and fundraising as in Ithaca's junior municipality or Milwaukee's newsboy republic. George's avowed desire to give kids greater autonomy in junior municipalities by lobbying police and judges to grant them legal powers thus was restricted to their practicing to fit rather than transform the social order of the greater republic. The Goo Goo worldview, which separated politics from administrative processes, helped to support this turn of events. Jacob Riis's early observations of Freeville presciently described the movement's longer-term influences on the broader field of youth activities. The Freeville experiment was "a practical effort to fit the boy to the things that are, rather than to such as might be in a millennium neither he nor we will live to see."[53]

Even George, who favored youthful leadership and hands-off management, ceded control only once confident that junior citizens had internalized the norms of rationalized civic procedures that the Goo Goos espoused rather than those of the boss rule or messier political protests many had seen firsthand. Freeville's shift from military to civilian operations, the turnover of the republic presidency to Jakey Smith, and George's expansion of the republic's disciplinary system in the mid-1910s from a jail to a series of graded citizenship statuses from 1 (free) to 4 (jailed) all made this clear. Initially hoping to reorganize so that each grade of citizen could inhabit a separate sub-republic, George's plan proved "impracticable in a place so small as the little colony at Freeville." So "instead, therefore, of having the actual separate enclosures, they became only theoretical." As the republic sheltered the youngest generation, then, equally it showed how a community might be transformed into an institution without walls, a "social sanitarium" as he called this institution made through social relations. George's later writings on the disciplinary system as both "prison walls without a prison," and a "jail inside yourself" highlighted the disciplinary capacities of democratic self-government in the environment and in the self.[54]

The disciplinary possibilities of the Goo Goos' vision of ideal democratic processes lay behind the introduction of worker and inmate governments and token economies in factories and prisons. They undergirded the enthusiasm from juvenile judges, police, and health and sanitation agencies for republics and their component activities—for example, on the sudden death of one Ford Republic child jurist, a judge from Michigan's supreme court traveled a hundred miles to attend the funeral, and the Wayne County Probate Court adjourned for two days in his honor. These possibilities equally explain why questions rarely arose about young people's performances of roles they could never play in real life. The Jewish mayors, African American judges, and female business owners who fascinated newspaper readers were learning the idealized character and behavioral norms associated with native-born middle-class whites, gaining empathy for those who aimed to rationally administer their world rather than learning alternative forms of democratic participation to advocate for change. Rare exceptions that flagged the possibility of alternative arrangements proved the rule: "Boys, I believe you did wrong to pattern your government after that of the United States," socialist Mayor Emil Seidel told the citizens of Milwaukee's YMCA boys republic in 1910, "I believe you ought to start a revolution right now.... You should make your own laws and not allow a set of officers to make them for you.... The present form of government of the United States is not the best after which to pattern yours."[55]

The educators and youth workers who guided these programs, like factory and prison management, thus were confident that friendly relations with subordinates would spawn eventual consensus despite the power differentials. That the junior municipality "works to the common advantage of the adult government, the boys and girls, and the whole community, has now been demonstrated in practice," asserted Stowe, noting how kids enjoyed the adult responsibilities and local officials saw the possibility of generating support from future voters. Junior police programs served "to eradicate the traditional enmity existing between the city boy and the policeman" and "to convert into law-abiding citizens many boys who might otherwise become toughs and gangsters." Youths' continued enthusiastic participation in their own disciplining—which included not only waitlists for republics and other youth programs but also later service as alumni volunteers and professionals in education and youth work—seemed to bear this out.[56]

The BBR's systematic efforts to advocate for youth perspectives, and occasionally activist strategies for so doing, thus highlighted the flexible possibilities of the civic role-plays that were so central to the modern youth experience—and yet, simultaneously, how most programs typically directed them toward a narrow set of applications. This suggests debates about reality versus make-believe ignored the narrow scope of so many carefully constructed models of reality—for example, republics had neither socialist politicians nor labor unions—and how the children's rights that educators and youth workers advocated were quite restricted in light of their primary ambition to persuade young people to conform to new norms associated with the social category "youth." That most youth activities aimed to convince young participants to diminish their own political interests and capacities and internalize adults' points of view created friction between Robbins and colleagues in his city. In 1921, BBR patron E. D. Hulbert confided to republic association member and former Sing Sing assistant warden Spencer Miller Jr. about "the almost universal hostility" to Robbins "among the other men in the same line of work" even though "Jack reaches a lot of boys that the others never would." The traditionalists were "almost unanimously opposed to the Boy's Brotherhood" because "self-government beyond a limited degree is harmful." The difficulty supporters encountered trying to establish BBRs beyond Chicago underscored how, in an era of proliferating republics, it was out of step with prevailing expectations.[57]

Histories of the emergence of the sheltered childhood already have noted the social control function of schools and youth-serving institutions through the programs of education and supervised leisure they supplied. Studies of home economics, vocational education, school banks, Scouting, and Camp Fire Girls attending to implicit curricula such as the importance of middle-class values and gendered identities in programs of "character development" have detailed how adults aimed to influence both how young people conceived of issues and the extent to which they should engage with them as part of the transition to the new youth ideal. Across these programs a network of prominent figures including Jacob Riis, Luther Gulick, and others built substantial ideological common ground.[58]

The evidence presented here confirms educators' and youth workers' interest in spreading such messages and identifies role-playing within a democratic self-government framework as a transcendent modern disciplinary technique. Like the living villages, dioramas, and wax museums which familiarized spectators with the "double position" that is said to define modern subjectivity and, simultaneously, encouraged their assimilation to contemporary conditions, the vicarious experiences of adulthood young people encountered in this period supplied a curriculum that communicated similar messages. As calls for suffrage and the new woman emerged, organizations like the Queens of Avalon and Camp Fire Girls gamified traditional domestic tasks and feminized community service rather than radically redefine expectations for the nation's future women—even as they offered girls citizenship training through voting and officeholding. Studying "the domestic life of the ladies of ancient courts" in the Queens of Avalon "encourage[d] the girls to housewifely tasks" both inside and outside the home, making this "play society" into "an effective instrumentality in developing a romanceful, pure, home-loving, serviceful type of womanhood," as William Forbush explained. Camp Fire Girls was even more explicit in its efforts. Taking the view that "one of the worst signs of the times ... is the restlessness of women, their dissatisfaction with home life ... directly due to the unfortunate fact that we have robbed home life in one way or another" of anything that was interesting to do, as Gulick put it, "training for femininity" was key to the organization. Although occasional headlines such as "Girls Take Up the Boy Scout Idea and Band Together" suggested gender-bending possibilities, a closer look reveals role-plays imposed new constraints.[59]

While the story of disciplinary developments inside classrooms and clubhouses is reasonably well known, equally significant were the many complementary activities taking place in community settings. The implications of the model of civic participation being promoted in these youth programs were particularly striking for the participants who were cause for concern not only because they were exposed to moral hazards on city streets or failed to attend school. In a period when labor unions were agitating for workers' rights and the firsthand effects of newsboy strikes were in recent public memory, these civic dramatizations offered alternatives to union membership and other forms of political organizing, suggesting even more meaningful ties between the programs of self-government embraced by educators and youth workers and the fashion for industrial democracy at the nation's factories and firms.[60]

From the junior police and junior sanitary inspectors who impersonated contemporary occupations to the Scouts and Knights of King Arthur who imitated historical and sometimes fictitious figures, these organizations had far more in common than not. All engaged young people in dramatizations that transformed participants' relations to public spaces and, in turn, transformed these spaces as well. Youth leaders, including New York City junior police organizer Arthur Woods and Boy Scout head James West, were in frequent contact with each other and with William George, engaged in a larger conversation about vicarious experiences of adulthood for educating and socializing youth. (Indeed, Woods became a trustee of George's association.)[61]

Although occasionally the subject of differentiation and dispute, statements of these activities' shared cause grew more common over time. Declaring, for example, in *Educational Problems* (1911), that service must be educators' highest ambition, Hall enthused about how Waring's New York City street cleaning brigade, Gunckel's Toledo newsboys, Scouts, Knights of King Arthur, and junior police—like George's republic and Boy City—contributed to the common good as they controlled the daily lives of boys. Forbush, who became head of the American Institute of Child Life, was a vocal spokesperson for these varied organizations and the commonalities they shared. In Scouting, each participant "thinks of himself as a pioneer and enacts...many of the resourceful habits of the early explorers." In the Queens of Avalon, "the girls think of themselves as the queens who in the King Arthur legend dwelt upon the magic Isle of Avalon for the healing of mankind." In junior republics and school cities, "the young people all the time realize a civic situation." His observations on the service orientation of Scouts, school cities, and newsboy republics together with the Knights of King Arthur and Waring's junior street cleaning brigade—and his recommendation that participants in his programs read Scouting manuals for inspiration—underscored this view. "The parent should crave, and the social worker plan, so that every child will have the opportunity during the 'gang' period of belonging to some social club whose scheme is based upon imaginative play," Forbush explained.[62]

By contrast, there was no equivalent reframing of these activities' economic implications. As educators and youth workers surveyed the growing roster of community-based republics and youth activities, they recognized how some of the benefits previously associated with youth programs at junior republics, schools, and youth-serving institutions were now accruing to the communities from which young people ostensibly were being removed. Yet the centrality of role-playing across these programs similarly extended interpretations that suggested how educators and youth workers were reducing rather than expanding the child labor pool. In short, the gamification of their public service ensured young people's contributions to American state building were understood not as economic activities but rather as character development and civic education.

The Gamification of Public Service

From the turn of the century, research investigations by developmental psychologists had made educators and youth workers anxious about the continued presence of children in public. And yet, simultaneously, this research tradition had raised their awareness as to some positive features of previously maligned activities. Ben Lindsey was among the prominent figures who offered public praise for the "voluntary delinquents" who brought other kids to court or the Denver gangs that had gone after "the men who were selling liquor and tobacco to boys," so they could be prosecuted. Adult-organized role-playing activities matched young people's energies to community needs more explicitly, and the results could be seen in the improvement of municipal operations.[63]

The newsboy republic in Milwaukee, for example, not only reduced the number of newsboys in reform school, it directly assisted the local street trades department and juvenile court, reducing the need to hire additional staff. "It has been a problem to enforce the street trades act with any effectiveness without employing a large corps of factory inspectors or other officers," one anonymous Milwaukee republic founder explained. "The results obtained by individual work of the supervisor in regulating and enforcing the street trades law was not effective, and it was impossible to extend the influence of the law all over the city, so a self-governing organization having the boys co-operate and enforce their own law, was devised." Annual newsboy republic expenses of $2,000 halved staff costs (estimated at $4,000 to $5,000) and saved $150,000 over a decade by diverting cases from the juvenile court. "The Republic has saved the taxpayers considerable money. During the past eleven years there have been approximately 7,500 complaints disposed of, and not more than twelve boys have been summoned to the Juvenile Court during this period for violating the street trades law." Echoing findings from George and Gill that young people were better at policing and prosecuting one another than were adults, and held one another to higher standards, Powell explained how "Tony of the Italian district, and Isidore of the Russian Jews, are far better able to look after their fellow 'newsies' than the adult policeman of American or Irish birth." In short, "the boys themselves enforce the street trades law better than ten state inspectors could."[64]

Single-agency role-playing programs provided similar aid to municipal coffers. The thousands of junior police who enforced bonfire ordinances "save the city thousands of dollars in asphalt," New York City police captain John Sweeney reported, noting how, "Since the force was formed" to "aid in enforcing" ordinances, "we have had few complaints about street bonfires, whereas we used to have a hundred a night sometimes." Similarly, "The daily destruction of public property in at least one of the parks" had been "stopped with no expense to the city at a time when it is absolutely essential to conserve every end and every piece of property now owned by the municipality," observed parks department assistant foreman Tim Sullivan after assigning junior police to patrol Bronx's Echo Park. "We have been shorthanded in this park for some time, so I didn't have enough men to watch twenty-four hours of the day—in fact, hardly enough to do the regular gardening work.... It is hard to estimate what amount of money they have saved the city, but every taxpayer should be grateful." In Council Bluffs, after kids took responsibility for enforcing fireworks ordinances, the Fourth of July "was quieter, more peaceful, and freer from accident than any other previous Fourth of July in the history of the city." Denver children's detective work proved vastly more effective than that of adults. Judge Lindsey described how the children "have prosecuted and convicted more men for selling liquor and tobacco to children, for selling them firearms, junk dealers for purchasing stolen property, men for circulating immoral literature, in one year of the Juvenile Court than the entire police department, sheriff's office and all other civil officers combined, have done in twenty years.'"[65]

Juvenile street cleaners, junior sanitary inspectors, and some junior civic leagues supplied vital information services and assisted officials from Birmingham and Atlanta to Cleveland and Detroit to San Diego and Denver with cleanup work. "The children are furnished blank form cards, on which to make out their reports," a journalist described Philadelphia's 8,000-strong Junior Sanitation League. "These cards have been carefully thought out and, when properly filled are remarkably complete records to teach the children the value of the system in civic affairs." Once indexed and placed on file at headquarters it became "possible for the municipal authorities, without leaving the city hall, to comb the town every 24 hours, and in a few moments tell as to the clean and unclean street conditions in any one as well as every section. The result is that Philadelphia is now, for the first time in its history, a clean and thoroughly sanitary city." Some junior police provided comparable services, for example a private squad organized at Indianapolis's Christamore Settlement. After training by local police and detectives, the kids wrote up reports on sanitation, card games, and law violations in their neighborhoods. "Those fellows are right up to the minute," one local police captain declared. "Our district men drop in at the boy's headquarters and read their reports and get many a tip as to what is happening in that neighborhood."[66]

As they continued to raise money to make their organizations self-supporting, participants in activities from Scouting to the Knights of King Arthur directed their role-playing toward complementary ends in a range of community service projects. Boy Scout troops aided citywide cleanup campaigns, as in Hartford, Connecticut, where they distributed 54,000 circulars to homes and inspected 15,225 yards. They formed fire patrols in communities lacking municipal fire departments. They helped maintain New York City parks. And they repaired roads in Savannah, Georgia, and other cities. Knights from "Castle Scrooby, Andover, Maine, started a campaign to paint the town white, calling it 'the white crusade.' They cleaned up and beautified the common and then did other things of service to the town." One Halloween, "the policemen in the section of the city near the headquarters of Castle Joyous Gard were suddenly encountered by huge Jack-o'-Lanterns and a bunch of hot coffee and sandwiches," provided by the boys.[67]

Ad hoc pairings of youth and government agencies yielded similar results. As the *Knickerbocker Press* reported of the child enumerators William George recruited to take New York's agricultural census, "The entire census was taken at virtually no cost to the State, whereas the Federal agricultural census taken every ten years is a big burden financially." The US Weather Bureau adopted the student-operated weather station at Boston's Farm and Trades School as an official reporting location.[68]

Yet as public figures recognized in growing numbers that, when faced with shortages of municipal workers, they could rely on children to play these roles, their discussions of these activities emphasized the dramatic nature and fun being had by participants so as to subordinate the immediate financial benefits to the future developmental benefits of recreation for participating youth. Junior municipalities, whose junior officials took up issues which senior officials "lacked time to look into personally" were the ur-example of how kids created value for local governments and yet how, by doing so in role as understudies, their contributions were linked to education and entertainment, playful virtual experiences rather than real work. Although there was ample precedent for young people making state contributions under the auspices of youth-serving institutions—for example, in the school cities in public schools or playground republics in cities with publically supported recreation—the breadth and depth of these youth activities' orientation toward community welfare was on a vastly larger scale. So too was the effort to conceal how activities adopted to teach the values lost with the erasure of work from children's lives provided more direct instruction than previously presumed.[69]

Thus, observers of newsboy republics in Boston and Milwaukee saw child labor exclusively in the boys' newspaper selling, while their street trades enforcement activities were part of the organization's recreational character-building scheme. Although "The Boston plan for enforcement seems to have given better results than the common system of intrusting the enforcement to officers already overburdened with other duties," reported the National Child Labor Committee's Edward Clopper, the program was nonetheless was a form of educational recreation "extending the [protective] influences of the schools" into city streets. Milwaukee's "figurative bluecoats" who reduced the numbers of youth in reform school, diminished the need for street trades inspectors, and eliminated the strain on the juvenile court were merely expanding club activities beyond the walls of schools and social centers, keeping the boys occupied with positive forms of recreation in an effort "to solve the child labor problem," as an unnamed republic founder put it. The match with kids' natural playtime activities was frequently cited. The "pleasure for boys to vote and to give speeches for their own candidates and to know that they have something directly to do with governing themselves," the founder explained. Observers used John Commons's language of "social agency" to suggest that the republic was a city-organized child welfare program that "puts street trades enforcement on educational lines," what P. O. "Pop" Powell later deemed a "permanent social agency of the city" rather than an organization of children doing the child protection work themselves. "This social agency has a peculiar saving power to the taxpayer," Pop observed, "actually saving dollars and cents and in the same turn of the wheel improving the standard of citizenship among the men of tomorrow." Alumni events decades later attest to the enjoyment and allegiances felt by participating youth.[70]

The broad awareness that children's "dramatic instinct" and zeal for impersonation could be put to positive or negative purposes frequently assisted in these rationalizations.

After noting how "New York City has long needed five or six thousand more men on its police force, but the cost of providing them has always remained prohibitory to the governing authorities," and that "The creation of a body of an equal number of boy police" was "much cheaper," Gregory Mason explained in *Labor Digest* how the junior police program offered an opportunity for civic dramatization. "The boyish love of adventure and mystery, which usually expresses itself in emulation of the exploits of criminal heroes of dime novels and the yellow press," would instead be "directed to the imitation of the deeds of the real heroes of American cities—the brave, honest, and unassuming members of the police force, in uniform and out." As a result, the "educational value of this junior police force is of more importance than its police value," observed the *National Municipal Review*. "This movement teaches the boys the principal municipal ordinances, encourages them to explain them to their parents who do not understand our language, and influences them to refrain from committing street offenses." In short, if "actual burglary and train wrecking by children are examples of dramatic instinct gone wrong," as G. Stanley Hall student Elnora Curtis explained, then directing kids at play to emulate police rather than criminals solved "the problem of the boy in the streets"—even as the program was "organized primarily to provide a supplementary force to aid in enforcing the ordinances as they related to the Health and Street Cleaning Departments."[71]

Related claims framed junior sanitation and junior civic leagues as observers who praised their efficiency lauded the child protection they supplied. Richard Welling's early suggestion "that the 'school city' branch out and take part in the affairs of the community" while describing youth participants, in keeping with his Goo Goo outlook, as "largely removed from politics" fit these later examples as well. So too did the view taken by observers of Waring's turn-of-the-century street cleaning brigades: "In a general way these were really boys clubs" run by city officials. "The education through voluntary organizations is self-insured and has large value as supplementing that of the schools," the president of Georgia's junior civic clubs explained. Assigning pupils to clean up the town playground and other public areas thus did not put them to work but instead was "organizing children for protective plays and occupations." Observing kids' routine play in the streets as police, detective, and fire brigade—indeed some programs took over squads previously organized by kids—they suggested this was the best kind of child-centered citizenship training. Republic affiliates, eager to ensure that George received credit for these proliferating organizations, wrote letters to the editor to "correct" newspaper coverage and publicize George's junior municipality work.[72]

Boy Scouts' public activities were also part of this story about "the dramatic instinct for the greatest entertainment and educational advantage." For the savings of $6,500,000 to the New York City parks department in 1916 dollars their assistance represented was nothing more than a "good turn." Aiding fire departments was "fun and valuable training." Scouting more generally was understood as informal and "recreational education," whatever the specific activity on hand. "It is a game to the boy who is in it," noted writer Harold Horne, a "huge, splendidly organized game, with all the fine zest of competition, the finer zest of co-operation, the keen testing of mind and muscle, the essential good sportsmanship of a football game. Only instead of just picking up a score, instead of winning for the sake of victory itself, it is constructive, progressive...therein lies the secret of Scouting's success." Professorships of Scouting and recreational leadership, for example held by J. C. Elsom at Wisconsin and Elbert Fretwell at Columbia's Teachers College, underscored these program's developmental benefits.[73]

Observing how "Within a few years there has been almost an epidemic of interest in dramatization," and praising these activities for channeling the imitative, dramatic instinct to positive ends, Elnora Curtis proposed more educators and youth workers follow suit. "I wish I had written it myself," G. Stanley Hall praised his former student's proposition in the preface to her book. By the 1910s, then, Forbush's observation that "some of the most successful clubs for boys and girls are those in which every activity is made a part of a play world, in which members live during, and to some extent, between, the sessions of the club," characterized common interpretations of these community-based youth programs. These activities were playful "miniatures of social life," as the American Public Health Association observed of junior sanitary squads, an "embryo" or "miniature" adult occupation—similar and yet distinct, "just like" but not the thing itself.[74]

Many youth themselves shared this view of their activities—with more than a few insisting that even non-cash remuneration compromised the learning experience. San Diego junior inspectors voted down the free movie admissions offered to members of the squad, believing it "beneath their dignity to have to be bribed into working for the welfare of San Diego." New York City junior police similarly rejected payment in chocolate. The Council Bluffs junior police force, who had "pretty nearly rendered unnecessary a juvenile court" in that city, stressed their reward came in "prestige." Even BBR citizens, despite their other disputes with public authorities, made no claims about the economic value of club activities.[75]

Thus, despite acknowledgements that the new breed of youth program responded to local governments' financial constraints and were associated with municipal efficiency advocates; despite the participation of child laborers and language of "work" describing these experiences; despite tallies of monies saved and prior traditions in some communities of paying youth who engaged in similar occupations; despite acknowledgments that real political life had come to be like a game and observations that "the school children are the most valuable asset to the state," young people were understood to be protected in civic dramatizations rather than exploited in actual civic work. As Alabama child labor committee chair Mrs. W. L. Murdoch explained, the newsboy republic there was "not unlike a child labor law. No newsboy can get a badge who is not in school." Even critics accepted this formulation, emphasizing the moral hazards of street-based youth programs rather than the economic exploitation of youth. In short, public officials and in turn the broader public followed the lead of developmental psychologists and educators to conclude that educational and recreational activities that duplicated adult occupations did not constitute work—even when these activities took place on public streets and financially benefitted the state.[76]

Municipal Housekeeping for Women, Public Role-Playing for Youth

Scholars such as Daphne Spain and Camilla Stivers have documented how, as the male-dominated Goo Goo movement rationalized administrative processes and procedures, middle-class women's voluntary associations organized other public improvements that, although uncounted in official tallies of community productivity, supplied value to urban populations. These public activities typically took place under the rubric of "municipal housekeeping" (sometimes called "public mothering") so as to maintain their social acceptability in light of the ideology of separate spheres. According to this view, when women established kindergartens and other youth programs, organized cleanup campaigns, and improved public safety and hygiene by building public baths and inspecting milk supplies, they merely extended their identities as housewives to new locations. That such activities were directed to public rather than private clients—and hence could be classified as expressions of citizenship—further undermined potential controversies. (This differential evaluation of public versus private sector clients was also present in discussions about prison labor; workshops in which prisoners made articles for government use were viewed with comparatively less hostility by organized labor.) Thanks to this framing the interpretation of women's public activities as unproductive and the sense of protection prevailed, despite the fact that when men assumed responsibility for these services they did so as paid public servants, and in some cases were seen to be tackling dangerous work. Like the housework that could be labeled "work" and yet not remunerated, then, municipal housekeeping followed suit.[77]

The evidence presented here attests to how young people similarly played vital yet hidden roles expanding local government capacity and how it was precisely the kids that common wisdom located outside the labor force who made the greatest contributions to state building. The dominant discourse that obscured the pioneering work of women and youth from inside such restrictive social categories differed for these two populations, however, as the "double lives" that characterized youth activities inside schools and youth-serving institutions held true in public as well. Echoing the factory and mill owners who employed women and children but suggested to potential adversaries how industrial betterment offered female workers a "finishing school" whereas it provided child laborers an education and protection from the streets, the educators and youth workers who organized these community-based programs proposed the new activities merely extended to new locations widely accepted ideals of play-based civic and character education. The distinction between reality and representation so central to dramatizations of adult life at schools and youth-serving institutions thus could also be found in the nation's communities, enabling celebrations rather than criticisms of the public activities of American youth.[78]

Like adults but not actual adults, young people accomplished much for themselves and their communities but were regularly reminded of their status as "only kids" who lacked the formal legal powers and protections of the adults they replaced and whose authority to perform their "occupations" was mostly informally granted by their elders. Educators and youth workers committed to republic principles had earlier expressed frustrations that too few supervisors gave children opportunities to do things themselves. The real-world status of virtual activities proved even more complicated as young people brought their role-plays into public settings, providing services rather than manufacturing goods. Many adults respected young people in these roles—for example, in one community the junior police were treated with admiration "not only by children of their own age but by careless janitors who disobey the Health Department regulations, pushcart peddlers who failed to maintain the traffic and health regulations and, in fact, any violator of the law or ordinances." Yet there were also stories of violators who refused to cooperate with the juvenile police who substituted for adult officers, such as the woman who, on being told she was violating a city ordinance, took a junior police lieutenant "over her knees and spanked him." The belief expressed by judges, police, and other authorities that youth role-playing activities should have real-world status was not universally persuasive.[79]

There were some cases in which interpretations of women's and young people's activities overlapped. When children participated in junior civic leagues sponsored by women's associations, the language of voluntarism and citizenship joined education, play, and simulation to underscore their noneconomic nature. Girls' organizations, including Camp Fire Girls, portrayed participants as junior municipal housekeepers. According to this view, public service built on domestic training, educating girls "to serve the community, the larger home, in the same ways that they have always served the individual home."[80]

These similarities and differences thus underscore the centrality of role-plays of adult life in understanding the modern youth experience and suggest that the unpaid contributions of youth were vital components of the efficiencies associated with local governments and the broader political economy of the welfare state. Like Daphne Spain's reappraisal of women's roles in public improvements, the story presented here of the public programs organized by educators and youth workers including government officials indicates that children too helped to "save the city." Although calls by William George and sponsors of the Milwaukee Newsboy Republic to make their programs a regular part of municipal government across the nation did not meet with success, other youth-run activities were eventually taken over by adult civil servants in greater numbers. To the story of public mothering activities professionalized and taken over by men, we can add an account of young people's dramatic instincts for playing roles as civil servants supervised and later superseded by adults. This evidence suggests the need to add to the literature on women's voluntary associations and young men's voluntary associations of a much earlier period a new literature on voluntarism by kids. It offers another reason for the growing interest among public officials in supervising youth activities. And in revealing how the view that schools and youth-serving institutions were non-market spaces carried over when children participated in educational and recreational activities beyond their borders, it confirms how age, like gender, plays a role in defining productivity.[81]

That these activities multiplied even as the long-fought battle for a federal youth agency concluded underscores the power of this now-dominant view. A Children's Bureau had become a reality within the US Department of Labor in 1913, its mandate to research the American youth experience and advocate for child protection across the nation. Preaching the importance of education and recreation from its debut, the agency geared up for a publicity blitz as US participation in World War I approached. Yet federal officials soon discovered what many of their colleagues in local government already knew. How they worked to bring the disciplinary and economic benefits of young people's occupational simulations to bear on a diversity of state building needs in war and peace and how, alongside the mass institutionalization of these activities the lexicon of double life began its slow disappearance, are the subjects of chapter 5.

III From Models and Dramatizations to Education and Recreation

5   Serving Community and Nation

"The George Junior Republic tries to avoid the danger incurred by many schools where a proper balance is not considered," Richard Welling told the *New York Times* in 1925. "Just as the body of citizens in any city is made up of all kinds, so the student body here is made up of all kinds," the republic board of trustees' president explained. Wealthy and poor were welcomed to the community for college preparatory coursework as well as learning trades. These "young citizens" were "paid for studying—the better their classwork the larger their paycheck"—and for their contributions to "village industries" there. "Learning by doing" was the mantra of the "school organized under the laws of the American republic" where pupils "run their own government after the fashion of any city government."[1]

Why, after years of George's fighting portraits of the republic as a school, reformatory, or other youth-serving "institution" would his close associate frame the republic in educational terms? And what might Freeville's choice to pay its citizen-students for their varied activities reveal about the broader field of schools and youth-serving institutions? This chapter follows the republic movement through World War I and the 1920s to document continuing enthusiasm for occupational role-playing at George's republic and beyond and how its assignment of monetary value to academic and trades training, together with George's private observation that the arrangement "was not only advantageous to the youth involved, but to the state as well," offers clues to a much larger story. As federal authorities faced a national security crisis, they favored occupational role-plays and civic simulations as means to economic and political ends. Continued confidence in these activities' broad benefits from educators and youth workers—a category that now included national as well as local officials—helped to sustain momentum for these techniques such that the "learning by doing" at the heart of the republic movement became a routine feature in the lives of American youth.[2]

Scholars have characterized World War I and the postwar period as tipping points for public acceptance of the sheltered childhood. In these accounts the expansion of high schools and recreational programs and the growing prosecution of "juvenile delinquency," together with the emergence of youth consumer culture, signal the achievement of reformers' ambitions for the lives of many, if not all, young people. Yet a closer look finds the persistence of other prewar patterns and trends. From inside ostensibly protected spaces and from supervised activities in public settings young people continued their value making activities, redirecting attention from local to national needs and remaking many junior republics, schools, and youth-serving institutions into economic engines of the wartime state. New postwar programs such as junior traffic patrols extended children's contributions to producing the sheltered childhood and their contributions to state building in the modern era. With the widespread institutionalization of activities from student government and vocational education to junior policing and Scouting, talk of "education" and "recreation" with more implicit association to some "real world" referent increasingly became the norm. Welling's simultaneous reference to the Freeville "citizens" and "students" signaled how the 1920s marked the final flowering of public commitment to the double life ideal—and how the coming of the sheltered childhood is more than a story about the institutionalization of adult-sponsored activities. Equally it is the story of these activities' changing meanings as "miniature" and "model" dramatizations of adult experiences came to be regarded as authentic educational and recreational experiences for American youth.

Schools and Youth-Serving Institutions as Shelters and Economic Engines in World War I

Educational historians' recognition that wartime needs helped to realize prewar proposals for curriculum reform, together with Joseph Kett's observation that "by World War I, boys were only playing at war," typify conventional understandings of youth participation in the conflict. These accounts contrast the Civil War and Spanish-American War, when children (mostly boys) fought on the front lines, with twentieth-century conflicts, when fewer enlisted or took war jobs and more remained in school and supervised activities or played with war-related toys and games at home. As military leaders redefined preparedness training away from the rote memorization of drill routines toward curricular methods that included vocational and physical education, they added powerful new voices in support of educators' and youth workers' long-standing efforts to place vicarious experiences of adulthood at the center of the curriculum.[3]

Activities such as Junior Reserve Officer Training Corps, Junior Army-Navy League, Junior Naval Reserve, and US Army Cadet Corps, which built on military role-plays such as boys brigades, military companies, broom drills, and sham battles, did attract thousands to play roles as uniformed service members—drilling, setting up camps, and practicing survival skills, updating a long tradition of military occupational role-plays with reference to "boy psychology," "the play and game instincts," and even learning by doing. Yet with the complexity and machine basis of modern warfare requiring forces to acquire broader skills, preparedness training and programming trends at schools and youth-serving institutions were increasingly well matched. US officials' testimonials contrasting their efforts to protect school-aged children from the dangers of wartime service with European allies—whose children participated in the conflict and thus were both exploited and consigned to a future of dead-end jobs—supply evidence for historians' assessment that the shift from family economy to sheltered childhood had been achieved for a majority of American youth by 1920.[4]

The discovery that many prewar educational and recreational programs were economically as well as developmentally productive invites another look at young people's wartime activities. Educators' and youth workers' recognition that many were eager to join the US mobilization, together with the military's revised definition of preparedness training, expanded and reoriented role-playing activities to address wartime needs. Schools and youth-serving institutions had already partnered with local authorities on service projects. Now these partnerships expanded to include federal agencies. As the conflict offered new opportunities to implement preexisting curricular visions, then, these programming choices provided value to the wartime state.

Such developments were apparent in Freeville, where times had been tough since reopening in 1914. Continuing financial problems had prompted George "to depend more on capable citizens ... and less upon high salaried adults" to supervise the cottages and industries. Older youth were also hired out to local industries as part of their trade education in light of the onsite school's increasingly academic curriculum.[5]

The war amplified these trends. The past year was "the most difficult in Junior Republic history," George wrote in the 1918 annual report. The enlistment of "82% of the eligible boys" had decimated its numbers and "left the republic practically a commonwealth of girls." This situation forced the closure of most onsite industries and cottages, raising questions about the institution's viability. As some youth enlisted and others sought government and industry work, George's National Republic at Annapolis had closed and most junior municipalities went on hiatus. In the wartime economy, the youth society needed to explore new fundraising possibilities.[6]

Initially brainstorming ideas for a Junior Republic Products Company that could profit from extant resources—like local berries or old rags, George abandoned this idea. Instead, he relocated the older girls (about twenty ages fifteen and up) along with a few boys to a donated house in Syracuse so they could work in government munitions factories there. In the "barracks" as they called it, citizens drilled in khaki garb and armbands that read "War Service," and lived by military schedule with reveille and taps. He enticed Atlantic Woolen Mills to open a "war industry" in Freeville for younger citizens to recycle wool suits for use in new uniforms. These children drilled with George's daughter Eleanor.[7]

In short, George revived practices of onsite hiring out and contracting that were once routine in child-saving institutions but had disappeared due to the belief they exploited youth. He reintroduced them with minor modifications: insisting that offsite

Figure 5.1
Syracuse Sector of the George Junior Republic.
Source: William R. George Family Papers, box 122, folder 4–9, envelope 8, "Girls, WWI." Courtesy Division of Rare and Manuscript Collections, Cornell University Library.

work be limited to government clients, that the republic industry had educational features, and that republic supervisors be allowed to observe anytime they wished. As "the Syracuse sector of the GJR" and "the war industry in the Republic" protected kids from actual military service, then, they simultaneously helped the nation's war effort and addressed the republic's financial problems by remunerating George's charges with money for room and board.[8]

The ambiguities of Freeville's wartime activities point to larger patterns shaping the American youth experience, nowhere more than the nation's public schools. As US participation in the conflict loomed, politicians and business owners discussed suspending child labor laws and converting school plants into war production centers. Educators like Teachers College vocational education professor Arthur Dean, who became supervising officer of the New York State Military Training Commission's Bureau of Vocational Education, rejected these proposals, believing that schools should protect pupils from wartime service while preparing them for future participation: "Our schools must be retained as educative plants, training munitions workers, if we will, but not making munitions; providing the government with skilled artisans and scientists, but by no means converting their function of education into industrial production." Fearing a national undoing of its campaigns for extended schooling, the US Children's Bureau declared 1918 a Children's Year.[9]

America's schools were not converted into factories. Yet their alternative path was more similar than most previous accounts have portrayed. Following Gary's lead of bringing apprenticeships into classrooms, many brought the war to kids. Inside woodworking shops, sewing rooms, and kitchens, students prepared

> canned goods and homemade articles for hospitals, training camps, and the front line...made posters; spoke as "Junior Four Minute Men"; wrote letters to the soldiers; assembled scrapbooks, and collected magazines for the training camps; sewed on dresses, rolled bandages, and canned food; constructed furniture and packing boxes; adopted war orphans; rendered assistance of various kinds to official boards, such as filling out and filing cards, tabulating questionnaires, addressing envelopes, and preparing signs and posters; held patriotic celebrations, parades, and pageants; and salvaged peach pits, nutshells, and tinfoil.[10]

Youth-led efforts to use school facilities for personal profit were now replaced by adult-organized efforts that benefited the wartime state. As educators guided students in military drill, making government-issue equipment, and farming the nation's food supply, prewar precedents enabled them to characterize such activities as pedagogical innovations rather than productive labor, "an opportunity for developing a closer relation between education and life, between life and service...no more revolutionary to introduce the war into our schools than it was to introduce" lab sciences, agricultural study, or millinery, as Dean explained. Although he saw the possibility to "incorporate useful labor into the educative process," production remained "subordinate" to educational needs so that no child labor was taking place. To stories of how federal officials urged youth to continue their future-oriented educations, then, must be added accounts of how their agencies helped to remake schools to supply more immediate contributions to national needs—and how the belief in such activities' educational benefits held even as they acknowledged the value produced.[11]

The US School Garden Army (USSGA), for example, transformed the school gardens that sustained nature study curricula, home economics courses, agricultural training, and junior civic leagues in nearly 80 percent of US school districts into war gardens to meet national food production goals. Administered by the federal agriculture and interior departments, the program supplied regionally oriented, seasonal handbooks and seed catalogs to maximize harvest yield by pupils organized into companies of privates sporting ensign bars with USSGA. Despite its militarism, USSGA taught democratic self-government to "Americanize" immigrants and counter antidemocratic regimes, with pupils selecting officers and making decisions about the gardens they cultivated. This was a valuable addition if, as one Chicago teacher put it in 1919, "We want to make American democracy a beacon light for the rest of the world" yet American schools remained largely autocratic in organization."[12]

Public discussions of the program attest to how federal officials agreed with educators and youth workers that wartime needs could enhance rather than disrupt the curriculum. "I am sure they would all like to feel that they are in fact fighting France,"

President Woodrow Wilson observed. "The movement to establish gardens, therefore, and to have the children work in them is just as real and patriotic an effort as the building of ships or the firing of cannon." Taking the view, as Clark University psychology fellow Ping Ling put it, that this approach prioritized "real life, instead of dead books," educators and youth workers who had been outspoken about such programs in peacetime took leadership roles to implement them during the war. Cyril Stebbins, whose community garden in Berkeley, California, was among the descendants of Rev. Floody's Worcester Garden Cities, became USSGA western regional director, writing manuals for the new federal program. Milwaukee street trades commissioner and republic supervisor P. O. "Pop" Powell led Milwaukee's Garden Army, encouraging newsboys to plant war gardens at home and in their communities as in schools. Thanks to his encouragement his city had more war gardens than any other.[13]

As the military campaign continued, school officials undertook further efforts to connect curricula to current affairs. For the youngest pupils, play cities such as Victory City directed all activities to patriotic goals. *Industrial Arts* magazine reported on the California school print shops that "rendered valuable service in promoting community and social war service work." In previous years, the priority was meeting institutional needs including

> school stationery...entertainment literature, programs, notices, tickets, etc.; reading lessons for the grades, and literature studies of the high school; syllabi outlines, laboratory guides; progressive directions for special supervisors; school songs, drawing instruction, physical training exercises; class and school bulletins; reference aids to the course of study, supplementary material, bibliographies, collateral assignments, hints for original studies, etc.

Now students across the state served a broader range of public clients: "Red Cross, community center, Liberty Loan and other war propaganda were effectively promoted through the printing contributed by the school shops." Indeed, "the entire responsibility for...composition, typing, making up forms, proofing, printing, binding, rests with pupils." (The California Junior Republic was listed here, suggesting how it, like its Freeville counterpart, was considered an educational institution.)[14]

US Treasury Department, US Food Administration, and US Fuel Administration staff also contacted school administrators with ideas for directing pupils' attention to their priorities, such as pupil savings banks to promote thrift activities. The Creel Committee on Public Information, which coordinated the nation's propaganda campaigns, enlisted students to spread its messages: delivering leaflets, speaking to public gatherings, and informing parents about voluntary canning and food rationing—building on prior efforts to use kids as conduits of government information to adults in their families and communities. As a bewildering array of proposals streamed in, some administrators and instructors became aggravated by the lack of interagency coordination. The Junior Red Cross stepped up to address these concerns. This quasi-public agency was a welcome intermediary in light of continued controversies about federal versus local

Figure 5.2
Students in World War I.
Source: Arthur Dean, *Our Schools in War Time—and After* (Boston: Ginn, 1918).

control of schools. More than half of all US school children joined the organization. (Some youthful pacifists rejected its war service orientation.)[15]

Directed by John Studebaker (who was concurrently pursuing a master's degree at Teachers College), the Junior Red Cross registered each participating school as a "junior auxiliary and a center for patriotic service." Working with federal officials, it provided lesson plans to connect academic subjects to news headlines. And it offered trades instructors precise specifications for the sweaters students knitted and the furniture they produced.

The Red Cross had been offering advice to schools even before this program debuted—for example in Los Angeles, where pupils had made, between April and June 1917, 925 pairs of pajamas, 800 hospital shirts, 100 bed slippers, 1,000 pillow cases, 505 pillows, 1,350 shoulder wraps, 1,320 comfort bags, 150 ambulance pillows, 50 surgeon caps, 180 napkins, 544 handkerchiefs, and 1,200 washcloths. Although the new organization encouraged pupils to undertake some community-oriented activities, its primary focus was making in-school activities of "real" usefulness to the war. "If all the boys and girls in their effort to be of service went to work making something for the soldiers without being told what was most needed or how it should be made, all sorts of mistakes would result," Studebaker explained. This was why "the Junior Red

Cross office at Washington sends out exact directions as to what is needed, how much is wanted, and how the articles are to be made." Under its auspices, pupils across the United States produced "surgical dressings, hospital supplies, hospital garments, refugee garments, articles for soldiers and miscellaneous items totaling 15,722,073 in number and valued at $10,152,461.96, or ten percent of the entire Red Cross production during the war."[16]

As the Junior Red Cross streamlined schools' contributions to national needs, it trumpeted the pedagogical importance of "reality" in the curriculum. The organization was merely, as cofounder and Vassar president Henry MacCraken explained to US education commissioner Philip Claxton, a means of putting into practice school teachers' long-standing educational ideals. Philadelphia School of Pedagogy professor and adviser James Lynn Barnard delighted in how it refreshed the civics curriculum in ways proponents of "the new civics" had espoused. The recognition that "young people learn much through observation and imitation…forces us to the conclusion that civics as a school subject must include…both a study of that social environment we call the community, and a practical training in good citizenship." Junior Red Cross activities and these activities' management by youth self-government (which included fundraisers so that the school auxiliaries could be largely self-supporting) were valuable curricular enhancements, enlisting "much of the splendid energy of the classes in cooking, sewing, and shopwork…added incentive for thrift clubs and for junior civic leagues—not to mention such auxiliary organizations as the Boy Scouts, the Girl Scouts, and the like." Developmental psychologists and educators backed these interpretations, with Hall supporting such activities over military role-playing and Claxton concurring that the organization's major contribution lay in the realm of education.[17]

From the USSGA to the Junior Red Cross, from print shops to home economics classrooms, when educators tallied the value of articles produced, they trumpeted the pedagogical rather than the financial contributions of the war-oriented curriculum. The school war gardens from which pupils routinely sold produce, were "a pedagogical measure" and "a national necessity," as Ping Ling put it. The Red Cross "insists that the emphasis of the movement is primarily on education; secondarily on production; and finally on financial support…[the 'juniors'] are strictly occupied with the two proper businesses of their lives—play and school." *Industrial Arts* magazine described how, "the primary purpose of installing printing" in schools was for educational ends, and that product should not be considered because

> It supplements and makes practical the usual English exercises, compels accuracy and alertness, stimulates to originality and effectiveness of expression, and appreciation of form and arrangement in composition…an effective means of arousing interest in otherwise unattractive exercises, and makes possible a stimulating and sound correlation of most academic subjects.

Los Angeles school administrators agreed that

> All of the so-called "war activities" became of themselves a valuable means of education...the extraordinary effort put forth by the pupils...not only served to vitalize the whole educational process, but that it also afforded actual experience in work performed in obedience to a direct emotional appeal, as evidenced in lessons which up to this time had tended to be rather formal in method and sterile in results.[18]

Thus while "the material contribution of the Los Angeles City Schools has been considerable"—indeed Los Angeles pupils' early collaborations with Junior Red Cross between April and June 1917 yielded $4,000 of goods, growing to nearly $25,000 of goods over seven months—it was the "educational value" that most impressed. "Boys and girls were engaged in the making of things which so happily reflected their powers of invention and industry, and which, because they were actually to be sold, afforded such a genuine sense of reality," reported another observer of the Los Angeles case. "At no time has there been any greater interest" in manual training "since the needs of the Red Cross were utilized to impress the content and method of education," school administrators reported:

> The benefits which have been derived...must not be measured wholly in dollars and cents, nor in materials produced and salvage reclaimed. The most significant results of these activities are the great benefits that shall accrue to the community through the training gained by the pupils in the schools. The ideal of service to the state and to their fellows, is being indelibly impressed upon the minds of the children in our schools.

Future citizenship would "find expression in actual performance. These school experiences are training them for such a service." A price could not be put on the value of democratic ideals.[19]

Educators endorsed these curricular adjustments for how they widened the possibilities for teachers to motivate students—for example, making articles for defense purposes rather than book racks and coat hangers for their own sakes—and how they achieved the modern military's vision of national preparedness. They did so despite greater public sensitivity to the possibility that schools could "be exploited in the great need for supplies" as MacCracken put it—or that "there is danger of laying too much stress upon the purely moneymaking end of the work [that] we must guard against" said Dr. E. G. Cooley, director of juvenile Red Cross work for the central division; despite the associations of some in-school activities with child labor—for example, printing, a trade the US Department of Labor long considered dangerous—and the acknowledgement that student-produced articles could be made at lower-than-market rates; despite the suggestion that "moving-picture reels of processes carried on according to the most modern methods of workroom procedure" be shown to pupils to teach them modern industrial techniques (and in some cases that new machines be installed in school shops); and despite the use of the terms "work" and "productive labor" for these in-school activities. Like the earlier Gary plan, the wartime curriculum represented "work," not work, because of its educational content and future orientation. "The idea of production, as such, has purposely not been emphasized because children are in school to learn, but the idea of producing and making things is already a part of our school work," Junior Red Cross cofounder Anna Hedges Talbot explained. The organization "affords a means of greatly extending such work into all the schools in this country which had been introduced long before many of us thought we would get into this war."[20]

Beyond the School Campus

Barnard's prediction that junior civic leagues and Scouts might find national needs amplifying their organizational missions proved prescient as these and other leisure-time groups reoriented their activities to the war. They, along with Camp Fire Girls, Knights of King Arthur, and the Milwaukee Newsboy Republic, adapted their public service promises to the new context, gathering scrap and salvage, growing and canning goods, making articles for soldiers, distributing war information, selling war bonds and stamps, learning first aid, and presenting patriotic entertainment. Even some organizations that ultimately disbanded during the war, such as New York City's junior police, collaborated with Scouts on home defense and preparedness activities. Other public campaigns recruited youth participation without adult supervision, such as California's crackdown on squirrels, which asked kids to place poison near the animals' burrows.[21]

For rural youth, the focus was food production and conservation through USDA organized boys and girls clubs as well as 4-H (established in 1911). O. H. Benson, a former teacher and later school superintendent who helped organize these programs, explained how the cost-efficiencies of USDA youth programming would have even greater wartime benefits. In 1916, for a cost of "79 cents per capita to supervise, direct, and instruct the boys and girls in our territory," the children had "made an average of $20.96 worth of food through their club activities" so "the net profit to the nation in food value was $20.17 per capita." The outlook for 1917 was even better. In Utah alone, "The total value of the pork produced within the state was $137,000.00 at a cost of $52,920.00. The average net profit per pound of pork produced was $.083." Given the eligible enrollees—"nearly 24,000,000 boys and girls of school age" across the nation—the possibilities for food production and conservation assistance looked bright.[22]

Scholars have acknowledged the service activities of several youth organizations and their integration into the merit badge system—for example, the Girl Scouts' relationship with USDA canning clubs. The government's most wide-ranging connections were with the Boy Scouts. During the war, as they continued community cleanup, residential fire inspections, and other "good turns," Scouts aided fire departments, harvested and canned fruit, performed tree censuses, and sold liberty loans. They distributed government literature en masse, including "government information bulletins to ten million homes in a single week." They trained in semaphore and wireless signaling and sleuthed out illegal radio outfits. As direct requests from the federal government came

Figure 5.3
Boy Scouts conduct a tree census.
Source: Harold Horne, "Why the Nation Supports the Boy Scouts," *Review of Reviews* 59 (1919).

into national headquarters, the boys responded with aplomb: "Take as an example their efforts to locate standing black walnut," critical in airplane manufacture. Shortages had made the War Department "desperate," so "the authorities turned to the Boy Scouts for help. They reasoned that if anybody could search out and find standing walnut it would be Scouts, because of their training in woodcraft and in observation, plus their patriotic zeal." The result? "The location of 20,758,660 board feet of standing walnut, equal to 5200 carloads."[23]

Missing from prior accounts, however, are the ways that public discussions of young people's contributions minimized their economic productivity—and how Scouts' wartime service fit a much larger and longer pattern of thinking about youth. Despite the tallies of man-hours worked and monies saved, these were "learning by doing" and the "daily good turn," and, in the case of locating walnut, "the consciousness that they had met the emergency like men," with future payoff: "a lasting ambition to shoulder responsible tasks and perform them well." Later historians followed suit, minimizing evidence that might offer alternative interpretations.[24]

Like the better-documented example of women, whose wartime activities largely maintained associations with the ideology of separate spheres that had enabled forays into municipal housekeeping, young people's contributions thus were described in language consistent with their earlier local public service activities. Assistance to government clients, rather than to the private sector, could be rationalized as civic participation. Some language of voluntarism, associated with women as well as with national service more generally, further undermined associations with labor, particularly in contexts when youth and adults worked side by side. More often, however, when young people made furniture, cultivated food, printed government documents, collected scrap metals, or sold school-produced articles to raise money under the auspices of junior republics, schools, and youth-serving institutions, the economic value for the state they created was typically explained away as a subsidiary benefit of role-playing activities that brought greater realism to educational and recreational programming. These new activities thus continued older patterns by suggesting that as young people enlisted in garden armies and thrift leagues they were being sheltered from the war while preparing for future civic participation. That junior republics, schools, and youth-serving institutions could contribute to national needs on a massive scale while maintaining their identities as agencies for child protection, a point of view the US Children's Bureau supported, makes clear that location influenced the definition of work and that these organizations stood outside the labor market in the popular mind.[25]

Figure 5.4
A lesson in service geography.
Source: Arthur Dean, *Our Schools in War Time—and After* (Boston: Ginn, 1918).

To be sure, not every proposal for young people's contributions under these organizations' auspices of received equal endorsement. MacCracken disapproved, for example, of enlisting pupils to collect money on the street in war drives (a stance with which the New York Child Labor Commission agreed). Girl Scout participation in Liberty Loan drives proved controversial to the organization's leadership, fearful about sending girls door-to-door or asking them to sell on public streets. Yet this objection appeared only in the fifth loan drive.[26]

The US Working Reserve attests to the broad reach of these views and their endorsement by the federal labor department. By the 1910s, the notion that farm labor uplifted youth had yielded to a more complex understanding that "the farmer is just as likely to exploit the child as the manufacturer." As a result, when the federal agency organized this program for students to aid farmers in meeting food needs, it cooperated with state education departments. More than 200,000 youth, mostly boys ages sixteen to nineteen, left schools for the planting and harvest seasons. With academic credit alongside wages to emphasize how the program supplemented rather than interrupted pupils' educations, an organization and recreational activities that encouraged comparisons to summer camps, and sponsorship from the same federal department whose Children's Bureau led the anti-child-labor campaign, the new "farm schools" attracted praise rather than charges of exploitation. "Farm work for older boys, carefully supervised," could teach "the new civics," Barnard declared. Occasional reports on the youth found "pulling weeds out of city roads," the programs that offered no academic credit, or the boys in one New York Working Reserve installation who struck for higher wages did not detract from broad support for these undertakings. Many Boy Scouts, Girl Scouts, newsboy republic citizens, and members of other youth organizations joined this food production effort or similar state and local equivalents (such as the New York Farm Cadets and Long Island Food Reserve Battalion).[27]

John Dewey, now at Teachers College, approved: "The school children of America can serve definitely, effectively and with educational results by helping in the plowing of Uncle Sam's acre." Concurring with Hall that "there will be better results from training drills with the spade and the hoe than parading America's youngsters up and down the school yard," he viewed food production as "important, valuable, and educational. It offers first of all an opportunity to educators and teachers to develop Constructive Patriotism.... there can never be any suspicion of a 'militaristic' influence." Consistent with his earlier view that payment could enhance some educational experiences, he observed farm programs "employ for economic production a great unused labor force which is too young to join the fighting forces," but "not interfere with the labor market or serve as 'scabs.'" Instead they "give the children healthful exercise, a sense of reality which means so much to children, and a sense of service in performance of work which is really useful." Colleague Arthur Dean agreed. While acknowledging "the farm labor

Figure 5.5
Girl Scout group with Mrs. Nicholas Longworth, selling Liberty Bonds, 1918.
Source: Library of Congress Prints and Photographs Division.

Figure 5.6
Girl Scout farmerettes harvesting crops.
Source: Harris & Ewing photograph collection, Library of Congress Prints and Photographs Division.

of the school boy" taking place, he contrasted these endeavors with work camps on account of their educational benefits and "play nature."[28]

Into the 1920s

Life for American youth experienced some changes after the armistice. Many in wartime employment were displaced by returning adults. Some popular programs were abruptly cancelled—for example, federally sponsored school gardens and American Junior Naval and Marine Scouts. Yet, by and large, trends in education and youth work that had culminated in students' contributions to the war effort continued into the postwar era. School administrators added curricular and extracurricular programs appealing to young people's leisure-time preferences as they pressed for further compulsory education legislation. And youth workers continued their efforts to design out-of-school outlets for young people's energies—especially "boy power"—to satisfy kids' desire for exciting play and simultaneously do good for their communities.[29]

"After the armistice," George described, came "a restoration period in the smallest Republic in the world just the same as in other governments affected by the hostilities." J. B. Kirkland, a former citizen who married George's daughter Eleanor, was helping with administration and was named superintendent in 1923. Unfortunately, Atlantic Woolen Mills had gone bankrupt and did not fulfill its obligation to improve the republic facilities it had used. Kirkland and George redoubled their efforts to bring industries to the republic so long as they "would not be operated on a strictly business basis" but rather were "closely allied or operated in conjunction with some educational plan." They hoped it might be "possible to obtain a very large part of the salary for each man and any necessary assistants for each type of work [as well as equipment costs], from the state and federal government" in light of public financing for commercial, industrial, and vocational education. Freeville's trustees also launched a major fundraising campaign.[30]

Former citizens now dominated Freeville's staff, among the numerous graduates who chose professions in education or youth work. A similar situation prevailed at George's other republics, as in Grove City, where there were no employees except "old republic boys" and the new barn was built entirely by the citizens. Alums or not, staff appeared to enjoy republic life almost as much as the citizens. Lester Babcock, an instructor and later superintendent at the Connecticut Junior Republic, was recruited to the prestigious St. Paul's School in 1919. Two years later he wrote to George of how the private school work was "beginning to grow irksome and unsatisfactory.... I should like to get back into something more active" he noted, asking George about employment opportunities "amongst the different Republics."[31]

Freeville celebrated its twenty-fifth anniversary in 1920 with the dedication of a cottage to former citizens killed in action and self-government promoters including board member Spencer Miller Jr. (now secretary-treasurer of Osborne's Welfare League Association) cheering George's broad influences on "factories, schools, prisons, community activities...boys clubs and the rest." George was unsatisfied, however, observing how for every supervisor who disliked staid environments there were others unable to let kids run the show. "I would have been able to have started a Junior Republic in every State of the Union," he wrote to Miller in 1920,

> but the tendency of the Board of Trustees or the Superintendant to depart from the principals [*sic*] caused it to be a very discouraging matter and I have refrained from starting new Junior Republics until there is some prospect of a guarantee that the idea of a self-governing democracy will be carried out literally instead of theoretically in every instance. At this point I may add that every one of these above mentioned Junior Republics have been a disappointment in this connection.[32]

Freeville's board, for example, while publically supporting George in fundraising excursions, was privately hostile to the hands-off supervision he preferred. (Miller,

Richard Welling, and ex-citizens such as Jacob Smith and William Dapping were exceptions.) "Imagine Edison, Burbank, Maconi [sic], Pasteur, working under a board of managers" he later lamented, suggesting that the delay in bringing republics to all the parties that eagerly contacted him was entirely his colleagues' fault. The contrast between an early George Junior Republic Association that had loudly defended George from public critics and a later incarnation that questioned the scheme's basic principles attests to changing ideas about youth capacities and how even George could not dissociate himself from these altered expectations. He asked the National Association of Junior Republics to temporarily suspend operations.[33]

George's frustrations guided his subsequent public presentations. "Some people may charge you with being young," he told high school students in Trenton, New Jersey in 1922. "Frequently they do this as an assumption of the superiority of years but do not let them fool you." The war experience had made clear how "at this very moment you are fit to assume all the responsibilities of citizenship quite as well as you will be when you are twenty-one years of age but the government will not give you the chance." Toward the goal of publically demonstrating these capacities and, still convinced that it was "too bad that every young man and woman cannot have a training like the citizens of the Junior Republic," George restarted the junior municipality program. Self-Government Inc.: A Council for Democratic Training backed his long-standing ambition that junior municipalities "soon become a recognized factor in the municipal government" of the US. The organization Welling had founded as the School Citizens Committee had changed its name once again, reflecting its broadened interest in self-government across factories and prisons alongside schools and its merger with the Council for Democratic Training. Targeting a demographic past the age limit served by schools, Scouts, and other youth organizations—young people ages sixteen to twenty-one—the group launched a campaign for one hundred junior municipalities by 1922.[34]

The postwar climate of intense concern about juvenile delinquency and the conviction that educational and recreational programming diverted youth from bad behavior prompted George to make crime control increasingly prominent in his efforts to recruit people and money to his cause. "American cities can reduce crime and gain a greater degree of obedience to law by paying more attention to the youth of the land, investing greater responsibility in boys between the ages of 16 and 21, and by perfecting a junior republic to extend from coast to coast," one reporter summarized his address to the Akron Kiwanis Club. Despite continued adamancy that his republics were not reformatories, George and his associates were greatly frustrated by the many instances he failed to receive credit for his ideas. As Mrs. Daddy scribbled on a clipping about the honor system at Delaware's New Castle Workhouse: "Some of Daddy's Prison ideas or Social Sanitarium Ideas but no credit given to Daddy."[35]

They were particularly annoyed when Thomas Osborne was hailed for inventing prison self-government. As early as 1914, when Sing Sing's Mutual Welfare League debuted, the *Ithaca Journal* accused Osborne of stealing the spotlight despite having previously scoffed at George's "plan to make the prisoners in a state institution self-governing." As prison self-government spread and inmates graduated to freedom, many helped Osborne with publicity and organized league reunions. George's essay "Prison Walls without a Prison" (1917) attempted to stake his claim for what was being called the Osborne system. The Creel Committee, much impressed by George's ideas of democracy and discipline, circulated the essay overseas. Yet while academic criminology texts at home cited George and penologists continued to visit Freeville, Osborne's name was better known in correctional contexts, particularly after Osborne became civilian commander of Portsmouth Naval Prison in 1917.[36]

As George sought public credit for behavioral improvements in Freeville and further afield, his explanations for juvenile delinquency departed from the era's common wisdom. Such behavior was not merely the result of young people who were bad or bored, he argued. Rather, it occurred on account of the excessive infantilization that organizations such as his junior republics and junior municipalities tried to address. "The same youth who would shout at a policeman at the drop of a hat... [if] sworn in as a policeman, would chase gangsters until his legs dropped off," he explained. The rare occasions when adult supervisors had to intervene in disciplinary matters were typically linked to young people's eagerness for harsh punishment, such as the Freeville legislator who threatened to starve those who chose not to work.[37]

Although the first junior municipalities in Ithaca and Cortland had encountered dwindling interest from area youth even before their wartime suspension, communities from Oswego, New York, to Glen Ridge, New Jersey, now embraced the program. Backing from the Daughters of the American Revolution helped to establish another in New York City's Bowling Green neighborhood. Simultaneously, Welling's organization selected the neighborhood around Columbia University, where Miller was an instructor in government, for a demonstration project. Teachers College faculty, including William Andrews and Elbert Fretwell, offered assistance, as did the local American Legion post. Yet university administrators' concerns that there would be too few Republican youth and that Columbia students wouldn't be the chief beneficiaries prompted them to abandon that plan in favor of reviving the junior municipality in East Orange, New Jersey.[38]

Wilson Gill, who had pushed for legislation to mandate school republics immediately before the war, also continued his efforts, now under the auspices of the Constitutional League of America (established 1920) and the School Republic Federation of the USA (established 1925). Although David Snedden joined critics of Gill's plans, school cities and republics regularly appeared in texts on classroom management and school discipline as well as civics instruction and progressive education, testaments to the many parties who endorsed their continued spread. From urban Washington, D.C., to rural Cook County, Illinois, from private institutions such as New York City's Ethical Culture School to public schools across Alaska, Gill's self-government scheme continued to spread. He too stepped up talk about its anticrime benefits while simultaneously touting its value as a tool for mutual understanding in an increasingly interconnected world. (Like some immigrants before them, for example, children in Kotzebue, Alaska, had banned the local language in favor of English in schools.) Despite the demonstrated support for bringing republic activities beyond classrooms and clubhouses into public settings, however, Gill never revived his plan for collaborations with local authorities.[39]

Now on the West Coast, Willis Brown attempted to reinstate himself as head of the Boy City movement, making use of media as publicity tools. Photoplays like "A Boy and the Law" (1914) spread the gospel of youth self-government and word of the "National Boy City" (which embarked on a round-the-world tour but never made it to the Panama-Pacific International Exposition). A few years later, Brown founded the Boy City Film Company in Culver City, California, and enlisted King Vidor to direct *Boy City*, the first of several delinquency prevention films Vidor made for his patron. Although in covering topics from peer pressure to race relations to immigrant patriotism, the films addressed subjects of national concern, Brown's efforts were unsuccessful. His own conduct continued to get him into trouble, and a mistress shot him dead in 1931.[40]

With junior Chautauqua reaching more than a million rural boys and girls in over 900 US towns in the 1920s, the junior town movement registered greater success. Movement leaders called in authorities on child development, including National Child Labor Committee general secretary Owen Lovejoy, New York City Bureau of Child Hygiene director Dr. S. Josephine Baker, Teachers College scouting and recreation professor Elbert Fretwell, and Junior Achievement Bureau director O. H. Benson, to get the weeklong summer programs on more permanent footing. From West Stockbridge, Massachusetts, to Buhl, Iowa, to Glendale, California, the organization partnered with schools and playgrounds to keep junior towns operating after the Chautauqua's departure. They soon functioned as community-oriented service programs under local supervision. The Junior Town of Cashmere, Washington, for example, was studying the city water system and the problem of typhoid fever, which had followed residents' use of ditch water and river water for drinking. It was "a thrilling experience" for children "to find they are a part of the show," particularly when these civic dramatizations aimed to expand community recreation opportunities: "Several junior towns are discussing the need for swimming pools and obtaining the co-operation of older folk in planning for them. Others are discussing the need for supervision of playgrounds during the summer, to protect apparatus and promote the right kind of leadership in games."[41]

At schools, playgrounds, reformatories, and summer camps, other postwar juvenile democracies proliferated separately from these ambitious organizations. In Philadelphia, the Smith Memorial Playgrounds operated three self-governing villages from 1921. A Progress City offshoot debuted in Utica, New York. Ford revived its dormant republic under a new director. Georgia's Juvenile State, which had sputtered, was rebuilt.

And the City of Newsboyville debuted in Boston from 1927. Although Milwaukee's Newsboy Republic continued (swelling to 7,000 members), Boston's ceased operations when Philip Davis left office. Harry Burroughs, a Russian immigrant and former Boston newsboy, organized its successor through the private "Burroughs newsboys club" in cooperation with local public schools. William George was in frequent touch with the leadership of these organizations, exchanging ideas and offering counsel. He even helped with job placement—for example, securing Lester Babcock a position working with Charles Bradley at the Boston Farm and Trades School. Other youth organizations that debuted after the war such as Model League of Nations took civic dramatizations in new directions.[42]

These and other youth democracies operated in a context in which female suffrage was now a nationwide reality—and the republic movement had played a part in this turn of events. "Girl suffrage" in Freeville was repeatedly referenced in women's franchise campaigns. As Harriet May Miles testified to a senate committee on suffrage in 1902,

> A few years ago the girls [at the GJR] thought, as some women think to-day, that they did not wish to vote, and there was a boy running for president who was very much opposed to the enfranchisement of the girls, and he said: "It would be unwomanly for you to vote. You do not wish to vote, do you?' And somebody foolishly said they did not. But a little while afterwards a tax was levied, and the girls found that they were taxed much more heavily in the republic than the boys, and then they began to open their eyes, and they thought if it was womanly for a girl to pay her taxes, and to pay such heavy taxes, it might be womanly for her to vote and decide what the taxes should be. That is the justice we ask at your hands to-day.

Women's clubs had also played at democracy to rehearse for political participation—for example Chicago women's clubs "played city." The American Women's Republic briefly emulated George's republic by setting up a model community in Missouri.[43]

William George, who told an audience at New York State woman suffrage headquarters he "never was a suffragist" until he saw how interested the girls were in the government of the republic, was among those converted after viewing female franchise holders and officials firsthand. Frustrated in his prewar programs that girls could only "vote from the time they are sixteen until they are twenty-one" and then "return to the status of idiots and criminals," he was excited by junior municipalities' revival after the Twentieth Amendment. Girls were also enthused: "It's lots more fun … to learn citizenship ourselves than have it taught to us through books and lectures. It's so much more like the real thing you know," said one junior councilwoman. Junior town clerk May C. McLaughlin explained, "It appeals to all types of girls. There is plenty of pep and excitement for the frivolous type, and the sincere debater finds outlet for her talents in many ways. Our meetings are never tiresome. It's so much more fun to work out problems of civic interest ourselves than to have older people tell us about them." Other political reformers contacted juvenile officials, asking them to try alternative government arrangements in the hopes of demonstrating the superiority of their policy proposals.[44]

Related activities continued—from student government and dramatic education to junior police and juvenile sanitary inspectors, to Camp Fire Girls and Queens of Avalon—as schools' embrace of extracurricular activities and membership in youth organizations sustained their growth patterns. In the postwar period, the educators, youth workers, and public officials who ran these activities would seek to maintain young people's interest in participation by finding novel challenges for youth. New undertakings such as junior traffic patrols, Boy Scout radio signaling, and Girl Scout cookie sales offered both developmental and economic benefits, underscoring how narratives of the growth in school attendance and leisure-time youth organizations must be expanded to include the stories of how a growing force of young people continued to help construct the sheltered childhood and in turn the American state.[45]

Cars, Communications, and Cookies

The surge of postwar automobility was a catalyst for major transformations to America's municipal environments, and a new source of fears. Children were frequent accident victims because their street behavior was less cautious than adults' and their smaller size made them harder for drivers to see. Particularly concerning were the many cases of pupils hurt or killed as they arrived or departed school. Frustrated that automobiles caused more fatalities than war or disease, police reminded the public to drive safely at back-to-school time. Yet these warnings were insufficient. President Herbert Hoover convened a conference on street and highway safety, which concluded that education was needed to address the new threat.[46]

At the center of what became known as "safety education" were juvenile traffic patrols. School administrators and police outfitted students with uniforms, badges, whistles, and placards; trained them to make road safety signage, direct traffic, and guide peers across streets; and delegated police powers for traffic management. Although some boys grumbled that girls distracted drivers, many squads were coed.[47]

Detroit, center of the auto industry, hosted one of the first in 1919. Other local governments followed, particularly in car-loving California. Massachusetts educators and police eagerly pushed their program through the state's education department, expanding youth activities to include traffic courts in which juvenile offenders were tried by their peers. Many of these organizations aimed to be self-governing, electing officers and establishing regulations. Statistics on traffic incidents soon confirmed accidents reduced and lives saved.[48]

Thanks to educators' growing interest in absorbing community-based youth organizations into extracurricular activities, schools now ran numerous Scout troops, and they took on responsibility for safety squads in many communities. Pupils in St. Louis, for example, elected the entire Scout organization as their junior safety cadet corps. To get the program off the ground, city officials took responsibility for testing the Scouts

Figure 5.7
Boy Scouts and radio.
Source: Arthur Lynch, "A Compact Portable Wireless Set: A Complete Wireless Telephone Transmitting and Receiving Station Which May Be Carried by a Single Boy Scout," *Radio Broadcast* 1 (1922).

who wished to receive safety merit badges. Troops in Buffalo and Hartford took on similar duties.[49]

Scouts' signaling expertise and the era's semaphore traffic signals were an obvious match. Federal authorities soon enlisted their facility with radio communications. Like automobility, radio was largely unregulated in its early years. Scouts were eager explorers of the airwaves from wireless communication's debut. Building sets was a regular troop activity so that Scouts could listen to and communicate with parties around the world. Government restrictions on spectrum use during the 1910s did not dull these amateurs' use. "It is doubtful if any one subject studied by Boy Scouts is as popular as radio," *Radio Broadcast* editor Arthur Lynch declared in 1922.[50]

Although accounts of boys' postwar engagements with radio communications typically focus on how their playful activities were largely restricted after interfering with government and corporate broadcasting interests, regulations did not place public officials and boys completely at odds. As the military transitioned from telegraphy to radio communications, leaders recognized that a reliable national wireless network required an infrastructure of humans as well as machines. Authorities thus set out to direct amateurs' radio activities to help make the new system work.[51]

Scouts were central in these efforts. The US Navy invited them to receive information from naval radio stations (mostly storm warnings and weather predictions) and relay them to local authorities by "radio; land telegraph, telephone, mail...semaphore, Morse with a flag or heliograph [mirror]." The combination "radio and messenger system" could reach most Americans within twenty-four hours with emergency information; by 1920 it was already in place in forty-two of the forty-eight US states. The US Army established its Army Amateur Radio System five years later, also for purposes of emergency communications and disaster relief, including backup communications for local, state, and federal agencies. Military officials coordinated youth engagement nationwide. Publications and hands-on training opportunities from military authorities and the Scouting organization set standards for boys' participation, such as making these activities the basis of a merit badge in 1925 and offering (through the navy) training as "pioneer scouts" or (through the army) a free two-week signaling camp for those who passed a correspondence course.[52]

Construction and maintenance took priority over use of these emergency communications systems, with a few exceptions. When a flood struck New England in 1927, Scouts sprang into action with radio alongside the other disaster relief methods they had previously employed. Seeing the network's value to colleagues in other agencies, administrators at the US Department of Agriculture began to use it as well.[53]

Although Girl Scouts had similarly demonstrated signaling skills in public performance from their organization's debut, a merit badge in radio was not created. (A telegrapher badge is listed in the 1925 handbook, however.) Cookie sales were a central focus of their postwar activities, offering funding and publicity for the growing organization.[54]

Established several years after Boys Scouts and more modern in its outlook on female identity than other girls' organizations, Girl Scouts operated a similar role-play-oriented program in which participants' natural inclinations were directed to developmental goals. This "democratic, self-governing and flexible" organization offered a learn-by-doing approach to domestic training while enabling girls to explore other identities. "A Girl Scout may be an artist, a beekeeper, a business woman, a craftsman, or a dancer; an electrician, a farmer, a musician, a scribe, a swimmer, or a star gazer," official publications declared. Participants drew inspiration from historical figures such as Sacajawea, whose skills as an explorer were critical in the Lewis and Clark mission; Louisa May Alcott, a proficient writer and homemaker; and Anna Shaw, a pioneer in learning by doing, for whom "The tests and sports for mastering which we earn badges were life's ordinary problems to her....She never knew it, but surely she was a real Girl Scout!"[55]

Despite these direct adaptations of the Boy Scout philosophy, and leaders' confidence that girls easily played such roles even when not being watched by somebody who "stands ready to report on her conduct," Girl Scouts were on shakier ground. The existence of a "girl problem" equivalent to concerns about boys remained an open question. Finding volunteers to lead all interested girls and funding program operations were continuing challenges. In the 1920s, as the national organization expanded leadership development opportunities for prospective troop leaders, it also discovered that making girls' training for the cooking merit badge a public event simultaneously bettered the girls and the organization's bottom line.[56]

The Scouts' first cookie sale predated the US entry into World War I, when an Oklahoma troop peddled homemade cookies in school to raise funds for its activities. In July 1922, the Scouting magazine published a cookie recipe from Chicago Scout leader Florence Neil that could be sold at seven times its cost. One year later, the cookie had become the chief symbol of the Girl Scouts.[57]

Early baking and selling tactics varied widely. Some used Neil's nationally published recipe; others used their own; still others gave recipes to local bakeries to assist in production. As girls in Boston hawked cookies on street corners and in public squares, New York City girls stationed themselves on Wall Street and in shopping districts. In Cambridge, Massachusetts, girls baked in shop windows to generate interest and sold cookies from cars driving through the city. In smaller communities such as Oak Park, Illinois, door-to-door delivery was the norm. Still other troops who "scoffed at…modern methods of distribution—cars, baskets, boxes, and bags," like those in Appleton, Wisconsin, delivered cookies from baby carriages.[58]

Valuing the Valueless Child

In her landmark *Pricing the Priceless Child*, Viviana Zelizer interprets school safety patrols as signals of modern norms ascribing pricelessness to youth. She also notes the comparative difficulty of controlling the dangers posed by adult drivers and the comparative ease of disciplining children to protect themselves. The evidence presented here about safety squads and other youth activities confirms her assessment while simultaneously identifying how, as they disciplined themselves to their priceless identity, young people made value for the public and private actors typically assigned credit for sheltering youth. Attending to the political economy of youth-serving institutions and the state in this period reveals how the role-plays that adjusted youth to new norms supplied vital assistance to both such that, in many cases, young people played pivotal roles constructing the sheltered childhood themselves.[59]

From the George Junior Republic to junior town service projects, such effects are widely apparent in the era's juvenile democracies, but the phenomenon could be seen farther afield. School-based traffic squads not only educated children about the need to be mindful in the modern transportation environment, these students addressed a municipal man-power shortage and served as future civil service recruits. Boy Scouts' collaborations with military authorities not only directed boys to use the airwaves in ways that minimized interference with government operations, they supplied "the only connecting link between the Navy radio stations and thousands of towns and cities" and enabled military authorities to establish "a large pool of volunteer radio operators without the expense of adding them to the Army's payroll." And Girl Scout cookie sales around the country did not merely expand girls' cooking practice; domestic education as public spectacle sold both cookies and the organization, recruiting volunteer leaders and raising funds for troop uniforms, conferences, camps, and buildings. Still other organizations, such as the National Child Welfare Association's school-based Knighthood of Youth (established 1924) underscored the belief that community service was an expression of good citizenship and character rather than unpaid labor.[60]

As in earlier eras, organizers acknowledged these contributions while finding new ways to highlight the benefits to youth. Yet alongside the mass institutionalization of so many role-plays of adult life in the 1920s, talk of "educational" and "recreational" programming increasingly replaced discussions about "models" of occupational experiences or civic dramatizations. With increasingly implicit reference to some "real world" adult activity, associations with schools and youth-serving institutions served as shorthand for child protection.

Thus the junior traffic patrols that compensated for municipalities' limited human resources by placing "trained boys" (and girls) in the middle of the streets long perceived as hazardous environments to "protect small pupils against the dangers of automobiles, trucks and other vehicles" were components of a learn-by-doing curriculum of safety education—even as junior safety officers were injured or killed in the line of duty. A National Safety Council promoted this interpretation through curricular resources that praised the patrols for appealing to pupils' zest for dramatization. Related activities were opportunities for improving child protection. In Birmingham, pupils conducted schools and home safety inspections. In Grand Rapids, they collected data on the numbers and sources of cars on the main streets to analyze and improve traffic flow. In Milwaukee, in addition to pupil Safety Cadets, newsboys issued circulars on the dangers of jaywalking, while Boy Scouts painted "Cross at Crossing" signs on sidewalks at busy intersections. Such activities provided a "suitable laboratory in which one may convert safety knowledge into safety habits."[61]

Similarly, Boy Scouts' roles in the federal-local radio communication system, which made each Scout troop "as necessary in its community as the local post office," were billed as a constructive recreational activity. Scout leaders and public officials recognized the arrangement recruited operators not yet of age for military service and exposed them to risks of electrocution, deafness, or unsavory public communications. Yet they hailed the arrangement as a positive influence, a mechanism for taking boys off the streets for "home study in tinkering," reducing their potential delinquent recreational activities, and vitalizing their education for modern careers, part of a larger emphasis on "learn by doing" in postwar Scouting.[62]

Girl Scout cookie sales benefited the Scouting organization rather than any government agency. Yet the sales which turned troops into factories to manufacture and sell thousands of cookies and publicize the organization were celebrated for vitalizing domestic training. In stark contrast to recent resistance to the girls' continued participation in Liberty Loan drives, Scout leaders and public officials largely supported these transactions on account of how they brought girls' domestic sensibilities onto public spaces. In baking and selling, Girls Scouts showed how they were learning to be like one of the many grandmothers who "knew an immense number of practical things that have been entirely left out of our town-bred lives"—an educational philosophy also being taught in demonstration kitchens and homes. Troop leaders further directed attention away from the monetary exchanges to the benefits girls earned from successful participation—for example, a new uniform, a week at camp, or in some cases a merit badge. (That the act of fundraising for organizational maintenance garnered a cooking badge was particularly noteworthy, because Girl Scouts could vie for a "business woman" badge at the time.)[63]

Participants shared with organizers the sense they were engaged in playful education or educational play rather than uncompensated work. "Just what do the members themselves of the [safety] patrol think of their duties?" inquired one journalist. Patrol captain Barney Millman "grinned broadly. 'Gee, I'll say it's great. It's got football licked to a frazzle.'" This writer's observation that the youthful officers were the envy of all their peers characterized the response across the US; so many wanted to participate in Boston's junior traffic forces, for example, that the Lion's Club raised money for uniforms the city could not afford. Radio became an obsession, yielding Scouts seriously committed to their new hobby, and the occasional boy so devoted to his amateur station that he neglected his schoolwork, prompting his parents to convince the federal radio commission to suspend his license. Girl Scouts relished the baking and selling season, with many disappointed it was not a year-round activity.[64]

By the end of the 1920s, then, decades of common wisdom in developmental psychology had been adapted to a wide range of programs of adult-directed activities at schools and youth-serving institutions, inside classrooms and on campuses and extending into broader spaces of communities and the airwaves, as well. This evidence supports scholars' previous contentions that the sheltered childhood had become a reality for many young people while simultaneously suggesting how role-plays of adulthood represented a second, equally essential pillar of the American youth experience. Chicago Boys Club administrator Walter Stone observed substantial changes in young people's lives since the turn of the century, in part because of cultural, social, and economic developments and in part because of deliberate interventions by adults. Praising the expansion of scientifically based "social engineering on the field of boyhood motivation," he singled out trends from the choice to tap natural groups in the community, to the effort to control youth by organizing activities around their interests, to the decision to let young people do things themselves, to the preference for "real living" rather than artificial activities, to "the shift from external control and discipline in the hands of adult authority to experimentation with self-government." Stone's review implicitly attested to how, despite George's frustration with many of the educators and youth workers he encountered, key tenets of the republic approach were being widely used.[65]

George had not yet succeeded in creating a national network of junior republics and junior municipalities, but his work had helped inspire the mass popularization of their component activities. Ironically, with the large-scale institutionalization of republic principles and practices came new ways of talking about them that concealed the very reasons for their mass popularization. The earlier sense that student governments, vocational education, home economics, Scouting, and junior policing offered access to vicarious experiences of adult life lost ground to the sense that these were authentic educational and recreational activities for youth. The new lexicon made young people's economic contributions more difficult to see.

Erving Goffman has observed that "real" is a "contrast term... 'unreal' phenomena equally can serve as the original of which something else is a mere mock-up, leading one to think that what is sovereign is *relationship, not substance.*" Histories of representational techniques from effigies to photography have established people's propensity to treat artifacts initially understood as copies as items with their own authenticity in the longer term. These accounts resonate with how perceptions of youth activities unfolded and how talk of double lives similarly disappeared. Trends in developmental psychology and the social sciences in the 1920s were a catalyst for this changing conversation as an earlier emphasis on imitation and suggestion in individual and societal development was replaced by attention to group-level processes and symbolic communication became the new focus for discussions about the educational and socialization potentials of simulation and subjectivity in the modern age.[66]

Reconstructing the Postwar Self

The consensus view of child development associated with G. Stanley Hall came under fire in the 1920s as researchers determined that biological explanations of self rooted in role-play were necessary but not sufficient. The University of Chicago's George Herbert Mead was a particularly influential exponent of the new interactionist view. Trained with Hall, Josiah Royce, and William James and moving in circles with Charles Horton Cooley and John Dewey, Mead agreed with his mentors that role-plays of adult life were critical to children's identity development. Yet impersonations of "specific others" were merely a first step. According to Mead, the self emerged only after a second, more complex form of game-based role-playing in which individuals internalized the roles of all others in the game together with its rules—the "generalized other." If the turn-of-the-century self was biological and made in role-plays of individuals, the 1920s self was too—but only as prelude to being socially made by groups. In this new framework, social sciences such as sociology and political science with understandings of human groupings now became relevant to understanding the American youth experience.[67]

Group studies had attracted interest in psychology from the early 1900s as the sense that personality was social became increasingly common. This analytic framework for understanding individual and societal development gathered strength after the war as notions of multiple identity were largely subsumed into assumptions about individuals in groups. As psychologists turned their attention to group processes they widened their definition of collective influence as well. Mead identified two major types: "concrete social classes or subgroups" in which "individual members are directly related to one another" versus "abstract social classes or subgroups" in which these members "are related to one another only more or less indirectly, and which only more or less indirectly function as social units, but which afford unlimited possibilities for the widening and ramifying and enriching of the social relations among all the individual members of the given society as an organized and unified whole."[68]

Other scholars, including L. L. Bernard, trained in sociology at University of Chicago and teaching there alongside Mead in the 1920s, labeled these direct versus indirect contacts, differentiating between in-person and mediated encounters on a spectrum of modes of communication and association that could be characterized as more or less vicarious. This formulation built on prior inquiries in the imitation-suggestion tradition, conceptualizing media environments and physical environments as parallel worlds, and observing that the "multiplication of psycho-social contacts or relationships" made possible by mass media was the defining feature of modern life. Contemporary humans were "brought in touch with a great many models representing all types of behavior," Bernard explained. These trends equally influenced Mead's quantitatively oriented psychology colleagues such as L. L. Thurstone who, in moving toward greater experimentalism and skeptical about earlier instinct-based studies, pioneered new mathematical techniques to measure the social dimensions of individual psychology—for example, how individual attitudes were influenced by peers or "measuring attitudes toward the movies."[69]

Group influence equally attracted research attention from sociologists and political scientists attending to questions about community cohesion and public opinion in mass society. The University of Chicago was a hub for these cross-disciplinary conversations and a center for efforts to make the social sciences more scientific and empirical. Mead's sociology colleagues, including Robert Park and Ernest Burgess, looked to plant and animal ecology as models for studying interactions between humans and their environments and the roles of individuals in groups, borrowing the vocabulary of conflict, accommodation, and succession to describe the general laws of community organization and disorganization. Together with Frederic Thrasher and Paul Cressey, they studied the social implications as media supplemented face-to-face encounters, such as how the newspapers reproducing village life supplied novel forms of interaction and virtual community for immigrants dispersed across cities as well as more proximate neighborhood groups. Political scientists Charles Merriam and Harold Lasswell set out to understand the public opinion shaping the collective behavior of "political animals," in particular, as journalist Walter Lippman put it in his bestselling *Public Opinion* (1922), how the vicarious "pictures in our heads" which served as the basis for action (rather than the reality of "the world outside") got made. The concept of propaganda, what Lasswell described as "the control of opinion by significant symbols...stories, rumors, reports, pictures and other forms of social suggestion" rather than "the control of mental states by changing such objective conditions as the supply of cigarettes or the chemical composition of food," was central to their interpretations. Early studies cataloged varied influence tactics toward analyzing their comparative effects; colleague Harold Gosnell's experiments on voter behavior (in which an experimental group received mailings whereas a control group did not) explored how attitudes and opinions could be manipulated on a broader scale in the absence of real-world change.[70]

In a context of greater attention to social environments in the development of self and society, scholarly work across the social sciences came to carry greater weight in efforts to understand child development. Equally, social scientists studied young people to shed light on their larger questions. Quantitative psychologists who found their experimental studies of attitudes and peer influence most easily conducted on the college populations they taught filled journals with accounts of student opinions and attitudes on topics from war to race under a range of experimental conditions. Sociologists' interest in the laws organizing communities prompted inquiries into the juvenile delinquency that manifested as "social disorganization," with Harvey Zorbaugh, Paul Cressey, Frederic Thrasher, Clifford Shaw, Henry McKay, and Walter Reckless discovering in the presence or absence of Scout troops, YMCAs, and boys and girls clubs clues to behavior patterns. Equally they studied media's influence on youth behavior, investigating newspapers, comics, tabloids, film, radio, and photography within a spectrum of activities and institutions they labeled as the "total situation" of environmental forces shaping modern life: the "bewildering and frequently conflicting behavior norms as set by movies, radio, magazines, schools, churches, social classes, and so forth." Political scientists seeking to understand the social bases of political cohesion and cultural reproduction investigated diverse modes of youth-oriented propaganda and persuasion techniques in textbooks, fairy tales, Scout troops, and church groups. Merriam, who proposed that children offered a compelling subject for study, assembled a team to prepare a comparison of civic education and public opinion in several nations.[71]

As this research into group processes revised the common wisdom about youth development and other subjects, it simultaneously offered novel interpretations for the successes of prior and ongoing educational initiatives and youth programs including junior republics, junior police, and Scouts. Frederic Thrasher's landmark dissertation *The Gang* attests to how youth-oriented studies of the 1920s supported such adult-supervised activities as antidotes to juvenile delinquency while simultaneously obscuring young people's contributions to the outcomes they tracked. Equally it makes clear how, alongside the reinterpretation of youth activities as authentic in their own right rather than dramatizations of something else, discussions of imitation, suggestion, and modern subjectivity shifted to the analysis of mass media in the lives of youth.

Thrasher's study of the quintessential "natural" grouping of young people (he called the gang a "play-group") exemplifies the new generation of research on child development. Going beyond biological mechanisms to attend to environmental factors in the broad community setting and the local context of the group, Thrasher made peer influence his focus for understanding youth gangs' "mechanisms of control." Each "individual member of a gang is almost wholly controlled by the force of group opinion," he explained.

> The way everybody in the gang does or thinks is usually sufficient justification or dissuasion for the gang boy...he is really feeling the pressure of public opinion in that part of his own social world which is most vital to him and in which he wishes to maintain status...opinion in the gang manifests its pressure in the variety of mechanisms.[72]

Such opinion could be directed to a variety of ends from law breaking to constructive activities, and it is here that Thrasher's analysis anchored a new interpretation of how programs like junior republics, junior police, and Scouts—each committed to transforming gangs rather than destroying them—actually worked. In agreement with earlier observers that directing rather than suppressing young people's natural energies was key to behavior management, and that peer influence could aid adults in these efforts, Thrasher departed from the view that such programs satisfied young people's developmental needs to recapitulate prior stages of the human race or expressed a more general dramatic or imitative instinct. He suggested instead such interventions worked by reshaping public opinion of the gang's natural democracy, building community cohesion as a counterforce to environmental disorganization.[73]

Echoing work from G. Stanley Hall and J. Adams Puffer complaining that public commentaries missed the more positive aspects of youth gangs, Thrasher's account provided new fuel for arguments about supervision without supervisors by assigning much of the responsibility for change to the group itself. According to this view, each gang was "a rudimentary society with a constructive tendency," with "the crude sort of democracy which is almost universal in such groups"—confirming earlier observers' view of "how deep the principles of republicanism strike into human nature, even when it is immature." These organizations' successes thus resulted from adult supervisors having tapped young people's abilities to help themselves, using group processes to reshape public opinion and create order in their rudimentary society. "It is group action—directed toward ends that are intelligible to the boy members themselves—through which order is established and habits are formed that are wholesome, or at least, harmless." As it cited work by William George, Lyman Beecher Stowe, and others, Thrasher's account provided an alternative lexicon for the long-standing finding that when young people were given greater responsibilities, infractions rapidly dwindled, and that kids were more effective at disciplining other youth than were adults.[74]

In short, as Thrasher championed a range of recreational youth activities first popularized around a philosophy of impersonation at a distance—for instance, recreation as some adult reality re-created—his analysis scarcely referenced the act of impersonation. (Under "imitation," for example, his index directed readers to "Social patterns and the gang.") At a time when the reference to some real world adult activity—senators and businesspeople in junior republics, heroic explorers for Scouts, police officers for junior police—was now implicitly understood in public talk about education and recreation, the focus on group processes in studies of youth development further deflected attention from these real world referents. Signs of the older language of mirroring were still apparent, for example, in the observation that each gang more generally "reflects in its activities the adult life and the customs of the particular community where it is found." Yet the earlier view that such programs provided kids the opportunity to simultaneously inhabit two times, places, or identities through the role-playing opportunities they supplied was largely superseded by attention to their roles as individuals within social groups, an experience dominated by what sociologist Emory Bogardus called "social mirrors" to refer to the socially reflected self rather than to reflections or mirrors of the adult social world.[75]

A growing flexibility across youth programs to organizational structures that did not seek to duplicate some adult activity helped to cement this shift. Early republic organizers' ambition was to copy some real world analog: the US, Chicago, New York State. The question of what constituted realistic versus fictitious simulations was paramount, sparking George's reflections on how the Freeville experience might be improved and his frustrations with efforts to duplicate it in other settings. In this context, departures from realism were typically rationalized in the service of making things more "real" for participants. The addition of town meetings to Freeville's federal system and Progress City's city manager plan, the opening of full suffrage to girls in many settings, and discussions of how to provoke controversies in the Ithaca junior municipality were decisions taken toward active engagement from greater numbers of youth—opportunities to keep their interest alive and make things more "republicky" in a conceptual sense to achieve the Goo Goo agenda. The choice to avoid recognizable political parties—such as the Rights and Lefts in Omaha's Kellom School City, the Optimus and Maximus parties in the State of Columbia, the Land and Water parties in Winona Boy City, and the complete lack of parties at the Hebrew Sheltering Guardian Society's republics—were deliberate efforts to be "free from all factionalism," as George put it, and "to name the various parties so that the ideals rather than the party name would form the attraction." The addition of unusual political offices such as Hamilton Fish Park's city departments of athletics and gymnastics or the Milwaukee Newsboys' secretary of athletics encouraged participants to bring self-government into their recreational activities.[76]

Now, from the republics that eschewed "adaptations of adult government organizations" in favor of "playground councils," "youth governments" and "boys towns" (much as in factories and prisons), to the growing preference for student councils and safety patrols over student senates and junior police, to the Scouts who were encouraged to be ideal boys rather than ideal men, the declining pressure to model or dramatize adult experiences was broadly apparent across a range of youth activities. "Authentic reproductions" persisted—such as student governments with public works and street cleaning departments or home economics classes in model kitchens. Yet now these were merely among the myriad options for educational and recreational programming. Performance-oriented approaches to youth development continued, but these specific activities (vocational education, Scouting, and so on)—with the exception of the Model League of Nations and later Model UN—lost their association with dramatization.[77]

As it shifted the conversation about youth activities away from dramatic impersonation, Thrasher's gang study revealed how interest in the educational and socialization potential of role-plays and vicarious experience, as well as modern subjectivity, did not entirely disappear. As some educators and youth workers turned to performance studies, these researchers moved their attention to question the extent to which young people were influenced, for better or for worse, by the media they consumed. The assumption that media shaped youth behavior had undergirded both reformers' anxious accounts of children's leisure activities and the industry of juvenile literature about heroic figures past and present. Although an earlier generation of analysts had theorized to some extent about symbolic communication—for example, William Forbush musing on the vicarious experience afforded by stereoscopic views—media studies were largely a postwar undertaking after the perceived wartime successes of the Creel Committee on Public Information drew attention to the influences of newspapers, film, and radio on group thought and action. Now evidence mounted that the content of comic books, dime novels, radio, and film supplied models for young people's behavior and actions, and that youthful audiences occasionally confused the stories they encountered with "real life." Despite evidence to the contrary—such as Thrasher's discovery that older youth strategically blamed media to excuse their misdeeds—media studies in subsequent decades would take a decidedly narrower media-centric view. In the social scientific framework of this period, however, such indirect contacts were merely one feature of what researchers called the "total situation."[78]

Revenge Effects

The scientific approaches to education and youth work that made gains "adjusting" young people to modern life by the 1920s showed signs of unraveling. Expanded numbers in prolonged schooling and afterschool activities—in evidence in the growth of public high school attendance from 110,000 in 1880 to 519,000 in 1900 to 2.2 million in 1920—created a mass youth culture that began to chafe at adult control. The contrast between Columbia Teachers College Professor George Coe's story "The Children's Republic" (1921), which juxtaposed children's purity and adults' corruption, and his subsequent pessimistic manifesto *What Ails Our Youth?* (1924) underscored this turn of events.[79]

Democratic approaches to management already had faced visible setbacks at factories and prisons. Alongside the public critics of industrial democracy who suggested it was too simplistic and opponents of prisoner self-government who charged it excessively coddled inmates, the dismantling of worker democracies and Mutual Welfare Leagues, together with more dramatic industrial strikes and prison riots at venues such as William Demuth and Co. (1919) and Auburn Prison (1929), highlight the limits of these methods for addressing institutions' structural deficiencies. The common interests that had brought educators and youth workers to these institutions before the war had continued into the 1920s to some extent (for example, establishing playgrounds and Scout troops at firms), and this turn of events soon had parallels for the nation's youth as peer influence increasingly mobilized the young people frustrated that adults were not taking seriously their political and economic concerns.[80]

As the cultural and economic optimism of the 1920s gave way to the Depression of the 1930s, a period when adult disenchantment with the American way of life expressed itself through activism, young people began to question the status quo: politics, economics, and their social positions within these systems. Updating complaints about reformatories' contributions to the crime problem, educators and youth workers now discovered that the schools and youth-serving institutions organized with attention to democratic group processes had become media for encouraging these trends. With his research having offered up the possibility that all youth were potential delinquents on account of how human groupings were always "in a condition of unstable equilibrium," as changing membership, interests, and other factors shaped their "continuous flux and flow," Thrasher observed how these environments created "opportunities for social contagion of undesirable social attitudes and patterns of conduct" as much as opportunities for social control.[81]

During the 1910s, BBR citizens' advocacy had seemed comparatively extreme. This had continued into the 1920s, with citizens investigating child labor conditions in eastern Pennsylvania in 1924, interviewing the US Secretary of Labor, and holding conferences with the governors of Pennsylvania and New York to improve the plight of their peers. Yet the sense that their advocacy was outside the bounds of typical youth

Figure 5.8
Boys Brotherhood Republic calls on Cook County warden.
Source: *Life of the Boys Brotherhood Republic* (Chicago: BBR, 1938).

behavior proved to be a short-lived state of affairs. The American Youth Congress, an umbrella organization of several hundred groups, issued a "Declaration of the Rights of American Youth" (1936) and subsequently rallied Congress to pass the American Youth Act, a complementary aid package. A World Youth Congress linked Americans with peers in other countries, offering close-up views of potential alternative political and economic systems.[82]

Although the extent to which training in the "new civics" supported such behavior rather than the more docile character development educators and youth workers espoused remains an open question, it is clear that these organizations together with the Southern Negro Youth Congress—comprised of local youth councils, model youth congresses, and youth legislatures—were radical alternatives to their self-government ideal. Issues of education, jobs, civil rights, and militarism were paramount for these and other groups. Identifying persistent gaps between schooling and the job market, these young activists suggested that despite the addition of subjects such as vocational education, extracurricular activities were of greatest relevance to students' employment needs. Surveys from such organizations as the American Youth Commission of the American Council on Education (directed by University of Chicago political scientist Floyd Reeves) reported on youth alienation and dissatisfaction and how, increasingly acquainted with dissent from adult organizations and alternative political and economic systems abroad, these activists' discussions about improving life in the US posed serious questions as to whether democracy and capitalism should survive.[83]

Even before the economic and political upheavals of the 1930s, youth workers like Walter Stone had worried about gaining "a modicum of control over behavior" in "this changed situation" of modernity "right at the point where old controls fall down." Now fears that disruptive ideas and activities like flapper fashion and flagpole sitting could be "catching" due to peer contagion were exacerbated by the social scientific work on group processes and symbolic communication. Too many young people were out of school or work, exposed to antidemocratic propaganda, and becoming politically active. A juvenile delinquency wave in 1933–1934 appeared to portend threats to national security if these problems were not addressed—prompting growing attention to young people by the FBI (such as files kept on the Southern Negro Youth Congress). Aware of youth frustrations with the current political and economic situation and cognizant of youth movements overseas mobilizing for fascist regimes, adult elites became greatly concerned about finding ways to improve young people's lives and morale.[84]

Presidents Herbert Hoover and then Franklin Delano Roosevelt invited scholars to Washington, D.C., to propose scientific solutions to the economic, political, and social problems at hand. Hall's foundational contributions had been questioned, but the commitment to linking theory and practice was not. Sharing Mead's view that "social reconstruction and self or personality reconstruction are the two sides of a single process—the process of human social evolution," academics advised political leaders, educators, and youth workers to address the youth crisis on parallel fronts: altering both the life experiences of American youth and what Lippman called the "pictures in their heads." Like the Goo Goos before them, many participants in these conversations were optimistic that applications of the latest research to politics would make government better and, in turn, improve citizen participation toward mutually beneficial ends.[85]

Drawing on the new socially situated understandings of youth behavior, their crisis management efforts directed special attention to two marginal groups. Older youth, lumped together with their younger brothers and sisters in literary societies and fire companies a century earlier, had gradually been separated as adult-supervised programming focused on younger kids. The sense that adolescence was lengthening (on account of both scientific discoveries and cultural transformation) prompted new awareness of the need to program for these populations, who had become increasingly visible during the Depression due to their widespread unemployment and vocal desire to work. African American youth of all ages, restricted by segregation and lack of investment by private and public organizations, had been stymied from large scale participation in educational and recreational programming even as they were long infantilized by whites (and even as vocational education rather than more academic subjects dominated offerings in African American institutions). These omissions became increasingly problematic in light of African Americans' contributions to World War I and increasingly visible in the wake of the Great Migration and restrictions on immigration after 1924. Kids had been involved in political protests in the 1920s, for example, over housing segregation in Detroit, and the NAACP was seeking to make young people more politically conscious. Continued evidence that "Negros" were more likely delinquents provided further motivation for rethinking ways to engage minority youth.[86]

In the 1930s, then, as young people complained about gaps between education and employment and wondered about the future of democratic industrial capitalism, they found support from some adults linked to left-wing movements. But mainstream and more conservative adult observers concerned with maintaining social stability saw a distinctly different set of youth problems regarding community organization and public opinion to be addressed. Self-governing communities for youth could tackle all of these challenges, junior republic advocates proposed. Older adolescents (sixteen to twenty-one) had been a focus in Freeville after its 1914 reopening; postwar junior municipalities explicitly enrolled older youth not served by existing organizations. Racial assimilation had been a central mandate of the republic movement from its debut, expanding from immigrants to Native Americans to the children in American possessions. How, during the 1930s, a massive expansion of republics offered older adolescents and African Americans access to now-common youth experiences and how, as all of these youthful populations took responsibility for helping to solve the nation's varied youth problems they made new kinds of economic contributions to youth-serving institutions and the state under the guise of educational and recreational programming, are the subjects of chapter 6.[87]

6   Expanding and Erasing the Republic Idea

In 1932, Warner Brothers announced it would make the film *Junior Republic*. The script characterized Freeville as a reformatory—and William George was appalled. Although "legally it *is* an institution," he admitted, "the Junior Republic in its every day practical operations is *not* an institution—in fact it is at the diametrically opposite pole from institutionalism." George mobilized citizens, alums, and board members in a letter-writing campaign to correct the script. Instead, the studio scuttled the project.[1]

What can a closer look at Freeville and related programs during the 1930s tell us about how, even after the "sheltered childhood" was widely accepted, popular ideas about appropriate activities for child-saving institutions remained closer to the older reformatory tradition than previously presumed? And how might citizens' efforts to shape this film portrayal reveal previously hidden dimensions of youth engagement with media and public relations in the period? This chapter follows the republic movement into the Depression and New Deal, when federal and local officials looked to republics and associated activities for young adults and African Americans to maintain social stability in a potentially explosive economic and political situation. Building community and shaping peer opinion were critical ambitions for the educators and youth workers who supplemented existing youth activities with new opportunities for media production toward these goals. Like so many predecessor programs, their efforts to address youth needs provided valuable service to sponsoring organizations and the nation, expanding our understanding of public works projects during this period of recovery from economic and political crisis. By the late 1930s, a lexicon of education and recreation had largely replaced an earlier framework of models and dramatization to describe such undertakings, and the sense of role-playing had all but disappeared. Yet the assumptions about protection and labor were sustained.

Histories of the emergence of the sheltered childhood have documented how, during the 1930s, young adults and African Americans previously excluded from broader cultural transformations were increasingly subject to the same expectations as white middle-class and working-class youth. Scholars identify responses to youth activism as critical catalysts for assigning sentimental rather than economic value to these populations. Advertisers' growing use of children as a protected class together with the consolidation of a youth market confirm these expectations' spread.[2]

Missing from these accounts, however, are the stories of how the newly anointed "youth" helped to build the organizations and programs that would protect them after the market crash and how, as the nation rebuilt, the full spectrum of populations that comprised this social category together advertised the sheltered childhood in ways that went far beyond the symbolic modes scholars have previously described. The National Youth Administration's Resident Training Centers, police-sponsored "Boystowns," and a range of programs at schools and youth-serving institutions confirm scholars' contention that older adolescents and African Americans came to be understood as youth during this period, while simultaneously proposing that they, too, played far more substantial roles creating this category than previously presumed. Guided by social scientific wisdom on human groups to address what Walter Lippmann called the "world outside" and the "pictures in our heads," these populations built facilities, administered programs, and improved the physical environment under the guise of youth protection. And together with many other young Americans, they now produced newspapers, radio broadcasts, and films to help organize their communities and manufacture public opinion—becoming public relations agents for a range of youth-oriented initiatives and in turn for democracy itself.[3]

Opportunity from Chaos: William George's Final Act

William George was aging and in poor health when the youth crisis exploded. J. B. Kirkland had left Freeville for the Boys Club Federation of America, replaced by Donald Urquart, George's daughter Esther's husband. "Daddy says Don has proven that someone else can run the Republic 'republicky' besides Daddy George," Mrs. Daddy wrote to ex-citizens in 1932. Malcolm Freeborn, married to George's daughter Edith, took over the junior municipality program, working in nearby Cortland to create "an object lesson for other cities." Jacob Smith stepped up his involvement with the association and as a correspondent for republic citizens seeking advice.[4]

The groundswell of youth radicalism, visible at nearby Cornell where the campus was "running wild with socialism and the usual accompanying -isms," recharged George's ambitions to scale up the republic idea. "Who said 21?" he routinely asked, calling for the nation to take seriously the sixteen to twenty-one year olds who were physically adults but legally infants except when it came to war. "What a pity…to consider this vast reserve army only in terms of warfare! Think of the potency of these millions during the years of peace were their strength to be directed toward natural solutions of local and national problems." Insisting that such attitudes were a chief cause of juvenile delinquency, George campaigned against anti-child-labor legislation, observing how "The country needs to be saved from the excessive reformer…as much as it does from an excessive exploiter of childhood." And he called for additional opportunities for youth participation in local government so that these "adult minors" could "feel themselves real, working members of the community in which they live" rather than face "the endless string of negatives...Don't, don't, don't!" These actions aligned conservative George with the radical youth who shared his frustrations about the "degrading infancy" foisted upon them. "There is one thing that our youth movement has in common with all other youth movements," he told one correspondent, "the belief that young people are capable of doing things."[5]

George now laid out his hopes for a posthumous legacy, one that would not merely continue junior republics and junior municipalities but would expand to reach all youth. He created two new organizations toward these ends. The League of Adult Minors, launched with Freeville president John Kinane, was "the right wing of youth movements," assembling sixteen to twenty-one year olds for projects to cultivate economic and civic responsibility: "youth participation, learning and earning, junior government, economic responsibility and self government, civic projects, social sanitarium, inmate participation and earning, social doctors, individual civic initiative." Phalanx: A League for the Promotion of Civic and Economic Responsibility (no apparent relation to Charles Fourier's Phalanxes) recruited adult helpers for this work. Representatives from programs that George hoped to scale up—for example, the New York City Merchant's Anti-litter Bureau, which assigned high school students to take over some police duties—addressed their meetings. "Dear Uncle Hotchie," he confided to Freeville's first instructor, now president of Chicago's Amour Institute. "I am having a lot of pleasure these days devising schemes for reforming the universe and am getting as much kick out of it as I did back in those days when we tried out sociological schemes in the Junior Republic." George hoped to make Syracuse his "social laboratory."[6]

He also joined the American Youth Congress, traveling with the Freeborns and Kinane to its first meetings in New York City in 1934. The Congress is typically remembered as the leading leftist US youth organization. Initially, however, it included a smaller conservative wing. The two younger men served on its board of governors, while George refused to stand for election so he would not be accused of being an old-timer trying to take control. Although George did not attend subsequent gatherings, the others participated in an effort to make space for conservative youth.[7]

The Depression thus had a silver lining for the republic movement. Even as Freeville felt its financial effects (in 1935, George and his wife could not afford to send their usual holiday greetings to friends and former citizens), George wrote to one correspondent that "Weathering the depression is very much like living again the 'pioneer days' in the little Republic. Not so bad after all!!!" Few republic graduates found themselves out of work during the crisis and George's records were "full of instances" of how former citizens had "learned to adjust their lives to the life of the community." Many were youth work leaders: Frank Searles, Children's Aid Society director; William

Gute, Spokane Parental School head; and Harris LeRoy, Boston Bunker Hill Boys Club superintendent. Junior municipalities were the kind of constructive leisure activities that James Rogers, now director of the US National Recreation Service, had called for in a recent report. Updating his analysis to match social scientists' attention to group processes and growing national concerns about community organization and public opinion, George and others dispensed with an earlier language of instincts and recapitulation and impersonation, instead proposing the programs he had pioneered were ideal solutions to contemporary youth problems insofar as they situated the natural force of social control in the public opinion of the group.[8]

Although George's ideas were decidedly right-wing, he remained optimistic about their appeal to adults seeking effective ideological management and to a broad range of youth. To support these projects he now insisted on the necessity of a federal youth department. "We have departments of agriculture, commerce, navy, army…Why not one for the guidance of youth, the business of which will be to study and plan for vocational, civic, and even social adjustments of rising generations?" Freeborn became spokesperson for these ideas. Observing how "youth seems to be running berserk" and "the number of young delinquents is rapidly increasing" and explaining how "communism and fascism are training their young men and women for political action," he asked: "If other systems look to their youth largely to perpetuate their system, can democracy do less?"[9]

Freeborn contacted federal officials in early 1935 with their proposals for programs the new agency should undertake. The "immediate action necessary to build a public opinion" to perpetuate the democratic way lay in encouraging American youth "to work in their own communities on their own problems." With George noting that the "complete development of adult-minor participation in community welfare can easily be seen at the Junior Republic," they were eager that "young people in a community, quite apart from all people in a Junior Republic," gain "training through practical experience." In short, "All youth must work either in a J.R. or outside." Freeborn laid out their vision of "Civic laboratories for Adult-Minor Citizenship…in several sections of the United States" where youth would "organize themselves." Freeborn emphasized the proposal's multiple beneficiaries, one of the most direct statements about the economic implication of George's ideas: "A program of participation in government by adult minors" would address "crime prevention, unemployment, and use of leisure time." Such projects would be "of economic value to the community" as youth would "assist in the elimination of governmental expenditures and cost" alongside their contributions to community stability and national security.[10]

Others also saw opportunity in crisis. Richard Welling, Lyman Beecher Stowe, and Spencer Miller Jr., affiliates of the National Self Government Committee (formerly Self Government, Inc.), promoted programs such as school cities and BBRs as antidotes to political radicalism, emphasizing their influences on community organization and bolstering group morale. While acknowledging that, as Philadelphia schools superintendent Oliver Cornman put it, "in such a civic dramatization" young people could become pupils in "a school of demagoguery and unscrupulous politics or of servile discipleship under the almost hypnotic leadership of a strong teacher" or youth worker, that adaptations abroad showed the potential modifications for use in other political systems (for example, German school city variants), and that "miniature social movements" at the Ford republic revealed it was not a perfect disciplinary scheme, they remained optimistic that such democratic tools could respond to the new national threats. Once on the fringes of the republic movement, BBR's longer-term record seemed to bear this out. The *Chicago Tribune*, reporting on a 1927 reunion of the boundary-line-gang-turned-BBR-citizens, observed how the

> former tough guys...had followed out the professions that had interested them as youngsters. The first judge of their court, for instance, Oscar M. Nudelman, is now a lawyer, So is the first prosecuting attorney, Harry Malkin....Benjamin Wernig, who was chairman of the first Boys' Job Day, April 19, 1916, is a manufacturer.[11]

Thriving during the Depression thanks to limited staffing needs, BBR opened a New York City branch in 1932. There to celebrate, Jack Robbins attended a Phalanx meeting. Miller and Welling joined the BBR board, bringing it into closer contact with the National Self Government Committee's networks (now including board members Henry MacCracken and John Dewey). The New York Police Department Crime Prevention Bureau offered BBR boys a field for sports, provided they cleared it themselves. The Chicago program expanded, adding a newspaper, store, and other programs, and eventually a facility for African Americans. "You are doing splendid work," wrote William George to BBR officials.[12]

To be clear, BBRs in both cities continued to advocate for non-member youth: investigating a reform school outside Chicago and prompting the removal of the warden and his assistants in 1933, and circulating petitions to create more neighborhood playgrounds in New York a few years later. Compared to the era's radical youth groups, however, their continued advocacy was tame. Recognized for their ongoing cooperation with adult agencies, the boys saved money to the public purse. "The republic has a record comparable to some adult civic reform committees in winning improved treatment of juveniles," noted a later observer, without mention of earlier citizens' view that youth and adults might differ on what that improved treatment meant.[13]

With BBR now appearing in criminology texts alongside other republics for its contributions to delinquency reduction, first mayor Ralph Goodman was appointed to Chicago's crime commission. In 1934, organizers of the National Crime Conference invited BBR citizens to share their stories with law enforcement. A few years later, New York Mayor Fiorello La Guardia named a BBR boy to his juvenile delinquency committee after reading a report the boys had produced. (Citizens subsequently prepared another on education, which proposed making schools more like republics.) Board members suggested that BBR's "modern method of treating the juvenile delinquency problem," which exemplified Dewey's "preparations for life in the midst of life" had broader implications. "At a time when dictatorships are widely heralded and democracy is being assailed," Miller explained, "a group of American youths, many of them underprivileged," was "not only defending democracy themselves but demonstrating it." The founding fathers "have no more conscious descendants in our day."[14]

Thus, the ample documentation that juvenile democracies helped maintain social stability at low cost and in ways that appealed to youth—for instance, there had been no newsboy strikes in Milwaukee even as the republic swelled to 7,000—prompted renewed interest in this child-saving technique. As junior republics, junior municipalities, and other youth-led organizations continued their operations, then, a new generation of closely related programs made their debuts. From the Resident Training Centers established by the National Youth Administration to the police-organized Boystowns in mostly African American neighborhoods, the late 1930s witnessed republics' further diversification, bringing older adolescents and African Americans into the social category of youth and broadening the sense of what it might be possible to achieve. William George celebrated his flagship republic's fortieth anniversary but did not live to see the resurgence of interest in his ideas. He died in 1936 of failing health. Wilson Gill died a few years later, in 1941.[15]

A New Deal for American Youth?

It was Franklin Delano Roosevelt's administration that realized William George's vision of a federal agency for youth (the National Youth Administration or NYA, established in June 1935) and graduated communities of responsibility for adult minors across the US (approximately 600 residential centers for sixteen to twenty-five year olds after 1937). The agency was established in the Works Progress Administration under the guidance of southern minister and social worker Aubrey Williams, with the mandate to address unemployment and excessive leisure time among the nation's under-twenty-fives and simultaneously to rally their commitment to the American way. It swiftly mobilized a range of programs to serve black and white, urban and rural, and later, European refugee youth. Educational initiatives that spanned vocational training, commercial education, and farm instruction provided student aid in exchange for institutional maintenance. Work relief enlisted young men and women to build and maintain public infrastructure and recreational facilities and perform survey research. These efforts, administered at state and local levels, aimed to enroll young people in extended training, delaying their full-time labor force participation so that, in the short term, competition between adults and youth for available private sector jobs would be reduced and, in the long term, the younger generation's employment prospects would be increased. Federal support for vocational guidance initiated in the Junior Employment Service continued here.[16]

With officials attuned to academic research on leisure's links to social (dis)organization, recreational programming also featured in agency activities. The NYA's Community Organization division gathered information on youth groups, promoting those they approved and keeping tabs on others such as the American Youth Congress. In communities with no prior programming, staff suggested activities from team sports to tie-dyeing, insisting on club constitutions, elected officers, and parliamentary procedures to organize the new groups. As Oklahoma NYA director William Campbell explained, the key to "learn to cooperate" was "actual participation in group organization," making recreational activities a "gateway to instruction in larger ideals." NYA staff also encouraged local youth councils (established in many communities to organize recreational activities) to add youth representatives and began vetting potential young adult members of a national advisory board.[17]

These programs paved the way for the agency's republic-like Resident Training Centers. The 595 facilities across forty-five states and Puerto Rico combined the "learning by doing" of agency vocational education programs with the civil service orientation of its public works programs, adding recreational activities and self-government toward complementary ends. Living, working, learning, and playing together, teaching trades and social skills, and offering medical and dental services, these total institutions for "the rebuilding of youth" brought the republic experience to regions around the US. Taking the view that "many of the problems of living at a resident center are very similar to those faced by people living in a small town," as NYA administrator Harry V. Gilson put it, the hope was for the experience to transfer into and improve "real" communities in the longer term. Gilson, who supervised the Quoddy Resident Training Center in Maine before rising to regional supervisor and then to the national office, was outspoken that "we can't have an enduring democratic government and economy without citizens who are acquainted with not only its theories but also its practice."[18]

Program cost was a constant concern. The centers used existing facilities where possible, assigning enrollees to improve these sites before transitioning to broader occupational training. Managing centers, building and repairing local public facilities, and producing goods and offering services for local government agencies earned them small salaries to pay for room and board. Exposure to varied experiences was a priority, with work training offered in classroom settings and "on the job;" vocational and personality tests supplemented these "try-outs" with further career guidance. Officials tracked and rated youth for their participation in approved recreational activities in recognition of "the value of an adequate recreational life in maintaining desirable attitudes and removing certain emotional maladjustments."[19]

Not every activity was organized from the top down, however. Quoddy enrollees published *Ye Village Crier* weekly to report on elections, club activities, and sports, introduce program participants to one another and to staff, and call out peers' behavior before administrators subsequently set up news production facilities. Other enrollees operated amateur radio stations. Radio's popularity—Washington headquarters' draft *NYA Amateur Radio Station Directory* cataloged hundreds—prompted administrators to make it a focus for some work projects. Among them, NYA youth built a network for the Maine Highway Patrol, set up a transmitter for municipal police in Waco, Texas, constructed twenty-five mobile units for the Colorado state police, and made receiving and transmitting equipment for NYA installations toward a nationwide emergency communications network.[20]

Optimistic that their comprehensive programs would benefit participants and nation because young people would be less likely to destroy communities they had built, administrators nonetheless insisted on more explicit training in communal and democratic living. "If democracy is going to survive," Gilson explained, "these youth, as citizens, are going to be compelled to put some effort into it." Charles Taussig, a member of Roosevelt's brain trust with ties to the National Self Government Committee, had been advocating for such practices from 1933. The president was familiar with self-government techniques; as assistant secretary of the navy, he had appointed Thomas Osborne warden at the Portsmouth Naval Prison, where Osborne organized a Mutual Welfare League. His administration's early relief programs including the Civilian Conservation Corps and Federal Emergency Relief Administration had encouraged, but did not require, self-government.[21]

Residential training centers required academic civics classes followed by learning by doing as enrollees applied self-government to their work training and recreational activities under the guidance of staff advisors and hired citizenship instructors. Most structured themselves as miniature cities although some chose nonspecific council forms. Thus, although federal officials urged "the youth government should be patterned as closely as possible after prevailing forms of local American government" to avoid "artificial government structures which might not be applicable in home communities," these centers followed increasingly common practice and did not duplicate any particular place. Regardless of the specifics, residents were expected to "formulate and enforce their own rules and regulations," Kenneth Osgood, director of the Concord, New Hampshire, center explained. Some created peer courts while others gave council members disciplinary responsibility. Their jurisdiction over "junior personnel" extended off campus. Enrollees exchanged ideas about self-government with peers in other centers through their newspapers and occasional conferences. Quoddy, an especially lively self-government program, circulated advice manuals to NYA staff across the US and hosted a meeting for them in 1938.[22]

It is important to understand that, despite efforts from Freeborn and others to call attention to their ongoing work and to George as the inventor of record, it was the broad enthusiasm for democratic group processes, rather than the expertise of specific individuals, that inspired self-government programs in the federal youth agency. In 1935, for example, before the centers debuted, representatives at the American Legion's Illinois

Figure 6.1
NYA youth court in session, Lima, NY.
Source: Gordon Halstead, *Work-Study-Live: The Resident Youth Centers of the NYA* (Lima, NY: NYA Resident Work Center, n.d.).

branch convened Boys State, a weeklong camp for teenaged boys. William George had addressed Legionnaires on numerous occasions, and affiliates had participated in junior municipalities in connection with their growing youth work. Now, the Legion organized a summer program modeled on the state administration, with athletics, newspaper production, and other recreational activities. The popular program spawned Boys States and Girls States across the US and, later, Boys Nation and Girls Nation. Alumni chapters followed. Public officials were eager to instruct the next generation of citizens—in Vermont, for example, junior citizens met the governor, lieutenant governor, attorney general, associate state supreme court justice, and others. Manuals on how state government worked served as program handbooks. Field trips to "visit the actual offices which they are to simulate," were included, and in Illinois and elsewhere youth used states' legislative chambers for some activities."[23]

Boys State was one of several educational and recreational organizations established in the 1930s for training in citizenship, many explicitly conceived of as defensive measures against propaganda from radical political groups. Junior American Statesmen, Boys and Girls Republics, YMCA Model Legislatures, United States Society, Junior

Citizens, and Youth Builders attest to the pervasive sense that, in a period of political and economic instability, young people needed to practice democracy to ensure its survival. "Instead of learning to goose-step to the dictates of an all-powerful leader, as in Germany; drilling with rifles at the age of 10, as in Italy; being drilled in use of the bayonet and the principles of Communism, as in Russia," reported a journalist for the *Washington Post*, "the boys and girls of America are to be united in a country-wide movement in support of the Bill of Rights and freedom under the law." These efforts, together with the junior republics, junior municipalities, and many descendants that continued their operations, offered a multiplicity of models for the NYA.[24]

Guided by theories of nondirective leadership, federal officials encouraged center staff to suggest rather than command, letting participants make mistakes and solve the resulting problems themselves. Supervisors proudly reported on the dictatorships residents set up and subsequently rejected, and the relaxed rules they tightened once the effects were felt. Certainly not all was smooth sailing. The Armor City youth government at South Charleston's Resident Training Center discontinued its public safety division after three months "because the youth had difficulty in interpreting and enforcing the rules in a new community where the citizens had not been accustomed to the types of control which were set up by the Youth Government."[25]

By and large, however, administrators were pleased with this approach. Gilson explained with reference to "mistakes" made at Quoddy when the youth government relaxed curfew regulations: "You see...that the experiment, even though it failed, was immeasurably helpful because it convinced the youth that their decisions would prevail even though questionable." Administrators "must have sufficient faith in the judgment of youth," he declared, admitting that, "in a number of instances when I have been skeptical of the results of certain measures adopted by the council, it actually turned out that their judgment was better than mine." Echoing William George in his comments on the superiority of youth judgment and "providing the workers with what they want as nearly as it can be supplied," the arrangement—which taught democracy as structure, process, and consensus rather than how to change the system—did not disrupt existing power relations. The youth government was fundamentally "an asset to the administration...a reliable source of information concerning the desires of the Junior Personnel" and a means by which "the Administration lays a guiding hand upon the Council's work." Even South Charleston staff viewed the community government as "an important factor in the promotion of harmony among the youth and between the youth and the administrative staff." At a time when American youth organizations were seeking greater voice in the NYA itself, these efforts directed participants' attention to governance in more restricted ways, adding more evidence about democracy's effectiveness as a disciplinary tool.[26]

Like so many republics before them, then, NYA Resident Training Centers appeared to adjust participating populations in an engaging way: "underprivileged youth received an experience in instructive group living and democratic self-government. Their general health and mental attitudes were improved; youth learned respect for public property because they were required to maintain the grounds and buildings in which they lived and worked. They earned their way while they learned," and many found employment on graduation. "It is very useful to us. It brings us the real things," said one Quoddy youth representative. Lima center director Gordon Halstead recounted how a third of his enrollees had police records and were there by court order. Yet "we had surprisingly few disciplinary problems." Indeed, "The youth themselves, where vested with authority in the management of projects, often proved more severe in their regulations than their supervisors." There was "a deadly seriousness about NYA youth" as they enforced behavioral controls from mealtime etiquette to dormitory cleanliness. Follow-up conversations confirmed that many enjoyed the experience, leading officials to conclude that, contrary to public protests, "young people prefer the traditional institutions and arrangements according to which their elders lived and into which they themselves expect and want to be tested for place and position."[27]

As these self-governing communities integrated new populations into common conceptions of "youth," they marked the migration beyond public schools of the common assumption that educational programming did not constitute work. Like Gary's "work-study-play" schools, the NYA centers with their "work-study-live" approach supplied experiences distinct from adult labor. In an economic context when cash-strapped state and local governments lacked funds for basic tasks, and a political context of some hostility to youth employment relief in light of high adult unemployment, NYA had to appease potentially activist youth while minimizing competition with adults—engaging young people in "a real job, not a 'set-up'" while simultaneously "not competing with existing agriculture, business, or industry" and "the great army of [adult] wage earners." The agency banked on the assumption, established over decades of school-based programs, that future-oriented vocational training and service to public rather than private interests lay outside the labor market, mollifying labor unions' fears of young people stealing adults' jobs at lower pay and differentiating them from adult work relief.[28]

Such activities kept an underresourced federal program operating, reducing operating costs and raising funds through contracts with other government agencies. While it had cost the WPA "over $25,000 a month to simply maintain the [Quoddy] property," the NYA did "a better job of maintenance" while "giving work experience to 380 boys for an additional cost of only $15,000 per month." Through self-government programs participants "enter[ed] into the field which is ordinarily reserved for supervisory staff," explained Gilson, noting how the youth government, "operated as an aid to the efficient functioning of this project and as a help to the administration in making the Village a pleasant place in which to live."[29]

As the Resident Training Centers assigned youth to administer programs and provide goods and services to local government agencies, some agency officials employed an older language of "realism" to describe their program. They noted, for example, how "The NYA wanted the center to offer realistic work through the actual production of articles for public purchase." And they described how the centers that "seemed like" industrial production facilities offered "a substitute for the practical work experience which in normal times they would have gained through work in private employment," as Gordon Halsted put it.[30]

More common, however, were references to the program's educational ambitions, its partnerships with state vocational education agencies, and the language of "school." They invoked Dewey's vision of miniature communities to underscore their centers' pedagogical orientation, environments separated from the real world, where students practiced skills needed in adulthood. His earlier observation that sometimes pay amplified the learning taking place inflected NYA officials' characterizations of their programs. Describing activities that earned or saved money as "educational opportunities," "work experience" and "learning by doing," their self-government programs as "student government" (despite some counsel to the contrary), and remuneration for center participants in some cases as "student aid" portrayed the economic aspects of the work-like activities as subsidiary to their educational agenda. This lexicon, which differentiated such activities from private sector employment and adult relief programs, drew attention away from how, once again, young people were producing institutions that sheltered them and creating value for the state.[31]

A similar vocabulary dominated NYA school-based programs where work-study participants remunerated for institutional maintenance at cash-strapped schools and colleges were classified as students receiving "scholarships" or "financial aid," emphasizing student learning rather than the benefits to sponsoring institutions. (George, still alive as these early programs were getting off the ground, saw resonance with his Phalanx platform for "learning and earning," such as offering wages for school attendance, which the republic had done with its publishing house scheme in 1896, and which John Kinane had promoted to the New York state legislature in recent years.) Even out-of-school work programs struck this tone, insisting projects be restricted to "work that could not have been undertaken under normal budgets of the agency they assisted" to avoid displacing adults. Yet ambiguities characterized the actual programs the authorities approved. Officially, "no construction projects for youth employment" were authorized, but "repairs such as painting and rehabilitating new youth centers" were deemed acceptable forms of "in service training," as were clearing and grading vacant lots and making equipment for recreation and youth center use. Young people's activities spanned landscaping and conservation, road work, installing traffic signs and signals, constructing and repairing schools, libraries, gyms, youth centers, courthouses, bridges, and sidewalks, providing clerical assistance, sewing, building furniture, and other tasks.[32]

The NYA's supervisory model amplified its self-conception as an educational agency. Briefly contemplating apprenticeships, officials subsequently characterized NYA staff as educators and youth workers. A "work program for youth demands a type of supervision which performs a training as well as a supervisory function," they insisted. Supervisors must be "counselors and advisors" to teach "good work habits and proper attitudes...teachers as well as foremen" noting that "wherever possible the facilities of local school systems are utilized to provide related training courses." College instructors as center supervisors, partnerships with state education agencies, and siting on college campuses publically sold this idea; behind-the-scenes cost estimates of center operations, which used nearby colleges as comparison points, underscore that agency personnel privately shared this view.[33]

To be sure, not all parties were completely persuaded. Labor unions initially resisted agency programs they viewed as cheap alternatives to adult employment. Roosevelt had responded to similar concerns about the Civilian Conservation Corps (CCC) by hiring a prominent union organizer to help administer the agency; now he encouraged union workers to supervise NYA projects. Radical youth organizations saw in agency programs the possibility for exploitation and called to organize unions at the NYA itself. A number of NYA Workers Unions were established in the 1930s but were not significant forces. Instead, the educational language, which persuaded unions that the agency's programs were not taking jobs from adults, incited school administrators' fears that an NYA-administered federal education system might replace the nation's existing public schools.[34]

Gamification in the Ghetto

National Youth Administration activities offer the most numerous examples of how William George's ideas closely continued to shape state-sponsored youth programs created even after his death in 1936. Yet they were not alone. For the young residents of African American neighborhoods, who had long lacked recreational facilities, activities, and even basic government services, programs resembling George's junior municipalities began cropping up in the late 1930s to address concerns about community disorganization and public opinion among these populations.[35]

Shifting immigration patterns that followed the 1924 Immigration Act, together with a new conception of race oriented to skin color rather than nationality, prompted social scientists of the 1920s and 1930s to compare the African American experience to that of other demographic groups. Sociologists identified how African Americans uprooted following the great migration typically clustered in ghettos whose conditions exemplified the concept of social disorganization, yet these populations were challenged to find hospitable alternatives. Psychologists' studies of racial attitudes confirmed that prejudice toward African Americans complicated generational assimilation patterns typically seen with immigrants. Political scientists observed the dearth of public resources to improve African Americans communities and the fears that residents might be attracted to communism as a result. Such studies, as well as housing and planning surveys, had brought to public attention the "national emergency" in African American neighborhoods across the US. It was in this context that African American police officers, following the social service model in white neighborhoods, took the lead to organize these self-governing "cities within a city" to encourage youth to help themselves and their communities. Many opened in cities where junior republics, junior municipalities, and related programs already served other populations.[36]

African American youth had not been completely excluded from republics and related activities. At Hart Farm and "colored" orphanages, at racially mixed institutions including Freeville and Progress City, and in some school cities and playground republics, African Americans had participated from the movement's early years, with William McKiernan observing, for example, how one integrated Newark playground republic "removes racial barriers," among other benefits. They had encountered occasional opportunities to participate in Scouting, junior civic leagues, junior safety programs, and junior policing as well. The 1930s witnessed the creation of recreational programs for African American youth on a much larger scale, however. From Cleveland's Boystown to Pittsburgh's Hill City to Youth Cities in Columbus and Philadelphia, police initiative expanded applications of the junior republic idea. Local governments led these efforts, but federal assistance followed as WPA and NYA assigned recreation and play supervisors to supplement their meager staffs.[37]

In these programs, Boys Towns joined the school republics, boy cities, junior towns, and other republic variations. A few years after George scuttled Warner Brothers' *Junior Republic*, Metro-Goldwyn-Mayer (MGM, which had purchased Willis Brown's film lot) produced *Boys Town* (1938), a fictionalized story of the republic in an Omaha boys' institution called Boys Town (established in 1926 and incorporated as a town in 1934).

Starring Spencer Tracy and Mickey Rooney, it was wildly popular; studio director Louis B. Mayer declared it his favorite MGM film. As a result of the film's wide reach and a sequel, *Men of Boys Town* (1941), "Boys Towns" became public shorthand for republic-like projects from the NYA's resident centers to police-organized republics for African American youth to George's own Litchfield Junior Republic. The films' popularity helps to explain such institutions' proliferation in African American communities absent the direct movement of specific people, further evidence of how the republic idea was in the air. (Notably, Omaha's Boys Town's first mayor had been African American.)[38]

Pittsburgh's Hill City Youth Municipality, headquartered in the New Granada theater, opened in 1939, expanding the police department Friendly Service Bureau's "junior crime prevention bureau" (itself modeled on a Columbus, Ohio, juvenile safety league). Pittsburgh was the closest big city to George's Grove City Republic; Carnegie Steel had opened a playground city in Pittsburgh after the first World War. Designed "to furnish worthwhile leisure time programs to combat anti-social tendencies," through activities such as band, Scouts, newspaper, radio broadcasting, and drama alongside

Figure 6.2
Boys Town movie poster.
Source: MGM/Album/Alamy Stock Photo.

crime prevention, Hill City served more than 4,000 mostly African American youth in the Hill District made famous by August Wilson's plays. Inspired by *Boys Town*, officer Howard McKinney persuaded local officials to participate in the self-government scheme: "Hill City officials and Pittsburgh officials holding the same positions are in close contact and cooperate on mutual problems."[39]

Pittsburgh's junior police program was not the first to scale up to a republic. George's Law and Order Gang was the kernel of Freeville's first police force; Portland, Oregon, boys who organized a junior police force in the 1910s subsequently expanded to a full youth government. Columbus, Ohio, officer Lesley Shaw followed McKinney's lead, transforming that city's juvenile safety league into Columbus Youth City a year later, an "exact duplicate of the Columbus municipal government," aiming to develop among 1,800 mostly African American youth "a keener appreciation of good citizenship, self reliance, self respect, and to generally develop character."[40]

Cleveland's Boystowns also opened in 1939, organized by municipal departments of recreation, health and welfare, and police. Aiming "to attract boys who might otherwise be engaged in anti social activities," it applied the latest thinking on gangs to redirect "talents for youthful leadership" formerly dissipated in "delinquent pursuits" to developing model communities in which boys would "learn good government, self-reliance, and respect for law and order," as journalist Fred Kelly explained. Six recently decommissioned police stations became "city halls" in neighborhoods where prior efforts to address juvenile delinquency had failed "because of a lack of community organization." While they adopted a variation on the movie title to attract local youth, Mayor Harold Burton and city safety director Eliot Ness had been inspired by Progress City, whose postwar leadership had stepped up crime prevention talk. "Progress City is a wonderful organization which should help to prevent further crime in America," Ness explained. Boystowns offered 6,000 youth lively programs of self-government and recreational activities—sports, summer camps, dancing, airplane and radio building, debate, and a shortwave radio network to interconnect program facilities and share information on political, cultural, and athletic programs. The boys patrolled their neighborhood toward delinquency prevention as well.[41]

The anxieties about African Americans behind these and related programs such as Philadelphia's Youth City equally shaped existing republics in changing neighborhoods. Central to ecological studies of group behavior was the notion that communities were in constant flux and that area institutions needed to adapt to changing conditions to survive. Administrators at Cleveland's Hiram House, for example, observing more African American neighbors, were addressing this issue. The story of one girl's confusion, in 1925, about the realism of Progress City confirmed staff concerns that local youth appeared increasingly ill-equipped to administer their juvenile government, prompting proposals to simplify its operations. "Girlie, you are in the right church, but you have the wrong spirit," a teller from Cleveland's Union Trust Bank informed her when she tried to cash a check in Progress City currency there (and confided that others had made the same mistake). As they streamlined the youth government, settlement staff created a satellite juvenile city they called Merryburgh at the Paul Revere Neighborhood Project in the city's main African American neighborhood.[42]

The new youth programs delivered to African American neighborhoods results familiar to other communities. As Hill City youth studied fingerprinting, implemented the police department's "area control plan" of beat patrols, and organized a better neighborhood drive, as Boystown citizens patrolled neighborhoods near their city halls, and as Philadelphia police enlisted Youth City participants to prevent petty crimes, they combated "social disorganization" and remade social norms. The manager of Pittsburgh's largest five-and-dime recounted how his staff used to "nab four or five Negro boys every day for stealing," but now there was barely one theft a month. "Pronty Ford, district attorney of Hill City, comes in here once a week to check up," he explained. "If we do catch a colored boy, we report to Pronty, not to the police." A visitor to Hill City's court found a similar situation. "Hill City has done such a remarkable job in bringing law and order the district, there was only one little insignificant case to be tried." The judges were sometimes "wrong on legal phraseology" but showed "plenty of common sense." Merryburgh became a case study in a 1931 book on community organization. Plummeting crime statistics prompted sociologists and police from other cities to take a closer look.[43]

Rooted in "friendly" supervision and group work techniques, these programs encouraged peers to pressure peers in new ways. In "sections [of Cleveland] where a boy's police record had been regarded as a mark of distinction, good citizenship is now fashionable," Ness observed. Library attendance in Pittsburgh was up as youth sought information on municipal codes. Intergroup relations and community morale similarly improved. "Here are youths flush with the prospects of a full life and the unrestricted opportunity of gratifying their sense of importance," Pittsburgh journalist James Reid described. The kids "feel that they belong—that they are part the community and as such they look out upon a new world full of hope." Even as young people took responsibility for reporting on their peers, boys and girls of different races were now "in complete harmonious relationship." As he talked with more and more neighborhood youth, one visitor from the *Pittsburgh Courier* reported,

> I became convinced that they were more social-minded than any group of elder people I have met... the entire staff of [youth] officials at Hill City were not at all concerned about their small personal problems, but each of them thought in terms of what aid they could render to other youths of the neighborhood. They believe it to be their obligation to direct the energies of misguided boys and girls in the path of proper social standards with emphasis on responsibilities to the community welfare.[44]

During a period when other youth activists were directly confronting structural racism—for example, the platforms of the American Youth Congress, Southern Negro Youth Congress, and NAACP highlighted discrimination in employment, housing, and

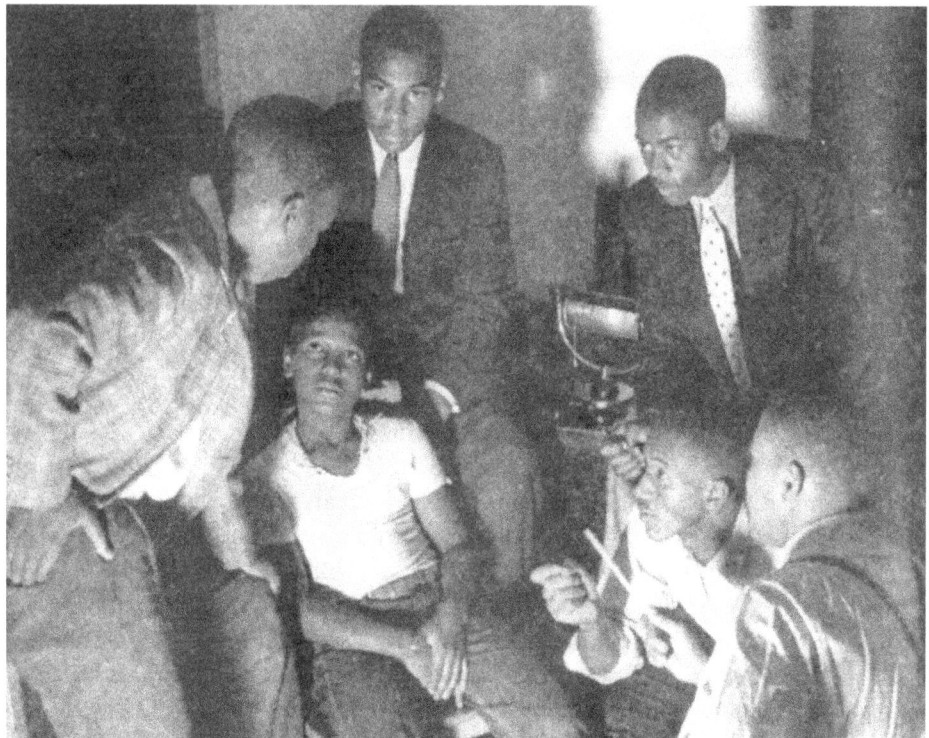

Figure 6.3
Hill City officials question a suspect.
Source: Webb Waldron, "Gang Goes Uphill: Story of Hill City Municipality of Negro Youth in Pittsburgh's Harlem," *Survey Graphic* 29 (March 1940).

recreation—these models of urban democracy directed young people to distinctly different kinds of community engagements. Hill City used politics to stay clear of politics, as New Granada theater owner Harry Henderson put it, simplifying government operations and punishing citizens for minor infractions, and improving race relations by self-control. The programs accomplished their aims, in part, because they were fun. "I was known as the menace of the neighborhood before the founding of Hill City and I was generally bad," Elmer James Boyd, chief of building police at city hall, reported. "Shortly after Hill City started Mr. McKinney sent for me and I was shown around. I took an interest in the work and now I am an officer. I like it and I have more fun here than I have ever had before…you don't get anything by being known as the menace but a bad name in the community."[45]

Reporting on improvements in Pittsburgh's Hill District, Reid described how Hill City shaped both the reality of the city and the pictures in participants' heads. On the

Figure 6.4
Judge Esther Ridley, Hill City.
Source: Webb Waldron, "Gang Goes Uphill: Story of Hill City Municipality of Negro Youth in Pittsburgh's Harlem," *Survey Graphic* 29 (March 1940).

one hand, the juvenile municipality was a "real democracy" at work "solving its own problems" so much so that McKinney had to combat some early misunderstandings of child control. And Wylie Avenue seemed unrecognizable: "No longer can they put this 'famous' thorofare [sic] in the same category with Chicago's State Street, Memphis' Beale Street, Philadelphia's South Street, Baltimore's Pennsylvania Avenue, Atlanta's Auburn Street, Birmingham's Eighth Avenue, New Orleans' Rampart Street, Washington's 12th street, St. Louis's Market Street or Los Angeles' Central Avenue." On the other hand, as "a psychological experiment station that seeks to adjust and make normal the warped and twisted minds of a generation that has felt the heavy hand of poverty and social denials of our system more than any other previous generation of young people," the youth democracy had done "much to inspire self-respect and obedience to the laws of the statute books and the rules of decency and fair play" even as "behind it lurks, untouched, the basic malady of the Hill—poverty, unemployment, dark, cold tenements, bleak, ugly streets." These youth democracies prioritized controlling youth in their communities rather than transforming these communities' relationships to the broader city, leaving untouched the social, economic, and political structures that had made African American neighborhoods the subjects of social scientists' and police concern.[46]

As African Americans gained recreational opportunities previously afforded only to whites, the common wisdom that participants were engaged in positive leisure-time activities rather than laboring to benefit youth-serving institutions or local governments also traveled. With the jail-based sentences common in earlier republics now on the decline, activities labeled "work" (usually cleanup) made only the rarest of appearances as a punishment for misbehavior, suggesting all other activities were recreation. Yet like better-known participatory crime prevention programs such as the Chicago Area Project, whose guiding principle was that experts were less necessary for community organizing than previously presumed, these programs insisted on limited roles for adults (for example, police in Cleveland and Pittsburgh adjudicated some disciplinary cases, and adults helped with some fundraising) and the majority of the community organizing done by neighborhood youth. Young participants raised funds to support programming (as at "self-financed" Columbus Youth City), persuaded donors to supply equipment (as at Cleveland Boystowns, provided only with heat, lighting, and water), and reduced operating costs by administering programs using self-government techniques. Their service on the front lines of delinquency prevention equally helped their cities' bottom lines by multiplying the powers of police. In an economic context where local governments were overstretched and structural reforms were not under way, then, these developments partially compensated, addressing public concern about economic depression and excessive leisure time by directing youth to address the juvenile crime problem themselves. As Philadelphia Youth City mayor Algie Nesbitt put it, "The Negro race can do a great deal more to wipe out crime and juvenile delinquency in the community than anyone else." Such programs underscore the era's widespread hope that youth would become the primary agents in solving the nation's youth problems—in the words of NAACP Philadelphia chapter president Theodore Spaulding, kids should "make themselves important factors in the community"—as well as the fact that, when they did, the full value of their activities did not register.[47]

To be clear, the economic benefits of youth activities linked to the "'deglamorization' of crimes and raising of moral standards"—for example, taxpayer dollars saved when Hill City citizens cleaned up neighborhood parks, policed playgrounds, reduced the number of kids in youth courts, and implemented the police department's area control plan to prevent and solve crimes—did not go entirely unnoticed. This "youth movement in which the young people themselves carry on a program designed to curb juvenile delinquency has already justified its existence" with successes that ranged from "keeping youngsters out of serious trouble" to "curbing anti-social acts which yearly cost the taxpayers millions of dollars" and it functioned with "no city, state or community fund support," one journalist described. Yet even as the group theories guiding these efforts explicitly recognized young people's responsibility for changing other young people's minds—for example, in reflections on how "Boystowns are organized to develop leadership from the community itself and from the boys taking part in the program... there was to be no outside influence or organization to influence the leadership"—no one suggested that the youthful participants were their cities' expert community organizers. They were instead regarded to be joining the "sheltered" experiences that had long been open to other populations. When Omaha Boys Town founder Father Edward Flanagan, visiting Hill City, counseled Pittsburgh's civic and business community to let kids "feel they are important," unstated by implication was that they were not.[48]

Media Making and Public Relations at Republics and Beyond

As NYA Resident Training Centers, republics for African Americans, and related programs applied enduring strategies to the nation's youth problem, a new focus on media making and public relations offered participants novel occupational explorations and produced supplemental value for these youth-serving institutions and the state. Both activities had been a feature of prior republics. *Junior Citizen* had circulated in Freeville from 1898, with children writing stories, taking photos, selling ads, and printing the paper, although George occasionally used it as a platform. Pioneer editor William Dapping, unofficially adopted by Thomas Osborne, became a journalist, winning a Pulitzer Prize for reporting on the 1929 Auburn Prison riots which, ironically, undermined George's and Osborne's ideas. Other Freeville writers also went into journalism, such as John Balderston, whose article at age nine about his republic experience appeared in an early issue. Citizens also assisted with republic publicity, leading visitors around the property and speaking to audiences in New York and other cities. Similar activities became standard fare from Progress City and Boy City to Milwaukee Newsboys Republic and Boys Brotherhood Republic and beyond.[49]

What set the proliferating youth-produced media and publicity in the 1930s apart from these earlier examples was the addition of radio and, in some cases, film, and the more nuanced theoretical understanding of what these symbolic communications achieved. Earlier efforts had received minimal commentary: Ludwig Bernstein's plans for a newspaper at his Boys and Girls Cities as "a periodical for the propaganda of the principles of self-government among other orphan asylums" was a rare exception. George's decision to enlist citizens to publicize his experiment was not elaborated like other republic principles. Later, framed by developmental psychology, these activities came to be understood as guiding young people's play instincts for making miniature panoramas, toy presses, and wireless radios, impersonating peddlers and shopkeepers, and giving illustrated lectures and performances to pedagogical ends.[50]

As postwar social scientific research together with the advertising industry's commercial achievements established that a successful persuasion effort depended on changing representations as much as reality, educators and youth workers discovered that media making and public relations organized along democratic lines and with the community as central subject could complement other occupational role-plays: achieving goals for youth and aiding their institutions. Not every new juvenile democracy in the interwar era undertook such efforts. Yet what stands out in this period is just how many did—from BBR's *Reporter* and American Boys Commonwealth's *Boy Citizen* to radio broadcasts from Cortland's Junior Municipality and Omaha's Boys Town, to the multimedia efforts at NYA resident centers and republics for African American youth.[51]

At the NYA's residential centers, for example, newspapers created "an esprit de corps and loyalty toward the project of inestimable value in promoting desirable attitudes toward the program and its objectives" among center youth and outside audiences. As these activities enhanced morale and supplied opportunities for professional development, they simultaneously served the federal agency's bottom line, selling the NYA as solution to the "youth problem" and building partnerships with local agencies and private employers critical to agency programs' ultimate success. Youth-made publications circulated to other centers and the surrounding communities whose local newspapers, such as Maine's *Eastport Sentinel*, often reprinted the young journalists' reports word for word. Radio programs written and dramatically presented by enrollees first in practice studios and subsequently on local commercial broadcast stations exposed participants to novel career options while also being "designed to publicize the work being done by the NYA." These activities complemented youth governments' other publicity efforts; many elected secretaries of public relations to make center programs "better known so that its graduates may find it easier to get jobs." Gilson's suggestion to colleagues that, "In public relations work and in general contacts with outside agencies, members of the youth government can be used to represent the resident center," reflected NYA headquarters' view that the agency's most compelling advertisers were its enrollees. At Washington, D.C., headquarters, young people were assigned to poll peers about their NYA project experiences, part of the agency's larger assignment of work-study students to public relations tasks. Not all coverage was hagiographic, but public relations was a priority.[52]

Juvenile democracies for African Americans followed a similar path, albeit with fewer resources and more pressing community relations needs as these programs depended on

Figure 6.5
New York BBR *Reporter* staff.
Source: *Life of the Boys Brotherhood Republic* (Chicago: BBR, 1938).

area adults agreeing to send young offenders to child police and judges for remediation. In the *Progress City News* and *Merryburgh Journal* and the neighborhood news sections of African American newspapers in Pittsburgh and Cleveland that offered column space to child journalists, reports on republics aimed to build public support. Crime prevention was central, with the *Pittsburgh Courier* offering young officials weekly space for their "publicity focus on crime prevention" and reminding readers how to help the organization meet its goals. Hill City citizens presented news and crime prevention programs on local radio stations WWSW and KQV. In one series of broadcasts, the Hill City Players (the group's drama club) aimed at "helping the public to understand the methods used by courageous youth…in their drive to save their companions from the ill effects of bad company and petty crimes" and encouraging adults to "become aware of the future that little children's pranks often lead to unless they are corrected immediately." Crystal radio building activities for Hill City youth ensured that households could listen in. Other efforts were lower-tech: Youth City Philadelphia elected a publicity secretary to guide its public relations efforts. Hill City citizens organized mock trials for visitors. Boystown youth offered open houses so visitors could see their operations first hand.[53]

Beyond Republics

As in prior decades, change and continuity at junior republics characterized the broader American youth experience. Educators and youth workers confronting the 1930s youth crisis added media making to the now-familiar activities at schools and youth-serving institutions. Across these diverse programs, the "educational" or "recreational" features were paramount in justifications for why the primary beneficiaries were youth, obscuring how, even after the "sheltered childhood" became the nation's new normal, young people expanded their value-making activities.

The Depression was an anxious period for educational administrators as families put their children to work, pupils questioned democratic ideals, strained resources prompted layoffs, and the NYA threatened local control. How, many wondered, could schools thrive in this political and economic context? To engage the era's pupils and conserve limited resources, educators drew on Dewey's vision of schools as small-scale democratic communities and the Gary Plan's activity coordination across schools. Community education, which bridged school and life and aspired to educational efficiency by centralizing local resources in schools and making communities into classrooms, was the most prominent rubric for these efforts. Wisconsin's Atwater School showcased the varied programs undertaken under its banner. Students there

> installed a public address system in the school; built their own gymnasium…built their tennis courts, out-door volley ball courts…[with some adult help] they constructed a ball park.…The students helped create a town park; have built and operated a materials' bureau; operate their own apiary, the honey from which is used in the school lunch room. They operate a hatchery of twenty thousand egg capacity. They built a ceramics' laboratory and large kiln. In this kiln they make of local clays, and glaze in fiesta style, all the dishes used in the school lunch program.…The students have constructed a cannery which is available to the entire community and which processes one hundred thousand cans annually. Other food for the school and community (for there is little distinction at Atwater) is perfectly kept in an eighty-unit zero locker planned and operated entirely by students. One-third less food has spoiled in the Atwater district since these means of preservation have been in use.…The school too is a center for the beautification of the homes, churches and other public buildings of the district. More than one-half million ornamentals have been grown in the school's three-acre nursery.…this project has added greatly to the beauty of the area without a penny's cost…there are in the school a barber shop and a beauty parlor, and the students installed their own shower and water-heating equipment.[54]

Elsewhere, teachers and administrators piloted other programs in a similar spirit. Millburn New Jersey's High School became "a legally established unit" of the municipal welfare department, with a home economics class preparing and serving lunch in the community's day nursery and making garments for needy kids, and pupils organizing an annual charity drive. New York City students made birdhouses and planted trees for the parks department. The weather club in one Allentown, Pennsylvania, junior high provided forecasts to the entire community. Science instructors across Pennsylvania enlisted pupils in an elm tree survey for the US forestry department. In schools around the country, community needs surveys became part of the social studies curriculum. And related organizations continued such as Knighthood of Youth, Young Citizens League, junior civic leagues, and junior citizens clubs; the project method and play cities for younger kids remained popular as well.[55]

Figure 6.6
Norfolk, Virginia, school safety patrol.
Source: 1934/Charles Borjes/Virginian-Pilot/TNS. Courtesy of TNS.

In connection with these efforts, the traffic patrols that debuted in the 1920s now expanded to operate in more than 1,000 cities and towns and enroll more than 200,000 youth. Originating on a school-by-school or district-by-district basis, they were increasingly coordinated at the state level, with legislation establishing the scope of participants' activities—for example, whether or not they were permitted to stand in the street—as well as schools' liability for injury. Reflecting the declining need to copy actual government agencies, "A great variety of names" now "applied to the pupil officers...members of the guard club, members of the safety patrol, members of the service club, junior police, marshals, pupil aids, student advisers, proctors, hall monitors, traffic patrolmen, and counselors." (The Freeville republic created its own safety club in 1936.)[56]

Youth workers of the interwar period, lacking the force of compulsory education legislation, searched for ways to maintain young people's interest in their organizations. Fearful of delinquency among unengaged youth and touched by group-work trends, many continued to back programming that assigned kids to reform themselves and their peers. The civics and character education offered in Scouting and junior police took on new meaning as young people questioned the future of democracy itself.[57]

Scouting membership soared in the 1930s, including African American troops in greater numbers. Originally established to mimic explorers and pioneers and expose boys to nature's healing effects, the program had reoriented around community needs and severed links to dramatic impersonation so that youth gained "a picture of the ideal boy" rather than the ideal man as a comparison between early and mid-twentieth-century *Handbooks for Scoutmasters* makes clear. The Depression-era natural resources crisis offered opportunities for Scouts to reengage their roots. Relationships with government agencies cultivated through prior programming from radio communications to residential fire inspection paved the way for troops to plant trees, rescue wildlife, maintain roads and trails, patrol recreation areas, and halt soil erosion.[58]

New badges deepened ties to local and national governments. Recognizing, like juvenile judges and police, young people's talent for disciplining their peers, the FBI had joined the growing list of government agencies involved in education and youth work in the 1930s, praising and in some cases assisting organizations that included Boy Scouts, Girl Scouts, 4-H, and YMCA. FBI director J. Edgar Hoover, anxious about youth crime, had reached out to educators and youth workers, including Junior States of America leader E. A. Rogers, for advice on delinquency reduction and subsequently recruited youth organizations to help the agency build a civil fingerprint database. Pupils, NYA enrollees, and Hill City junior citizens were trained in fingerprinting. Scouts were the FBI's most enthusiastic partner after the national council voted in 1936 to fingerprint all Scouts and create a fingerprinting merit badge in 1938.[59]

Growing out of the city's long tradition of juvenile street cleaners, the New York City Junior Inspectors Club debuted in 1934 to enlist multiracial populations of youth in street cleaning in exchange for a recreational program of self-government, athletics, field trips, drama, a band, and weekend and summer programs. Replicating its sponsoring agency was not a priority, although the group established a self-governing Children's Congress in 1940. Staffed at first by the sanitation department and later assisted by WPA recreation workers, the program enrolled more than 150,000 participants in its early years. David Rosser, who had organized a junior city government at Christadora House, helped run the program.[60]

Junior policing surged, with African Americans participating in greater numbers. New York City's suspended program restarted as the Junior Police Athletic League, a testament to the declining importance of mirroring adult agencies or impersonating officers—also apparent in the variation among what constituted the "policework" done by youth. In Spring Lake, New Jersey, for example, boys tailed suspects: "Unsuspecting housewives, business men and even the chief himself are often shadowed by the youngsters for hours at a time." In Essex, Massachusetts, they managed traffic and patrolled streets to report misdemeanors like biking on sidewalks or breaking streetlights. Newark's had the authority to confiscate contraband. Denver's created a bike patrol and boy-administered court. By contrast, youth in Boston and in Inglewood, California, participated exclusively in sports, camps, and drills. (Like Cleveland's Boys-towns, Boston's initially used police stations' squad rooms as recreation halls but later changed venues.) Patrol activities were minimal, although physical and mental tests were sometimes conditions of participation.[61]

Across these diverse organizations, media production became increasingly common, complementing other opportunities for career explorations and directing peer pressure to build community and public opinion within these groups. Philip Cox, whose *Creative School Control* (1927) took pupils' maladjustment to modern society and the sense that democracy remained an as-yet unproven regime as its points of departure, was an early example of the many educators and youth workers who shared this view. Leaning on an older vocabulary for school activities he described how, from republics and congresses to assemblies and newspapers, school-based activities "that parallel community activities" or "reproduce within itself typical situations of social life" could improve social control inside schools in the short term and make democracy work in the longer term. Influenced by Dewey's vision of schools as miniature communities, educators' sociological emphasis on peer influences, and Lippman's distinction between "the world outside" and "the pictures in our heads," Cox reviewed activities at progressive schools where young people ordered school supplies in commercial courses and raised money to build gymnasiums. He reframed them as instruments of community building and public opinion making and, in turn, proposed that student journalism became part of a complementary "laboratory" approach.[62]

Of course, media had some history in schools and youth-serving institutions. New technologies had entered US classrooms to vitalize learning and channel kids' leisure-time interests to pedagogical ends. Pierce Fleming's 1912 observation that the cinematograph was a "substitute for that heretofore remedial weakness" of textbooks—"namely the absence of reality"—underscores how classroom technologies and role-plays shared common aims, an idea still circulating in the 1920s. From the school papers whose content was chiefly literary, to the classroom poster projects and school print shops that published government documents for school officials and local authorities during World War I, to the wireless clubs for radio building and communications, students had been making media for some time. Among youth organizations, Knights of King Arthur, Queens of Avalon, junior civic leagues, boys clubs, and playgrounds had printed newspapers and magazines such as the *King's Herald* and *Queen's Messenger*. James Rogers described the lively press club in one town where 736 child contributors published 72 issues of a playground newspaper in 1927. Scouts had formalized their radio activities with a merit badge in the 1920s, but radio building and wireless communications were widely found among the era's boys organizations.[63]

Cox's book was a harbinger of how youth media production attracted increasing attention from educators and youth workers and how their ideas about its uses drew on an older tradition of occupational role-playing even as talk of impersonation disappeared. (The movement of educators and youth workers like Harry McKown and Harry Potamkin into the media field, like William Forbush's earlier peregrinations, underscores the sense of these affinities was widely shared.) According to this view, when young people collaborated as editors, writers, printers, and production managers, the publications they produced built community and shaped public opinion among peers and bridged the campus and community. "Faculties look to the school publications as most potent instruments for stimulating and popularizing the forms of activity that are of most value to individuals and groups if they are undertaken voluntarily," Cox explained.

> If the paper capitalizes on ... a club or a home-room group in developing a library, or in contributing an original assembly program, members of other groups are stimulated to propose and carry through similar projects for their groups. Through the paper's editorials, if honest and sincere, popular sentiment and public opinion can be molded ... editorials, articles, stories, and illustrations express the community's approval of desirable behaviors and scorn of undesirable conduct.[64]

In the coming years, more educators made media part of the larger conversation about building school morale and methods of organizing the school. From the 1930s, school radio activities refocused around the technology's broadcasting applications. (Surveys put school broadcasting in at least 10 percent of city schools as of 1938.) Vocational education, engineering, English, safety, and drama instructors incorporated it into their lesson plans, with extracurricular clubs supplying further learning opportunities. Young people built equipment and studios, wrote scripts, and served as announcers and performers. Radio workshops (occasionally called radio laboratories) could be found in many institutions. Schools lacking broadcast facilities—for example in Boise, Idaho—set up "lifelike" mock studios for "imitation broadcasting" to prepare, updating the long history of simulated occupational environments such as model kitchens in educational settings.[65]

Filmmaking, which relied on equipment that young people could not easily build themselves, lacked a comparable amateur tradition. Introduced in English, drama, safety, and vocational education courses as well as through extracurricular clubs, students learned directing, publicity, and production, promoted with now-familiar rationales. "It takes teaching out of the narrow confines of the school room, and gives to the students valuable experience in 'learning to do by doing,'" Louisville, Kentucky, teacher and filmmaker Lillian McNulty explained. "One of the real purposes of a school produced motion picture is not to 'play like Hollywood' but to help vitalize some piece of literature, historical event, or community problem."[66]

Contrasting textbook learning with film, educators postulated that, by connecting with students' out-of-school interests, "the mental hygiene of the non-academic pupil can be much improved if the motion picture is utilized as an essential mode of school

Figure 6.7
Junior high students make movies, Long Beach, CA.
Source: Eleanor Child and Hardy Finch, *Producing School Movies: A Manual for Teachers and Students Interested in Producing Amateur Films* (National Council of Teachers of English, 1941).

experience...personality adjustment may well become more than a verbal objective when modern tools" were used. Most school filmmaking programs made silent 16mm films which they supplemented with live or recorded sound.[67]

Recreational youth organizations also embraced media production in light of the enthusiasm with which participants greeted these modern "occupations." The Boy Scouts expanded their media making capacities from the late 1920s when the Lone Scouts, a separate organization that later merged with the Boy Scouts of America, created press clubs across the troop network, forming a national Boy Scout Press Association and holding annual conferences from 1928. Updating earlier advice to study heroes as models for behavior, troop leaders now proposed Scouts learn about great journalists and editors. From 1927, a journalism badge required boys to publish at least one article and write many more, a goal generally achieved by serving as "a volunteer or paid reporter for a period of six weeks or until six of his items have been accepted. As a substitute for newspaper experience he may conduct an authorized amateur publication." Local papers such as Salt Lake City's *Deseret News* and the national Scouting magazine, *Boys' Life*, offered column space to the budding journalists.[68]

Scouts' radio activities, previously oriented around emergency communications, also turned to broadcasting. From the 1920s, Scout camps constructed temporary radio stations for communication and broadcasting; troops with many licensed amateurs operated stations year-round (and some even built commercial stations). These activities sparked the development of a Boy Scout Radio Network. Covering troop activities from camping trips to the national jamboree, these media shared information and created community across the network of troops and, in some cases, between Scouts and their local communities. (Notably, O. H. Benson organized some merit badge classes broadcast via radio for rural Scouts.)[69]

As national youth organizations beyond Boy Scouts, including Girl Scouts and 4-H, embraced newspaper production and radio broadcasting, some local programs such as the New York City Junior Inspectors Club did the same. From 1937, the *Spic and Span* (also called *Junior Citizen*) built morale across the network of neighborhood chapters and publicized the program. The children produced plays, music, and a variety show for municipal station WNYC. They held meetings not only in person but also over the air. Highly regarded for channeling gang energies to positive outlets and for teaching decorum and manners to urban youth, the program inspired copies in Pittsburgh and Boston.[70]

These youth-produced media covered diverse terrain—dramatizations, news and features on community organizations, and subject-related instruction. Safety education was especially popular, with on-air patrol club meetings for school safety squads and pupil police. Although a few student-produced radio programs such as Denver's *Too Young to Vote* and Pittsburgh's *Your Government* tackled current events, more often these media covered activities in schools and local settings toward cohesion at the organizational and community levels. Educators and youth workers were confident that

Figure 6.8
Junior Inspectors Club, Department of Sanitation and Street Cleaning, New York City, performing on WNYC.
Courtesy NYC Municipal Archives.

radio and film could inculcate democratic values not merely through their content but also in the production process. Radio and film clubs at schools and youth-serving institutions regularly elected officials and used parliamentary procedure. The kinds of cooperation required to plan and produce programs offered important training for "social living in a democracy," as one teacher put it.[71]

A 1942 conference on radio in informal education looked back on radio's uses in youth organizations and the value of youth engagement beyond audience roles, particularly in an era when some feared that boys' and girls' "clubs of the air" (organized around radio programs like *Junior Police Patrol*) might render traditional youth organizations obsolete. Troops of Boy Scouts and Girl Scouts, settlements, Jewish recreational groups, and YMCAs were among the many organizations giving youth production experience, Ohio State professor and radio education researcher I. Keith Tyler explained, observing how, "Radio now constitutes the common man's body of literacy. It is his newspaper, his theater, his forum, his school, his music hall, and his vaudeville." Training in media production yielded many more benefits than occupational skill building, fellow presenters declared. Building on the characterization of radio production "as a resource for the group leader" that Columbus area Scouting representative Robert Hiestand had offered, Sherman Lawton from Stephens College explained how production, even more than listening, "could help indoctrinate your members" and accomplish organizational aims. "The Mormon Church has long recognized the value of asking their own young people to act as missionaries," he noted. "Even when the young missionaries get no converts, they come back to the Mother Church full of their own teachings." Similarly, "A boy who writes a script on how to raise hogs becomes a spiritual life member of the 4-H. This chance for indoctrination of your own members through a radio workshop is a very real one."[72]

Education, Recreation, and the Continued Erasure of Work

By the 1930s, as educators and youth workers adjusted their programming to address a new generation's economic and political concerns, their interest in models and dramatizations had disappeared. A more flexible range of organizational structures for these programs was apparent as well. In this context the occasional return to an older rhetoric—for example, descriptions of Boys State as a "mythical" and "miniature" government" (or as a "medium," a turn of phrase also applied to Youth City) and BBR a "miniature civic government"—now functioned to elaborate operating structures of an "educational program" (Boys State) or "recreation program" (BBR) rather than theoretically justify a program's efficacy as a youth management tool. As youth-produced media coverage of activities such as vocational education, student senates, Scouting, and junior policing assisted in "interpreting" educational and recreational programs by reproducing situations inside classrooms and further afield, it underscored Erving Goffman's observations about the comparative nature of reality. Youth activities once regarded as mediated experiences of adulthood were now understood as authentic realities in the lives of youth, while the media employed to reproduce them eclipsed role-playing as the focus for talk about simulation in educating and socializing the next generation. These changes highlight the decline of role-plays of adulthood as a constitutive practice of the modern American youth experience as well as the narrowed public definition of media. Yet, as in earlier decades, at the same time that schools, youth-serving institutions, and the state assisted in improving the lives of the nation's youngest citizens, the benefits flowed in the other direction as well.[73]

School programs connecting students and their communities became critical public assets. Thus, when Atwater School pupils partnered with local farmers, the Farm Security Administration, the County Farm Agent, the Soil Conservation Service, and the State Forest Service, their conservation efforts "rendered twenty-eight thousand dollars worth of service within the district." Junior traffic patrols, occasionally defying state and local regulations by stationing kids in roadways, offered complementary benefits. "Ten years old and 'earning' $25,000 a year," was the 1933 estimate from the Berkeley Traffic Safety Commission that "it would require 30 policeman working several hours a day to take the place of the boys...the young policemen save $25,000 a year to the taxpayers." Activities undertaken by youth organizations in the name of civic and character education similarly served local needs. Scouts' action on natural resource protection provided vital assistance to state agencies. Florida Scouts undertook a reforestation project "in cooperation with the State Forest Service." Schenectady Scouts received 300,000 trees from the state conservation department to plant near their camp. One Albany County troop helped the Soil Conservation Service, persuading 109 property owners "to sign an agreement not to burn grassland in the spring and early summer, earning praise from the state conservation commissioner." Junior police multiplied eyes on the street and enforced laws, raising property values and freeing adult police to devote their attention to serious matters.[74]

Media making supplemented such now-familiar outcomes. As young people manufactured and maintained radio equipment and facilities; raised funds to purchase filmmaking equipment; wrote and edited newspaper stories, radio, and film scripts; served as radio and film announcers, directors, and performers; and charged fees to enjoy the media they made, they managed costs and rallied public support for schools' and youth-serving institutions' local agendas and continued operations. In Fargo, North Dakota, for example, public school radio programs director Clarence B. Wright described how

> the great numbers of children appearing on these programs throughout the year help to create an interest in the schools and their problems. These children call attention at home to the broadcasts and the parents form the habit of listening to the school programs. This fact was demonstrated several years ago when the radio programs helped markedly in bringing out a near record vote in a special school election which gave the schools an additional two mills to the regular school levy at a time when the general sentiment was in favor of lowering taxes rather than raising them.

Films served similar purposes, as articles such as "School Made Motion Pictures for Public Relations in Ohio," "Interpreting the Public Schools through Motion Pictures," and "Student Production of a Newsreel, Movie Record, or Propaganda Film" made clear.[75]

Of course, this was not the first time that young people beyond the republic movement performed service for public relations duties on behalf of schools, youth-serving institutions, and the state. Junior police and the Juvenile City League in New York City had publicized local ordinances to neighborhood adults. Pupils and Scouts had distributed government information and sold federal programs from Liberty Loans to food conservation during World War I. In the 1920s, junior chambers of commerce and junior civic leagues had enlisted participants to boost their cities, as in Madison, Wisconsin, where they published *Madison: An Interpretation by the Youth of the City* (1927). And Girl Scout cookie sales had memorably advertised that organization.

Yet media making amplified young people's voices. Thus, alongside the pupils who lobbied local politicians to finance specific educational activities were larger-scale persuasion efforts. Recognizing this subsidiary benefit, media boosters urged students and teachers to offer to produce publicity films for school administrations.

> A well-managed film of this type is ideal as a beginning, for it does have a wide audience appeal. Students are interested in seeing themselves on the screen and will pay money to do so. Parents like to see the school and their children in action. School officials like to have some graphic means of showing people what is being done in the schools. They welcome a well-planned publicity film…they are generally more interested in helping a film group make other motion pictures if the first is helpful to them. That might mean additional equipment, or money for supplies.[76]

Useful for youth-serving institutions, such developments proved vitally important for schools. In his best-selling *Propaganda* (1928), Edward Bernays had encouraged educators to embrace public relations, a proposal with greater urgency in the Depression as educators heard talk of a need to modernize despite stretched resources and felt threatened by the NYA's popular educational offerings. Lacking public relations staffs, schools depended on student media to recruit audiences to school events and rally local populations to help finance institutional needs. A tradition of community newspapers offering column space to pupil journalists, now joined by commercial radio stations offering airtime to school groups and local theaters mounting student films, supplied platforms that took kids into the community and brought the community into the classroom toward mutual understanding. Although a few questioned the value of such student productions, more common were texts such as William Yeager's *Home-School-Community Relations: A Textbook in the Theory and Practice of Public School Relations*, confirming administrators' enthusiasm for reasons beyond simply improving pupil morale.[77]

Ample evidence thus attests to the continuation, during the 1930s, of young people's value making activities, and indeed their expansion into new domains. Taking place under the auspices of schools, these varied activities were said to illustrate modern methods of experiential education following John Dewey and his student and later colleague William Kilpatrick, bridging school and community to train pupils for democratic citizenship, learn respect for the law, and improve friendly relations with local officials. Millburn pupils who administered the town's welfare programs were receiving education in citizenship. Junior traffic squads in Seattle operating in 118 schools from eight a.m. to seven p.m. daily and supervising more than 34,000,000 crossings by children each year, were "bring[ing] democracy to the classroom." And the Atwater School students' conservation efforts were paradigmatic examples of "work experience" and "study-action." This framework equally applied to their media production; Philip Cox had noted how the "popular sentiment and public opinion" touched by student media could reach beyond schools, giving the example of the *Daily Illini*, Champaign, Illinois's high school newspaper, which served as that community's paper. This suggested that when student journalists covered school activities they could achieve Dewey's ambitions for schools as embryonic communities and bridging school and life. Such curricular and extracurricular programs were decidedly not exploitative, wrote Morris Mitchell in *Progressive Education*, because "children like to do hard things if they can really do them well" and had "suffered more from the frustration of not being invited to share in solving real problems than from being overtaxed in working at them."[78]

In earlier eras, pupils who conducted health inspections, tracked down truants, took their communities' agricultural censuses, or improved neighborhoods were regarded as merely playing roles. Now a lexicon of educational benefit undercut the sense of economic exchange. Acknowledgement of the mutual gains for pupils and community institutions were typically accompanied by declarations of the careful selection of projects that prioritized learning objectives, reminders that young people were rewarded for their contributions with merit badges, free movies, and football games, or commentary on the fun had by participating youth. "Youth have a part to play," declared one compendium of 167 such programs, without mention of role-playing.[79]

When youth-serving institutions supplied the guidance, young people's economic contributions more often were seen to embody the latest knowledge on recreation, character building, and juvenile delinquency prevention—examples of how constructive leisure time and the future of US democracy were linked. Scouts engaged in conservation projects were returning to the organization's roots, demonstrating the service and patriotism that were Scouting's hallmarks. Junior police who targeted urban environments in their improvement efforts drew similar praise for altering peer norms around play. Although reports of boys playing police could still be found, more common were descriptions of the fun of supervised recreation, undercutting the economic implications in communities from Las Cruces, New Mexico, to Bauxite, Arizona, and to St. Louis, Missouri, where junior forces were paid. "I have not yet made up my mind which is more exciting—a good game of football or a good game of policing," Las Cruces football captain and junior officer Windy Hall told one reporter. Even critics took this view—for example, critical of Boston police involvement in the junior police program because it was "non police work." Media making was framed in similar terms. As dramatizations, musical performances, humor and news helped to "acquaint the public with Scouting's many phases," it was characterized by the *New York Times* as "hobby news."[80]

To be sure, public observers acknowledged community benefits from these recreational activities, sometimes with reference to work. The New Jersey Scouts who received seedlings from the Cumberland County Board of Agriculture supplied "the tools and labor—one solid week of the latter" to beautify area highways. Yet discussions of public gains were balanced with descriptions of participating youth as equal or greater beneficiaries of these programs, from the notion of "saving trees and saving boys" to the eager junior police squads who lobbied to patrol during school vacations. Thus the Florida Scouts who partnered with the State Forest Service had an explicit "double objective" to save the forest and to offer "Scouts themselves a worthwhile outdoor program to supplement camping activities and merit badge study along similar lines." According to this view, reductions in juvenile delinquency were not chiefly attributable to the actions taken by these kids to improve their environment but rather to the diversions this recreational programming supplied. The Russell Sage Foundation's later study of public relations in Scouting, which focused on adults in the organization—despite the appearance of a public relations merit badge—echoed these assessments.[81]

Taken together, this evidence underscores how age and the environments associated with it continued to shape common wisdom about the meaning of work. Activities interpreted at the time by scholars and the public and by later historians as educational and recreational alternatives to labor force participation were far more ambiguous than such descriptions suggest. Comparing the Boy Scouts' conservation activities with those of their slightly older brethren in the Civilian Conservation Corps (CCC) make this clear. CCC participants were paid for their efforts, unlike Scouts remunerated with merit badges, public praise, and access to campsites. The similarities and differences across these programs suggest the need to reread Scouts' voluntary activities, like those of so many women before them, as uncompensated work based on age-related rather than gender-related assumptions about labor force participation.[82]

Debates about the appropriateness of junior traffic patrols underscore how the meaning of work was tied to age. For even as adults overlooked the full impact of young people's activities, some expressed discomfort about the street protection services these populations undertook. A few questioned the social work orientation of police; others denounced being turned in by kids for violations. More numerous were public queries about whether young people should be policing adults—much like discussions about the suitability of women supervising men. Observers differentiated as to "whether the patrol organization attempts to have the child function as an adult or a child," critical of organizations that had children "acting as junior police," rather than "as a child in a miniature social environment" like pupil patrols who policed peers within a school building or on school playgrounds. Others raised similar questions on legal grounds. In 1926, a Boston area man took the young officer who had issued him a traffic ticket to court. The judge ruled the boy "was assuming an authority...to stop traffic as a traffic policeman" that he did not legally possess. "He assumed an authority by reason of some custom in the school to provide for the safety of children crossing the street." This judgment acknowledged that youth authority in Boston was only informal—but did not end the program with his ruling.[83]

Of course, this was not the first time adults had questioned children's public authority. From the woman who spanked a New York City junior officer to discussions about the legality of junior juvenile courts, young people's status vis-à-vis one another and adults were not settled matters. Now reports from some communities noted adult compliance with young people's informal powers—for example, in San Francisco where "the upraised hand of a student traffic officer will halt traffic...as quickly as a red light." But elsewhere legal questions were raised with greater frequency. This was the impetus for the state legislation that spelled out pupils' authority and schools' liability and in other cases prompted new complaints. Confronted with the proposal for a school patrol in 1931, San Diego School Superintendent Walter Hepner said he "does not feel like accepting the responsibility of having the children in the streets," but was overruled by other city officials. The Santa Barbara board of education rejected a similar proposal on grounds that its liability for pupils injured in the line of duty was unclear. "Patrolling of streets for the reduction of hazards to pedestrians is a function of the police department," one school board member declared. Parents were similarly reluctant—but police commissioners backed the plan.[84]

The focus of these debates on questions of legal authority and liability rather than remuneration makes clear how the work that pupils performed, like Scouts' contributions to conservation, carried a different status from the same activities when assigned to adults. A few years later when student traffic patrols were being used in more than 3,100 US cities, labor leaders from the Congress of Industrial Organizations joined the conversation as forty-five California municipalities met to discuss the matter, "demanding that able-bodied men be employed." But this exception proved the rule.[85]

The invisibility of young people's media making and public relations activities in addressing the era's youth crisis and promoting the importance of schools and youth organizations is striking in light of the widespread recognition, at the time, of the significance of peer influence, of media making and public relations as increasingly common career choices, and of paid child performers. It is particularly notable when the recognition among later media scholars of the panoply of media betterment and propaganda literacy programs for young people that followed the Payne Fund Studies is taken into account. As surveys reported young people preferred to *produce* rather than to *listen* or *watch*, several organizations that scholars associate with "media betterment" helped young people learn media making, from Young Reviewers and 4-Star clubs (also called Scholastic Photoplay Clubs) to Scholastic Radio Guilds. Payne Fund Study participants, including Edgar Dale and Frederic Thrasher, promoted these activities. "Perhaps one of the greatest contributions of the school-made film is that those who produce them are in a real-life situation," Ohio State University professor Dale observed. Thrasher, eager to avoid merely the "passive absorption of the spectacular and dramatic actions of others," undertook similar media making experiments to reduce "the universal American disease of 'spectatoritis'" with slightly older students after joining the NYU faculty. In short, young people's directed engagements with media went far beyond learning to be savvy audiences; equally they learned to make media as persuasive tools, persuading themselves and their communities about the benefits of a range of youth programming and the value of democracy itself.[86]

Histories of the New Deal have detailed the Roosevelt administration's expansive efforts to market its alphabet soup of programs, from the placement of projects around the country to the launch of a US Film Service, and the growing importance in this period of "interpreting" government and social service agencies' problem definition and solutions for clients and taxpayers alike. The stories of young people's activities in the NYA Resident Training Centers, police-sponsored republics, public schools, and Scouts makes clear how vital to the government's publicity strategy—as well as the strategies of nongovernmental youth organizations—were the many local efforts that assigned young people responsibility for interpretation. As public-relations broadcasting became the most common type of radio and film activity at schools and youth agencies, other government officials sought ways to work with kids. From the Department of the Interior, which encouraged schools in one conservation area "to write and produce radio programs dealing with the local conservation project," to the Texas Agricultural Extension Agency, which assigned youth to inform farmers about novel conservation methods, to one small Western town, which "turned over the work of advertising the city to the younger generation" as part of its "juvenile city" activities, a few federal and local agencies were even more direct in these ambitions to use young people to interpret their programs—updating a longer history of young people's community-based information work. In an era when, as Mary Swain Routzahn of the Russell Sage Foundation Department of Social Work later explained, public relations work was "widely accepted as an essential accompaniment to any public service" and yet "many agencies are unable or reluctant to seek funds to provide for necessary staffs and materials," educators, youth workers, and local officials followed long-standing precedent and turned to young people instead.[87]

Conclusion: The Legacies of William R. George

This book has argued that the history of the junior republic movement recasts our understanding of the transformation from family economy to sheltered childhood in the United States by placing performance at the center of the story. New evidence about individuals and institutions including Wilson Gill and Willis Brown, school cities and school republics, Boy Cities and Boystowns, together with rereadings of familiar subjects from G. Stanley Hall's recapitulation theory of child development and John Dewey's vision of experiential education, to the shared priorities of schools, juvenile courts, playgrounds, and police, bring to light how developmental psychologists, educators, and youth workers applied the theory and practice of role-playing to defining and managing young people in the modern age. Although scholars have recognized that, with assistance from an interconnected network of experts, these populations acquired a new sense of self and circumscribed their actions during this period, previous accounts have missed how dramatic encounters with adult occupations figured alongside more protected experiences in the story to comprise the "double lives" of modern youth. The popularity of William George's total simulated societies for youth—junior republics and, later, junior municipalities—makes clear how a broad range of activities with dual status as real and not real that included student congresses, children's gardens, vocational education, model cottages, junior street cleaning leagues, and juvenile traffic patrols figured in the construction and maintenance of modern childhood and adolescence in America.

Situating the discourse of "miniature" and "reproduction" that linked these youth activities to a cultural context in which living villages, winter gardens, and historical reenactments proliferated and human scientists viewed imitation as a central feature of individual and societal development helps to explain their mass popularity over several decades and why young people were drawn to programming that aimed to copy life experiences from which they were being separated in the real world. Recognizing the affinities between educational entertainments and the discourses about impersonating adults in child development that guided these programs equally calls attention to how the claims about the proximity and distance between reality and representation that popularized homemaking in model cottages and policing delinquency in city streets worked to produce the category of youth. Indeed, it was these activities that were the most common genre of mediated activity with which youth engaged: participatory performances of adulthood that offered instruction in white, middle-class values, gendered social expectations, and models of democracy and citizenship that obscured as much as they revealed. These pairings of virtual adulthood and sheltered childhood proved popular in a period when expectations about youth behavior were changing, when psychologists recognized a developmental imperative for children to impersonate adults and when vicarious experiences were viewed as real enough to adjust young people to society as it was but unreal enough to reassure adults that kids were not actually undertaking adult activities.

In light of the dominant sheltered childhood narrative, such activities' common features with better-documented educational entertainments have not been part of previous accounts. Yet prominent developmental psychologists, educators, and youth workers saw equivalencies between Scouting, in which "the lad thinks of himself as a pioneer and enacts through a skillful variety of exercises many of the resourceful habits of the early explorers," and the stereoscope which "enables the imaginative youth, or adult even, to enter so vividly into foreign experiences and customs as to constitute, if but briefly, actual experiences of travel." Later social scientists similarly clumped youth organizations, including Scouts, with radio and film as techniques of "propaganda" and "mediums of education." The shifting lexicon that accompanied the spread of these youth activities—from "models" and "dramatizations" to "education" and "recreation"—made it difficult to see these links. Revisiting the alternative worldview of a bygone era points us to how people, activities, and institutions that have traditionally been the province of historians of childhood equally belong in histories of performance and media toward a broader understanding of these fields. This plethora of dramatic techniques mediating experience that existed in parallel with the print, radio, and film technologies—what Edgar Dale later referred to as the "cone of experience"—are methods that persist to the present day even as their full histories remain to be told.[1]

As important as the contributions to young people's self-disciplining were the ways that the routinization of role-playing grew the capacities of youth-serving institutions and the state. From within the confines of restricted settings and identities, children and adolescents produced economic value for the people and institutions most closely associated with removing them from the economy and public life and subsequently did the same for their communities, revealing that with the spread of role-plays of adult life came the spread of assumptions that activities with chiefly developmental value were taking place. Late nineteenth-century reformatories had been criticized for exploiting youth for free labor; in this constellation of organizations and activities, by contrast, young people were celebrated for engaging in variations on occupations that they would be criticized for doing for pay in the "real world." When these populations built facilities, prepared meals, administered programs, disciplined peers, and made media for public relations purposes under adult supervision at junior republics, schools, and youth-serving institutions, they and their supervisors were applauded for implementing the latest scientific theories of learning and play—preparing for the future and learning values lost from the erasure of work. Rare were the occasions when the possibility of exploitation was entertained. Even when observers employed the language of "work" and "production" to describe these goods and services, such activities did not hold the status of child labor.

Discovering the ways in which child labor was redirected and redescribed, these findings thus complicate conventional understandings of how actors in the story of the transition from family economy to sheltered childhood behaved. They reveal economic implications of the contributions to performance theory and practice from developmental psychologists, educators, and youth workers such as G. Stanley Hall and John Dewey who circumscribed the boundaries of work as much as play as they shaped public understandings of relationships between reality and representation in modern life. They document how the schools and youth-serving institutions ostensibly devoted to child protection depended on young people for their construction and maintenance and how the professionalization of experts in education and youth work was inseparable from the "deskilling" of youth—that the populations these experts aimed to free from the labor force shared much in common with workers encouraged to become less proficient over time. And, in identifying public officials' contributions to youth programs and ambiguous positions on child labor, they point to how the histories of child reform and government reform were closely intertwined.

In short, this history of youth and the state flips the narrative to reveal not only how the welfare state constructed youth but also how youth constructed the welfare state, identifying schools and playgrounds, courts and police, street cleaning and street trades among the myriad agencies that developed symbiotic relationships with youth to their mutual benefit. Recuperating the deep history of state interest in everyday performance makes clear how the influences of young people's experiences at the George Junior Republic on what George called the "greater republic" went far beyond what he and his colleagues anticipated. Of course, activities such as health inspection, truant tracking, traffic management, food conservation, and public relations offered the citizenship training that program organizers claimed. Yet these activities' systematic adoption to compensate for a lack of resources, and in many cases the later replacement of kids by paid adults, underscores how civic education was neither their sole nor primary rationale. Moving beyond stories of how citizen participation can become political cooptation, the evidence presented here reveals its hidden economic dimensions.

Continuity and Change in World War II

Resonances between life inside George's junior republic and the American republic continued into World War II. With the sheltered childhood as national norm, wartime propaganda trumpeted how America was protecting its precious youth, and educational and recreational activities increasingly emphasized future preparation. Yet in Freeville and beyond, the nation's educators, youth workers, and public officials chose to scale back rather than eliminate young people's economic contributions to the institutions that sheltered them and in turn to the American state.[2]

Over the four decades of his involvement in the junior republic movement, George had been a public booster for American youth. His attitudes to their capacities had evolved, however, as in his decisions to replace Freeville's citizen-hoteliers with adult cottage "parents" and to increase voting age from 12 to 16. During the dustup with Warner Brothers, George had used Richard Welling's formulation of "citizen-student" to counter the suggestion the institution was a reformatory, continuing this educational talk in the last years of his life. This framework shaped the republic's retooling during World War II as it lost many male citizens to war industries and military service, recruited more female citizens, expanded athletics, and added vocational training for war industries, including mechanics, aviation, woodworking, and electricity. Describing the "student controlled…educational town" in 1943, the *Christian Science Monitor* reported how the republic's emphasis on learning by doing rather than academic training alone was well suited to postwar reconstruction. The importance of civic education in ensuring a solid future for American democracy was also stressed. "Indifferent and useless citizens are responsible for today's chaotic world situation," explained Lyman Beecher Stowe. "France was a victim of sleeping sickness, and that must not happen here." Although, during the conflict, republic programming was less directly war-related and more future-focused than in World War I, when Atlantic Woolen Mills opened a war industry on campus and older girls moved to Syracuse for government munitions work, Freeville's junior citizens continued to participate in an economic system—in particular, increasing farm output by one-third to bring in additional income and helping nearby farmers on account of a local labor shortage. Fewer differences than previously presumed separated the young people who chose to work in war industries or jobs vacated by adults from those who remained in supervised settings—even as these institutions' economic activities were reduced.[3]

Developments in Freeville point to subtle shifts across other republics, schools, and youth-serving institutions during the war. African American republics reorienting their programs to the national emergency added new activities that highlighted their commitment to American democracy while sustaining their earlier sense of purpose supplying supervised recreation. Policing gave way to civil defense as the priority for Cleveland's Boystowns, heralded during the conflict as a leading "leisure time organization" for minority youth. Hill City added first aid training and raised funds for an ambulance to serve neighborhood populations. Youth City, Philadelphia's first "recreation center for black youth," was most vocal in its patriotism, arranging vocational training for war jobs, a bugle and drum corps, and entertainment for African American servicemen. Director Samuel Evans, who insisted that African Americans could love their country without loving its wrongs, became coordinator of "colored activities" for the city's branch of the US Department of Physical Training of the US Office of Civilian Defense. Unfortunately, continuing financial difficulties led Youth City to shut down in 1943, one of several republics (including Cottage Row and Progress City) that collapsed around World War II.[4]

Police and housing agencies organized several new juvenile democracies for African American and racially mixed neighborhoods in the early 1940s, and their programming aligned with these broad-brush trends. (Still more were planned, but never fully operational.) First aid training and civil defense were less common than traditional recreational activities, delinquency prevention efforts that organizers believed helped a nation at war, as mothers entered the labor force leaving many youth unsupervised and as race relations came to be understood in national security terms. Washington, DC, police officer Oliver Cowan, seeing boys "getting in trouble because they had nothing better to do," devoted himself to creating "better" leisure activities by organizing the Junior Police and Citizens Corps. His federation of more than 150 small groups transformed gangs into junior police squads and subsequently into juvenile democracies whose main activities centered on a buffet of recreational options including athletics, drill corps, orchestra, chorus, and newspaper (the *Youthtown News*), and crime prevention. Trained in sociology at Howard and NYU, Cowan was guided by academic theory, using spot maps of criminal activity to site the groups and persuading gang leaders to participate, with the expectation they would recruit other youth. More than 10,000 participated. The personal and community improvement that followed even as the corps operated "with "no money, no buildings, and no outside support"—for example, a 50 percent drop in crime in one precinct over four months—attracted substantial publicity and copies in other locations.[5]

Chicago officials, eager to build community in the city's recently constructed housing projects, were first to install youth self-government to enhance these institutions' self-conception as "children's cities" and reduce potential delinquency on site. Like the Junior Police and Citizens Corps, in the Junior Municipality of Wellstown (at the Ida B. Wells Homes public housing project), Altgeld Junior State (at Altgeld Gardens), Cabrini Junior City (at Cabrini Green), and Lathrop Junior City (at the Julia Lathrop homes), organizers and participants focused not on duplicating some adult referent so much as on recreation and the need for "something better to do." Wellstown mayor Adolf Slaughter explained to a meeting of the National Association of Housing Officials how that "junior city is not run so much to punish the kids in their own courts, as to give them something to do so that they won't have to be punished."[6]

California housing officials followed with San Francisco Junior City for the children of war workers populating the Hunters' Point housing project and surrounding neighborhoods, more than a thousand in all. "The kids like to keep busy," reported African

Figure 7.1
Jelna Carr opening the meeting of the Wellstown aldermen 1942. Ida B. Wells Homes housing project, Chicago, Illinois. J. Delano, photographer.
Source: Library of Congress Prints and Photographs Division.

American child mayor Horace Peppers on the rich activity program that included a newspaper (*Junior City News*), a radio program hosted by the local CBS affiliate ("Mayor of the Air," a case study for the textbook *Interpreting Social Welfare*), and a Junior Employment Service to place older youth in part-time jobs. "There's always something to interest us here, and we know what we do will be appreciated. We're treated like adults and we work like adults." Peppers's comments about work aside, the value made was chiefly in its delinquency prevention, because according to one report, more than two years into its operation, police had little to do, the city attorney had never had a case, and the judges had not yet had occasion to hold a session of court. Program administrator Burt Kebric prepared a bibliography on boystowns and junior cities for the National Association of Housing Officials to help get similar projects off the ground.[7]

Not every republic fit this pattern. Residential training centers, initially created to advance the NYA's ambition "to fit youth into the world about them" and to diffuse "social dynamite," shifted their attention to war production when the Federal Security Administration

Figure 7.2
"Mayor of the Air," San Francisco Junior City mayor Horace Peppers (left).
Source: Helen Cody Baker and Mary Brayton Swain Routzahn, *How to Interpret Social Welfare: A Study Course in Public Relations* (New York: Russell Sage, 1947). Courtesy Russell Sage Foundation.

assumed operational responsibilities in 1939. Education for preparedness and democratic living continued across agency programs with the language of learning by doing, vocational education, and student government as points of pride in the fight against totalitarian states. At the centers, opportunities for self-governance expanded to include a federation of youth governments, worker leadership, and youth representatives to a national advisory committee. Keeping equipment in continuous use lest it be reallocated to war production and manufacturing articles to military specification, these communities of older youth made economic contributions to national needs on a comparatively outsized scale. Staff, enrollees, and labor leaders shared the understanding that the centers broke bottlenecks in the labor supply by reducing on-the-job education required when youth "graduated" to actual wartime industry employment while manufacturing goods that private industry was "unable to supply in sufficient quantities to meet current needs." Although the agency failed in its effort to push the analogy to schools to its logical conclusion and avoid paying taxes, most opponents did not doubt its "educational" orientation; they merely called for transferring its activities to the nation's schools. (The

Figure 7.3
National Youth Administration girls and their citizenship instructor at the Good Shepherd community center, Chicago (south side), Illinois, April 1941. Russell Lee, photographer.
Source: FSA-OWI Collection, Library of Congress Prints and Photographs Division.

American Youth Congress was an exception, taking issue with what it called the FSA's "forced labor battalions" and offering a counter-proposal for a "real program for jobs and training.") School administrators' fears of an NYA takeover proved unfounded when the agency collapsed on just these grounds in 1943.[8]

FBI director J. Edgar Hoover, whose agency was actively investigating radical youth organizations, enthusiastically supported the republic movement during the military conflict. This was part of his broader interest in how organized youth programs could complement FBI objectives. (Hoover was elected a national director of the Boys Clubs of America in 1943.) He spoke at Omaha Boys Town's commencement exercises about its valuable programs. The FBI sponsored film screenings for the Junior Police and Citizens Corps and called for their expansion to every community in the country. Agents worked with boys in several chapters of Boys State, and trained the San Francisco Junior

City police squad. The agency even hired republic organizers to its staff. For example, James Robinson, who replaced Howard McKinney as Hill City director when McKinney left for army service in 1943, was added to the FBI payroll the following year.[9]

From Prisons and Factories to Internment Camps

Drawing praise over five decades for helping immigrants, Native Americans, and African Americans adjust to the "American way of life," sponsored by judges, police, and the FBI, and still a point of reference for criminology and corrections professionals, during World War II the junior republics that had inspired adult programs at prisons and factories also provided a blueprint for the internment camps that detained thousands of Japanese Americans. These influences did not result from personal contacts but rather underscore how ideas about democracy and discipline remained in the air. The US War Relocation Authority's (WRA) insistence that the camps become self-governing and self-sufficient (and, in some cases, that the schools inside them teach youth self-government) underscores federal officials' continuing embrace of principles and practices made popular by William George. Equally it points to how economic factors were never far from disciplinary ones in motivating state interest in the republic idea. From the program's inception, WRA staff took the approach that Navy Surgeon General Ross McIntire called "the liberal democratic way of management" to "show that the United States could carry out a program of evacuation and relocation in a democratic manner that would provide the greatest possible contrast to population shifts in Axis countries." And because "the more efficient and self regulating the administration makes the community, the fewer guards and soldiers will be needed," this left more men free for frontline action.[10]

Federal officials' initial vision for these total institutions was model communities that could "convert the Center from an item of government expense into an asset." Evacuees' community governments would take "responsibility for the civic management of the colony," administering local agencies, including courts, fire, and police, businesses, and recreational activities such as newspaper, athletics, Scouts, and entertainment. Federal officials detailed these plans:

> Through agriculture and industry these communities would become nearly self-supporting, and that there would be a measurable degree of local government.... The economic development would include the production of agricultural products not only for internal consumption, but also for distribution through regular market channels, and the establishment of factories that would engage entirely in war production. The necessary social services would be provided largely through recruitment from the evacuees. The hospitals, schools, police, fire, maintenance, and other activities would be largely evacuee staffed and directed.

This arrangement was to offer "an equitable substitute for the life, work, and homes given up, and to facilitate participation in the productive life of America both during and after the war."[11]

Legal obstacles thwarted the plan to give camp governments the status of local governments outside the camps—like Native American reservations in the 1930s or Omaha's Boys Town. Officials subsequently restricted voting and office holding to US citizens, and made community governments subsidiary to federal administrators. Later, work programs placing evacuees in jobs outside the camps replaced camp-based industries. With authority resting outside of their group, and work programs compensating them at unfairly low rates when compared with local staff wages, evacuees followed the precedents of prison inmates and protested these conditions. Government officials were disheartened but simultaneously fascinated by how the comparative robustness of self-government organizations affected how these disturbances played out. At Manzanar, with a weak community government, the administration called in military police. At Poston, by contrast, the community organization negotiated peacefully with administrative staff. These developments vivified the disciplinary powers of democracy and highlight persistent similarities between American strategies for managing prisoners and educating and socializing youth.[12]

Beyond Republics

The experiences of participants across the field of junior republics during World War II underscore both continuity and change in the lives of American youth. At the same time that beliefs persisted that the best way to ensure a stable future democracy was to enable young people to practice it and that peers did more to influence behavioral norms than adults, duplicating some adult referent in the organization of programming for these populations became subsidiary to actively engaging them—with the result that young people's economic activities were much reduced. Compared to the American youth experience during World War I, or the women of World War II, for whom the reality of taking on male jobs conflicted with the rhetorical redefinition of these positions as feminine, domestic service for the nation, at Freeville and beyond the rhetoric and reality of child protection grew more closely aligned. These trends were apparent across the broader landscape of educational and recreational programming as well.[13]

Although, at first glance, students' experiences in World War II shared much in common with those of the generation in school during the World War I, key differences highlighted transformations in social expectations. Certainly, once again students of all ages encountered the war in the curriculum, with younger students finding problems in math, geography, and other subjects framed in terms of war, and vocational subjects for war industries dominated the upper grades from 1942. Community school projects reoriented to wartime needs, for example with students taking on responsibility for publicizing conservation measures to local populations. And civic education and "world mindedness" were also stressed.[14]

Yet a closer look at how the curriculum brought the war inside schools finds teachers and administrators prioritized future-oriented training and scaled back the production of military supplies. John Studebaker's shift from heading the Junior Red Cross in the 1910s (which hijacked classrooms to produce millions of articles) to his leadership of the US education commission's newly organized High School Victory Corps in the 1940s (which asked students to pledge commitment to further their educations) encapsulated the changing common wisdom about the ideal youth experience. Students' economic activities did not entirely disappear, but as the older view that such adult-like activities vitalized the curriculum was superseded by growing unease among educators that these additions to the school day were incompatible with schools' basic mission, value production—for example, selling war bonds and stamps, collecting salvage, competing in poster-making contests for federal agencies, and producing public opinion in student newspapers—increasingly shifted to extracurricular and vacation activities. (The Junior Red Cross, which had coordinated school activities during World War I, became largely associated with weekend or school break projects in World War II.) Radio and film making programs dropped off substantially; those that survived covered subjects such as "the dangers of loose talk in a democracy" and "interpreting the news.") This paralleled developments at the NYA, which reduced radio broadcasting in its centers so that national security needs could take priority for spectrum use.[15]

The wartime activities of junior police, Boy Scouts, Girl Scouts and Girl Reserves, and new organizations such as the American Youth Reserves (established by the US Office of Civil Defense) and the Junior Citizens Service Corps (established by the Civilian Defense Corps), also initially appeared to replicate youth participation in the first World War as these organizations directed participants to sell liberty loans, bonds, and stamps; cultivate war gardens and farms; entertain and feed service members; distribute posters and deliver messages for government agencies; collect paper and metal for recycling; serve as hospital aids and junior air raid wardens; cook meals and babysit for female war workers; raise money for soldiers and kids in war areas; and help with harvesting during school vacations. Indeed, when compared to in-school activities, their economic contributions to the wartime economy were more readily apparent. Boy Scouts and junior police stepped up "to assist short-handed regular police and Senior Auxiliary Police in handling crowds and traffic" and serve as poll watchers. Girl Reserves filled places of older workers in "making black-out candles, knitting afghans, tending children, serving as clinical aides, and performing innumerable other wartime tasks into which their teenage zest and ingenuity lead them." The Girl Scouts presented President Roosevelt with a "check" for "15,430,000 hours service in war work." In fact, the nation faced a youth worker shortage as hordes of eager boys and girls found a dearth of available adults to supervise their out-of-school activities. (The number of Boy Scout leaders and former Scouts in military service was a source of frequent comment.) Youth participation in organizations that simulated military occupations was, by contrast, reduced; from the late 1930s youth organizations lacking formal endorsement from the armed forces had been forced to drop terms like "navy" from their names.[16]

Yet as these recreational activities offered young people opportunities to make contributions to the war, they too were touched by changing social expectations. Despite occasional claims of history repeating itself—for example, observations of Scouts' long history of service, or that youth were substitutes for adults—young people's out-of-school wartime participation looked distinctly different from adults' voluntary service and from the experiences of youth in World War I. Raising questions about the appropriateness of such undertakings with greater frequency, adults restricted many programs to older teens fifteen or sixteen and above, limiting younger boys and girls to "preparedness" activities: learning first aid skills, improving physical fitness, knowing what to do in an emergency, and training for service as junior air raid wardens, or "to act as messengers in the event of communication failures"—in short, endorsing future-oriented programming as inside the nation's schools. Simultaneously they stressed the importance to the war effort of young people's more indirect contributions, from learning about the democratic system to cultivating world-mindedness and improved race relations, to just being kids. As a Girl Scouts spokesperson told the *New York Times*, "Sending a little girl out to do a big girl's job is a pitfall into which the national Girl Scout organization is determined not to fall in adapting the Scout program to the war."[17]

Of course, there were exceptions to these larger patterns. Although the civic training such activities supplied typically reinforced the status quo, some groups for predominantly African American youth protested racial conditions in a context of African American service overseas and at home—for example, the Harlem-based junior police troops who demanded the federal government do more to prevent lynchings. There were schools that opted for curricular activities that hewed more closely to older precedents of war production, such as sewing and woodshop classes in several communities that made military articles or Junior Red Cross programs integrated into the curriculum, as in Hartford, Connecticut. Schoolboy patrols in Los Angeles directly replaced the adult crossing guards who left for war work with more than 14,000 eleven and twelve year olds. Yet if during the earlier conflict educators and youth workers had used the rhetoric of models and dramatizations to obscure how the activities they embraced were building their institutions and American state capacity, now more prioritized youth protection. As a result, some who made other choices—like Sabra Holbrook of New York City's Youth Builders, which rallied kids to learn how to stop rumors, make films and radio programs, and include themselves "in work which the government has already defined as necessary"—were forced to scale back their ambitious wartime programming on account of how it conflicted with changing social expectations.[18]

Rethinking the Sheltered Childhood

The recognition that it was under the auspices of precisely those institutions associated with child protection that young people produced value and that such ambiguities remained long after the sheltered childhood became the norm invites new questions about the economic implications of youth programs in the decades since World War II. Histories of household labor that articulate the economic value of women's uncompensated activities have called attention to the lasting legacy of the century-old decoupling of productivity from domesticity. For example, the value created by full-time homemakers and caregivers inside spaces that once defined national productivity remain unaccounted for in present-day official figures which separate caregiving from home-based businesses for purposes of taxation and GDP. What, then, of the activities inside schools and youth-serving institutions and the supervised programs beyond their borders in recent years?[19]

Young Americans may not prepare cafeteria meals, perform community maintenance activities, serve as crossing guards, discipline peers, or make publicity with the same frequency as in earlier decades. Yet evidence suggests that adult administrators and staff are not the only ones making value in educational and recreational contexts. From to unpaid internships for academic credit to contemporary configurations of junior police, teen courts, school patrols, youth councils, and student media; from the cookie sales that sustain the Girl Scouts organization to the college athletes who bring in millions to their universities; from student service learning projects at schools of design and public administration that supply free consulting to local governments, to beta testing software in schools and after-school programs, from the controversies around unionizing graduate teaching assistants, to Boy Scouts' extensive service projects to the US National Park Service, educational and recreational programs that develop young people's human capital for later application are not without present-day value. Century-old assumptions that work is defined by who is doing it and where it is taking place persist, however—for example, the idea that a distinction should be drawn between schools or other preparatory experiences and the "real world." Armed with historical insights, we can begin a new conversation about the state of childhood in America in which young people's capabilities and accomplishments take center stage.[20]

Epilogue: What Happened to Junior Republics?

At a 1956 meeting of the US Senate Judiciary Committee, officials heard a proposal to transform the decommissioned naval air station at Squantum, Massachusetts, into a Boys Town. Twelve veterans had organized as Massachusetts Boys Town, Inc., six years earlier but lacked a site to implement their plans. A national program for preventing delinquency through "citizenship training" and "good group activities" would greatly assist needy youth, the men argued, reviewing the history of George Junior Republics, Omaha's Boys Town, and similar institutions as they explained how putting former military bases to use for youth self-government programs across the United States would reduce future crime and strengthen community stability. Each boy would "[play] a part in the actual administration of security, justice, welfare, and so on in his own community" and "learn at firsthand through participation something about the governmental processes." And since, in such an organization, "a good deal of the work could be done under the shop man with the boys participating," taxpayer costs would be limited.[1]

This proposal for a nationwide network of state-sponsored communities for boys was not the only evidence of interest in the republic movement's postwar expansion. As part of the American occupation of Germany, the US State Department, with assistance from Richard Welling, exported self-government as it restructured the educational system to be more democratic. In the worlds of George Junior Republic business advisor Donald Stralem, the republic idea was "being used now...to rehabilitate the young in conquered areas." The United Nations Educational, Scientific, and Cultural Organization (UNESCO) organized several self-governing children's communities to ease the psychological and economic adjustment for war orphans—among them, Pestalozzi Children's Village and Gaudiopolis.[2]

Yet as these developments signaled the possibility that George might garner posthumous acclaim, the fading memory of his contributions already apparent before the war blunted the long-term impact of the republic movement in the US and farther afield. George had long faced difficulties controlling the movement he started on account of the proliferation of school republics, boy cities, junior towns, and other variations on his republic idea. His perfectionist critiques of such adaptations, together with his criticisms of public interpretations of his work—for example, that Freeville was not a reformatory—had further undermined his efforts to garner credit for the basic principles that influenced practices from schools to prisons. Once a household name, by the mid-twentieth century George was increasingly forgotten, even among those who followed his work.[3]

Memories of George faded further after World War II, particularly following the 1946 death of Welling, one of his greatest boosters. Stralem was among the few Americans to publicize connections between Europe's postwar schools and youth-serving institutions and George's stateside activities. With rare exceptions, most citing Father Flanagan's Boys Town, the organizers of Europe's children's communities claimed themselves inheritors of a European tradition originating with Johann Heinrich Pestalozzi and Friedrich Froebel, even as that "tradition" was first chronicled thanks to junior republics' broad diffusion including earlier European experiments to copy William George's work. Although, like the Creel Committee before it, the US Information Agency publicized the Freeville republic in materials circulating overseas, its efforts did not rebalance public assessments.[4]

Figure 8.1
Boys Republic, Italy.
Source: *La Repubblica dei Ragazzi* (Il Villagio del Fanciullo a Santa Marinella), 1948.

Epilogue

In this context, the 1956 hearings—and the Senate's rejection of the veterans' proposal—underscore how William George's popular standing had further diminished and how efforts to establish additional republics on US soil, even under the auspices of the Boys Towns which had superseded republics in public dialog, had grown increasingly rare. Although, amidst the conflict, the anticipation of a postwar juvenile delinquency crisis had mobilized new republics like San Francisco Junior City, this argument had limited traction after the war—and not merely on account of popular amnesia about the movement's founders. With the decline of imitative play and the popularity of mass media alternatives to other youth activities, with changing neighborhoods surrounding campuses and clubhouses and changing ideals of citizenship in which consumption rather than production was a dominant value, aspects of the American youth experience were shifting even before the war accelerated, making junior republics less appealing to adults and youth than in earlier years. Other developments—for example, mental health professionals' reorientation to treating "problem" youth in shorter outpatient programs rather than longer residential stays, as well as legal controversies about inmates doing institutional maintenance as part of treatment regimens—compounded incentives against expanding the republic idea. More general social expectations about the limited capacities of youth that characterized the sheltered childhood, some based on generational change in young people's skill set, were contributing factors as well.[5]

As a result, US educators and youth workers witnessed the republic movement's fadeout in the postwar period. Few new republics were started, and a number of those created before or during the war closed their doors. Chicago's Boys Brotherhood Republic, facing financial troubles and changing neighborhood demographics, was absorbed by the Young Men's Jewish Council in 1946 and merged a decade later with two organizations for mostly African American youth to create Chicago Youth Centers, a recreational institution for whom civic dramatization was not a priority. Youth self-government programs in Chicago and San Francisco housing projects, with the exception of Altgeld Junior State, ceased their operations in the late 1940s.[6]

Other US-based republics continued—the George Junior Republics in New York, Connecticut, California, and Pennsylvania; the New York City Boys Brotherhood Republic; Boys Towns in Omaha and Cleveland; San Jose's Boys City Boys Club; Pittsburgh's Hill City; Washington, D.C.'s Junior Police and Citizens Corps; and Boys and Girls States around the country—albeit with changes to their programming in many instances. Some followed prewar trends in Freeville to remake themselves into specialized educational institutions. Learning by doing continued, for example at Grove City, where, after administrators purchased buildings from the War Assets Administration, the youth dismantled them, transported the material to the republic, and subsequently reassembled them there. Litchfield Junior Republic, now regarded as the "only boarding trade school in Connecticut," was widely admired for organizing "the ultimate in effective student government." Staff and students shared their expertise with peers from across Connecticut when they hosted the first statewide conference on student government in 1951.[7]

Back in Freeville, however, the institution's educational orientation was joined by the welfare orientation that superintendent Donald Urquart preferred. Psychiatrists were a growing presence there as administrators retooled as an alternative to public schooling for "disturbed" and "troubled" teens. Although these new personnel endorsed William George's founding principles of self-government and a token economy, the republic's practical operations looked very different in a context where the staff-to-citizen ratio stood at 50 to 120, and later 85 to 185—responding both to the changing population and to changing ideas about kids. On hiring a social worker as its new director the Litchfield republic took steps in the same direction, adding specialized services such as a social work department, psychiatric and psychological counseling, and case workers to its staff. Similar trends could be seen in Detroit's Ford Republic and Omaha's Boys Town as these institutions deepened relationships with welfare and medical professionals.[8]

Even as George's remaining republics maintained earlier ambitions to duplicate American society on a smaller scale, with economic activities at the center, local attention from media, scholars, and other observers to the surviving individual institutions grew detached from talk of a broader movement as well as from the component and allied activities such as vocational education and junior policing that once had been seen as programs based on common principles to be discussed in an integrated conversation. Europe's children's communities sustained the most active conversations on youth self-government—albeit largely without attention to William George. In the coming decades, a few prominent educators would offer proposals to model future schools on the George Junior Republic. Scattered miniature communities—from Kinderspielstadt in Germany to Safety Villages in Canada—continued aspects of the idea in camps, playgrounds, and other educational and recreational contexts.[9]

As Freeville staff continued their work with increasingly troubled youth, they suspended the self-government that had brought the republic worldwide renown. A name change in 2005, to the William George Agency for Children's Services, cemented the shift in emphasis. The "village like any other" thus no longer exists. But even in its absence, George's lasting impact on childhood in America remains.

Notes

Introduction

1. James Muirhead, *The United States, with Excursions to Mexico* (Leipzig: Karl Baedeker, 1904), 236–237; Muirhead, *The United States, with Excursions to Mexico* (Leipzig: Karl Baedeker, 1909), 146. Baedeker guides were published in several European languages.

2. Muirhead (1909), 146.

3. William George, "Self-Government as a Means of Moral Education," *Junior Republic Citizen* 17, no. 4 (1915): 7; William George, *The George Junior Republic, Its History and Ideals* (New York: Appleton, 1910), 180–181; Frances Keefe, "The Development of (Daddy) George's Educational Ideas and Practices from 1866 to 1914," EdD dissertation, Cornell University, 1967, 116; "Boys Who Play at Government," *Washington Post*, September 28, 1897; "Boys Hold Election To-day: Free City Government in Miniature in Hebrew Asylum a Success," *New-York Tribune*, July 4, 1910; "Community's 'Boys' Town Elects City Officials,'" *Cleveland Call and Post*, February 23, 1939; "Columbus 'Youth City' Gets Ready for Annual Elections," *Cleveland Call and Post*, November 1, 1941; "Girls Not to Vote," *New-York Tribune*, August 15, 1905; "Election in the 'Playground City,'" *New-York Tribune*, August 10, 1905; "Boys Brotherhood Installs New Mayor," *New York Times*, September 25, 1937; "Kramer New Mayor of Newsboyville," *Daily Boston Globe*, April 5, 1934; "Park Mayor Sworn in," *New York Times*, September 2, 1905; G. W. Harris, "Playground City," *Review of Reviews* 32 (November 1905): 574–580; "Boy Mayor Elected," *Chicago Daily Tribune*, June 18, 1918; "Indian Youth Taught Citizenship as Well as Agriculture at Chilocco in Oklahoma," *Christian Science Monitor*, August 28, 1912; "He's a Real Mayor; New York Lad Made Boss of a Playground. Energetic Business Methods," *Grand Rapids Press*, published as the *Evening Press*, August 16, 1905; Helen Keep and M. Agnes Burton, *Guide to Detroit* (Detroit: Detroit News Company, 1916) [mention of Ford Republic]; Federal Writers' Project, *Illinois: A Descriptive and Historical Guide* (Chicago: McClurg, 1939) [mention of Boys Brotherhood Republic]; Jerry Stiller, *Married to Laughter: A Love Story Featuring Anne Meara* (New York: Simon & Schuster, 2000); William Osborne Dapping, *The Muckers: A Narrative of the Crapshooters Club*, ed. Woody Register (Syracuse, NY: Syracuse University Press, 2016).

4. Johannes-Martin Kamp, *Kinderrepubliken: Geschichte, Praxis und Theorie radikaler Selbstregierung in Kinder- und Jugendheimen* (Berlin: Springer, 1995); Clara Engelen, "An American Children's

Republic," *Tijdschrift voor Armenzorg en Kinderbescherming* 363 (1908): 170–172; Georges Nestler-Trioche, "Une république d'enfants avec gravures et photos dans le texte (membres du Congrès de la Junior Republic, jeunes prisonniers en tenue de travail)," *Le Magasin Pittoresque* 15 (August 1, 1898), 252–254; Marjorie Wilson, "France Sends a Call for Help to 'Daddy George': It Has Many War Orphans on Its Hands and Thinks the Methods of the Junior Republic at Freeville, N. Y., Might Start Them in Life Properly," *Atlanta Constitution*, March 4, 1923; "Self-Government Adopted: Armenian Relief Workers Apply Principle to Thousands," *Indianapolis Star*, December 12, 1920; "Boy Republic for England," *Washington Post*, January 30, 1911; H. Caldwell Cook, *The Play Way: An Essay in Educational Method* (New York: Stokes, 1917); Wilhelm F. K. Guderjahn, *Kampf gegen die Verwahrlosung und Entartung der Jugend in USA Erlebnisse in nordamerikanischen Knaben-erziehungsheimen und Jugendrepubliken* (Leipzig: Universitätsverlag von Robert Noske, 1935); "Une colonie de vacances Americaine," *Revue philanthropique* 15 (1904): 627; Elsie Bazeley, *Homer Lane and the Little Commonwealth* (London: Allen and Unwin, 1965); Robert H. Gault, "Junior Republics in England," *Journal of the American Institute of Criminal Law and Criminology* 3 (September 1912): 470–472; "Junior Republics Abroad: England to Adopt American Plan of Helping Delinquent Boys," *New York Times*, April 7, 1912; "Little Cubans Like It: Junior Republic Appeals to Their Pride," *Washington Post*, May 7, 1905; "To Help Bad Filipino boys," *Washington Post*, March 17, 1905.

5. William Forbush, *The Coming Generation* (New York: Appleton, 1912), 19.

6. Kriste Lindenmeyer, *"A Right to Childhood": The U.S. Children's Bureau and Child Welfare, 1912–46* (Urbana: University of Illinois Press, 1997). The exact origin of the common terms "sheltered" and "protected" childhood is not clear. Notably, aspects of the story recounted in this book are hidden in plain sight in the work of prominent historians of childhood. Joseph Kett, for example, describes a number of youth activities, including the college extracurriculum, as "a form of surrogate involvement, a substitute for attendance at comparable activities in the world outside the college." Kett, *Rites of Passage: Adolescence in America, 1790 to the Present* (New York: Basic, 1977), 174.

7. John Demos, *A Little Commonwealth: Family Life in Plymouth Colony* (New York: Oxford University Press, 1970); Holly Brewer, *By Birth or Consent* (Chapel Hill: University of North Carolina, 2005); Robert Bremner, *Children and Youth in America: A Documentary History* (Cambridge, MA: Harvard University Press, Volume 1: 1600–1865 (1970); Volume 2: 1866–1932 (1971); Volume 3: 1933–1973 (1974); John Modell, *Into One's Own: From Youth to Adulthood in the United States, 1920 to 1975* (Chapel Hill: University of North Carolina, 1989); John Demos, "Infancy and Childhood in the Plymouth Colony," in *The American Family in Social/Historical Perspectives*, ed. M. Gordon (New York: St. Martins, 1973), 180–191; Thomas Hine, *The Rise and Fall of the American Teenager* (New York: Bard, 1999); Elizabeth Kolbert, "Spoiled Rotten: Why Do Kids Rule the Roost?" *New Yorker*, July 2, 2012, https://www.newyorker.com/magazine/2012/07/02/spoiled-rotten; Richard Brody, "Kids These Days," *New Yorker*, June 27, 2012, https://www.newyorker.com/culture/richard-brody/kids-these-days; B. K. Barber, *Intrusive Parenting: How Psychological Control Affects Children and Adolescents* (Washington, DC: American Psychological Association Press, 2003); David Deming and Susan Dynarski, "The Lengthening of Childhood," *Journal of Economic Perspectives* 22, no. 3 (Summer 2008): 71–92; J. J. Arnett and S. Taber, "Adolescence Terminable and Interminable: When Does Adolescence End?" *Journal of Youth and Adolescence* 23, no. 5 (2003): 517–537; J. J.

Arnett, "Learning to Stand Alone: The Contemporary American Transition to Adulthood in Cultural and Historical Context," *Human Development* 41 (1998): 295–315.

8. Peter Baldwin, "'Nocturnal Habits and Dark Wisdom': The American Response to Children in the Streets at Night, 1880–1930," *Journal of Social History* 35, no. 3 (2002): 593–611; Richard Busch, *The Making of American Audiences* (Cambridge: Cambridge University Press, 2000); Marta Gutman and Ning de Coninck-Smith, *Designing Modern Childhoods: History, Space, and the Material Culture of Children* (New Brunswick, NJ: Rutgers University Press, 2008); Howard Chudacoff, *Children at Play: An American History* (New York: New York University Press, 2007); Viviana Zelizer, *Pricing the Priceless Child* (Princeton, NJ: Princeton University Press, 1994); David MacLeod, *The Age of the Child: Children in America 1890–1920* (New York: Twayne, 1998); Kett, *Rites of Passage*; Brewer, *By Birth or Consent*; Anthony Platt, *The Child Savers* (Chicago: University of Chicago Press, 1977); Paula Fass, *The Damned and the Beautiful: American Youth in the 1920s* (New York: Oxford University Press, 1977); Jennifer Light, "Putting Our Conversation in Context," in *From Voice to Influence*, ed. D. Allen and J. Light (Chicago: University of Chicago Press, 2015); Susan Bartoletti, *Kids on Strike* (Boston: Houghton Mifflin Harcourt, 1999); Joseph Hawes, *The Children's Rights Movement* (New York: Twayne, 1991); Julia Grant, "Children versus Childhood: Writing Children into the Historical Record, or Reflections on Paula Fass's *Encyclopedia of Children and Childhood in History and Society*," *History of Education Quarterly* 45, no. 3 (2005): 468–490; Patricia Clement, *Growing Pains, Children in the Industrial Age* (New York: Twayne, 1997); Daniel Rodgers, "Socializing Middle-Class Children: Institutions, Fables, and Work Values in Nineteenth-Century America," *Journal of Social History* 13, no. 3 (1980): 354–367; Susan Miller, *Growing Girls* (New Brunswick, NJ: Rutgers University Press, 2007); Alice Smuts, *Science in the Service of Children, 1893–1935* (New Haven, CT: Yale University Press, 2009); Steven Schlossman, *Love and the American Delinquent: The Theory and Practice of "Progressive" Juvenile Justice, 1825–1920* (Chicago: University of Chicago Press, 1977); Dominic Cavallo, *Muscles and Morals: Organized Playgrounds and Urban Reform, 1880–1920* (Philadelphia: University of Pennsylvania Press, 1981); Michael Grossberg, "A Protected Childhood: The Emergence of Child Protection in America," in *American Public Life and the Historical Imagination*, ed. Wendy Gambler, Michael Grossberg, and Hendrik Hartog (Notre Dame, IN: University of Notre Dame Press, 2003); Courtney Weikle-Mills, *Imaginary Citizens: Child Readers and the Limits of American Independence* (Baltimore: Johns Hopkins University Press, 2012); William Graebner, "Outlawing Teenage Populism: The Campaign against Secret Societies in American High Schools, 1900–1960," *Journal of American History* 74 (1987): 411–435; Jeffrey Miral, "From State Control to Institutional Control of High School Athletics: Three Michigan Cities, 1883–1905," *Journal of Social History* 16 (Winter 1982): 82–99; Sanford Gaster, "Historical Changes in Children's Access to U.S. Cities: A Critical Review," *Children's Environments* 9, no. 2 (1992): 23–36; Mary Lou O'Neil, "Youth Curfews in the United States: The Creation of Public Spheres for Some Young People," *Journal of Youth Studies* 5, no. 1 (2002): 49–67. Notably, as Robert Enright et al. explain, this was not an entirely linear transformation. "Do Economic Conditions Influence How Theorists View Adolescents?" *Journal of Youth and Adolescence* 16, no. 6 (1987): 541–559.

9. On the earlier era of exploitation, see Barry Krisberg, "The Legacy of Juvenile Corrections," *Corrections Today* 57, no. 5 (1995): 122; and David Rothman, *Conscience and Convenience: The Asylum and Its Alternatives in Progressive America* (Boston: Little, Brown, 1980).

10. On the uneven arrival, see Clement, *Growing Pains*; Zelizer, *Pricing the Priceless Child*; Schlossman, *Love and the American Delinquent*; Rebecca de Schweinitz, *If We Could Change the World* (Chapel Hill: University of North Carolina Press, 2009); John L. Rury, "Vocationalism for Home and Work: Women's Education in the United States, 1880–1930," *History of Education Quarterly* 24, no. 1 (1984): 21–44; Herbert Kliebard, *Schooled to Work* (New York: Teachers College Press, 1999); Helga Zeiher, "Children's Islanding in Space and Time: The Impact of Spatial Differentiation on Children's Ways of Shaping Social Life," in *Childhood in Europe: Approaches, Trends, Findings*, ed. Manuela du Bois-Reymond, Heinz Sünker, and Heinz-Hermann Krüger (New York: Peter Lang, 2001); Gutman and de Coninck-Smith, *Designing Modern Childhoods*.

11. In so doing, it builds on T. J. Jackson Lears's perceptive interpretation of how anti-modernism paradoxically paved the way for modernity. Yet, if in Lears's account youth activities such as the Knights of King Arthur, farm schools, and domestic and manual education are "nostalgic," this book instead sees them as paradigmatic examples of the virtual adulthoods that came to dominate young people's' experiences, activities that, together with vocational training, thrift education, scouting, youth congresses, and guided reenactments of the lives of knights, pilgrims and native Americans, simultaneously served as gateway experiences to the subjectivity that characterized the new age. See T. J. Jackson Lears, *No Place of Grace* (Chicago: University of Chicago Press, 1994). For examples from earlier periods, see Clement, *Growing Pains*.

12. On the cultural fascination with simulations in this period, see Miles Orvell, *The Real Thing: Imitation and Authenticity in American Culture, 1880–1940* (Chapel Hill: University of North Carolina Press, 1989); Vanessa Schwartz, *Spectacular Realities: Early Mass Culture in Fin-de-Siècle Paris* (Berkeley: University of California Press, 1998); Barbara Kirschenblatt-Gimblett, *Destination Culture* (Berkeley: University of California Press, 2008); Timothy Mitchell, *Rules of Experts* (Chicago: University of Chicago Press, 2002); Alison Griffiths, *Shivers Down Your Spine: Cinema, Museums, and the Immersive View* (New York: Columbia University Press, 2013); Tom Gunning, "The World as Object Lesson: Cinema Audiences, Visual Culture and the St. Louis World's Fair, 1904," *Film History* 6, no. 4, "Audiences and Fans" (Winter 1994): 422–444; Anne Friedberg, *Window Shopping: Cinema and the Postmodern* (Berkeley: University of California Press, 1993); Susan Tenneriello, *Spectacle Culture and American Identity, 1815–1940* (New York: Palgrave Macmillan, 2013); Ruth Leys, "Mead's Voices: Imitation as Foundation, or, the Struggle against Mimesis," *Critical Inquiry* 19, no. 2 (Winter 1993): 277–307; American Institute of Child Life, *The Dramatic Instinct in Children* (New York: Abingdon Press, 1914), 18. G. Stanley Hall earlier discussed the dramatic instinct in *Adolescence* (New York: D. Appleton, 1904). See also Victor Turner, *From Ritual to Theater: The Human Seriousness of Play* (New York: PAJ, 1982); Erving Goffman, *The Presentation of Self in Everyday Life* (New York: Anchor, 1959); Judith Butler, *Gender Trouble: Feminism and the Subversion of Identity* (New York: Routledge, 1990); Michel Foucault, *Discipline and Punish: The Birth of the Prison* (New York: Vintage, 1995). Susan Glenn recognizes the history of scientific backing for the "performative model of personality" that emerged in this period; Glenn, *Female Spectacle: The Theatrical Roots of Modern Feminism* (Cambridge, MA: Harvard University Press, 2000), 88. On child actors, see Zelizer, *Pricing the Priceless Child*, 94; Marah Gubar, "The Cult of the Child and the Controversy over Child Actors," in *Artful Dodgers: Reconceiving the Golden Age of Children's Literature* (New York: Oxford University Press, 2009); Patrick Tuite, "Assimilating Immigrants through Drama: The Social

Politics of Alice Minnie Herts and Lillian Wald," *Youth Theatre Journal* 12, no. 1 (1998): 10–18. Robin Bernstein's *Racial Innocence: Performing American Childhood from Slavery to Civil Rights* (New York: New York University Press, 2011) is one of the very few studies of performativity and childhood to date. This book's focus is on a different kind of performance—how performing adulthood defined youth and is equally keen to uncover the theoretical tradition behind it. Studies of the state's interest in performance include David Glassberg, *American Historical Pageantry: The Uses of Tradition in the Early Twentieth Century* (Chapel Hill: University of North Carolina Press, 1990); Leslie Frost, *Dreaming America* (Athens: Ohio State University Press, 2013); and Tracy Davis, *Stages of Emergency: Cold War Nuclear Civil Defense* (Durham, NC: Duke University Press, 2007).

13. On the migratory instinct, see J. Adams Puffer, *"The Boy and His Gang"* (New York: Houghton Mifflin, 1912); and L. W. Kline, "Truancy as Related to the Migratory Instinct," *Pedagogical Seminary* 5, no. 3 (1898). Classic studies of the transformation to work include David Hounshell, *From the American System to Mass Production, 1800–1932: The Development of Manufacturing Technology in the United States* (Baltimore: Johns Hopkins University Press, 1985); Daniel T. Rodgers, *The Work Ethic in Industrial America 1850–1920* (Chicago: University of Chicago Press, 1979); and Alfred Chandler, *The Visible Hand: The Managerial Revolution in American Business* (Cambridge, MA: Harvard University Press, 1977).

14. Nancy Folbre, "The Unproductive Housewife: Her Evolution in Nineteenth-Century Economic Thought," *Signs* 16, no. 3 (1991): 463–484; Jeanne Boydston, *Home and Work: Housework, Wages, and the Ideology of Labor in the Early Republic* (New York: Oxford University Press, 1994); Daphne Spain, *How Women Saved the City* (Minneapolis: University of Minnesota, 2000); John Dewey, *The School and Society* (Chicago: University of Chicago Press, 1899); Edward Devine, "The New View of the Child," *Proceedings of the Fourth Annual Meeting of the National Labor Committee* (Philadelphia: American Academy of Political and Social Science, 1908), 4–10.

15. Celia Pearce, "Productive Play: Game Culture from the Bottom Up," *Games and Culture* 1, no. 1 (January 2006): 17–24; Edward Castronova, *Exodus to the Virtual World* (New York: Macmillan, 2008); Jane McGonigal, *Reality Is Broken* (New York: Random House, 2010); Paul Saettler, *History of Instructional Technology* (New York: McGraw-Hill, 1968); Larry Cuban, *Teachers and Machines* (New York: Teachers College Press, 1986); Marsha Orgeron, *Learning with the Lights Off* (New York: Oxford University Press, 2011); Ian Bogost, *Persuasive Games: The Expressive Power of Videogames* (Cambridge, MA: MIT Press, 2007); Sherry Turkle, *Simulation and Its Discontents* (Cambridge, MA: MIT Press, 2009); Paul Leonardi, *Car Crashes without Cars* (Cambridge, MA: MIT Press, 2012); Brian Morton, "Larps and Their Cousins through the Ages," in *Lifelike*, ed. Jesper Donnis, Morten Gade, and Line Thorup (Copenhagen: Projektgruppen KP07, Landsforeningen for Levende Rollespil, 2007); Sara de Freitas, "Are Games Effective Learning Tools? A Review of Educational Games," *Educational Technology and Society* 21, no. 2 (2008): 74–84; Greg Castowka, *Virtual Justice* (New Haven, CT: Yale University Press, 2011); Richard Heeks, "Real Money from Virtual Worlds," *Scientific American*, January 2010, 68–73; Julian Dibbel, *Play Money* (New York: Basic, 2006); James Grimmelmann, "Virtual Worlds as Comparative Law," *New York Law School Law Review* 147 (2004); Jack Balkin, "Virtual Liberty," *Virginia Law Review* 90, no. 8 (2004): 2043–2098; Marina Umaschi Bers, "Virtual Worlds as Digital Playgrounds," *EDUCAUSE Review* 43, no. 5: 80–81; Farnaz Alemi, "An Avatar's Day in Court," *UCLA Journal of Law and Technology* 11, no. 2

(2007); Laura Beals and Marina Bers, "A Developmental Lens for Designing Virtual Worlds for Children and Youth," *International Journal of Learning and Media* 1, no. 1 (2009): 51–65; Eric Lee, "Online Picket Line, Virtual Worlds, Real Exploitation," *Industrial Worker*, April 1, 2005; Constance Steinkuhler and Kurt Squire, "Virtual Worlds and Learning," *Educational Research* 52, no. 2 (June 2012); Frances Bell, "Learning and Teaching in Immersive Virtual Worlds," *Research in Learning Technology* 16, no. 3 (2008); Julian Kucklich, "Virtual Worlds and Their Discontents," *Games and Culture* 4 (2009), 340; Clark Aldrich, "Virtual Worlds, Simulations, and Games for Education," *Innovate* 5, no. 5 (2009); Finn Juul, *Half Real* (Cambridge, MA: MIT Press, 2005); Karen Yeung, "Algorithmic Regulation: A Critical Interrogation," *Regulation and Governance* 12, no. 4 (2017): 505–523; Trebor Scholz, *Digital Labor: The Internet as Playground and Factory* (New York: Routledge, 2013); Jacob Smith, *Eco-sonic Media* (Berkeley: University of California Press, 2015); F. Gregory Lastowka and Dan Hunter, "The Laws of the Virtual Worlds," *California Law Review* 92, no. 1 (2004); Anna McCarthy, "Cyberculture or Material Culture? Computers and the Social Space of Work," *Etnofoor* 15, no. 1/2 (2002): 47–63; Nick Dyer Witherford and Grieg de Peuter, eds., *Games of Empire: Global Capitalism and Video Games* (Minneapolis: University of Minnesota Press, 2009); Nick Yee, "The Labor of Fun: How Video Games Blur the Boundaries of Work and Play," *Games and Culture* 1, no. 1 (2006): 68–71; Tiziana Terranova, "Free Labor: Producing Culture for the Digital Economy," *Social Text* 18, no. 2 (2000): 33–58. Notably there are efforts in many of the discussions about contemporary technologies to reflect on history, for guidance or legitimation. Yet, as this book suggests, it is necessary to destabilize categories and look historically using actors' categories to inform our sense of antecedents. The history of media and youth has largely emphasized unidirectional instructional technology; with this story we begin to recover the deep history of immersive and interactive media in child development, which in turn extends a growing body of scholarship in media studies documenting the roots of mass-mediated society beyond the development of film, audio, and other technologies.

16. On the fringe status, see Joseph Hawes, *Children in Urban Society* (New York: Oxford University Press, 1971). Jack Holl, *Juvenile Reform in the Progressive Era: William R. George and the Junior Republic Movement* (Ithaca, NY: Cornell University Press, 1971) is the only full-fledged historical study of the movement, yet it recognizes only a small set of the wide influences of the republic on the American youth experience. Johannes-Martin Kamp's *Kinderrepubliken* says more about its non-US influences. Kevin Murphy, *Political Manhood* (New York: Columbia University Press, 2010) has some coverage as well. Other scholars describe the histories of specific republics, including the Ford Republic, Allendale, and Boy City, albeit with limited reference to the larger junior republic movement. See, for example, Gay Pitman Zieger, *For the Good of the Children* (Detroit: Wayne State University Press, 2003); LeRoy Ashby, *Saving the Waifs: Reformers and Dependent Children, 1890–1917* (Philadelphia: Temple University Press, 1984); Ronald D. Cohen and Raymond A. Mohl, *The Paradox of Progressive Education: The Gary Plan and Urban Schooling* (Port Washington, NY: Kennikat, 1979). During the period itself, however, comparisons to Freeville were widespread, as I discuss in "Building Virtual Cities, 1895–1945," *Journal of Urban History* 38, no. 2 (2012): 336–371. See, for example, Boys Brotherhood Republic, *Life of the Boys Brotherhood Republic* (Chicago: BBR, 1938); "Junior Municipality," *Los Angeles Times*, March 21, 1914; "Governing Themselves," *Youth's Companion* 79, no. 37 (1905): 426; "South's George Junior Republic: To Be Called the Juvenile State When Completed, Near Athens, Ga.," *New-York Tribune*, July 21, 1907; Duane R.

Dills, "A Successful Form of Self-Government for Boys," *Association Boys* (October 1908): 188–194; "Miniature Republic Created by Pupils. Ceremonies at Washington Duplicated. Superintendent Oliver W. Best of Echo Park Playground Finally Puts Novel Plan into Operation," *Los Angeles Herald*, March 5, 1909; "Vacation School Exercises," *New-York Tribune*, August 18, 1897; T. H. MacQueary, "Schools for Dependent, Delinquent, and Truant Children in Illinois," *American Journal of Sociology* 9, no. 1 (1903): 1–23; Anna Pratt, "The Junior Republic of the San Francisco Boys Club," *San Francisco Chronicle*, September 7, 1902; "The Chicago Woman's Club Discusses Self-Government in Schools," *Kindergarten Primary Magazine*, vol. 15, 1899; "An Educational Novelty," *Current Literature* 27, no. 2 (1900): 98; "Swearing Has Stopped; School in North Salem Has a City Government with Boys and Girls Acting as Mayor, Common Council and Police Officers. Juvenile Judge Presides over the Court. Which Tries Offenders—Many Arrests at Firsts, but Now They Are Very Few—Teachers Are No Longer Kings and Queens—The School Republic Maintains a High Standard of Citizenship—Cigarette Smoking Has Been Abolished," *Boston Daily Globe*, April 22, 1906; Winifred Buck, *Boys Self-governing Clubs* (New York: Macmillan, 1903); Lyman Beecher Stowe, "Good Citizens in the Making," *Lexington Herald*, October 5, 1913. In fact, as a sign of the republic's broad reach, there were also some institutions that called themselves or their programs "republics" when a closer look finds limited adoption of the republic's core principles.

17. A. E. Winship, "Looking about the California Junior Republic," *Journal of Education*, June 6, 1912; A. E. Winship to William George, June 8, 1908, box 4, folder 20, William R. George Family Papers, 1750–1989, Division of Rare and Manuscript Collections, Cornell University Library [hereafter WG Papers]; "Modern Reform Methods: Work of Junior Republic Contrasted with That of Reformatory Schools," *Washington Post*, May 13, 1901; "'International' Text Study," *Friends' Intelligencer* 59, no. 3 (1902): 36. Bernard Wishy, *The Child and the Republic* (Philadelphia: University of Pennsylvania Press, 1968) and John Kasson, *Civilizing the Machine* (New York: Grossman, 1976) elaborate how anxieties about youth and anxieties about democracy were entangled during this period.

18. *All-round Route and Panoramic Guide of the St. Lawrence* (Montreal: Canada Railway News Co., 1881), 45.

19. William Byron Forbush, *Dramatics in the Home* (Philadelphia: American Institute of Child Life, 1914), 14, 27.

20. John Dewey, *School and Society*, 15–16; Katherine Camp Mayhew and Anna Camp Edwards, *The Dewey School* (New York: Appleton, 1936).

21. *The Dramatic Instinct in Children* (Philadelphia: American Institute of Child Life, 1914), 15.

22. Ruth McIntire, review of *The Gary Schools* series, *Child Labor Bulletin* 7 (1919): 289–291.

23. Gregory Mason, "The Boy Police of New York," *Labor Digest* 8, no. 7 (1915): 31; Elwood Street, "Going the Juvenile Court One Better," *Survey* 33, no. 4 (1915): 83; W. B. Seymour, "Junior Deputy Sanitary Inspectors," *American City* (December 1916): 696–698.

24. *Life of the Boys Brotherhood Republic*.

25. Forbush, *Dramatics in the Home*, 26; Spain, *How Women Saved the City*; "To Have Juvenile Police," *Municipal Journal and Engineer* 30, no. 12 (1911): 422; "Portland, Ore., to Have Police

Force of Boys," *Municipal Journal* 34, no. 21 (1913): 722; Mrs. George Zimmerman, "Children's Leagues of Good Citizenship," *American City* 7 (1912): 443–446; Reuben Simons, "The Juvenile Street Cleaning Leagues of New York," *American City* 3 (October 1910), 163–166.

26. Ronald Bauer, "The Utilization of the Junior Red Cross as an Enrichment Program in the Schools," MS thesis, University of North Dakota, 1943, 8. See also Lewis Todd, *Wartime Relations of the Federal Government and the Public Schools: 1917–1918* (New York: Columbia University Teachers College. 1945).

27. "Junior Police Will Keep Order in School Yards: 600 Boys Are Organized Just Like Real Cops," *Chicago Daily Tribune*, March 10, 1924.

28. Richard Reiman, *The New Deal and American Youth* (Athens: University of Georgia, 1992); Britt Haas, "As They Saw the Thirties," PhD diss., State University of New York at Albany, 2011. Although there is a larger literature on the history of the college experience, this book's primary focus is youth under twenty-one in an era when few attended college.

29. National Youth Administration, *Final Report, 1936–1943* (Washington, DC: Federal Security Agency, War Manpower Commission, 1944); Light, "Building Virtual Cities, 1895–1945," 336–371.

30. Harry McKown, *The Student Council* (New York: McGraw-Hill, 1944); Boy Scouts of America, *Handbook for Scoutmasters: A Manual of Leadership* (New York: Boys Scouts of America, 1947 edition).

Chapter 1

1. J. W. Jenks, "The George Junior Republic," *Journal of Social Science* (December 1897): 65–68.

2. Jack Holl, *Juvenile Reform in the Progressive Era: William R. George and the Junior Republic Movement* (Ithaca, NY: Cornell University Press, 1971). This is the only full-fledged historical study. Kevin Murphy, *Political Manhood* (New York: Columbia University Press, 2010). Murphy devotes significant attention to George's republic in this study of political masculinity.

3. Miles Orvell, *The Real Thing: Imitation and Authenticity in American Culture, 1880–1940* (Chapel Hill: University of North Carolina Press, 1989), 33–34. John Kasson has characterized the antebellum era as one of institution building to deal with the emergent complexities of life in the US as an industrializing and urbanizing nation, making the absence of junior republics from histories of the period particularly noteworthy. Kasson, *Civilizing the Machine* (New York: Macmillan, 1976), 63.

4. Leo Marx, *The Machine in the Garden* (Oxford: Oxford University Press, 1964); Matthew Fry Jacobsen, *Whiteness of a Different Color* (Cambridge, MA: Harvard University Press, 1998); Jack Holl, *Juvenile Reform in the Progressive Era: William R. George and the Junior Republic Movement* (Ithaca, NY: Cornell University Press, 1971), 69; William George, *The Adult Minor* (New York: Appleton Century, 1937); Bernard Wishy, *The Child and the Republic* (Philadelphia: University of Pennsylvania Press, 1968).

5. Robert Wiebe, *The Search for Order* (New York: Farrar, Straus and Giroux, 1966); Camilla Stivers, *Bureau Men, Settlement Women: Constructing Public Administration in the Progressive Era*

(Lawrence: University Press of Kansas, 2000); John Jordan, *Machine-Age Ideology: Social Engineering and American Liberalism, 1911–1939* (Durham: University of North Carolina Press, 2010); Richard Hofsteder, *The Age of Reform* (New York: Vintage, 1955); Kenneth Fox, *Better City Government: Innovation in American Urban Politics, 1850–1937* (Philadelphia: Temple University Press, 1978); Martin J. Schiesl, *The Politics of Efficiency: Municipal Administration and Reform in America 1800–1920* (Berkeley: University of California Press, 1977); Gerald McFarland, *Mugwumps, Morals, and Politics 1884–1920* (Amherst: University of Massachusetts Press, 1975); Mordecai Lee, *Bureaus of Efficiency: Reforming Local Government in the Progressive Era* (Milwaukee: Marquette University Press, 2008); Samuel Haber, *Efficiency and Uplift: Scientific Management in the Progressive Era, 1890–1920* (Chicago: University of Chicago Press, 1964).

6. Richard Welling, *The Twig Is Bent* (New York: Putnam, 1942). There was ample precedent for youth gang participation in politics in New York City and beyond. See Joseph Kett, *Rites of Passage: Adolescence in America, 1790 to the Present* (New York: Basic, 1977), 93; James Howell and John P. Moore, "History of Street Gangs in the United States," *National Gang Center Bulletin* 4 (2010); Frederic Thrasher, *The Gang* (Chicago: University of Chicago Press, 1927).

7. Kevin Murphy, *Political Manhood* (New York: Columbia University Press, 2010), 137–138; William Welling, *East Side Story* (New York: BBR, 1982), 1; Lyman Beecher Stowe, "What to Do with a Boy: How to Turn His Energy, His Loyalty, His Gang into Helpful Paths," *World's Work* 26 (June 1913): 190–195; William George, *The Adult Minor* (New York: Appleton Century, 1937), 179–181.

8. Fresh air camps typically involved placing out, but George was unable to find sufficient families to take the kids. See Julia Guarneri, "Changing Strategies for Child Welfare, Enduring Beliefs about Childhood: The Fresh Air Fund, 1877–1926," *Journal of the Gilded Age and Progressive Era* 11, no. 1 (2012): 27–70; and Sharon Wall, ed., *The Nurture of Nature: Childhood, Antimodernism, and Ontario Summer Camps, 1920–55* (Vancouver: University of British Columbia Press, 2009). On the social gospel, see Joseph Kett, *Rites of Passage: Adolescence in America, 1790 to the Present* (New York: Basic, 1977); David MacLeod, *Building Character in the American Boy* (Madison: University of Wisconsin Press, 2004); Jack Holl, *Juvenile Reform in the Progressive Era: William R. George and the Junior Republic Movement* (Ithaca, NY: Cornell University Press, 1971), 66; Lyman Beecher Stowe and William George, *Citizens Made and Remade* (Boston: Houghton Mifflin, 1912), 32.

9. John Commons, "The Junior Republic," *American Journal of Sociology* (1897): 282. US Commissioner of Education, *Report of the Commissioner of Education, Volume 1* (Washington, DC: US Office of Education, 1902), 239.

10. On changing attitudes toward poor relief in this period and the issue of whether benevolence exacerbated the problem it was adopted to solve, see David Rothman, *The Discovery of the Asylum* (Boston: Little, Brown, 1971); and Alice O'Connor, *Poverty Knowledge* (Princeton, NJ: Princeton University Press, 1991).

11. William George, *The Junior Republic: Its History and Ideals* (New York: Appleton, 1910), 48–49; John Commons, "The Junior Republic," *American Journal of Sociology* (1897): 281–296.

12. John Commons, "The Junior Republic," *American Journal of Sociology* (1897): 284.

13. The constitution can be found in William George, *Nothing Without Labor* (Freeville, NY: George Junior Republic, 1902). The republic was variously referred to as the George Industrial Camp and the Young America Republic in its early days. George Crittenden, "Sociological Light on the Hilltop: The George 'Industrial Camp' and 'Junior Republic,'" *Self Culture* 8, no. 3 (1898): 307–311; "To Start a Republic," *Sun*, September 1, 1895, 7; "Camp of Boys and Girls—Industrial Farm in Tompkins County for City Children—Conducted by William R. George—Influences for Good which Surround the Citizens of this Miniature Republic—Have Their Own Congress and Police," *New York Times*, August 25, 1895; "Ran a Small Republic," *New York Times*, September 6, 1895.

14. "From Bad to Good," *Chicago Daily Tribune*, September 9, 1895; William Orton, "The Boys' Republic," *Outlook*, September 21, 1895, 477; "Citizens for the Young Republic," *New York Times*, July 7, 1896; "A Wee Republic Ended," *New York Sun*, September 6, 1895. Lists of helpers can be found in the William George Family Papers, Cornell University Archives (hereafter WG Papers).

15. William George, "Teach Obedience and Self-Control," *Harper's Bazaar*, March 1910, 204.

16. Barry Krisberg, "The Legacy of Juvenile Corrections," *Corrections Today* 57, no. 5 (1995): 122–154; William Orton, "The Boys' Republic," *Outlook*, September 21, 1895, 477; Theodore L. Cuyler, "The Junior Republic," *New York Evangelist* 67 (September 3, 1896): 36; "The George Junior Republic," *Harper's Weekly*, May 23, 1896, 513; Albert Shaw, "Vacation Camps and Boys Republics," *Review of Reviews*, May 1896, 575; "A Wee Republic Ended," *New York Sun*, September 6, 1895.

17. Charles Loring Brace, "Vacations for the Poor," *Independent*, June 4, 1896, 12.

18. "Young American Republic at George Industrial Camp," *School Journal* (September 14, 1895): 222; "Ran a Small Republic," *New York Times*, September 6, 1895. Alexander Keyssar, *The Right to Vote* (New York: Basic, 2009) describes American women's ability to cast votes on a limited number of topics such as school issues before the Twentieth Amendment gave them full suffrage.

19. "The George Junior Republic," *Harper's Weekly*, May 23, 1896, 513. E. Lawrence Hunt, "A Boys and Girls Republic," *Congregationalist*, October 1, 1896, 482. Girls' access to voting was briefly restricted.

20. "The George Junior Republic," *Harper's Weekly*, May 23, 1896, 514; "A Child Republic in Tents," *Christian Herald* 18 (September 4, 1895): 17–19. For a vivid account of the political goings-on, see "Ran a Small Republic," *New York Times*, September 6, 1895.

21. "The George Junior Republic," *Harper's Weekly*, May 23, 1896, 513–514; "'Jakey' and the Junior Republic: Some of the Good Results of Mr. George's Experiment, and Its Needs," *New-York Tribune*, April 11, 1897; John Commons, "The Junior Republic," *American Journal of Sociology* (1897). According to George's later writings, he hired a cook partway through the winter, but no other participating adults are mentioned. See William George, *The Junior Republic: Its History and Ideals* (New York: Appleton, 1910).

22. Adele Fielde, "The George Junior Republic," *Independent*, July 23, 1896, 1; John Commons, "The Junior Republic," *American Journal of Sociology* (1897); Waldorf Hotel contract, August 30, 1897, WG Papers, box 2, folder 7; Contract for dining room, likely from 1898, WG Papers, box 3, folder 7.

23. William Hull, "The George Junior Republic," *Annals of the American Academy of Political and Social Science* 10, no. 1 (1897): 80–82; John Commons, "The Junior Republic," *American Journal of Sociology* (1897): 281–296.

24. Adele Fielde, "The George Junior Republic," *Independent*, July 23, 1896, 989–990; William Hull, "The George Junior Republic," *Annals of the American Academy of Political and Social Science* 10, no. 1 (1897): 80–81.

25. Mary Gay Humphreys, "The Smallest Republic in the World," *McClure's Magazine*, July 1897, 737; "In the GJR: Children as Citizens," *Current Literature* 135 (August 1896); US Commissioner of Education, *Report of the Commissioner of Education, Volume 1* (Washington, DC: US Office of Education, 1902), 246; Abigail Powers, "The George Junior Republic," *Puritan* 9 (1901): 737–756; "Civic and Educational Notes," *Gunton's Magazine*, November 1898, 362–364.

26. John Commons, "The Junior Republic," *American Journal of Sociology* (1897): 281–296; William Hull, "The George Junior Republic," *Annals of the American Academy of Political and Social Science* 10, no. 1 (1897). For greater details on a range of financial problems in Freeville's republic, see Fielde. "Back from the Junior Republic," *New-York Tribune*, September 6, 1896; "A Republic Run by Youngsters," *New-York Tribune*, March 29, 1897. Although this was regarded at the time as the moment when George passed the torch to youth, there were continuing examples of adult involvement in the political system. For example, the *Junior Republic Citizen* in 1898 mentioned Thomas Osborne and George Waring standing for election to government posts.

27. Members of Advisory Council, box 2, folder 9, WG Papers; "Environment and Christian Duty," *New York Evangelist*, July 30, 1896; "Home News," *New-York Tribune*, November 14, 1895; "To Found a Home in Freeville," *New-York Tribune*, July 22, 1896; "New Charities Incorporated," *New York Times*, July 16, 1896; Washington Gladden, "The Junior Republic at Freeville," *Outlook*, October 31, 1896, 778; "Citizens for the Young Republic," *New York Times*, July 7, 1896; "Back from the Junior Republic," *New-York Tribune*, September 6, 1896; Adele Fielde, "The George Junior Republic," *Independent*, July 23, 1896, 1; "In the George Junior Republic," *Current Literature* 20, no. 2 (August 1896): 135; Theodore L. Cuyler, "The Junior Republic," *New York Evangelist*, September 3, 1896, 36.

28. John Commons, "The George Junior Republic," *American Journal of Sociology* (1897): 281–296; "Gift for Mrs. McKinley," *New-York Tribune*, November 18, 1896; "'Jakey' and the Junior Republic: Some of the Good Results of Mr. George's Experiment, and Its Needs," *New-York Tribune*, April 11, 1897; "Help the Boys' Republic," *New York Times*, March 25, 1897; "Junior's President Talks," *New York Times*, March 29, 1897; John Commons, "The Junior Republic II," *American Journal of Sociology* (1898): 435; "A Republic Run by Youngsters," *New-York Tribune*, March 29, 1897. This phenomenon was repeated in later years: "A Republic in Miniature," *New York Times*, May 5, 1897; "A Unique Institution: Operation of the Junior Republic in New York," *Oregonian*, June 28, 1898.

29. "Camp of Boys and Girls—Industrial Farm in Tompkins County for City Children—Conducted by William R. George—Influences for Good which Surround the Citizens of this Miniature Republic," *New York Times*, August 25, 1895; Washington Gladden, "The Junior Republic at Freeville," *Outlook*, October 31, 1896, 778; Mary Gay Humphreys, "The Smallest Republic in the World," *McClure's Magazine*, July 1897, 742; Agnes Boyle O'Reilly Hocking (wife of Harvard's

Ernest Hocking), "Glimpse of the George Junior Republic Taken from Letters Written in 1905," box 4, folder 7, WG Papers; William Hull, "The George Junior Republic," *Annals of the American Academy of Political and Social Science* 10, no. 1 (1897): 73–86. On popularity among sociologists, see "Summer School of Sociology," *New-York Tribune*, June 26, 1898; "Institutions," *New York Evangelist*, August 31, 1899, 21.

30. Mary Gay Humphreys, "The Smallest Republic in the World," *McClure's Magazine*, July 1897, 735–747; "A Republic in Miniature," *New York Times*, May 5, 1897; T. M. Osborne, "The George Junior Republic," *New York Evangelist*, August 11, 1898, 23; Thomas Osborne, "The George Junior Republic," *Journal of Social Science* 36 (December 1898): 135; "Daddy's prophecy, made New Year's Eve just before the hour of 12m 1899," box 3, folder 17, WG Papers; "Prayer and Self-Government," *Outlook*, August 18, 1900, 906; "Our 'Junior Republics,'" *New York Times*, December 26, 1898; "The George Junior Republic," *New York Evangelist*, March 11, 1897, 19; William George, *The Junior Republic: Its History and Ideals* (New York: Appleton, 1910), 164; "The George Junior Republic," *New-York Tribune*, January 31, 1899.

31. Delavan Pierson, *The Boys and Girls Republic at Freeville* (New York: Dickie, 1899); Thomas Osborne, "The George Junior Republic," *Journal of Social Science* 36 (December 1898): 134; "A Republic in Miniature," *New York Times*, May 5, 1897; Adele Fielde, "The George Junior Republic," *Independent*, July 23, 1896, 1; "The George Junior Republic," *New-York Tribune*, January 31, 1899; "George Junior Republic: Dr. Van Dyke and Ex-Secretary Fairchild Address the Association at Brick Presbyterian Church," *New York Times*, November 18, 1899; J. W. Jenks, "The George Junior Republic," *Journal of Social Science* 35 (December 1897): 65; E. Lawrence Hunt, "A Boys and Girls Republic," *Congregationalist*, October 1, 1896, 482; Thomas Osborne, "The George Junior Republic," *New York Evangelist*, August 11, 1898, 23; "In the George Junior Republic Romance," *Current Literature* 20, no. 2 (August 1896): 135.

32. "A Republic in Miniature," *New York Times*, May 5, 1897; "Reclaiming the Ragamuffin," *American Hebrew* 59 (1896): 294; Abigail Powers, "The George Junior Republic," *Puritan* (1901): 743.

33. "Camp of Boys and Girls—Industrial Farm in Tompkins County for City Children—Conducted by William R. George—Influences for Good which Surround the Citizens of this Miniature Republic," *New York Times*, August 25, 1895, 21; E. Lawrence Hunt, "A Boys and Girls Republic," *Congregationalist*, October 1, 1896, 482; "The George Junior Republic," *New York Evangelist*, March 11, 1897, 19.

34. James Price, "The Junior Republic," *Friend* 72 (1898): 55; "George Junior Republic: Dr. Van Dyke and Ex-Secretary Fairchild Address the Association at Brick Presbyterian Church," *New York Times*, November 18, 1899; Abigail Powers, "The George Junior Republic," *Puritan* (1901): 753.

35. US Commissioner of Education, *Report of the Commissioner of Education, Volume 1* (Washington, DC: US Office of Education, 1902), 243; E. Lawrence Hunt, "A Boys and Girls Republic," *Congregationalist*, October 1, 1896, 482.

36. "The George Junior Republic: Its System of Operation and Plans for the Future," *New York Times*, January 20, 1900; "Smoking," December 4, 1898, box 3, folder 5, WG Papers; Cases of smoking, chewing tobacco, "obscene language" noted, n.d., box 3, folder 5, WG Papers; "To the

citizens of the GJR," June 26, 1899, box 3, folder 12, WG Papers; William Hull, "The George Junior Republic," *Annals of the American Academy of Political and Social Science* 10, no. 1 (1897): 83; Frederic Almy, "Juvenile Courts in Buffalo," *Annals of the American Academy of Political and Social Science* 20 (1902): 284.

37. William Hull, "The George Junior Republic," *Annals of the American Academy of Political and Social Science* 10, no. 1 (1897): 79; William George, *The Junior Republic: Its History and Ideals* (New York: Appleton, 1910), 73, 97–98.

38. "The George Junior Republic," *Harper's Weekly,* May 23, 1896; John Commons, "The George Junior Republic II," *American Journal of Sociology* (1898); Washington Gladden, "The Junior Republic at Freeville," *Outlook*, October 31, 1896, 779; Allen Sangree, "Boy rulers: The Freeville citizens discuss their summer republic. The Views of ex-Policemen. Senators, Jail Keepers and Bank Presidents Who Helped to Govern. Several Hundred Boys and Girls from the Tough Districts. Regrets and aspirations. Practical politicians needed. The new woman at Freeville. Mr. George's experiment. What it taught the boys. Workings of the Republic. Size counts," *Los Angeles Times*, September 29, 1895; Thomas Osborne, "The George Junior Republic," *Journal of Social Science* 36 (December 1898): 134.

39. John Commons, "The George Junior Republic II," *American Journal of Sociology* (1898): 434; Washington Gladden, "The Junior Republic at Freeville," *Outlook*, October 31, 1896, 781.

40. Adele Fielde, "The George Junior Republic," *Independent* July 23, 1896, 2; Mary Gay Humphreys, "The Smallest Republic in the World," *McClure's Magazine*, July 1897, 739. John Commons, "The Junior Republic," *American Journal of Sociology* (1897) also describes these guardianships.

41. Washington Gladden, "The Junior Republic at Freeville," *Outlook*, October 31, 1896, 781.

42. William George, *The Junior Republic: Its History and Ideals* (New York: Appleton, 1910); Catherine Claxton Dong, "The Struggle to Define Childhood: Resistance to the Private Sphere from the Junior Republic Movement, 1894–1936" (PhD diss., Cornell University, 1995); Washington Gladden, "The Junior Republic at Freeville," *Outlook*, October 31, 1896, 781; William Orton, "The Boys' Republic," *Outlook*, September 21, 1895, 477; "List of graduates and citizens of the George Junior Republic," c. 1903, box 4, folder 3, WG Papers.

43. "We the undersigned for the privilege of remaining at the Junior Republic make the following agreement," included promises of manual labor, no smoking, evenings at the library, attending lectures and religious services, and staying on campus except in cases of permission to leave, February 16, 1898, box 3, folder 6, WG Papers; L. L. Harris, "Republic of Young Boys: A Story of the Junior Republic Founded by *New York Journal*—Its Great Growth and Prosperity a Marvel of the Century," *Atlanta Constitution*, July 18, 1897; E. Lawrence Hunt, "A Boys and Girls Republic," *Congregationalist* October 1, 1896, 482; L. S. H., "The George Junior Republic," *New York Evangelist*, April 1, 1897, 8; "Camp of Boys and Girls—Industrial Farm in Tompkins County for City Children—Conducted by William R. George—Influences for Good which Surround the Citizens of this Miniature Republic," *New York Times*, August 25, 1895; William Hull, "The George Junior Republic," *Annals of the American Academy of Political and Social Science* 10, no. 1 (1897): 79; "The Boys' Republic," *Washington Post*, October 15, 1895; Theodore L. Cuyler, "The Junior Republic,"

New York Evangelist, September 3, 1896, 4; "A Republic in Miniature," *New York Times*, May 5, 1897; Alexander Woollcott, "A Practical Laboratory of Citizenship," *American Legion Weekly*, October 7, 1921, 7–8; Thomas Osborne, foreword in William George, *The Junior Republic: Its History and Ideals* (New York: Appleton, 1910); Theodore Roosevelt, "The Junior Republic," *New Outlook*, January 20, 1912, 117; Mary Wager Fisher, "Daddy's Boys—A Factory of Good Citizenship," *Rural New Yorker*, June 17, 1899, 445–446; John Kasson, *Civilizing the Machine* (New York: Grossman, 1976), 41; "'International' Text Study," *Friends' Intelligencer* 59, no. 3 (1902): 36; Minna Norriss, "The History of the California Junior Republic" (MA thesis, University of Southern California, 1931), 125, citing A. E. Winship, "Looking about the California Junior Republic," *Journal of Education*, June 6, 1912; Ralph Black, "A miniature republic: The interesting experiment at Freeville, NY. A government of, for and by the children. They come from the tenements of the Metropolis. The scheme is developing into a fine success," *Detroit Free Press*, August 2, 1896.

44. US Commissioner of Education, *Report of the Commissioner of Education, Volume 1* (Washington, DC: US Office of Education, 1902), 243; "Mr. George and the Freeville Republic," *Outlook*, March 21, 1914, 623; J. H. P., "George Junior Republic," *New York Evangelist*, August 12, 1897, 25; Charles Burr Todd, "Civics and Education, A Novel Educational Experiment," *Gunton's Magazine*, November 1898, 349; Thomas Osborne, "The George Junior Republic," *Journal of Social Science* 36 (December 1898): 137; Elizabeth Van Nortwick, "Significance and Influence of the Junior Republic," *Young Woman's Journal* 28 (1917): 251–257.

45. Thomas Osborne, "The George Junior Republic," *Journal of Social Science* 36 (December 1898): 134; "Citizens for the Young Republic," *New York Times*, July 7, 1896; "One Kind of Vacation Camp," *Detroit Free Press*, May 23, 1896.

46. Susan Stewart, *On Longing* (Durham, NC: Duke University Press, 1992); John Mack, *The Art of Small Things* (Cambridge, MA: Harvard University Press, 2008); Curtis Hinsley, "The World as Marketplace: Commodification of the Exotic at the World's Columbian Exposition, Chicago, 1893," in *Exhibiting Cultures*, ed. Steven Lavine and Ivan Karp (Washington, DC: Smithsonian Institution, 1991); Marina Benjamin, "Sliding Scales: Microphotography and the Victorian Obsession with the Miniscule," in *Cultural Babbage: Technology, Time and Invention*, ed. Francis Spufford and Jenny Uglow (London: Faber & Faber, 1997); Alison Griffiths, *Shivers Down Your Spine: Cinema, Museums, and the Immersive View* (New York: Columbia University Press, 2013); Alison Griffiths, "Journeys for Those Who Cannot Travel," *Wide Angle* 18, no. 3 (1996): 53–84; "Boer War Spectacle, Coney Island's Latest Show," *New York Times*, May 21, 1905, 5; Eric Ames, *Carl Hagenbeck's Empire of Entertainments* (Seattle: Washington University Press, 2009); Susan Tenneriello, *Spectacle Culture and American Identity, 1815–1940* (London: Palgrave Macmillan, 2013); Lauren Rabinovitz, "More Than the Movies: A History of Somatic Visual Culture through Hale's Tours, IMAX, and Motion Simulation Rides," in *Memory Bytes: History, Technology, and Digital Culture*, ed. Lauren Rabinovitz and Abraham Geil (Durham, NC: Duke University Press, 2004); Anne Whiston Spirn, "Constructing Nature: The Legacy of Frederick Law Olmsted," in *Uncommon Ground: Toward Rethinking the Human Place in Nature*, ed. William Cronon (New York: Norton, 1995); Virginia Jenkins, *The Lawn* (Washington, DC: Smithsonian Institute, 2015); Donna Haraway, "Teddy Bear Patriarchy: Taxidermy in the Garden of Eden, New York City, 1908–1936," *Social Text* 11 (Winter 1984–1985): 20–64; Jonathan Crary, "Géricault, the Panorama and Sites of

Reality in the Early 19th Century," *Grey Room* 9 (Autumn 2002): 5–25; Katrin Mauer, "Archaeology as Spectacle: Heinrich Schliemann's Media of Excavation," *German Studies Review* 32, no. 2 (2009): 303–317; Robert Rydell, *All the World's a Fair* (Chicago: University of Chicago Press, 1984); Timothy Mitchell, "The World as Exhibition," *Comparative Studies in Society and History* 31, no. 2 (1989): 217–236; Vanessa Schwartz, *Spectacular Realities: Early Mass Culture in Fin-de-Siècle Paris* (Berkeley: University of California, 1998); Michael Taussig, *Mimesis and Alterity: A Particular History of the Senses* (New York: Routledge, 1993); Erkki Huhtamo, *Illusions in Motion: Media Archaeology of the Moving Panorama and Related Spectacles* (Cambridge, MA: MIT Press, 2013); Brendan Edward Gregory, "The Spectacle Plays and Exhibitions of Imre Kiralfy, 1887–1914" (PhD diss., 1988, University of Manchester); Steven Lavine and Ivan Karp, eds., *Exhibiting Cultures* (Washington, DC: Smithsonian Books, 1991); Tom Gunning, "The World as Object Lesson: Cinema Audiences, Visual Culture and the St. Louis World's Fair, 1904," *Film History* 6, no. 4, Audiences and Fans (1994): 422–444; Miles Orvell, *The Real Thing: Imitation and Authenticity in American Culture, 1880–1940* (Chapel Hill: University of North Carolina Press, 1989); T. J. Jackson Lears, *No Place of Grace* (Chicago: University of Chicago Press, 1994); Wolfgang Schivelbusch, *The Railway Journey* (Oakland: University of California Press, 1980); Lisa Gitelman, *Scripts, Grooves, and Writing Machines: Representing Technology in the Edison Era* (Stanford, CA: Stanford University Press, 1999); Stephen Kern, *The Culture of Time and Space 1880–1918* (Cambridge, MA: Harvard University Press, 1983); Jonathan Crary, *Suspensions of Perception: Attention, Spectacle and Modern Culture* (Cambridge, MA: MIT Press, 2000); Anson Rabinbach, *The Human Motor: Energy, Fatigue, and the Origins of Modernity* (Berkeley: University of California Press, 1992); Timothy Mitchell, *Colonising Egypt* (Berkeley: University of California Press, 1988); Anne Friedberg, *Window Shopping: Cinema and the Postmodern* (Berkeley: University of California Press, 1993); Susan Glenn, *Female Spectacle: The Theatrical Roots of Modern Feminism* (Cambridge, MA: Harvard University Press, 2002); Vanessa Schwartz, "Cinematic Spectatorship Before the Apparatus: Early Mass Culture in Fin-de-Siècle Paris," in *Viewing Positions*, ed. Linda Williams (New Brunswick, NJ: Rutgers University Press, 1994), 87–113; Lauren Rabinovitz and John Belton, eds., *Electric Dreamland: Amusement Parks, Movies, and America*; Alison Griffiths, *Wondrous Difference* (New York: Columbia University Press, 2002); Maren Stange, "Jacob Riis and Urban Visual Culture: The Lantern Slide Exhibition as Entertainment and Ideology," *Journal of Urban History* 15, no. 3 (1989): 274–303; Samuel Batzli, "The Visual Voice: 'Armchair Tourism,' Cultural Authority, and the Depiction of the United States in Early Twentieth-Century Stereographs" (PhD diss., University of Illinois, 1997); Judith Babbitts, "Stereographs and the Construction of a Visual Culture in the United States," in *Memory Bytes: History, Technology, and Digital Culture*, ed. Lauren Rabinovitz and Abraham Geil (Durham, NC: Duke University Press, 2004); Barbara Kirschenblatt-Gimblett, "Objects of Ethnography," in *Exhibiting Cultures*, ed. Steven Lavine and Ivan Karp (Washington, DC: Smithsonian Books, 1991); Gertrude Scott, "Village Performance: Villages at the Chicago World's Columbian Exposition, 1893" (PhD diss., New York University, 1991).

47. "Panorama of a European Tour," *Hartford Courant*, January 13, 1853; "Perrine's Panorama of the Holy Land," *Chicago Tribune*, March 15, 1861; William Byron Forbush, *Dramatics in the Home* (Philadelphia: American Institute of Child Life, 1914); "The Council of Seventy," *The Biblical World* 13, no. 6 (1899); Jean Baudrillard, "Simulacra and Simulations," in *Jean Baudrillard, Selected Writings*, ed. Mark Poster (Stanford, CA: Stanford University Press, 1988), 166–184.

48. "Darkest Africa: Real African Life in a Real African Village," souvenir guide cited in Robert Rydell, *All the World's a Fair* (Chicago: University of Chicago Press, 1984), 268n40; "Cairo Street Open," *Chicago Sunday Tribune*, May 28, 1893; Rosalyn R. LaPier and David R. M. Beck, *City Indian: Native American Activism in Chicago, 1893–1934* (Lincoln: University of Nebraska Press, 2015); L. G. Moses, "Indians on the Midway: Wild West Shows and the Indian Bureau at World's Fairs, 1893–1904," *South Dakota History* 21, no. 3 (1991). "The Midway Plaisance of the Chicago World's Fair—Its Reproduction in Toronto Next Week under the Auspices of the Queen's Own Rifles—Scenes and Amusements of this Wonderful Thoroughfare," *Globe*, June 2, 1894. This included "identical reproductions" and "facsimiles" of their traditional practices from the past. "Iroquois Are Coming," *Chicago Daily Tribune*, June 21, 1893; Gertrude Scott, "Village Performance: Villages at the Chicago World's Columbian Exposition, 1893" (PhD diss., New York University, 1991), 77, quoting *A Week at the Fair* (Chicago: Rand, McNally, 1893), 242. Also quoted by Scott, Isabel Aberdeen, "Ireland at the World's Fair," *North American Review* (1893), described "an exact reproduction (on a scale of two-thirds) of the stronghold of the old McCarthys...Each cottage is the copy of an actual cottage now existing in some part of Ireland." Also quoted by Scott, T. Dean, *White City Chips* (Chicago: Warren Publishing, 1895), 273; Caroline Malloy, "Irish Villages, Pavilions, Cottages, and Castles at International Exhibitions, 1853–1939" (PhD diss., University of Wisconsin–Madison, 2013, 786); Chauncey M. Depew, "Wonders at the Fair's Magnitude," *Chicago Tribune*, June 19, 1893; John Eastman "Village Life at the World's Fair," *Chautauquan* 17 (1893) 602–604; "Looked Like Real War," *Nashville American*, August 15, 1897.

49. Luke Sharp, "The Big Show: An Account of a Cheap Trip to the New Orleans Exposition," *Detroit Free Press*, April 12, 1885.

50. Chauncey M. Depew, "Wonders at the Fair's Magnitude," *Chicago Tribune*, June 19, 1893; Ruth Oldenziel, *Making Technology Masculine: Men, Women, and Modern Machines in America, 1870–1945* (Amsterdam: Amsterdam University Press, 1999); Robert Rydell, *All the World's a Fair* (Chicago: University of Chicago Press, 1984); "Prison Life Illustrated by Dolls," *Chicago Tribune*, April 23, 1893; Benjamin Truman, *History of the World's Fair*, 1898; Luke Sharp, "The Big Show: An Account of a Cheap Trip to the New Orleans Exposition," *Detroit Free Press*, April 12, 1885; "Fair as a Textbook for Coeds," *St. Louis Post-Dispatch*, August 30, 1904; Nicholas Murray Butler, "The Educational Influence of the Exposition," *Cosmopolitan* 31 (1901): 540; Minnie Reynolds, "Exposition as an Educator," *New York Times*, October 6, 1901; Alison Griffiths, "Journeys for Those Who Cannot Travel," *Wide Angle* 18, no. 3 (1996): 53–84.

51. Gertrude Scott, "Village Performance: Villages at the Chicago World's Columbian Exposition, 1893" (PhD diss., New York University, 1991). Scott reports on some of the anxieties about authenticity versus fraud at the fairs. Lears offers an account of broader concerns about the breakdown of authentic experience in the period. T. J. Jackson Lears, *No Place of Grace* (Chicago: University of Chicago Press, 1994). Barbara Kirschenblatt-Gimblett, "Objects of Ethnography," in *Exhibiting Cultures*, ed. Steven Lavine and Ivan Karp (Washington, DC: Smithsonian Institution, 1991); "Great Aid to Education," *New York Times*, March 4, 1894; Melissa Rinehart, "To Hell with the Wigs! Native American Representation and Resistance at the World's Columbian Exposition," *American Indian Quarterly* 36, no. 4 (2012): 403–442; James Bartlett Campbell, *Campbell's Illustrated History of the World's Columbian Exposition, March 1892–March 1893* (Chicago: J. B.

Campbell, 1893); "A Wee Republic Ended," *New York Sun*, September 6, 1895; William Fremont Blackman, review, *"The Junior Republic: Its History and Ideals* by William R. George," *Economic Bulletin* 3, no. 4 (1910): 445–447.

52. Catherine Claxton Dong, "The Struggle to Define Childhood: Resistance to the Private Sphere from the Junior Republic Movement, 1894–1936" (PhD diss., Cornell University, 1995); Jack Holl, *Juvenile Reform in the Progressive Era: William R. George and the Junior Republic Movement* (Ithaca, NY: Cornell University Press, 1971); Thomas Osborne, "The George Junior Republic," *New York Evangelist*, August 11, 1898, 23; "Junior Republic at Freeville," *New York Times*, October 15, 1897; J. H. B., "The George Junior Republic Vindicated," *Friend*, February 1, 1902, 226; "Official Investigation of the George Junior Republic," *American Journal of Sociology* 3 (1898): 708–710; "Its work well done; the George Junior Republic commended by a committee of experts; An Investigation Made into its Methods and the Conditions at Freeville—Report to the State Board of Charities," *New-York Tribune*, February 5, 1898; Adele Fielde, "The George Junior Republic," *Independent*, July 23, 1896, 1; William Hull, "The George Junior Republic," *Annals of the American Academy of Political and Social Science* 10, no. 1 (1897): 77; William George, *The Junior Republic: Its History and Ideals* (New York: Appleton, 1910), 98.

53. "Its work well done; the George Junior Republic commended by a committee of experts; An Investigation Made into its Methods and the Conditions at Freeville—Report to the State Board of Charities," *New-York Tribune*, February 5, 1898; Colin A. Scott, *Social Education* (Boston: Ginn, 1908); Article 2, no title, *Independent*, November 11, 1897, 13; J. H. B., "The George Junior Republic Vindicated," *Friend*, February 1, 1902, 226; "Report upon the George Junior Republic, Freeville, NY," *Quarterly Record* 1, no. 4 (1900): 364–369.

54. J. W. Jenks, "The George Junior Republic," *Journal of Social Science* 35 (December 1897): 67; John Commons, "The Junior Republic," *American Journal of Sociology* (1897); Washington Gladden, "The Junior Republic at Freeville," *Outlook*, October 31, 1896, 778, 782; "Civic and Educational Notes," *Gunton's Magazine*, November 1898, 363–364.

55. "The Midway Plaisance of the Chicago World's Fair—Its Reproduction in Toronto Next Week under the Auspices of the Queen's Own Rifles—Scenes and Amusements of This Wonderful Thoroughfare," *Globe*, June 2, 1894; "Iroquois Are Coming," *Chicago Daily Tribune*, June 21, 1893; J. W. Jenks, "The George Junior Republic," *Journal of Social Science* 35 (December 1897): 65; Curtis Hinsley, "The World as Marketplace: Commodification of the Exotic at the World's Columbian Exposition, Chicago 1893," in *Exhibiting Cultures*, ed. Steven Lavine and Ivan Karp (Washington, DC: Smithsonian Institute, 1991); Melissa Rinehart, "To Hell with the Wigs! Native American Representation and Resistance at the World's Columbian Exposition," *American Indian Quarterly* 36, no. 4 (2012): 403–442; Brian Hochman, *Savage Preservation* (Minneapolis: University of Minnesota, 2014), 117; Miles Orvell, *The Real Thing: Imitation and Authenticity in American Culture, 1880–1940* (Chapel Hill: University of North Carolina Press, 1989), 86, 96–98; Erkki Huhtamo, *Illusions in Motion: Media Archaeology of the Moving Panorama and Related Spectacles* (Cambridge, MA: MIT Press, 2013); "Cairo Street Open," *Chicago Sunday Tribune*, May 28, 1893.

56. "President's Letter 1897," box 2, folder 8, WG Papers; "A Republic Run by Youngsters," *New-York Tribune*, March 29, 1897.

57. William Hull, "The George Junior Republic," *Annals of the American Academy of Political and Social Science* 10, no. 1 (1897); "Personals," *Independent*, April 1, 1897, 31; "Ministers and Churches," *New York Evangelist*, June 10, 1897, 26; "The Boys Not Forgotten," *New-York Tribune*, May 15, 1897; Adele Fielde, "The True Story of a Life Sixteen Winters Long," *Independent*, August 26, 1897, 27; William Dapping, "Report from the criminal court judge," cover letter appended to cases from summer 1897, box 2, folder 5, WG Papers.

58. John Commons, "The Junior Republic II," *American Journal of Sociology* (1898): 447; Mrs. George to Dr. Foote, listing winter citizens, September 13, 1897, box 2, folder 7, WG Papers.

59. Mrs. George to Dr. Foote, explains the financial circumstances of several youth, October 4, 1897, box 2, folder 8, WG Papers; "Report of the business manager of the GJR association for the summer of 1897," describes the kinds of preparations made in the absence of kids that she hoped to reassign to citizens, box 2, folder 2, WG Papers.

60. Charles Burr Todd, "Civics and Education," *Gunton's Magazine*, November 1898, 349; "A Few Words to the Rich Citizens of New York About the Junior Republic," *New York Journal*, July 15, 1896; Abigail Powers, "The George Junior Republic," *Puritan* 9 (1901): 737–756; "Good Work for Bad Boys," *Atlanta Constitution*, July 8, 1900; Jack Holl, *Juvenile Reform in the Progressive Era: William R. George and the Junior Republic Movement* (Ithaca, NY: Cornell University Press, 1971), 13–14. "Citizens for the Young Republic," *New York Times*, July 7, 1896; "Summer School of Sociology," *New-York Tribune*, June 26, 1898; "Institutions," *New York Evangelist*, August 31, 1899, 21; "The Religious World: Theology and Sociology," *Outlook*, March 6, 1897, 706. "Women's League of the GJR," organized in 1899 is mentioned in Elizabeth Cady Stanton et al., *History of Woman Suffrage* (National American Woman Suffrage Organization, multiple dates); "George Junior Republic: Dr. Van Dyke and Ex-Secretary Fairchild Address the Association at Brick Presbyterian Church," *New York Times*, November 18, 1899.

61. "The George Junior Republic," *New-York Tribune* January 31, 1899; "New York," *New York Observer*, May 23, 1901; "George Junior Republic," *Boston Daily Globe*, April 19, 1899; David Rothman, *The Discovery of the Asylum* (Boston: Little, Brown, 1971), 258–259; Patricia Clement, *Growing Pains: Children in the Industrial Age* (New York: Twayne, 1997), 213; F. A. King, "Self-Government and 'the Bunch,'" *Charities* 13 (October 1, 1904): 36–41; "Town Meeting Day at Freeville," *Charities* 10 (June 6, 1903): 573–575.

62. "Daddy's prophecy, made New Year's Eve just before the hour of 12m 1899," box 3, folder 17, WG Papers.

63. "Reclaiming the Ragamuffin," *American Hebrew* 59 (1896); J. H. P., "George Junior Republic," *New York Evangelist*, August 12, 1897, 25; Andrew Hargadon, *How Breakthroughs Happen* (Cambridge, MA: Harvard Business School Press, 2003).

64. John Commons, "The Junior Republic," *American Journal of Sociology* (1897): 281; "A Wee Republic Ended," *New York Sun*, September 6, 1895; Henry Davidson Sheldon, *Student Life and Customs* (New York: Appleton, 1901); *Official Proceedings of the Board of Commissioners of Cook County, Illinois* (Chicago: The Commissioners, 1895); "Junior Congress of the United States," in *Encyclopedia of the History of St. Louis* (St. Louis: Southern History, 1899); "America's Junior Congress,"

Washington Post, October 25, 1903; "Discussed Woman Suffrage," *Washington Post*, February 1, 1903; "Junior Congress Hot," *St. Louis Post-Dispatch*, April 10, 1898; "Will Discuss Prohibition," *St. Louis Post-Dispatch*, April 21, 1898; "Miniature Congress," *Chicago Press and Tribune*, October 29, 1859; Ashley Van Storm, "Discipline as the Result of Self-Government, *Proceedings of the National Education Association* 33 (1894): 764–772; W. K. Wickes, *A Youth-Congress Manual* (Syracuse, NY, 1893); Courtney Weikle-Milles, *Imaginary Citizens* (Baltimore: Johns Hopkins University Press, 2002); Glen Wallach, *Obedient Sons* (Amherst: University of Massachusetts Press, 1997); Thomas Harrison, *The Career Reminiscences of an Amateur Journalist and the History of Amateur Journalism* (Indianapolis: Author, 1883); Eleanor Eells, *History of Organized Camping* (American Camping Association, 1996); Joseph Hawes, *Children in Urban Society* (New York: Oxford University Press, 1971); Charles B. Morrell, *Handbook of the Boys' Brigade, Containing Full Directions for Organizing and Conducting Military Companies in Churches* (Cincinnati: Pettibone, 1893); Joseph Barnett, *Barnett's Broom Brigade Tactics and Fan Drill: Suitable for School, Church, Social, or Military Entertainment for Boys and Girls* (Springfield, MA: M&M, 1890); Sally Gregory Kohlstedt, "A Better Crop of Boys and Girls: The School Gardening Movement, 1890–1920," *History of Education Quarterly* 48, no. 1 (2008): 58–93; Brian Trelstad, "Little Machines in Their Gardens: A History of School Gardens in America, 1891 to 1920," *Landscape Journal* 16, no. 2 (1997): 161–173; Marie Warsh, "Cultivating Citizens: The Children's School Farm in New York City, 1902–1931," *Buildings & Landscapes: Journal of the Vernacular Architecture Forum* 18, no. 1 (2011): 64–89; "Camp of Boys and Girls—Industrial Farm in Tompkins County for City Children—Conducted by William R. George—Influences for Good which Surround the Citizens of this Miniature Republic," *New York Times*, August 25, 1895; Charles Loring Brace, "Vacations for the Poor," *Independent*, June 4, 1896; J. H. Thiry, "School Savings Banks in the United States," *Proceedings of the International Congress of Education of the World's Columbian Exposition, Chicago, July 25–28, 1893* (New York: National Education Association, 1895), 286–287; Joseph Kett, *Rites of Passage: Adolescence in America, 1790 to the Present* (New York: Basic, 1977); Lisa Jacobsen, *Raising Consumers* (New York: Columbia University Press, 2005); Anthony Rotondo, *Manhood in America* (New York: Basic, 1994); "The Working of School Banks," *Nineteenth Century* 22 (1887): 415; John Henry Thiry, "School Savings Banks in the United States," *American Banker* (1890); LeRoy Ashby, *Saving the Waifs: Reformers and Dependent Children, 1890–1917* (Philadelphia: Temple University Press, 1984); Patricia Clement, *Growing Pains, Children in the Industrial Age* (New York: Twayne, 1997); E. R. B. Gordon, *The History and Growth of Vocational Education in America* (Boston: Allyn & Bacon, 1999); Marvin Lazerson and W. Norton Grubb, eds., *American Education and Vocationalism: A Documentary History 1870–1970* (New York: Teachers College Press, 1974); John L. Rury, "Vocationalism for Home and Work: Women's Education in the United States, 1880–1930," *History of Education Quarterly* 24, no. 1 (1984): 21–44; Harry McKown, *The Student Council* (New York: McGraw-Hill, 1944); "School Children as Officials," *Chicago Daily Tribune*, February 19, 1895; "It Ends in Disorder: Pandemonium Reigns at Junior Republic's Meeting," *Chicago Daily Tribune*, March 31, 1895; "Junior City Council Is Sworn In," *Chicago Daily Tribune*, May 12, 1895; "Mass Meeting for a Junior Mayor," *Chicago Daily Tribune*, April 4, 1895; "Organ of Junior American Republic. Young Citizens Issue the First Number of a Creditable Semi-Monthly," *Chicago Daily Tribune*, May 6, 1895. See "He Won't Agree Not to Blot It," *Chicago Daily Tribune*, April 10, 1895, about mail-in ballot; notes that membership roll was 2,000 at latest count. "Junior City Council Ticket," *Chicago Daily Tribune*,

January 12, 1896; "For Junior American Republic," *Chicago Daily Tribune*, July 4, 1896; Jennifer S. Light, "Putting Our Conversation in Context: Youth, Old Media, and Political Participation, 1800–1971," in *From Voice to Influence*, ed. Danielle Allen and Jennifer S. Light (Chicago: University of Chicago Press, 2015); Augustine E. Costello, *Our Firemen: A History of the New York Fire Departments, Volunteer and Paid, from 1609 to 1887* (New York: Knickerbocker, 1887); George W. Sheldon, *The Story of the Volunteer Fire Department of the City of New York* (New York, Harper, 1882); David Nasaw, *Children of the City: At Work and at Play* (New York: Anchor, 1985); Susan Campbell Bartoletti, *Kids on Strike* (New York: Houghton Mifflin, 1999); Martin Greenberg, *Citizens Defending America* (Pittsburgh: University of Pittsburgh Press, 2005); Paula Petrik, "Desk-Top Publishing: The Making of the American Dream," *History Today* 39 (1989): 12–19; Paula Petrik, "The Youngest Fourth Estate: The Novelty Printing Press and Adolescence, 1870–1876," in *Small Worlds: Children and Adolescence, 1850–1950*, ed. Elliott West and Paula Petrik (Lawrence: University of Kansas Press, 1992); Anthony Platt, *The Child Savers* (Chicago: University of Chicago Press, 1977); Robert S. Fogarty, *All Things New: American Communes and Utopian Movements, 1860–1914* (Chicago: University of Chicago Press, 1990); Clara Maria Liepmann, *Die Selbstverwaltung der Gegenfang*, reviewed by Thorsten Sellin, *Journal of the American Institute of Criminal Law and Criminology* 20, no. 1 (May 1929): 152–153; Gregory Singleton, "Protestant Voluntary Associations and the Shaping of Victorian America," *American Quarterly* 7, no. 5 (1975): 549–560; "A Bold Sedition," *National Amateur* (June 1880): 2; "Back from Their Outing: Happy Recruits from the George Industrial Camp Reach Home," *New-York Tribune*, September 6, 1895; David Rothman, *Conscience and Convenience: The Asylum and Its Alternatives in Progressive America* (Boston: Little, Brown, 1980); Richard Welling, *As the Twig Is Bent* (New York: Putnam's, 1942); William Welling, *East Side Story* (New York: BBR, 1982).

Chapter 2

1. G. Stanley Hall, "Some Social Aspects of Education," *Pedagogical Seminary* 9 (1902): 82–89. According to Jack Holl, the Carlisle Indian School borrowed methods from the Freeville republic. See Holl, *Juvenile Reform in the Progressive Era: William R. George and the Junior Republic Movement* (Ithaca, NY: Cornell University Press, 1971). Colin Scott's *Social Education* (Boston: Ginn, 1908) similarly profiled the Freeville republic and Dewey's school, among others.

2. "W. R. George, 69, Dead; Founded Junior Republic," *New York Herald Tribune*, April 26, 1936.

3. On the republic as an educational institution, see "Organized Work with Boys," *New-York Tribune*, November 1, 1900; Chicago Board of Education, *Annual Report* (1901), 15.

4. John Commons, "The Junior Republic," *American Journal of Sociology* (1897): 281; William George, *The Junior Republic: Its History and Ideals* (New York: Appleton, 1910); William George, *Nothing Without Labor* (Freeville, NY: George Junior Republic, 1902), 23–24; "Peterboro Avenue," *Junior Republic Citizen*, July 1899, 1–3; "Junior Republic Meeting; T. M. Osborne and Billy Zavenski to Speak this Evening," *Buffalo Courier*, March 8, 1901. George's papers are filled with correspondence from interested parties eager for his counsel to start new republics, such as Thomas Chew [superintendent Fall River Boys Club] to William George, May 30, 1898, box 3, folder 6, WG Papers.

5. "Environment and Christian Duty," *New York Evangelist*, July 30, 1896; "Back from the Junior Republic," *New-York Tribune*, September 6, 1896; "Camp of Boys and Girls—Industrial Farm in Tompkins County for City Children—Conducted by William R. George—Influences for Good which Surround the Citizens of this Miniature Republic," *New York Times*, August 25, 1895; Charles Loring Brace, "Vacations for the Poor," *Independent*, June 4, 1896; Adele Fielde, "The George Junior Republic," *Independent*, July 23, 1896; "Successful Boys' Republic," *Los Angeles Times*, May 20, 1899. On debates about biology versus environment, see Catherine Claxton Dong, "The Struggle to Define Childhood: Resistance to the Private Sphere from the Junior Republic Movement, 1894–1936" (PhD diss., Cornell University, 1995); Karin Calvert, *Children in the House* (Boston: Northeastern University Press, 1992); Joseph Kett, *Rites of Passage: Adolescence in America, 1790 to the Present* (New York: Basic, 1977). On the positive associations with exposure to nature, see Conevery Bolton, *The Health of the Country: How American Settlers Understood Themselves and Their Land* (New York: Basic, 2002); Galen Cranz, *The Politics of Park Design: A History of Urban Parks in America* (Cambridge, MA: MIT Press, 1989); and Anne Whiston Spirn, "Constructing Nature: The Legacy of Frederick Law Olmsted," in *Uncommon Ground: Toward Rethinking the Human Place in Nature*, ed. William Cronon (New York: Norton, 1995).

6. Listing for Rev. Edward Bradley in *A Score of Years, the Record of the Class of 1884, Princeton* (Princeton, NJ: Princeton University, 1904); "Boys Who Govern a City," *Chicago Daily Tribune*, November 21, 1896, 10; Euphemia Holden, "Where They Make Good Boys," *Good Housekeeping*, June 1904, 583; "Chicago's Junior Republic," *Chicago Daily Tribune*, August 16, 1896; Gladys Priddy, "School on Lake Gives 100 Lads Big Start in Life," *Chicago Daily Tribune*, March 10, 1949; Edward L. Bradley and Maud Menefee Bradley, *Allendale Annals* (Lake Villa, IL: Allendale, 1926); Josephine Raymond, "The Social Settlement Movement in Chicago" (ML thesis, University of Wisconsin, 1897); "A Miniature City, Lake Villa Junior Municipality Idea for Boys," *Cass City Enterprise*, December 24, 1896; May Henrietta Morton, "Allendale—A Social Experiment with Chicago Boys," *Kindergarten Magazine*, January 1898. On the era's widely held idea of democracy being more healthy in rural areas, see Susan Tenneriello, *Spectacle Culture and American Identity, 1815–1940* (London: Palgrave Macmillan, 2013); US National Resources Committee, *Our Cities*. (Washington, DC: US National Resources Committee, 1937).

7. "Boys Who Govern a City," *Chicago Daily Tribune*, November 21, 1896; "A Boys' Municipality," *Charities Review* 9 (1899): 284; "Chicago's Junior Republic," *Chicago Daily Tribune*, August 16, 1896; "A Miniature City: Lake Villa Junior Municipality Idea for Boys," *Cass City Enterprise*, December 24, 1896, also in *Idaho Falls Times*, January 21, 1897; "Allendale Farm," *Chicago Daily Tribune*, May 28, 1905.

8. "Chicago's Junior Republic," *Chicago Daily Tribune*, August 16, 1896; Josephine Raymond, "The Social Settlement Movement in Chicago" (ML thesis, University of Wisconsin, 1897); "Boys Who Govern a City," *Chicago Daily Tribune*, November 21, 1896. Financial problems appeared at other, later republics, for example, the Litchfield George Junior Republic, organized in 1904. See "Snake in Boys' Utopia," *Chicago Daily Tribune*, August 10, 1906.

9. "Boys Who Govern a City," *Chicago Daily Tribune*, November 21, 1896; Josephine Raymond, "The Social Settlement Movement in Chicago" (ML thesis, University of Wisconsin, 1897).

10. "Boys Who Govern a City," *Chicago Daily Tribune*, November 21, 1896; Euphemia Holden, "Where They Make Good Boys," *Good Housekeeping*, June 1904, 583; Listing for Rev. Edward Bradley in *A Score of Years, the Record of the Class of 1884, Princeton* (Princeton, NJ: Princeton University, 1904); LeRoy Ashby, "'Recreate This Boy': Allendale Farm, the Child, and Progressivism," *Mid-America* 58 (1976): 31–53; LeRoy Ashby, *Saving the Waifs: Reformers and Dependent Children, 1890–1917* (Philadelphia: Temple University Press, 1984); "A Miniature City: Lake Villa Junior Municipality Idea for Boys," *Cass City Enterprise*, December 24, 1896, also in *Idaho Falls Times*, January 21, 1897; "Chicago's Junior Republic," *Chicago Daily Tribune*, August 16, 1896; Dwight Goddard, "Allendale Farm—a Real Home for Homeless Boys," *Congregationalist and Christian World*, August 23, 1902, 260–261; Edward L. Bradley and Maud Menefee Bradley, *Allendale Annals* (Lake Villa, IL: Allendale, 1926); Clifford Jones, *Allendale: A Boy's World* (Lake Villa, IL: Allendale, 1986).

11. "Gardiner's Industrial Colony: An Interesting Experiment in Juvenile Local Government Now in Operation," *New-York Tribune*, August 17, 1897; "Farm Education for Boys," *New York Times*, March 21, 1897; "Farm Republics," *Boston Globe*, May 6, 1897; "A 'County-Plan' Colony," *New-York Tribune*, September 5, 1897; William Byron Forbush, "The USA," *Congregationalist*, January 28, 1897, 125; John Johnson, "Rudimentary Society among Boys," *Johns Hopkins University Studies in Historical and Political Science* 1, no. 1 (1884): 495–496; J. W. Jenks, "The George Junior Republic," *Journal of Social Science* (December 1897): 65; "The GJR," *New York Evangelist*, March 11, 1897, 19. Notably, G. Stanley Hall also mentioned McDunough alongside the Freeville republic in his 1902 speech.

12. *New Charter of Cottage Row, Farm School* (Boston: Farm and Trades School, 1901); "News and Notes," *Charities Review* 7 (1898): 711; Max Bennett Thrasher, "A Government of Boys, for Boys, by Boys: Cottage Row at Thompson's Island," *New England Magazine* 22 (1900): 204 [reprinted as "A Government of Boys," *School Journal* 60, no. 18 (1900): 473–474]; H. Addington Bruce, "A Vocational School a Hundred Years Old," *The Outlook*, July 28, 1915, 734; *Annual Report of the Commissioner of Education, US Office of Education*, 1902, 247; Max Bennett Thrasher, "A Boys' City," *New York Evangelist*, March 16, 1899, 19; Mary Winslow, "Our Schools," *Beacon* 1, no. 3 (August 1897); "Visiting Day," *Beacon* 3, no. 4 (August 1899); "Bright Boys and Busy," *Boston Daily Globe*, May 28, 1902; obituary of Charles Henry Bradley, *Proceedings of the Vermont Historical Society* (1924), 272; Max Bennett Thrasher, "A Government of Boys," from *New England Magazine*, condensed in *Public Opinion*, April 26, 1900, 525. Whether the two Bradleys were related is not clear.

13. William George, *The Junior Republic: Its History and Ideals* (New York: Appleton, 1910), 318–319; John Commons, "The Junior Republic II," *American Journal of Sociology* (January 1898): 433–448; Untitled document, c. 1898, box 3, folder 5, WG Papers; "Boy Republic's Needs," *Washington Post*, January 21, 1901; Mary Lockwood, "A Day at National Junior Republic," *Washington Post*, October 15, 1900; "Making Good Citizens," *Washington Post*, March 12, 1900; "To Start a Republic: Superintendant Rogers and 'Citizen' Jackson arrive," *Baltimore Sun*, September 1, 1899; HJT, "National Junior Republic," *Friends' Intelligencer* 57, no. 13 (March 31, 1900): 253; "New Superintendant Appointed," *Washington Post*, September 1, 1899; Ned D. Heindel, *Iron, Armor, and Adolescents: The History of Redington and the Carter Junior Republic* (Bethlehem, PA: Northampton County Historical and Genealogical Society, 1982).

14. Jack Holl, *Juvenile Reform in the Progressive Era: William R. George and the Junior Republic Movement* (Ithaca, NY: Cornell University Press, 1971), 195; Albert Shaw, "The School City—A Method of Pupil Self Government," *Review of Reviews* 20 (1899): 673–686; Richard Welling, *As the Twig Is Bent* (New York: Putnam, 1942); "Sons of the American Revolution," *New-York Tribune*, March 29, 1891; "Sons of Patriot Fathers," *New-York Tribune*, December 8, 1889; Wilson Gill, *The Gill System of Moral and Civic Training* (New Paltz, NY: Patriotic League, 1901); Wilson Gill, *Young People's Society to Promote Practical Patriotism* (New York: Author, 1891); Wilson Gill, *A Social and Political Necessity* (New York: Patriotic League, 1902); Wilson Gill, "A Children's Palace for the World's Fair," *The Christian at Work*, April 28, 1892; "A Children's Palace," *New-York Tribune*, March 27, 1892; Wilson Gill, "Engineering versus Evolution in the Moral and Civic Uplift of Nations," *Congressional Record* [appendix] (1917), 283, also published in *Case and Comment* (1917), 871. Gill's organization is to be distinguished from the American Patriotic League, an anti-immigration organization with chapters across the United States.

15. Daphne Spain, *How Women Saved the City* (Minneapolis: University of Minnesota, 2000); Molly Ladd-Taylor, *Mother Work: Women, Child Welfare, and the State, 1890–1930* (Urbana: University of Illinois Press, 1995); Alice Smuts, *Science in the Service of Children, 1893–1935* (Chicago: University of Chicago Press, 2008).

16. "A Children's Palace at the World's Fair," *New York Evangelist*, July 14, 1892, 6; "Children's Department at the Fair," *Washington Post*, May 8, 1891; Louis Owens, "The Children's Building at the Worlds Fair," *Detroit Free Press*, November 4, 1893; "For the Little Ones," *Chicago Tribune*, February 11, 1893; "For a Kitchen-Garden Exhibit," *World's Columbian Exhibition Illustrated*, December 1892, 210; Wilson Gill, "Toys and the World's Fair," *Union Signal*, February 23, 1893; "Little Kitchen Garden Maids," *Chicago Tribune*, October 29, 1893; "Success of the Children's Building," *World's Columbian Exhibition Illustrated*, December 3, 1893, 264–266; Wilson Gill, "Children's Toys and the Fair," *Christian Work* 74 (February 23, 1892); "A Children's Palace," *Current Opinion* 10 (1892): 222; "Women at the Fair," *Chicago Tribune*, January 22, 1893; "A Children's Home," *Detroit Free Press*, September 25, 1892. Separately, the fair also included a World Youth Congress, organized by Rev. Frederick Bliss, although it was a gathering of youth representatives rather than a model government. "The World's Youth Congress," *Globe and Mail*, June 10, 1893. Bliss introduced youth congresses into schools in Detroit and Chicago as the Junior American Republic shortly thereafter. See "Boys and Girls Meet: They Assemble as Representatives of the World's Youth," *Chicago Daily Tribune*, July 18, 1893; "Young People the Delegates: World's Congress of Representative Youth—Children Invited to Attend," *Chicago Daily Tribune*, July 16, 1893; "Under All Flags," *San Francisco Chronicle*, September 15, 1893.

17. Bernard Cronson, *Pupil Self-Government* (New York: Macmillan, 1907). See also B. O. Flower, "Wilson L. Gill: The Apostle of Democracy in Education," *Arena* 35, no. 195 (February 1906): 176; Wilson Gill, *A New Citizenship* (Philadelphia: Patriotic League, 1913); Lyman Beecher Stowe, "School Republics," *New Outlook* 90 (December 26, 1908): 939–948; Wilson Gill, *The Gill System of Moral and Civic Training* (New Paltz, NY: Patriotic League, 1901); "Mimic Cities in Schools," *Sun*, September 12, 1897; Lucy Yendes, "School Children Who Govern Themselves," *Chautauquan* 30, no. 2 (November 1899): 135.

18. "School Cities," *Youth's Companion* 73, no. 49 (December 7, 1899): 650; Wilson Gill, *The Gill System of Moral and Civic Training*. (New Paltz, NY: Patriotic League, 1901); "A Helper of the Needy," *New York Times*, January 29, 1898; "Gold Medal for School City," *Chautauquan* 38, no. 2 (October 1903): 178; "School Cities Proposed," *New-York Tribune*, September 12, 1897; Lucy Yendes, "School Children Who Govern Themselves," *Chautauquan* 30, no. 2 (November 1899): 135.

19. "Vacation School Exercises," *New-York Tribune*, August 18, 1897; "Vacation Schools Close," *New York Times*, August 18, 1897; Wilson Gill, *The Gill System of Moral and Civic Training*. (New Paltz, NY: Patriotic League, 1901); Wilson Gill, *A Social and Political Necessity* (New York: Patriotic League, 1902); "A Helper of the Needy," *New York Times*, January 29, 1898; Lucy Yendes, "School Children Who Govern Themselves," *Chautauquan* 30, no. 2 (November 1899): 135; Carl Zimring, *Clean and White: A History of Environmental Racism in the United States* (New York: New York University Press, 2016). Notably, Gill had advocated for expanding vocational education during his time in Ohio.

20. "The Gill School City," *New York Evangelist*, September 23, 1897, 27; "The Gill School System: A New Educational Idea," *Public Opinion*, August 26, 1897, 278; "School Cities," *Youth's Companion* 73, no. 49 (December 7, 1899): 650.

21. "The Gill School City," *New York Evangelist*, September 23, 1897, 27.

22. James Collins, *The Art of Handling Men* (Philadelphia: Henry Altemus, 1910), 17–18; "Children as Improvement Workers," *Journal of Education* 60, no. 8 (August 25, 1904): 142; "Junior Street Cleaning Leagues," *Public Opinion*, April 1, 1897; George Edwin Waring, *Street-Cleaning and the Disposal of a City's Wastes* (New York: Doubleday & McClure, 1898); "Col. Waring's Young Aids: Receive Badges and Compliments from the Commissioner: Told They Are a Part of the Municipal Government, and Have Important Obligations Resting on Their Young Shoulders—Special Praise for the Youngster Who Dared Tackle 'Silver Dollar' Smith's Bartender–Orators Among Them," *New York Times*, May 24, 1896; "Col. Waring Their Guest: Juvenile Street Cleaners Have a Reception," *New York Times*, November 14, 1896; Martin Melosi, *Garbage in the Cities* (Pittsburgh: University of Pittsburgh Press, 1981); "Vacation Schools Close," *New York Times*, August 18, 1897; "Mimic Cities in Schools," *Sun*, September 12, 1897; Albert Shaw, "The School City—A Method of Pupil Self Government," *Review of Reviews* 20 (1899): 673–686. *Junior Republic Citizen* (September/October 1897), 7, mentions Waring standing for state engineer.

23. Wilson Gill, *The Gill System of Moral and Civic Training* (New Paltz, NY: Patriotic League, 1901); "The Gill School City," *New York Evangelist*, September 23, 1897; James White, "The Gill School City," *Gunton's Magazine*, June 1902, 535; "The Gill School City," *Municipal Affairs* 1 (1897): 564; "Mimic Cities in Schools," *Sun*, September 12, 1897; "The Outlook," *Zion's Herald*, September 15, 1897, 1; Charles Richmond Henderson, "Social Elements, Institutions, Character, Progress: The Gill School City," *Public Opinion*, August 26, 1897; "School Cities Proposed," *New-York Tribune*, September 12, 1897; "City in a School," *Boston Daily Globe*, September 12, 1897; "The Gill School System—A New Educational Idea," *Wisconsin Journal of Education* 27 (1897): 278.

24. "Mimic Cities in Schools," *Sun*, September 12, 1897.

25. Wilson Gill, *The Gill System of Moral and Civic Training* (New Paltz, NY: Patriotic League, 1901); E. B. Sherman, "Civic Training in the Public Schools, Past, Present and Future," *Proceedings*

of the Thirty-Third Annual Meeting of the Nebraska State Teachers' Association, 70; Harriet Dynan, "An Experiment in Civics in the Eighth Grade Room," *Child Study Monthly* 3 (1897–1898): 87–94, 98; "Progress of the Schools," *Omaha Daily Bee,* November 26, 1899; article on Kellom School City, no title, *Omaha Illustrated Bee,* January 7, 1900, 22; "Cities Ruled by Tots," *Washington Post,* September 10, 1905; B. O. Flower, "Wilson L. Gill: The Apostle of Democracy in Education," *Arena* 35, no. 195 (February 1906): 176; Albert Shaw, "The School City—A Method of Pupil Self Government," *Review of Reviews* 20 (1899): 673–686; Anna McCormick, "The School City," paper given at Philadelphia Civic Club, undated, box 59, folder 6, WG Papers.

26. Delos Wilcox and Wilson Gill, *Outline of American Government* (New Paltz, NY: Patriotic League, 1899).

27. Delos Wilcox and Wilson Gill, *Outline of American Government* (New Paltz, NY: Patriotic League, 1899), 99; William George, *The Junior Republic: Its History and Ideals* (New York: Appleton, 1910); Catherine Claxton Dong, "The Struggle to Define Childhood: Resistance to the Private Sphere from the Junior Republic Movement, 1894–1936" (PhD diss., Cornell University, 1995). Gill's later work drops the suggestion to work with local officials.

28. "Cities Ruled by Tots," *Washington Post,* September 10, 1905; "An Educational Novelty," *Current Literature* 27, no. 2 (February 1900): 98; James White, "The Gill School City," *Gunton's Magazine,* June 1902, 535; Albert Shaw, "The School City—A Method of Pupil Self Government," *Review of Reviews* 20 (1899): 673–686; "Municipal Reform Progress," *City and State,* September 26, 1901, 201; "The Gill School System: A New Educational Idea," *Public Opinion,* August 26, 1897, 278; Myron Scudder, "The Civic Idea in Work with Boys," *The Aims of Religious Education: The Proceedings of the Third Annual Convention of the Religious Education Association, Boston, February 12–16, 1905,* 436; Wilson Gill, *The Gill System of Moral and Civic Training.* (New Paltz, NY: Patriotic League, 1901); "Miniature City Government Conducted by Public School Pupils in New York," *Washington Post,* March 25, 1906; Thomas Slicer, "The School City as a Form of Student Government," *Proceedings of the National Conference for Good City Government* (National Municipal League, 1904); "Men and Movements that Are Making for Progress: Democracy in Education; or, the School City in Practical Operation," *Arena* 35, no. 198 (May 1906): 512; Charles S. Drum, "Moral and Civic Training: The Gill School Republic," *Instructor* 17 (December 1907): 13–15.

29. "A Miniature City: Lake Villa Junior Municipality Idea for Boys," *Cass City Enterprise,* December 24, 1896; "Chicago's Junior Republic," *Chicago Daily Tribune,* August 16, 1896.

30. "Cities Ruled by Tots," *Washington Post,* September 10, 1905; Wilson Gill, *The Gill System of Moral and Civic Training* (New Paltz, NY: Patriotic League, 1901), 144–145; Bernard Cronson, *Pupil Self-Government* (New York: Macmillan, 1907).

31. "Plan a School City," *Washington Post,* February 5, 1906; "Chicago's Junior Republic," *Chicago Daily Tribune,* August 16, 1896.

32. Albert Shaw, "The School City—A Method of Pupil Self Government," *Review of Reviews* 20 (1899): 679; "Self-Government in Schools," *Herald of Gospel Liberty* 95, no. 31 (July 30, 1903): 500; Max Bennett Thrasher, "A Boys' City," *New York Evangelist,* March 16, 1899, 19; William Byron Forbush, "The U.S.A.," *Congregationalist,* January 28, 1897, 125; Euphemia Holden, "Where They

Make Good Boys," *Good Housekeeping*, June 1904, 583; Dwight Goddard, "Allendale Farm—a Real Home for Homeless Boys," *Congregationalist and Christian World*, August 23, 1902, 260; "Boys Who Govern a City," *Chicago Daily Tribune*, November 21, 1896; Josephine Raymond, "The Social Settlement Movement in Chicago" (ML thesis, University of Wisconsin, 1897).

33. Thomas Slicer, "The School City as a Form of Student Government," *Proceedings of the National Conference for Good City Government* (National Municipal League, 1904), 61; "Boy Republic's Needs," *Washington Post*, January 21, 1901.

34. George H. Martin, "Student Self-Government," *Proceedings of the National Conference for Good City Government* (National Municipal League, 1904), 278–282; J. H. P., "George Junior Republic," *New York Evangelist*, August 12, 1897, 25; Frank Parsons, "The School City: A New Experiment in Self-Government of the Young," *Century*, January 1906, 496; "The School City," *Christian Observer*, February 21, 1906, 21; M. C. Craft, "The School City a Success," *Atlanta Constitution*, May 5, 1901; Lucy Yendes, "School Children Who Govern Themselves," *Chautauquan*, November 1899, 135; Thomas Slicer, "The School City as a Form of Student Government," *Proceedings of the National Conference for Good City Government* (National Municipal League, 1904), 284.

35. "A Miniature City: Lake Villa Junior Municipality Idea for Boys," *Cass City Enterprise*, December 24, 1896, also in *Idaho Falls Times*, January 21, 1897; "A Successful Boys' Home," *Chicago Daily Tribune*, December 4, 1901; "George Junior Republic: Dr. Van Dyke and Ex-Secretary Fairchild Address the Association at Brick Presbyterian Church," *New York Times*, November 18, 1899; "The School City," *Congregationalist*, December 14, 1899, 927; Mary Lockwood, "A Day at National Junior Republic," *Washington Post*, October 15, 1900; Albert Shaw, "The School City—A Method of Pupil Self Government," *Review of Reviews* 20 (1899): 679. For other discussions of the dual status of republic life, see "Chicago's Junior Republic," *Chicago Daily Tribune*, August 16, 1896; "News and Notes," *Charities Review* 7 (1898): 711; Wilson Gill, *A New Citizenship* (Philadelphia: Patriotic League, 1913); "School Cities Proposed," *New-York Tribune*, September 12, 1897; "The Gill School City," *New York Evangelist*, September 23, 1897, 27; "Gill School City Rules," *New-York Tribune*, March 31, 1899; James White, "The Gill School City," *Gunton's Magazine*, June 1902, 535; "The Smallest Republic in the World," *Ohio Farmer* 100, 4 (July 25, 1901): 62; "The Educational Outlook," *Forum* 35, no. 3 (January 1904): 429; "What It Teaches: Workings of the George Junior Republic Duties of Citizenship, Dignity of Labor and Wholesomeness of Law. Not a Playhouse, but Actual Life for Boys and Girls," *Boston Daily Globe*, November 30, 1902; Alice Weldon Wasserbach, "Boys Control Boys: Government in Miniature and How It Is Conducted," *Washington Post*, November 9, 1902; Lucy Yendes, "School Children Who Govern Themselves," *Chautauquan*, November 1899, 135. Nonetheless, some depictions continued to emphasize the appeal of pastoral settings. These include Edward L. Bradley and Maud Menefee Bradley, *Allendale Annals* (Lake Village, IL: Allendale, 1926); "Allendale Farm," *Chicago Daily Tribune*, May 28, 1905; Dwight Goddard, "Allendale Farm—a Real Home for Homeless Boys," *Congregationalist and Christian World*, August 23, 1902, 260; "Successful Boys' Republic," *Los Angeles Times*, May 20, 1899; F. S. Key Smith, "Our New Problem—An Old Idea Enlarged Upon," *Albany Law Journal* 63, no. 12 (December 1901): 451.

36. Whether the ties between Gill's vision for republics and the field of child study were deliberate or coincidental remains an open question. Gill himself, motivated more by a vision of scientific

governance than scientific management of youth, did not speak explicitly about developmental psychology, although according to William Welling, Gill had been a student in one of the nation's first kindergartens, taught by Louisa Frankenburgh, an assistant to Froebel. Yet the resonances with this field are apparent on deeper inspection. Welling, *East Side Story* (New York: BBR, 1982).

37. Alice Smuts, *Science in the Service of Children, 1893–1935* (Chicago: University of Chicago Press, 2008); Kathleen Jones, *Taming the Troublesome Child: American Families, Child Guidance, and the Limits of Psychiatric Authority* (Cambridge, MA: Harvard University Press, 1999); Kriste Lindenmeyer. *"A Right to Childhood": The U.S. Children's Bureau and Child Welfare, 1912–46* (Urbana: University of Illinois Press, 1997); James Dale Hendricks, "The Child-Study Movement in American Education 1880–1910: A Quest for Educational Reform through a Scientific Study of the Child" (PhD diss., Indiana University, 1968); Sara Wiltse, "A Preliminary Sketch of the History of Child Study," *Pedagogical Seminary* 3 (1885): 189–212; Ian Hacking, *Rewriting the Soul: Multiple Personality and the Sciences of Memory* (Princeton, NJ: Princeton University Press, 1995); Eric Caplan, *Mind Games: American Culture and the Birth of Psychotherapy* (Berkeley: University of California Press, 1998); Stephen Schlossman, "G. Stanley Hall and the Boys' Club: Conservative Applications of Recapitulation Theory," *Journal of the History of the Behavioral Sciences* 9, no. 2 (1973): 140–147; T. S. Crosswell, "Amusements of Worcester School Children," *Pedagogical Seminary* 6 (1898): 314–371; A. C. Ellis and G. S. Hall, "A Study of Dolls," *Pedagogical Seminary* 4 (1896): 129–175; Henry D. Sheldon, "The Institutional Activities of American Children," *American Journal of Psychology* 9 (July 1898): 425–448; G. Stanley Hall and T. R. Crosswell, "Spontaneously Invented Toys and Amusements," *Child Study Monthly* 3 (1897): 75–77; Henry D. Sheldon, *The History and Pedagogy of American Student Societies* (New York: Appleton, 1901); Genevra Sisson, "Bibliography of Children's Plays," *Studies in Education* 5 (November 1896); Zach McGee, "A Study in the Play Life of Some South Carolina Children," *Pedagogical Seminary* 7 (1900): 459–478. Notably, anthropologists and sociologists were also studying children's games. See, for example, William Wells Newell, *Games and Songs of American Children* (New York: Harper and Brothers, 1884); W. I. Thomas, "The Gaming Instinct," *American Journal of Sociology* 6 (1901): 750–763.

38. Ruth Leys, "Mead's Voices: Imitation as Foundation, or, the Struggle against Mimesis," *Critical Inquiry* 19, no. 2 (1993): 277–307; Susan Glenn, *Female Spectacle: The Theatrical Roots of Modern Feminism* (Cambridge, MA: Harvard University Press, 2002); Brian Hochman, *Savage Preservation* (Minneapolis: University of Minnesota, 2014); Lee Grieveson, "Cinema Studies and the Conduct of Conduct," in *Inventing Film Studies*, ed. Lee Grieveson and Haidee Wasson (Durham, NC: Duke University Press, 2008); Michael Taussig, *Mimesis and Alterity: A Particular History of the Senses* (New York: Routledge, 1993); Gabriel Tarde, *The Laws of Imitation*, trans. Elsie Clews Parsons (New York: Holt, 1903), xiv, 82–87; William T. Harris, "The Imitative Faculty in Education," *Public-School Journal* 14, no. 6 (February 1895); W. T. Harris, *Psychological Foundations of Education* (New York: Appleton, 1898), 301. Another early source on the social importance of imitation is Walter Bagehot, *Physics and Politics* (New York: Appleton, 1875), 89–111.

39. James Mark Baldwin. *The Mental Development of the Child and the Race* (New York: Macmillan, 1895), 487–488; Charles Ellwood, "The Theory of Imitation in Social Psychology," *American Journal of Sociology* 6, no. 6 (May 1901): 723, 740, citing Gabriel Tarde, *The Laws of Imitation*, trans. Elsie Clews Parsons (New York: Holt, 1903), 40–41; Lee Grieveson, "Cinema Studies and the

Conduct of Conduct," in *Inventing Film Studies*, ed. Lee Grieveson and Haidee Wasson (Durham, NC: Duke University Press, 2008). On mimesis in subject formation, see also Susan Glenn, "'Give an Imitation of Me': Vaudeville Mimics and the Play of the Self," *American Quarterly* 50, no. 1 (1998): 47–76; L. L. Bernard, *Introduction to Social Psychology* (New York: Holt, 1926). On the era's ideas about reality existing in the observer, see Jonathan Crary, *Suspensions of Perception: Attention, Spectacle and Modern Culture* (Cambridge, MA: MIT Press, 2000).

40. Ian Hacking, *Rewriting the Soul: Multiple Personality and the Sciences of Memory* (Princeton, NJ: Princeton University Press, 1998), 222; Lee Grieveson, "Cinema Studies and the Conduct of Conduct," in *Inventing Film Studies*, ed. Lee Grieveson and Haidee Wasson (Durham, NC: Duke University Press, 2008); Ruth Leys, "Mead's Voices: Imitation as Foundation, or, the Struggle against Mimesis," *Critical Inquiry* 19, no. 2 (1993): 277–307; William James, *The Principles of Psychology* (New York: Holt, 1890), 294. These ideas were also manifested in cultural practices, including literature, theater, and art. Stephen Kern, *The Culture of Time and Space 1880–1918* (Cambridge, MA: Harvard University Press, 1983); Jonathan Crary, *Suspensions of Perception: Attention, Spectacle and Modern Culture*. (Cambridge, MA: MIT Press, 2000); Susan Glenn, *Female Spectacle: The Theatrical Roots of Modern Feminism* (Cambridge, MA: Harvard University Press, 2002); Vanessa Schwartz, *Spectacular Realities: Early Mass Culture in Fin-de-Siècle Paris* (Berkeley: University of California, 1998); J. Herdman, *The Double in Nineteenth-Century Fiction* (London: Macmillan, 1990).

41. Schools of thought beyond Hall made related claims. See, for example, James Sully, "The Imaginative Side of Play," *Popular Science Monthly* (September 1894); James Sully, "Studies of Childhood," *Popular Science Monthly* (multiple issues between 1894 and 1896); Karl Groos, *The Play of Animals*, trans. Elizabeth L. Baldwin (New York: Appleton, 1898); Karl Groos, *The Play of Man*, trans. Elizabeth L. Baldwin (New York: Appleton, 1901).

42. Caroline Frear Burk, "Play: A Study of Kindergarten Children," *North-western Monthly* 9 (March-April 1899): 349–355; Miriam Formanek-Brunell, *Made to Play House* (Baltimore: Johns Hopkins University Press, 1998); Patricia Clement, *Growing Pains, Children in the Industrial Age* (New York: Twayne, 1997); Caroline Frear, "Imitation: A Study Based on E. H. Russell's Child Observations," *Pedagogical Seminary* 4 (1897): 382–386; Henry D. Sheldon, "The Institutional Activities of American Children," *American Journal of Psychology* 9 (July 1898): 425–448; Genevra Sisson, "Children's Plays (reprinted from *Pacific Educational Journal*, June 1894), *Studies in Education* 5 (November 1896); T. S. Crosswell, "Amusements of Worcester School Children," *Pedagogical Seminary* 6 (1898): 314–371; G. Stanley Hall, "Children's Lives," *American Journal of Psychology* 3 (January 1890): 59–70; Zach McGee, "A Study in the Play Life of Some South Carolina Children," *Pedagogical Seminary* 7 (1900), 459–478; A. C. Ellis and G. S. Hall, "A Study of Dolls," *Pedagogical Seminary* 4 (1896): 129–175. On the use of machines as research tools, see "Topical Syllabi for Child Study," *Transactions of the Illinois Society for Child-Study* 1 (1894): 44; G. Stanley Hall, "Put the Children on Record," *Youth's Companion* 68 (February 28, 1895): 106; Brian Hochman, *Savage Preservation* (Minneapolis: University of Minnesota, 2014); Erika Brady, *A Spiral Way: How the Phonograph Changed Ethnography* (Jackson: University Press of Mississippi, 1999); Alison Griffiths, *Wondrous Difference* (New York: Columbia University Press, 2002); Michael Taussig, *Mimesis and Alterity: A Particular History of the Senses* (New York: Routledge, 1993); Ian Hacking, *Rewriting the Soul: Multiple Personality and the Sciences of Memory* (Princeton, NJ: Princeton University Press, 1998).

43. Arthur Allin, "Play," *University of Colorado Studies* 1 (1902): 65, 59; Louis Hartson, *Psychology of the Club* (Worcester, MA: Clark University Press, 1911).

44. Gabriel Tarde, *The Laws of Imitation*, trans. Elsie Clews Parsons (New York: Holt, 1903), 82; James Mark Baldwin, *Mental Development of the Child and the Race* (New York: Macmillan, 1895), 487–488; William James, *Principles of Psychology, vol. 2* (New York: Holt, 1890), 409; Josiah Royce, "The Imitative Functions, and Their Place in Human Nature," *Century*, May 1894, 137, 142. See also E. A. Ross, *Social Control* (New York: Macmillan, 1901), which described youth as especially suggestive.

45. Susan Blow, *Symbolic Education: A Commentary on Froebel's "Mother Play"* (New York: Appleton, 1894), 114.

46. Thomas Benjamin Atkins, *Out of the Cradle into the World: or Self Education through Play* (Boston: Sterling, 1895). See also similar phrasing in Gladys Williams, "The Use of Myths in the Primary," *School Journal* 65 (1902). Arthur Allin, "Play," *University of Colorado Studies* 1 (1902): 61.

47. G. Stanley Hall, *Youth, Its Education, Regimen and Hygiene* (New York: Appleton, 1912), 80; George Johnson, "Child Study on the Playground," *Proceedings of the National Education Association Annual Meeting* (Winona, MN, 1908), 917–924; Stephen Kern, *The Culture of Time and Space 1880–1918* (Cambridge, MA: Harvard University Press, 1983); Stephen Jay Gould, *Ontogeny and Phylogeny* (Cambridge, MA: Harvard University Press, 1985); Lilla Estelle Appleton, "A Comparative Study of the Play Activities of Adult Savages and Civilized Children," *American Journal of Sociology* 16, no. 2 (1910): 269–270; Karl Groos, *Play of Animals*, trans. Elizabeth Baldwin (New York: Appleton, 1898); Edward Tylor, *Primitive Culture* (New York: Holt, 1889); Joshua Garrison, "A Problematic Alliance: Colonial Anthropology, Recapitulation Theory, and G. Stanley Hall's Program for the Liberation of America's Youth," *American Educational History Journal* 35, no. 1 (2008): 131–147. "Social embryology" was a closely related term.

48. Henry D. Sheldon, "The Institutional Activities of American Children," *American Journal of Psychology* 9 (July 1898): 436; G. Stanley Hall, *Adolescence* (New York: Appleton, 1907), 398.

49. G. Stanley Hall, *Youth, Its Education, Regimen and Hygiene* (New York: Appleton, 1912), 2; Alexander Caswell Ellis, "Suggestions for a Philosophy of Education," *Pedagogical Seminary* 5 (1897): 158–201; James Mark Baldwin, *Mental Development in the Child and the Race* (New York: Macmillan, 1895).

50. G. Stanley Hall, "The Story of a Sand-Pile," *Scribner's Magazine*, June 1888, 690–696.

51. G. Stanley Hall, "Children's Lies," *American Journal of Psychology* (January 1890); G. Stanley Hall, *Educational Problems* (New York: Appleton, 1911); G. Stanley Hall, *Adolescence* (New York: Appleton, 1907); G. Stanley Hall, Adolescence (New York: D. Appleton, 1904), see chapter on social instincts and institutions; J. Adams Puffer, "A Study of Boys' Gangs," *Pedagogical Seminary* 12 (1905); Donald Mrozek, "The Natural Limits of Unstructured Play, 1880–1914," in *Hard At Play: Leisure in America, 1840–1940*, ed. K. Grover (Amherst: University of Massachusetts Press and the Strong Museum, 1992); Bernard Mergen, "The Discovery of Children's Play," *American Quarterly* 27, no. 4 (1975): 399–420; G. Stanley Hall, "A Medium in the Bud," *American Journal of Psychology* 29, no. 2 (1918): 147, 153–154. Hall's earlier investigations of hypnosis included G.

Stanley Hall, "Reaction-Time and Attention in the Hypnotic State," *Mind* 8, no. 30 (1883): 170–182; G. Stanley Hall, "Recent Researches on Hypnotism," *Mind* 6, no. 21 (1881): 98–104. Notably, Hall was not alone in his view that youth at play at imitative activities generated a near-hypnotic state. Karl Groos, a German researcher, had come to similar conclusions in his 1896 book *The Play of Animals*, although he framed these developments in darker terms.

52. G. Stanley Hall, *Youth: Its Education, Regimen, and Hygiene* (New York: Appleton, 1908), 114. His colleague H. A. Carr predicted the work/play distinction might disappear. Carr, *The Survival Values of Play* (Boulder: University of Colorado, 1902).

53. Lillian McLean, "Kindergarten Metaphysics," *Mind* 6 (1900): 133; also cited in Ida Dusenberry, "The Kindergarten and Its Educational Value," *Improvement Era* 18 (1914): 348. M. B. Thrasher, "A Government of Boys, for Boys, by Boys," *New England Magazine*, April 1900, 198; M. B. Thrasher, "A Boys' City," *New York Evangelist*, March 16, 1899, 19. Later observations on how Cottage Row self-government grew up "naturally" further suggested that it aligned with the instincts of youth. See "The Thompson's Island School," *Oregonian*, August 6, 1915.

54. "Official Investigation of the George Junior Republic," *American Journal of Sociology* 3 (1898): 709; W. T. Harris, *Psychologic Foundations of Education* (New York: Appleton, 1898), 301; William T. Harris, "Discussion," *Journal of Social Science* 39 (1901): 81; William T. Harris, "The Imitative Faculty in Education," *Public-School Journal* 14, no. 6 (February 1895), 301–304; U.S. Bureau of Education, "Educational Pathology, or Self-Government in School," *Report of the Commissioner*, 1901, 235–262.

55. Ellen Lagemann, *An Elusive Science: The Troubling History of Education Research* (Chicago: University of Chicago Press, 2000); John Dewey, *The School and Society* (Chicago: University of Chicago Press, 1899); Lawrence Cremin, *American Education, the Metropolitan Experience, 1876–1980* (New York: Harper & Row, 1988); Herbert Kliebard, *Schooled to Work: Vocationalism and the American Curriculum, 1876–1946* (New York: Teachers College Press, 1999); David Nasaw, *Schooled to Order: A Social History of Public Schooling in the United States* (New York: Oxford University Press, 1981); Tracy L. Steffes, *Schools, Society, and State* (Chicago: University of Chicago Press, 2012); Ellen Berg, "Citizens in the Republic of Childhood: Immigrants and the American Kindergarten, 1880–1920" (PhD diss., University of California, Berkeley, 2004); James R. Robarts, "The Quest for a Science of Education in the Nineteenth Century," *History of Education Quarterly* 8, no. 4 (1965): 431–446; Frank Leavitt, "Cooperation of the Schools in Reducing Child Labor," *Child Labor Bulletin* 3 (1914): 141–147. Professionalizing teachers was part of the conversation, as was replacing instructors with modern machines. John Matthew Sloan, *The Duployan Phonographic Instructor* (Paris: Sloan, 1883); Epinetus Webster and Andrew Jackson Graham, *The Phonographic Teacher* (New York: Fowler and Wells, 1857).

56. Barbara Finkelstein, *Governing the Young: Teacher Behavior in Popular Primary Schools in Nineteenth-Century United States* (London: Falmer, 1989); Meredith Bak, "Democracy and Discipline: Object Lessons and the Stereoscope in American Education, 1870–1920," *Early Popular Visual Culture* 10, no. 2 (2012): 147–167; Tom Gunning, "The World as Object Lesson: Cinema Audiences, Visual Culture and the St. Louis World's Fair, 1904," *Film History* 6, no. 4 (1994): 422–444; Meredith Bak, "Perception and Playthings: Optical Toys as Instruments of Science and Culture" (PhD diss., University of California, Santa Barbara, 2012); Katie Day Good, "Bring the World to

the Child: Grassroots Media and Global Citizenship in American Education, 1900–1965" (PhD diss., Northwestern University, 2015); Sarah Anne Carter, "On an Object Lesson, or Don't Eat the Evidence," *Journal of the History of Childhood and Youth* 3, no. 1 (2010): 7–12; Louisa Hopkins, *The Spirit of the New Education* (Boston: Lee and Shepard, 1892); Tracy L. Steffes, *School, Society, and State* (Chicago: University of Chicago Press, 2011), 159–160; Ashley Van Storm, "Discipline as the Result of Self-Government," *Proceedings of the National Education Association* 33 (1894): 764–772; W. L. Wickes, *A Youth-Congress Manual* (Syracuse, NY: Author, 1893); William A. Comstock, "Syracuse High School Republic Scrapbook: Speeches, Constitution and By-laws, and Minutes of the Republic," 1892; "Fads in the Public Schools," *Michigan Farmer* 38, no. 21 (1900): 386; Joel H. Spring, *The American School, 1642–2000* (Boston: McGraw-Hill, 2001); Homer C. Bristol, "The Use of the Stereopticon in Teaching" *School Journal* 59, no. 6 (1898): 145–146; Alexander Urbiel, "The Making of Citizens: A History of Civic Education in Indianapolis, 1900–1950" (PhD diss., University of Indiana, 1996); "Evolution of School Health Programs," in *Schools and Health: Our Nation's Investment*, ed. Diane Allensworth, Elaine Lawson, Lois Nicholson, and James Wyche (Washington, DC: National Academies Press, 1997); Sally Gregory Kohlstedt, "A Better Crop of Boys and Girls: The School Gardening Movement, 1890–1920," *History of Education Quarterly* 48, no. 1 (2008): 58–93; J. S. Taylor, "Methods of Teaching Self Government," in *Art of Class Management and Discipline* (New York: Kellogg, 1903); Kimberly Tolley, *The Science Education of American Girls* (New York: Routledge, 2002); E. R. B. Gordon, *The History and Growth of Vocational Education in America* (Boston: Allyn & Bacon, 1999); Marvin Lazerson and W. Norton Grubb, eds., *American Education and Vocationalism: A Documentary History 1870–1970* (New York: Teachers College Press, 1974); John Rury, "Vocationalism for Home and Work: Women's Education in the United States, 1880–1930," *History of Education Quarterly* 24, no. 1 (1984): 21–44; Patricia Clement, *Growing Pains: Children in the Industrial Age* (New York: Twayne, 1997); Dominick Cavallo, "The Politics of Latency: Kindergarten Pedagogy, 1860–1930," in *Regulated Children/Liberated Children*, ed. Barbara Finkelstein (New York: Psychohistory Press, 1979); Brian Trelstad, "Little Machines in Their Gardens: A History of School Gardens in America, 1891 to 1920," *Landscape Journal* 16, no. 2 (1997): 161–173; Marie Warsh, "Cultivating Citizens: The Children's School Farm in New York City, 1902–1931," *Buildings and Landscapes* 18, no. 1 (2011): 64–89; Richard Welling, *As the Twig Is Bent* (New York: Putnam's, 1942); C. H. Thurber, "High School Self-Government," *School Review* 5, no. 1 (1897): 32–35; F. E. C. Robbins, "The Greenport Experiment," *Youth's Companion* 73, no. 41 (1899): 494; "Junior City of Detroit," *Detroit Free Press*, October 24, 1900; David Glassberg, *American Historical Pageantry* (Durham: University of North Carolina Press, 1990); Courtney Weikle-Milles, *Imaginary Citizens* (Baltimore: Johns Hopkins University Press, 2002); "The High School—Its Government," *Pennsylvania School Journal* 51 (March 1903): 414–422.

57. G. Stanley Hall, *The Story of a Sand Pile* (New York: Kellogg), 17–19; G. Stanley Hall, "The Ideal School as Based on Child Study (Address to the NEA Conference)," *Review of Education*, Illinois Society for Child Study, 1901–1902, 88–94; G. Stanley Hall, "Child Study: The Basis of Exact Education," *Forum* 16 (December 1893): 429–441; G. Stanley Hall, "Child Study and Its Relation to Education," *Forum* 29 (August 1900): 688–702; G. Stanley Hall, "Some Criticisms of High School Physics and of Manual Training and Mechanic Arts High Schools, with Suggested Correlates," *Manual Training Magazine*, July 1902, 189–200; G. Stanley Hall and John Mansfield, *Hints toward a Select and Descriptive Bibliography of Education* (Boston: Heath, 1886); Joseph Kett, "Curing the

Disease of Precocity," in *Turning Points*, ed. John Demos and Sarane Spence Boocock (Chicago: University of Chicago Press, 1978).

58. Ida Dusenberry, "The Kindergarten and its Educational Value," *Improvement Era* 18 (1914), 348; Gabriel Tarde, *The Laws of Imitation*, trans. Elsie Clews Parsons (New York: Holt, 1903): 82–83; Susan Blow, *Letters to a Mother on the Philosophy of Froebel* (New York: Appleton, 1899), 112; Bureau of Education, "The Kindergarten Curriculum," *Bulletin* 16 (1919): 22; Maurice H. Small, "The Suggestibility of Children," *Pedagogical Seminary* 4 (December 1896); G. Stanley Hall, "Child Study at Clark University: An Impending New Step," *American Journal of Psychology* (1903), 98, mentions G. Stanley Hall and M. H. Small, "Suggestion and Imitation," topical syllabus, Clark University, Worcester, MA, February 1896; Katherine Beebe, "Games and Plays for the Schoolroom," *Primary Education* (September 1897): 278; Katherine Beebe, *The First School Year: For Primary Workers* (Chicago: Werner, 1895). It should be noted there were some tensions between dueling visions of kindergarten, with one school of thought focused on it as a domestic practice versus another as science—and both embracing role-playing. See Dominick Cavallo, "The Politics of Latency: Kindergarten Pedagogy, 1860–1930," in *Regulated Children/Liberated Children*, ed. Barbara Finkelstein (New York: Psychohistory Press, 1979).

59. Ida Dusenberry, "The Kindergarten and Its Educational Value," *Improvement Era* 18 (1914): 348; Gabriel Tarde, *The Laws of Imitation*, trans. Elsie Clews Parsons (New York: Holt, 1903), 82–83; E. R. Snyder, "Manual Training," in *Arithmetic and Manual Training*, Bulletin of State Normal School, San Jose, California, March 1903; F. D. Crawshaw, "Organization of Teaching Material—Examples for the Teacher of Manual and Industrial Arts," *Industrial-Arts* 2 (1914): 151; G. Stanley Hall, "Some Social Aspects of Education," *Pedagogical Seminary* 9, no. 1 (1902).

60. Charles A. Ellwood. "The Theory of Imitation in Social Psychology," *American Journal of Sociology* 6 (1901): 740; William James, *Principles of Psychology* (New York: Macmillan, 1890); Arthur Allin, "Play," *University of Colorado Studies* 1 (1902): 61. James Sully concurred, as Frederick Bolton explained: "Sully tells us that children, when pretending to live another life, frequently resent any intrusion that seems to contradict the harmony of the simulated world." Frederick Elmer Bolton, *Principles of Education* (New York: Scribner's, 1910), 408. Sully writes: "A little girl of four was playing 'shops' with her younger sister. 'The elder one' (writes the mother) 'was shopman at the time I came into her room and kissed her. She broke out into piteous sobs, I could not understand why. At last she sobbed out: "Mother, you never kiss the man in the shop."' I had with my kiss quite spoilt her illusion." James Sully, *Children's Ways* (New York: Appleton, 1897), 23.

61. Gabriel Tarde, *The Laws of Imitation*, trans. Elsie Clews Parsons (New York: Holt, 1903), 62; "Plan for Toy Legislation: Mimic Congresses and Councils to be Tried in Schools," *Chicago Daily Tribune*, November 6, 1904; "Inspired by a Girl," *Chicago Daily Tribune*, March 3, 1895; Ida Dusenberry, "The Kindergarten and Its Educational Value," *Improvement Era* 18 (1914): 348. On suggestion in education and other professions, see Louis Waldstein, *The Subconscious Self and Its Relation to Education and Health* (New York: Scribner's, 1897); "Hypnotism in Education," *Colorado School Journal* 12 (1896); R. Osgood Mason, *Hypnotism and Suggestion in Therapeutics, Education, and Reform* (New York: Holt, 1901); Jasper Newton Deahl, *Imitation in Education: Its Nature, Scope and Significance* (New York: Macmillan, 1900); William Arthur Clark, *Suggestion in Education* (Chicago:

University of Chicago Press, 1903); Bureau of Education, "The Kindergarten Curriculum," *Bulletin* 16 (1919): 22; Maurice H. Small, "The Suggestibility of Children," *Pedagogical Seminary* 4 (December 1896); "Juvenile Politics," *Chicago Eagle*, February 20, 1904, 7; G. Stanley Hall, "Child Study at Clark University: An Impending New Step," *American Journal of Psychology* (1903).

62. Anne Durst, *Women Educators in the Progressive Era* (New York: Palgrave Macmillan, 2010), 118; John Dewey, *The School and Society* (Chicago: University of Chicago Press, 1899); John Dewey, "My Pedagogic Creed," *School Journal* 54 (January 1897): 77–80. Hall had trained Dewey at Johns Hopkins University, and both worked briefly at the University of Michigan, but Dewey disliked him intensely. Nonetheless, the imprint of Hall's ideas are clear. Thomas Fallace, "John Dewey and the Savage Mind: Uniting Anthropological, Psychological and Pedagogical Thought, 1894–1902," *Journal of the History of the Behavioral Sciences* 44, no. 4 (2008): 335–349. Dewey's intellectual networks included many of the same figures, for example, Royce, alongside whom he presented at the 1893 World's Fair Philosophical Congress, and Baldwin, with whom he collaborated on a dictionary of philosophy and psychology.

63. John Dewey, *The School and Society* (Chicago: University of Chicago Press, 1899; 1915 ed.), 15–16, 27, 131, 135; John Dewey, "My Pedagogic Creed," *School Journal* 54 (January 1897): 77–80; John Dewey, *Democracy and Education* (New York: Macmillan, 1916), 237, 240; R. D. Lakes, "John Dewey's Theory of Occupations: Vocational Education Envisioned," *Journal of Vocational and Technical Education* 2, no. 1 (1985): 41–45; Bernard Wishy, *The Child and the Republic* (Philadelphia: University of Pennsylvania Press, 1968).

64. John Dewey, *Democracy and Education* (New York: Macmillan, 1916), 239.

65. John Dewey, *The School and Society* (Chicago: University of Chicago Press, 1899; 1915 ed.), 41, 91, 125–126; John Dewey, *The Early Works of John Dewey, 1882–1898*, ed. Joanne Boydston (Carbondale: Southern Illinois University Press, 1969); William Arthur Clark, *Suggestion in Education* (Chicago: University of Chicago Press, 1903), 32.

66. G. Stanley Hall, "Some Social Aspects of Education," *Pedagogical Seminary* 9 (1902): 89, John Dewey, "My Pedagogic Creed," *School Journal* 54 (January 1897): 77–80. Dewey's proposals for the teaching of history are described in *School and Society*, and their practice is further elaborated in Katherine Camp Mayhew and Anna Camp Edwards, *The Dewey School* (New York: Appleton, 1936), 19; and Anne Durst, *Women Educators of the Progressive Era* (New York: Palgrave Macmillan, 2010). See also Thomas Fallance, "John Dewey and the Savage Mind," *Journal of the History of the Behavioral Sciences* 44, no. 4 (2008): 335–349. This approach was called the culture epoch theory. See John Dewey, "The Interpretation of the Culture Epoch Theory," *Public School Journal* 15, no. 5 (1896); Cephas Guillet, "Recapitulation and Education," *Pedagogical Seminary* 7 (1900): 397–445; C. C. Wan Liew, "The Educational Theory of the Culture Epochs," *Year Book of the Herbart Society* 1 (1899); B. O. Flower, "Fostering the Savage in the Young," *Arena* 10 (1894): 422–432; Charles Everett Strickland, "The Child and the Race: The Doctrines of Recapitulation and Culture Epochs in the Rise of the Child Centered Ideal in American Educational Thought, 1875–1900" (PhD diss., University of Wisconsin, 1963). Role-playing proved such a popular mode of instruction at Dewey's school that teachers expanded its uses beyond impersonating adults; for example, in Katherine Camp's science class, students impersonated the solar system.

67. Patricia Clement, *Growing Pains: Children in the Industrial Age* (New York: Twayne, 1997); David Rothman, *The Discovery of the Asylum* (Boston: Little, Brown, 1971), 258–259; Joseph Hawes, *The Children's Rights Movement* (New York: Twayne, 1991), 14. G. Stanley Hall mentions the GJR and many of its offshoots throughout his works. See, for example, "Some Social Aspects of Education" (1902); *Adolescence* (1904); *Educational Problems* (1911); and "Social Phases of Psychology," *Proceedings of the American Sociological Society* 7 (1912): 38–46, among others. In addition, it also appeared in passing in his students' research. See, for example, T. S. Crosswell, "Amusements of Worcester School Children," *Pedagogical Seminary* 6 (1898): 314–371. Taking the view that all schools were already in some sense miniature republics, one school superintendent in Reading, Pennsylvania, called for making every school a junior republic. E. Mackey, "Misfit Pupils," *Pennsylvania School Journal* 48 (March 1900): 399–407.

68. James White, "The Gill School City," *Gunton's Magazine*, June 1902, 536–537. Activities in Freeville and other republics were similarly reframed as part of this historical trajectory. See "In the George Junior Republic: Children as Citizens," *Current Literature* 20, no. 2 (August 1896): 135; Jack Holl, *Juvenile Reform in the Progressive Era: William R. George and the Junior Republic Movement* (Ithaca, NY: Cornell University Press, 1971), 192; Daniel Murray, "Report of an Address by William Byron Forbush to the Boys of Cottage Row," *Beacon* 4, no. 2 (June 1900).

69. M. C. Craft, "The School City a Success," *Atlanta Constitution*, May 5, 1901; John T. Ray, "Democratic Government of Schools," booklet produced by John Crerar Grammar School, Chicago, 1901; Wilson Gill, *A Social and Political Necessity* (New York: Patriotic League, 1902); "The First Gill School City," *Canada Educational Monthly*, June-July 1898; "An Experiment in Civics in Eighth Grade Room," *Child-Study Monthly* 8 (1897–1898); Jane Brownlee, *A Plan for Child Training* (Toledo, OH: Author, 1905); John T. Ray, "Pupil Self-Government," *Journal of Education* (October 25, 1906); John T. Ray, "Pupil Self-Government and Training for Good Citizenship," *School Journal* 73, no. 15 (October 27, 1906): 339; Waldo Sherman, *Civics: Studies in American Citizenship* (New York: Macmillan, 1905); Ernest Hamlin Abbott, "Collegeville—A Community in Miniature," *Outlook*, April 25, 1903, 965; John Commons, "Referendum, Initiative, Proportional Representation," in Wilson Gill, *The Gill System of Moral and Civic Training* (New Paltz, NY: Patriotic League, 1901).

70. "Our 'Junior Republics,'" *New York Times*, December 26, 1898; T. M. Osborne, "The George Junior Republic," *New York Evangelist*, August 11, 1898, 23; "Daddy's prophecy, made New Year's Eve just before the hour of 12m 1899," box 3, folder 17, WG Papers; "Prayer and Self-Government," *Outlook*, August 18, 1900, 906; "Self-Government in Schools: Benefits Which the School City Idea Has Proved in Cuba," *New York Times*, June 11, 1906; Wilson Gill, *Carta municipal de la ciudad escolar* (Havana: Secretaria de Instrucción Publica, 1901); "Little Cubans Like It: Junior Republic Appeals to Their Pride," *Washington Post*, May 7, 1905; George Kennan, "Cuban Character," *Outlook*, December 30, 1899, 1016; "Cities Ruled by Tots," *Washington Post*, September 10, 1905; "Instruction in Municipal Government," *Chautauquan* 38, no. 6 (February 1904): 594; Wilson Gill, *A Social and Political Necessity* (New York: Patriotic League, 1902); Wilson Gill, "The School City," *Journal of the Franklin Institute* (July 1903); Leonard Wood, *Report of the Military Governor of Cuba on Civil Affairs*, 1901.

71. Thomas J. McEvoy, *The Science of Education* (Brooklyn: Author, 1911), 177; Wilson Gill, *The Gill System of Moral and Civic Training* (New Paltz, NY: Patriotic League, 1901), 15; "Reports by

American Teachers and Educationists on the School City System of Government and Discipline," in Llewellyn Wynn Williams, *Education: Disciplinary, Civic and Moral* (London: Simpkin, Marshall, Hamilton, Kent, 1903), 120; Charles S. Drum, "Moral and Civic Training: The Gill School Republic," *Instructor* 17 (December 1907): 14; Great Britain Board of Education, "The Teaching of Civics in American Schools," *Special Reports on Educational Subjects* 10, no. 1 (1902); "Editorials," *Arena* 33, no. 186 (May 1905): 537; Wilson Gill, "Have a Republic in Every Schoolroom," *Boston Daily Globe*, August 6, 1916; Albert Shaw, "The School City—A Method of Pupil Self Government," *Review of Reviews* 20 (1899): 673–686; William R. Ward, *Student Participation in School Government: Six Years Experience with the School City* (Poughkeepsie, NY: Haight, 1906); M. C. Craft, "The School City a Success," *Atlanta Constitution*, May 5, 1901; "Gill School City Rules," *New-York Tribune*, March 31, 1899; A. Walker, "Self-Government in the High School," *Elementary School Teacher* 7, no. 8 (April 1907): 451–457; Wilson Gill, *A Social and Political Necessity* (New York: Patriotic League, 1902). Branch Normal School City is mentioned in *Salt Lake Herald*, October 7, 1900, 27. "At the Humboldt School," *St. Paul Globe*, March 7, 1898; B. O. Flower, "Wilson L. Gill: The Apostle of Democracy in Education," *Arena* 35, no. 195 (February 1906): 176; "Omaha High School Notes," *Omaha World Herald*, November 7, 1902; "The Gill School City: A Novel Educational Experiment Tried in New York," *Oregonian*, October 2, 1897; "Self-Ruling Schools: The Junior Republic Idea in Common Education," *Sun*, December 11, 1899; "A School City Organized at New York Under Government of a Mayor and City Council," *Jackson Citizen Patriot*, April 11, 1900; "They Make Laws. Novel Method of Teaching the Science of Political Economy to Children," *Grand Forks Herald*, February 3, 1901; "The School City a Success," *Kalamazoo Gazette*, May 12, 1901; "How the Gill School Works," *Dallas Morning News*, June 18, 1902; "Educational Club's Season," *Philadelphia Inquirer*, March 21, 1903; W. L. Gill, "The 'School City' in Connection with 'Pupil Self-Government,'" *Annual Report of the State Superintendant, New York Department of Public Instruction* 49 (1903); Richard Welling, *As the Twig Is Bent* (New York: Putnam's, 1942); Jack Holl, *Juvenile Reform in the Progressive Era: William R. George and the Junior Republic Movement* (Ithaca, NY: Cornell University Press, 1971), 199n54; Richard Welling, "The Teaching of Civics and Good Citizenship in the Public Schools," National Education Association, *Journal of Proceedings and Lectures* 42 (1903).

72. Great Britain Board of Education, "The Teaching of Civics in American Schools," *Special Reports on Educational Subjects* 10, no. 1 (1902): 136; "Gill School City Rules," *New-York Tribune*, March 31, 1899; Thomas Slicer, "The School City as a Form of Student Government," *Proceedings of the National Conference for Good City Government* (National Municipal League, 1904); William Torrey Harris, *The School City* (Syracuse, NY: Bardeen, 1907), 15; Wilson Gill, "Principles and Methods of Pupil Government: Child-Citizenship and the School City," *Proceedings of the Annual Conference of the National Education Association of the United States* 47 (1908): 285–294; Mabel Hill, *The Teaching of Civics* (Boston: Houghton Mifflin, 1914).

73. Lawrence Cremin describes the importance of these organizations as educational institutions in the period. Cremin, *American Education: The Metropolitan Experience, 1876–1980* (New York: Harper and Row, 1988).

74. Gail Bederman, *Manliness and Civilization: A Cultural History of Gender and Race in the United States, 1880–1917* (Chicago: University of Chicago Press, 1996); Joseph Kett, *Rites of Passage:*

Adolescence in America, 1790 to the Present (New York: Basic, 1977); Stephen Schlossman, "G. Stanley Hall and the Boys' Club: Conservative Applications of Recapitulation Theory," *Journal of the History of the Behavioral Sciences* 9, no. 2 (1973): 140–147; Cromwell Child, "New York's School Cities," *Los Angeles Times*, September 12, 1897; William Forbush, "The Social Pedagogy of Boyhood," *Pedagogical Seminary* 7 (1900): 307–346; William Forbush, *The Boy Problem* (Boston: Pilgrim, 1901); Walter Stone, *The Development of Boys' Work in the United States* (Nashville: Cullom and Ghertner, 1935); Ronald Tuttle Veal and J. T. Bowne, *Classified Bibliography of Boy Life and Organized Work with Boys* (New York: International Committee of Young Men's Christian Associations, 1919); Kevin Murphy, *Political Manhood* (New York: Columbia University Press, 2010); Wilson Gill, "Principles and Methods of Pupil Government: Child-Citizenship and the School City," *Proceedings of the Annual Conference of the National Education Association of the United States* 47 (1908): 286.

75. Frederic Thrasher, *The Gang* (Chicago: University of Chicago Press, 1927); Sidney Peixotto, *The Simple Tale of a Ten Years' Work for and among City Boys* (San Francisco: Columbia Park Boys' Club, 1905); Henry Gibson, *Boyology: or, Boy Analysis* (New York: Association Press, 1918); Thomas J. Browne, "The Clan or Gang Instinct in Boys," *Association Outlook* 9 (1900): 223–274; James Rogers, "The Theory of a Boys Club," *Education* 30 (1909): 40–44; Ronald Tuttle Veal and J. T. Bowne, *Classified Bibliography of Boy Life and Organized Work with Boys* (New York: International Committee of Young Men's Christian Associations, 1919); Dominic Cavallo, *Muscles and Morals: Organized Playgrounds and Urban Reform, 1880–1920.* (Philadelphia: University of Pennsylvania Press, 1981); Stephen Schlossman, "G. Stanley Hall and the Boys' Club: Conservative Applications of Recapitulation Theory," *Journal of the History of the Behavioral Sciences* 9, no. 2 (1973): 140–147; Maxine Seller, "G. Stanley Hall and Edward Thorndike on the Education of Women," *Educational Studies* 11, no. 4 (1981): 365–374; Lesley Diehl, "The Paradox of G. Stanley Hall," *American Psychologist* 41, no. 8 (1986); G. Stanley Hall, "Some Social Aspects of Education," *Pedagogical Seminary* 9 (1902): 83; J. Adams Puffer, "A Study of Boys' Gangs," *Pedagogical Seminary* 12 (1905); J. Adams Puffer, *The Boy and His Gang* (Boston: Houghton Mifflin, 1912); William Byron Forbush, "Boys Clubs," *Proceedings of the Child Conference for Research and Welfare* (1909), 25–31; Edgar James Swift, "Some Criminal Tendencies of Boyhood," *Pedagogical Seminary* 8 (1901): 87.

76. "The Real Day of the Real Boy," *San Francisco Chronicle*, October 16, 1904; A. J. Todd, "Experiment in Man Making: Boytown," *Charities* 17 (1906): 131–137; "Boys Found a Model City," *San Francisco Chronicle*, June 18, 1904; Sidney Peixotto, *The Simple Tale of a Ten Years' Work for and among City Boys* (San Francisco: Columbia Park Boys' Club, 1905), 12; James Rogers, *The State of Columbia, a Junior Republic* (San Francisco: Recorder, 1903); James Rogers, "'City of Telhi,' a Junior Republic or, How a Boys Club Mixed a Bit of Sociology with Their Sport, During Their Summer School Vacation, in California," *Education* 27 (1907): 271–280; "A Californian Junior Republic," *School Journal* 68 (1904): 333; Anna Pratt, "The Junior Republic," *San Francisco Chronicle*, September 7, 1902; James Rogers, "The State of Columbia, a Junior Republic," *Charities* 12 (1904): 245–250; "Boys' Club Returns from Summer Camp," *San Francisco Chronicle*, July 13, 1904; Eustace M. Peixotto, "The Columbia Park Boys' Club, a Unique Playground," *Annals of the American Academy of Political and Social Science* 35, no. 2 (1910): 220–224; Sidney Peixotto, "The Columbia Park Boys Club," *Out West* 24, no. 4 (April 1906).

77. James Rogers, *State of Columbia: A Junior Republic* (San Francisco: Recorder, 1903); James Rogers, "The State of Columbia, a Junior Republic," *Charities* 12 (1904): 246.

78. James Rogers, *State of Columbia: A Junior Republic* (San Francisco: Recorder, 1903); "A Californian Junior Republic," *School Journal* 68 (1904): 333; "The Real Day of the Real Boy," *San Francisco Chronicle*, October 16, 1904; "Boys Found a Model City," *San Francisco Chronicle*, June 18, 1904.

79. For side-by-side comparison of school cities and GJR, see Wilson Gill, *A New Citizenship* (Philadelphia: Patriotic League, 1913), 82–83; "Talk of Junior Republic," *Washington Post*, April 15, 1901; Jack Holl, *Juvenile Reform in the Progressive Era: William R. George and the Junior Republic Movement* (Ithaca, NY: Cornell University Press, 1971); Thomas Osborne to William George, May 31, 1904, box 4, folder 6, WG Papers; "Junior Republic's Work: Problem Now Is to Accommodate All Applicants for Admission," *Washington Post*, May 9, 1904; "The 'Junior Republic' Movement," *Los Angeles Times*, December 1, 1898; "The School City," *New York Observer and Chronicle*, January 15, 1903; "The School-City Movement as a Factor in Civic Development," *Arena* 34 (1905); "Men and Movements That Are Making for Progress," *Arena* 35, no. 198 (May 1906): 512; "Chief Executives Meet: President, Cabinet, and Judiciary of George Junior Republic Make a State Visit to Mr. McKinley," *New York Times*, March 11, 1900; Connecticut Junior Republic, *A Century of Caring for Youth: Connecticut Junior Republic, 1904–2004* (Litchfield, CT: Connecticut Junior Republic, 2004); Connecticut Junior Republic, *Fifty Years of Self-Government* (Litchfield, CT: Connecticut Junior Republic, 1954).

80. "Children to Run Miniature Cities. Franklin Institute Indorses Plan to Establish Municipalities in Schools," *Philadelphia Inquirer*, June 1, 1904; "Seeks $25,000 Fund for School City. Franklin Institute Believes Method Would Educate Children to Duties of Citizenship," *Philadelphia Inquirer*, June 12, 1904; "The School City," *Christian Observer*, February 21, 1906, 21; Wilson Gill, "The School City," *Journal of the Franklin Institute* (July 1903): 19–31; "The School City: The Report of the Franklin Institute, through its Committee on Science and the Arts, on the System of Civic Education Devised by Wilson L. Gill, of New Paltz, N.Y.," *Journal of the Franklin Institute* 156 (December 1903): 401–412; Wilson Gill, "The 'School City' in Connection with 'Pupil Self-Government,'" *Annual Report of the State Superintendant for the School Year* 49 (1903): 49; Wilson Gill, *A New Citizenship* (Philadelphia: Patriotic League, 1913).

81. DeLancey M. Ellis, "Thomas A. Edison, Inc., Sham Battle at the Pan-American Exposition," in *New York at the Louisiana Purchase Exposition, St. Louis 1904* (Albany, NY: Lyon, 1907); Tom Gunning, "The World as Object Lesson: Cinema Audiences, Visual Culture and the St. Louis World's Fair, 1904," *Film History* 6, no. 4 (1994): 422–444; Robert Rydell, *All the World's a Fair* (Chicago: University of Chicago Press, 1984); "Junior Republic Meeting," *Buffalo Courier*, Friday March 8, 1901.

Chapter 3

1. Nina Carter Marbourg, "George Junior Republic, the Juvenile Colony; Place where erring boys and girls from New York City streets reform themselves; novel experiment in self-government successfully prepares children for useful lives," *Los Angeles Herald*, December 4, 1904. See also Emmie Parker, "Making Model Citizens at the George Junior Republic," *Washington Post*, October

22, 1905. For a similar depiction of the National Junior Republic, see "In the City of Juniors," *Baltimore Sun*, May 18, 1913.

2. John Dewey, *The School and Society* (Chicago: University of Chicago Press, 1899, 1915 ed.), 15.

3. Historians of architecture and urbanism support such interpretations of the construction of the sheltered childhood as well. See, for example, Marta Gutman and Ning de Coninck-Smith, *Designing Modern Childhoods: History, Space, and the Material Culture of Children* (New Brunswick, NJ: Rutgers University Press, 2008).

4. On these earlier stories of reformatories, contract labor, and placing out, see Barry Krisberg, "The Legacy of Juvenile Corrections," *Corrections Today* 57, no. 5 (1995): 122; and David Rothman, *Conscience and Convenience: The Asylum and Its Alternatives in Progressive America* (Boston: Little, Brown, 1980). Patricia Clement observes some economic implications of youth activities in an earlier period—for example, efforts by orphanages and reformatories to train girls in domestic skills. Clement, *Growing Pains, Children in the Industrial Age* (New York: Twayne, 1997), 20.

5. "School City a Failure," *Sun*, May 1, 1899; "A Believer in Boys," *New-York Tribune*, May 28, 1899; "School Republic Unsuccessful," *Atlanta Constitution*, June 7, 1903; C. W. French, "The School City," *School Review* 13, no. 1 (1905): 33–41; Albert Shaw, "The School City—A Method of Pupil Self Government," *Review of Reviews* 20 (1899): 673–686; "The School City," *Municipal Affairs* (March 1906): 8; Caroline Murphy, "Report of School City Committee," *Daughters of the American Revolution Magazine* 29 (1906): 415–417; Edward Bradley, *Allendale Annals* (Lake Villa, IL: Allendale Association, 1926); Bernard Cronson, *Pupil Self-Government* (New York: Macmillan, 1907); US Bureau of Education, "Educational Pathology, or Self-Government in School," in *Report of the Commissioner*, 1901, 235–262.

6. Anthony Platt, *The Child Savers* (Chicago: University of Chicago Press, 1977); Ronald Cohen, "Child Saving and Progressivism, 1885–1915," in *American Childhood*, ed. Joseph Hawes and N. Ray Hiner (Westport, CT: Greenwood, 1985); Joseph Kett, *Rites of Passage: Adolescence in America, 1790 to the Present* (New York: Basic Books, 1977); Kate Bradley, "Growing Up with a City: Exploring Settlement Youth Work in London and Chicago, c. 1880–1940," *London Journal* 34, no. 3 (2009): 285–298; Daphne Spain, *How Women Saved the City* (Minneapolis: University of Minnesota, 2000); Walter Stone, *The Development of Boys' Work in the United States* (Nashville: Vanderbilt University, 1933), 102; Richard Butsch, *The Making of American Audiences* (Cambridge: Cambridge University Press, 2000); Edward Chandler, "How Much Children Attend the Theater, the Quality of the Entertainment They Choose and Its Effect upon Them," *Pedagogical Seminary* 16 (1909): 367–371; J. E. Wallace Wallin, "The Moving Picture in Relation to Education, Health, Delinquency and Crime," *Pedagogical Seminary* 17 (1910): 129–142; J. Pierce Fleming, "Moving Pictures As a Factor in Education," *Pedagogical Seminary* (September 1911): 336–352; Michael Davis, *The Exploitation of Pleasure: A Study of Commercial Recreations in New York City* (New York: Russell Sage Foundation Department of Child Hygiene, 1911); Jane Addams, *The Spirit of Youth and City Streets* (New York: Macmillan, 1909); Sidney Peixotto, *The Simple Tale of a Ten Years' Work for and among City Boys* (San Francisco: Columbia Park Boys Club, 1905); *A Historical Report of the Sixteen Years' Work at Hiram House* (Cleveland: Hiram House, 1912); Winifred Buck, *Boys Self Governing Clubs* (New York: Macmillan, 1903); Joan C. Tonn, *Mary Follett: Creating Democracy,*

Transforming Management (New Haven, CT: Yale University Press, 2008); Mina Carson, *Settlement Folk* (Chicago: University of Chicago Press, 1990); T. S. Crosswell, "Amusements of Worcester School Children," *Pedagogical Seminary* 6 (1899): 314–371; "Youthful Misdoing As Misapplied Energy," *Puritan* 9 (1901): 743. Jonathan Crary, *Suspensions of Perception: Attention, Spectacle and Modern Culture* (Cambridge, MA: MIT Press, 2000), whose focus is Europe, offers the richest study of anxieties about attention in this period.

7. Arthur Leland, "Playground Self Government," *Charities* 12 (June 4, 1904): 588. On sports teaching democracy, see Luther Gulick, "Psychological, Pedagogical, and Religious Aspects of Group Games," *Pedagogical Seminary* 6 (March 1899): 135–151. On playgrounds and democracy, see Sarah Jo Peterson, "Voting for Play: The Democratic Potential of Progressive Era Playgrounds," *Journal of the Gilded Age and Progressive Era* 3, no. 2 (2004): 145–175. On the notion that self-government is the aim of the playground in general, see Joseph Lee, "What Has Been Learned," *Mind and Body* 15, no. 7 (1908): 181. The miniature cities were not exact duplicates; one playground notably created several novel positions for its junior citizens, including a city librarian who could lend books to local children and a board of trade whose child staff showed visitors around the park.

8. "A Young Republic: Girls and Boys of Hebrew Asylum Comprise It," *New-York Tribune*, March 20, 1907; *Annual Report of the Hebrew Sheltering Guardian Society*, box 1, folder 4, Annual Reports (bound) 1905–1909, Records of the Hebrew Sheltering Guardian Society of New York, Center for Jewish History; Ludwig Bernstein, "Modern Tendencies in Jewish Orphan Asylum work," in *Annual Report of the Hebrew Sheltering Guardian Society*, 50, box 1, folder 4, Annual Reports (bound) 1905–1909, Records of the Hebrew Sheltering Guardian Society of New York, Center for Jewish History; Samuel Levy, "A Study in Child-Rearing," in *Annual Report of the Hebrew Sheltering Guardian Society*, 37, box 1, folder 4, Annual Reports (bound) 1905–1909, Records of the Hebrew Sheltering Guardian Society of New York, Center for Jewish History; Annual Report 1909/1911, box 2, folder 2, Annual Reports 1909–1913, Center for Jewish History, Records of the Hebrew Sheltering Guardian Society of New York, undated, 1879–1970, I-43; "Boys Hold Election To-day: Free City Government in Miniature in Hebrew Asylum a Success," *New-York Tribune*, July 4, 1910; "Boys to Operate Bank: Hebrew Guardian Society back of the scheme; it will do a regular banking business on a small scale and hopes to make money—has a list of depositors already," *Detroit Free Press*, August 12, 1907; "Brownieland Fills Orphans' Coffers," *New York Times*, May 23, 1910.

9. John Grabowski, "*From Progressive to Patrician: George Bellamy and Hiram House Social Settlement, 1896–1914*," *Ohio History Journal* 87 (Winter 1978): 37–52; *Pioneering on Social Frontiers, 1896–1936* (Cleveland: Hiram House Social Settlement, 1937); John J. Grabowski, "A Social Settlement in a Neighborhood in Transition: Hiram House, Cleveland, Ohio, 1896–1926" (PhD diss., Case Western Reserve, 1976); Daphne Spain, "Make-Believe Municipalities: A Settlement House Experiment in Promoting Citizenship," paper presented at the annual conference of the Society of American City and Regional Planning History, St. Louis, Missouri, November 2003; [George Bellamy presumed speaker], speech, "Progress City: An Answer to the Demand for a Civic Education," folder 3, Progress City ca. 1906–1920, Hiram House Records MS 3319, Western Reserve Historical Society [hereafter HH Records]; George Albert Bellamy, *A Historical Report of the Sixteen Years' Work at Hiram House, Cleveland, Ohio* (Cleveland: Hiram House, 1912); "Mayor Lost in the

Foot Race, Chief Executive of 'Progress City' Not So Fleet As His Constituent, Wheels of Government Run Smoothly in Miniature Municipality," *Cleveland Plain Dealer*, July 8, 1906; Bertha Johnston, "Some Educational Forces Supplementary to the Public Schools," *Kindergarten Magazine* 19 (1907): 214–227; Cleveland Foundation Committee, *The Sphere of Private Agencies* (Cleveland: Cleveland Foundation, 1920), 105; Frank Koos, "Progress City: A Citizenship Laboratory," n.d., no page, container 36, folder 3, Progress City ca. 1906–1920, HH Records; Frank Koos, "Progress City: A Model Juvenile City," undated speech c. 1909–1912, container 36, folder 3, Progress City ca. 1906–1920, HH Records; "WANTED A Citizen to Foretell the Weather, Apply at Progress City Weather Bureau," *Progress City News*, July 27, 1906, container 53, bound volume 1, Hiram House Publications, Newsletters, HH Records; "Children Will Have Own City. Model Municipalities Soon to Be Opened for Hiram House Colony," *Cleveland Plain Dealer*, May 24, 1907; Charles Bushnell, "Progress City" (Fall 1906), container 36, folder 3, Progress City ca. 1906–1920, HH Records; Charles Bushnell, "Progress City," *World To-Day* 12 (May 1907): 532–535; "Progress City: An Answer to the Demand for a Civic Education," container 36, folder 3, Progress City ca. 1906–1920, HH Records; Ethel Rogers, "Playing at Citizenship," *American City* 9 (1913): 445; Josiah Strong, Appendix B, "The Hiram House, Cleveland, Ohio," in *The Challenge of the City* (New York: Young People's Missionary Movement, 1907). Records of the visiting students are available in the Hiram House Archives.

10. [George Bellamy presumed speaker], speech, "Progress City: An Answer to the Demand for a Civic Education," folder 3, Progress City ca. 1906–1920, HH Records.

11. Rev. R. J. Floody, "Worcester's Garden City," *Work with Boys: A Magazine of Methods*, April 1912, 209, 214; "Children's Meeting, Saturday, February 13, 1909," *Transactions of the Worcester County Horticultural Society* (Worcester: Worcester County Horticultural Society, 1909), 122; R. J. Floody, "Worcester Garden City Plan; or, the Good Citizens' Factory," *Nature Study Review* 8 (1912): 145–150; R. J. Floody, "Good Citizens Factory, and Law School: What the Garden City has been called by some who have observed the workings of this plan for civic betterment among the little men and women of the Island district," *Worcester Magazine* 13 (1910): 35–37; Charles Nutt, *History of Worcester and Its People* (New York: Lewis Historical, 1919); "Garden City, The Great Social Settlement in Worcester: Established Three Years Ago for the Betterment of Poor Children in an Unlovely, Marshy, Mosquito-Breeding Place Long Used As a Dump for the Debris of the Streets and the Castaway Things of the Homes—Hundreds of Boys Girls Plant and Care for Sections of Land Allotted to Them, and Strive with Great Diligence to Win Prizes Offered for Bounteous, Well Kept Gardens—Tremendous Growth of the Little City Since the First Sowing of Seed, Given the Children by the Government—Neighborhood Greatly Improved—Boy Police and Other Officials Elected by the Boys," *Boston Daily Globe*, May 22, 1910; "Garden City Boys and Girls Rewarded," *Boston Daily Globe*, October 14, 1910; "Globe Provides a Pilot for Youngsters from Worcester," *Boston Daily Globe*, October 12, 1911; "A Girl May Run This Garden City: Maidens Are Judge and Police Chief," *Boston Post*, August 9, 1910, from Clippings File, WG Papers.

12. Frank Koos, "Progress City: A Citizenship Laboratory," n.d., no page, container 36, folder 3, Progress City ca. 1906–1920, HH Records. Progress City operated with a slightly altered understanding of its "laboratory environment" from Dewey's formulation, for here it was youth who did the experimenting.

13. *A Historical Report of the Sixteen Years' Work at Hiram House* (Cleveland: Hiram House, 1912), 78; Cleveland Federation for Charity and Philanthropy, *The Social Year Book* (1913), 142. See also Laura Gifford, "The Hiram House Model Cottage and Its Influences," *Survey* 33 (October 17, 1914): 70–71; Laura Gifford, "The Hiram House Model Cottage: A Social Settlement," *Journal of Home Economics* 15 (April 1915): 185–188.

14. Mabel Kittredge, "Housekeeping Centers in Settlements and Public Schools," *Survey* (May 3, 1913): 190–191.

15. Mabel Kittredge, "Housekeeping Centers in Settlements and Public Schools," *Survey* (May 3, 1913): 188–189; Jeanne Boydston, *Home and Work* (New York: Oxford, 1990). This was distinct from the focus of earlier reformers in teaching American standards to immigrant populations. See also Mabel Kittredge, "Home-Making in a Model Flat: The Next Step in Public School Extension," *Survey* (1905): 176–181; and "Duplicating the Home in the School," *Journal of Home Economics* 6 (1914): 236.

16. Lawrence Cremin, *History of Teachers College* (New York: Columbia University Press, 1954), 12; Emily Huntington, *Little Lessons for Little Housekeepers* (New York: Randolph, 1875); Emily Huntington, *How to Teach Kitchen Garden: or, Object Lessons in Household Work Including Songs, Plays, Exercises and Games, Illustrating Household Occupations* (New York: Doubleday, Page, 1901; Daphne Spain, *How Women Saved the City* (Minneapolis: University of Minnesota, 2000), 219; *The Kitchen Garden* (newsletter, Cincinnati Kitchen Garden Association); *Household Economy: A Manual for Use in Schools* (New York: Kitchen Garden Association, 1882); Annie Prescott Bull, "The 'Kitchen Garden,'" *Harper's Bazaar*, September 23, 1899, 38; "The Kitchen Garden," *New York Sun*, cited in *Current Literature* 30, no. 2 (February 1901): 186; Laura Winnington, "The Kitchen-Garden," *Outlook*, May 4, 1901, 52; "For a Kitchen-Garden Exhibit," *World's Columbian Exhibition Illustrated*, December 1892, 210; "Little Kitchen Garden Maids," *Chicago Tribune*, October 29, 1893.

17. On developmental psychology in youth work, particularly with boys, see David MacLeod, *Building Character in the American Boy* (Madison: University of Wisconsin Press, 2004); Stephen Schlossman, "G. Stanley Hall and the Boys' Club: Conservative Applications of Recapitulation Theory," *Journal of the History of the Behavioral Sciences* 9, no. 2 (1973): 140–147. On the philosophy of play as education, see Dominic Cavallo, *Muscles and Morals: Organized Playgrounds and Urban Reform, 1880–1920* (Philadelphia: University of Pennsylvania Press, 1981) and Henry Curtis, *Education through Play* (New York: Macmillan, 1914).

18. "Jackson Speaks at Chautauqua: Promoter of Juvenile State Will Visit George Junior Republic," *Atlanta Constitution*, July 5, 1907; "Gossip from the Summer Resorts," *Cleveland Plain Dealer*, July 14, 1907; Harry Chalfant, "Chautauqua Notes," *Zion's Herald* 85, no. 33 (August 14, 1907): 1038; "Classified Program" [see session on "The Juvenile Problem"], *Chautauquan* 47, no. 2 (July 1907): 239.

19. "Politicians Try to Oust Brown," *Salt Lake Herald*, January 27, 1907.

20. "Politicians Try to Oust Brown," *Salt Lake Herald*, January 27, 1907; A Canyon Crester, "What Canyon Crest Did for a Loafer," *Salt Lake Herald*, October 15, 1906; "Buy Farm for Homeless

Boys," *Salt Lake Herald*, March 27, 1906; "Visitors Are Welcome," *Salt Lake Herald*, July 12, 1906; "Canyon Crest Election," *Inter-Mountain Republican*, March 20, 1907; "Notes," *Survey* 16 (August 11, 1906): 517; "Canyon Crest Is Like a Paradise," *Inter-Mountain Republican*, May 5, 1906; "Society Women Cook for the Boys at Canyon Crest Ranch," *Salt Lake Telegram*, July 11, 1907.

21. Robert Mennel, *Thorns and Thistles* (Lebanon, NH: University Press of New England, 1973); Ellen Ryerson, *The Best Laid Plans* (New York: Farrar, Straus and Giroux, 1978); Jonathan Simon, "Punishment and the Political Technologies of the Body," in *SAGE Handbook of Punishment and Society*, ed. Jonathan Simon and Richard Sparks (Newbury Park, CA: SAGE Publishing, 2013); Samuel Barrows, *Children's Courts in the United States* (International Penal and Prison Commission, 1904), xvii; Ben Lindsey, *The Problem of the Children and How the State of Colorado Cares for Them* (Denver: Juvenile Court of the City and County of Denver, 1904), 101–102; Steven Schlossman, "End of Innocence: Science and the Transformation of Progressive Juvenile Justice, 1899–1917," *History of Education* 7, no. 3 (1978): 207–218; Alice Smuts, *Science in the Service of Children, 1893–1935* (Chicago: University of Chicago Press, 2008), 107; Thomas Eliot, *The Juvenile Court and the Community* (New York: Macmillan, 1914); Steven L. Schlossman, *Love and the American Delinquent: The Theory and Practice of "Progressive" Juvenile Justice, 1825–1920* (Chicago: University of Chicago Press, 1977); Paul Colomy and Martin Kretzmann, "Projects and Institution Building: Judge Ben B. Lindsey and the Juvenile Court Movement," *Social Problems* 42, no. 2 (1995): 191–215; Lincoln Steffens, "Ben B. Lindsey: The Just Judge," *McClure's* 27 (October 1906): 563–582; Lincoln Steffens, "Ben B. Lindsey: The Just Judge, II—The Opposition," *McClure's* 28 (November 1906): 74–88; Charles Larsen, *The Good Fight: The Life and Times of Ben B. Lindsey* (Chicago: Quadrangle, 1972; Henry Haskell, "The 'Kid Judge' of Denver," *Outlook*, June 24, 1905, 497. According to Thomas D. Eliot, "The report of the Hotchkiss committee on the juvenile court of Chicago (1911–1912) contains perhaps the best statement of the thesis that the juvenile court is an educational institution." Eliot, "The Trend of the Juvenile Court," *Annals of the American Academy of Political and Social Science* 52 (1914): 149.

22. William Hull, "The George Junior Republic," *Annals of the American Academy of Political and Social Science* 10, no. 1 (1897): 85; Ben Lindsey to T. M. Osborne (then president of GJR association), April 21, 1908, box 4, folder 17, WG Papers; *Annual Report of the Hebrew Sheltering Guardian Society*, box 1, folder 4, Annual Reports (bound) 1905–1909, Records of the Hebrew Sheltering Guardian Society of New York, Center for Jewish History; Lincoln Steffens, "Ben B. Lindsey: The Just Judge," *McClure's*, October 1906, 563–581; "Will Fight for Social Purity," *Los Angeles Times*, March 17, 1907; "Parental Republic: Unique Educational Experiment in Connection with Public School Is Visited by Class," *Los Angeles Times*, April 6, 1910; A. J. Todd, "Experiment in Man Making: Boytown," *Charities* 17 (1906): 131–137; "Here Playing Is the Thing," [Omaha] *Sun*, September 10, 1908; Harriet Hickox Heller, "The Playground As a Phase of Social Reform," *Proceedings of the Second Annual Playground Conference* (1909): 177–185; "Children Elect Officers," *Washington Post*, August 3, 1907; LeRoy Ashby, *Saving the Waifs: Reformers and Dependent Children, 1890–1917* (Philadelphia: Temple University Press, 1984); "Georgia to Have Juvenile State," *Charities and the Commons* (April 25, 1908): 13; "South's George Junior Republic: To Be Called the Juvenile State When Competed, Near Athens, Ga.," *New-York Tribune*, July 21, 1907; "Jackson Pushing Work on the Juvenile State," *Atlanta Constitution*, November 12, 1907; "Men of Distinction Do Honor to Dead Waif, Judge of Ford Republic," *Kalamazoo Gazette*, October 15, 1911; R. H. Stevens,

"Democracy as an Educational Principle," *The Public: A Journal of Democracy* 14 (May 19, 1911): 464; "A Successful Boys' Home," *Chicago Daily Tribune*, December 4, 1901.

23. "Boys' City Plan Strongly Backed. Project Started in Indianapolis for Benefit of Young America. Provides Civic Training. Will Have Municipal Government and Be Modern in Every Respect," *Washington Times*, January 2, 1907; "Waifs to Make Merry," *Salt Lake Herald*, December 20, 1906; "Great Promise of Canyon Crest Ranch," *Salt Lake Herald*, June 10, 1906; "Politicians Try to Oust Brown," *Salt Lake Herald*, January 27, 1907; "Scenes at Canyon Crest Ranch," *Salt Lake Herald*, June 18, 1906; "Farm Home for Boys Is Inspected: Plans Are Laid to Carry on Work of the Juvenile Betterment League," *Salt Lake Herald*, May 5, 1906; "Money Is Needed for Canyon Crest; Director of Boys' Farm Wants to Raise $20,000 in Ten Days," *Inter-Mountain Republican*, June 7, 1906; "Will Talk to Boys," *Indianapolis Morning Star*, May 12, 1907; "Judge Brown Returns. Chief of Juvenile Court Will Probably Accept Leadership of Winona Assembly," *Salt Lake Herald*, November 14, 1906; "State Owns the Child," *Detroit Free Press*, December 7, 1908; "Gossip from the Summer Resorts," *Cleveland Plain Dealer*, July 14, 1907; "A City for Boys Only," *New-York Tribune*, November 25, 1906; "Boyville to Be Reality: Town with 5,000 Population Planned at Lake Winona, Ind. Goods held in common. Youths will conduct city government and own all stores. Stores to be boys' property. Telephone system a feature. Band and chorus planned," *Chicago Daily Tribune*, February 10, 1907; "Judge Willis Brown," promotional pamphlet, Hollister Press, 1904, http://digital.lib.uiowa.edu/cdm/ref/collection/tc/id/38078; "To Visit Boys Farm," *Inter-Mountain Republican*, May 1, 1906. There are conflicting stories of his departure. See "Works for Boys City," *Indianapolis Star*, October 27, 1907; "Judge Brown Returns: Chief of Juvenile Court Will Probably Accept Leadership of Winona Assembly," *Salt Lake Herald*, November 14, 1906; Ronald D. Cohen and Raymond A. Mohl, *The Paradox of Progressive Education: The Gary Plan and Urban Schooling* (Port Washington, NY: Kennikat, 1979); *Mill v. Brown*, 88, *Pacific Reporter* 609 (Utah, 1907); Steven L. Schlossman, *Love and the American. Delinquent: The Theory and Practice of "Progressive" Juvenile Justice, 1825–1920* (Chicago: University of Chicago Press, 1977); "Warrant Is Served on Judge Brown," *Inter-Mountain Republican*, January 29, 1907; Ben Lindsey to Mrs. William George, May 23, 1907, box 4, folder 10, WG Papers; Steven L. Schlossman and Ronald D. Cohen, "The Music Man in Gary: Willis Brown and Child-Saving in the Progressive Era," *Societas* 7 (1977): 1–17. Brown rarely acknowledged a debt to others and routinely took credit for others' ideas, from republics to the Anti-Cigarette League. The next Canyon Crest superintendent discontinued self-government, but the nearby industrial school at Ogden launched a Boy City. See "The Boys' City at Ogden," *Salt Lake City Herald-Republican*, November 11, 1909. He was not alone in taking credit for borrowed ideas; the head of Missouri's Kemper School claimed he had invented the school city. See "How a Missouri Idea," *St. Louis Post-Dispatch*, February 25, 1906.

24. "Works for Boys City," *Indianapolis Star*, October 27, 1907; "Many Joys Planned for Boys of Indiana: Thousand Youngsters Will Camp at Winona Lake in Novel Way. 'Boyville' Is Real Town. Will Elect Mayor and Postmaster and Operate Bank Just Like Grownups," *Indianapolis Star*, July 16, 1907; "Magical Boys City Will Rise in Woods: Municipal Elections Will Be Held in Boyville, and Youths Will Rule Camp. Winona Plans Innovation. Cheap Vacation at Summer Resort Will Draw Hundreds," *Indianapolis Morning Star*, June 2, 1907; "Will Talk to Boys," *Indianapolis Morning Star*, May 12, 1907.

25. "Pastor Heads Twenty Boys to Boyville," *Indianapolis Star*, July 26, 1907; "Place Is Given to Judge Brown: Presiding Genius of the Juvenile Court to Supervise Boys' Town. A City for Youngsters. They Will Run Things Absolutely with Their Own Laws and Officers to Enforce Them," *Deseret Evening News*, November 5, 1906; "Law Is Hard on Boy," *Indianapolis Star*, February 24, 1908; "Boys' City Plan Strongly Backed. Project Started in Indianapolis for Benefit of Young America. Provides Civic Training. Will Have Municipal Government and Be Modern in Every Respect," *Washington Times*, January 2, 1907; Andrew Rieser, *The Chautauqua Moment: Protestants, Progressives, and the Culture of Modern Liberalism* (New York: Columbia University Press, 2003). This movement of reforms from urban to rural areas could be found in educational programs more generally. See Tracy L. Steffes, *School, Society, and State* (Chicago: University of Chicago Press, 2012); James Delzell, "The Betterment of Rural Schools through Boys' and Girls' Clubs: The Nebraska Plan," *APNEA* (1912): 1373–1375.

26. "Many Joys Planned for Boys of Indiana: Thousand Youngsters Will Camp at Winona Lake in Novel Way. 'Boyville' Is Real Town. Will Elect Mayor and Postmaster and Operate Bank Just Like Grownups," *Indianapolis Star*, July 16, 1907; "Pastor Heads Twenty Boys to Boyville," *Indianapolis Star*, July 26, 1907.

27. "Out for Mayor of Boyville," *Indianapolis Star*, June 19, 1907; "A City for Boys Only," *New-York Tribune*, November 25, 1906.

28. "Many Joys Planned for Boys of Indiana: Thousand Youngsters Will Camp at Winona Lake in Novel Way. 'Boyville' is Real Town. Will Elect Mayor and Postmaster and Operate Bank Just Like Grownups," *Indianapolis Star*, July 16, 1907; "Juvenile Court at Winona, 'Citizens of Boys' City Will Pose As the 'Culprits,'" *Indianapolis Star*, July 14, 1907; "Gossip from the Summer Resorts," *Cleveland Plain Dealer*, July 14, 1907; "Boys' City to Give Circus August 10," *Indianapolis Star*, August 4, 1907; "Swayzee Girl Gets Medal at Winona," *Indianapolis Star*, August 8, 1907; "Boys of America to Own a City," *Reading Eagle*, February 24, 1907; "Place Is Given to Judge Brown: Presiding Genius of the Juvenile Court to Supervise Boys' Town. A City for Youngsters. They Will Run Things Absolutely with Their Own Laws and Officers to Enforce Them," *Deseret Evening News*, November 5, 1906; "Merchants Boys' Guests," *Indianapolis Star*, August 5, 1908; "Boys Greet Visitors. Entertain South Bend Men. Youth's Settlement at Winona Lake Inspected by Commercial Committee—DAR Plans Program Friday," *Indianapolis Star*, August 6, 1908; "Out for Mayor of Boyville," *Indianapolis Star*, June 19, 1907; "Pastor Heads Twenty Boys to Boyville," *Indianapolis Star*, July 26, 1907; "Boys Form Two Political Parties. Land Organization and Water Forces Will Fight Municipal Battles at Winona. Postmaster Is a Russian. Four Hundred Lads Present and Big Mass Meeting Will Be Held Today," *Indianapolis Star*, July 28, 1907; "The Badger of Canyon Crest, by W. Eckstein, Mayor of Canyon Crest Ranch" *Salt Lake Herald*, September 2, 1906; "Utah Delegate Is Now at Boyville," *Indianapolis Star*, July 26, 1907; "Boy's Mayor Gives Inaugural Address," *Indianapolis Star*, August 1, 1907; "A City for Boys Only," *New-York Tribune*, November 25, 1906; "'Boyville' to Be Reality," *Chicago Daily Tribune*, February 10, 1907; "More News of Boy City," *Salt Lake Telegram*, August 13, 1908; "Boys' City Grows in Woods," *Chicago Daily Tribune*, July 26, 1907; "Snap Shots at Home, Judge Brown Remains There," *Salt Lake Telegram*, August 19, 1907.

29. "Tent City for Boys Only: Five Thousand Will Live in It and Run Its Government," *Washington Herald*, November 6, 1906; Ronald D. Cohen and Raymond A. Mohl, *The Paradox of Progressive*

Education: The Gary Plan and Urban Schooling (Port Washington, NY: Kennikat, 1979), 77; Steven L. Schlossman and Ronald D. Cohen, "The Music Man in Gary: Willis Brown and Child-Saving in the Progressive Era," *Societas* 7 (1977): 1–17; "Will Talk to Boys," *Indianapolis Morning Star*, May 12, 1907; "Boys' City Plan Strongly Backed. Project Started in Indianapolis for Benefit of Young America. Provides Civic Training. Will Have Municipal Government and Be Modern in Every Respect," *Washington Times*, January 2, 1907; "Boys' City to Be Larger This Year Than Before," *Indianapolis Star*, July 12, 1908; "Boys Choose Tickets," *Indianapolis Star*, July 31, 1908; "Boy's City Opens July 27," *Indianapolis Star*, March 31, 1908; "Been in Boy City? Here Is a Town No Traveler Should Miss. It's Just Organized," *Grand Rapids Press (Evening Press)*, July 31, 1909; Steven L. Schlossman and Ronald D. Cohen, "The Music Man in Gary: Willis Brown and Child-Saving in the Progressive Era," *Societas* 7 (1977): 1–17; "Miniature Boy City for Michigan," *Norfolk Weekly News-Journal*, June 18, 1909; "Worth While Folk: Boss of a Citizen Factory," *New-York Tribune*, November 9, 1913; "Election to Be Held in Model 'Boy City,'" *Hopkinsville Kentuckian* [and many other newspaper reprints], May 25, 1909; "Residents of Boy City See New Head Take Oath," *Indianapolis Star*, August 1, 1909; "Charlevoix Will Have 'Boy City,'" *Detroit Free Press*, July 4, 1909; "'Boy City' Has Been Moved to Michigan," *Salt Lake Herald*, May 21, 1909; "At The Resorts," *Kalamazoo Gazette*, July 25, 1909, 7; "Pith of News from the Middle West," *Los Angeles Times*, May 21, 1909: 2 under the heading "Model Boy City [Associated Press Day Report]"; "Boy City in Michigan," *Carbon County News*, May 27, 1909; "Insurgents Win at Boy City; Bosses Annihilated," *Tacoma Times*, August 12, 1910; "Boy's City Wins Fame," *Indianapolis Star*, July 17, 1910; "Expert Will Pick Teachers," *Chicago Daily Tribune*, January 12, 1908; "At the Resorts," *Kalamazoo Gazette*, July 25, 1909; "Juvenile Court Judge Conducts a Boy City," *Inter-Mountain Republican*, May 30, 1909; "Founder of the Boy City Here," *Detroit Free Press*, December 6, 1908; H. M. H., "Winona Lake Incidents," *Friends' Intelligencer* 65, no. 39 (September 26, 1908): 602; "Driven from Boys City," *Indianapolis Star*, August 16, 1908.

30. "Boy City Will Be Formed in Oregon: Method of Teaching Boys to Control Themselves Has Been Success," *Oregonian*, December 25, 1910; Boys' Club Association of Indianapolis, *A Glimpse into Boyville* (Indianapolis: Boys' Club Association, 1910); "Hundred Boys Registered to Get a Vote in 'Boyville': Will Have Part in Self-Government Plan to Be Installed on Jan. 1 at 3757 Wentworth Avenue," *Chicago Daily Tribune*, December 8, 1912; "Boys of St. Paul's Church to Form Miniature 'City,'" *Chicago Daily Tribune*, November 28, 1908; "Boys' Friend to Speak Here," *Chicago Daily Tribune*, December 12, 1908; "The Founder of Boyville," *Marion Daily Mirror*, April 22, 1910; "Life in Boytown," *Indianapolis Star*, January 7, 1912; "Insurgents Win at Boy City; Bosses Annihilated," *Tacoma Times*, August 12, 1910; "Works for Boys City," *Indianapolis Star*, October 27, 1907; "Will Act As Mayor of Indiana Boy City," *Grand Rapids Press*, May 23, 1912; "Our Boys' Band Makes Big Hit," *Salt Lake Telegram*, August 14, 1907.

31. "Boys of Anderson Will Cast Ballots," *Indianapolis Star*, February 16, 1908; Herbert Wright Gates, "The History, Scope and Success of Organizations for Boys and Girls," *Religious Education* 7 (1912): 230; "Members of Boyville Colony at Anderson Meet at Banquet," *Indianapolis Star*, December 9, 1907; "Boys to Take Vows on Easter Sunday," *Indianapolis Star*, April 12, 1908; "Election Arouses Boys," *Indianapolis Star*, February 23, 1908.

32. Henry W. Thurston, "Review of *The Junior Republic: Its History and Ideals* by William R. George," *School Review* 18, no. 8 (1910): 566–567; Katie Brannigan, "Changes," *Junior Republic*

Citizen (September 1899): 4–5; Jeanne Robert, "Republic for Boys and Girls—After Twenty Years," *Review of Reviews* 42 (December 1910): 705–712; "Our Boys' Republic Getting to Work," *Los Angeles Times*, September 3, 1907; Multiple letters from citizens departing for California, box 4, folder 20, WG Papers; Minna Norriss, "The History of the California Junior Republic" (master's thesis, University of Southern California, 1931); "Will Fight for Social Purity," *Los Angeles Times*, March 17, 1907; "Simmering in New Republic. Real Life Is Led by George Junior Citizens; Regular Superintendent Will Soon Take Charge; Teaching Handicrafts Is an Important Item," *Los Angeles Times*, October 30, 1908; "Miniature Ranchos," *Los Angeles Times*, January 4, 1915; "President Is Inaugurated: George Junior Republic Is Born at San Fernando," *Los Angeles Times*, March 20, 1908. Box 4, folders 19–24 in WG Papers contain early correspondence back and forth between George and the leadership at the new California republic, noting personnel problems centered on Nat Bedford's wife. Bedford resigned in July 1908. Other efforts to duplicate republics are detailed in: R. Gabel to Calvin Derrick, regarding the Texas Industrial School for Boys, September 26, 1908, box 4, folder 26, WG Papers; W. B. Buck (superintendent) to William George, regarding the Children's Village of the Seybert Institution in Meadowbrook, PA, October 26, 1908, box 4, folder 28, WG Papers.

33. Lew Allen Chase, *The Government of Michigan* (New York: Scribner's, 1919), 65; "National Republic of Boys and Girls," *Hartford Courant*, June 3, 1908; "Federate Junior Republics," *Washington Post*, January 7, 1908; "'George Junior Nation' Founded," *Zion's Herald* 86, no. 24 (June 10, 1908): 739; L. B. Stowe to Homer Lane, June 14, 1912, box 12, folder 10, WG Papers; Homer Lane to L. B. Stowe, June 11, 1912, box 12, folder 9, WG Papers; L. B. Stowe to Mr. G. A. Lightner, June 14, 1912, box 12, folder 9, WG Papers; L. B. Stowe to Homer Lane, June 14, 1912, box 12, folder 10, WG Papers; "Juvenile State Thriving; Now Has Bank and Courts," *Atlanta Constitution*, August 7, 1910; Clifford L. Anderson, "Juvenile State Will Make Wayward Boys Govern Selves," *Atlanta Constitution*, April 22, 1909; "Governor Gentle to Be Inaugurated," *Atlanta Constitution*, November 22, 1909; "Formally Open Juvenile State," *Atlanta Constitution*, November 25, 1909; "Juvenile State Will Be Unique," *Atlanta Constitution*, March 22, 1907; "Constitution Adopted for the Juvenile State," *Atlanta Constitution*, March 25, 1907; "For Reformatory People Declare," *Atlanta Constitution*, March 23, 1905; Peter Rice, "What Juvenile State Will Do for Society," *Atlanta Constitution*, April 28, 1909; Clifford L. Anderson, "Builders of Boys and Boys As Builders," *Atlanta Constitution*, April 28, 1909; Clifford L. Anderson, "What a Juvenile State Does for Society and the Child," *Atlanta Constitution*, April 20, 1909; Gay Pitman Zieger, *For the Good of the Children* (Detroit: Wayne State University Press, 2003); LeRoy Ashby, *Saving the Waifs: Reformers and Dependent Children, 1890–1917* (Philadelphia: Temple University Press, 1984); "Scene in Boys' Court: Citizens of Ford Republic Make Own Laws and Enforce Them," *Beaumont Enterprise*, August 21, 1910; Frederick Mather Caldwell, "Boy Power Applied," *Everybody's Magazine* 23 (1910): 183; "Democracy as an Educational Principle," *The Public: A Journal of Democracy* 14 (1911); F. James Clatworthy, "Homer T. Lane's Legacy of Self-Government: An Inquiry into Organizational Synecology at the Boys Republic, 1909–1982," November 5, 1982, ERIC ED225965; "Fresh Air Boys Govern Own Camp: 'Live Ones' of Gas House District Organize in Self-Rule Test. Court Administers Impartial Justice. One Lad Sentenced to Peel Potatoes—Apple Connoisseurs Take Their Loot Back," *New-York Tribune*, July 31, 1914; Lyman Beecher Stowe, "Junior Citizens in Action," *Outlook*, November 18, 1914, 654. These republics are listed as affiliated organizations in

Hastings Hornell Hart, "List of George Junior Republics in the Order of Their Founding Reported by Mr. William R. George, August 29, 1910," in *Preventive Treatment of Neglected Children* (New York: Charities Publications Committee, 1910). Notably, other excited groups were unsuccessful in launching their republic bids. See, for example, "Mrs. McKim Helps Boys," *New York Times*, May 16, 1910; "Educational News and Comment," *American Education* (1911): 414; "The Spread of the Junior Republic Idea," *Outlook,* July 6, 1912, 516.

34. William George, *The Junior Republic: Its History and Ideals* (New York: D. Appleton, 1910), Osborne preface, xii; Emmie Parker, "Making Model Citizens at the George Junior Republic," *Washington Post*, October 22, 1905.

35. "Boys Open Tent City: Mayor issues proclamation. Declares only those who will obey rules are wanted as citizens at Winona Lake camp," *Indianapolis Star,* July 28, 1908; G. Stanley Hall, *Educational Problems* (New York: Appleton, 1911); G. Stanley Hall, "Some Social Aspects of Education," *Educational Review* (May 1902): 433–445; G. Stanley Hall, *Adolescence* (New York: Appleton, 1904); G. Stanley Hall and Some of His Pupils, *Aspects of Child Life and Education* (Boston: Ginn, 1907); Harry McKown, *The Student Council* (New York: McGraw-Hill, 1944); "School City a Panacea: Inventor Explains It to N. Y. U. Pedagogy Students," *New-York Tribune*, November 4, 1911; Richard Welling, *As the Twig Is Bent* (New York: Putnam's, 1942), 99; "In the Mirror of the Present: Progress of the School-City Movement," *The Arena* 35, no. 195 (February 1906): 201; Samuel Keeble, *The Citizen of Tomorrow: A Handbook on Social Questions* (London: C H Kelly, 1906); "The Junior City Council [Manchester, England]," *Municipal Journal* 17 (December 25, 1908): 1050; R. H. G., "Junior Republics in England," *Journal of Criminal Law and Criminology* 3 (1912): 470; E. Stagg Whitin, "Review of *Citizens Made and Remade* by W. R. George" *Annals of the American Academy of Political and Social Science* 47 (May 1913): 299; Lyman B. Stowe, *Annals of the American Academy of Political and Social Science* 47 (May 1913): 299; New Zealand Department of Education, *Report* (1908), 41. Regionally and locally, other republics with no immediate ambitions for replication also became models for duplication. Cleveland's municipal and Jewish Alliance playgrounds installed eight playground democracies fashioned after Progress City in 1908 and 1909; Allendale became the template for a republic in Kalamazoo, Michigan. See Mary Humphrey, "Helping the Poor Boy," *Detroit Free Press*, June 14, 1908; Frank Koos, "Progress City: A Model Juvenile City," undated speech c. 1909–1912, container 36, folder 3, Progress City ca. 1906–1920, HH Records.

36. Caroline Murphy, "Report of the School City Committee," *Daughters of the American Revolution Magazine* 29 (1906); Wilson Gill, *City Problems* (New York: Patriotic League, 1909); "Plan a School City," *Washington Post*, February 5, 1906; Frank Parsons, "The School City: A New Experiment in Self-Government of the Young," *Century Illustrated Magazine*, January 1906, 496; "In the Mirror of the Present: Progress of the School-City Movement," *The Arena* 35, no. 195 (February 1906): 201; "Chicago Newsletter," *School Journal*, September 16, 1905; "Plan a School City: Pupils to Be Its Governing Authority," *Washington Post*, February 5, 1906; B. O. Flower, "Wilson L. Gill: The Apostle of Democracy in Education," *The Arena* 35, no. 195 (February 1906); Wilson Gill, "Principles and Methods of Pupil Government, Child-Citizenship and the School City," *Journal of Proceedings and Addresses of the National Education Association Annual Meeting* 47 (1908); "A Schoolboy Court: Where Pupils Are Trained in Administering Justice," *New-York*

Tribune, February 12, 1905; "Based on Child Pride," *Washington Post*, January 26, 1906; "Pupil Self Government Called a Success: School Citizens' Committee's Canvass Refutes Objections to Junior Republics," *New York Times*, February 12, 1911; William Ward, *Student Participation in School Government, Six Years Experience with the School City* (New York: Haight, 1906); Wilson L. Gill, *The Boys' and Girls' Republic* (Philadelphia: Patriotic League, 1913); School Citizens Committee, *Some Facts about Pupil Self-Government* (New York: SCC, 1904); M. Friedman, Superintendant, US Indian Service, Indian Industrial School at Carlisle to William George, May 29, 1908, box 4, folder 19, WG Papers; "Proposed to Have Indian Boys Build Their Own Homes," *Christian Science Monitor*, May 29, 1912; "Indian Youth Taught Citizenship As Well As Agriculture at Chilocco in Oklahoma," *Christian Science Monitor* August 28, 1912; Wilson Gill, *A New Citizenship: Democracy Systematized* (Philadelphia: Patriotic League, 1913); Wilson Gill, *The School Republic in Indian Schools* (Chemawa, OR: Salem Indian Training School, 1912); "New Plan for Indian Schools," *Christian Science Monitor*, May 4, 1911; "Indians and the School City," *Christian Science Monitor*, August 3, 1912; "Indian Students to Rule Selves: Chemawa School Has Plan Like Junior Republic; Government Supervisor Seeks to Interest State in Scheme—Redskins to Make Own Laws," *Oregonian*, February 22, 1912; "School Plan Gaining: Junior Republic Methods Adopted in Salem; Success Already Shown at Chemawa Institution, and Adoption May Lead to Development," *Oregonian*, March 3, 1912; "Self-Rule for Indian Schools," *Christian Science Monitor*, May 10, 1911; "School City Organized at Carlisle," September 29, 1911, ARROW, https://home.epix.net/~landis/hauser.html.

37. B. O. Flower, "Wilson L. Gill: The Apostle of Democracy in Education," *The Arena* 35, no. 195 (February 1906): 176; Wilson Gill, "Laboratory Method of Teaching Citizenship," *American City* 4 (1911): 173; Wilson Gill, "The School City," *Journal of the Franklin Institute* 156, no. 1 (July 1903): 19–31; Wilson Gill, "The School City," *Journal of the Franklin Institute* 156, no. 6 (December 1903): 401–412; "School City Methods," *Outlook*, April 3, 1909, 777; "Child Citizenship and International Peace," *Washington Post*, March 2, 1908; "Judge Lindsey: A Typical Builder of a Nobler State," *The Arena* 35, no. 197 (1906): 350; "Little Republics in the Public Schools: Patriotic League's Idea of Teaching Self-Government to the Youth of the Land," *Oregonian*, July 3, 1910; "'School Republics' Popular with Girls and Boys" *San Francisco Call* [*Junior Call*], July 31, 1910; Wilson Gill, *City Problems* (New York: Patriotic League, 1909); Wilson Gill, "Have a Little Republic in Every Schoolroom; Civic Activities of Children a Necessary Factor in the New Civilization—Through the School-Republic System the Boys and Girls Practice Self-Government Under Instruction—Results of the Laboratory Method—How the Youngsters Helped to Clean the City of New York and the Island of Cuba," *Boston Daily Globe*, August 6, 1916; Thomas Jefferson McEvoy, *The Science of Education* (Brooklyn: McEvoy, 1911), 176; Delos Franklin Wilcox, *The American City: A Problem in Democracy* (New York: Macmillan, 1909), 104; Wilson Gill to L. B. Stowe, January 14, 1913, box 14, folder 6, WG Papers.

38. "The Founder of Boyville," *Marion Daily Mirror*, April 22, 1910, referred to Charles Hahn as "The King of the Kids." "Selling Cigarettes to Boys, Court Contempt," *Detroit Free Press*, April 3, 1910; "Gary School Forces Name Parental Judge," *Indianapolis Star*, March 29, 1911; "Judge Brown Drafts Parental Court Bill: Announces Reform Measure Is Ready for Introduction in Indiana Assembly," *Indianapolis Star*, February 26, 1912; Rheta Childe Dorr, "Keeping the Children in School," *Hampton Magazine*, July 1911, 55–66. Brown's title closely resembled that of Gill's position in Cuba.

39. Ronald D. Cohen and Raymond A. Mohl, *The Paradox of Progressive Education: The Gary Plan and Urban Schooling* (Port Washington, NY: Kennikat, 1979); Andrea Tone, *The Business of Benevolence* (Ithaca, NY: Cornell University Press, 1997); Daniel Rodgers, *The Work Ethic in Industrial America 1850–1920* (Chicago: University of Chicago Press, 1978); Roy Rosenzweig, *Eight Hours for What We Will* (Cambridge: Cambridge University Press, 1985); William Tolman, *Social Engineering* (New York: McGraw, 1909), 5; Nicholas Paine Gilman, *A Dividend to Labor* (New York: Houghton Mifflin, 1899), 268, 353; New Jersey Bureau of Industrial Statistics, *Industrial Betterment Institutions in New Jersey Manufacturing* (Trenton, NJ: MacQuellish and Quigley, 1905). Human scientists had long made passing references to resemblances between people and machines; the changing nature of work ignited such comparisons in greater detail.

40. William Tolman, *Social Engineering* (New York: McGraw 1909), 1; Budgett Meakin, *Model Factories and Villages: Ideal Conditions of Labour and Housing* (London: Unwin, 1905), 203; *A Dividend to Labor* (New York: Houghton Mifflin, 1899), 203; National Civic Federation, *Conference on Welfare Work, Held at the Waldorf Astoria*, March 16, 1904; Mary McDowell, "The Right to Leisure," *Playground* 4 (1910): 328–331. It is "only where high spirits and enthusiasm enter the human machine that, like a well-oiled engine, all the parts work smoothly and produce the greatest effect with the least friction," journalist Budgett Meakin concurred.

41. Andrea Tone, *The Business of Benevolence* (Ithaca, NY: Cornell University Press, 1997); Bradley Ruding, "Industrial Betterment and Scientific Management As Social Control, 1890–1920," *Berkeley Journal of Sociology* 17 (1972–73): 59–77; National Cash Register, "The Human Side of Industry," pamphlet, n.d.; Susan Porter Benson, *Counter Cultures* (Champaign: University of Illinois Press, 1987); Colorado Fuel and Iron Co., *Report of the Medical and Sociological Department of the Colorado Fuel and Iron Co*, 1902; Roland Marchand, *Creating the Corporate Soul* (Berkeley: University of California Press, 1998); Chas. M. Steele, "Welfare Work: The New Industrial Policy," *Facts Magazine* (July 1905), online at https://www.daytonhistorybooks.com/page/page/2705417.htm; Rev. H. R. Miles, "Solving 'the Industrial Problem,'" in *Industrial Betterment Institutions in New Jersey Manufacturing* (Trenton, NJ: MacQuellish and Quigley, 1905); "New Department Is Established: Mr. Palmer Is Appointed Director of NCR Physical Culture," *NCR Outing*, August-September 1905, 219–220; N. P. Gilman, *Dividend to Labor* (New York: Macmillan, 1899); William Tolman, *Social Engineering* (New York: McGraw, 1909), 1909; Truman Vance, "Welfare Work As a Way to Prevent Labor Disputes," *American Academy of Political and Social Science* 36 (1910): 127–136. Some have suggested these activities provided the satisfaction and moral benefits that had disappeared from work itself.

42. Gertrude Beeks, "Welfare Work and Child Labor in Southern Cotton Mills," *National Civic Association Review*, July-August 1906, 21; John Kasson, *Civilizing the Machine* (New York: Macmillan, 1976); Budgett Meakin, *Model Factories and Villages* (London: Unwin, 1905), 259*ff.*; E Wake Cook, *Betterment* (New York: Stokes, 1906); New Jersey Bureau of Industrial Statistics, *Industrial Betterment Institutions in New Jersey Manufacturing* (Trenton, NJ: MacQuellish and Quigley, 1905).

43. "The Public School System of Gary, Indiana," *Bulletin: United States. Bureau of Education* (1914), 55; Elliott Flower, "Gary, The Magic City," *Putnam's Magazine* 5, no. 6 (March 1909), 643–653; Roland Marchand, *Creating the Corporate Soul* (Berkeley: University of California, 1998); "Welfare Work of Steel Corporation Discussed at Chairman Gary's Dinner," *Industrial World* 45, no. 1 (1911):

575; "Aid for Steel Workers," *New-York Tribune*, April 27, 1911; "Steel Men Hear Gary," *New-York Tribune*, May 18, 1912; "Messrs. Frick and Gary Should Be Summoned Before the Senate Committee," *Sun*, February 11, 1909; "Judge Gary Replies to Attacks on U.S. Steel Corporation," *Wall Street Journal*, January 17, 1912; H. E. Doty, "Betterment Work in American Industries" (master's thesis, University of Illinois, 1918); William Dealey, "The Theoretical Gary," *Pedagogical Seminary* 23 (June 1916): 269–282; William Wirt, "Utilization of the School Plant," *Proceedings of the National Education Association*, 1912, 492–497; "Cities for Young Is Wirt's Plan. Superintendant of the Schools of Gary, Ind., Would Rebuild Towns for Children," *New York Times*, June 15, 1915; William Wirt, "Preventive Agencies," *Indiana Bulletin of Charities and Correction*, 1909, 315; Burton Hendrick, "Children of the Steel Kings," *McClure's* 41, no. 5 (1913): 61–69; Randolph Siliman Bourne, *The Gary Schools* (Boston: Houghton Mifflin, 1916); George Dayton Strayer and Frank P. Bachman, *The Gary Public Schools: Organization and Administration* (New York: General Education Board, 1918); William Paxton Burris, *The Public Schools [The Public School System] of Gary*, US Bureau of Education no. 18 (Washington, DC: GPO, 1914); Ronald D. Cohen and Raymond A. Mohl, *The Paradox of Progressive Education: The Gary Plan and Urban Schooling* (Port Washington, NY: Kennikat, 1979); Ronald Cohen, *Children of the Mill: Schooling and Society in Gary, Indiana, 1906–1960* (New York: Routledge, 2002); Michael Knoll, "From Kidd to Dewey: The Origin and Meaning of 'Social Efficiency,'" *Journal of Curriculum Studies* 41, no. 3 (2009): 361–391; Samuel Hays, *Conservation and the Gospel of Efficiency: The Progressive Conservation Movement, 1890–1920* (Pittsburgh: University of Pittsburgh Press, 1999); Camilla Stivers, *Bureau Men, Settlement Women: Constructing Public Administration in the Progressive Era* (Lawrence: University Press of Kansas, 2000); John Jordan, *Machine Age Ideology* (Durham: University of North Carolina Press, 2010); Raymond Callahan, *Education and the Cult of Efficiency: A Study of the Social Forces That Have Shaped the Administration of the Public Schools* (Chicago: University of Chicago Press, 1962). The company's initial vision for its "city without slums" had eschewed amenities for most workers, setting aside recreational sites for only its small group of well-to-do and middle-class managers. Already in operation at other US Steel plants, according to Roland Marchand (*Creating the Corporate Soul*) "by the second decade of the century" the company "was approaching expenditures of $10 million per year on welfare programs" to boost worker productivity, forestall government regulation of corporate consolidation, and to burnish its public image. Gary's plant created a welfare committee in 1911, boosting its work after 1912 as a response to a congressional investigation of labor practices there. Although at first public schools exclusively served youth (including evening classes for those who worked), Wirt's longer-term plan was to expand services for adults. Gary schools would become municipal "opportunity centers" that integrated library, museum, playground, theater, police, and clubs for all ages—an efficient route to supplying city services and maximizing use of the school buildings that would ultimately increase worker efficiency as well. United States Steel Corporation, Bureau of Safety, Relief, Sanitation and Welfare, *Bulletin* (1913, multiple issues) has amazing photographs of Scout troops, school gardens, and other welfare programs sponsored by affiliates across the United States.

44. William Dealey, "The Theoretical Gary," *Pedagogical Seminary* 23 (June 1916): 297; Ronald D. Cohen and Raymond A. Mohl, *The Paradox of Progressive Education: The Gary Plan and Urban Schooling* (Port Washington, NY: Kennikat, 1979); Ronald Cohen, *Children of the Mill: Schooling and Society in Gary, Indiana, 1906–1960* (New York: Routledge, 2002); "Cinderella, Wonder Why Our Chicago Schools Don't Try This," *Chicago Daily Tribune*, January 25, 1917; Horace Hollister,

"Relation of the High School to the Community Life," *School and Home Education* 30 (1911): 349–355, 404–408; John Palmer Garber, *A Report on Education throughout the World* (Philadelphia: Lippincott, 1912); William Wirt, "Utilization of the School Plant," *Proceedings of the National Education Association,* 1912, 494; Burton Hendrick, "Children of the Steel Kings," *McClure's* 41, no. 5 (1913): 61–69; Rheta Childe Dorr, "Keeping the Children in School," *Hampton Magazine*, July 1911, 55–66; "No Waste Motion in Wirt System. Mrs. Welling Continues Her Discussion of Educational Reform in New Jersey," *Trenton Evening Times*, October 12, 1911; Henry Curtis, *Education through Play* (New York: Macmillan, 1914); Michael Knoll, "From Kidd to Dewey: The Origin and Meaning of 'Social Efficiency,'" *Curriculum Studies* 41, no. 3 (2009): 361–391.

45. George Ellis Jones, *Training in Education*, University of Pittsburgh Bulletin, General series, 1916 [originally prepared as PhD diss. at Clark University], 104; "Life in Boytown," *Indianapolis Star*, January 7, 1912; "Boyville and Boytown: Civic Training Schools," *San Francisco Chronicle*, June 16, 1912. Brown's Boy Cities in Gary were occasionally confused with Gill's School Cities, as in William Paxton Burris, *The Public Schools [The Public School System] of Gary*, US Bureau of Education no. 18 (Washington, DC: GPO, 1914).

46. Horace Hollister, "Relation of the High School to the Community Life," *School and Home Education* 30 (1911): 353; "Boyville and Boytown: Civic Training Schools," *San Francisco Chronicle*, June 16, 1912; "New Child Law Urged by Brown. 'Boy Town' Founder Would Make All Minors Under 18 Immune from Arrest," *Indianapolis Star*, November 18, 1911; "Lad Fights Cigaret [sic] Sale: Mayor of Gary's 'Boyville' asks city council if it is 'on the square,'" *Chicago Daily Tribune*, December 7, 1910, p, 1; William Paxton Burris, *The Public Schools [The Public School System] of Gary*, US Bureau of Education no. 18 (Washington, DC: GPO, 1914), 55; "Judge Brown Drafts Parental Court Bill," *Indianapolis Star*, February 26, 1912.

47. "No Waste Motion in Wirt System. Mrs. Welling Continues Her Discussion of Educational Reform in New Jersey," *Trenton Evening Times*, October 12, 1911; Horace Hollister, "Relation of the High School to the Community Life," *School and Home Education* 30 (1911): 353; "Boyville and Boytown: Civic Training Schools," *San Francisco Chronicle*, June 16, 1912; "Life in Boytown," *Indianapolis Star*, January 7, 1912; William Paxton Burris, *The Public Schools [The Public School System] of Gary*, US Bureau of Education no. 18 (Washington, DC: GPO, 1914), 27. See also the "work card" for Boytown in John Franklin Bobbitt, "The Elimination of Waste in Education," *Elementary School Teacher* 12, no. 6 (1912): 269.

48. Raymond Callahan, *Education and the Cult of Efficiency: A Study of the Social Forces That Have Shaped the Administration of the Public Schools* (Chicago: University of Chicago Press, 1962), 143; William Paxton Burris, *The Public Schools [The Public School System] of Gary*, US Bureau of Education no. 18 (Washington, DC: GPO, 1914), 8; David Tyack, "Review of Ronald Cohen, *Children of the Mill: Schooling and Society in Gary, Indiana, 1906–1960*" [1st ed. 1990], *History of Education Quarterly* 31, no. 1 (Spring 1991): 93–97; Ronald D. Cohen and Raymond A. Mohl, *The Paradox of Progressive Education: The Gary Plan and Urban Schooling* (Port Washington, NY: Kennikat, 1979); William Dealey, "The Theoretical Gary," *Pedagogical Seminary* 23 (June 1916): 269–282; John L. Rury, *Education and Social Change: Themes in the History of American Schooling* (Mahwah, NJ: Erlbaum, 2002). For an account of specific efforts to duplicate the Gary system, see "The

Gary System in Troy," *National Association of Corporation Schools Bulletin* 2, no. 9 (1915): 31; and "Studying Gary to Help New York," *National Association of Corporation Schools Bulletin* 1, no. 9 (1914): 36. Not all evaluations were positive, however. See "1000 School Children Strike: Hold Parade Against Gary Plan," *New-York Tribune*, October 17, 1917.

49. William Dealey, "The Theoretical Gary," *Pedagogical Seminary* 23 (June 1916): 276; Rheta Childe Dorr, "Keeping the Children in School," *Hampton Magazine*, July 1911, 63; William Wirt, *The Official Wirt Reports to the Board of Education of New York City*, 1916, 30; William Frederick Howat, *A Standard History of Lake County, Indiana and the Calumet Region*, vol. 1 (Chicago: Lewis, 1915), 405; "General Educational Notes," *National Association of Corporation Schools Bulletin* (December 1915), 42; "Studying Gary to Help New York," *National Association of Corporation Schools Bulletin* 1, no. 9 (1914): 37; Doris E. Fleischman, "Every Child Should Learn a Manual Art Says William Wirt, Explaining Vocational and Avocational Training in Public Schools," *Bulletin of the National Association of Corporation Schools* 2, no. 6 (1915): 39; "Educational Engineer, Constructive Genius of the Gary System," *Current Opinion* 59 (October 1915): 235–236; Ronald D. Cohen and Raymond A. Mohl, *The Paradox of Progressive Education: The Gary Plan and Urban Schooling* (Port Washington, NY: Kennikat, 1979); Henrietta Rodman, "Makes Pupils Aid in School Repairs: Wirt Explains Process in Vocational Training for Boyhood. Doing Real Work Is Best, He Says. Has Lads Get Jobs As Helpers to Actual Workmen Engaged on Educational Buildings," *New-York Tribune*, March 15, 1915; William Wirt, "Utilization of the School Plant," *Proceedings of the National Education Association*, 1912, 493; William Wirt, "Preventive Agencies," *Indiana Bulletin of Charities and Correction*, 1909, 315–319; *First Annual Report of the Heads of Municipal Departments Gary, Indiana*, 1909, 50–51; Horace Hollister, "Relation of the High School to the Community Life," *School and Home Education* 30 (1911): 350; John Dewey and Evelyn Dewey, *Schools of Tomorrow* (New York: Dutton, 1915); Alice Barrows Fernandez, "What Is the Gary Plan? Professor Dewey, of Columbia, Says Value of Work-Study-and-Play Has Already Been Established—Should Be Extended to Other Schools—Richer Opportunities for Children," *New-York Tribune*, December 16, 1915.

50. Tracy Steffes, *School, Society, and State* (Chicago: University of Chicago Press, 2012); David Samuel Snedden and Ellwood Patterson Cubberley, *Vocational Education: Its Theory, Administration and Practice* (New York: Houghton Mifflin, 1912); Rheta Childe Dorr, "Keeping the Children in School," *Hampton Magazine*, July 1911, 64; Walter H. Drost, *David Snedden and Education for Social Efficiency* (Madison: University of Wisconsin Press, 1967); "Vocational Guidance an Aid to Social Efficiency," in Irving King, *Education for Social Efficiency* (New York: Appleton, 1913), 219–231; Burton Hendrick, "Children of the Steel Kings," *McClure's* 41, no. 5 (1913): 63, 69; *First Annual Report of the Heads of Municipal Departments Gary, Indiana*, 1909, 50–51; Will H. Moore, *"If I Had Known" About Gary in 1909* (Chicago: Barnard and Miller, 1909); George Ellis Jones, *Training in Education*, University of Pittsburgh Bulletin, General series, 1916 [originally prepared as PhD diss. at Clark University]; William Wirt, *Newer Ideals in Education: The Complete Use of the School Plant, an address delivered before the Public Education Association in the New Century drawing room January 30, 1912* (Philadelphia: Public Education Association of Philadelphia, 1912); "Studying Gary to Help New York," *National Association of Corporation Schools Bulletin* 1, no. 9 (1914): 36; "What Your Child Is Best Fitted to Do," *National Association of Corporation Schools Bulletin* 2, no. 3 (1915): 9.

51. David Labaree, "How Dewey Lost: The Victory of David Snedden and Social Efficiency in the Reform of American Education," *Pragmatism and Modernities* 57 (2010): 165–166; Walter H. Drost,

"Social Efficiency Reexamined: The Dewey-Snedden Controversy," *Curriculum Inquiry* 7, no. 1 (1977): 19–32; Jasper T. Palmer, "The Democratizing Influences of the Schools of Today," *Elementary School Journal* 24, no. 6 (1924): 464–467; Herbert Kliebard, *Schooled to Work: Vocationalism and the American Curriculum, 1876–1946* (New York: Teachers College Press, 1999), 43; William Dealey, "The Theoretical Gary," *Pedagogical Seminary* 23 (June 1916): 269–282; David Snedden, *The Problem of Vocational Education* (New York: Houghton Mifflin, 1910), 9, 36, 38; "What Your Child Is Best Fitted to Do," *National Association of Corporation Schools Bulletin* 2, no. 3 (1915): 9; G. Stanley Hall, "The Age of Efficiency," *Youth's Companion* 84 (November 17, 1910): 639–640. Hall expressed enthusiasm about both approaches.

52. Edward Devine, "The New View of the Child," *Proceedings of the Fourth Annual Meeting of the National Labor Committee* (Philadelphia: American Academy of Political and Social Science, 1908), 9; Burton Hendrick, "Children of the Steel Kings," *McClure's* 41, no. 5 (1913): 61–69; William Paxton Burris, *The Public Schools [The Public School System] of Gary*, US Bureau of Education no. 18 (Washington, DC: GPO, 1914), 18; William Wirt, "Preventive Agencies," *Indiana Bulletin of Charities and Correction*, 1909, 315–319; "Studying Gary to Help New York," *National Association of Corporation Schools Bulletin* 1, no. 9 (1914): 37; Herbert Kliebard, *Schooled to Work: Vocationalism and the American Curriculum, 1876–1946* (New York: Teachers College Press, 1999), 128; A. F. Levins, "Gary School Plan As a City Campaign Issue: Advantages of the System Upheld by Mayor Mitchel's Supporters, While Tammany Insists It Has Been a Failure," *New York Times*, October 21, 1917; Raymond Callahan, *Education and the Cult of Efficiency: A Study of the Social Forces That Have Shaped the Administration of the Public Schools* (Chicago: University of Chicago Press, 1962); "Worth While Folk: Boss of a Citizen Factory," *New-York Tribune*, November 9, 1913; Mary Wager Fisher, "Daddy's Boys—A Factory of Good Citizenship" *Rural New Yorker*, June 17, 1899, 445–446; Theodore Roosevelt, "The Junior Republic," *New Outlook*, January 20, 1912, 117; John Kasson, *Civilizing the Machine* (New York: Macmillan, 1976) Even when Dewey disagreed with Snedden and others as to the pedagogical aims of vocational activities, he did not believe it constituted child labor. See John Dewey, "Some Dangers in the Present Movement for Industrial Education" *Child Labor Bulletin* 1, no. 4 (February 1913): 69–74. "Preventive Agencies," *Indiana Bulletin of Charities and Correction*, 1909, can also be considered here.

53. Raymond Callahan, *Education and the Cult of Efficiency: A Study of the Social Forces That Have Shaped the Administration of the Public Schools* (Chicago: University of Chicago Press, 1962); William Paxton Burris, *The Public Schools [The Public School System] of Gary*, US Bureau of Education no. 18 (Washington, DC: GPO, 1914), 20–21; A. J. McKelvey, "Welfare Work and Child Labor in Southern Cotton Mills," *Charities* 17 (November 10, 1906): 271–273, responding to Gertrude Beeks, "Welfare Work and Child Labor in Southern Cotton Mills," *National Civic Association Review*, July-August 1906; Abraham Flexner and Frank Bachman, *The Gary Schools: A General Account* (New York: General Education Board, 1918), 198, 202–203; Ruth McIntire, "Reviews of New Books…Published by General Education Board" [Abraham Flexner and Frank Bachman, *The Gary Schools: A General Account*; George D. Strayer and Frank Bachman, *Organization and Administration*; Charles R. Richards, *Industrial Work*; Frank Bachman and Ralph Bowman, *Costs, School Year 1915–1916*], *Child Labor Bulletin* (1917), 289.

54. "Junior's President Talks," *New York Times*, March 29, 1897; William George, *Nothing Without Labor* (Freeville: GJR, 1902); Abigail Powers, "The George Junior Republic," *Puritan* 9 (1901):

756; "Junior Republic Meeting; T. M. Osborne and Billy Zavenski to Speak This Evening," *Buffalo Courier*, March 8, 1901; "A Republic in Miniature," *New York Times*, May 5, 1897; "A Unique Institution: Operation of the Junior Republic in New York," *Oregonian*, June 28, 1898; "Talk of Junior Republic," *Washington Post*, April 15, 1901; "George Junior Republic: Citizens Number About 50, One-Fourth Being Girls—How the Work Is Conducted," *Boston Daily Globe*, April 19, 1899; "Notes on the Philadelphia Trip," *Junior Citizen*, January 16, 1899, 5–8; "Boy Republic's Needs," *Washington Post*, January 21, 1901; David Preston to William George, July 21, 1914, box 16, folder 11, WG Papers; "Junior Republic Assured Fact," *Los Angeles Times*, October 12, 1907; "Our Boys' Republic Getting to Work," *Los Angeles Times*, September 3, 1907; "In the City of Juniors," *Sun*, May 18, 1913; Jack Holl, *Juvenile Reform into the Progressive Era: William R. George and the Junior Republic Movement* (Ithaca, NY: Cornell University Press, 1971); Rev. R. J. Floody, "Worcester's Garden City," *Work with Boys: A Magazine of Methods*, April 1912, 208–214; Ethel Rogers, "Playing at Citizenship," *American City* 9 (1913): 445–448; William J. McKiernan, "The Intelligent Operation of Playgrounds," *Proceedings of the Second Annual Playground Congress, New York City, September 8–12, 1908* (New York: Playground Association of America, 1908), 101–112; Duane R. Dills, "A Successful Form of Self-Government for Boys," *Association Boys* (October 1908): 188–194; "Proposed to Have Indian Boys Build Their Own Homes," *Christian Science Monitor*, May 29, 1912; Wilson Gill, *The Gill System of Moral and Civic Training* (New Paltz, NY: Patriotic League, 1901); "Miniature City Government Conducted by Public School Pupils in New York," *Washington Post*, March 25, 1906; "Men and Movements That Are Making for Progress: Democracy in Education; or, The School City in Practical Operation," *The Arena* 35, no. 198 (May 1906): 512; Myron Scudder, "The Civic Idea in Work with Boys," *The Aims of Religious Education: The Proceedings of the Third Annual Convention of the Religious Education Association, Boston, February 12–16, 1905*, 436; "Boyville to Be Reality," *Chicago Daily Tribune*, February 10, 1907; "More News of Boy City," *Salt Lake Telegram*, August 13, 1907; James Rogers, "Military Dept. Columbia Park Boys Club," *How to Help Boys: A Journal of Social Pedagogy* [precursor to *Work with Boys*] 3, no. 3 (July 1903): 232; Anna Pratt, "The Junior Republic," *San Francisco Chronicle*, September 7, 1902; A. J. Todd, "Experiment in Man Making: Boytown," *Charities* 17 (1906): 131–137; James Rogers, "'City of Telhi,' a Junior Republic or, How a Boys Club Mixed a Bit of Sociology with Their Sport, During Their Summer School Vacation, in California," *Education* 27 (1907): 271–280; "Chicago's Junior Republic," *Chicago Daily Tribune*, August 16, 1896; *Annual Report of the Hebrew Sheltering Guardian Society*, box 1, folder 4, Annual Reports (bound) 1905–1909, Records of the Hebrew Sheltering Guardian Society of New York, Center for Jewish History.

55. "Reports by American Teachers and Educationists on the School City System of Government and Discipline," in Llewellyn Wynn Williams, *Education: Disciplinary, Civic and Moral* (London: Simpkin, Marshall, Hamilton, Kent, 1903), 120; Charles S. Drum, "Moral and Civic Training: The Gill School City," *Instructor* 17 (December 1907): 13–15; Wilson Gill, *The Gill System of Moral and Civic Training* (New Paltz, NY: Patriotic League, 1901); B. O. Flower, "Wilson L. Gill: The Apostle of Democracy in Education," *The Arena* 35, no. 195 (February 1906); Wilson Gill, "Principles and Methods of Pupil Government, Child-Citizenship and the School City," *Journal of Proceedings and Addresses of the National Education Association Annual Meeting* 47 (1908): 285; Samuel T. Dutton, *School Management: Practical Suggestions Concerning the Conduct and Life of the School* (New York: Scribner's, 1904), 93; A. Walker, "Self-Government in the High School," *Elementary School Teacher*

7, no. 8 (April 1907): 451–457; Arthur Leland and Lorna Higbee Leland, *Playground Technique and Playcraft* (New York: Doubleday, 1909), 105; "Report of the Supervisor of the Playgrounds," *Annual Reports of the City Officers and City Boards* (St. Paul, MN, 1905), 96; "Report of the Supervisor of the Playgrounds," *Annual Reports of the City Officers and City Boards* (St. Paul, MN, 1906), 352; David Snedden, "A Practical Agency in Moral and Civic Education," October 18, 1910, address to Headmasters' School Republic Banquet, cited in Wilson Gill, *A New Citizenship: Democracy Systematized* (Philadelphia: Patriotic League, 1913); David Snedden, "Administration and Educational Work of American Juvenile Reform Schools" (PhD diss., Columbia University, 1907), 144; Samuel Train Dutton and David Snedden, *The Administration of Public Education in the United States* (New York: Macmillan, 1909); Wilson Gill, *More Efficient Citizenship* (Washington, DC: GPO, 1915); A. E. Winship, "Projected Efficiency of the Junior Republics," *Journal of Education*, September 18, 1913; Wilson Gill, *The School Republic in Indian Schools* (Chemawa, OR: Salem Indian Training School, 1912). Snedden singled out the George Junior Republic, Cottage Row, and School Cities.

56. Katherine Camp Mayhew and Anna Camp Edwards, *The Dewey School* (New York: Appleton, 1936), 29, 44; "Report of Riverside School, California, September 1, 1904," in US Department of Interior, *Annual Reports of the Department of the Interior*, 1905; Philip Cox, *Creative School Control* (Philadelphia: Lippincott, 1927); Jenny Snow, "The Luncheon As a Project in Elementary and Secondary Education," *Journal of Home Economics* 9 (1917), 361–4; Eleanor Eells, *History of Organized Camping* (American Camping Association, 1996); Walter Stone, *The Development of Boys Work in the United States* (Nashville: Vanderbilt University, 1933), 102; William George, *The Junior Republic: Its History and Ideals* (New York: Appleton, 1910), 67; "Report of the business manager of the George Junior Republic Association for the summer of 1897," Mrs. George to Dr. Foote, October 4, 1897, box 2, folder 2, WG Papers; Helen Louise Johnson, "Learning by Doing: How some little girls planned built and furnished a house thereby learning arithmetic and many other things," *Good Housekeeping*, March 1903, 232; Benjamin Andrew, "Education for the Home," *US Bureau of Education Bulletin* (1915); Judith Pasch, "Changing Curriculum and the Practice Cottage," in *The Challenge of Constantly Changing Times*, ed. Rima Apple (Madison, WI: Parallel, 2003); Booker T. Washington, *Working with the Hands* (New York: Doubleday, Page, 1904); Laura Gifford, "The Hiram House Model Cottage and Its influences," *Survey* 33 (October 17, 1914): 70–71; Albert Leake, *The Vocational Education of Girls and Women* (New York: Macmillan, 1920), 54; Mabel Kittredge, "Housekeeping Centers in Settlements and Public Schools," *Survey* (May 3, 1913): 188–192; Theodore Roosevelt, "The Junior Republic," *New Outlook*, January 20, 1912, 117.

57. Ethel Rogers, "Playing at Citizenship," *American City* 9 (1913): 445; "The Boy and the Law," *New-York Tribune*, September 20, 1908; Rev. R. J. Floody, "Worcester's Garden City," *Work with Boys: A Magazine of Methods* 12 (1912): 213; William McKiernan, "Newark Playgrounds," *Playground* 2 (1907): 5; William J. McKiernan, "The Intelligent Operation of Playgrounds," *Proceedings of the Second Annual Playground Congress, New York City, September 8–12, 1908* (New York: Playground Association of America, 1908), 109, 105; George Butler, *Playgrounds: Their Administration and Operation* (New York: Barnes, 1936), 97; "Indiana Boys Run a Model City," *New York Times*, August 9, 1908; H. Addington Bruce, "A Vocational School a Hundred Years Old," *Outlook*, July 28, 1915, 734–742; Bertha Johnston, "Some Educational Forces Supplementary to the Public Schools," *Kindergarten Magazine and Pedagogical Digest* 19 (1907): 214; "Appeal from the

Playground Commission," *New Jersey Review of Charities and Corrections* 6 (1907): 230; "Many Joys Planned for Boys of Indiana: Thousand Youngsters Will Camp at Winona Lake in Novel Way. 'Boyville' Is Real Town. Will Elect Mayor and Postmaster and Operate Bank Just Like Grown-ups," *Indianapolis Star*, July 16, 1907; "A City for Boys Only" *New-York Tribune*, November 25, 1906; "Worth While Folk: Boss of a Citizen Factory," *New-York Tribune*, November 9, 1913; Anna Pratt, "The Junior Republic," *San Francisco Chronicle*, September 7, 1902; "A Californian Junior Republic," *School Journal* 68 (1904): 333; "'City of Telhi,' a Junior Republic or, How a Boys Club Mixed a Bit of Sociology with Their Sport, During Their Summer School Vacation, in California," *Education* 27 (1907): 271–280; "The Real Day of the Real Boy," *San Francisco Chronicle*, October 16, 1904; James Rogers, "The State of Columbia, a Junior Republic," *Survey* 12 (1904); Sidney Peixotto, *The Simple Tale of a Ten Years' Work for and among City Boys* (San Francisco: Columbia Park Boys Club, 1905); A. J. Todd, "Experiment in Man Making: Boytown," *Charities* 17 (1906): 131–137; James Rogers, "Military Dept. Columbia Park Boys Club," *How to Help Boys: A Journal of Social Pedagogy* 3, no. 3 (July 1903): 232.

58. "Plan for Toy Legislation: Mimic Congresses and Councils to Be Tried in Schools," *Chicago Daily Tribune*, November 6, 1904; Edward H. Reisner, *A Descriptive List of Trade and Industrial Schools in the United States* (New York: National Society for the Promotion of Industrial Education, 1910); David Snedden, *The Problem of Vocational Education* (New York: Houghton Mifflin, 1910), 61; Jenny Snow, "The Luncheon as a Project in Elementary and Secondary Education," *Journal of Home Economics* 9 (1917): 361–364; "Cities Ruled by Tots," *Washington Post*, September 10, 1905.

59. Oscar Chrisman, "Paying Children to Attend School," *The Arena* 37, no. 207 (February 1907): 166–167; William Wirt, "Utilization of the School Plant," National Education Association 1912, 493; Roy Rosenzweig, *Eight Hours for What We Will* (Cambridge: Cambridge University Press, 1985), 142–143; *Playground* (special issue, May 1910); Herbert Kliebard, *Schooled to Work: Vocationalism and the American Curriculum, 1876–1946* (New York: Teachers College Press, 1999); Raymond Callahan, *Education and the Cult of Efficiency: A Study of the Social Forces That Have Shaped the Administration of the Public Schools* (Chicago: University of Chicago Press, 1962); "Reformers Who Misuse Children," *St. Louis Post-Dispatch*, September 1, 1907; Willis Brown, "The Boy Problem," *Los Angeles Times*, December 24, 1915; Grant Hyde, "The New Idea in Playgrounds," *Popular Mechanics*, October 1913, 476; Harriet Hickox Heller, "The Playground as a Phase of Social Reform," *American Physical Education Review* 13, no. 9 (1908): 498–505; Rev. R. J. Floody, "Worcester's Garden City," *Work with Boys: A Magazine of Methods*, April 1912, 208–214; Theodore Roosevelt, "The Junior Republic," *New Outlook*, January 20, 1912, 117; H. M. P., letter to the editor, "The Child Labor Bill," *Baltimore Sun*, February 16, 1906, making reference to the National Junior Republic. G. Stanley Hall observed the potentials for overwork "in the school factory." Hall, *Youth: Its Education, Regimen and Hygiene* (New York: Appleton, 1909), 308. Even opponents of the new curricular approaches shared this view. William Huber, president of the United Brotherhood of Carpenters and Joiners, thus declared he was against industrial education because "there is nothing like rubbing up against the real thing" to educate for a career in the trades. According to this view, then, simulations might have their own realities, but these were not the reality of the thing they aimed to copy. When Gill observed how "Whatever government a child is under at school" or in similar settings "is a real government, governing him during a

large and important portion of his life," and the US Bureau of Education could describe students in Gary "doing real work under the direction of real workmen," they made a similar point. "Cities Ruled by Tots," *Washington Post*, September 10, 1905; Wilson Gill, *The Gill System of Moral and Civic Training* (New Paltz, NY: Patriotic League, 1901); William Paxton Burris, *The Public Schools of Gary*, US Bureau of Education no. 18 (Washington, DC: GPO, 1914).

60. Ethel Rogers, "Playing at Citizenship," *American City* 9 (1913): 446; "'City of Telhi,' a Junior Republic or, How a Boys Club Mixed a Bit of Sociology with Their Sport, During Their Summer School Vacation, in California," *Education* 27 (1907): 271; James Rogers, *The State of Columbia, a Junior Republic* (San Francisco: Recorder, 1903); "A Californian Junior Republic," *School Journal* 68 (1904): 333; *The Story of the State of Columbia: A Summer Government Camp, 1906-1907-1908* (San Francisco: Columbia Park Boys Club, 1908).

61. Mrs. George to Dr. Foote, October 4, 1897, box 2, folder 8, WG Papers; "Good Business Boys," *Boys' Life*, September 1913, 28.

62. Jeanne Boydston, *Home and Work* (New York: Oxford University Press, 1990); Nancy Folbre, "The Unproductive Housewife: Her Evolution in Nineteenth-Century Economic Thought," *Signs: Journal of Women in Culture and Society* 16, no. 3 (Spring 1991): 463–484.

63. Jeanne Boydston, *Home and Work* (New York: Oxford University Press, 1990); Nancy Folbre, "The Unproductive Housewife: Her Evolution in Nineteenth-Century Economic Thought," *Signs: Journal of Women in Culture and Society* 16, no. 3 (Spring 1991): 463–484; Andrea Tone, *The Business of Benevolence* (Ithaca, NY: Cornell University Press, 1997); Ruth Cowan, *More Work for Mother* (London: Free Association, 1989); Dolores Hayden, *The Grand Domestic Revolution: A History of Feminist Designs for American Homes, Neighborhoods and Cities* (Cambridge, MA: MIT Press, 1981); Viviana Zelizer, *The Social Meaning of Money* (New York: Basic Books, 1995); Florence Marshall, "Industrial Training for Women," *National Society for the Promotion of Industrial Education Bulletin* 4 (October 1907).

64. To be sure, there were some connections between women's experience and that of youth. Viviana Zelizer describes, for example, how "instructions to census enumerators specified that 'children who work for their parents at home merely on general household work, on chores, or at odd times on other work, should be reported as having no occupation.'" Zelizer, *Pricing the Priceless Child* (Princeton, NJ: Princeton University Press, 1994), 83. New evidence from developmental psychologists and other observers about young people building youth democracies on their own backed these claims. "Boy City Falls in a Police Raid," *Cleveland Plain Dealer*, December 5, 1907; Harry Carr, "Los Angeles Twenty Years Ago," *Los Angeles Herald*, December 25, 1910; "New City Builded in Just Six Days," *Los Angeles Times*, September 11, 1902; "Bryan to the Boys," *Salt Lake Herald*, August 8, 1908; Josiah Strong, *The Challenge of the City* (New York: Young People's Missionary Movement, 1907).

65. William Jennings Bryan was on the Winona Board that issued the invitation to Willis Brown to organize a boy city at its summer program. Longtime friend to William George, Teddy Roosevelt stopped in Freeville during his vice presidential and later presidential campaigns. President William Taft and Vice President Charles Fairbanks wrote to the children of Boy City while William

Jennings Bryan was on the Winona board; Taft was behind Gill's appointment as supervisor of Indian Schools. Interior secretary James Garfield, a native of Hiram, Ohio, came to speak to Progress City youth. Ethel Rogers, "Playing at Citizenship," *American City* 9 (1913): 445; "YMCA Boys Republic; with Harmon," *Grand Rapids Press*, May 23, 1912; "At the Resorts," *Kalamazoo Gazette*, July 25, 1909; "Playgrounds' Mayor Takes Lesson from Real Mayor," *Plain Dealer*, July 31, 1910; "Metz Talks to Boy Republic," *New-York Tribune*, February 1, 1909; Duane R. Dills, "A Successful Form of Self-Government for Boys," *Association Boys* (October 1908): 188–194; *Annual Report of the Hebrew Sheltering Guardian Society*, box 1, folder 4, Annual Reports (bound) 1905–1909, Records of the Hebrew Sheltering Guardian Society of New York, Center for Jewish History; "The City of Boys," *Case & Comment* 17 (1911): 418; "Residents of Boy City See New Head Take Oath," *Indianapolis Star*, August 1, 1909; "Boy Mayor in Office," *New-York Tribune*, September 2, 1905; "National Junior Republic," *Oregonian*, March 12, 1900; "Roosevelt at Boy Republic," *New York Times*, November 4, 1911; "Roosevelt at Freeville," October 29, 1900, news clipping, box 46, folder 29, WG Papers; Theodore Roosevelt telegram to William George, October 27, 1900, box 3–24, WG Papers; "Taft Talks to the Boys, Answers Letter of Greeting from Winona City Lads," *Washington Herald*, August 5, 1908; "Thousand Boys in a Camp City, Form Municipal Government—Come from Twenty Towns in Four States," *New-York Tribune*, August 1, 1908.

66. Frederick Elmer Bolton, *Principles of Education* (New York: Scribner's, 1910), 408; Randolph Bourne, "The Natural School," *New Republic*, May 1, 1915, 327; "New Junior Republic," *Washington Post*, May 18, 1899; Emmie Parker, "Making Model Citizens at the George Republic," *Washington Post*, October 22, 1905; Colin Scott, *Social Education* (Boston: Ginn, 1908); Randolph Silliman Bourne, *The Gary Schools* (New York: Houghton Mifflin, 1916), 137.

67. T. R. Crosswell, "Amusements of Worcester School Children," *Pedagogical Seminary* 6, no. 3 (1898): 358; "Review of Henry E Bourne, *The Teaching of History and Civics*," *Congregationalist and Christian World* 87, no. 31 (August 2, 1902): 171; "Civic and Educational Notes," *Gunton's Magazine*, November 1898, 363; Colin Scott, *Social Education* (Boston: Ginn, 1908), 60, 66; "Discussion" following W. H. Whittaker, "Criminals: Their Punishment and Reformation, Report of Committee," *The Social Welfare Forum: Official Proceedings [of the] Annual Forum* 35 (1908): 189; William Fremont Blackman, "Review of *The Junior Republic, Its History and Ideals* by William R. George," *Economic Bulletin* 3, no. 4 (1910): 445–447; Wilson Gill, "Principles and Methods of Pupil Government, Child-Citizenship and the School City," *Journal of Proceedings and Addresses of the National Education Association Annual Meeting* 47 (1908): 285–294; Oliver Cornman, "Principles and Methods of Pupil Government, School Cities," *Journal of Proceedings and Addresses of the National Education Association Annual Meeting* 47 (1908), 293.

68. "Pupil Government Called a Success: School Citizens' Committee Canvass Refutes Objections to Juvenile Republics; Power Never Is Abused," *New York Times*, February 12, 1911; "Cities Ruled by Tots," *Washington Post*, September 10, 1905; "One Kind of Vacation Camp," *Detroit Free Press*, May 23, 1896; "Place Is Given to Judge Brown. Presiding Genius of the Juvenile Court to Supervise Boys' Town. A City for Youngsters. They Will Run Things Absolutely with Their Own Laws and Officers to Enforce Them," *Deseret Evening News*, November 5, 1906; "Miniature City Government Conducted by Public School Pupils in New York," *Washington Post*, March 25, 1906; George Walter Fiske, *Boy Life and Self-Government* (New York: Association Press, 1912), 23. Notably, some

supervisors spoke of "limited self-government." See Samuel Levy, "A Study in Child-Rearing," *Annual Report of the Hebrew Sheltering Guardian Society*, box 1, folder 4, Annual Reports (bound) 1905–1909, Records of the Hebrew Sheltering Guardian Society of New York, Center for Jewish History; Ludwig Bernstein, "Modern Tendencies of Jewish Orphan Asylum Work," *Annual Report of the Hebrew Sheltering Guardian Society*, box 1, folder 4, Annual Reports (bound) 1905–1909, Records of the Hebrew Sheltering Guardian Society of New York, Center for Jewish History; "Progress of the Schools" *Omaha Daily Bee*, November 26, 1899; Wilson Gill, *The Gill System of Moral and Civic Training* (New Paltz, NY: Patriotic League, 1901), 129.

69. "Its Work Well Done; the George Junior Republic Commended by a Committee of Experts; An Investigation Made into Its Methods and the Conditions at Freeville—Report to the State Board of Charities," *New-York Tribune*, February 5, 1898, box 2, folder 10, WG Papers; William McKiernan to William George, March 21, 1913, box 14, folder 14, WG Papers; William J. McKiernan, "The Intelligent Operation of Playgrounds," *Proceedings of the Second Annual Playground Congress, New York City, September 8–12, 1908* (New York: Playground Association of America, 1908), 108; Arthur Leland, "Playground Self Government," *Charities* 12 (June 4, 1904): 586–590; William Cummings, "Cottage Row," *Thompson's Island Beacon*, June 1897. McKiernan and George stayed close over the years. "Newark Man Here to Watch Junior Election," *Ithaca Daily News*, November 5, 1913.

70. Josiah Royce, "The Imitative Functions, and Their Place in Human Nature," *Century*, May 1894, 138; Frances Margaret Keefe, "The Development of William Reuben (Daddy) George's Educational Ideas and Practices from 1866 to 1914" (PhD diss., Cornell University, 1967), 164; J. Adams Puffer, "Study of Boys' Gangs," *Pedagogical Seminary* 12 (1905): 207; Frederick Elmer Bolton, *Principles of Education* (New York: Scribner's, 1910), chap. 6; Donald Mrozek, "The Natural Limits of Unstructured Play, 1880–1914," in *Hard at Play: Leisure in America, 1840–1940*, ed. K. Grover (Amherst: University of Massachusetts Press and the Strong Museum, 1992).

71. Agnes Boyle O'Reilly Hocking, "Glimpse of the George Junior Republic Taken from Letters Written in 1905," box 4, folder 7, WG Papers; F. S. Key Smith, "Our New Problem—An Old Idea Enlarged Upon," *Albany Law Journal* 63, no. 12 (December 1901): 451; Wilson Gill, *A New Citizenship: Democracy Systematized* (Philadelphia: Patriotic League, 1913), 93; "Pupil Self Government Called a Success: School Citizens' Committee's Canvass Refutes Objections to Junior Republics," *New York Times*, February 12, 1911.

72. William George, *The Junior Republic: Its History and Ideals* (New York: Appleton, 1910), 319; William Gute to William George, June 30, 1913, box 14, folder 28, WG Papers. Ludwig Bernstein, "Superintendant's Report," 33, and "Modern Tendencies in Jewish Orphan Asylum Work," 50, *Annual Report of the Hebrew Sheltering Guardian Society*, box 1, folder 4, Annual Reports (bound) 1905–1909, Records of the Hebrew Sheltering Guardian Society of New York, Center for Jewish History; also published as Ludwig Bernstein, "Social and Civic Activities in Orphan Asylums," *Ninth New York State Conference of Charities and Correction. Proceedings, Elmira, New York, November 16–20, 1908*, Annual Report of the New York State Board of Charities, 1909. On older managerial and disciplinary approaches at youth-serving institutions, see Patricia Clement, *Growing Pains, Children in the Industrial Age* (New York: Twayne, 1997); Jacqueline S. Reiner, *From Virtue*

to Character: American Childhood, 1775–1850 (New York: Twayne, 1996); David B. Wolcott, Cops and Kids: Policing Juvenile Delinquency in Urban America, 1890–1940 (Columbus: Ohio State University Press, 2005); Paula Fass, The Damned and the Beautiful: American Youth in the 1920's (New York: Oxford University Press, 1977); Dominick Cavallo, "The Politics of Latency: Kindergarten Pedagogy, 1860–1930," in Regulated Children/Liberated Children, ed. Barbara Finkelstein (New York: Oxford University Press, 1977); Bernard Wishy, The Child and the Republic (Philadelphia: University of Pennsylvania Press, 1968); William Graebner, The Engineering of Consent: Democracy and Authority in Twentieth-Century America (Madison: University of Wisconsin Press, 1987). On other former citizens in youth work, see WG Papers: Hervey Miller to William George, July 15, 1904, box 4, folder 6; William Gute to L. B. Stowe, June 13, 1914, box 16, folder 6; Billy Childs to Mrs. Daddy George, June 14, 1914, box 16, folder 6; Syria [H. G. LeRoy] and LeRoy to William George, July 19, 1914, box 16, folder 9.

73. Edgar Robinson, "Self-Government for Boys," Association Boys 7, no. 2 (1908): 109.

74. David MacLeod, Building Character in the American Boy (Madison: University of Wisconsin Press, 2004), 270; "A Boys' Republic," New York Times, November 18, 1906; Harvey L. Smith, "The TUXIS System of Character Building," in Reaching the Boys of an Entire Community (New York: YMCA Press, 1909), 130; William J. McKiernan, "The Intelligent Operation of Playgrounds," Proceedings of the Second Annual Playground Congress, New York City, September 8–12, 1908 (New York: Playground Association of America, 1908), 106; Wilson Gill, "Principles and Methods of Pupil Government, Child-Citizenship and the School City," Journal of Proceedings and Addresses of the National Education Association Annual Meeting 47 (1908): 286; Samuel Train Dutton and David Snedden, The Administration of Public Education in the United States (New York: Macmillan, 1909), 516; Arthur Leland and Lorna Higbee Leland, Playground Technique and Playcraft (New York: Doubleday, 1909); Arthur Leland, "Playground Self Government," Charities 12 (June 4, 1904): 587; Caroline Murphy, "Report of School City Committee," Daughters of the American Revolution Magazine, 29 (1906).

75. E. J. Swift, "Some Criminal Tendencies of Boyhood," Pedagogical Seminary 8 (1901): 87; Edward James Swift, "Juvenile Delinquency and Juvenile Control," Psychological Bulletin 6 (1909): 127–129; "Insurgents Win at Boy City," Tacoma Times, August 12, 1910; "Life in Boytown," Indianapolis Star, January 7, 1912; Patricia Clement, Growing Pains, Children in the Industrial Age (New York: Twayne, 1997); Harvey L. Smith, "The TUXIS System of Character Building," in Reaching the Boys of an Entire Community (New York: YMCA Press, 1909); Wilson Gill, "Principles and Methods of Pupil Government, Child-Citizenship and the School City," Journal of Proceedings and Addresses of the National Education Association Annual Meeting 47 (1908): 285–294; "Modern Reform Methods: Work of Junior Republic Contrasted with That of Reformatory Schools," Washington Post, May 13, 1901; William Graebner, The Engineering of Consent: Democracy and Authority in Twentieth-Century America (Madison: University of Wisconsin Press, 1987); Theodore Roosevelt, "The Junior Republic," New Outlook, January 20, 1912, 118; Sarah Converse, "Redemption of Youthful Criminals Solved by the George Junior Republic," Atlanta Constitution, September 29, 1907. The alternative subtitles of Ludwig Bernstein's 1914 book (Studies in Modern Child Caring: How Six Hundred Children Are Trained for Intelligent Co-operation and Citizenship and Studies in Modern Child Caring: How Six Hundred Children Are Trained to Co-operate and to Respect Law and Order) provide supporting testimony for the disciplinary benefits of democratic processes.

76. Caroline Murphy, "Report of School City Committee," *Daughters of the American Revolution Magazine* 29 (1906): 419; "Ban on Bribes in Kids' City, Some Citizens Acting Suspiciously on the Eve of an Election," *Cleveland Plain Dealer*, June 30, 1906; William George, *The Junior Republic, Its History and Ideals* (New York: Appleton, 1910), ix–x; Wilson Gill, *More Efficient Citizenship* (Washington, DC: GPO, 1915), 10; Harriet Hickox Heller, "The Playground as a Phase of Social Reform," *American Physical Education Review* 13, no. 9 (1908): 498–505. Steffes (2012) notes this shift in management style could be found among middle managers in schools as well. On visions of democracy as a disciplinary force in the period, see Stanley K. Schultz, "The Morality of Politics: The Muckrakers' Vision of Democracy," *Journal of American History* 52 (December 1965): 527–547.

77. Alexander Pisciotta, *Benevolent Repression: Social Control and the American Reformatory-Prison Movement* (New York: New York University Press, 1994); Michel Foucault, *Discipline and Punish* (New York: Vintage, 1995); Andrea Tone, *The Business of Benevolence* (Ithaca, NY: Cornell University Press, 1997); Rebecca McLennan, *The Crisis of Imprisonment: Protest, Politics, and the Making of the American Penal State, 1776–1941* (New York: Cambridge University Press, 2008); William Graebner, *The Engineering of Consent: Democracy and Authority in Twentieth-Century America* (Madison: University of Wisconsin Press, 1987); Jonathan Simon, "Punishment and the Political Technologies of the Body," in *SAGE Handbook of Punishment and Society*, ed. Jonathan Simon and Richard Sparks (Newbury Park, CA: SAGE Publishing, 2013); David Garland, *Punishment and Welfare: A History of Penal Strategies* (Aldershot, UK: Gower, 1985).

78. Alexander Pisciotta, *Benevolent Repression: Social Control and the American Reformatory-Prison Movement* (New York: New York University Press, 1994), 14; Alexander Pisciotta, "Child Saving or Child Brokerage? The Theory and Practice of Indenture and Parole at the New York House of Refuge, 1825–1935," in *History of Juvenile Delinquency*, ed. Albert Hess and Priscilla Clement (Aalen, Germany: Scientia Verlag, 1993); Jack Holl, *Juvenile Reform in the Progressive Era: William R. George and the Junior Republic Movement* (Ithaca, NY: Cornell University Press, 1971); Orlando Lewis, "Inmate Self-Government a Century Ago," *The Delinquent* 8 (January 1918); J. E. Baker, "Inmate Self-Government," *Journal of Criminal Law, Criminology, and Police Science* 55, no. 1 (March 1964): 39–47; Maurice Parmelee, *Criminology* (New York: Macmillan, 1918); "New York State Asylums for the Insane Are Now Passing Under a New System of Management," *New-York Tribune*, March 9, 1902; Rebecca McLennan, *The Crisis of Imprisonment: Protest, Politics, and the Making of the American Penal State, 1776–1941* (New York: Cambridge University Press, 2008); Orlando Lewis, "The New Freedom at Auburn Prison," *Outlook* August 15, 1914; James McGrath Morris, *Jailhouse Journalism: The Fourth Estate Behind Bars* (Jefferson, NC: McFarland, 1998); Frederick Wines and Winthrop Lane, *Punishment and Reformation* (New York: Crowell, 1919); "Osborne Sets Up Convict Republic," *New York Times*, December 9, 1914; Philip Klein, "Prison Methods in New York State," *Proceedings of the Annual Congress of the American Prison Association*, 1920; B. G. Lewis, *The Offender* (New York: Harper, 1917); Thomas Osborne, *Society and Prisons* (New Haven, CT: Yale University Press, 1916); Howard Davidson, "Political Processes in Prison Education: A History," *Journal of Correctional Education* 47, no. 3 (September 1, 1996): 133; Howard Davidson, "An Alternative View of the Past: Re-visiting the Mutual Welfare League (1913–1923)," *Journal of Correctional Education* 46, no. 4 (1995): 169–174.

79. Budgett Meakin, *Model Factories and Villages: Ideal Conditions of Labour and Housing* (London: Unwin, 1905), 233–234; Andrea Tone, *The Business of Benevolence* (Ithaca, NY: Cornell University

Press, 1997); James Collins, *The Art of Handling Men* (Philadelphia: Altemus, 1910); Frank Herrmann Timken, *General Factory Accounting* (Chicago: Trade Periodical, 1914); Charlotte Albina Aikens, *Hospital Management* (Philadelphia: Saunders, 1911), 193; *Library of Factory Management*, vol. 4 (Chicago: A.W. Shaw Company, 1915), 215; Stephen Meyer, *The Five Dollar Day: Labor Management and Social Control in the Ford Motor Company, 1908–1921* (Albany: State University of New York Press, 1981); Olivier Zunz, *Making America Corporate, 1870–1920* (Chicago: University of Chicago Press, 1990); Daniel Rodgers, *The Work Ethic in Industrial America 1850–1920* (Chicago: University of Chicago Press, 1978); Roy Rosenzweig, *Eight Hours for What We Will* (Cambridge: Cambridge University Press, 1985); John Kasson, *Civilizing the Machine* (New York: Macmillan, 1976); N. P. Gilman, *A Dividend to Labor* (New York: Houghton Mifflin, 1899); Nelson Lichtenstein and Howell John Harris, eds., *Industrial Democracy in America: The Ambiguous Promise* (New York: Cambridge University Press, 1993); Roland Marchand, *Creating the Corporate Soul* (Berkeley: University of California, 1998); David Montgomery, "Industrial Democracy or Democracy in Industry? The Theory and Practice of the Labor Movement, 1870–1925," in *Industrial Democracy in America: The Ambiguous Promise*, ed. Nelson Lichtenstein and Howell John Harris (New York: Cambridge University Press, 1996); William Graebner, *The Engineering of Consent: Democracy and Authority in Twentieth-Century America* (Madison: University of Wisconsin Press, 1987). For other discussions of self-government in industry, see New Jersey Bureau of Industrial Statistics, *Industrial Betterment Institutions in New Jersey Manufacturing* (Trenton, NJ: MacQuellish and Quigley, 1905); Frank P. Walsh, "We Must Democratize Industry," *Square Deal* (August 1914): 6–8; E. Wake Cook, *Betterment: Individual, Social, and Industrial* (New York: Stokes, 1906). In a context where even authoritarian factory managers saw the factory as a government or a state within a state, the idea of bringing democratic processes inside their institutions seemed a natural fit. See, for example, Frank Vosburgh and Walter Ames, *Instructions to Foremen and How to Become a Foreman* (Chicago: Teich, 1904), which has a first chapter on government.

80. Thomas Osborne, "New Methods at Sing Sing Prison," *Review of Reviews* (October 1915): 449–450; Thomas Osborne, "Prison Efficiency" *Efficiency Society Journal* (November 1915); Thomas Osborne, *Society and Prisons* (New Haven, CT: Yale University Press, 1916); Jennifer Alexander, *The Mantra of Efficiency: From Waterwheel to Social Control* (Baltimore: Johns Hopkins University Press, 2008), 93; Andrea Tone, *The Business of Benevolence* (Ithaca, NY: Cornell University Press, 1997); Jack Holl, *Juvenile Reform in the Progressive Era: William R. George and the Junior Republic Movement* (Ithaca, NY: Cornell University Press, 1971); Frederick Wines and Winthrop Lane, *Punishment and Reformation* (New York: Crowell, 1919); "Social Economics of the Weston Electrical Instrument Co.," in New Jersey Bureau of Industrial Statistics, *Industrial Betterment Institutions in New Jersey Manufacturing* (Trenton, NJ: MacQuellish and Quigley, 1905), 145; Maurice Parmelee, *Criminology* (New York: Macmillan, 1918); Peter Scharf and Joseph Hickey, "Thomas Mott Osborne and the Limits of Democratic Prison Reform," *Prison Journal* 57 (October 1977): 3–15.

81. Jack Holl, *Juvenile Reform in the Progressive Era: William R. George and the Junior Republic Movement* (Ithaca, NY: Cornell University Press, 1971); Roy Rosenzweig, *Eight Hours for What We Will* (Cambridge: Cambridge University Press, 1985); "Substitute for Spanking: Teach Children Self-Government Is Advice of Dr. Elliot," *New-York Tribune*, March 24, 1908; *Playground* (special

issue, May 1910); Arthur Todd, "The Organization and Promotion of Industrial Welfare through Voluntary Efforts," *Annals of the Association of Political and Social Science* (January 1923); Joseph Lee, *Play in Education* (New York: Macmillan, 1915); Andrea Tone, *The Business of Benevolence* (Ithaca, NY: Cornell University Press, 1997); James Collins, *The Art of Handling Men* (Philadelphia: Altemus, 1910); Jane Addams, *Newer Ideals of Peace* (New York: Macmillan, 1907); Spencer Miller [for Thomas Osborne], "Recreation and Prison Reform," *Playground* 10 (1910): 438–444; Adolph Lewisohn, HSGS, to William George, November 4, 1915, lecture invitation, box 17, folder 10, WG Papers; O. F. Lewis to William George, April 9, 1915, box 17, folder 4, WG Papers; "Good Work for Bad Boys," *Atlanta Constitution*, July 8, 1900; Franklin Clark, "Osborne, Millionaire 'Prisoner': The Graphic Report of the Penology Expert Who Set Out to See New York Prison Abuses for Himself," *Boston Evening Transcript*, May 29, 1914; Winthrop Lane, "Pioneer in Prison Reform," *New York Herald Tribune*, March 31, 1935; Thomas Osborne, "Within Prison Walls," *Proceedings of the Annual Congress of the National Prison Association of the United States*, 1904; Rebecca McLennan, *The Crisis of Imprisonment: Protest, Politics, and the Making of the American Penal State, 1776–1941* (New York: Cambridge University Press, 2008); Calvin Derrick, "Self-Government," *Survey* 38 (September 1, 1917): 473–479; Thomas Osborne, "Common Sense in Prison Management," *Journal of the American Institute of Criminal Law and Criminology* 8 (1918); Thomas Osborne, *Society and Prisons* (New Haven, CT: Yale University Press, 1916); E. S. Martin, "Warden Osborne's Idea," *Life*, April 8, 1915; Frank Marshall White, "Thomas Mott Osborne, a Practical Prison Idealist," *Outlook*, December 23, 1914, 920; Orlando Lewis, "The New Freedom at Auburn Prison," *Outlook*, August 15, 1914, 917; Harold M. Helfman, "Antecedents of Thomas Mott Osborne's 'Mutual Welfare League' in Michigan," *Journal of Criminal Law and Criminology* 40, no. 5 (1950): 597–600; J. E. Baker, "Inmate Self-Government," *Journal of Criminal Law, Criminology, and Police Science* 55, no. 1 (1964): 39–47; Calvin Derrick, *Institutional Management* (Ione, CA: Preston School of Industry, 1915); Calvin Derrick, *The Constitution and the Penal Code of the Preston School of Industry* (Ione, California: Preston School, 1913); Walter Given Martin, "A Study of Self-Government in the Preston School of Industry" (master's thesis, University of California, Berkeley, 1917); William Gute to William George, June 30, 1913, box 14, folder 28, WG Papers; "Writes Praise of Osborne," *New York Times*, December 24, 1915; Burdette Gibson Lewis, *The Offender and His Relations to Law and Society* (New York: Harper, 1917); Frederick Wines and Winthrop Lane, *Punishment and Reformation* (New York: Crowell, 1919); J. E. Baker, *The Right to Participate: Inmate Involvement in Prison Administration* (Methuen, NJ: Scarecrow, 1974); Calvin Derrick, *Training Delinquent Boys for Citizenship*, (Ione, California: Preston School,1914). Reform schools were mostly for boys, but Miriam Van Waters subsequently implemented a girls' reformatory, El Retiro, near Los Angeles. See W. I. Thomas and Dorothy Thomas, *The Child in America* (New York: Knopf, 1928).

82. "Good Work for Bad Boys," *Atlanta Constitution*, July 8, 1900; Franklin Clark, "Osborne, Millionaire 'Prisoner': The Graphic Report of the Penology Expert Who Set Out to See New York Prison Abuses for Himself," *Boston Evening Transcript*, May 29, 1914; Jack Holl, *Juvenile Reform in the Progressive Era: William R. George and the Junior Republic Movement* (Ithaca, NY: Cornell University Press, 1971); Winthrop Lane, "Pioneer in Prison Reform," *New York Herald Tribune*, March 31, 1935; Thomas Osborne, "Within Prison Walls," *Proceedings of the Annual Congress of the National Prison Association of the United States*, 1904; Rebecca McLennan, *The Crisis of Imprisonment: Protest,*

Politics, and the Making of the American Penal State, 1776–1941 (New York: Cambridge University Press, 2008); Frank Tannenbaum, *Osborne of Sing Sing* (Chapel Hill: University of North Carolina Press, 1933); Rudolph W. Chamberlain, *There Is No Truce: A Life of Thomas Mott Osborne* (New York: Macmillan,1935); Calvin Derrick, "Self-Government," *Survey* 38 (September 1, 1917): 473–479; Thomas Osborne, "Common Sense in Prison Management," *Journal of the American Institute of Criminal Law and Criminology* 8 (1918); Thomas Osborne, *Society and Prisons* (New Haven, CT: Yale University Press, 1916); E. S. Martin, "Warden Osborne's Idea," *Life*, April 8, 1915, 626–627; Frank Marshall White, "Thomas Mott Osborne, a Practical Prison Idealist," *Outlook*, December 23, 1914, 920; Orlando Lewis, "The New Freedom at Auburn Prison," *Outlook,* August 15, 1914, 917; Harold M. Helfman, "Antecedents of Thomas Mott Osborne's 'Mutual Welfare League' in Michigan," *Journal of Criminal Law and Criminology* 40, no. 5 (1950): 597–600; J. E. Baker, "Inmate Self-Government," *Journal of Criminal Law, Criminology, and Police Science* 55, no. 1 (March 1964), 39–47; "Writes Praise of Osborne," *New York Times,* December 24, 1915.

83. Gina Lombroso-Ferrero, *Criminal Man, According to the Classification of Cesare Lombroso* (New York: Putnam's, 1911); Enoch Wines, *The State of Prisons and of Child-Saving Institutions in the Civilized World* (Cambridge: University Press and John Wilson and Son, 1880); Erving Goffman, *Asylums* (New York: Doubleday, 1961); Rebecca McLennan, *The Crisis of Imprisonment: Protest, Politics, and the Making of the American Penal State, 1776–1941* (New York: Cambridge University Press, 2008); Alexander Pisciotta, *Benevolent Repression: Social Control and the American Reformatory-Prison Movement* (New York: New York University Press, 1994), 105; Robert Weiss. "Humanitarianism, Labour Exploitation, or Social Control? A Critical Survey of Theory and Research on the Origin and Development of Prisons," *Social History* 12, no. 3 (1987): 331–350; Alex Lichtenstein, *Twice the Work of Free Labor* (New York: Verso, 1995); David Rothman, *Conscience and Convenience: The Asylum and Its Alternatives in Progressive America* (Boston: Little, Brown, 1980); Noah Zatz, "Prison Labor and the Paradox of Paid Non-Market Work," in *Economic Sociology of Work* (Research in the Sociology of Work, vol. 18), ed. Nina Bandelj (Bingley, UK: Emerald Group, 2009); Noah Zatz, "Working at the Boundaries of Markets: Prison Labor and the Economic Dimensions of Employment Relationships," *Vanderbilt Law Review* 61 (2008): 857.

84. Jack Holl, *Juvenile Reform in the Progressive Era. William R. George and the Junior Republic Movement* (Ithaca, NY: Cornell University Press, 1971); J. R. Commons to WG, March 13, 1897, box 2, folder 5, WG Papers; "Honor Among Thieves," *Outlook*, July 19, 1913, 599; C. R. Henderson, "Review of *Methods of Penal Administration in the United States* by Edward Grubb," *American Journal of Sociology* 10, no. 6 (1905): 840; Thomas Osborne, introductory remarks in William George, *The Junior Republic: Its History and Ideals* (New York: Appleton, 1910); Frederick Almy, "The George Junior Republic," in *Correction and Prevention*, ed. Charles Richmond Henderson, Eugene Smith, and Hastings Hornell Hart (New York: Charities Publication Committee, 1910), 42; "Call on Junior Republic: English Students of Criminology at Maryland Institution," *Washington Post*, September 9, 1910; "Junior Republic Is Commended: Juvenile Offenders to Be Sent There for Training," *Los Angeles Times*, January 29, 1911; "Modern Reform Methods: Work of Junior Republic Contrasted with that of Reformatory Schools," *Washington Post*, May 13, 1901; J. E. Baker, "Inmate Self-Government," *Journal of Criminal Law, Criminology, and Police Science* 55, no. 1 (1964): 39–47; Beate Kreisle, "Punishment or Self-Discipline? Early Roots of Reform," *Reclaiming*

Children and Youth 19, no. 3 (2010): 14–15; L. B. Stowe, "Remaking Men in the Philippines," 1914, box 16, folder 29, WG Papers; "The Growth of the Junior Republic Idea," *Outlook,* July 5, 1913, 500; "George Junior Republic Plan to Help Criminals Reform: Founder of the Boy Communities Believes a Similar Idea Would Accomplish Better Results with Some Adults than Imprisonment for Crime," *New York Times,* July 7, 1912. The colony's director was W. Cameron Forbes, whose brother Alexander, a Harvard Medical School professor, became involved with the George Junior Republic. Books like Enoch Wines's *The State of Prisons and of Child-Saving Institutions in the Civilized World* or criminologist Cesare Lombroso's praise for the George Junior Republic and Hebrew Sheltering Guardian Society underscore the sense of common purpose across these institutions.

85. Tracy Steffes, *School, Society, and State* (Chicago: University of Chicago Press, 2012).

86. "To Organize 'Kid' Republic: Famous 'George Junior' Man Here in January; Juvenile Self-Government Instead of Reform," *Los Angeles Times,* November 25, 1906; "President Is Inaugurated: George Junior Republic Is Born at San Fernando," *Los Angeles Times,* March 20, 1908; A. J. Todd, "Experiment in Man Making: Boytown," *Charities* 17 (1906): 131–137; Frederick Almy, "The George Junior Republic," in Hastings Hornell Hart, *Preventive Treatment of Neglected Children* (New York: Charities Publications Committee, 1910); R. H. Stevens, "Democracy as an Educational Principle," *The Public: A Journal of Democracy* 14 (May 19, 1911): 464; Edward Bradley, *Allendale Annals* (Lake Villa, IL: Allendale Association, 1926). William Byron Forbush, *The Coming Generation* (New York: Appleton, 1913). On graduates' career choices, see "George Junior Republic Results," *Journal of Education* 64, no. 4 (1906): 115.

87. "Pupil Self Government Called a Success: School Citizens' Committee's Canvass Refutes Objections to Junior Republics," *New York Times,* February 12, 1911; "Self-Government in Schools: The School City in Operation—Good Results in Philadelphia and Cuba," *Public Opinion* 34 (1903): 332–333; "Self-Government in Schools," *Herald of Gospel Liberty* 95, no. 31 (July 30, 1903): 500; William Torrey Harris, *The School City* (Syracuse, NY: Bardeen, 1907); "School Plan Gaining: Junior Republic Methods Adopted in Salem; Success Already Shown at Chemawa Institution, and Adoption May Lead to Development," *Oregonian,* March 3, 1912; Albert Shaw, "The School City—A Method of Pupil Self Government," *Review of Reviews* 20 (1899): 673–686; "Life in Boytown," *Indianapolis Star,* January 7, 1912; A. J. Todd, "Experiment in Man Making: Boytown," *Charities* 17 (1906): 137; H. Bruce Addington, "A Vocational School a Hundred Years Old," *Outlook,* July 28, 1915, 740; "'School Republics' Popular with Girls and Boys," *San Francisco Call,* July 31, 1910; "Playground 'City,'" *Playground* 3 (1909): 18; William J. McKiernan, "The Intelligent Operation of Playgrounds," *Proceedings of the Second Annual Playground Congress, New York City, September 8–12, 1908* (New York: Playground Association of America, 1908); Lillian A. Robinson, "The City of Hawthorne," *Charities and the Commons* 15 (November 4, 1905): 182–185; Lillian Robinson, *Children's House: A History of the Hawthorne Club* (Boston: Marshall Jones, 1937); Los Angeles Playground Commission, *Report* (1907), 6; Arthur Leland and Lorna Higbee Leland, *Playground Technique and Playcraft* (New York: Doubleday, 1909); G. W. Harris, "Playground City," *Review of Reviews* 32 (November 1905): 574–580; "He's a Real Mayor, New York Lad Made Boss of a Playground, Energetic Business Methods," *Grand Rapids Press (Evening Press),* August 16, 1905; "Kase Elected Mayor," *New-York Tribune,* August 16, 1905; "Boy Mayor in Office," *New-York Tribune,* September 2, 1905; "Girls Not to Vote," *New-York Tribune,* August 15, 1905; "Election in the

'Playground City,'" *New-York Tribune*, August 10, 1905; "Help Form Character," *Washington Post*, January 11, 1909; "Park Mayor Sworn In," *New York Times*, September 2, 1905; "Boys Organize Government for Playground," *Chicago Daily Tribune*, August 17, 1905; G. W. Harris, "Playground City," *Review of Reviews* 32 (November 1905): 574–580; "Turns Light Upon Play City Graft: Director Proves Youthful Officials of Playground Stone Ball Outfit," *Cleveland Plain Dealer*, August 25, 1909; "Playground's Mayor Takes Lesson from Real Mayor," *Cleveland Plain Dealer*, July 31, 1910; Bessie Stoddart, "Recreative Centers of Los Angeles, California," *Annals of the American Association of Political and Social Science* 35 (1910); "Children Elect Officers," *Washington Post*, August 3, 1907; Harriet Hickox Heller, "The Playground as a Phase of Social Reform," *Proceedings of the Playground Association of America Proceedings of the Second Annual Playground Congress, New York City, September 8–12, 1908* (New York: Playground Association of America, 1908), 182; "Echo Park Republic," *Los Angeles Times*, February 24, 1910; J. F. B. Tinling, "Juvenile Self Governing Communities," *Progress: Civic, Social, Industrial* 4 (January 1909): 1–12; "Here Playing Is the Thing," *Sun*, September 10, 1908; "Miniature Republic Created by Pupils, Ceremonies at Washington Duplicated, Superintendent Oliver W. Best of Echo Park Playground Finally Puts Novel Plan into Operation," *Los Angeles Herald*, March 5, 1909; "Republic to Hold Annual Election," *Los Angeles Herald*, February 24, 1910; "New Republic Junior Kind," *Los Angeles Times*, February 26, 1909; "Playground Self Government," *Annual Reports of the City Officers and City Boards* (St. Paul, MN, 1906), 352; John ver Mehren, "Attorney Frank Heller Dies of Pneumonia," *Omaha Morning World-Herald*, January 3, 1907; "Closes His Lecture Series," *Washington Post*, August 22, 1907; "Playground Finals Soon," *Washington Post*, August 23, 1907; "Junior Republic at Playground: Violet Street Center Elects Mayor and Council; Most of the Officials Are of Age and Honors Are Divided Between White Persons and Negroes—Another Election Next Saturday for Two Offices," *Los Angeles Times*, November 12, 1911; "Playground Self Government," *Palestine Daily Herald*, October 7, 1905; William McKiernan, "Newark Playgrounds," *Playground* 2 (1907): 6; "Children Elect Officers," *Washington Post*, August 3, 1907.

88. Graham Romeyn Taylor, "The Chicago Conference on Truancy—Causes and Prevention," *Survey* 17 (1906): 537. Box 4, folder 9, WG Papers contains numerous invitations to George to speak at public and private schools, settlements and prisons, showing he was widely in demand. "Publishing House Scheme," c. 1913, described how junior republic principles could be applied to boarding schools, preparatory schools, and finishing schools, box 14, folder 2, WG Papers; Tracy Steffes, *School, Society, and State* (Chicago: University of Chicago Press, 2012) is about how, in focusing on marginal youth in educational history, scholars miss seeing the expansion of disciplinary power to all youth; the story of junior republics expands on these themes.

89. Michel Foucault, *Discipline and Punish* (New York: Vintage, 1995); Roy Rosenzweig, *Eight Hours for What We Will* (Cambridge: Cambridge University Press, 1985); Lee Grieveson, "The Work of Film in the Age of Fordist Mechanization," *Cinema Journal* 51, no. 3 (2012): 25–51; Rebecca McLennan, *The Crisis of Imprisonment: Protest, Politics, and the Making of the American Penal State, 1776–1941* (New York: Cambridge University Press, 2008); Alexander Pisciotta, *Benevolent Repression: Social Control and the American Reformatory-Prison Movement* (New York: New York University Press, 1994); Steven L. Schlossman, *Love and the American Delinquent: The Theory and Practice of "Progressive" Juvenile Justice, 1825–1920* (Chicago: University of Chicago Press, 1977). For discussion of the regulation of youth behavior in public settings, see Tracy Steffes, *School, Society, and*

State (Chicago: University of Chicago Press, 2012); and Peter Baldwin, "'Nocturnal Habits and Dark Wisdom': The American Response to Children in the Streets at Night, 1880–1930," *Journal of Social History* 35, no. 3 (2002): 593–611. They have, however, noted schools' efforts to intervene in youth and family life, for example, by providing medical or social services, while saying little about how young people themselves facilitated these developments, performing the work eventually incorporated into regular school programs as jobs done by adults. George Shrafte, "Health Inspection of Schools in the United States," *Pedagogical Seminary* 18, no. 3 (September 1911): 273–314; David B. Tyack and Michael Berkowitz, "The Man Nobody Liked: Toward a Social History of the Truant Officer, 1840–1940," *American Quarterly* 29, no. 1 (1977); Larry Cuban, "Why Some Reforms Last: The Case of the Kindergarten," *American Journal of Education* 100, no. 2 (February 1992): 166–194; Larry Cuban, "What Happens to Reforms that Last? The Case of the Junior High School," *American Educational Research Journal* 29, no. 2 (1992): 227–251.

90. "Flock to Play at Hiram House, Children Swarm Over Grounds Where Merrymaking Is the Rule," *Cleveland Plain Dealer*, July 10, 1907; Josiah Strong, Appendix B, "The Hiram House, Cleveland, Ohio," in *The Challenge of the City* (New York: Young People's Missionary Movement, 1907); "Boyville and Boytown: Civic Training Schools," *San Francisco Chronicle*, June 16, 1912.

Chapter 4

1. William George to Carl Kelsey, November 26, 1914, box 16, folder 24, WG Papers; Lyman Beecher Stowe, "Junior Citizens in Action," *Outlook*, November 18, 1914, 654; "Boys Hold Elections Like Their Elders," *New York Times*, November 9, 1913; "Junior Municipality to Handle Cases of Truancy," *Syracuse Post-Standard*, June 22, 1914; "Elmer Hook Gets Filter Plant Job," *Ithaca Daily News*, April 16, 1914; "'Daddy' George Greeted by Junior Officials," *Ithaca Daily News*, March 25, 1914; "Jr. Mayor Names Standing Committees," *Ithaca Daily News*, March 18, 1914; "Time to Get Busy for Playgrounds," *Ithaca Daily News*, March 26, 1914; "Mayors Discuss Their City Problems," *Auburn Citizen*, June 4, 1914; "Ithaca Children to Have Fine New Playgrounds," *Syracuse Post-Standard*, June 2, 1914; "Mayor Reamer Urges Order at All Costs," *Ithaca Daily News*, December 6, 1913; "One Junior Mayor in Fact One Junior City Under This Plan," *Auburn Citizen*, December 11, 1913; "Want Junior Police to Have Power at Arrest," *Ithaca Daily News*, December 13, 1913; "Juniors to Have a Juvenile Court: New Department of Junior Government Will Relieve the City Court of Many Trivial Cases and Do Much Good—City Officers to Cooperate," *Ithaca Daily News*, June 6, 1914; "Charges Italians Assaulted Him," *Ithaca Daily News*, June 16, 1914; "Junior Municipality Mayor Names Committees," *Ithaca Daily News*, March 10, 1914; "Junior Officers Have Had Success: Boy and Girl Political Parties? Now Making Preparations for the Fall Election—Accomplishments of Juvenile Government," *Ithaca Daily News*, July 9, 1914; "Jersey Juveniles Start Government: 'Daddy' George's novel plan of training children in real life affairs is taken up by the officials of Jersey City—started in Ithaca," *Ithaca Daily News*, July 28, 1913; Henry van Brocklin (Cortland Junior Mayor) to L. B. Stowe, June 19, 1914, box 16, folder 7, WG Papers; "Mayors Discuss Their Problems," *Auburn Citizen*, June 4, 1914; "Junior Municipality Mayor Names Committees" *Ithaca Daily News*, March 10, 1914; Lyman Beecher Stowe, "Junior Citizens in Action, " *Outlook*, November 18, 1914, 654–656; "Juvenile Idea in Ithaca: Boys and Girls Ready to Help Govern the City," *New-York Tribune*, July 2, 1913; "Register for the Charter

Election," *Ithaca Daily News,* September 26, 1913; "Girls Rival Youths in Make Believe Politics," *New-York Tribune,* October 4, 1913; "One Junior Mayor," *Auburn Citizen,* December 11, 1913.

2. Lyman Beecher Stowe, "Junior Citizens in Action," *Outlook,* November 18, 1914, 654; "Juvenile Idea in Ithaca: Boys and Girls Ready to Help Govern the City," *New-York Tribune,* July 2, 1913; Herman Hagedorn, "Citizens through Understanding," *Survey* (September 16, 1921): 677; "'Daddy' George Greeted by Juvenile Officials," *Ithaca Daily News,* March 18, 1914; "'Daddy' George Pleased with Work of Juniors; Young Men Gave Assistance to Police Officers in Subduing Woman," *Syracuse Post-Standard,* June 1, 1914; "Ithaca to Try Out Junior Municipality Plan Proposed by 'Daddy' George—Will Be Adopted Here—No Expense Attached," *Ithaca Daily News,* June 5, 1913; "Junior Mayor Names Standing Committees: Juvenile Officers Outline Ways Whereby They Can Be of Assistance to Regular City Administration," *Ithaca Daily News,* March 25, 1914; "Boys Hold Elections Like Their Elders," *New York Times,* November 9, 1913; "The Sewerage System of the N.J.R.," *Republic News* [Annapolis], January 1913, box 100, folder 2, WG Papers; William George, "The Publishing House Scheme," *Republic News* [Annapolis], June 1913, box 100, folder 2, WG Papers; "The G.J.R. of W.P.," *Pioneer Citizen* [Grove City, PA], n.d., box 100, folder 9, WG Papers.

3. Ronald D. Cohen and Raymond A. Mohl, *The Paradox of Progressive Education: The Gary Plan and Urban Schooling* (Port Washington, NY: Kennikat Press, 1979), 12; Delavan Pierson, "The Little Republic at Freeville," *Missionary Review* (November 1899): 801. Tracy Steffes, *School, Society, and State* (Chicago: University of Chicago Press, 2012) is one of the few studies of how, during this period, schools gained legal powers to regulate students' public behaviors. My focus here is complementary influences of schools and youth-serving institutions on more informal social norms. Alexandra Rutherford has described the expansion of Skinnerian psychology "beyond the box"; this account suggests a related set of applications for an earlier psychological tradition. Rutherford, *Beyond the Box: B.F. Skinner's Technology of Behavior from Laboratory to Life, 1950s–1970s* (Toronto: University of Toronto Press, 2009).

4. William McKiernan to William George, March 28, 1913, box 14, folder 14, WG Papers; Jennifer Light, "Building Virtual Cities, 1895–1945," *Journal of Urban History* 38, no. 2 (2012): 336–371; *Catalog and Annual Report Chemawa Indian School* (Chemawa, OR: Chemawa Indian School, 1914); "Willis Brown and Child Saving in Gary," in Ronald Cohen, *Children of the Mill: Schooling and Society in Gary, Indiana, 1906–1960* (New York: Routledge, 2002) ; "Hold 'Boy Cities' Founder as Swindler," *Trenton Evening Times,* December 15, 1915.

5. "American Boys Keep Going," *Chicago Daily Tribune,* July 13, 1913; William Paxton Burris, *The Public Schools [The Public School System] of Gary* US Bureau of Education no. 18 (Washington, DC: GPO, 1914); Randolph Siliman Bourne, *The Gary Schools* (Boston: Houghton Mifflin, 1916); "Garyville Boys Are Helping to Run Their Town, Boyville Corporation Elects Mayor and Board of Aldermen and Make laws," *Montgomery Advertiser,* January 31, 1915; "Hundred Boys Registered to Get a Vote in 'Boyville': Will Have Part in Self-government Plan to Be Installed on Jan. 1 at 3757 Wentworth Avenue (1912)," *Chicago Daily Tribune,* December 8, 1912; "Boys' City at Winona Lake to Open This Week," *Indianapolis Star,* June 20, 1920; *Chicago Boys Club Annual Report* (Chicago: Chicago Boys Club, 1914); Dorothy Sauer, "Educational Activities of the Chicago Boys Club" (master's thesis, DePaul University, 1950); "Wants City to Have Boyville on Heath Site,

Mayor Donnelly Finds Judge Gnichtel and Probation Officer in Favor of Plan," *Trenton Evening Times*, May 21, 1914; "Boys Enjoy a Day in Church Camp," *Indianapolis Star*, August 11, 1917; "Boyville to Open Tomorrow," *Indianapolis Star*, August 1, 1915; "Crowd Is Large on Boyville Day," *Indianapolis Star*, August 12, 1914; "Credit Prizes Given Battle Ground Boys: 'Boyville' at Methodist Camp Meeting Presented with Winning Trophies—Church Program Still Continues," *Indianapolis Star*, August 16, 1914; "Boyville Camp Opens," *Indianapolis Star*, August 3, 1920; "Events at Boyville Entertain Campers," *Indianapolis Star*, August 12, 1916 ; "Boyville Camp Ousts Officers," *Indianapolis Star*, August 14, 1916; O. M. Brundson, "A Boys' City," in Albert M. Chesley, *Social Activities for Men and Boys* (New York: Association Press, 1916), 247; Glenn Uminowicz, "Chautauqua Week on the Eastern Shore," *Tidewater Times* (June 2008), https://tidewatertimes.com/GlennUminowicz-June2008.htm.

6. "Boyville Head Coming: Judge Willis Brown to Lecture Here Twice January 30," *Oregonian*, January 26, 1912; "Judge Willis Brown to Speak: Noted Utah Philanthropist Will Give Illustrated Talk in Union Tomorrow," *Harvard Crimson*, November 4, 1913; "Boy City to Be Ruled by Boys," *Salt Lake Telegram*, May 18, 1912; "Boy City Will Be Formed in Oregon: Method of Teaching Boys to Control Themselves Has Been Success," *Oregonian*, December 25, 1910; "Judge Former Oregonian: Willis Brown, Founder of 'Boy City,' Lived Here 20 Years Ago," *Oregonian*, January 30, 1912; "Worth While Folk: Boss of a Citizen Factory," *New-York Tribune*, November 9, 1913; "Boys Will Build and Govern City Near Reno, Nev.," *San Francisco Chronicle*, June 29, 1916, 15; "Talk Juvenile Problems," *Detroit Free Press*, June 18, 1910; "Willis Brown Will Open Boys' Camp," *Salt Lake Telegram*, June 28, 1916; "Juvenile Courts Are Given a Rap," *San Francisco Chronicle*, March 22, 1914; "City for Boys to Be Built. Judge Willis Brown, Author of Juvenile Laws of Utah, Starts Movement in Reno. To Teach Trades. Boy Citizens to Enact Own Laws, Conduct Bank, Post-office, Library and Civic Center," *Ogden Standard*, June 28, 1916, 10; "To Have Chance to Go Around World Some Local Lad Booked for Place in American Achievement Band," *Grand Rapids Press*, March 1, 1913; "$1,000,000 for a Great Boy City, Boys of the World Will Take Part," *Cleveland Gazette*, June 28, 1913; "Boy City's Work Described Here," *Washington Times*, November 27, 1916; "National Boy City Will Be One of Features at Big Exposition," *Oregonian*, March 16, 1913; "Picks Ideal Boy for World Tour," *Chicago Daily Tribune*, April 13, 1913; "Achievement Boy to Be Received at White House by Pres. and Mrs. Wilson," *Jackson Citizen Patriot*, April 28, 1913; James M. Hamill, *The Major and His Boys: The Story of Major Sidney Peixotto and the Columbia Park Boys' Club* (Los Angeles: Anderson, Ritchie, and Simon, 1972).

7. Wilson Gill, "Have a Little Republic in Every Schoolroom; Civic Activities of Children a Necessary Factor in the New Civilization—Through the School-Republic System the Boys and Girls Practice Self-Government Under Instruction—Results of the Laboratory Method—How the Youngsters Helped to Clean the City of New York and the Island of Cuba," *Boston Daily Globe*, August 6, 1916; "School Republics Advocated by SAR," *Boston Daily Globe*, June 21, 1916; "Boys and Girls of Passaic Have Government All Their Own, With Commission Rule," *Trenton Evening Times*, December 1, 1913; "Robert Cyril Stebbins," *Copeia* 3 (2006): 563–572; Matthew Crenson, *Building the Invisible Orphanage* (Cambridge, MA: Harvard University Press, 2009), 116; "Chicago Hebrew Institute," *Advocate: America's Jewish Journal* 44 (1912): 112; Grant Hyde, "The New Idea in Public Playgrounds," *Popular Mechanics*, October 1913, 476; LeRoy Ashby, *Saving the Waifs:*

Reformers and Dependent Children, 1890–1917 (Philadelphia: Temple University Press, 1984); Nurith Zmora, "A Rediscovery of the Asylum: The Hebrew Orphan Asylum through the Lives of Its First Fifty Orphans," *American Jewish History* 77, no. 3 (March 1, 1988): 452; R. D. Leigh, "Portland, Ore.–City Manager Plan in a Boy City," *American City* 15 (October 1916): 380–381; Nurith Zmora, *Orphanages Reconsidered: Child Care Institutions in Progressive Era Baltimore* (Philadelphia: Temple University Press, 1994), 221; *Ninety Years of Changing Lives: Starr Commonwealth: for Children Since 1913* (Albion, MI: Starr Commonwealth, 2003); "Boys' Cabinet Is Planned by Y. M. C. A," *Salt Lake Telegram*, September 29, 1913; "Equipping Boys for Factories: George Junior Republic to Increase Vocational Departments," *Los Angeles Times*, December 4, 1915; "Novel Republics May Revolutionize Care of Orphans," *New York Times Sunday Magazine*, May 12, 1912; "Can Have Home Named for You: Be One of Seventeen Sought by Hebrew Sheltering Society to Endow Cottages," *New-York Tribune*, March 8, 1915; "Town of Orphans Only: Hebrew Guardian Society to Adopt Cottage Plan—Another Junior Republic Six Hundred Children to Enjoy Country Life at Pleasantville, N. Y.—Curriculum Practical," *New-York Tribune*, June 8, 1912; "Ask Help for Orphans," *New York Times*, March 1, 1915; "School Children Run This Store," *Boston Daily Globe*, June 3, 1917; "Junior City Council," *Boston Daily Globe*, October 22, 1916; Wallace J. Atwood, "Habitat Groups in the Teaching of Geography," *Visual Education* 1 (1920): 30–36; New York Board of Education, "Thrift as Taught in One of the City High Schools," in *High Points of the Work of the High Schools of New York City* (1920); James Hilton Manning, *Century of American Savings Banks* (New York: Buck, 1917), 177; Herbert Kliebard, *Schooled to Work: Vocationalism and the American Curriculum, 1876–1946* (New York: Teachers College Press, 1999); Philip Cox, *Creative School Control* (Philadelphia: Lippincott, 1927); "In Lighter Vein: In the Meantime," *San Francisco Chronicle*, August 15, 1912; S. J. Vaughn, "Some Fundamentals in Manual Training," *Industrial Arts and Vocational Education* (1914): 13–15; Annual report 1911–1913, Records of the Hebrew Sheltering Guardian Society of New York, 1879–1970, I-43, box 2, folder 2, Annual Reports 1909–1913, Center for Jewish History.

8. William George, *Nothing Without Labor* (Freeville, NY: George Junior Republic, 1902); Lyman Beecher Stowe to Dr. V. Hattingberg, Munich, box 16, folder 10, WG Papers; Untitled document listing citizens and current professions, box 12, folder 22, WG Papers; Jeanne Robert, "A Republic for Boys and Girls—After Twenty Years," *Review of Reviews* 42 (1910): 708; "Junior Republics Grow: National Association Hears of the Success of Former Citizens," *New York Times*, June 7, 1914; James Price, "The Junior Republic," *The Friend*, September 3, 1898; H. Addington Bruce, "A Vocational School a Hundred Years Old," *Outlook*, July 28, 1915, 734–742; Minna Norriss, "The History of the California Junior Republic" (master's thesis, University of Southern California, 1931). On statistical data gathered by George's imitators, see "Editorial: Bulwarking Democracy through Practical Education," *Arena* 33, no. 186 (May 1905): 537; Wilson Gill, *A Social and Political Necessity: Moral, Civic and Industrial Training, Experiences, Reports and Proposed Legislation* (New York: Patriotic League, 1902); "You Cannot Change Human Nature," *Outlook*, March 18, 1911, 578. Assertions about the translatability of republic experiences into the "real" world include: Edgar Robinson, "Self-Government for Boys," *Association Boys* 7, no. 2 (1908): 109; Robert Bingham, "Progress City Report, 1914," container 36, folder 3, Progress City ca. 1906–1920, HH Records; "The Boy and the Law," *New-York Tribune*, September 20, 1908; E. B. French, "Lombroso's *Criminal Man*," *The Bookman: A Review of Books and Life* 34, no. 4 (December 1911): 424;

Theodore Roosevelt, "The Junior Republic," *New Outlook*, January 20, 1912, 117; Alissa Frank, "An Orphan Asylum with a Real Idea," *New-York Tribune*, April 6, 1919; James Hilton Manning, *Century of American Savings Banks* (New York: Buck, 1917), 177; "Boys Burn Bricks for Institution," *Los Angeles Times*, October 22, 1916; *Report of the Board of Managers of the Farm and Trades School, Thompson's Island* (Boston: Farm and Trades School, Thompson's Island, 1915), 24.

9. L. W. Kline, "The Migratory Impulse vs. Love of Home," *American Journal of Psychology* (October 1898); L. W. Kline, "Truancy as Related to the Migratory Instinct," *Pedagogical Seminary* 5 (1898): 381–420; David Nasaw, *Children of the City: At Work and at Play* (Oxford: Oxford University Press, 1986); Milwaukee City Club, *Amusements and Recreation in Milwaukee* (Milwaukee: City Club of Milwaukee, 1914), 10; Rowland Haynes and Stanley Davies, *Public Provision for Recreation* (Cleveland: Cleveland Foundation Committee, 1920), 23–24; John Collier and Edward Barrows, *The City Where Crime Is Play* (New York: People's Institute, 1914), 11; Maurice Hexter, "The Newsboys of Cincinnati," *Studies from the Helen S. Trounstine Foundation* 1, no. 4 (1919): 113–177; G. Walter Fiske, "Prolonging the Period of Adolescence for Employed Boys," *Association Yearbook* 14 (1915): 241–243; Edward Nicholas Clopper, *Child Labor in City Streets* (New York: Macmillan, 1912); Susan Campbell Bartoletti, *Kids on Strike* (Boston: Houghton Mifflin, 1999).

10. "Flock to Play at Hiram House, Children Swarm over Grounds Where Merrymaking Is the Rule," *Cleveland Plain Dealer*, July 10, 1907; Appendix B, "The Hiram House, Cleveland, Ohio," in Josiah Strong, *The Challenge of the City* (New York: Missionary Education Movement of the United States and Canada, 1907), 291; "Boyville and Boytown: Civic Training Schools," *San Francisco Chronicle*, June 16, 1912; Walter Stone, *The Development of Boys' Work in the United States* (Nashville: Vanderbilt University, 1933), 132; Willis Brown, "The Boy Problem," *Los Angeles Times*, December 24, 1915; J. Adams Puffer, "Study of Boys Gangs," *Pedagogical Seminary* 12 (1905): 175–212; J. Adams Puffer, *The Boy and His Gang* (Boston: Houghton Mifflin, 1912); David Nasaw, *Children of the City: At Work and at Play* (Oxford: Oxford University Press, 1986); Henry Gibson, *Camping for Boys* (New York: Association Press, 1911); John Boardman, "Probation from the Standpoint of the Boy Scout Movement," in *Report of the New York State Division of Probation* vol. 12 (Albany: Lyon, 1919), 211–218.

11. Duane R. Dills, "A Successful Form of Self-Government for Boys," *Association Boys* (October 1908): 188–194.

12. "George Quits Republic," *New-York Tribune*, September 5, 1912; "Spread of the Junior Republic Idea," *Outlook*, July 6, 1912, 516; "Germans to Make Study of Freeville Institution," *Syracuse Post-Standard*, October 8, 1913; Theodore Roosevelt, "The Junior Republic," *New Outlook*, January 20, 1912, 117; *Junior Citizen* (1913, multiple issues); William George, speech to New York State Probation Commission, published in *Eleventh Annual Report of New York State Probation Commission* (1918), 344; "George Republic near Bankruptcy," *New-York Tribune*, June 19, 1914; William George, "A Junior Republic in a City," *Junior Citizen* 14, no. 12 (1912): 246; "Hopes to Form Republic in City of Any Size," *Syracuse Post-Standard*, August 27, 1914; William George, "The City Junior Republic," *Ithaca Journal*, August 26, 1914; William George, *The Adult Minor* (New York: Appleton, 1937), 51; "New Republic Junior Kind: Playground Nation Elects First Officers, Square Deal for All is Its Citizens' Motto. Youngsters Take Up Work of Self-Government," *Los Angeles*

Times, February 26, 1909. The following are in WG Papers: William George to W. C. LeGendre, July 29, 1914, box 16, folder 13; L. B. Stowe to Alexander Forbes, September 8, 1914, box 16, folder 16; William George to Hon. Ben Conger of Groton, NY, 1914, box 16, folder 19; "A Junior Republic in a City," box 16, folder 17; Lyman B Stowe to Mrs. Ensor Chadwick, September 21, 1914, mentions the pamphlet "Junior Republics—What They Are and How to Start Them," box 16, folder 16.

13. "Boys Hold Elections Like Their Elders," *New York Times*, November 9, 1913; "Ithaca to Try Out Junior Municipality: Plan Proposed by 'Daddy' George Will Be Adopted Here—No Expense Attached," *Ithaca Daily News*, June 5, 1913; "Junior Officers Are Inaugurated: 'Daddy' William R. George Administers Oath of Office to J. Bert Wilson, Mayor—City Officials Make Short Speeches," *Ithaca Daily News*, December 2, 1913; "Junior Government in Every City," *New York Times*, April 8, 1913; "Spread of the Junior Republic Idea," *Outlook*, July 6, 1912, 516–517; "Register for the Charter Election, Every Boy and Girl Between 16 and 21 Will Be Given Chance to Assert Junior Citizenship at the City Hall Tomorrow," *Ithaca Daily News*, September 26, 1913; "Junior Municipality System; One Devised by Founder of George Jr. Republic to Be Tried in Ithaca," *Utica Daily Press*, June 6, 1913; "Boys' Government: 'Petition for Independence' Signed by Forty Boys and Six Girls in City of Ithaca," *Geneva Daily Times*, July 22, 1913; "New Plan by 'Daddy' George," A Junior Municipal Government, Every City of the Land Is the Plan," *Auburn Semi Weekly Journal*, April 11, 1913; "Girls Secure the Right to Vote," *Ithaca Daily News*, October 2, 1913; Lyman Beecher Stowe, "Good Citizens in the Making: How the Boys' and Girls' New 'Junior Municipality' Was Organized," *Illustrated Buffalo Express*, August 17, 1913; "Juvenile Idea in Ithaca: Boys and Girls Ready to Help Govern the City," *New-York Tribune*, July 2, 1913; "Daddy George Will Attend Board Meeting," *Ithaca Daily News*, March 23, 1914; "Junior City Judge Shumer Resigns; Gives Up Position in Junior Municipality to Return to Freeville Republic as Head of Laundry Work," *Ithaca Daily News*, April 3, 1915; "Will Have Chance to Study Junior Republic," *Ithaca Daily News*, July 7, 1914; "Plan to Extend Junior City," *Ithaca Daily News*, August 12, 1913; Lyman Beecher Stowe, "Good Citizens in the Making," *Ogden Standard*, November 19, 1913; "Working Youths Show Interest: Those Not in School See Opportunity of Securing Practical Training in Citizenship—Much Excitement Expected in November Election," *Ithaca Daily News*, September 8, 1913. What separated George's scheme from the republics that already called themselves "junior municipalities" or "dual governments" was that local governments were the sponsoring organizations. See "Boy City Officers Urge Track Elevation," *Indianapolis Star*, December 4, 1911; "Juniors to Have a Field Day," *Elmira Daily Gazette and Free Press*, May 13, 1897; "Jews Plan to Educate Young Men and Women," *Brooklyn Daily Eagle*, November 3, 1916; "Junior Municipality to Be City-Wide among Boys of Indianapolis Schools," *Indianapolis Star*, October 27, 1912; "Junior Municipality: Students in Venice Grammar School Establish Miniature City Government with Complete Set of Officers," *Los Angeles Times*, March 21, 1914; "New Junior Mayor of Richmond Faces Army of Job Hunters," *Indianapolis Star*, July 30, 1916; "Complete Boy Government in City of Hammond, Ind.," *Ithaca Daily News*, April 1, 1910; "School Municipality," *Morning Olympian*, March 10, 1910.

14. "Juniors to Have a Juvenile Court," *Ithaca Daily News*, June 6, 1914; "Junior Officers Are Inaugurated: 'Daddy' William R. George Administers Oath of Office to J. Bert Wilson, Mayor—City Officials Make Short Speeches," *Ithaca Daily News*, December 2, 1913; "'Daddy' George Conducts

Inauguration Ceremonies," *Syracuse Post-Standard*, November 29, 1913; "Junior Municipality Installs Its Officers," *Syracuse Post-Standard*, December 2, 1913; "Mayor Makes Bid for Cooperation," *Ithaca Daily News*, March 5, 1914; Lyman Beecher Stowe, "Good Citizens in the Making: How the Boys' and Girls' New 'Junior Municipality' Was Organized," *Illustrated Buffalo Express*, August 17, 1913; "Sixteen Try for Jobs with the City," *Ithaca Daily News*, March 21, 1914; "Ithaca Children to Have Fine New Playgrounds," *Syracuse Post-Standard*, June 2, 1914; Lyman Beecher Stowe, "Junior Citizens in Action," *Outlook*, November 18, 1914, 654–656; "'Daddy' George Greeted by Junior Officials," *Ithaca Daily News*, March 25, 1914; "Ithaca Women's Clubs Plan Historic Pageant," *Syracuse Post-Standard*, June 26, 1914; "Junior Judge to Hold Court," *Ithaca Daily News*, June 13, 1914; "Charges Italians Assaulted Him," *Ithaca Daily News*, June 5, 1914; "Juniors to Have a Juvenile Court: New Department of Junior Government Will Relieve the City Court of Many Trivial Cases and Do Much Good—City Officers to Cooperate," *Ithaca Daily News*, June 6, 1914; "Offenders Held for Grand Jury" *Ithaca Daily News*, June 16, 1914; "Only Two Tickets for Junior Election," *Ithaca Daily News*, October 15, 1913; "Junior Mayoralty Seekers Make a Canvass for Voters," *Syracuse Post-Standard*, October 7, 1913; "Junior Policemen to Be Appointed," *Ithaca Daily News*, September 24, 1913; "Junior Officers Have Had Success: Boy and Girl Political Parties? Now Making Preparations for the Fall Election—Accomplishments of Juvenile Government," *Ithaca Daily News*, July 9, 1914; "Young Politicians Prepare Platform: Pledge Junior Municipality to Assist Enforcement of Laws Pertaining to Gambling, Pool Rooms and Regular School Attendance," *Ithaca Daily News*, October 16, 1913; "Young Woman Is the Prime Mover: Miss Bates Takes Active Part in Junior Municipality—'Daddy' George Says County, State and National Government May Develop," *Ithaca Daily News*, August 5, 1913; "'Daddy' George Has Brand New Scheme; Would Form Junior Municipal Government in All Cities Allowing Boys and Girls to Vote for Their Own Officers at the Age of 16," *Ithaca Daily News*, April 7, 1913; "Girls Rival Youths in Make Believe Politics," *New-York Tribune*, October 4, 1913.

15. "Steigerwald Is Assessor," *Auburn Citizen*, December 17, 1913; "To Tell Auburn about Junior Municipality," *Ithaca Daily News*, December 16, 1913; "Well Organize New Junior Republics," *Syracuse Post-Standard*, July 16, 1914; "Newark Man Here to Watch Junior Election," *Ithaca Daily News*, November 5, 1913; "Junior City Will Help Municipality Ithaca, New York, to Let Boys and Girls Learn Practical Government," *Trenton Evening Times*, July 8, 1913; "Citizens in the Making: How the Boys' and Girls' New 'Junior Municipality' Was Organized," *Times-Picayune*, August 17, 1913; "Good Citizens in the Making: How the Boys' and Girls' New 'Junior Municipality' Was Organized," *Lexington Herald*, October 5, 1913; "Buffalo Interested in Junior Municipality," *Ithaca Daily News*, February 11, 1914; "Made a Good Start: New Council Started First Meeting Right on Time," *Auburn Citizen*, January 7, 1914; "'Daddy' George Greeted by Junior Officials," *Ithaca Daily News*, March 25, 1914; "Others Will Follow Ithaca's Lead: Many Requests Come to 'Daddy' George for Junior Municipality Ideas—Founder Busy on Road," *Ithaca Daily News*, October 4, 1913; "May Organize Municipality: Batavia Men Interested in New Scheme for Making Citizens," *Sunday Times* [Batavia, NY], August 24, 1913; "Wroath Once More Will Have Charge of the City's Playgrounds," *Auburn Citizen*, June 24, 1914; "After the Fourth Come Playgrounds," *Auburn Citizen*, July 2, 1914; "Request George to Offer His Visit to Auburn," *Ithaca Daily News*, July 23, 1914; "No Junior Municipality in Auburn, at Least Not for the Present, Says Mayor Brister," *Auburn Citizen*, July 24, 1914; "New officers for the Junior Municipality," *Albany Evening Journal*, November 18, 1916; "Plans for

Boys; Central YMCA to Have Socials and Junior Municipality," *Albany Evening Journal*, October 3, 1916; "Dormitory Men Have Self-Government Fun," *Ithaca Daily News*, October 7, 1913; "Jersey Juveniles Start Government: 'Daddy' George's Novel Plan of Training Children in Real Life Affairs Is Taken Up by the Officials of Jersey City—Started in Ithaca," *Ithaca Daily News*, July 28, 1913; "Junior Municipal Government," *Bulletin of the Public Affairs Information* Service 1 (1915), 143; "'Daddy' George Greeted by Junior Officials," *Ithaca Daily News*, March 25, 1914; "Junior Charter Now Completed. Constitution Committee Sings Doxology. When Work Is Ended Juvenile Government Will Have Board of Education and Supreme Court," *Ithaca Daily News*, September 6, 1913; "Cortland Adopts Junior Municipality: Constitutional Committee, Composed Mostly of Boys, Has Its First Meeting," *Ithaca Daily News*, August 20, 1913; "Boys Hold Elections Like Their Elders" *New York Times*, November 9, 1913; "Propose Training School for Voters; Plan Suggested Whereby Members of Junior Municipality Would Understudy City Officials to Be Considered at Early Meetings," *Ithaca Daily News*, August 22, 1913; "Junior Municipality Makes Its Nominations," *Syracuse Post-Standard*, October 31, 1913; "Juvenile Voters Register for Election at Cortland," *Syracuse Post-Standard*, October 19, 1913; "The George Junior Municipality Was Recently Organized in Cortland," *Richfield Mercury*, January 22, 1914; "George Creates Sentiment for Junior Municipality: Addresses Gathering of Forty Young People Together with City Officials at Cortland," *Syracuse Post-Standard*, July 5, 1913; "Plan to Extend 'Junior City,'" *Ithaca Daily News*, August 12, 1913; "Additional brevities—Junior Municipality registrations were held in Cortland last night, with W. R. George officiating. Junior Mayor J. Bert Wilson of this city attended and was called upon for an address," *Ithaca Daily News*, December 9, 1913; "Urges Juvenile Judges," *New-York Tribune*, April 8, 1913; "New Officials of Junior Municipality," *Oregonian*, July 14, 1914; "Spread of the Junior Republic Idea," *Outlook*, July 6, 1912, 516–517; Lyman Beecher Stowe, "Boy Judges in a Boys' Court," *Outlook*, May 1 1913, 485–496; Lyman Beecher Stowe, "Junior Citizens in Action," *Outlook*, November 18, 1914, 654–656; Lyman Beecher Stowe, "What to Do with a Boy," *World's Work* 26 (June 1913): 190–195; "Would Imitate the Junior Municipality," *Ithaca Daily News*, January 23, 1915.

16. "Boys Republic Exhibit: Three Buildings to Be Reproduced at Woman's Industrial Show," *New York Times*, February 26, 1912. George's national association also contemplated an exhibit at the Panama-Pacific International Exposition. See National Association of Junior Republics, brief summary of meeting, June 15, 1914, box 16, folder 6, WG Papers. "Echo Park Republic," *Los Angeles Times*, February 24, 1910; J. F. B. Tinling, "Juvenile Self Governing Communities," *Progress: Civic-Social-Industrial* (January 4, 1909): 1–12; "Here Playing Is the Thing," *Sun*, September 10, 1908; "Miniature Republic Created by Pupils, Ceremonies at Washington Duplicated, Superintendent Oliver W. Best of Echo Park Playground Finally Puts Novel Plan into Operation," *Los Angeles Herald*, March, 5, 1909; "Republic to Hold Annual Election" *Los Angeles Herald*, February 24, 1910; "New Republic Junior Kind," *Los Angeles Times*, February 26, 1909; "Junior Republic Founder Offers to Visit Fort Worth," *Fort Worth Star-Telegram*, April 21, 1915; "Play City Will Work Says Expert Explanation of Plan Satisfies Miss Van Buren at Wednesday's Conference," *Fort Worth Star-Telegram*, April 22, 1915; "'Mayor' Wilson Home from East Side Camp," *Ithaca Daily News*, August 7, 1914; "Fresh Air Boys Govern Own Camp, 'Live Ones' of Gas House District Organize in Self-Rule Test," *New-York Tribune*, July 31, 1914; E. T. Baneley, *Homer Lane and the Little Commonwealth* (London: Allen and Unwin, 1928); Homer Lane, *Talks to Parents and Teachers* (London: Allen and

Unwin, 1928); "Junior Republics Abroad," *New York Times*, April 7, 1917. The following are in WG Papers: "Suggestions regarding a training school for republic workers and pioneer citizens," c. 1912, box 14, folder 2; John Bauer to William George, May 25, 1914, box 16, folder 4; Earl Bruner to William George, January 15, 1913, box 14, folder 6; William Gute to L. B. Stowe, June 13 1914, box 16, folder 6; William George to William A Gute, January 4, 1914, box 21, folder 19 or box 21, folder 20; Letter from Gerald Waterhouse of the California Junior Republic, June 1, 1914, box 16, folder 5; L. B. Stowe to Walter Brooks, July 17, 1914, box 16, folder 9; Auburn Mayor C. W. Brister to William George, July 6, 1914, box 16, folder 8; C. Spencer Richardson to John Clyde Oswald, box 16, folder 8; Principal of PS 83 to William George, April 1, 1914, box 16, folder 1; Charles Pekor Jr. to William George, April 10, 1915, box 17, folder 4. George also sent Wilson to Flemington Junction to train more kids; that republic shut down soon after. "'Mayor' Wilson Home from East Side Camp," *Ithaca Daily News*, August 6, 1914.

17. "Plot is Alleged in George Case," *New-York Tribune*, December 2, 1913; "Made a True Republic: George Leaves Freeville to Let Juniors Be Supreme," *New-York Tribune*, September 8, 1912; "How Daddy George Scandal Started," *Ithaca Daily News*, July 15, 1914; "Find George Guilty on Two Charges, Investigators Report Head of Junior Republic Involved with Inmates," *Grand Rapids Press*, March 3, 1914; *Report of the Special Committee on the George Junior Republic Submitted to, and Unanimously Adopted by, the State Board of Charities, at Its Meeting of December 17*, 1913, box 15, folder 23, WG Papers; "Brogan: Lands on George," *Cincinnati Enquirer*, December 19, 1913; "Junior Republic Head Dismissed," *San Francisco Call*, December 18, 1913; "Good, Bad and Daddy George," *Survey* 30 (August 2, 1913): 565–566; "Grave Charges Against William R. George," *Survey* 31 (March 14, 1941): 755–756; Frederick Hankinson, "The George Junior Republic and Its Lessons," *Parents Review* (October 1913): 754–762; "Demand George Quit 'Republic,'" *New-York Tribune*, December 19, 1913; "George Junior Republic Closed," *New-York Tribune*, September 11, 1914; "Close Junior Republic Daddy George's Project Lacks Funds to Continue," *Cleveland Plain Dealer*, September 11, 1914; "Crisis in the George Junior Republic," *Outlook*, September 14, 1912, 53–54.

18. William George to William Gute, May 27, 1914, box 16, folder 4, WG Papers; "Judge Lindsey Upholds National Junior Republic," *Ithaca Daily News*, January 4, 1914; "Citizens Rally to George's Defense," *Syracuse Journal*, December 29, 1913; "Still Have Faith in George," *Monroe County Mail*, January 1, 1914 [reprinted in numerous local papers]; "Still Trust in WR George," *Sun*, December 29, 1913; "Will Send Testimonial to 'Daddy' George," *Ithaca Daily News*, December 22, 1913; "Send Resolutions to Daddy George: Founder of Republic at Freeville Told of Esteem in Which He Is Held by the Citizens of That Institution—He Sends Reply," *Ithaca Daily News*, December 27, 1913; *Report of the Special Committee on the George Junior Republic Submitted To, and Unanimously Adopted By, the State Board of Charities, at Its Meeting of December 17*, 1913, box 15, folder 23, WG Papers; Petition praising William George prepared by junior citizens, box 15, folder 27, WG Papers; Letters of support for George from former citizens, judges, trustees of other republics and Interior Secretary Franklin K. Lane—see Lane to William George, April 11, 1914, box 16, folder 1, WG Papers; "How Daddy George Scandal Started," *Ithaca Daily News*, July 15, 1914; "Junior Republic Growing Rapidly, 'Daddy' George Says Census High Water Mark of Old Republic Will Soon Be Reached," *Ithaca Daily News*, January 18, 1915; "Will Continue Work of Junior Republic," *Trenton Evening Times*, October 20, 1914; William George to Archie Stephenson c/o Mr. Bruk,

October 31, 1914, box 16, folder 19, WG Papers; William George to Joe Butterfield, October 21, 1914, box 16, folder 19, WG Papers; "That Junior Municipality: No Move Made as Yet Here and No Word Received from Daddy George. What effect the charges recently made against William R. George of the George Junior Republic may have upon the proposed Junior Municipality in this city is not known," *Auburn Citizen*, March 6, 1914; "Word from George: He Can't Come to Auburn at the Present Time. But Hopes to Come Later. Strain through Which He Has Passed Makes It Necessary for Him to Give Up Work," *Auburn Citizen*, March 24, 1914; "A Change in Policy," *Outlook*, August 4, 1915, 779; "Junior Republic Method Planned," *Christian Science Monitor*, September 16, 1914; "$10,000 Gift Saves Freeville Republic," *New York Times*, June 20, 1914; "George Republic Head Is Given an Exoneration," *Arizona Republican*, March 12, 1914; "Junior Republics Ask George to Stay," *New York Times*, March 12, 1914; "Founder May Take Over Junior Republic," *Indianapolis Star*, September 16, 1914.

19. Minna Norriss, "The History of the California Junior Republic" (master's thesis, University of Southern California, 1931), 125, citing A. E. Winship, "Looking About the California Junior Republic," *Journal of Education* (June 6, 1912); Delos Wilcox and Wilson Gill, *Outline of American Government* (New Paltz, NY: Patriotic League, 1899), 98; "Camp of Boys and Girls—Industrial Farm in Tompkins County for City Children—Conducted by William R. George—Influences for Good which Surround the Citizens of This Miniature Republic—Have Their Own," *New York Times*, August 25, 1895; William Hull, "The George Junior Republic," *Annals of the American Academy of Political and Social Science* 10, no. 1 (1897): 73–86; "The School City," *New York Evangelist*, September 23, 1897, 27; Bernard Cronson, *Pupil Self-Government* (New York: Macmillan, 1907); Wilson Gill, "The 'School City' in Connection with Pupil Self-Government," *Annual Report of the State Superintendant, New York Department of Public Instruction* 49 (1903): 47–58; Lyman Beecher Stowe, "School Cities," *American Educational Review* 29 (1907): 213; Wilson Gill, *The System of Moral and Civic Training* (New Paltz, NY: State Normal School at New Paltz, 1901); "The Gill School City," *New York Evangelist*, September 23, 1897, 27; "In the Mirror of the Present: Progress of the School-City Movement," *Arena* 35, no. 195 (February 1906): 201; M. C. Craft, "The School City a Success," *Atlanta Constitution*, May 5, 1901; Wilson Gill, "Have a Republic in Every Schoolroom," *Boston Daily Globe*, August 6, 1916; "The Public School System of Gary Indiana," *Bulletin: United States. Bureau of Education* (1914); "Garyville Boys Are Helping to Run Their Town. Boyville Corporation Elects Mayor and Board of Aldermen and Make Laws," *Montgomery Advertiser*, January 31, 1915; "Lad Fights Cigaret Sale: Mayor of Gary's 'Boyville' Asks City Council If It Is 'on the Square,'" *Chicago Daily Tribune*, December 7, 1910; Duane R. Dills, "A Successful Form of Self-Government for Boys," *Association Boys* (October 1908): 188–194. Youth-produced newspapers from the Boston Farm and Trades School's Cottage Row and Cleveland Hiram House settlement's Progress City are among those filled with accounts of these field trips and site visits.

20. LeRoy Ashby, *Saving the Waifs: Reformers and Dependent Children, 1890–1917* (Philadelphia: Temple University Press, 1984); *In Memory of John E. Gunckel: Founder and Life President of the National and Toledo Newsboys Association*, Trustees of Toledo Newsboys Association, Toledo, Ohio, 1915; "Boyville," *New York Times*, February 17, 1906; A. E. Winship, "Successful Work for Wayward Boys," *Missionary Review of the World* 32, no. 2 (1909): 856; Edgar James Swift, *Youth and the Race* (New York: Scribner's, 1912), 161; Philip Davis, *Street-Land: Its Little People and Big*

Problems (Boston: Small, Maynard, 1915), 217; "Newsboys' Judges," *Boston Daily Globe*, November 21, 1912; Lewis E. Palmer, "Horatio Alger, Then and Now," *Survey* 27 (December 2, 1911): 1276; T. D. A. Cockerell, "Children of the City," *The Dial*, August 15, 1915, 103; "Four Scholarships," *Boston Daily Globe*, February 12, 1911; "Philip Davis, Supervisor of Licensed Boy Workers, Boston," *Boston Daily Globe*, June 11, 1911; "Newsboys' Elections," *Boston Daily Globe*, November 12, 1911; "Newsboys Elect Judges to Preside Over Court," *Christian Science Monitor*, November 8, 1910; "Newsboy's Republic Poll," *Christian Science Monitor*, November 9, 1910; "School Citizens Committee," *Psychological Clinic* 4 (1911): 280; "227,201 Enrolled in 296 Boys' Clubs," *New York Times*, January 15, 1928. Newsboys had previously participated in other self-government programs, for example, summer camps through William Forbush's Society for Christian Endeavor. (See "Newsboys Camp: Youngsters Having a Good Time in Harford County," *Sun*, June 24, 1899.) Eagerly watching these developments, the School Citizens Committee made plans to organize a New York newsboy state with assistance from Richard Welling. See "School Citizens Committee," *Psychological Clinic* 4 (1911): 280.

21. "School City a Failure," *Sun*, May 1, 1899; "A Believer in Boys," *New-York Tribune*, May 28, 1899; William Torrey Harris, *The School City* (Syracuse: Bardeen, 1907); "Scores Government of the United States: Milwaukee's Socialist Mayor in Address to Boys' Republic Says Model Is Poor," *San Francisco Chronicle*, October 22, 1910; Wilson Gill, *A New Citizenship: Democracy Systematized* (Philadelphia: Patriotic League, 1913). Wilson Gill, *The Gill System of Moral and Civic Training* (New Paltz, NY: State Normal School at New Paltz, 1901) lists John Commons as a Patriotic League instructor book chapter contributor. John Commons, "The George Junior Republic," *American Journal of Sociology* (1897): 281–296; John Commons, "The George Junior Republic II," *American Journal of Sociology* (1898): 433–448; John Commons, *The Newsboys of Milwaukee* (Milwaukee: Bureau of Economy and Efficiency, 1911); Edgar James Swift, *Youth and the Race* (New York: Scribner's, 1912), 164; Lillian McLean, "Kindergarten Metaphysics," *Mind* 6 (1900): 133; Philip Davis, *Street-Land: Its Little People and Big Problems* (Boston: Small, Maynard, 1915), 274; T. D. A. Cockerell, "Children of the City," *The Dial*, August 15, 1915, 103.

22. "Working Rules Approved: Milwaukee Newsboys' Republic Formally Approves Constitution and Forms Two Parties" *Milwaukee Sentinel*, October 26, 1912; "Plan Newsboys' Republic: State Industrial Commission Seeks to Organize Workers," *Milwaukee Sentinel*, October 3, 1912; "Getting Hold of Milwaukee's Newsboys. Report on Effectiveness of Street Trades Law and of Newsboys' Republic in Milwaukee, P. O. Powell, Supervisor of Street Trades, Milwaukee, Wisconsin," *Playground* 10 (November 1914): 296–299; David Steenberg, "Book of Revelations: A Farce on Biblical Book Dealing with Newsies," *Newsboys' World*, November 1916; "Newsboys Republic Officers Installed the New Officers of the News Boys Republic Were Inaugurated," *Milwaukee Sentinel*, February 5, 1916; "Inauguration Best Ever Inauguration of New Newsies Officers," *Newsboys' World*, March 1917; "Newsboys' Republic to Inaugurate Friday" *Milwaukee Sentinel*, January 22, 1915; "Reitman Made Head of Newsboy Republic" *Milwaukee Sentinel*, November 20, 1912; "Inaugurate Officers of Newsboys' Republic: Gov. McGovern Commends Boys' Movement, Saying It Will Enable Them to Understand Laws," *Milwaukee Sentinel*, December 20, 1912; B. E. Kuechle, "Newsboys' Republic, Milwaukee, Wis.," *Survey* (March 22, 1913): 859; "Ignore Agitators, Plea to Newsboys," January 31, 1914, *Milwaukee Sentinel*; Gerhard A. Bading, Mayor, to *Newsboys' World*,

September 1915; "The Milwaukee Republic, by One of Its Founders" *Work with Boys* (1914): 25–26. Some documents are also available in James Marten, *Childhood and Child Welfare in the Progressive Era: A Brief History with Documents* (New York: Bedford/St. Martins, 2004).

23. "At Last," *Newsboys' World*, November 1915; "Notes on Street Trades Department and Milwaukee Newsboys' Republic, P. O. Powell, Supervisor of Street Trades, Milwaukee Public Schools," *Proceedings of the National Conference on Social Work* (1921), 297; "Pop Tells of Results Accomplished by Newsboys' Republic and the Future Needs, Update on the Newsies Republic and How It Affects the City of Milwaukee," *Newsboys' World*, June 1923; "Campaign to Start May 15th, Newsies Try to Raise Money to Help Sick Members," *Newsboys' World*, April-May 1917; "Milwaukee's Newsboys' Republic," *Outlook*, April 15, 1913, 743–744; "James Clifford Elected President of 16th Avenue School: An Update on Some of the Newsies," *Newsboys' World*, April 1916; "Getting Hold of Milwaukee's Newsboys: Report on Effectiveness of Street Trades Law and of Newsboys' Republic in Milwaukee, P. O. Powell, Supervisor of Street Trades, Milwaukee, Wisconsin," *Playground* 10 (November 1914): 296–299. Notably, the social centers they used were connected to the efficiency movement. See Edward W. Stevens Jr., "Social Centers, Politics, and Social Efficiency in the Progressive Era," *History of Education Quarterly* 12, no. 1 (Spring 1972): 16–33; "Make the Most of School Life: Education Is Important to All," *Newsboys' World*, December 1921.

24. "Working Rules Approved: Milwaukee Newsboys' Republic Formally Approves Constitution and Forms Two Parties" *Milwaukee Sentinel*, October 26, 1912; "Milwaukee's Newsboys' Republic," *Outlook*, April 15, 1913, 743–744; "Strange Milwaukee Newsboys: The Milwaukee 'Newsies,'" *Youth's Companion* 87, no. 28 (1913): 358; Esther Lee Rider, "Newsboys in Birmingham," *American Child* 3 (February 1922): 316; "A Voice from Dixie," *Newsboys' World*, November 1915; "New Officials of Junior Municipality," *Oregonian*, July 14, 1914; W. L. Murdoch, "Child Labor Reform in Alabama," *Child Labor Bulletin* 3 (1914): 82; "Newsboys' Republic to Inaugurate Friday," *Milwaukee Sentinel*, January 22, 1915; "Newsboys Republic Officers Installed: The New Officers of the News Boys Republic Were Inaugurated," *Milwaukee Sentinel*, February 5, 1916; John R. Commons, *The Newsboys of Milwaukee* (Milwaukee: Bureau of Economy and Efficiency, 1911); "The Milwaukee Republic, by One of Its Founders," *Work with Boys* (1914): 21–27; B. E. Kuechle, "Newsboys' Republic, Milwaukee, Wis.," *Survey* (March 22, 1913): 859; "Milwaukee's Newsboys' Republic," *Outlook*, April 5, 1913, 743–744; "Notes on Street Trades Department and Milwaukee Newsboys' Republic, P. O. Powell, Supervisor of Street Trades, Milwaukee Public Schools," *Proceedings of the National Conference on Social Work* (1921), 297.

25. Kevin Murphy, *Political Manhood* (New York: Columbia University Press, 2010), 138; "Allies for Col. Waring," *New York Times*, August 1, 1895; "Junior Street Cleaning Leagues," *Public Opinion*, April 1, 1897; David Willard, "The Juvenile Street Cleaning Leagues," in George Edwin Waring, *Street-Cleaning and the Disposal of a City's Wastes* (New York: Doubleday and McClure, 1897); "St. Louis Swept by an Army of Children," *St. Louis Post-Dispatch*, May 3, 1903; "Children for Clean Streets," *New York Times*, August 1, 1899; "Gill School City Rules," *New-York Tribune*, March 31, 1899; "The Boy Street Cleaning Brigade," *New-York Tribune*, September 20, 1903; "Juvenile Street Cleaners," *New York Times*, August 23 1903; Martin V. Melosi, *Garbage in the Cities: Refuse, Reform, and the Environment* (College Station: Texas A&M University Press, 1981); "For the East Side's Health," *New York Times*, September 7, 1895; Richard Welling, "The Teaching of Civics and

Good Citizenship in the Public Schools," *Journal of Proceedings and Lectures, National Education Association* 42 (1903); "Current Topics: Juvenile Inspectors," *Sun*, October 23, 1897; "The Young Citizens' League: Work That Is Being Done in the Schools in the Oranges," *New York Times*, May 11, 1903; *Keep Our City Clean: How the Children of St. Louis May Assist in Making It a Clean, Healthy, Beautiful City* (St. Louis: Gottschalk, 1903); "St. Louis Swept by an Army of Children," *St. Louis Post-Dispatch*, May 3, 1903; "Children as Improvement Workers," *Journal of Education* 60, no. 8 (August 25, 1904): 142; "Children to Beautify City," *St. Louis Post-Dispatch*, December 7, 1902; "Ald. Scully and His Juvenile Street Cleaning Brigade at Work," *Chicago Daily Tribune*, April 20, 1903; "Children as Street-Cleaners," *Ladies' Home Journal*, January 1897, 4; "Boy Protectors of Streets: Careful As to Membership and Enthusiastic in Work," *New York Times*, May 21, 1896; "Child Street Cleaners: System Adopted by Several Eastern Cities," *San Francisco Chronicle*, January 24, 1897; "Juvenile Street Cleaners: Boys Encouraged to Assist in Work of Removing Rubbish by Being Given Membership in Circulating 'Sporting Goods Library'—Several Clubs Open," *New York Times*, August 23, 1903; "The Juvenile League," *New-York Tribune*, November 9, 1897; "Precocious Reformers," *New-York Tribune*, November 16, 1896; "Col. Waring's Young Aids: Receive Badges and Compliments from the Commissioner: Told They Are a Part of the Municipal Government, and Have Important Obligations Resting on Their Young Shoulders—Special Praise for the Youngster Who Dared Tackle 'Silver Dollar' Smith's Bartender—Orators Among Them," *New York Times*, May 24, 1896; "Col. Waring Their Guest: Juvenile Street Cleaners Have a Reception," *New York Times*, November 14, 1896.

26. Leroy Peterson, "Social Service in the New York Police Department," *Delinquent* (March 1916): 6–7; "The 'Boy Cops,'" *Work with Boys* 16 (1916): 41; "The Sturdy Boy Police Force of Echo Park," *New-York Tribune*, February 28, 1915; Gregory Mason, "The Boy Police of New York," *Outlook*, July 28, 1915, 706–708; Arthur Woods, "Police Administration," *Proceedings of the Academy of Political Science in the City of New York* 5, no. 3 (April 1915): 54–61; "The Telephone Boy Sleuth," *St. Louis Post-Dispatch*, July 26, 1893; "Edmond, 'Boy Detective,' Fearing Spanking by Ma, Is Terribly Embarrassed," *Detroit Free Press*, October 18, 1913; "Boy Police Patrol This New York School," *St. Louis Post-Dispatch*, December 7, 1902; "Back to the Farm for Boy Detective," *St. Louis Post-Dispatch*, October 13, 1904; "Heller's Moral Obligation," *Washington Post*, February 21, 1896; "Thugs Cut Throat of Boy Detective," *Detroit Free Press*, December 27, 1909; "Boy 'Detective' in Hands of Police," *Arizona Republican*, April 2, 1910; "Boy Detective in Tears," *New York Times*, May 27, 1884; "Local Criminal Items," *Chicago Daily Tribune*, April 5, 1881; "A Boy Detective Shot," *New-York Tribune*, September 5, 1881; Gayle Olsen Raymer, "The American System of Juvenile Justice" in *History of Juvenile Delinquency*, vol. 2, ed. Albert Hess and Patricia Clement (Aalen, Germany: Scientia Verlag, 1993); David B. Wolcott, *Cops and Kids: Policing Juvenile Delinquency in Urban America, 1890–1940* (Columbus: Ohio State University Press, 2005); "Boy Cops Will March in Parade with Police: Lads Organized by Captains Sweeney and Sexton Will Wear Copies of Regular Uniform Provided by Their Benefactors, Black and Spencer," *New-York Tribune*, March 8, 1915; "The Junior Police of New York City, Captain John F. Sweeney, 'Commissioner' of the Kid Cops," *Survey* 33 (March 13, 1915): 652–653; "Beat It, Here Comes the Cop," *Modern City* 2 (September 1917): 32; "Junior Police Aid Marjorie's Fund," *New-York Tribune*, March 30, 1916; "Boy Fire Brigade Formed: Brownsville Lady to Get Co-operation of Adamson," *New-York Tribune*, August 19, 1917; "Boy Police Check Cigarette Sales to West End Minors," *St. Louis Post-Dispatch*, January 12,

1919; "Two Squads of Juvenile Police at Odds over Merger," *St. Louis Post-Dispatch*, January 16, 1916; "Boys Trail 2 Suspects," *Detroit Free Press*, September 1, 1908; Courtland Holdom, "Training Efficient Police: Chief August Vollmer, Who Began to Instruct Policemen Early in the Century, Believes that the Preservation of American Democracy Demands Widespread Education for Public Service," *Christian Science Monitor*, February 5, 1936; "The Kid Cops," *Literary Digest* 50 (February 20, 1915): 396–397; "Wants Boy Police in All Precincts: Woods Says Idea Is Good, and Plans to Organize," *New-York Tribune*, March 26, 1915; "Boy of 11 Years a 'Policeman': Frank Williams to Keep Boys Off McGann's Roof, Judge Sturtevant's Ruling in Somerville Court, 'Junior Officer' Will Use His Fists for a Club," *Boston Daily Globe*, July 21, 1923; Gregory Mason, "The Boy Police of New York," *Labor Digest* 8, no. 7 (1915): 31; Arthur Woods to L. B. Stowe, May 27, 1914, box 16, folder 4, WG Papers; "Boy City Falls in a Police Raid, Bluecoats Wipe Out Promising Municipality in Election Booths," *Cleveland Plain Dealer*, December 5, 1907; Harry Carr, "Los Angeles Twenty Years Ago," *Los Angeles Herald*, December 25, 1910; "New City Built in Just Six Days," *Los Angeles Times*, September 11, 1902.

27. "Young Sleuths to Scour East Side," *New-York Tribune*, March 30, 1914; "Shopkeepers Obey Boy Police Orders," *New York Times*, June 1, 1914; "Boy Police," *Americana Supplement: A Comprehensive Record of the Latest Knowledge and Progress of the World* 1 (1911): 189; "Council Bluffs Kid Police Force," *Westminster* 33 (August 2, 1908): 9; "Boy Police Stop Noise," *New York Times*, June 30, 1907; "Council Bluffs Boy Police," *Christian Science Monitor*, January 7, 1911; "Flock to Play at Hiram House, Children Swarm Over Grounds Where Merrymaking Is the Rule," *Cleveland Plain Dealer*; July 10, 1907; Appendix B, "The Hiram House, Cleveland, Ohio," in Josiah Strong, "The Hiram House, Cleveland, Ohio," in Josiah Strong, *The Challenge of the City* (New York: Missionary Education Movement of the United States and Canada, 1907), 291; "Boy Police in Council Bluffs," *Christian Science Monitor*, December 3, 1908; "Boy Police Make an Orderly Fourth," *New York Times*, July 1, 1907.

28. Martin Melosi, *Garbage in the Cities* (College Station: Texas A&M Press, 1981); "Teaching Children to Help Their City," *New York Times*, November 9, 1913; "Children Again Form Clean Streets League," *New York Times*, June 22, 1906; *Junior Citizen* (September–October 1898): 7; "The School City" *Congregationalist*, December 14, 1899, 84, 50, 927; "Editorial: Bulwarking Democracy through Practical Education," *Arena* 33, no. 186 (May 1905): 537; "Boys Aid in Making a City Clean," *Christian Science Monitor*, September 2, 1915; "In Interest of Clean Streets," *New-York Tribune*, December 18, 1906; George William Hunter and Walter George Whitman, *Civic Science in the Community* (New York: American Book, 1922); "R. S. Simons Dies," *New York Times*, April 12, 1929. Notably, the early observers of the Juvenile City League saw resonance with Gill's School Cities. See William Langdon, "The Juvenile City League of New York," *The Aims of Religious Education: Proceedings of the Third Annual Convention of the Religious Education Association, Boston* 3 (1905): 442; William Chauncy Langdon, "Ideas for Civic Education from the Juvenile City League," *Chautauquan* 43, no. 4 (June 1906): 370.

29. William Seymour, "Junior Deputy Sanitary Inspectors," *American City* 15, no. 5 (1916): 696–697; Frances Gulick Jewett, *Town and City* (Boston: Ginn, 1906) [chapter on juvenile street cleaning leagues]; Reuben Simons, "The Juvenile Street Cleaning Leagues of New York," *American City* 3 (October 1910): 163–166; L. B. Stowe, letter to the editor, *NY Globe and Commercial Advertiser*, June 20, 1914, box 16, folder 7, WG Papers.

30. "A Boyville Court Handling Cleveland's Juvenile Crooks: Special Youthful Officers and Judges Work Under Jurisdiction of Social Center and Regular Courts," *Colorado Springs Gazette*, September 27, 1914; LeRoy Ashby, *Saving the Waifs: Reformers and Dependent Children, 1890–1917* (Philadelphia: Temple University Press, 1984); Lyman Beecher Stowe, "What to Do with a Boy," *World's Work* 26 (June 1913): 190–195; Lewis Meriam, "Child Welfare," *American Year Book: A Record of Events and Progress, 1914* (New York: Appleton, 1915), 377; "Jottings," *Survey* 34 (May 15, 1915): 168; "Boy Judges Pass on Offenses in Juvenile Court," *Christian Science Monitor*, November 28, 1915; "Junior Juvenile Court Idea Is Welcomed," *Sun*, May 2, 1915; "Oyez Oyez, Junior Juvenile Court Is Now in Session," *St. Louis Post-Dispatch*, November 18, 1914; "Koch Blames Movies," *Sun*, April 22, 1915; "A Junior Juvenile Court," *Sun*, April 27, 1915; "End of an Outing," *Los Angeles Times*, February 16, 1917. In some cities youth police and courts were a single program; see, for example, "Brookline Tries Boy Police," *Boston Daily Globe*, February 20, 1917.

31. Delos Wilcox and Wilson Gill, *An Outline of American Government* (New Paltz, NY: Patriotic League, 1899), 99.

32. Boy Scouts of America, *Handbook for Scoutmasters* (New York: BSA, 1913), 280; David MacLeod, *Building Character in the American Boy* (Madison: University of Wisconsin Press, 2004); "Boy Scouts Must Be Like Daring Men," *New York Times*, October 9, 1910; Louis Dunton Hartson, "Psychology of the Club: A Study in Social Psychology," *Pedagogical Seminary* 18 (1911), 408; Elnora Whitman Curtis, *The Dramatic Instinct in Education* (Boston: Houghton Mifflin, 1914), 102; Norman Egbert Richardson and Ormond Eros Loomis, *The Boy Scout Movement Applied by the Church* (New York: Scribner's, 1916), 291.

33. Boy Scouts of America, *Handbook for Scoutmasters* (New York: BSA, 1913), 51; Winifred Buck, *Boys Self Governing Clubs* (New York: Macmillan, 1912); "Group Organization," *Playground* 11 (1917): 170–171; Boy Scouts of America, *Handbook for Boys* (New York: BSA, 1911), 7; "Boy Scouts of America," *New International Year Book*, ed. Frank Moore Colby (New York: Dodd and Mead, 1921), 96; H. S. Curtis, "Scouts: The Salvation of the Village Boy," *Pedagogical Seminary* 20 (1913).

34. William Byron Forbush and Frank Lincoln Masseck, *The Boys' Round Table* (Potsdam, NY: Frank Lincoln Masseck, 1908), 30–31; William Byron Forbush, "The Social Pedagogy of Boyhood," *Pedagogical Seminary* 7 (1900): 318; William Byron Forbush and Frank Masseck, *Queens of Avalon* (Potsdam, NY: Frank Lincoln Masseck, 1911), https://d.lib.rochester.edu/camelot/publication/forbush-queens-of-avalon; James Franklin Page, *Socializing for the New Order* (Rock Island, IL: James F. Page, 1919), 83; Frank B. Arthur, "Boy Scouts Building for Manhood," *Outing Magazine* 57 (October 1910–March 1911): 276–284; Brian Morris, "Ernest Thompson Seton and the Origins of the Woodcraft Movement," *Journal of Contemporary History* 5, no. 2 (1970): 189–190; Boy Scouts of America, *Scoutmasters Handbook* (New York: BSA, 1913); Ernest Seton, *Book of Woodcraft* (Garden City, NY: Doubleday, Page, 1912); Ernest Seton, *How to Play Indian* (Philadelphia: Curtis, 1903); Philip Joseph Deloria, "Playing Indian: Otherness and Authenticity in the Assumption of American Indian Identity" (PhD diss., Yale University, 1994); "Young Knights of Arthur: An Order of Chivalry for American Boys," *New-York Tribune*, November 21, 1897; Jeanne Fox Friedman, "Howard Pyle and the Chivalric Order in America: King Arthur for Children," *Arthuriana* 6, no. 1 (Spring 1996): 77–95; Mary Bronson Hartt, "A Boy Specialist: William Byron Forbush, A

Wizard with the Youngsters," *New-York Tribune,* July 26, 1908; "Knights of King Arthur," *Detroit Free Press,* May 5, 1907; William Byron Forbush, *The Coming Generation* (New York: Appleton, 1912); William Byron Forbush, *The Boys' Round Table* (Albany: Men of Tomorrow, 1903); Elnora Whitman Curtis, *The Dramatic Instinct in Education* (Boston: Houghton Mifflin, 1914), 101; Barbara and Alan Lupack, *King Arthur in America* (Rochester, NY: Boydell and Brewer, 1999); William Byron Forbush, *Knights of King Arthur: The Merlin's Book of Advanced Work* (Oberlin, Ohio: Knights of King Arthur, 1916); "Knights in Convention: Boy Emulators of King Arthur Meet to Systematize the Work of the Order," *Boston Daily Globe,* October 14, 1910; William Forbush and Frank Masseck, *The Queens of Avilion or Ladies of the Court of King Arthur* (Potsdam, NY: Frank Lincoln Masseck, 1908); William Byron Forbush and Frank Masseck, *Queens of Avalon* (Potsdam, NY: Frank Lincoln Masseck, 1911), https://d.lib.rochester.edu/camelot/publication/forbush-queens-of-avalon; "Young Knights of Arthur: An Order of Chivalry for American Boys," *New-York Tribune,* November 21, 1897; William Byron Forbush and Dascomb Forbush, *The Knights of King Arthur: How to Begin and What to Do* (Oberlin, Ohio: Knights of King Arthur, 1915); David MacLeod, *Building Character in the American Boy* (Madison: University of Wisconsin Press, 2004); Joseph Kett, *Rites of Passage: Adolescence in America, 1790 to the Present* (New York: Basic Books, 1977); William Byron Forbush, *The Merrye Yeoman of King Arthur, A Happy Church Organization for Junior Boys* (Oberlin, Ohio: Knights of King Arthur, 1916). To be clear, adults continued to participate in these role-playing schemes much as they had when Osborne was George Junior Republic supreme court chief justice or Bradley was Allendale's. For example, adults could serve as head chief or chief medicine man or medicine woman in Woodcraft Indians, or as Merlins in the Knights of King Arthur.

35. William Byron Forbush, "The USA," *Congregationalist,* January 28, 1897, 125; William Byron Forbush, *Dramatics in the Home* (Philadelphia: American Institute of Child Life, 1914), 15 [also in his *Manual of Play* (1914), 141–142 in the second chapter, on Plays of Impersonation]; Elnora Whitman Curtis, *The Dramatic Instinct in Education* (Boston: Houghton Mifflin, 1914), 94; Minnie Herts Heniger, *The Kingdom of the Child* (New York: Dutton, 1917), 17–18. William Byron Forbush, "The Travel Lessons on the Life of Jesus," (1905) and "The Travel Lessons on the Old Testament" (1909) were both published by Underwood and Underwood.

36. William Bryon Forbush, *The Boys' Round Table: A Manual of the International Order of the Knights of King Arthur* (Detroit: Knights of King Arthur, 1910), 27; William Byron Forbush and Dascomb Forbush, *The Knights of King Arthur: How to Begin and What to Do* (Oberlin, Ohio: Knights of King Arthur, 1915); William Byron Forbush, *Queens of Avalon,* 4th ed. (Boston: Forbush, 1925); Norman Egbert Richardson and Ormond Eros Loomis, *The Boy Scout Movement Applied by the Church* (New York: Scribner's, 1916).

37. Ernest Seton, *Book of Woodcraft* (Garden City, NY: Doubleday, Page, 1912); Daniel Carter Beard, *The Boy Pioneers: Sons of Daniel Boone* (New York: Scribner's, 1909); William Byron Forbush and Dascomb Forbush, *The Knights of King Arthur: How to Begin and What to Do* (Oberlin, Ohio: Knights of King Arthur, 1915); "Boys from All Over the State Gather in Cambridge Today," *Boston Daily Globe,* February 15, 1913; Boy Scouts of America, *Official Handbook for Boys* (New York: BSA, 1912); William Byron Forbush, *The Coming Generation* (New York: Appleton, 1912), 378; "Civic Associations," *Yonkers Statesman,* May 11, 1921; "Notes on Street Trades Department and Milwaukee Newsboys' Republic, Perry O. Powell, Supervisor of Street Trades, Milwaukee Public Schools,"

Proceedings of the National Conference on Social Work (1921), 297; "Visit of General Baden Powell to the George Junior Republic," 1912, box 14, folder 2, WG Papers; William George and Lyman Beecher Stowe, *Citizens Made and Remade* (Boston: Houghton Mifflin, 1912); Wilson Gill, *A New Citizenship* (Philadelphia: Patriotic League, 1913).

38. William Dealey, "The Theoretical Gary," *Pedagogical Seminary* 23 (June 1916): 278; "Hold Conclave in Taunton," *Boston Daily Globe*, February 23, 1915; "Play at Spring Festival," *Washington Post*, May 4, 1912; "Boys from All Over the State Gather in Cambridge Today," *Boston Daily Globe*, February 15, 1913; "Join Knights of King Arthur," *Washington Post*, December 18, 1914; "Plan for Young Folk," *Washington Post*, March 16, 1912; "Form First-Aid Band," *Washington Post*, March 19, 1912; "Miss Taft a Teacher," *Washington Post*, March 23, 1912; "Camp Fire Girls Will Brave Sylvan Terrors," *Atlanta Constitution*, May 31, 1912; "YMCA Roof Garden Party," *Boston Daily Globe*, June 27, 1915; H. S. Curtis, "Scouts: The Salvation of the Village Boy," *Pedagogical Seminary* 20 (1913); "To Have Juvenile Police," *Municipal Journal and Engineer* 30, no. 12 (1911): 422; T. R. Porter, "A Squad of Boy Police," *St. Nicholas* 35, Part 2 (1908): 1107; "Boy Police," *Native American*, November 14, 1908, 763; "Portland, Ore., to Have Police Force of Boys," *Municipal Journal* 34, no. 21 (1913): 722; "Would Have East Side Boy Police," *New-York Tribune*, October 9, 1908; "Shopkeepers Obey Boy Police Orders," *New York Times*, June 1, 1914; "Inaugurates Boy Police: Portland, Me., Will Equip Band of Youths as Peace Preservers," *Detroit Free Press*, May 11, 1913; "Plan Boy Police for Portland," *San Francisco Chronicle*, May 16, 1913; "Boy Police Force for Portland, OR," *Boston Daily Globe*, May 11, 1913; "Brookline Tries Boy Police," *Boston Daily Globe*, February 20, 1917; "Sanitary Workers Talk Over Plans," *Detroit Free Press*, July 25, 1916; Mrs. George Zimmerman, "Children's Leagues of Good Citizenship," *American City* 7, no. 5 (November 1912): 443–446; "In Only Two Innings," *Boston Daily Globe*, June 25, 1905; "Boston Castle Wins," *Boston Daily Globe*, May 24, 1914; "King Arthur's Knights Meet," *Washington Post*, June 22, 1916; "Wilmington Knights of King Arthur as Thespians," *Boston Daily Globe*, May 23, 1924; "Scouts and Camp Fire Girls Working for Woman's Edition," *Atlanta Constitution*, March 30, 1913; "Amateur Ball Clubs," *Sun*, February 18, 1909; William Seymour, "Junior Deputy Sanitary Inspectors," *American City* 15 (1916): 696; "39th Precinct Is Victor: Gets First Honors in Five of Six Events at Junior Police Games," *New York Times*, September 9, 1917; Clifton Lisle, Ward Macauley, and Raymond Marshall Robinson, *Boy Scout Entertainments* (Philadelphia: Penn, 1918); David P. Setran, "Developing the 'Christian Gentleman': The Medieval Impulse in Protestant Ministry to Adolescent Boys, 1890–1920," *Religion and American Culture: A Journal of Interpretation* 20, no. 2 (2010): 165–204; "Some Jersey 'Braves,'" *New-York Tribune*, February 22, 1903; Sarah Addington, "Woodcraft Girls and the Kingdom of Outdoors," *New-York Tribune*, July 18, 1915; Philip Joseph Deloria, "Playing Indian: Otherness and Authenticity in the Assumption of American Indian Identity" (PhD diss., Yale University, 1994); David MacLeod, *Building Character in the American Boy* (Madison: University of Wisconsin Press, 2004); M. K. Smith, "Ernest Thompson Seton and Woodcraft," *Encyclopedia of Informal Education* (2002), http://www.infed.org/thinkers/seton.htm; "News of the Shipping: Boy Scouts' Sisters Organize Camp Fire Girls of America," *Sun*, April 11, 1911; Susan A. Miller, *Growing Girls: The Natural Origins of Girls' Organizations in America* (New Brunswick, NJ: Rutgers University Press, 2007); "Boy Fire Brigade Formed: Brownsville Lady to Get Co-operation of Adamson," *New-York Tribune*, August 19, 1917; "St. Paul Junior Civic Association," *Christian Science Monitor*, July 21, 1917; Ida Treadwell Thurston, *The Torch*

Bearer: A Camp Fire Girls' Story (New York: Revel, 1913); Sherrie A. Inness, "Girl Scouts, Camp Fire Girls, and Woodcraft Girls: The Ideology of Girls' Scouting Novels, 1910–1935," in *Nancy Drew and Company* (Madison: University of Wisconsin Press, 1997); M. Paul Holsinger, "A Bully Bunch of Books: Boy Scout Series Books in American Youth Fiction, 1910–1930," *Children's Literature Association Quarterly* 14, no. 4 (Winter 1989): 178–182; James Franklin Page, *Socializing for the New Order* (Rock Island, IL: James F. Page, 1919).

39. William Forbush, *The Boys' Round Table: A Manual of the International Order of the Knights of King Arthur* (Detroit: Knights of King Arthur, 1910); Lyman Beecher Stowe, "What to Do with a Boy," *World's Work* 26 (June 1913): 190–195; William Forbush, *Queens of Avalon*, 4th ed. (Boston: Forbush, 1925); William Forbush and Frank Masseck, *The Queens of Avilion or Ladies of the Court of King Arthur* (Potsdam, NY: Frank Lincoln Masseck, 1908); William Forbush, *Queens of Avilion* (Detroit: Knights of King Arthur, 1911); "Young Knights of Arthur: An Order of Chivalry for American Boys," *New-York Tribune*, November 21, 1897; Jeanne Fox Friedman, "Howard Pyle and the Chivalric Order in America: King Arthur for Children," *Arthuriana* 6, no. 1 (Spring 1996): 77–95; William Byron Forbush and Dascomb Forbush, *The Knights of King Arthur: How to Begin and What to Do* (Oberlin, Ohio: Knights of King Arthur, 1915); David MacLeod, *Building Character in the American Boy* (Madison: University of Wisconsin Press, 2004).

40. Sonja Dümpelmann, *Seeing Trees* (New Haven, CT: Yale University Press, 2019); *The Junior Citizen: An Account of the Activities of the Junior Civic and Industrial League, Lincoln, Nebraska, 1917–18* (Lincoln: Junior Civic and Industrial League, 1918); Jesse Hinton Binford and Ellis Urban Graff, *The Young American Citizen: Civics for Grammar Grades* (Richmond, VA: Johnson, 1922); "Civics and Social Settlements," *Chautauquan* 47 (1906): 88; *Welfare Work for Policy-Holders* (New York: Metropolitan Life Insurance, 1915), 15; Henry Hyde, "Young and Old Use Gary school," *Bulletin, the National Association of Corporation Schools* (1916), 36–38; Joseph Lee, *Play in Education* (New York: Macmillan, 1915); Alvord Baker to William George, October 19, 1914, includes reports of farm conditions made by fifth and sixth graders, box 16, folder 19, WG Papers; Farm census taken by pupils with hand-drawn maps and charts, box 16, folder 27, WG Papers; J. D. Bigelow to Mrs. Leo (Vera) Rockwell, May 30, 1935, box 35, folder 32, WG Papers; "School Children as Census Takers," *Ithaca Daily News*, February 3, 1916; William George, "School Children as Census Takers," box 16, folder 28, WG Papers; William George to Thomas Osborne, February 24, 1915, box 17, folder 2, WG Papers; Census data, box 17, folders 10, 17–11, 17–12, WG Papers; Hand-drawn maps, box 17, folder 25, WG Papers; "School Children as Census Takers," *Outlook*, August 11, 1915; "West End Children Believe in the Beautiful," *Atlanta Constitution*, March 9, 1913; "Throng Rides in Parade of Junior Civic League," *Detroit Free Press*, May 3, 1914; Ella White, "State President Commends Leagues," *Atlanta Constitution*, April 14, 1912; "Junior Civic Leagues," *Atlanta Constitution*, June 4, 1913; "Junior Civic Club of Peeples Street School," *Atlanta Constitution*, June 4, 1913; "Report of Civic War Clubs of City Organized through Efforts of City Federation," *Atlanta Constitution*, June 4, 1913; Mary Pressly, "Peeples Street School," *Atlanta Constitution*, December 7, 1913; "A Junior Civic League Formed," *Atlanta Constitution*, June 11, 1911; "Stirring Creed of New Junior Civic Leagues," *Atlanta Constitution*, June 25, 1911; Ben Lindsey, *Report of the Juvenile Court of Denver*, 1904; Ben Lindsey, *The Problem of the Children and How the State of Colorado Cares for Them* (Denver: Juvenile Court of the City and County of Denver, 1904),

108; Henry Haskell, "The 'Kid Judge' of Denver," *Outlook,* June 24, 1905; *Welfare Work for Policy-Holders* (New York: Metropolitan Life Insurance, 1915), 15.

41. Robert Bingham, "Report of the Director of Progress City–Hiram House, Season 1913 June 23-August 8"; Robert Bingham, "Progress City Report, 1914"; "Progress City: An Answer to the Demand for a Civic Education," container 36, folder 3, Progress City ca. 1906–1920, HH Records MS 3319; *A Historical Report of the Sixteen Years' Work at Hiram House* (Cleveland: Hiram House, 1912); Cleveland Federation for Charity and Philanthropy, *The Social Year Book* (1913); *Progress City News,* August 1, 1912, container 54, Hiram House Publications, newsletters and promotional pamphlets, folder 2, HH Records MS 3319 container 36; Graham T. Taylor, "Civic Activities of Social Settlements," *Chautauquan* 47, no. 1 (1907): 86; "One City Actually 'Fly-Less' Last Summer: St. Louis Can Do What Cleveland Did," *St. Louis Post-Dispatch*, February 15, 1914; Ethel Rogers, "Playing at Citizenship," *American City* 9 (1913): 445–448; Jean Dawson, "Civic or Social Biology," *School Science and Mathematics* 16 (1916): 691. Hiram House had sponsored a Boys Brigade from 1904, a Knights of King Arthur Castle from 1906, a Scout troop in 1911 (that appears to have replaced the Boys Brigade), and a Camp Fire Girls unit shortly afterward (around 1913).

42. "A Boyville Court Handling Cleveland's Juvenile Crooks: Special Youthful Officers and Judges Work under Jurisdiction of Social Center and Regular Courts," *Colorado Springs Gazette*, September 27, 1914; Robert Bingham, "Progress City Report, 1914," container 36, folder 3, Progress City ca. 1906–1920, HH Records MS 3319; Ellwood Street, "Going the Juvenile Court One Better," *Survey* 33 (October 24, 1914): 83; George Bellamy, "The Culture of the Family from the Standpoint of Recreation," *Proceedings of the National Conference of Charities and Corrections* (Memphis, 1914), 103–107.

43. William Byron Forbush and Frank Masseck, *The Boys' Round Table* (Detroit: Knights of King Arthur, 1910), 22; Frank B. Arthur, "Boy Scouts Building for Manhood," *Outing Magazine* 57 (October 1910–March 1911): 281; "The Thompson's Island School," *Oregonian*, August 6, 1915; Charles Zueblin, "The Civic Renascence," *Chautauquan* 38, no. 2 (October 1903): 373–384; "Men and Movements That Are Making for Progress," *Arena* 35, no. 198 (May 1906): 512; "Survey of Civic Betterment," *Chautauquan* 38, no. 2 (October 1903): 178; Brian Morris, "Ernest Thompson Seton and the Origins of the Woodcraft Movement," *Journal of Contemporary History* 5; no. 2 (1970): 189–190; Boy Scouts of America, *Scoutmasters Handbook* (New York: BSA, 1913); Ernest Seton, *Book of Woodcraft* (Garden City, NY: Doubleday, Page, 1912); Philip Joseph Deloria, "Playing Indian: Otherness and Authenticity in the Assumption of American Indian Identity" (PhD diss., Yale University, 1994); Stephen Schlossman, "G. Stanley Hall and the Boys' Club: Conservative Applications of Recapitulation Theory," *Journal of the History of the Behavioral Sciences* 9, no. 2 (1973): 140–147; Frederick Bolton, *Principles of Education* (New York: Charles Scribner's Sons, 1910); Percy Davidson, *The Recapitulation Theory and Human Infancy* (New York: Columbia Teachers College, 1914), 69; Charles Ellwood, *Sociology in Its Psychological Aspects* (New York: Appleton, 1912); Mrs. Howard S Braucher, "Problems of Dramatic Play," *Playground* 6 (1912): 319–324; William Byron Forbush, *The Dramatic Instinct in Children* (Philadelphia: American Institute of Child Life, 1914).

44. "Life in Boytown," *Indianapolis Star*, January 7, 1912.

45. Jane Lincoln Hoxie, *Hand Work for Kindergartens and Primary Schools* (Springfield, MA: Milton Bradley, 1903); S. J. Vaughn, "Some Fundamentals in Manual Training," *Industrial Arts and Vocational*

Education 1/2 (1914): 13–15; "Now for the Campfire Girls," *Detroit Free Press*, March 24, 1912; Susan A. Miller, *Growing Girls: The Natural Origins of Girls' Organizations in America* (New Brunswick, NJ: Rutgers University Press, 2007); Arthur Woods, "Crime Prevention: A Lecture on the Spencer Trask Foundation," delivered at Princeton University (Princeton University Press, 1918), 108–109; "Boy Police Display Mature Favoritism," *New York Times*, September 13, 1915; "Would Have East Side Boy Police," *New-York Tribune*, October 9, 1908; William Forbush, *Child Study and Child Training* (New York: Charles Scribner's Sons, 1915); "Boy Police," *Americana Supplement: A Comprehensive Record of the Latest Knowledge and Progress of the World* 1 (1911): 189; William Seymour, "Junior Deputy Sanitary Inspectors," *American City* 15 (1916): 696; William Langdon, "The Juvenile City League of New York," *The Aims of Religious Education, Proceedings of the Third Annual Convention of the Religious Education Association, Boston* 3 (1905): 442; James Albert Woodburn and Thomas Francis Moran, *The Citizen and the Republic* (New York: Longmans, Green, 1921), 29.

46. O. H. Benson and George Fitch, "Educational Forum," *Journal of Education* 96, no. 24 (December 28, 1922): 665–666; "Boy Scouts to Form Junior Police Force," *Detroit Free Press*, January 26, 1918; "Junior Police Force of Ann Arbor," *Detroit Free Press*, March 12, 1922; Charles-Edward Amory Winslow, *Healthy Living* (New York: Merrill, 1917), 326; "Newsboys Offer Aid to Health Department," *Milwaukee Journal*, April 6, 1915; "Clean-up Day in Charge of Junior Municipality," *Syracuse Post-Standard*, May 1, 1914; "Clean City Saturday; Members of Junior Municipality Take Charge at Cortland," *Syracuse Post-Standard*, April 21, 1914; "Word from George: He Can't Come to Auburn at the Present Time. But Hopes to Come Later. Strain Through Which He Has Passed Makes It Necessary for Him to Give Up Work," *Auburn Citizen*, March 24, 1914; "That Junior Municipality, No Move Made as Yet Here and No Word Received from Daddy George," *Auburn Citizen*, March 6, 1914; "WR George Requested to Defer Auburn Visit," *Syracuse Post-Standard*, July 23, 1914; G. Stanley Hall, "Social Phases of Psychology," *Proceedings of the American Sociological Society* 7 (1912): 38–46; "Davis Street School Children Have Done Wonderful Work through Civic League," *Atlanta Constitution*, December 1, 1912; Agnes Pound, "Junior Civic Leagues and Playgrounds," *Atlanta Constitution*, September 10, 1911; G. Stanley Hall, "Some Social Aspects of Education," *Pedagogical Seminary* 9 (1902): 84; "Boy Bandits Made to Order," *St. Louis Post-Dispatch*, June 14, 1903. Superintendent Wirt was an affiliate of the local Scouting organization, so prior to Brown's departure Boyville hosted a Scout troop over his objections.

47. *Life of the Boys Brotherhood Republic* (Chicago: BBR, 1938); "Boys' Republic to Honor Its Original 16 Members," *Chicago Daily Tribune*, January 27, 1935; "Do Chicago Boys Want a Boys' Republic Club?" *Chicago Defender*, October 15, 1921; Jack Robbins to William George, April 4, 1918, box 21, folder 6, WG Papers; *Life of the Boys Brotherhood Republic* (Chicago: BBR, 1938); William Welling, *East Side Story: The Boys Brotherhood Republic's First Fifty Years on New York's Lower East Side* (New York: BBR, 1982).

48. *Life of the Boys Brotherhood Republic* (Chicago: BBR, 1938); William Welling, *East Side Story: The Boys Brotherhood Republic's First Fifty Years on New York's Lower East Side* (New York: BBR, 1982); "C.H.I. Boys Win Junior Title in Wrestling Meet," *Chicago Daily Tribune*, March 20, 1919; James Franklin Page, *Socializing for a New World Order* (Clarksville, Missouri: J. F. Page, 1919); "Do Chicago Boys Want a Boys' Republic Club?" *Chicago Defender*, October 15, 1921; "Boys' Republic

Seeks $50,000 for New Home: Start Drive as Part of Week's Activities," *Chicago Daily Tribune*, May 20, 1925; "Boys Republic Chief Gives Up Wife for 'Pals,'" *Chicago Daily Tribune*, October 28, 1920.

49. *Life of the Boys Brotherhood Republic* (Chicago: BBR, 1938); William Welling, *East Side Story: The Boys Brotherhood Republic's First Fifty Years on New York's Lower East Side* (New York: BBR, 1982); Webb Waldron, "B. B. R.—Of, By, and For Boys," *Rotarian* (April 1936), 21; "Telling it to them! Boyville ruler outlines his ideas of reforming wayward youth to his police 'aids' in Maxwell Street district. Boyville to try 'pal' system. 'Brotherhood Republic' to take charge of erring youth in its district," *Chicago Daily Tribune*, December 20, 1915; Mrs. Jule F. Brower, "News of the Chicago Women's Clubs," *Chicago Daily Tribune*, December 29, 1918.

50. *Life of the Boys Brotherhood Republic* (Chicago: BBR, 1938); James Page, *Socializing for the New World Order* (Clarksville, Missouri: J. F. Page, 1919), 91–92; William Welling, *East Side Story: The Boys Brotherhood Republic's First Fifty Years on New York's Lower East Side* (New York: BBR, 1982).

51. James Page, *Socializing for the New World Order* (Clarksville, Missouri: J. F. Page, 1919), 90–92; "500 Boys Given Jobs, 57 Positions Unfilled," *Chicago Daily Tribune*, April 11, 1916; "Boys Blank File at Saddle Club," *Chicago Daily Tribune*, August 6, 1917; "Pennies Pledged by Boys Here to Aid 'Kids' Judge,'" *Chicago Daily Tribune*, August 30 1919; *Life of the Boys Brotherhood Republic* (Chicago: BBR, 1938); "Little 'Big' Stories: Boys 'Mayor' Protests to Olson on Fingerprints," *Chicago Daily Tribune*, October 22, 1915; "Scheme to Oust Juvenile Court Judge Exposed," *Chicago Daily Tribune*, October 1, 1919; "Boys Advise Chapman to Demand Liberty or Death," *New-York Tribune*, December 18, 1918; "Mass Meetings to Be Held in Chicago to Aid Paul Chapman," *New-York Tribune*, November 27, 1918; "Mayor to Proclaim April 10 'Job Finding Day,'" *Chicago Daily Tribune*, March 14, 1917; "Boys' Republic Would Convict Club Gardener," *Chicago Daily Tribune*, July 26, 1916; "Boy's Death May Open Club's Beach to Public," *Chicago Daily Tribune*, July 29, 1916; "Seek to Save Slayer," *New-York Tribune*, May 22, 1918; "Telling it to them! Boyville ruler outlines his ideas of reforming wayward youth to his police 'aids' in Maxwell Street district. Boyville to try 'pal' system. 'Brotherhood Republic' to take charge of erring youth in its district," *Chicago Daily Tribune*, December 20, 1915; "Boys Start Drive to Pay Fine of Lindsey Denver Juvenile Court Judge," *Twin Falls News*, August 30, 1919; "The Boy Problem," *Kalamazoo Gazette*, May 20, 1918; "Brotherhood Helps Bat Nelson," *Times-Picayune*, October 20, 1918; "Judge Lindsey's Story Written by Himself 'I Wouldn't Betray the Confidence of a Boy!'" *Trenton Evening Times*, October 20, 1918; "Boys' Republic 'Indicts' City for Negligence," *Chicago Daily Tribune*, January 21, 1917; "Scheme to Oust Juvenile Court Judge Exposed," *Chicago Daily Tribune*, October 1, 1919; "Acquired Traits Not Hereditary, Boy Expert Says," *Chicago Daily Tribune*, April 27, 1919; Frederic Thrasher, *The Gang* (Chicago: University of Chicago Press, 1927); "City's Lawyer Hears Boys Ask Right to Beach: Brotherhood Republic Wants Saddle and Cycle Club's Land Condemned," *Chicago Daily Tribune*, August 2, 1916; "'Boy Job' Day Would Produce Steady Citizens: Members of Brotherhood Republic Propose Solution of Their Problem," *Chicago Daily Tribune*, March 19, 1916; "Strike of School Boys Planned to Aid Doomed Boy," *Chicago Daily Tribune*, November 24, 1918; "Boy Demands Saddle & Cycle Open Grounds: Brotherhood Republic's 'City Clerk' Asks Winston to Throw Open Gates," *Chicago Daily Tribune*, August 1, 1916.

52. "Citizens' Seek Meeting Place; Junior Municipality, Ithaca, Handicapped by Lack of Funds; Large Quarters Wanted," *Syracuse Post-Standard*, December 31, 1913; "Boy Police on Peace Jaunt,"

Los Angeles Times, December 2, 1916; Christopher Capozolla, *Uncle Sam Wants You* (New York: Oxford University Press, 2008).

53. Frances Margaret Keefe, "The Development of William Reuben (Daddy) George's Educational Ideas and Practices from 1866 to 1914" (PhD diss., Cornell University, 1967), 214; Jacob Riis cited in William George, *Nothing without Labor* (Freeville, NY: George Junior Republic, 1902), 29; Minna Norniss, "The History of the California Junior Republic" (master's thesis, University of Southern California, 1931), 124. This greater conservatism is consistent with the broader history of educational reform. See Larry Cuban, "Why Some Reforms Last: The Case of the Kindergarten," *American Journal of Education* 100, no. 2 (February 1992): 166–194; Larry Cuban, "What Happens to Reforms that Last? The Case of the Junior High School," *American Educational Research Journal* (1992): 227–251.

54. William George, "Practical Working of the Social Sanitarium," late 1919 to 1920 according to Mrs. George's notes, box 21, folder 25, WG Papers; William George, "Prison Walls without a Prison," *Survey* (November 3, 1917); *Report of the New York State Department of Probation* 11 (1918): 343; "George Republic Plan to Help Criminals Reform," *New York Times*, July 7, 1912, SM9; William George, "Social Sanitariums and social doctors," *Outlook*, January 5, 1921, 18; William George, "Social Sanitariums and Social Doctors," *Outlook*, January 5, 1921, 18–21; William George, "Jail Inside Yourself," *Survey* 49 (October 15, 1922): 82–84.

55. William Graebner, *The Engineering of Consent: Democracy and Authority in Twentieth-Century America* (Madison: University of Wisconsin Press, 1987); Rebecca McLennan, *The Crisis of Imprisonment: Protest, Politics, and the Making of the American Penal State, 1776–1941* (New York: Cambridge University Press, 2008); Winthrop D. Lane, "Judge Frederick Bloman," *Times-Picayune*, October 22, 1911, 38; "Scores Government of the United States: Milwaukee's Socialist Mayor in Address to Boys' Republic Says Model Is Poor," *San Francisco Chronicle*, October 22, 1910.

56. Lyman Beecher Stowe, "Junior Citizens in Action," *Outlook*, November 18, 1914, 656; "Junior Police in New York City," *National Municipal Review* (July 1915): 481; "Junior Police," *The American Year Book* (New York: Appleton, 1915), 238; "Ex-Hawkers Hold a Reunion," *Milwaukee Journal*, October 21, 1983. The popularity of programs led to waitlists well beyond the George Junior Republic, as kids were turned away from participating in junior police forces in Council Bluffs, Iowa, and Portland, Oregon. Facing such circumstances, some youth organized similar programs in the hopes of joining adult-supervised forces. See "Council Bluffs Kid Police Force," *Westminster* 33 (August 2, 1908): 9; "Captain John F. Sweeney, 'Commissioner' of the Kid Cops," *The American Year Book* (New York: Appleton, 1915), 6; "Junior Policemen Win Wood's O.K.," *New-York Tribune*, June 5, 1915; "Plan Boy Police for Portland: Chief Slover Is Swamped by Youngsters of the City Who Would Become Officers," *San Francisco Chronicle*, May 16, 1913; "Boy Police Force for Portland, OR," *Boston Daily Globe*, May 11, 1913.

57. E. D. Hulbert to William George, August 3, 1921, box 23, folder 2, WG Papers; William George to E. D. Hulbert, July 26, 1921, box 23, folder 2, WG Papers; E. D. Hubert to Spencer Miller Jr., box 22, folder 30, WG Papers. On efforts to duplicate the BBR, see William Welling, *East Side Story: The Boys Brotherhood Republic's First Fifty Years on New York's Lower East Side* (New York: BBR, 1982); *Life of the Boys Brotherhood Republic* (Chicago: BBR, 1938); William J. Robinson, "BBR Republic Run by Boys Themselves," *Boston Daily Globe*, May 9, 1920; "Boys 'Republic'

Planned: Self-Governing Body to Be Formed Here by American War Mothers," *Indianapolis Star*, May 10, 1920; "Members of 'Boys Republic,'" *Schenectady Gazette*, May 22, 1920; "Youthful Orleanians Form Boys' Brotherhood Republic Organization Is Self-Governing and Will Help Youth of City," *Times-Picayune*, December 5, 1920; "Members of 'Boys Republic,'" *Schenectady Gazette*, May 22, 1920. Although adult and youth observers occasionally looked askance at BBR's unorthodox approach, most assessments of the Chicago republic were positive in tone even if communities did not duplicate the organization. One exception was in Milwaukee where the worst boy campaign stirred up a negative response from newsboys. "Seek Worst Boy in US to Make Him 100% Good," *Chicago Daily Tribune*, January 4, 1918; "Nuf Said," *Newsboys' World*, May/June 1918, 10. The closest that republic came to replicating itself in the short term was the creation of the more staid American Boys' Commonwealth by a former BBR citizen, Chicago's Harry Branovitz, in 1919. See "Scheme to Oust Juvenile Court Judge Exposed," *Chicago Daily Tribune*, October 1, 1919, which mentions his name and occupation; "Chicago Boys Rule Selves in Mimic States" *Chicago Daily Tribune*, November 21, 1920. At the time of its founding Branovitz was a probation officer for Chicago's juvenile court. Some earlier examples of youth activism are detailed in Jennifer Light, "Putting Our Conversation in Context," in *From Voice to Influence*, ed. D. Allen and J. Light (Chicago: University of Chicago Press, 2015); "Protest of Young America: Boys Petition the Legislature Against Passage of a Curfew," *Chicago Daily Tribune*, March 20, 1896; William Walling, "A Children's Strike on the East Side," *Charities* 13 (1904–1905): 305; "For the East Side's Health: A Committee of Boys Urges that More Care Should Be Taken in the Regulation of Pushcart Trade," *New York Times*, September 7, 1895; "Junior Municipality to Be City-Wide Among Boys of Indianapolis Schools," *Indianapolis Star*, October 12, 1912; Anthony Platt, *The Child Savers* (Chicago: University of Chicago Press, 1977), 100.

58. Mina Carson, *Settlement Folk* (Chicago: University of Chicago Press, 1990); Anthony Platt, *The Child Savers* (Chicago: University of Chicago Press, 1977); Steven L. Schlossman, *Love and the American. Delinquent: The Theory and Practice of "Progressive" Juvenile Justice, 1825–1920* (Chicago: University of Chicago Press, 1977); David MacLeod, *Building Character in the American Boy* (Madison: University of Wisconsin Press, 2004); Susan A. Miller, *Growing Girls: The Natural Origins of Girls' Organizations in America* (New Brunswick, NJ: Rutgers University Press, 2007); Harvey Kantor, "Work, Education, and Vocational Reform: The Ideological Origins of Vocational Education, 1890–1920," *American Journal of Education* 94, no. 4 (1986): 401–426; Herbert Kliebard, *Schooled to Work: Vocationalism and the American Curriculum, 1876–1946* (New York: Teachers College Press, 1999); David Nasaw, *Schooled to Order: A Social History of Public Schooling in the United States* (New York: Oxford University Press, 1981); William Graebner, *The Engineering of Consent: Democracy and Authority in Twentieth-Century America* (Madison: University of Wisconsin Press, 1987); Lisa Jacobsen, *Raising Consumers* (New York: Columbia University Press, 2005); Ellen Ryerson, *The Best Laid Plans* (New York: Farrar, Straus & Giroux, 1978); Marvin Lazerson and W. Norton Grubb, eds., *American Education and Vocationalism: A Documentary History 1870–1970* (New York: Teachers College Press, 1974); Raymond Wolters, *The New Negro on Campus* (Princeton, NJ: Princeton University Press, 1975).

59. William Byron Forbush and Frank Masseck, *Queens of Avalon* (Potsdam, NY: Frank Lincoln Masseck, 1911), https://d.lib.rochester.edu/camelot/publication/forbush-queens-of-avalon; "Now

for the Campfire Girls," *Detroit Free Press*, March 24, 1912; Edward Marshall, "Girls Take Up the Boy Scout Idea and Band Together," *New York Times,* March 17, 1912; Susan A. Miller, *Growing Girls: The Natural Origins of Girls' Organizations in America* (New Brunswick, NJ: Rutgers University Press, 2007); Laurie Finke and Susan Aronstein, "The Queens of Avalon: William Byron Forbush's Arthurian Antidote," *Arthuriana* 22 (2012): 21–40; William Byron Forbush, *Queens of Avalon*, 4th ed. (Boston: Forbush, 1925); Miriam Formanek-Brunell, *Made to Play House: Dolls and the Commercialization of American Girlhood, 1830–1930* (New Haven, CT: Yale University Press, 1993); Laura Starr, "The Educational Value of Dolls," *Pedagogical Seminary* 16 (1909): 566–567; "Form First-Aid Band," *Washington Post*, March 19, 1912; "Camp Fire Girls Organized," *Washington Post*, March 16, 1912; Philip Joseph Deloria, "Playing Indian: Otherness and Authenticity in the Assumption of American Indian Identity" (PhD diss., Yale University, 1994) cites "A Happy Thought and Its Development," *Human Factor* 1 (September 1913): 5; Lena Beard and Adelia Beard, *Girl Pioneers of America, Official Manual* (New York: Pioneers, 1914); "Camp Fire Girls Learn How to Form Their Own Characters," *Boston Daily Globe*, October 22, 1912; "Gulick Chosen Chief of 36,000 Camp Fire Girls," *New-York Tribune*, January 23, 1913; "Wants More Nurses," *Washington Post*, January 19, 1913; "What Campfire Girls Are Doing," *Atlanta Constitution*, June 9, 1912; "Problems Women Face In and Out of Home," *Atlanta Constitution*, April 15, 1911; "Camp Fire Girls Rival Boy Scouts," *Atlanta Constitution*, May 12, 1912; "Now for the Campfire Girls," *Detroit Free Press*, March 24, 1912; Charles Eastman, *Indian Scout Talks: A Guide for Boy Scouts and Camp Fire Girls* (Boston: Little Brown, 1914); "Aim of the Girl Pioneers," *New-York Tribune*, June 11, 1911; "Prizes for Campfire Girls," *Washington Post*, May 22, 1915; "Work in Thomasville for the Needy Ones," *Atlanta Constitution*, December 26, 1914; "Girls Send Free Ice Money," *Chicago Daily Tribune*, June 3, 1914; "Untrammeled Wilds Reclaimed for Girls," *New-York Tribune*, June 21, 1914; "Shut-ins Visited," *Boston Daily Globe,* December 25, 1913; "Need More Missions," *Washington Post*, October 8, 1913; "Camp Fire Girls' First Lesson in the Secrets of Woodcraft," *Washington Post*, July 26, 1912; "Seek Aid of Children: Hygiene Experts Look to Obey Scouts and Campfire Girls," *Washington Post*, September 15, 1912.

60. National Civic Federation, *Conference on Welfare Work, Held at the Waldorf Astoria*, March 16, 1904 (New York: Press of Andrew D. Kellogg, 1904); Robert Bruere, "Industrial Democracy: A Newsboy Labor Union and What It Thinks of a College Education," *Outlook* 81 (1906): 879–883; James Hardin, "The History of the Little Merchant System," *International Circulation Managers Association*, cited in David Nasaw, *Children of the City: At Work and at Play* (Oxford: Oxford University Press, 1986); Susan Campbell Bartoletti, *Kids on Strike* (Boston: Houghton Mifflin, 1999); "Notes on Street Trades Department and Milwaukee Newsboys' Republic, Perry O. Powell, Supervisor of Street Trades, Milwaukee Public Schools," *Proceedings of the National Conference on Social Work* (1921); "The Milwaukee Republic, by One of Its Founders," *Work with Boys* (1914): 21; "Getting Hold of Milwaukee's Newsboys," *Playground* 10 (November 1914): 296–299.

61. Arthur Woods to L. B. Stowe, May 27, 1914, box 16, folder 4, WG Papers; James West to L. B. Stowe, box 12–18, WG Papers; "Visit of General Baden Powell to the George Junior Republic," 1912, box 14, folder 2, WG Papers; Wicks Warnholdt to William George, December 2, 1914, box 16, folder 21, WG Papers; O. M. Phelps to William George, April 6, 1918, box 21, folder 6, WG Papers. Letterhead (box 16, folder 8) indicates that in 1912 Arthur Woods was a trustee of the George Junior Republic Association.

62. G. Stanley Hall, *Educational Problems* (New York: D. Appleton, 1911), 303; William Byron Forbush, *Dramatics in the Home* (Philadelphia: American Institute of Child Life, 1914), 26–27, 29; Mary Bronson Hartt, "A Boy Specialist: William Byron Forbush, A Wizard with the Youngsters," *New-York Tribune*, July 26, 1908; Elnora Whitman Curtis, *The Dramatic Instinct in Education* (Boston: Houghton Mifflin, 1914), 94; Minnie Herts Heniger, *The Kingdom of the Child* (New York: Dutton, 1917), 17–18.

63. Ben Lindsey, *Report of the Juvenile Court of Denver*, 1904; Ben Lindsay, *The Problem of the Children and How the State of Colorado Cares for Them* (Denver: Juvenile Court of the City and County of Denver, 1904).

64. "The Milwaukee Republic, by One of Its Founders," *Work with Boys* (1914): 22; "Pop Tells of Results Accomplished by Newsboys' Republic and the Future Needs. Update on the Newsies Republic and How It Affects the City of Milwaukee," *Newsboys' World* (June 1923); "Milwaukee's Newsboys Republic," *Outlook*, April 5, 1913, 743; "Newsboys' Republic, Reducing Delinquency, Saves City Big Sum," *Milwaukee Journal*, July 14, 1916; "Getting Hold of Milwaukee's Newsboys. Report on Effectiveness of Street Trades Law and of Newsboys' Republic in Milwaukee. P. O. Powell, Supervisor of Street Trades, Milwaukee, Wisconsin," *Playground* 10 (November 1914): 296–299; "Newsboys; Republic Saved 250 of 300 Cases Handled from Juvenile Court," *Milwaukee Journal*, March 8, 1914. Indeed, more common were observations that it was rare for youth to appeal to adults for further adjudication. At the Brooklyn YMCA's City of Tuxis, where children unhappy with peer justice could appeal to association staff, there had been only three appeals in four years. See Harvey L. Smith, "The TUXIS System of Character Building," in *Reaching the Boys of an Entire Community* (New York: YMCA Press, 1909), 130.

65. "Captain John F. Sweeney, 'Commissioner' of the Kid Cops," *Survey* (March 13, 1915): 653; "Junior Police Force Disbanded by Enright," *New-York Tribune*, July 10, 1918; "The Sturdy Boy Police Force of Echo Park," *New-York Tribune,* February 28, 1915; "Boy Police," *Americana Supplement: A Comprehensive Record of the Latest Knowledge and Progress of the World* 1 (1911): 189; Ben Lindsey, *Report of the Juvenile Court of Denver*, 1904; Ben Lindsey, *The Problem of the Children and How the State of Colorado Cares for Them* (Denver: Juvenile Court of the City and County of Denver, 1904), 108; "Boy Police Installed in Park: 'Headquarters' Opened by Commissioner Stover, and Now Youthful Patrolmen Are Equipped to Help Regulars in Making Populace Behave," *New-York Tribune*, August 21, 1913; Gregory Mason, "The Boy Police of New York," *Outlook*, July 28, 1915, 706–708; "Junior Police Aid Marjorie's Fund," *New-York Tribune*, March 30, 1916; "Wirt and Woods to Discuss Problems: Educator and Police Head to Attend Nat Charities Conference," *New-York Tribune*, March 6, 1916; "Boy of 11 Years a 'Policeman,'" *Boston Daily Globe*, July 21, 1923; "Boy Police Make an Orderly Fourth," *New York Times*, July 1, 1907; "Junior Police See to Closing Orders," *Christian Science Monitor*, January 18, 1918; "Boy Police in Collinsville: Twelve Lads Appointed to Help Adult Patrolmen," *St. Louis Post-Dispatch*, September 22, 1916; "Council Bluffs Kid Police Force," *Westminster* 33 (August 2, 1908): 9; "Shopkeeper Obey Boy Police Orders," *New York Times*, June 1, 1914; "Boy Police Stop Noise," *New York Times*, June 30, 1907; "Council Bluffs Boy Police," *Christian Science Monitor*, January 7, 1911; "Young Sleuths to Scour East Side," *New-York Tribune*, March 30, 1914; "Social Service in the NY Police Department: The Junior Police of the City of New York," *The Delinquent* 6, no. 3 (March 1916): 6–7; "The 'Boy

Cops,'" *Work with Boys* 16 (1916): 41; "Boy Cops Will March in Parade with Police," *New-York Tribune*, March 8, 1915; "Boy Police Display Mature Favoritism," *New York Times*, September 13, 1915; "New York's Junior Police Force," *Work with Boys* 16 (1916): 232. The New York Edison Company invited the kids to protect its property in and around Echo Park but were stymied by a lack of adequate uniforms and badges (for which each boy forked over a dime). "We could get a dozen more boys if we only had badges," company officials explained.

66. "Junior League Has Helped Make a Clean City," *Christian Science Monitor*, August 23, 1915; Martin Melosi, *Garbage in the Cities* (College Station: Texas A&M Press, 1981), 106n62; Hubert Robertson, "The Moral Value of Junior Sanitation Leagues," *Public School Journal* 37 (1918): 39; Williard Price, "'Head 'Em Off' Campaign in Spring Better than 'Swat the Fly' in Summer," *Atlanta Constitution*, August 24, 1913; "One City Actually 'Fly-Less' Last Summer: St. Louis Can Do What Cleveland Did," *St. Louis Post-Dispatch*, February 15, 1914; "Junior Sanitary Force to Continue Efforts," *Detroit Free Press*, October 12, 1916; William Seymour, "Junior Deputy Sanitary Inspectors," *American City* 15, no. 5 (1916): 696; "Student Leagues to Be: Women's Federation to Junior Civic Work in Schools," *Detroit Free Press*, October 12, 1916; "Member of Civic League Is Guilty," *St. Louis Post-Dispatch*, May 16, 1907; Sanford Bell, "Hill Street School," *Atlanta Constitution*, April 27, 1913; Clara Wyatt, "Letters from the Schools," *Atlanta Constitution*, April 6, 1913; "Davis Street School Children Have Done Wonderful Work through Civic League," *Atlanta Constitution*, December 1, 1912; "Women Teaching Citizenship," *Indianapolis Star*, October 27, 1913; "What Women's Clubs Are Doing in State of Kansas," *Christian Science Monitor*, November 13, 1914; J. O. Engleman, "The Junior Sanitation League and Its Work in Decatur," *School and Home Education* 36, no. 5 (January 1917): 132–134; "Women's Clubs: Omitting Feasts in Order to Help the Needy—Junior Sanitary Inspectors," *Sun*, November 30, 1914; "'Swat the Fly,' Slogan of Youths," *Detroit Free Press*, June 20, 1916; "Second and Third Ward Junior Civic Leagues," *Atlanta Constitution*, May 20, 1917; Effie Power et al., *A List of Books and Articles on Child Welfare, and A Reading List for Use with the Junior Civic League* (St. Louis: Public Library, 1912); Virginia Public Schools, *Junior Civic League Booklet* (Richmond: Junior Civic League, 1913; "Junior Civic Leagues Organized at Rome," *Atlanta Constitution*, February 22, 1914; Lyman Amsden, "Report of State of Junior Civic Leagues," *Atlanta Constitution*, December 12, 1915; "Best Time to Form Junior Civic Leagues," *Atlanta Constitution*, September 14, 1913; Wm. B. Margaret Young, "Will Organize Junior Civic Leagues in Florida," *Atlanta Constitution*, December 26, 1915; "Stirring Creed of New Junior Civic Leagues," *Atlanta Constitution*, June 25, 1911; "Women in the News of the Day: Children to Help in Bettering City," *Detroit Free Press*, November 14, 1912; "South End Girls Form a Junior Civic League," *Christian Science Monitor*, January 27, 1912; "Christamore Boy Police Department Also on Duty," *Indianapolis Star*, May 7, 1919; "Coffin Reviews Junior Police," *Indianapolis Star*, July 5, 1918; "Junior Civic Organization Is Proposed by Park Head," *Indianapolis Star*, February 21, 1917; "Boy Police Force Organized by Advancement Association," *San Francisco Chronicle*, November 17, 1905; "Junior Citizens Club, Altoona, Pa.," *American City* (August 1917): 171; "Children's Club Active: Newspaper Teaches Gardening and Landscape Improvement," *American Printer* (December 20, 1916): 56.

67. William and Dacsomb Forbush, *Knights of King Arthur: How to Begin and What to Do* (Oberlin, Ohio: Knights of King Arthur, 1915); "Young Knights of Arthur: An Order of Chivalry for American

Boys," *New-York Tribune*, November 21, 1897; George Gladden, "Boy Scouts as Naturalists," *Review of Reviews* 59 (1919): 627; William Ashley, "Harnessing Boy Power," *Scientific American* (February 1919); "'A Scout Is Helpful' Reports from Everywhere Prove It," *Boys' Life*, December 1915, 40.

68. William George, *The Adult Minor* (New York: Appleton, 1937), 99, mentioning the September 4, 1916, issue of the *Knickerbocker Press;* H. Addington Bruce, "A Vocational School a Hundred Years Old," *Outlook* (July 28, 1915), 739.

69. Lyman Beecher Stowe, "Junior Citizens in Action," *Outlook*, November 18, 1914, 655.

70. John R. Commons, "The Newsboys of Milwaukee," *Milwaukee Bureau of Economy and Efficiency Bulletin* 8 (November 15, 1911); "Strange Milwaukee Newsboys: The Milwaukee 'Newsies,'" *Youth's Companion* 87, no. 28 (1913): 358; "The Prestige of Being a Newsboy Has Gone Up," *Newsboys' World*, March 1916; "Getting Hold of Milwaukee's Newsboys. Report on Effectiveness of Street Trades Law and of Newsboys' Republic in Milwaukee. P. O. Powell, Supervisor of Street Trades, Milwaukee, Wisconsin," *Playground* 10 (November 1914): 293, 296–299; "Newsboys' Republic Saved 250 of 300 Cases Handled from Juvenile Court," *Milwaukee Journal*, March 8, 1914; Edward Nicholas Clopper, *Child Labor in City Streets* (New York: Macmillan, 1912), 209; Edgar James Swift, *Youth and the Race* (New York: Charles Scribner's Sons, 1912), 164; James K. Paulding, "Enforcing the Newsboy Law in New York and Newark," *Charities* 14 (1905): 836–837; B. E. Kuechle, "Newsboys' Republic, Milwaukee, Wis.," *Survey* (March 22, 1913): 859; Philip Davis, *Street-Land: Its Little People and Big Problems* (Boston: Small, Maynard, 1915), 217; Madeleine Appe, "Enforcement of the Street Trades Law in Boston, Paper Read at the 17th National Conference on Child Labor," *American Child* 4 (1922); "Milwaukee's Newsboys Republic," *Outlook*, April 5, 1913, 743; "The Milwaukee Republic, by One of Its Founders," *Work with Boys* (1914): 21, 27; "Notes on Street Trades Department and Milwaukee Newsboys' Republic, Perry O. Powell, Supervisor of Street Trades, Milwaukee Public Schools," *Proceedings of the National Conference on Social Work* (1921): 297; "Getting Hold of Milwaukee's Newsboys. Report on Effectiveness of Street Trades Law and of Newsboys' Republic in Milwaukee. P. O. Powell, Supervisor of Street Trades, Milwaukee, Wisconsin," *Playground* 10 (November 1914): 293; "Newsboys' Republic, Reducing Delinquency, Saves City Big Sum," *Milwaukee Journal*, July 14,1916; "Ex-hawkers Hold a Reunion," *Milwaukee Journal*, October 21, 1983; "Working Children Well Cared For: Milwaukee Does More for Youth in Industry than Other Cities," *Milwaukee Sentinel*, February 12, 1922.

71. Gregory Mason, "The Boy Police of New York," *Labor Digest* 8, no. 7 (1915): 31; "Junior Police in New York City," *National Municipal Review* (July 1915): 481; Elnora Whitman Curtis, *The Dramatic Instinct in Education* (Boston: Houghton Mifflin, 1914), 94; "Junior Police Force Disbanded by Enright," *New-York Tribune*, July 10, 1918; Arthur Woods, "Police Administration," *Proceedings of the Academy of Political Science in the City of New York* 5, no. 3 (April 1915): 54–61. The "natural" inclination of kids to play cops and robbers, including children's imitation of crime stories, was widely documented. See F. Fenton, "The Influence of Newspaper Presentations upon the Growth of Crime and Other Antisocial Activity" (PhD diss., University of Chicago, 1911); "The Telephone Boy Sleuth," *St. Louis Post-Dispatch*, July 26, 1893; "Edmond, 'Boy Detective,' Fearing Spanking by Ma, Is Terribly Embarrassed," *Detroit Free Press*, October 18, 1913; "Back to the Farm for Boy Detective," *St. Louis Post-Dispatch*, October 13, 1904; "Thugs Cut Throat of Boy Detective," *Detroit*

Free Press, December 27, 1909; "Boy 'Detective' in Hands of Police," *Arizona Republican*, April 2, 1910; "Boy Detective in Tears," *New York Times*, May 27, 1884; "Local Criminal Items," *Chicago Daily Tribune,* April 5, 1881; "A Boy Detective Shot," *New-York Tribune,* September 5, 1881; "Boys Trail 2 Suspects," *Detroit Free Press*, September 1, 1908; "Thieving Mystery Solved," *Los Angeles Times*, August 11, 1905; "Arrest of Rosen," *Boston Daily Globe*, July 22, 1905; "Boy Detective Recognizes Escaped Convict in Store," *St. Louis Post-Dispatch*, October 23, 1907; "S. Holmes Pupil Outdoes Teacher," *St. Louis Post-Dispatch*, February 23, 1904; "Boy Detective Nabs His Father," *Detroit Free Press*, July 29, 1909; "Boy Detective," *Boston Daily Globe*, August 22, 1908; "Bold Ruse of a Sleuth," *Los Angeles Times*, February 4, 1909; "Boy Sleuth on Auto," *New-York Tribune*, October 2, 1909; "Boy Sleuth to Get a Medal of Honor," *New York Times*, October 3, 1909; "Chased by Boy Sleuth," *Sun*, December 31, 1912; "Boy Sleuth Causes Arrest of Burglar," *San Francisco Chronicle*, July 9, 1907; "A Boy Sleuth Foiled," *New York Times,* February 24, 1906; "Boy Sleuth Nips a Robbery," *New York Times*, October 1, 1905; "Boy Sleuth Has Newsey Held on 'Bunco' Charge," *St. Louis Post-Dispatch*, February 19, 1908; "Boy Sleuth on Trail," *New-York Tribune*, September 26, 1913; "John Kelly, Messenger Boy, Has Dime Novel Adventure," *Chicago Daily Tribune*, January 20, 1914; "Thugs Sleep Well and Boy Sleuth Quits Watch," *San Francisco Chronicle*, June 21, 1913; "Boy Sleuth Is a Wonder," *Los Angeles Times*, June 30, 1913; "Boy Detectives Seize Burglar Fleeing School," *Chicago Daily Tribune*, May 16, 1917; "Messenger Boy Detective," *Sun*, August 15, 1915; "Boy Detective, Accused of Theft, Clears Self," *New-York Tribune*, June 23, 1919; "Boy Detective Traces Loot," *Sun*, June 25, 1912; "Newest 'Boy Detective' and First 'Pinch,'" *Chicago Daily Tribune*, May 17, 1913; "'Boy Detective' Held at Bay," *Chicago Daily Tribune*, May 17, 1913.

72. Richard Welling, "The Teaching of Civics and Good Citizenship in the Public Schools," *Journal of Proceedings and Lectures*, *National Education Association* 42 (1903): 99; Ella White, "State President Commends Leagues," *Atlanta Constitution*, April 14, 1912; "Junior Civic League Formed at Mt. Airy," *Atlanta Constitution*, July 20, 1911; Frances Gulick Jewett, *Town and City* (Boston: Ginn, 1906), 39; "One City Actually 'Fly-Less' Last Summer," *St. Louis Post-Dispatch*, February 15, 1914; Lucy Stewart, "Annual Reports of Individual Clubs," *Atlanta Constitution*, January 17, 1909; E. Mabel Skinner, "Training for Citizenship," *Journal of Education* 85, no. 16 (April 19, 1917): 437–439; George Bellamy, "A Community Recreation Program for Juveniles," *Proceedings of the National Conference of Social Work* 45 (1918): 65–68; William Seymour, "Junior Deputy Sanitary Inspectors," *American City* 15, no. 5 (1916): 696–698; L. B. Stowe, letter to the editor, *NY Globe and Commercial Advertiser*, June 20, 1914, box 16, folder 7, WG Papers.

73. Rowland Haynes, "Social and Economic Problems: Recreation," in *The American Yearbook* (New York: Appleton, 1914), 392; William Ashley, "Harnessing Boy Power," *Scientific American*, February 1919, 100–101; Boy Scouts of America, *Handbook for Scoutmasters* (New York: BSA, 1913), 67; Harold Horne, "Why the Nation Supports the Boy Scouts," *Review of Reviews* (1919), 625; Louis Dunton Hartson, "Psychology of the Club: A Study in Social Psychology," *Pedagogical Seminary* 18 (1911): 353–414; Elnora Whitman Curtis, *The Dramatic Instinct in Education* (Boston: Houghton Mifflin, 1914), 102; Lawrence Cremin, *History of Teachers College* (New York: Columbia University Press, 1954); "Fire Call for Scouts," *Boys' Life*, September 1916.

74. Elnora Whitman Curtis, *The Dramatic Instinct in Education* (Boston: Houghton Mifflin, 1914), 38, xvii; William Byron Forbush, *Dramatics in the Home* (Philadelphia: American Institute of Child

Life, 1914), 26. Examples of this "epidemic" include Elnora Whitman Curtis, "The Dramatic Instinct in Education," *Pedagogical Seminary* 15 (September 1908): 301–311; B. O. Flower, "The Theater as a Potential Factor for Higher Civilization and a Typical Play Illustrating Its Power," *Arena* (May 1907): 497–509; William Ordway Partridge, "Relation of the Drama to Education," *Journal of Social Science* (September 1886): 188–206; Helen Purcell, "Children's Dramatic Instinct and How This May Be Utilized in Education," *Elementary School Teacher*, May 1907, 510–518; Alice Herts, "Dramatic Instinct: Its Use and Misuse," *Pedagogical Seminary* 15 (December 1908): 550–562; Madge Jenison, "A Hull House Play," *Atlantic Monthly*, July 1906, 83–92; Mrs. George Spencer Morris, "The Educational Value of the Drama," *Child Welfare*, September 1913, 14–15; Alice Herts, "The Children's Educational Theater," *Atlantic Monthly*, December 1907, 798–806; Sidney Peixotto, "The Ideal Dramatics for a Boys' Club," *Charities and Commons*, October 3, 1908, 64–66; Karl Groos, *The Play of Man, translated by Elizabeth L. Baldwin* (New York: Appleton, 1901); Ben Lindsey, "Public Playgrounds and Juvenile Delinquency," *Independent*, August 20, 1908, 421–423; Marie Shedlock, "Dramatic Instinct in the Social Life of the Child," *Social Education Quarterly* 1 (1908): 61–68; F. M. Bjorkman, "A Nation Learning to Play," *World's Work* (September 1909): 12038–12045; Percy McKaye, "American Pageants and Their Promise," *Scribner's*, July 1909, 28–34; Ira S. Wile, "Public Health Publicity and Education through Public Schools," *American Journal of Public Health* 8 (1918): 339.

75. William Seymour, "Junior Deputy Sanitary Inspectors," *American City* 15, no. 5 (1916): 697; "Council Bluffs Kid Police Force," *Westminster* 33 (August 2, 1908): 10; "Boy Police," *Americana Supplement: a comprehensive record of the latest Knowledge and Progress of the World* 1 (1911), 189; *Life of the Boys Brotherhood Republic* (Chicago: BBR, 1938).

76. "Third Ward Civic Club," *Atlanta Constitution*, May 8, 1913; W. L. Murdoch, "Child Labor Reform in Alabama," *Child Labor Bulletin* 3 (1914): 82; "Working Children Well Cared For: Milwaukee Does More for Youth in Industry than Other Cities," *Milwaukee Sentinel*, February 12, 1922; "Christamore Boy Police Department Also on Duty," *Indianapolis Star*, May 7, 1919; "Coffin Reviews Junior Police," *Indianapolis Star*, July 5, 1918; "New York's Junior Police Force," *Work with Boys* 16 (1916): 232; Lyman Beecher Stowe, "Good Citizens in the Making: How the Boys' and Girls' New 'Junior Municipality' Was Organized," *Illustrated Buffalo Express*, August 17, 1913; "Boys Hold Elections Like Their Elders," *New York Times*, November 9, 1913; "Metz Talks to Boy Republic," *New-York Tribune*, February 1, 1909; Geoffrey Parsons, *The Land of Fair Play* (New York: Scribner's, 1920); "Boy Detectives: Called to 'Spot' the Breakers of the Prohibition Law in Rhode Island," *Chicago Daily Tribune*, July 20, 1886; "Byrnes' Boy Detectives," *Boston Daily Globe*, February 16, 1890; "Juvenile Detectives: Smart Children Who Trap Crafty Criminals," *Boston Daily Globe*, August 2, 1891; "Boy Detectives," *St. Louis Post-Dispatch*, May 17, 1884; "Field Day for Cigaret Foes, "*Chicago Daily Tribune*, April 17, 1904; "Cigaret War Is Revived with Boy Detectives Used," *Chicago Daily Tribune*, April 7, 1904; "Cigaret Crusade Is Active," *Chicago Daily Tribune*, April 8, 1904; "News from Southern California Towns," *Los Angeles Times*, October 6, 1898; "Debate Using Boy Detectives," *Chicago Daily Tribune*, June 17, 1903; "Boy Detectives Work for City," *Chicago Daily Tribune*, April 21, 1901; "Chicago Has Boy Sleuths: Their Work Is Hard and Their Pay Small," *Detroit Free Press*, April 22, 1901; "Boy Detective Works as Girl," *Los Angeles Times*, July 28, 1909; "Boy Detective Aids the City," *Chicago Daily Tribune*, May 17, 1908; Joe

Miller, "Government of the Gallery," *Indianapolis Morning Star*, February 25, 1906; "'Boy Sleuth' Is Foiled," *Chicago Daily Tribune*, December 9, 1904; "Council Bluffs Kid Police Force," *Westminster* 33 (August 2, 1908): 9; "Captain John F. Sweeney, 'Commissioner' of the Kid Cops," *The American Year Book* (New York: Appleton, 1915), 6; "Junior Policemen Win Wood's O.K," *New-York Tribune,* June 5, 1915; "Plan Boy Police for Portland: Chief Slover Is Swamped by Youngsters of the City Who Would Become Officers," *San Francisco Chronicle*, May 16, 1913; "Boy Police Force for Portland, OR," *Boston Daily Globe*, May 11, 1913; "Stubborn Girl Pacifist Wins Fight with School Principal," *New-York Tribune*, March 11, 1918; "The Milwaukee Republic, by One of Its Founders," *Work with Boys* (1914): 21; "Getting Hold of Milwaukee's Newsboys," *Playground* 10 (November 1914): 296–299; Esther Lee Rider, "Newsboys in Birmingham," *American Child* 3 (February 1922): 316; "A Voice from Dixie," *Newsboys' World*, November 1915; "Ex-hawkers Hold a Reunion," *Milwaukee Journal*, October 21, 1983; "Kill Flies to Protect the City from Disease," *Newsboy's World*, November 1915; William Seymour, "Junior Deputy Sanitary Inspectors," *American City* 15, no. 5 (1916): 696; "Milwaukee's Newsboys' Republic," *Outlook*, April 15, 1913, 743–744; William Byron Forbush and Dascomb Forbush, *The Knights of King Arthur: How to Begin and What to Do* (Oberlin, Ohio: Knights of King Arthur, 1915); Gregory Mason, "The Boy Police of New York," *Outlook*, July 28, 1915, 706–708; "Boy Police," *Americana Supplement: A Comprehensive Record of the Latest Knowledge and Progress of the World* 1 (1911): 189; "Reformers Who Misuse Children," *St. Louis Post-Dispatch*, September 1, 1907; "Held for Using Boy Sleuth: Policeman Accused of Impairing the Morals of a Minor," *New-York Tribune*, August 29, 1912; "Municipality for Minors Favored by Auburn Mayor," *Syracuse Post-Standard*, December 12, 1913; Wm. W. B. Seymour, "Junior Deputy Sanitary Inspectors," *American City* (December 1916): 696–698; LeRoy Ashby, *Saving the Waifs: Reformers and Dependent Children, 1890–1917* (Philadelphia: Temple University Press, 1984).

77. Camilla Stivers, *Bureau Men, Settlement Women: Constructing Public Administration in the Progressive Era* (Lawrence: University Press of Kansas, 2000); Daphne Spain, *How Women Saved the City* (Minneapolis: University of Minnesota, 2000); Juliann Sivulka, "From Domestic to Municipal Housekeeper: The Influence of the Sanitary Reform Movement on Changing Women's Roles in America, 1860–1920," *Journal of American Culture* 22, no. 4 (December 1999): 1–7; Rebecca McLennan, *The Crisis of Imprisonment: Protest, Politics, and the Making of the American Penal State, 1776–1941* (New York: Cambridge University Press, 2008); Adam Rome, "'Political Hermaphrodites': Gender and Environmental Reform in Progressive America," *Environmental History* 11 (July 2006): 440–463; Susan Rimby, "Better Housekeeping Out of Doors: Mira Lloyd Dock, the State Federation of Pennsylvania Women, and Progressive Era Conservation," *Journal of Women's History* 17, no. 3 (Fall 2005): 9–34; Agnes Gottlieb, *Women Journalists and the Municipal Housekeeping Movement, 1868–1914* (Lewiston, NY: Mellen, 2001); Molly Ladd-Taylor, *Mother Work: Women, Child Welfare, and the State 1890–1930* (Champaign: University of Illinois Press, 1994); Sheila Rothman, *Woman's Proper Place: A History of Changing Ideals and Practices, 1870 to the Present* (New York: Basic Books, 1980); Shailer Matthews, ed., *The Woman Citizen's Library. A Systematic Course of Reading in Preparation for the Larger Citizenship*, multiple dates; Mary Pattison, *Principles of Domestic Engineering* (New York: Trow Press, 1915).

78. Compare Andrea Tone, *The Business of Benevolence* (Ithaca, NY: Cornell University Press, 1997) on women to Gertrude Beeks, "Welfare Work and Child Labor in Southern Cotton Mills,"

National Civic Association Review (July-August 1906): 14–21. On continued enthusiasm for play-based education, see Samuel Hamilton, "Plea for Play as a Method of Education," *Pennsylvania School Journal* 5 (April 1917): 454–462; Walter le Burley Wood, *Children's Play and Its Place in Education* (London: Keegan Paul, 1915).

79. "Boy Police," *Americana Supplement: A Comprehensive Record of the Latest Knowledge and Progress of the World* 1 (1911): 189; "Boy Cops Will March in Parade with Police," *New-York Tribune*, March 8, 1915; Arthur Woods, "Crime Prevention: A Lecture on the Spencer Trask Foundation," delivered at Princeton University (Princeton University Press, 1918), 107–108; "Plan Boy Police for Portland," *San Francisco Chronicle*, May 16, 1913; "Boy Police Force for Portland, OR," *Boston Daily Globe*, May 11, 1913; William Langdon, "The Juvenile City League of New York," *The Aims of Religious Education, Proceedings of the Third Annual Convention of the Religious Education Association, Boston* 3 (1905): 442.

80. "Report of Camp-Fire Girls, Thomasville, October 1912–13," *Atlanta Constitution*, January 18, 1914; "South End Girls Form Junior Civic League," *Christian Science Monitor*, January 27, 1912; "Work in Thomasville for the Needy Ones," *Atlanta Constitution*, December 26, 1914; "Girls Send Free Ice Money," *Chicago Daily Tribune*, June 3, 1914; "Shut-ins Visited," *Boston Daily Globe*, December 25, 1913; "Need More Missions," *Washington Post*, October 8, 1913; "Camp Fire Girls' First Lesson in the Secrets of Woodcraft," *Washington Post*, July 26, 1912; "Seek Aid of Children: Hygiene Experts Look to Boy Scouts and Camp Fire Girls," *Washington Post*, September 15, 1912; "Now for the Campfire Girls," *Detroit Free Press*, March 24, 1912; Miriam Formanek-Brunell, *Made to Play House: Dolls and the Commercialization of American Girlhood, 1830–1930* (New Haven, CT: Yale University Press, 1993).

81. Health inspections and truancy management were two examples of jobs from which children were eventually removed. George Shrafte, "Health Inspection of Schools in the United States," *Pedagogical Seminary* 18 (September 1911): 273–314; David B. Tyack and Michael Berkowitz, "The Man Nobody Liked: Toward a Social History of the Truant Officer, 1840–1940," *American Quarterly* 29, no. 1 (1977); Tracy Steffes, *School, Society, and State* (Chicago: University of Chicago Press, 2011). On young men's voluntary associations, see Albrecht Koschnik "Fashioning a Federalist Self: Young Men and Voluntary Association in Early Nineteenth-Century Philadelphia," *Explorations in Early American Culture* 4 (2000): 220–257; R. T. Anderson, "Voluntary Associations in History," *American Anthropologist* 73, no. 1: 209–222; Elisabeth S. Clemens and Doug Guthrie, eds., *Politics and Partnerships: The Role of Voluntary Associations in America's Political Past and Present* (Chicago: University of Chicago Press, 2010); Glenn Wallach, *Obedient Sons* (Amherst: University of Massachusetts Press, 1997); Wallace Kenneth Schoenberg, "The Young Men's Association, 1853–1876" (PhD diss., New York University, 1962).

Chapter 5

1. "George Junior Republic Has Citizens of All Types," *New York Times*, September 27, 1925.

2. "WR George, 69, Dead; Founded Junior Republic," *New York Herald Tribune*, April 26, 1936; William George, "The Junior Municipality," 1921, box 23, folder 21, WG Papers. "'The George Junior

Republic is neither an institution nor a school,' said President George, 'although, of course, it has schools. The Republic is a village incorporated under the laws of the State of New York.'" From "Votes for Boys, 16, Urged by George in YMHA Talk," *Utica Morning Telegram,* December 6, 1920.

3. Joseph Kett, *Rites of Passage: Adolescence in America, 1790 to the Present* (New York: Basic Books, 1977); *American Education and Vocationalism: A Documentary History 1870–1970,* ed. Marvin Lazerson and W. Norton Grubb (Columbia: Teachers College Press, 1974); Ellen Lagemann, *An Elusive Science: The Troubling History of Education Research* (Chicago: University of Chicago Press, 2022); Herbert Kliebard, *Schooled to Work: Vocationalism and the American Curriculum, 1876–1946* (New York: Teachers College Press, 1999); Lewis Todd, *Wartime Relations of the Federal Government and the Public Schools, 1917–1918* (New York: Teachers College Press, 1945); Stephen F. Brumberg, "New York City Schools March Off to War: The Nature and Extent of Participation of the City Schools in the Great War, April 1917-June 1918," *Urban Education* 24, no. 4 (1990): 440–475; Frederick Camp, "Physical Education and Military Drill: What Should Be Our Policy?" *School Review* 25, no. 8 (1917): 537–545; W. R. Burgess et al., "Military Training in the Public School: An Annotated Bibliography," *Teachers College Record* 18 (March 1917): 141–160; "Teachers Split on School Drill," *New-York Tribune,* July 6, 1916; Susan Zeiger, "The Schoolhouse vs. the Armory: US Teachers and the Campaign Against Militarism in the Schools, 1914–1918," *Journal of Women's History* 15, no. 2 (2003): 150–181; Timothy P. O'Hanlon, "School Sports as Social Training: The Case of Athletics and the Crisis of World War I," *Journal of Sport History* 9 (1982): 4–29; Ronald D. Cohen and Raymond A. Mohl, *The Paradox of Progressive Education: The Gary Plan and Urban Schooling* (Port Washington, NY: Kennikat Press, 1979); "New York's Answer to Preparedness Riddle," *New York Times,* April 15, 1917; Arthur Dean, *Our Schools in War Time—and After* (Boston: Ginn, 1918).

4. Miriam Warren Hubbard, "The Soldier-Girls at the National Service School," *St. Nicholas,* April 1917, 519–520; Nathan Andrew Long, "The Origins, Early Developments, and Present-Day Impact of the Junior Reserve Officers' Training Corps on the American Public Schools" (EdD diss., University of Cincinnati, 2003); U.S. Junior Naval Reserve, *The Significance of the U.S. Junior Naval Reserve,* 1917; Edgar Steever, "The Wyoming Plan of Military Training for the Schools," *School Review* 25, no. 3 (March 1917): 145–150; Lewis Todd, *Wartime Relations of the Federal Government and the Public Schools, 1917–1918* (New York: Teachers College Press, 1945), 93; "Boys 16 to 18 Must Enroll," *New York Times,* November 20, 1918; Edgar Steever and J. L. Fink, *The Cadet Manual: Official Handbook for High School Volunteers of the United States* (Philadelphia: Lippincott, 1918), ix; Arthur Sears Henning, "Chicago to Get Student Army of 14,500 Boys: Fifty Army Officers Will Train Them," *Chicago Daily Tribune,* January 28, 1919; "Make Chicago's Military Plan National," *Chicago Daily Tribune,* March 30, 1919; *Military Training in High Schools of the United States,* (Washington, DC: Civilian Military Educational Fund, 1938); Ping Ling, "Military Training in the Public Schools," *Pedagogical Seminary* 25 (September 1918): 251–275; Ross F. Collins, *Children, War and Propaganda* (New York: Peter Lang, 2011), 38; Elsie Clews Parsons, "The Dragon's Teeth," *Harper's Weekly,* May 8, 1915, 449; "Government Policies toward Schools in War Time," *History Teacher's Magazine,* May 1, 1918, 5; Anna Rochester, *Child Labor in Warring Countries: A Brief Review of Foreign Reports* (Washington, DC: National Child Labor Committee, 1917); Owen Lovejoy, "Safeguarding Childhood in Peace and War," *Child Labor Bulletin* 6 (May 1917), 72–77; W. D. Lane,

"Schooling and Child Labor," *Survey* 38 (August 4, 1917): 383–386. Notably, despite the use of "Navy" and "Army," and former soldiers and sailors as youth leaders, these organizations were chiefly privately organized rather than state-sanctioned groups. Exceptions could be found in the school districts that mandated military training for boys—for example, across New York State.

5. William George, Speech to New York State Probation Commission, published in *Eleventh Annual Report of New York State Probation Commission* (1918). The following are in WG Papers: Untitled document, October 20, 1914, box 16, folder 23; William George to Milton Baldwin, April 26, 1915, box 17, folder 8; "Concerning the Admittance of Citizens to the George Junior Republic," c. 1918, box 21, folder 16.

6. The following are in WG Papers: Annual report 1918 typescript, box 21, folder 19; Mrs. George to Estell Forscheimer August 1, 1918, box 21, folder 12; Mrs. Daddy to Lieutenant Timothy O'Connor, September 1, 1918, box 21, folder 13; multiple letters to Henry Curtis, box 21, folder 1; multiple letters, box 21, folder 4. "Junior Republic Grounds Once Directed by Boys, Now Given Up to Weeds: Annapolis Junction Community Was Active Decade Ago with Youths Living Golden Rule," *Sun,* November 1924; John and Mary Baer, "New Relevance for the Junior Republic," *Washington Post,* March 19, 1995; "Child Guardians Propose to Sell Home," *Washington Post,* November 14, 1923; "By the Way," *Outlook,* August 21, 1918, 638; *Child Workers in America* 1937 noted a sharp increase in child labor between 1915 and 1919. On the decline of the school population and increase in child labor more generally, see "Hope for War Profits Increases Child Labor," *New York Times,* November 24, 1918, in Robert Bremner et al., *Children and Youth in America,* vol. 2 (Cambridge: Harvard University Press, 1971), 719–720; "Outside Employment Among School Pupils," *New York Times,* October 21, 1917; "Many Children in War Jobs," *Washington Post,* July 31, 1918; "School Classes Show Falling Off from 1917," *New-York Tribune,* September 10, 1918.

7. The following are in WG Papers: Mrs. George to Rebecca Osler, July 7, 1918, box 21, folder 10; William George to Leonard Levin, July 11, 1918, box 21, folder 11; Untitled document, with cover note from Mrs. Daddy that it was drafted in early 1918, box 21, folder 17; "Concerning the Admittance of Citizens to the George Junior Republic," c. 1918, box 21, folder 16; Annual report 1918 typescript, box 21, folder 19; Contract between Atlantic Woolen Mills of Dryden and GJR of Freeville, October 17, 1918, box 21, folder 14; Mrs. Daddy to Lieutenant Timothy O'Connor, September 1, 1918, box 21, folder 13.

8. Mrs. George to Rebecca Osler, July 7, 1918, box 21, folder 10, WG Papers; Annual report 1918 typescript, box 21, folder 19, WG Papers; Barry Krisberg, "The Legacy of Juvenile Corrections," *Corrections Today* 57, no. 5 (August 1995): 122–154.

9. Arthur Dean, *Our Schools in War Time—and After* (Boston: Ginn, 1918), 5–6; "Education in the Garden," *Moderator-Topics* 39 (1918): 229; Ross F. Collins, *Children, War and Propaganda* (New York: Peter Lang, 2011), 63; "Says Gary Plan Will Aid US: H.E. Miles of National Defense Council Praises Board of Education," *New York Times,* September 17, 1917; "Child Saving Crusade Launched for Georgia," *Atlanta Constitution,* May 19, 1918; Franklin Lane, "Use of Schools in War Time," *School and Society* (April 6, 1918): 404; Owen Lovejoy, "Future of American Childhood in Relation to the War," *Proceedings of the National Conference of Social Work,* 1917, 268–273.

10. Lewis Todd, *Wartime Relations of the Federal Government and the Public Schools, 1917–1918* (New York: Teachers College Press, 1945), 7.

11. Francis R. North, "The Relation of the Public High School to the System of Which It Is a Part," *School Review* 27, no. 2 (February 1919): 81–89; Arthur Dean, *Our Schools in War Time—and After* (Boston: Ginn, 1918), 2, 4, 66, 309; Ping Ling, "School Children and Food Production," *Pedagogical Seminary* 25 (September 1918): 163–190; Ping Ling, "Public Schools and Food Conservation," *Pedagogical Seminary* 25 (September 1918): 101–210; Ping Ling, "Military Training in the Public Schools," *Pedagogical Seminary* 25 (September 1918): 251–275; "Government Policies Involving the Schools in War Time," 6 p. Wash. Govt. April 1918 (Teachers' leaflet no. 3), also in *Survey* 39 (March 9, 1918): 626–628; US Office of Education secondary school circular, "Secondary Schools and the War," Circular 1, 1918; Colorado Department of Public Instruction, *A War-Modified Course of Study for the Public Schools of Colorado* (Denver: Eames Brothers, 1918); "High School Cadets to Get Real Rifles in Spring Drill," *Chicago Tribune*, April 19, 1918; Claude Walker, "War Service by the High Schools: How They Could Be Mobilized to Be Centers of National and Community Influence," *New-York Tribune*, January 4, 1918; *Suggestions for the conduct of educational institutions during the continuance of the war to the end that their educational efficiency may not be lowered, that they may render the largest amount of service both for the present and for the future*, 8 p. Wash. Govt. 1917 (US Office of Education Pamphlet 89). There were some cases when schools were commandeered by military for production but chiefly employed adults. See "Training for Citizenship through Service," *School and Society* 8 (September 7, 1919): 273.

12. Ping Ling, "School Children and Food Production," *Pedagogical Seminary* 25 (September 1918): 163–190; William McKeever, "A Better Crop of Boys and Girls," *Nature Study Review*, December 1911; E. Reed, "Nature Study and Gardening in Indian Schools," *Nature Study Review*, April 1906; Sally Gregory Kohlstedt, "A Better Crop of Boys and Girls: The School Gardening Movement, 1890–1920," *History of Education Quarterly* 48, no. 1 (2008): 58–93; Brian Trelstad, "Little Machines in Their Gardens: A History of School Gardens in America, 1891 to 1920," in *Landscape Journal* 16, no. 2 (1997): 161–173; R. L. Templin, *Information and Suggestions on School Gardens, Children's Home Gardens, Junior Clean-up Work and How to Make Your Home and Community a More Desirable Place to Live* (Cleveland: Children's Flower Mission, 1915); James Ralph Jewell, "The Place of Nature Study: School Gardens and Agriculture in Our School System," *Pedagogical Seminary* 13 (1906): 213–292; "Eleven Thousand Gardeners in the USDA School Garden Army," *Newsboys World*, March/April 1918; J. H. Francis, *The United States School Garden Army* (Washington, DC: GPO, 1919); *The Fall Manual of the United States School Garden Army* (Washington, DC: GPO, 1918); *The Spring Manual of the United States School Garden Army* (Washington, DC: GPO, 1919); United States School Garden Army, *Courses in School-Supervised Gardening for the Northeastern States* (Washington, DC: GPO, 1919); Ethel Murphy, *The Victory of the Gardens, a Pageant in Four Episodes* (Washington, DC: United States School Garden Army, 1919); United States School Garden Army, *Lessons in Gardening for the Central States Region* (Washington, DC: GPO, 1919); P. P. Claxton, *Home Gardening for Town Children* (Washington, DC: GPO, 1919); Arthur Dean, *Our Schools in War Time—and After* (Boston: Ginn, 1918); "Education in the Garden," *Moderator-Topics* 39 (1918), 229; Ross F. Collins, *Children, War and Propaganda* (New York: Peter Lang, 2011), citing Frances Harder, "A Plea for Greater Democracy in Our Public Schools," *NEA Addresses and Proceedings 57th Annual Meeting, Milwaukee 1919*, 391.

13. *Fall Manual of the US School Garden Army* (Washington, DC: GPO, 1918), 3–4; Ping Ling, "School Children and Food Production," *Pedagogical Seminary* 25 (September 1918): 174; "President Wilson Approves School Garden Campaign," *Educational Foundations* 29 (May 1918): 542; Colorado Department of Public Instruction, *A War-Modified Course of Study for the Public Schools of Colorado* (Denver: Eames Brothers, 1918); "Robert Cyril Stebbins," *Copeia* 3 (2006): 563–572; *History of Agricultural Education of Less Than College Grade in the United States: A Cooperative Project of Workers in Vocational Education in Agricultural and in Related Fields* (Washington: FSA, 1942); Robert Cyril Stebbins, *United States School Garden Army: A Manual of School-Supervised Gardening for the Western States* (Washington, DC: Department of the Interior, Bureau of Education, United States School Garden Army, 1920); Robert Cyril Stebbins, *Connecting with Nature* (Arlington, VA: NSTA Press, 2012), 52; "Milwaukee Leads the List," *Newsboys' World*, December 1918; "Proclamation from the Newsboys Republic Stating that They Will Be Good Citizens," *Newsboys' World*, April/May 1917; "Newsboys' Republic Lead Garden Campaign, *Milwaukee Sentinel*, June 2, 1917; "The Newsboys Republic and the War," *Newsboys' World*, November 1917; "Newsboys Patriotic Service League: Newsies Establish a Patriotic Club for Its Members," *Newsboys' World*, May/June 1918; "Republic to Conduct Campaign for Better Gardens," *Newsboys' World*, July 1917; "My Boy: Are You Doing Your Bit," *Newsboys' World*, November 1917; "Eleven Thousand Gardeners in the USA School Garden Army," *Newsboys' World* March/April 1918; W. A. McRae, "The Home Garden and Its Advantages," *Bulletin of the Florida Department of Agriculture*, July 1, 1919, 7; "Ruth Pyrtle of Lincoln," *Journal of Education* (April 29, 1915): 462; Ruth Pyrtle, "Juvenile Food Producers for Uncle Sam," *Journal of Education* (May 2, 1918): 494.

14. "Printing in California Schools," *Industrial-Arts Magazine* 8 (1919): 460; Colorado Department of Public Instruction, *A War-Modified Course of Study for the Public Schools of Colorado* (Denver: Eames Brothers, 1918); Margaret Wells, *A Project Curriculum* (Philadelphia: Lippincott, 1921).

15. Ross F. Collins, *Children, War and Propaganda* (New York: Peter Lang, 2011); Lewis Todd, *Wartime Relations of the Federal Government and the Public Schools, 1917–1918* (New York: Teachers College Press, 1945), 137; Arthur Dean, *Our Schools in War Time—and After* (Boston: Ginn, 1918); Andrew Price, "Teaching Thrift as a Branch of Public Instruction," *Education* 37 (October 1916): 116–121; "Schools and War-Savings Work," *School Life* 1, no. 2-3 (September 16, 1918); United War Work Campaign Victory Boys, *How Boys Can Earn Money* (New York: United War Work Campaign, 1918); *Victory Girls Earn and Give* (New York: United War Work Campaign, 1918); "Red Cross Begins School Campaign," *Washington Post*, September 3, 1917; "Red-Cross Work for School Girls," *Literary Digest* 55 (September 15, 1917), 32; "Junior Red Cross Work Is Defined," *Detroit Free Press*, May 8, 1918; "Junior Red Cross, American Maker," *Detroit Free Press*, February 16, 1918; "Children Will Help in Thrift Campaign," *New-York Tribune*, January 10, 1918; "Junior Red Cross Now Hard at Work," *Detroit Free Press*, March 20, 1918; "Junior Red Cross Outstrips Seniors," *Boston Daily Globe*, March 19, 1918; "Junior Red Cross Shop Is Popular," *Los Angeles Times*, March 15, 1918; "To Mobilize the Schools," *Los Angeles Times*, March 3, 1918; "Junior Red Cross Will Start Work in Schools," *Atlanta Constitution*, February 27, 1918; "143,472 School Children Enroll in Junior Red Cross," *Boston Daily Globe*, February 15, 1918; "Will Enroll School Buildings as Junior Red Cross Auxiliaries," *Atlanta Constitution*, January 19, 1918; "War Service by the High Schools," *New-York Tribune*, January 4, 1918; *Suggestions on Organization of School Societies*

and Junior Red Cross Work in the Public Schools (Madison: Wisconsin Department of Public Instruction, 1918); John Studebaker, "The Junior Red Cross: Its Accomplishments and Future Plans," *Educational Administration and Supervision* 4 (January 1, 1918): 437–439; "Junior Red Cross Work in a High School," *Industrial-Arts Magazine* 7 (January 1, 1918): 224; "A Junior Red Cross," *Youth's Companion* (November 15, 1917): 658; "Wilson Greets the Littlest Army: 22,000,000 Kids," *Chicago Daily Tribune*, September 19, 1917; "Red Cross Asks Children's Aid," *Detroit Free Press*, September 19, 1917; "School Children's Junior Red Cross," *Boston Daily Globe*, September 3, 1917; "Stubborn Girl Pacifist Wins Fight with School Principal," *New-York Tribune*, March 11, 1918.

16. *Los Angeles City Schools and the War* (Los Angeles City School District, 1918), 29; John Studebaker, *Our Country's Call to Service: A Manual of Patriotic Activities through the Schools* (Chicago: Scott, Foresman, 1918), 50; Ronald Bauer, "The Utilization of the Junior Red Cross as an Enrichment Program in the Schools" (master's thesis, University of North Dakota, 1943), 8; Lewis Todd, *Wartime Relations of the Federal Government and the Public Schools, 1917–1918* (New York: Teachers College Press, 1945); Arthur Dean, *Our Schools in War Time—and After* (Boston: Ginn, 1918); "Civic Activities of the Junior High Grades," *History Teachers' Magazine* 9 (1918); John Studebaker, "The Junior Red Cross: Its Accomplishments and Future Plans," *Educational Administration and Supervision* 4 (1918): 437–439; "Junior Red Cross Now Hard at Work: Auxiliary to Major Society Will Explore New Fields in Helping Cause, Boys Will Collect Waste Material to Sell, While Girls Make Articles," *Detroit Free Press*, March 20, 1918; American National Red Cross, *A Program of Junior Red Cross Service Outlined in Proceedings of the Educational Conference January 7, 1918* (New York: University Printing Office, 1918); C. P. Gary, *Suggestions on Organization of School Societies and Junior Red Cross Work in the Public Schools* (Madison: Wisconsin Department of Public Instruction, 1918); *Junior Red Cross Activities: Teachers Manual* (Washington, DC: American Junior Red Cross, 1918); *Agriculture for Junior Red Cross* (Washington, DC: American Junior Red Cross, 1918); *Junior Red Cross Activities in the Pittsburgh Public Schools* (Washington, DC: American Junior Red Cross, 1919); "Junior Red Cross Shop Is Popular," *Los Angeles Times*, March 15, 1918; "Praise System Here Supt. Shiels Asked to Give Plans of Junior Red Cross for National Adoption," *Los Angeles Times*, December 18, 1917; "Wilson Greets the Littlest Army: 22,000,000 Kids," *Chicago Daily Tribune*, September 19, 1917; "143,472 School Children Enroll in Junior Red Cross," *Boston Daily Globe*, February 15, 1918; "Junior Red Cross Outstrips Seniors," *Boston Daily Globe*, March 19, 1918; Henry MacCracken, "Red Cross Ideals for American Schools," *Red Cross Magazine* 13 (April 1918): 3; "Civic Activities of the Junior High Grades," *History Teachers' Magazine* 9 (1918): 497; "Junior Red Cross Work Is Defined," *Detroit Free Press*, May 8, 1918; Florence Taylor, *Physical Welfare of Employed Children* (Washington, DC: National Child Labor Committee, 1918); American National Red Cross, *A Program of Junior Red Cross Service Outlined in Proceedings of the Educational Conference January 7, 1918* (New York: University Printing Office, 1918).

17. Lewis Todd, *Wartime Relations of the Federal Government and the Public Schools, 1917–1918* (New York: Teachers College Press, 1945), 195; J. Lynn Barnard, "A Program of Civics Teaching for War Times, and After," *Historical Outlook* (December 1918): 492, 498; "Red Cross Begins School Campaign," *Washington Post*, September 3, 1917; "Red-Cross Work for School Girls," *Literary Digest* 55 (September 15, 1917), 32; "Junior Red Cross Work Is Defined," *Detroit Free Press*, May

8, 1918; "Junior Red Cross, American Maker," *Detroit Free Press,* February 16, 1918; "Children Will Help in Thrift Campaign," *New-York Tribune,* January 10, 1918; "Junior Red Cross Now Hard at Work," *Detroit Free Press,* March 20, 1918; "Junior Red Cross Outstrips Seniors," *Boston Daily Globe,* March 19, 1918; "Junior Red Cross Shop Is Popular," *Los Angeles Times,* March 15, 1918; "To Mobilize the Schools," *Los Angeles Times,* March 3, 1918; "Junior Red Cross Will Start Work in Schools," *Atlanta Constitution,* February 27, 1918; "143,472 School Children Enroll in Junior Red Cross," *Boston Daily Globe,* February 15, 1918; "Will Enroll School Buildings as Junior Red Cross Auxiliaries," *Atlanta Constitution,* January 19, 1918; "War Service by the High Schools," *New-York Tribune,* January 4, 1918; *Suggestions on Organization of School Societies and Junior Red Cross Work in the Public Schools* (Madison: Wisconsin Department of Public Instruction, 1918); John Studebaker, "The Junior Red Cross: Its Accomplishments and Future Plans," *Educational Administration and Supervision* 4 (January 1, 1918): 437–439; "Junior Red Cross Work in a High School," *Industrial-Arts Magazine* 7 (January 1, 1918): 224; "A Junior Red Cross," *Youth's Companion* (November 15, 1917): 658; "Wilson Greets the Littlest Army: 22,000,000 Kids," *Chicago Daily Tribune,* September 19, 1917; "Red Cross Asks Children's Aid," *Detroit Free Press,* September 19, 1917; "School Children's Junior Red Cross," *Boston Daily Globe,* September 3, 1917; Arthur Dean, *Our Schools in War Time—and After* (Boston: Ginn, 1918); *Los Angeles City Schools and the War* (Los Angeles City School District, 1918); G. Stanley Hall, "Some Educational Values of War," *Pedagogical Seminary* 25 (1918): 112–113; G. Stanley Hall, "Unexpected Moral Changes Produced by the War," *Washington Post,* September 10, 1916; "Sees in Psychology Means to Win War," *New York Times,* December 29, 1916; "Civic Activities of the Junior High Grades," *History Teachers' Magazine* 9 (1918); J. Lynn Barnard, *A Program of Civics Teaching for War Times, and After Historical Outlook* (December 1918): 492–500; "Praise System Here Supt. Shiels Asked to Give Plans of Junior Red Cross for National Adoption," *Los Angeles Times,* December 18, 1917.

18. Ping Ling, "School Children and Food Production," *Pedagogical Seminary* 25 (September 1918): 171, 190; Henry MacCracken, "Red Cross Ideals for American Schools," *Red Cross Magazine* 13 (April 1918): 3; "Printing in California Schools," *Industrial-arts Magazine* 8 (1919): 460; *Los Angeles City Schools and the War* (Los Angeles City School District, 1918), 5.

19. *Los Angeles City Schools and the War* (Los Angeles City School District, 1918), 8, 25, 27, 29, 55; Ping Ling, "Moral Training of School Children in War Time," *Pedagogical Seminary* 25 (1918): 292.

20. Henry MacCracken, "Red Cross Ideals for American Schools," *Red Cross Magazine* 13 (April 1918): 3; "Junior Red Cross Work Is Defined," *Detroit Free Press,* May 8, 1918; Arthur Dean, *Our Schools in War Time—and After* (Boston: Ginn, 1918), 200; Anna Hedges Talbot, "Junior Red Cross Ideals," in American National Red Cross, *A Program of Junior Red Cross Service Outlined in Proceedings of the Educational Conference January 7, 1918* (New York: University Printing Office, 1918), 105; Florence Taylor, *Physical Welfare of Employed Children* (Washington, DC: National Child Labor Committee, 1918); John Studebaker, "The Junior Red Cross: Its Accomplishments and Future Plans," *Educational Administration and Supervision* 4 (January 1, 1918): 437–439; Ronald Bauer, "The Utilization of the Junior Red Cross as an Enrichment Program in the Schools" (master's thesis, University of North Dakota, 1943), 8. The title of Studebaker's call to action for students was "Work—Save—Give," but as in the Gary schools this "work" was different from adult

occupations. See John Studebaker, *Our Country's Call to Service through Public and Private Schools: Work—Save—Give* (New York: Scott, Foresman, 1918); John Studebaker, "The Junior Red Cross; Its Accomplishments and Future Plans," *Educational Administration and Supervision* 4 (1918), 438. Along with his suggestion of showing industrial films to pupils, Dean also proposed putting new machines (such as knitting machines) into school shops.

21. "Junior Police Disbanded by Enright," *New-York Tribune*, July 10, 1918; Hermann Hagedorn, *You Are the Hope of the World: An Appeal to the Boys and Girls of America* (New York: Macmillan, 1917); Ross F. Collins, *Children, War and Propaganda* (New York: Peter Lang, 2011), 159; Susan A. Miller, *Growing Girls: The Natural Origins of Girls' Organizations in America* (New Brunswick, NJ: Rutgers University Press, 2007); David MacLeod, *Building Character in the American Boy* (Madison: University of Wisconsin Press, 2004); Camp Fire Girls, *Manual of Activities and War Program for the Girls of America: The Book of the Camp Fire Girls,* 1918; "Thousands Cheer Junior Patriots and Preparedness," *New-York Tribune,* March 26, 1917; "Proclamation from the Newsboys Republic Stating that They Will Be Good Citizens," *Newsboys' World,* April-May 1917; "Newsboy's Patriotic Service League," *Newsboys' World,* May-June 1918; Henry Rood, "The New York Police: An Object-Lesson in Wise Municipal Government," *Century Illustrated Magazine* 93 (1917): 762; "Junior War Stamp Campaign," *Christian Science Monitor,* February 2, 1918; "Malden Youth Active in War Activities," *Boston Daily Globe,* February 17, 1918; "Soldiers Are Fed from Bronx War Gardens," *New-York Tribune,* September 14, 1918; "Many Children in War Jobs: Children's Year Committee Favors New Child Labor Law," *Washington Post,* July 31, 1918, 12; William B. Ashley, "Harnessing Boy Power," *Scientific American,* February 1, 1919, 100–101, 106; "Again the Boy Scouts and Militarism," *Survey* 35 (December 25, 1915): 342; Harold Horne, "Why the Nation Supports the Boy Scouts," *Review of Reviews* 59 (1919): 623–626; Frank Crane, "What Boys Can Do to Win the War," *Golden Cross Journal* (August 1918): 2; Superintendent Carroll, "War Times, in the Middle Atlantic District," *American Missionary* 71 (1917): 398; M. S. M., "The "Squirrel Is a Hun," *California Blue Bulletin,* Issued by the State Department of Education (June 1918), 16. In contrast to their UK equivalents, US Scouts were avowedly nonmilitary, although US Army officials complained about the Scouts' "artificial soldiering" much as Hall complained about it more generally, and Ernest Seton resigned from the organization because he found it too closely aligned with national defense.

22. O. H. Benson, "Cooperation with Extension Service of the Department of Agriculture," in American National Red Cross, *A Program of Junior Red Cross Service Outlined in Proceedings of the Educational Conference January 7, 1918* (New York: University Printing Office, 1918), 95–96; Arthur Dean, *Our Schools in War Time—and After* (Boston: Ginn, 1918); O. H. Benson, "Accomplishments of Boys' and Girls' Clubs in Food Production and Conservation," *Annals of the American Academy of Political & Social Science,* November 1917, 74, 147–157; O. H. Benson, "Boys' and Girls' Extension Work," in *Farm Knowledge,* vol. 4, ed. Edward Seymour (New York: Doubleday, 1919), 287; Charles Pack, *The War Garden Victorious: Its War-Time Need and Its Economic Value in Peace* (Philadelphia: Lippincott, 1919); Ping Ling, "School Children and Food Production," *Pedagogical Seminary* 25 (1918).

23. Susan A. Miller, *Growing Girls: The Natural Origins of Girls' Organizations in America* (New Brunswick, NJ: Rutgers University Press, 2007), 55; Juliette Gordon Low, *How Girls Can Help Their Country, Adapted from Agnes Baden-Powell and Sir Robert Baden-Powell's Handbook* (Savannah, GA:

Byck, 1916); "War Work of Girl Scouts," *Washington Post,* August 25, 1918; Armstrong Perry, "Farm Boys to Be Government Messengers," *Farm Boys and Girls Leader* (July 1920), 13; Harold Horne, "Why Our Nation Supports the Boy Scouts," *American Review of Reviews* 59 (1919): 624–625; David MacLeod, *Building Character in the American Boy* (Madison: University of Wisconsin Press, 2004); Joseph Kett, *Rites of Passage: Adolescence in America, 1790 to the Present* (New York: Basic Books, 1977); William B. Ashley, "Harnessing Boy Power," *Scientific American,* February 1, 1919; Ross F. Collins, *Children, War and Propaganda* (New York: Peter Lang, 2011).

24. Harold Horne, "Why Our Nation Supports the Boy Scouts," *American Review of Reviews* 59 (1919): 625. Lewis Todd was one of the few observers to recognize the students' productive labor, although he seemed unable to comprehend it within social expectations about youth. "Strange as it may seem," he continued, "perhaps the greatest contribution made to the war effort by the vocational training organization of the public schools was the actual production of finished articles for the war machine." Todd, *Wartime Relations of the Federal Government and the Public Schools, 1917–1918* (New York: Teachers College Press, 1945), 192.

25. Ida Clyde Clarke, *American Women and the World War* (New York: Appleton, 1918); Kimberly Jensen, *Mobilizing Minerva: American Women in the First World War* (Urbana: University of Illinois Press, 2008); "Energetic Women Do Club and War Work," *Atlanta Constitution,* October 1918; Harriot Stanton Blatch, *Mobilizing Woman-Power* (New York: Woman's Press, 1918); Christopher Capozolla, *Uncle Sam Wants You* (New York: Oxford University Press, 2008); Ross F. Collins, *Children, War and Propaganda* (New York: Peter Lang, 2011).

26. Arthur Frothingham, *Handbook of War Facts and Peace Problems*, (New York: National Security League, 1919), 102; "Children and War Drives," *New-York Tribune,* September 15, 1918; E. Ruth Pyrtle, "Juvenile Food Producers for Uncle Sam," *Journal of Education* 87, no. 18 (2178) (May 2, 1918): 494; J. W. Studebaker, "The Junior Red Cross: Its Accomplishments and Future Plans," *Educational Administration and Supervision* 4 (1918): 437–439; George Hall, "The Use of Children in War Drives Disapproved," *Child Labor Bulletin* 7 (1919), 88. See also Edith Howes, "Girls in War Drives," (letter to the editor), *Survey* 41 (October 19, 1918), 76; George Hall to Miss Julia Lathrop, "Regarding children on the streets during war drives," May 25, 1918 (Records of the Children's Bureau, online); Ross F. Collins, *Children, War and Propaganda* (New York: Peter Lang, 2011); Susan A. Miller, *Growing Girls: The Natural Origins of Girls' Organizations in America* (New Brunswick, NJ: Rutgers University Press, 2007). Students had done similar campaigns, for example, in Detroit.

27. "Farm Colonies for Misdemeanants (a Bibliography)," *Journal of the American Institute of Criminal Law and Criminology* 17, no. 4 (February 1927): 626–639; Ping Ling, "School Children and Food Production," *Pedagogical Seminary* 25 (1918), 183, 187; J. L. Barnard, "Program of Civics Teaching for War Times, and After," *Historical Outlook* (December 1918), 498; "Will Enlist Boys to Work on Farm," *Atlanta Constitution,* March 15, 1918; "Will Mobilize 25,000 Boys for Illinois Farms; Plan to Organize New Supply of Labor by Spring," *Chicago Daily Tribune,* November 10, 1917; "Jersey Begins Recruiting Farm Army from Schools," *New-York Tribune,* April 15, 1917; "To Train a Million Boys for War Work," *New York Times,* August 11, 1918; Arthur Dean, *Our Schools in War Time—and After* (Boston: Ginn, 1918); "1,000 Chicago Boys Report on Their Farm Jobs: War Work Makes Youths Healthy, Happy, and Prospers," *Chicago Daily Tribune,* July 26,

1917; "Training Boys for Farm Work," *US Employment Service Bulletin*, February 25, 1918, 2; Lewis Todd, *Wartime Relations of the Federal Government and the Public Schools, 1917–1918* (New York: Teachers College Press, 1945); "Soldiers of the Soil," *Newsboys' World*, October 1917; "Work Is Profitable: Work or Fight Law in Miniature Is Adopted in City," *Milwaukee Sentinel*, June 23, 1918; "Jersey Begins Recruiting Farm Army from Schools," *New-York Tribune*, April 15, 1917; "Milwaukee Boys Go over the Top," *Newsboys' World*, March/April 1918; "Conference on Boy Power in Washington this Week," *US Employment Service Bulletin*, September 17, 1918, 3; "Junior Industrial Army of New Jersey," *Manual Training Magazine* 18 (1917), v; W. I. Hamilton, "Mobilizing Boys for Farm Labor," *School and Society* (June 16, 1917); Arthur Dean, *Our Schools in War Time—and After* (Boston: Ginn, 1918); Frank Victor Thompson, *Report of the Committee on Mobilization of High School Boys for Farm Service* (Massachusetts Committee on Public Safety, 1917); *Making Boy Power Count* (United States Boys' Working Reserve, 1919); "The Labor Problem Among Fruit Growers," *Agricultural Digest* 2 (1917): 937; "Farm Labor and Boy Camps," *Country Life in America* 32 (August 1917): 68; "Proclamation from the Newsboys Republic Stating that They Will Be Good Citizens," *Newsboys' World*, April–May 1917; "Newsboy's Patriotic Service League," *Newsboys' World*, May-June 1918; National Child Labor Committee, *Children in Food Production: A Summary of the Results of These Children in Food Production in the United States in 1917 with Suggestions for the Coming Year* (Washington, DC: NCLC, 1917); William McKeever, *Child Welfare in War Time* (Lawrence: University Press of Kansas, 1918); "Million Boys and Girls in Farm Clubs: War's Impetus to the Movement Is Expected to Result in Permanent Benefit to Agriculture and Betterment of Rural Life," *New York Times*, December 30, 1917; Walter Irving Hamilton, "Mobilizing Boys for Farm Labor," *School and Society* 5 (June 16, 1917): 714–717; "Boys Rescue the Crops," *St. Nicholas* 44 (August 1917): 881–882; "What Farmers Think of Boy Labor," *Survey* 38 (May 12, 1917): 142; Ross F. Collins, *Children, War and Propaganda* (New York: Peter Lang, 2011); Eugene Davenport, *Farm Craft Lessons, Issued by the Educational Section of the U.S. Boys' Working Reserve, U.S. Employment Service, Department of Labor* (Washington, DC: US Department of Labor, Boys Working Reserve, 1919); "Schools Must Train for War," *Detroit Free Press*, February 4, 1918; John Dewey, "Vocational Education in the Light of the World War," *Bulletin of the Vocational Education Association of the Middle West* (January 1918).

28. "School Children Can Serve America," *Nebraska Teacher* 19 (1916): 459 [reprinted widely]; John Dewey, "Enlistment for the Farm," *Columbia War Papers* 1, no. 1 (1917): 4–6; John Dewey, "Enlist School Boys for the Farm: Drill Them at Once in the Use of the Hoe and the Spade for Real Service," *Detroit Free Press*, April 21, 1917; Arthur Dean, *Our Schools in War Time—and After* (Boston: Ginn, 1918), 245.

29. "Back-to-School Drive Under Way," *New York Times*, February 16, 1919; "Millions Sought to Make Schools Attract Children," *New-York Tribune*, February 8, 1919; "Urges Pupils: Return," *Washington Post*, November 21, 1918; "Schools Will Feature Vocational Training," *Los Angeles Times*, August 25, 1918; "Sees Need to Keep Children in School," *New York Times*, June 8, 1919; "Pleads for Thrift Among The Young: Treasury Sees in Boys and Girls Nation's Economic Strength in Years to Come," *New York Times*, October 5, 1919; "Home Aid Corps of Girl Scouts: Manhattan Organization Plans an Employment Bureau to Help Solve The Problem of Part-Time and Emergency Domestic Service," *New York Times*, October 26, 1919; "Labor vs. Schoolroom," *Atlanta*

Constitution, December 1, 1920; "Defect in Schools Drives Children to Work, Says Expert," *New-York Tribune*, March 4, 1919; Harry McKown, *School Clubs* (New York: Macmillan, 1929); Harold D. Meyer, *A Handbook of Extra-Curricular Activities in the High School* (New York: Barnes, 1926); Elbert K. Fretwell, *Extra-Curricular Activities in Secondary Schools* (Boston: Houghton, Mifflin, 1931). Certainly not all young people departed the labor force. In recognition, the US labor department established "junior employment service" bureaus in several cities to promote part-time work and vocational guidance as a happy medium. Anna Reed and Wilson Woelpper, *Junior Wage Earners* (New York: Macmillan, 1920); "The Child Problem," *New York Times*, July 18, 1920; Dorothea De Schweinitz, "The Junior Employment Service," (master's essay, Columbia University, 1929); "Indiana Puts B.W.R. On Permanent Basis with Adequate Funds and Establishes Junior Section of Employment Service," *Boy Power*, April 21, 1919, 7; "The Children's Year and After," *Proceedings of the National Conference of Social Work* 45 (1920), 62–64. Several junior republic affiliates were leading figures in vocational education and guidance, from the George Junior Republic's Frank Parsons to the State of Columbia's John Brewer.

30. The following are in WG Papers: William George to Rector Francis M. Wetherill, May 30, 1921, box 23, folder 1; J. B. Kirkland to Bernard Gluck, May 18, 1920, box 22, folder 1; William George to Mrs. Andrew D. White, January 25, 1919, box 21, folder 21; "Industries," January 25, 1919, box 21, folder 21; William George to Albert Bushell Hart, April 15, 1921, box 22, folder 26. "George Junior Republic Fund Reaches $39,865," *Boston Daily Globe*, April 30, 1926; "George Junior Republic Has Citizens of all Types," *New York Times*, September 27, 1925; "Founder of Junior Republic in Boston, W. R. George Will Pass 10 Days in Speaking," *Boston Daily Globe*, March 3, 1924; "Tells About George Junior Republic: Effort to Raise $200,000 in Boston," *Boston Daily Globe*, April 22, 1926; "Big Endowment Sought," *New York Times*, February 14, 1926; "Republic Celebrates: George Juniors Mark 25th Year—Have Helped 4,000," *New York Times*, July 11, 1920; "Big Endowment Sought," *New York Times*, February 14, 1926.

31. The following are in WG Papers: J. B. Kirkland to Bernard Gluck, May 18, 1920, box 22, folder 1; William George to Mrs. Andrew White, January 25, 1919, box 21, folder 21; "Industries," January 25, 1919, box 21, folder 21; William George to Albert Bushell Hart, April 15, 1921, box 22, folder 26; "Alumni Notes," for *Advocate* (May, 1920s), box 22, folder 11; Earle Bruner to William George, December 19, 1921, box 23, folder 19; Lester Babcock to William George, June 4, 1921, box 22, folder 28.

32. The following are in WG Papers: Samuel Tatnall to William George, January 24, 1921, box 22, folder 16; Samuel Tatnall to William George, June 13, 1921, box 22, folder 28; William George to Samuel Tatnall, June 15, 1921, box 23, folder 1; "Written by William R. 'Daddy' George in 1919," box 21, folder 28; "Relating to the extension of the J.R., J.M., & other ideas," n.d., box 22, folder 8; "What the Junior Republic Needs to Extend Its Growth" n.d., box 22, folder 9; William George to Spencer Miller Jr., August 30, 1920, box 22, folder 12; William George to Samuel Tatnall, February 9, 1921, box 22, folder 20; Spencer Miller Jr. to William George, July 9, 1920, box 23, folder 3. "Republic Celebrates: George Juniors Mark 25th Year—Have Helped 4,000," *New York Times*, July 11, 1920. Despite George's criticisms, his other republics also were widely admired. See "New Chapel Is Republic Plan," *Los Angeles Times*, May 9, 1920; R. T. Lyans, "Establishment That Raises Good Stock and Good Boys," *Los Angeles Times*, August 29, 1920; "Junior Republic Helps Lads,"

Los Angeles Times, September 26, 1928. Clippings and letters show public interest in starting new republics was undiminished.

33. The following are in WG Papers: William George to Richard Welling, October 14, 1921, box 23, folder 9; William George, "The Social Doctor," 1919, box 21, folder 15; William George to Rector Francis M. Wetherill, May 30, 1921, box 23, folder 1; William George to Arthur Morgan, June 15, 1921, box 23, folder 1; untitled notes by William George, August 20, 1935, box 35, folder 31.

34. The following are in WG Papers: William George, "The Delinquent Child and Education," written between 1916–1918 according to cover note by Mrs. George, February 18, 1948, box 21, folder 16; William George, "Dear Friends, to the young men and women, Senior High School of Trenton, NJ," March 10, 1922, box 23, folder 30; William George, "The Junior Municipality," n.d., box 21, folder 16; March 1921, Bulletin No. 18, "Self Government: A Council for Democratic Training," box 22, folder 22; William George to Richard Welling, proposing "Vacation Jr. Republic" at Freeville for junior municipality officials, April 26, 1922, box 23, folder 25; William George, "To the Council for Democratic Training" and paper William George presented to the group, July 28, 1920, box 22, folder 3; Self-Government Inc.: A Council for Democratic Training Bulletin 32, September 1, 1921, box 23, folder 5; Spencer Miller, Jr., "Confidential Memorandum," 1921, box 23, folder 21. "'Daddy' George Pleased with Work of Juniors; Young Men Gave Assistance to Police Officers in Subduing Woman," *Syracuse Post Standard,* June 1, 1914; Herman Hagedorn, "Citizens through Understanding," *Survey* 46 (1921): 676–678. A testament of the group's continued close relations to William George is evident insofar as the self-government group hired George Junior Republic youth to print its brochures. See Self-Government Committee, *Some Suggestions Regarding the Organization and Conduct of a Plan of Pupil Co-operation in School Management,* (Freeville, NY; George Junior Republic, n.d.)

35. "Junior Republic Urged for Boys," *Cleveland Plain Dealer,* January 7, 1921; "Every Convict on Parole in Model Prison," article with cover note by Mrs. George dated 1921, box 23, folder 21, WG Papers. On fears of delinquency, see "Less Juvenile Delinquency," *New York Times,* March 15, 1927; Frederic Thrasher, *The Gang* (Chicago: University of Chicago Press, 1927); James Gilbert, *A Cycle of Outrage: America's Reaction to the Juvenile Delinquent in the 1950s* (New York: Oxford University Press, 1986); G. Abbott, "Trend in Juvenile Delinquency Statistics," *Journal of Criminal Law and Criminology* 17 (1926): 167–172; K. M. B. Bridges, "Factors Contributing to Juvenile Delinquency," *Journal of Criminal Law and Criminology* 17 (1927): 531–580; Percival Symonds, "Causes and Prevention of Delinquency," *Journal of Educational Psychology* 18, no. 2 (February 1927): 129–131; Leta Hollingsworth, "Causes and Treatment of Juvenile Delinquency," *Journal of Educational Psychology* 17, no. 4 (April 1926): 281–282; "Offer Plan to Curb Child Delinquency: Baumes's Investigators Would Coordinate Recreation in Congested Districts," *New York Times,* April 1, 1928; M. Healy, *The Practical Value of the Scientific Study of Juvenile Delinquents,* US Department of Labor [Children's Bureau] Publication 96 (1922); "Murasky Discusses Gang Spirit in Boys: Always There, Needs Directing Rightly Boy Scouts, Neighborhood Clubs, Y. M. C. A., Potent Agencies for Good Their Pep, Energy Often Misleads Them into Wrongdoing," *San Francisco Chronicle,* December 26, 1920; "Board Tells How Boy Gangs Rise in New York Slums," *New York Times,* March 20, 1927; Joint Committee on Methods of Preventing Delinquency, *Three Problem*

Children: Narratives from the Case Records of a Child Guidance Clinic (New York: Joint Committee on Methods of Preventing Delinquency, 1926); Benjamin Gruenberg, "Clubs and Gangs," in *Outlines of Child Study: A Manual for Parents and Teachers*, ed. Benjamin Gruenberg (New York: Macmillan, 1922); "Juvenile Criminality," *Detroit Free Press,* March 13, 1920; Lucy Calhoun, "Survey Reveals Boy Bandit Zone Still Lawless," *Chicago Daily Tribune,* January 31, 1919; "Baseball to End Gang Fights," *Boston Daily Globe,* April 20, 1919; A. F. Payne, "Vocational Education as a Preventative of Juvenile Delinquency," *School and Society* 10 (1919): 509–514; "Offer Plan to Curb Child Delinquency," *New York Times,* April 1, 1928; "Juvenile Criminality," *Detroit Free Press,* March 13, 1920; "Written by William R. 'Daddy' George in 1919," box 21, folder 28, WG Papers; "Junior Republic Urged for Boys," *Cleveland Plain Dealer,* January 7, 1921.

36. The following are in WG Papers: "Stealing Daddy George's Thunder," *Ithaca Journal,* December 19, 1914, box 16, folder 21; Henry W. Thurston to William George, December 23, 1914, box 16, folder 21; "Every Convict on Parole in Model Prison," article with cover note by Mrs. George dated 1921, box 23, folder 21; L. B. Stowe, memorandum on the application of the Junior Republic idea to other institutions, n.d., box 16, folder 29; George W. Kercteney [name unclear] to William George, June 9, 1920, box 22, folder 2; Frank Kiernan to L. B. Stowe, June 2, 1914, re: "Problem of Pennsylvania Commission" with list attached to letter: "Self government organizations other than schools and colleges, known to the Self Government Committee, 2 Wall Street, New York," box 16, folder 5; Arthur St. John, "A New Way with Criminals," *Sociological Review* 21, no. 3 (1929): 233–240; Burdette Gibson Lewis, *The Offender and His Relations to Law and Society* (New York: Harper, 1921), 164; "Training School Head to Study Eastern Prisons," *Atlanta Constitution,* July 31, 1922; "Self Government in Prison Opposed," *Christian Science Monitor,* September 18, 1923; "Osborne Says Self-Government for Convicts," *St. Louis Post-Dispatch,* June 15, 1921; "Osborne Would Bar Prison Sweatshops," *St. Louis Post-Dispatch,* June 22, 1921; A. C. H., "Letters to the Editor: A Definition of the 'Honor System,'" *Christian Science Monitor,* November 6, 1924; "Lack of Stated Dry Law Held to Aid Police," *Sun,* December 10, 1928; William George, "Prison Walls without a Prison," *Survey* (November 3, 1917): 120–123; "Self-Rule in Prison Is Found a Success," *New York Times,* November 11, 1921; "Notables Praise Junior Republic," *Hartford Courant,* October 3, 1925; "Woman Reformatory Executive Is Winning Wide Recognition," *Christian Science Monitor,* May 11, 1925; Mayme Peak, "Prison without Walls for Women, without Even Name of 'Prison,'" *Boston Daily Globe,* April 26, 1925; "Jennings Uses War Experience in Rilling Prison," *New York Herald Tribune,* December 12, 1929; "Prison Ideals," *Manchester Guardian,* September 13, 1922; "Prison Problems Bring 1000 Delegates Here," *Boston Daily Globe,* September 9, 1923; "A Prison Reformer," *New York Times,* October 22, 1926; "Prison Colony Successfully Governs Itself," *Christian Science Monitor,* October 10, 1928; Herbert Carpenter, "Thomas Mott Osborne," *New York Times,* October 22, 1926; L. H. Robbins, "Where Prisoners Help to Run a Prison," *New York Times,* March 2, 1930; "Stone Walls Do Not Make This Maryland Test Prison," *Christian Science Monitor,* July 28, 1932; "Jail within a Jail One of Features That Make Norfolk Prison Different," *Christian Science Monitor,* January 11, 1932; William Bilevitz, "Higher Education in the Prison," *Sun,* August 30, 1931; Louis Lyons, "Job and Hobby for Each Prisoner," *Boston Daily Globe,* July 3, 1932; "Teaching Convicts Community Life," *Boston Daily Globe,* January 11, 1932; "Reduced Terms Urged as Pay for Prisoners," *New York Herald Tribune,* January 5, 1931; *The Prison and the Prisoner: A Symposium* (Boston: Little, Brown, 1917); Rodney Watterson, *Whips to Walls:*

Naval Discipline from Flogging to Progressive Era Reform at Portsmouth Prison (Annapolis, MD: Naval Institute Press, 2014); "Sing Sing Ready for Emergency, Lawes Asserts," *New York Herald Tribune,* July 30, 1929; "Self-Rule in Prison Is Found a Success," *New York Times,* November 11, 1921; "Osborne Says Self-Government for Convicts," *St. Louis Post-Dispatch,* June 15, 1921; "Bedford Cruelty Charges Against Officials Upheld," *New-York Tribune,* March 19, 1920. The following are in WG Papers: Paul Kennaday to William George, April 11, 1916, box 21, folder 6; William George, "Concerning discipline," c. 1918, box 21, folder 17; WG, no title, a recasting of "Prison Walls Without a Prison" from *Survey* (November 3, 1917), box 22, folder 4. Notably, there is some evidence that Osborne was mulling over the concept of prisoner self-government as early as 1904. See *Proceedings of the Annual Congress of the National Prison Association of the United States* from that year. Osborne died in 1926.

37. "'Daddy' George gives 'Crime wave' cause," *Boston Daily Globe,* March 30, 1926; Spencer Miller Jr. to William George, August 25, 1920, box 22, folder 4, WG Papers; "Written by William R. 'Daddy' George in 1919," box 21, folder 28, WG Papers.

38. "Light Registration for the Junior Election," *Ithaca Daily News,* October 18, 1913; "Wilson Elected as Junior Mayor," *Ithaca Daily News,* November 6, 1913; "Citizens Seek Meeting Place; Junior Municipality, Ithaca, Handicapped by Lack of Funds; Large Quarters Wanted," *Syracuse Post Standard,* December 31, 1913; "Only 196 Juniors Are Registered. Managers Surprised at Lack of Interest Now Shown in Junior Municipality Affairs—Think Poll Tax Had Some Effect," *Ithaca Daily News,* November 3, 1913; "Matson, Junior Mayor, Resigns. Gives as Reason, Lack of Time Because of University Studies—Has Been Active Worker Since Organization of Junior Municipality," *Ithaca Daily News,* March 16, 1915; "Junior Municipality Idea Spreading in New York," *Syracuse Post Standard,* April 3, 1921; Arthur Leland, "Junior City Government Meets Regularly in City Hall," *American City* (September 1919): 232; "'Daddy' George at Ford Hall Forum," *Boston Daily Globe,* October 16, 1922; "Another Junior Government," *Tampa Morning Tribune,* November 1, 1921; "For Our Inevitable Citizens," *Outlook,* October 5, 1921, 160; Richard Welling, *As the Twig Is Bent* (New York: Putnam's, 1942), 154–157; "Civic Associations," *Yonkers Statesman,* May 11, 1921; "Oswego People to Remember Poor," *Binghamton Press,* December 23, 1921; Herman Hagedorn, "Citizens through Understanding," *Survey* 46 (1921): 676–678; "Walks Right into Jail Wearing Pair of Brand New Shoes," *Binghamton Press,* November 23, 1921; "Kiwanis Hear Boys Champion," *Auburn Citizen,* December 1, 1920; "Society in the Suburbs," *New York Evening Post,* August 27, 1925; "Council of Civic Associations," *Yonkers Statesman,* June 8, 1921; "Junior Republic Head at UFA Assembly," *Utica Morning Telegram,* April 9, 1921; "Urges Civic Training of Youth of the City," *Utica Daily Press,* July 22, 1921; "Junior Republic Urged for Boys," *Cleveland Plain Dealer,* January 7, 1921; "Junior Municipalities," *New York Times,* July 24, 1921; "Junior Municipality at Glen Ridge, New Jersey," *Playground* (September 1921): 358; "Junior Republics Doings Heard by Academy Boys," *Utica Morning Telegram,* December 4, 1920; "Founder Tells of the Work of George Junior Republic," *Amsterdam Evening Recorder,* January 26, 1921; "Binghamton May Have Junior Municipality," *Binghamton Press,* February 7, 1921; "Votes for Boys, 16, Urged by George in YMHA Talk," *Utica Morning Telegram,* December 6, 1920; "Junior Republic's Aides Meet," *New York Times,* September 30, 1928; "Juvenile Republic Here: George to Found Another Freeville for

Bowling Green Youths," *New York Times,* February 25, 1927; Ida Clyde Clarke and P. P. Claxton, *The Little Democracy: A Text-Book on Community Organization* (New York: Appleton, 1918). The following are in WG Papers: "Juniors in Glen Ridge in Government Move," *Newark Evening News,* March 4, 1921, box 100, folder 6; Ida Clyde Clarke, "Heard About the Junior City Plan?" *Pictorial Review,* July 1922, box 100, folder 6; Correspondence with National Council for Democratic Training, box 22, folder 5; Notes on starting postwar junior republics and junior municipalities, box 22, folder 7; William George to Spencer Miller Jr., August 13, 1920, box 22, folder 12; William George to Spencer Miller, November 20, 1920, box 22, folder 13; William George to Harold Yetman, October 19, 1921, box 23, folder 12; Bulletin 12, National Council for Democratic Training and "Meeting Report January 1921," box 22, folder 16; Bulletin 14, National Council for Democratic Training and "Meeting Report Feb 1921," box 22, folder 18; Bulletin 23, April 1921, "Self-Government Inc.: A Council for Democratic Training," box 22, folder 24; William George to Hamilton McArthur, July 8, 1921, box 23, folder 2.

39. Lillian Billups, "How to Handle Classroom Discipline in an Elementary School" (master's thesis, University of Southern California, 1929); George Willard Frasier and Winfield Dockery Armentrout, *An Introduction to Education* (Chicago: Scott, Foresman, 1927); Charles Hubbard Judd, *Psychology of Secondary Education* (Boston: Ginn, 1927); John Franklin Bobbitt, *Curriculum Investigations* (Chicago: University of Chicago, 1929); Margaret Berry and Samuel Burnett Howe, *Actual Democracy: The Problems of America* (New York: Prentice Hall, 1923); John Montgomery Gambrill, *Experimental Curriculum-Making in the Social Studies* (Philadelphia: McKinley, 1924); James Albert Woodburn et al., *The American Community: An Elementary Text in Community Civics* (New York: Longmans Green, 1924); "The 'School Republic' Idea," *Constitutional Review* 5 (1921): 246; Thomas Marion Deam and Olive May Bear, *Socializing the Pupil through Extra-Curriculum Activities* (Chicago: Sanborn, 1928); Walter Bodle Munson, "Pupil Participation in the Management of an Intermediate School" (master's thesis, University of California, 1920); William Chandler Bagley, *Classroom Management: Its Principles and Technique* (New York: Macmillan, 1926); Pickens Elmer Harris, *Changing Conceptions of School Discipline* (New York: Macmillan, 1928); Fredric Philip Woellner, *Education for Citizenship in a Democracy* (New York: Scribner's, 1923); Joseph Roemer and Charles Forrest Allen, *Extra-Curricular Activities in Junior and Senior High Schools* (New York: Heath, 1926); Walter Robinson Smith, *Constructive School Discipline* (New York: American Book, 1924); Raymond Drewrey, *Pupil Participation in High School Control* (New York: Harcourt, Brace, 1928); Ira S. Wile, "Civics in the Schools," *School and Society* 6 (September 8, 1917): 311–316; "Statement of Wilson L. Gill in relation to more efficient citizenship, through direct training for it in the schools, and in support of an amendment intended to be proposed by Mr. Owen, to the bill (H.R. 19909) making appropriations for the legislative, executive, and judicial expenses of the government for the fiscal year ending June 30, 1916, and for other purposes," printed as Wilson Gill, *More Efficient Citizenship* (Washington, DC: US GPO, 1915); Wilson Gill, *A Social and Political Necessity: Moral Civic and Industrial Training* (New York: Patriotic League, 1902); Elizabeth Pendry, *Organizations for Youth: Leisure Time and Character Building Procedures* (New York: McGraw-Hill, 1935); Wilson Gill, *American Citizenship in Schools* (New York: Constitutional League of America, 1920); Wilson Gill, *The Third Act of the American Revolution* (New York: Constitutional League of America, 1921); Wilson Gill, *Youth's Commonwealth* (Philadelphia: Patriotic League, 1928);

Wilson Gill, *Children and the Constitution* (Philadelphia: Patriotic League, 1928); Eskimo Language Banned: Children of Far North Adopt English in the United States," *Oregonian,* May 28, 1918; John Leo Coontz, "The Three R's at Sixty Below!" *Washington Post,* August 25, 1929; William Atherton du Puy, "Work of the Schools in Our Furthest North," *New York Times,* September 30, 1928; "U.S. Government Is Civilizing the Eskimos: School at Point Barrow and Wainwright Have Town Councils and—How the Girls Learn to Cook and Sew," *Boston Daily Globe,* January 28, 1917; Frank G. Carpenter, *Alaska: Our Northern Wonderland* (New York: Doubleday, Page, 1923), ch. 28; "'Course in Living' of County Schools Is Shown to Public," *Chicago Daily Tribune,* March 24, 1927; "Child-City Run on Adult Basis," *New York Times,* June 12, 1927; Wilson Gill, *American Citizenship at the Beginning of Life, Not Prison or Electric Chair at Its End, Can Stop Crime; The Civic Life of Children* (Philadelphia: Patriotic League, 1932); Wilson Gill, *International Peace and Progress through Child Citizenship* (Philadelphia: Patriotic League, 1926); Wilson Gill, *Charter of the School City,* 1925, printed in *Ohio Archaeological and Historical Publications* 29; "School 'Cities' Ruled by Pupils' Authority," *Sun,* October 13, 1920; Myrtle L. Wright, "The City of Make Believe: A Project in Character-Building and Citizenship," *Elementary School Journal* 26, no. 5 (January 1926): 376–386; L. H. Wagenhorst, "The Development of a School City in the Slippery Rock Junior High School," *Junior High Clearing House* 3, no. 5 (November 1928): 28–31; David Snedden, *Educational Applications of Sociology* (New York: Century, 1924), 282; "Teaching Citizenship," *Educational Review* (October 1922): 246–248; Cheesman Herrick, "Are Schools Successfully Preparing for Citizenship?" *Proceedings of the 37th Annual Convention of the Association of Colleges and Preparatory Schools of the Middle States and Maryland* (1923), 25; "Alumni Notes," *Teachers College Record* 31, no. 6 (1929): 598. Progressive educators also continued to espouse the "play city" for younger kids. Katharine Keelor, *"Making a Play City," Progressive Education 1, no. 2 (1924):* 78–83; Katharine Louise Keelor, *Curriculum Studies in the Second Grade* (New York: Columbia University, Teachers College, 1925); Caroline Pratt and Lucile C. Deming, *The Play School, Bulletin Number Three* (New York: Bureau of Educational Experiments, 1917). Other less enthusiastic educators included George Alonzo Mirick, *Progressive Education* (New York: Houghton Mifflin, 1923), 158.

40. "A Boy and the Law," *Grand Rapids Press,* December 10, 1914; "Judge Says His Stories Are Designed for Adult Appeal," *Moving Picture World,* June 1, 1918, 1304; Greg Merit, *Celluloid Mavericks: The History of American Independent Film* (Boston: Da Capo, 1999), 34; "The Motion Picture Lyceum Bureau," *Motography* (July–December 1915); "See Child Courts as 'Crime Plants,':" Former Judge Brown Says All Juvenile Tribunals Have Proved to Be Failures," *Washington Post,* June 6, 1921; Myra Nye, "Commercializing Goodness in Films," *Los Angeles Times,* November 2, 1919; "Photo-play of New Sort," *Boston Daily Globe,* November 7, 1913; "Willis Brown, You Are Wanted," *Chicago Defender,* August 31, 1918; "Willis Brown Under Arrest," *Ogden Standard,* December 15, 1915; "Prize Boys on World Tour," *Interior* (May 15, 1913): 678; Sidney S. Peixotto, "Plea for Columbia Park Boys' Club: Sidney S. Peixotto Declares People Do Not Realize Its Importance," *San Francisco Call,* April 8, 1913; "The American Boys," *The Age* [Australia], November 18, 1913; "California Boys Coming: Party from San Francisco on Self-Supporting Trip Round the World Due Here May 5," *Boston Evening Transcript,* April 28, 1913; "Achievement Boy to Be Received at White House by Pres. and Mrs. Wilson," *Jackson Citizen Patriot,* April 28, 1913; "Wilson Greets Boys," *Boston Evening Transcript,* April 28, 1913; "Boys City at Ogden," *San Diego*

Union, July 29, 1915; "Great Boy City Will Be a Feature of Fair: American Juveniles to Compose Community and Show Superiority," *San Francisco Call,* March 10, 1913; "Boy City Film Corporation," in Anthony Slide, ed., *The American Film Industry: A Historical Dictionary* (Lanham, MD: Scarecrow, 1990); "Judge Brown as Producer; Children's Advocate to Release Characteristic 'Stories of Youth' Through General Film," *Motion Picture World,* December 29, 1917, 1; "Read the Synopsis of Judge Willis Brown's 'A Boy and the Law' Then See It at the American Tomorrow and Wednesday," *Salt Lake Telegram,* June 29, 1914; "Willie Eckstein, Hero of the Photoplay, 'A Boy and the Law,' to Be Shown Here, a Tough Customer When He Landed in Salt Lake City," *Salt Lake Telegram,* June 24, 1914; "'A Girl and the Law' Built Around Juvenile Court Case: Youth Photoplay Company with Its General Headquarters in Judge Brown's Famous Boy City in Michigan and Organized to Produce True Films Largely Dealing with His World Famed Work, Completed the Fourth Judge Brown Film in This City, Where He Accomplished Much," *Salt Lake Telegram,* June 6, 1914. Tag Gallagher, *King Vidor Critical Filmography* has a complete list of the films made by the Boy City Film Company. "Urges Boys' Town in East," *Washington Post,* June 21, 1922; "Lads and 'Dads' Invited," *Washington Post,* November 1, 1921; "Next President Up to 4 Million Boys, Says Judge Brown," *New-York Tribune,* February 23, 1920; "For First Voters' League," *New York Times,* February 23, 1920; "Judge Cites Judge in Contempt Case," *Washington Post,* July 11, 1922; "'Boy-Problem' Talk Is Scouted by Judge," *Washington Post,* November 2, 1921; "The Pledge for the Future," *Salt Lake Telegram,* May 4, 1921; "Look Out Mister for Boy City Bosses. Lads Search Out Merry Blacknesses," *Salt Lake Telegram,* May 2, 1921; "Boy City's Work Described Here," *Washington Times,* November 27, 1916. The interest in media for publicity was long-standing. During his time at Winona, Brown's public lectures so impressed businessman William Selig that Selig helped Brown produce a film about Boy City, *The City of Boys* (1910), to encourage audiences to start programs in their communities. See *"The City of Boys,* Globe Theatre Next Week," *Ogden Standard,* December 18, 1910; "Moving Pictures of Boys' Town," *The Start,* December 5, 1910, 6.

41. "Chautauqua Picks Junior Advisors: Committee Named to Cooperate in Children's Feature Program," *Trenton Evening Times,* September 6, 1922; P. W. Wilson, "Chautauqua Movement Now Fifty Years Old," *New York Times,* June 15, 1924; "Junior Town Receives Its Charter," *Los Angeles Times,* March 26, 1927; "Hightstown Ready for Chautauqua," *Sunday Time-Advertiser* [Trenton], June 13, 1915; "Hightstown Has Chautauqua Week," *Trenton Evening Times,* June 18, 1919; "Children of Three Rivers Organize City," *Kalamazoo Gazette,* August 28, 1919; "Chautauqua 'Kids' Organize and Hold Picnic," *Olympia Record,* August 3, 1921; Georgene Faulkner [National Association of Junior Chautauquas], *Through Story-Land with the Children* (New York: Revell, 1924); National Association of Junior Chautauqua Directors, *Fun Folk and Fairy Tales* (New York: Revell, 1923); Mrs. William John Hall, *Junior Music Clubs and the Chautauquas: A Guide for the Junior Chautauqua Worker and the Local Music Club Leader, with Reference Lists and Program Suggestions* (New York: National Bureau for the Advancement of Music, 1925); "Portland Woman Chosen for Chautauqua Work," *Sunday Oregonian,* January 28, 1923; "Chautauqua Plans Work for Youths," *San Francisco Chronicle,* September 10, 1922; "Chautauqua to Give Drama to Masses," *New York Times,* March 21, 1927; James R. Schultz, *The Romance of Small-Town Chautauquas* (Columbia: University of Missouri Press, 2002); "Pageant Today at Chautauqua: It Will Be Given by Children of Junior Town—Session to Close Today at Chautauqua," *Hartford Courant,* July 9, 1923; "Junior

Government for Berlin Children: Mrs. George E. Green to Have Charge," *Hartford Courant,* July 23, 1922; Grace Gearing, "Girl to Rule One Hour as Head of City: Mayor Wade Will Turn Over Office to Chief Executive of Junior Town," *Hartford Courant,* July 28, 1926; *Annual Report of the Glendale City Schools* (Glendale, CA, 1929), 35; "MarBain Again Chosen Mayor of Glendale," *Los Angeles Times,* April 20, 1927; "Junior Chautauqua Plans," *Lyceum Magazine,* November 1922, 24; "A Junior Chautauqua," *Playground* (July 1921): 247; Harry Hibschman, "Chautauqua 'Pro' and 'Contra,'" *North American Review* 225, no. 843 (May 1928): 597–605; "West Stockbridge," *Springfield Republican,* February 15, 1928; "Chautauqua Boys Run City for Full Hour; Mayor George Otis, 13, Refuses Postmaster Potter's Request to Be Fire Chief," *Springfield Daily Republican,* July 15, 1925; "Aiken [SC] Boys Run Own for House: Boys Arrest Many and Fine Them; Ride Fire Truck," *Augusta Chronicle,* May 28, 1929; Junior Town Reporter, "Junior Towners Program Planned: Second Meeting Held; Welfare Commissioners Named," *Augusta Chronicle,* April 29, 1930, 8.

42. "Memorials That Live," *Playground* 18 (1922): 331; Phoebe Hall Valentine, *Smith Memorial Playgrounds and Playhouses and the Martin School Recreation Center* (Philadelphia: Fidelity-Philadelphia Trust, 1936); Phoebe Hall Valentine, *The Village: An Experiment in Educational Play Conducted by the Smith Memorial Playgrounds in Philadelphia: Being a Report Made to Fidelity Trust Company, Trustee* (Philadelphia: n.p., 1925); Harrison Grey Otis, "Cultivate the Coming Crop (Clarksburg, W. Va.)," *American City* (December 1923): 630–631; "Student City Formed at Holy Cross Summer School; Elects Today. Children over Fourth Grade Now Citizens of Progress City Modeled on Lines of Utica Government—Russell Osgood to Supervise Activities," *Utica Observer-Dispatch,* July 3, 1924; *Progress City News,* August 15, 1924, container 36, folder 7, Progress City 1924, HH Records; Arthur Leland, "Junior City Government Meets Regularly in City Hall," *American City* (September 1919): 232; "Newport Children Engage in City Government," *Municipal Record* [San Francisco Board of Supervisors] 12 (1919); "YMCA Expands Boys' Camp in Ramapos to Serve 600," *New York Times,* May 24, 1925; Madeleine Appel, "Enforcement of the Street Trades Law in Boston," *American Child* (1922): 104–106; "Notes on Street Trades Department and Milwaukee Newsboys' Republic, Perry O. Powell, Supervisor of Street Trades, Milwaukee Public Schools," *Proceedings of the National Conference on Social Work* (1921); "Average Newsboy Not Poor Orphan," *Boston Daily Globe,* July 19, 1928; Hanno Hardt, *Newsworkers: Toward a History of the Rank and File* (Minneapolis: University of Minnesota Press, 1995), 207–208; "Boston Newsboys Learn While They Earn: Free Scholarships Training for Citizenship," *Christian Science Monitor,* July 17, 1930; Albert H. Davis, "Boston's Newsboys," *[Massachusetts] Law Society Journal* 1–5 (1929); "Newsboy Republic Leaders Take Office," *Milwaukee Sentinel,* October 29, 1927; "Newsies Republic Adds States," *Newsboys' World,* March 5, 1926; "Newsboys' Republic to Give Scholarship to Worthy Members," *Milwaukee Sentinel,* June 16, 1923; "227,201 Enrolled in 296 Boys' Clubs," *New York Times,* January 15, 1928; Craig Gingold, "A Republic of Their Own," *Cobblestone* 14, no. 10 (December 1993); "The 'Tiny Town' Gives Impetus to Building Campaign," *American City* 21 (September 1919): 265; Etta V. Leighton, "Our Little Citizens," *Primary Education* 27, no. 8 (October 1919): 483–485; Gordon Cummings, "A Tiny Town Under City Manager Plan," *City Manager,* 7 (1925), 13; Supt. W. W. Thomas, Springfield, Missouri, "Build 'Tiny Town' as a Civic and Industrial Arts Problem," *Industrial Arts and Vocational Education* 8 (1919): 397; "Playground Clubs Are Urged by Young," *Atlanta Constitution,* June 12, 1916; "Chicago Boys Rule Selves in Mimic States," *Chicago Daily Tribune.* November 21, 1920; "To Ask $100,000 for Junior State: Juvenile Protective Association

Plans Campaign to Revive Boys' and Girls' Republic," *Atlanta Constitution,* April 16, 1922; "'Junior Republic' Organized," *Oregonian,* November 23, 1923; Ethel Armes, "Results of the Recreation Movement in City Manager Cities," *City Manager Bulletin* 4 (1922): 83; "Of Children, by Children, for Children: How Juvenile Government Is Working in Omaha," *Red Cross Magazine,* December 1919, 80; A. H. Wyman, "Community Recreation as Part of Americanization Work," *Annual Proceedings of the National Association of Corporation Training* (1921), 888–892; A. H. Wyman, "Recreation in Industrial Communities," *American Physical Education Review* 24, no. 9 (1919): 477; George Butler, *Introduction to Community Recreation* (New York: McGraw-Hill, 1940), 125; "Playground Clubs Are Urged by Young: Children Will Benefit Greatly by Formation of 'Republics' in Atlanta," *Atlanta Constitution,* June 2, 1916; "Any American Boy May Be President One of These Days and These Promising Young Officials of the Playground City of the Mingo Steel Works of the Carnegie Steel Company, Mingo, Ohio, Are Getting Good Training for Citizenship Either in Office or Out," photograph in *Playground* (December 1922): 394; "Junior Town Receives Its Charter," *Los Angeles Times,* March 26, 1927; "Columbia Park Boys' Club Will Have New Home," *San Francisco Chronicle,* May 30, 1920; "Georgia 'Junior State' Planned on Site Near City," *Atlanta Constitution,* April 7, 1922; "To Aid Southern Boys," *New York Times,* December 15, 1912; "Georgia 'Junior State' Planned on Site Near City," *Atlanta Constitution,* April 7, 1922; "Parent-Teachers Indorse Plan for Junior Republic," *Atlanta Constitution,* October 22, 1922; William I. Thomas and Dorothy Swaine Thomas, *The Child in America* (New York: Knopf, 1928), 111, 121; Myrtle L. Wright, "The City of Make Believe: A Project in Character-Building and Citizenship," *Elementary School Journal* 26, no. 5 (January 1926): 376–386; "May Form Citizen Groups for Young," *Washington Post,* October 29, 1920; Courtlandt Van Vechten Jr., "A Study of Success and Failure of One Thousand Delinquents Committed to a Boys' Republic" (PhD diss., University of Chicago, 1935); Clyde Reed, "Self-Government for Problem Boys," *Delinquency News Letter,* 1936; Gay Pitman Zieger, *For the Good of the Children* (Detroit: Wayne State University Press, 2003); "Much Interest Shown in Junior Republic: Funds Are Needed by Organization to Erect the Several Buildings," *Atlanta Constitution,* December 22, 1922; "Georgia 'Junior State' Planned on Site Near City: Training School for Boys Also Will Be Located There," *Atlanta Constitution,* April 7, 1922; Harry Burroughs, *Boys in Men's Shoes* (New York: Macmillan, 1944); George William Hunter and Walter George Whitman, *Civic Science in the Community* (New York: American Book, 1922); Charles Anspach, *An Experiment in Character Development of Pupils through Their Participation in the Management of an Elementary School* (University of Wisconsin–Madison, 1929); *Outline for Model Assemblies* (New York: League of Nations Non-Partisan Association, 1928); Myrtle Hege, "Junior City Organization: A Valley Falls High School English Class Is Organized as Junior City for the Study of Their City Government," *Kansas Municipalities* 8 (1923): 18–19; C. H. Bradley to William George, July 27, 1921, box 22, folder 31, WG Papers; William George to Charles Bradley, July 29, 1921, box 23, folder 2, WG Papers.

43. "Tompkins to Have Suffrage Campaign," *Ithaca Daily News,* November 8, 1913; "Talk Woman Suffrage: New-Jersey Association Convention—Protest Against Statehood Bill," *New-York Tribune,* November 22, 1904; "Girls Working as Politicians: First Exhibit of Junior Equal Suffrage Occurs in Mass Meeting When the Equalist Party Is Formed by the Burns Backers," *Ithaca Daily News,* October 14, 1913; "Professor Schmidt to Address Suffrage Clubs," November 6, 1913; "Junior Municipality Adopts Its Charter: Ithaca Girls Win Contest for Suffrage by Vote of 144 to 63,"

Syracuse Post Standard, October 2, 1913; Representative of the women's political union to William George, November 3, 1913, box 15, folder 18, WG Papers; Mrs. Oliver A. Belmont [Political Equality Association] to L. B. Stowe, December 27, 1913, box 15, folder 26, WG Papers; "Women Play City, Name a Council," *Chicago Daily Tribune,* September 3, 1907; "Women Will 'Play City,'" *Chicago Daily Tribune,* April 21, 1907; "In the Women's Clubs," *Brooklyn Daily Eagle,* April 18, 1908; "Junior Municipalities Mean Equal Suffrage, Such Training Would Give Women Ballot Says Prof. Nathaniel Schmidt," *Cornell Daily Sun,* November 8, 1913; *Brief Prospectus of the American Woman's Republic: Its Declaration and Constitution* (St. Louis: n.p., 1912); *Keep Your Face to the Sunshine; The American Woman's Republic: Founded by the American Woman's League* (St. Louis: People's Savings Trust Company, 1911). Elizabeth Cady Stanton et al., *History of Woman Suffrage 1883–1900* (1902), mentions a Women's League of the GJR organized in 1899.

44. "Girls Rival Youths in Make Believe Politics," *New-York Tribune,* October 4, 1913; "Juniors in Glen Ridge in Government Move" *Newark Evening News,* March 4, 1921, box 100, folder 6, WG Papers; Ida Clyde Clarke, "Heard About the Junior City Plan?" *Pictorial Review,* July 1922, box 100, folder 6, WG Papers; "Junior Republic's Aides Meet," *New York Times,* September 30, 1928; "Juvenile Republic Here: George to Found Another Freeville for Bowling Green Youths," *New York Times,* February 25, 1927; Robert Bingham, "Progress City Report, 1914," container 36, folder 3, Progress City ca. 1906–1920, HH Records MS 3319; William P. Halenkamp, Secretary of the Ohio Site Value Taxation League, to the Hon. James Siciliano, Mayor, Progress City, 2550 E. 30th St., Cleveland, Ohio, July 9, 1919 [misfiled], container 36, erroneously filed with folder 7, Progress City 1924, HH Records MS 3319. Other adults also played Congress; the Washington, D.C., "little congress" was comprised of secretaries and clerks of members of house and senate. See "Mimic Congress Rejects 9% Beer and War Training," *New-York Tribune,* February 4, 1920.

45. "Honor Evanston Boy Police for Safety Record," *Chicago Daily Tribune,* June 23, 1929; Ollie Croucher, "Evanston Play Program Draws Eyes of World," *Chicago Daily Tribune,* December 9, 1928; Susan A. Miller, *Growing Girls: The Natural Origins of Girls' Organizations in America* (New Brunswick, NJ: Rutgers University Press, 2007); William Byron Forbush, *Queens of Avalon* (Boston: Knights of King Arthur, 1925); Charles Smith, *Games and Game Leadership* (New York: Dodd, Mead, 1932); "The Policeman and the Juvenile," *Broad Ax,* December 4, 1926, 1; "Chicago's Health," *Broad Ax,* May 21, 1927, 2; O. J. Bauman, "Home Aid Corps of Girl Scouts," *New York Times,* October 26, 1919; "Junior Patrol to Aid Police," *Washington Post,* August 17, 1924; "Officers of Junior Police Hold Meeting," *Chicago Daily Tribune,* March 13, 1924; "A Junior Police Force Is Formed," *Christian Science Monitor,* July 20, 1921; "St. Louis Plans Junior Police: Boys Between 12 and 18 to Be Enrolled to Prevent Crime," *Detroit Free Press,* July 8, 1921; "Junior Police Will Keep Order in School Yards: 600 Boys Are Organized Just Like Real Cops," *Chicago Daily Tribune,* March 10, 1924; "Omaha's 500 Worst Boys to Police City on Halloween," *New York Times,* October 29, 1923; "Boy Police Force," *Sun,* June 13, 1926; "Boy Detectives Catch Runaway Who Foiled Cops," *Chicago Daily Tribune,* July 26, 1927; "Boy Sleuth's Plea," *New York Times,* June 20, 1924; "Campaign in Schools Succeeds," *Los Angeles Times,* December 18, 1927; "Merchants to Help Parks," *New York Times,* March 31, 1926; "Newspapers Demand Clean Streets and Parks," *Greater New York,* July 31, 1922, 13; "Junior League Is Organized at Grove Park," *Atlanta Constitution,* March 6, 1921; Olivia Pound, *Extra Curricular Activities of High School Girls* (New York: Barnes, 1931);

"School Court Instituted," *Los Angeles Times*, December 4, 1924; "National and Self-Government Ideals through School Court," *Christian Science Monitor*, August 23, 1927; Harold D. Meyer, *A Handbook of Extra-Curricular Activities in the High School* (New York: Barnes, 1926); Elbert K. Fretwell, *Extra-Curricular Activities in Secondary Schools* (Boston: Houghton, Mifflin, 1931); Philip Cox, *Creative School Control* (Philadelphia: Lippincott, 1927); "Boy of 11 Years a 'Policeman,'" *Boston Daily Globe*, July 21, 1923; "Boys Save Long Beach Parade," *New York Times*, June 1, 1926; "Our Boys Form Honor Guard in Big Parade," *Chicago Defender*, May 31, 1924; Mabel Skinner, "The Junior Citizen and His Municipal Government: Shall We Give Him a Share in It, and If So, How Shall We Do It?" *Journal of Education* 95 (1922): 231–234.

46. *An Outline of Safety Education for Elementary Schools and Junior Safety Council Organization* (Birmingham: School Safety Council, 1928); "Prepare to Cut Auto Accidents," *Boston Daily Globe*, September 2, 1927; Harold D. Meyer, "A Program of Safety Activities," in *A Handbook of Extra-Curricular Activities in the High School* (New York: Barnes, 1926).

47. "Forty Boys Sworn in as Wilmette's Junior Police," *Journal of the Illinois State Historical Society* 17, no. 1/2 (April–July 1924); "To Guard Pupils from Accidents Junior Safety Council Is Being Organized in Schools," *Grand Rapids Press*, October 7, 1921; "Guarding Lives at School and Elsewhere Is Purpose of Junior Safety Council," *Dallas Morning News*, September 23, 1930; "Junior Chamber Undertaking Reduction of Accidents with Direction of Safety Engineer," *Dallas Morning News*, August 5, 1928; "Junior Safety Council Will Meet with Lions," *Dallas Morning News*, March 13, 1926; "Junior Safety Patrol Accorded Credit for Reduction of Noises," *Dallas Morning News*, May 1, 1925; "Junior Chamber Holds Safety First Meeting," *Dallas Morning News*, January 17, 1924; "Children Told of Vacation Dangers: Junior Safety News Warns of Risks in Skating and Coasting," *Grand Rapids Press*, December 19, 1922; "Pupils Band for Safety, Thirty-Seven Schools, 25,000 Enrollment Have Junior Councils," *Kansas City Star*, December 17, 1922; "A Junior Safety at Scarritt. Council Chooses Irwin Hurwitt President—Staff Outlines List of 'Don'ts,'" *Kansas City Star*, November 24, 1922; "More Junior Safety Councils, Bancroft and Bryant School Pupils Unite to Prevent Accidents," *Kansas City Star*, November 16, 1922; "Junior Safety Council Officers Hear Traffic Discussed," *Dallas Morning News*, March 29, 1925; "Ten Schools in Safety Drive," *Kansas City Times*, November 12, 1922; "Best Essay on Traffic Safety Will Win Prize, Contest Is Open to Senior, Junior High," *Salt Lake Telegram*, October 15, 1922; "Trentonian Wins National Award, Teacher at Junior High School Is Honored in Safety-First Contest," *Trenton Evening Times*, August 3, 1922; "Place 25 Safety Signs, Junior Chamber Is Making Corners Dangerous for Autoists," *Tulsa World*, July 25, 1922; "Interest Pupils in Safety First Junior C. Campaign Results in Education of 3,000 Children," *Tulsa World* June 7, 1922; "Members of Junior Safety Council, 1200 Strong, Take Pledge at Meeting in Lincoln High School to Guard Against Accidents," *Oregonian*, April 30, 1922; "Pupils Aid Safety Cause, 1200 Attend Rally of Junior Council, Three of 72 Accidents to School Children in Last 18 Months," *Oregonian*, April 28, 1922; "Safety Rally Is Planned, Portland Junior Council to Hold Annual Exercises Today," *Oregonian*, April 26, 1922; "Urges a 'Safety First' Campaign May Become an Objective of Junior Chamber for This Year," *Tulsa World*, April 12, 1922; "To Guard Pupils from Accidents Junior Safety Council Is Being Organized in Schools," *Grand Rapids Press*, October 7, 1921; "Form Junior Safety Council for Children," *Grand Rapids Press*, September 26, 1921; "Danger to Children Less, Junior Safety Committees Cut Down

Accidents," *Oregonian,* June 2, 1921; "Safety Meeting Today, Junior Council to Hear Lectures and See Motion Pictures," *Oregonian,* May 31, 1921; Walter Collins, "The Teaching of Citizenship in the Elementary Schools with Special Reference to Civics, Health Education, Morals and Manners, and Thrift Education" (PhD diss., University of Cincinnati, 1928); "Latest Bests in Elementary Schools," *Journal of Education* 95, no. 14 (April 6, 1922): 379–380; "Girls Cause Traffic Troubles, Is Charge," *Washington Post,* March 27, 1927. There were a few precedents for such activities. For example, Ithaca's junior municipality had assigned child police as crossing guards near the Buffalo Hill East playground. In 1915, after a pupil's death in Rochester, New York, students self-organized as a "safety first" group to assist younger children in crossing streets. See "Rochester Council no. 9," *Safety Engineering* 29 (1915): 447; "An Experiment in Safety First," *Outlook,* October 20, 1915, 395. Yet it was only with the massive growth of private vehicle traffic that local governments systematized such programs and delegated police powers for traffic management to youth.

48. Peter D. Norton, *Fighting Traffic: The Dawn of the Motor Age in the American City* (Cambridge, MA: MIT Press, 2011); Helen M. Rocca, *Council-Manager Government in Berkeley, California: 1923–1935* (Berkeley: Gillick, 1935); Kansas City Safety Council, *Rules and Regulations Governing the Junior Safety Council Street Patrols: A Handbook Issued by Kansas City Safety Council,* 1926; Birmingham (Ala.). Board of Education and Birmingham Safety Council, *An Outline of Safety Education for Elementary Schools and Junior Safety Council Organizations,* 1925; Kansas City Safety Council and Kansas City Junior Safety Council Organization, *Safety Instruction for Kansas City Elementary Schools,* 1922; Martin Alan Greenberg, *American Volunteer Police: Mobilizing for Security* (Boca Raton: CRC Press, 2014); John Leo Coontz, "The West Coast's Model Policeman," *Washington Post,* November 17, 1929; "Berkeley Proud of Service of the Junior Traffic Police: They Spell Safety to Thousands of Students," *Christian Science Monitor,* December 23, 1940; "School Pupils Have Own Court for Violators of Safety Rules," *Boston Daily Globe,* December 8, 1926; "Is Your Town Safer than St. Louis?" *Independent,* August 7, 1920; "Danger to Children Less, Junior Safety Committees Cut Down Accidents," *Oregonian* June 2, 1921; "The Present Status of Safety Education," *The Twenty-Fifth Yearbook of the National Society of the Study of Education, Part 1* (Bloomington, IL: Public School Publishing, 1926); F. M. Rossland, "Nine Years without an Injury to Children on Their Way to or from School," *American City,* November 1926, 684; Gene Carte and Elaine Carte, *Police Reform in the United States: The Era of August Vollmer, 1905–1932* (Berkeley: University of California Press, 1975), 34. Esteemed Berkeley, California, police chief August Vollmer was often credited with the first junior traffic patrol among his contributions to police force modernization but he was adamant it was not his idea.

49. Harold D. Meyer, *A Handbook of Extra-Curricular Activities in the High School* (New York: Barnes, 1926); "School Pupils Have Own Court for Violators of Safety Rules," *Boston Daily Globe,* December 8, 1926; "Boy Scouts," *New York Times,* October 2, 1921; Boy Scouts of America, *Annual Report of the Boy Scouts of America,* 1930; "Boy Scouts as Leaders," *State Center Enterprise* [November 9, 1922 or July 19, 1923]; "10,000 Children Join Safety March," *New York Times,* October 10, 1922; "Boy Scouts," *New York Times,* May 13, 1923; "Boy Scouts," *New York Times,* October 9, 1921; "Boy Scouts: Fix Date for Paris Conference," *New York Times,* October 9, 1921. On enlisting Girl Scouts in road safety campaigns, see Charles Upham, "American Road Builders Association Launches Safety Campaign," *Michigan Roads and Pavements,* August 25, 1927, 3–4.

50. "Pioneer Radio Man Says Radio Will Help Form International Boy Scout Order," *Harrison Times* [Arkansas], January 26, 1915; Arthur Lynch, "A Compact Portable Wireless Set: A Complete Wireless Telephone Transmitting and Receiving Station Which May Be Carried by a Single Boy Scout," *Radio Broadcast*, May 1922, 54; "Scout Activity Threatened," *Centralia Evening Standard*, April 16, 1919; "Boys' Club Exhibit of Home-made Radios Opens," *Chicago Daily Tribune*, April 17, 1924; "Nearly Every Boy Scout Has Radio Receiver," *Chicago Daily Tribune*, August 17, 1924; "Radio Raid on Maj. Dillon," *Los Angeles Times*, June 18, 1922; Robert Heinl, "Youth Predominant in Developing Radio Activities of World," *Washington Post*, July 24, 1927; W. E. Downey, "Amateurs' Work Promotes Radio," *New York Times*, September 9, 1928; "US Has 14,902 Hams as Radio Reserve Force," *Chicago Daily Tribune*, October 31, 1926; "Amateurs in Radio Are Experimenting with Short Waves," *Washington Post*, April 15, 1928; Kristen Haring, *Ham Radio's Technical Culture* (Cambridge, MA: MIT Press, 2006); Department of Commerce, *Amateur Radio Stations of the US* (Washington: GPO, 1924 and other years).

51. Susan J. Douglas, "The Navy Adopts the Radio, 1899–1919," in *Military Enterprise and Technological Change*, ed. Merritt Roe Smith (Cambridge, MA: MIT Press, 1985); V. F. Greaves, "The Radio Operator Problem," *Proceedings of the Institute of Radio Engineers* 2, no. 3 (1914): 195–210; Susan Douglas, "Amateur Operators and American Broadcasting: Shaping the Future of Radio," in *Imagining Tomorrow: History, Technology, and the American Future*, ed. Joseph Corn (Cambridge, MA: MIT Press, 1986), 35–57.

52. "Boy Scouts: Scout Radio Commodore Perry's Plan," *New York Times*, January 1, 1922; Armstrong Perry, "Farm Boys to Be Government Messengers," *Farm Boys and Girls Leader* 2 (1920): 13; "Naval Radio Sends Boy Scout Messages Daily" *Electronics World* 3 (1921): 42; Noah Arceneaux, "Paul Reveres of Early Radio: The Boy Scouts and the Origins of Broadcasting," *Studies in Popular Culture* 31, no. 2 (2009): 81–100; "A Volunteer Radio Corps," *QST*, January 1916, 16; Edgar Felix, "Department of Defense," *QST*, February 1917, 20; Scott Hedberg, "The Army Amateur Radio System, 1925–1941," School of Advanced Military Studies, Fort Leavenworth, Kansas, 2010; "Great Radio Link in United States Is Approved by War Department: Communication Net from Coast to Coast Will Prove of Value in Time of National Emergency," *Albert Lea* [Minnesota] *Evening Tribune*, February 8, 1926; John Gray, "Boy Scout Radio," *QST*, January 1922, 22; "News of Boy Scouts: Wireless Class at Work. Troop One Makes Record. New Eagle Scouts. Scouts Advance in Rank. Receive Merit Badges. New Troop Papers. Camp Roosevelt Banquet. Among the Troops," *Washington Post*, December 18, 1921; "Radio Unit Entertains: Navy Instructors Aiding Long Beach Boys in Their Work; Now Planning Heliograph Tests," *Los Angeles Times*, March 4, 1923; A. H. Lynch, "What Radio Holds for Boy Scouts," *Radio Broadcast*, July 1923, 251–254; "Scout Membership Grows: Youth Presses National Champion for Archery Honors—Jury of Boys Sits in Wyoming Court, Scouts to Run Own Hospital," *Los Angeles Times*, September 2, 1923; Boy Scouts of America, *Merit Badge, Scout Radio* (1925); "Boy Scouts Will Get Radio Message from Navy Stations," *Los Angeles Times*, June 24, 1920; Armstrong Perry, "Scout Work," *QST*, November 1921, 58; "Are You Copying NAH Scout News?" *Boys' Life*, August 1920, 38; "Local Amateurs Hold Successful Convention," *Boston Daily Globe*, April 29, 1928; Thomas Stevenson, "Bureau Circulars Make Home Radio Set Building Easy," *Washington Post*, November 2, 1924; "Amateur Commends Navy's Radio Service," *New York Times*, December 25, 1922; "Attention, Boys of District," *Washington Post*, April 2, 1922. Previously, military officials had informally guided Scouts' radio

activities. For example, a Washington, D.C., Signal Corps instructor offered training to a local troop (see "Boy Scouts Begin Wireless Studies Under US Signal Corps Instructor," *Washington Post,* January 4, 1914). In Long Beach, navy officers assisted with youth training. Ad hoc efforts could be found in the postwar period, for example, in San Diego, where a radio school was set up in collaboration with ARRL to standardize the equipment and the people participating and to give them "real traffic to handle" while "not tying up the air with useless hamming." Many Scouts applied for radio operator licenses, but the arrangement required only radio receivers.

53. "Attention, Boys of District," *Washington Post,* April 2, 1922; "Boy Scouts: Scout Radio Commodore Perry's Plan," *New York Times,* January 1, 1922; "Boy Scouts," *New York Times,* April 8, 1923; "Boy Scouts Aid New England During Flood," *New York Times,* November 20, 1927; David Boydon, "Amateur Radio Work in New England Flood," *QST,* January 1928, 1–4; Scott Hedberg, "The Army Amateur Radio System, 1925–1941," School of Advanced Military Studies, Fort Leavenworth, Kansas, 2010; "Radio Amateurs and a Tornado," *Boys' Life,* December 1928, 37, 64; "Boy Scouts' Drill Thrills Big Crowd," *New York Times,* November 21, 1915; Armstrong Perry, "The Boy Scout's Place in the Radio Game," *Radio Broadcast,* February 1923), 275; Boy Scouts of America, *Merit Badge, Scout Radio,* 1925; "10,000,000 Boys Keen for Radio Wonders," *Washington Post,* May 18, 1924; "Boy Scouts' Receiving Contest," *Radio Broadcast,* July 1, 1923; Arthur Lynch, "What Radio Holds for Boy Scouts," *Radio Broadcast,* July 1, 1923, 251; Uthai Wilcox, "Making Home Interesting to the Boy," *Better Homes and Gardens,* November 1926, 11, 31–32; "Boy Scouts," *New York Times,* October 9, 1921; Noah Arceneaux, "Paul Reveres of Early Radio: The Boy Scouts and the Origins of Broadcasting," *Studies in Popular Culture* 31, no. 2 (2009): 81–100.

54. Henrietta Jessup, "These Recipes Earn Money," *Ladies' Home Journal,* September 1925, 129; "Hingham Girl Scouts Will Launch Drive for Purchase of Own Home," *Boston Daily Globe,* August 11, 1929; *Scouting for Girls: Official Handbook of the Girl Scouts,* 6th reprint, 1925 (copyright 1920); Girl Scouts of the United States of America, *Campward Ho! A Manual for Girl Scout Camps, Designed to Cover the Need of Those Undertaking to Organize and Direct Large, Self-Supporting Camps for Girls* (New York: Girl Scouts, 1920). Cookie sales were not Scouts' only fundraising technique: they put on Christmas markets, sold homemade and store-bought candy, and entertained with dramatic performances and fortune telling.

55. *Scouting for Girls: Official Handbook of the Girl Scouts,* 1920, 26; "Educational Work of the Girl Scouts," *Bulletin, US Bureau of Education* (1921), 11; "The Girl Scouts," *New York Times,* October 18, 1923.

56. *Scouting for Girls: Official Handbook of the Girl Scouts,* 1927, 5; "Educational Work of the Girl Scouts," *US Bureau of Education Bulletin* (1921), 11; "The Girl Scouts," *New York Times,* October 18, 1923; Elizabeth Kemper Adams and Eleanor Perry Wood, *A Five Year Experiment in Training Volunteer Group Leaders, 1922–27, Conducted by the Girl Scout National Organization* (New York: Girl Scouts of America, 1927); Boy Scouts of America, *Commission Report on Dividends of Scouting as Revealed by Established Facts,* 1928, in *Official Report of the Fifth National Training Conference of Scout Executives* (Ithaca, NY: BSA, 1928), 599–606; Boy Scouts of America, *Commission Report on Building Up Adequate Volunteer and Institutional Support,* in *Official Report of the Fifth National Training Conference of Scout Executives* (Ithaca, NY: BSA, 1928), 148–172; "Annual Scout Exhibit

Opens," *Los Angeles Times,* March 26, 1929; "Cookies for Clothes Is Girl Scout Motto," *Appleton Post-Crescent,* March 18, 1930; Boy Scouts of America, *Commission Report on Council Finance,* 1928, in *Official Report of the Fifth National Training Conference of Scout Executives* (Ithaca, NY: BSA, 1928); *Campward Ho!: A Manual for Girl Scout Camps* (New York: Girl Scouts of America, 1920), 21. (A Lone Scout program was available but not widely publicized for girls.)

57. Susan A. Miller, *Growing Girls: The Natural Origins of Girls' Organizations in America* (New Brunswick, NJ: Rutgers University Press, 2007), 58; "News of the Girl Scouts," *Washington Post,* March 28, 1926; "Pertinent Paragraphs on Atlanta Girl Scout Work," *Atlanta Constitution,* December 12, 1926; "Girls Scouts' Cookies Will Be Sold Today," *Boston Daily Globe,* November 3, 1923.

58. "Local Girl Scouts in New Activities," *Boston Daily Globe,* December 3, 1925; "New Jersey Girl Wins Scout Recipe Contest," *Detroit Free Press,* October 29, 1926; "Bought Cookies and 'Were Boys' Again," *Boston Daily Globe,* November 4, 1923; "Girl Scouts to Sell Cookies Today," *Detroit Free Press,* May 7, 1927; "Girl Scouts to Sell Cookies on Saturday," *Boston Daily Globe,* October 31, 1923; "Girls to Sell Cookies: Scouts start $439,703 Campaign for New Home Tomorrow," *New York Times,* October 19, 1923; "Cambridge Girl Scouts Have 'Cookie Day' for Camp Fund," *Boston Daily Globe,* February 6, 1926; "Girl Scouts' Cookies Will Be Sold Today," *Boston Daily Globe,* November 3, 1923; "Girl Scout Cookie Day," *Oak Parker,* December 2, 1927; "Cookies for Clothes Is Girl Scout Motto," *Appleton Post-Crescent,* March 18, 1930.

59. Viviana Zelizer, *Pricing the Priceless Child* (Princeton, NJ: Princeton University Press, 1994).

60. "Boy of 11 Years a 'Policeman,'" *Boston Daily Globe,* July 21, 1923; "Junior Police Force of Ann Arbor," *Detroit Free Press,* March 12, 1922; "St. Louis Plans Junior Police," *Detroit Free Press,* July 8, 1921; "Prepare to Cut Auto Accidents," *Boston Daily Globe,* September 2, 1927; "Call Radio Experts to Map Air Rules," *Washington Post,* February 10, 1922; Scott Hedberg, "The Army Amateur Radio System, 1925–1941," School of Advanced Military Studies, Fort Leavenworth, Kansas, 2010, 27; "The Signal Corps Affiliation with the Transmitting Radio Amateur," *Signal Corps Bulletin* 34 (May 1926): 41; "Here's a Big Wireless Opportunity," *Boys' Life,* December 1921, 26; Spark Gap, "For the Wireless Amateur," *Boys' Life,* June 1920, 42; V. F. Greaves, "The Radio Operator Problem," *Proceedings of the Institute of Radio Engineers* 2, no. 3 (1914): 195–210; "Radio Amateurs and a Tornado," *Boys' Life,* December 1928; "Girl Scouts Parade, Hold Review, and Plan Cookie Sale for 'Nest Egg,'" *Boston Daily Globe,* October 21, 1923; "Cambridge Girl Scouts Have 'Cookie Day' for Camp Fund," *Boston Daily Globe,* February 6, 1926; "Mrs. Coolidge Greets Girl Scouts," *New York Times,* October 18, 1923; "Cookies for Clothes Is Girl Scout Motto," *Appleton Post-Crescent,* March 18, 1930; "Girl Scouts of Hamilton," *Hamilton* [Ohio] *Evening Journal,* December 27, 1930; "Atlanta Girl Scouts Will Study Good Manners and Social Form," *Atlanta Constitution,* February 3, 1929; "Girl Scouts Plan Annual Cookie Day," *Detroit Free Press,* May 7, 1927; "Girls to Sell Cookies: Scouts Start $439,703 Campaign for New Home Tomorrow," *New York Times,* October 19, 1923; "Hingham Girl Scouts Will Launch Drive for Purchase of Own Home," *Boston Daily Globe,* August 11, 1929; Herbert Allen, "The Knighthood of Youth: The Story of a New Age of Chivalry," *Social Progress* 10-11 (1926): 28; Mary Haviland, "The Knighthood of Youth," *Child Welfare* 20 (1925): 149; "Nationwide Movement to Be Known as 'Knighthood of Youth' Inaugurated," *Brooklyn Standard Union,* January 2, 1925; *Knighthood of Youth: Order of Character* (New York: National

Child Welfare Association, 1925); *Self-Government in Education: A Digest of Ideas Favoring the Principle* (New York: National Child Welfare Association, 1925).

61. "Junior Traffic Police," *Boys' Workers Round Table* (1924); "Pupils as Traffic Police," *American School Board Journal* 65 (1922): 133; George L. Baker, "Portland School Boys Sign Up for Safety," *National Safety News*, June 1924, 17–18; Charles A. McCall, "Knights of the Crossroads," *National Safety News*, March 1925, 21–23; George B. Masslich, "Results of Safety Teaching in Chicago Schools," *National Safety News*, October 1924, 35–63; "Officer McBride and the Safety Scouts of Trenton," *National Safety News*, March 1923, 9–10; George Earl Wallis, "The Junior Safety Councils of Kansas City," *National Safety News*, February 1924, 5–9; George Earl Wallis, "Juniors Set the Pace in Louisville Safety Derby," *National Safety News*, August 1924, 11–12; Idabelle Stevenson, "Safety Education in Massachusetts," *Journal of Education* 102, no. 10 (2546) (September 24, 1925): 261–262; "Education in Action," *Journal of Education* 103, no. 8 (2568) (February 25, 1926): 218–220; *The Junior Safety Council: A Handbook of Extra-Curricular Safety Activities Containing Practical Program Suggestions and Information on Junior Safety Patrol Organization* (Chicago: National Safety Council, n.d.); "Auto Kills Boy Policeman in School Traffic; Hit as He Aids Pupils at Crossing," *Chicago Daily Tribune*, April 24, 1930; "School Pupils Have Own Court for Violators of Safety Rules," *Boston Daily Globe*, December 8, 1926; "School Board to Hear Safety Officer Shea," *Boston Daily Globe*, October 2, 1929; "Boy Scouts," *New York Times*, October 9, 1921; Louis Resnick, "Milwaukee Conducts Successful 'No Accident Week,'" *American City* 23 (1920): 531–535; *An Outline of Safety Education for Elementary Schools and Junior Safety Council Organizations* (Birmingham: School Safety Council, 1928), 5; Albert Whitney, "Safety Education in the Public Schools," *American Architect*, March 3, 1920, 297; "Let Us Make the Roads Safe," *Youth's Companion* (November 2, 1922): 628; James Franklin Chamberlin, "What Do You Think About It?" *Overland Monthly and Out West Magazine*, April 1928, 110; Fritz Blocki, "The Most Dangerous Job in the World," *Independent* (May 30, 1925, 605; "Boy Scouts: Fix Date for Paris Conference," *New York Times*, October 9, 1921.

62. "The Boy Scout Radio Operator's Place in the National Radio Systems," *Merit Badge Series, Radio* (New York: Boy Scouts of America, 1925), 17; Armstrong Perry, "Farm Boys to Be Government Messengers," *Farm Boys and Girls Leader* 3, no. 13 (1920); O. K. Sadtler, "Radio in the American Army," 10, 1930 research paper cited in Scott Hedberg, *The Army Amateur Radio System, 1925–1941*, School of Advanced Military Studies, Fort Leavenworth, 2010; "Youth Killed by Short Circuit at Radio Plant," *Chicago Daily Tribune*, February 18, 1928; "Radio Boon to American Boy," *Los Angeles Times*, June 15, 1924; "Boy Scouts: No Scouts in Juvenile Courts," *New York Times*, August 14, 1921; "Merit Badges Won by Scouts Grew in Number Last Year: Prison Commission's President Says Movement Should Be Used to Offset Criminal Influences," *New York Times*, February 20, 1927; "Prizes of $5,000 Offered by Radio Corporation," *Washington Post*, February 28, 1926; "Youth and Radio Join in Progress of New Science," *Atlanta Constitution*, March 29, 1925; "Declares Radio Is Farmers' Friend," *New York Times*, September 17, 1925; "News of the Scouts; Happenings in Radio Field: Troop 94 Is Praised by Scoutmaster, Attendance at Meetings and Ability in Work Lauded," *San Francisco Chronicle*, July 23, 1922; "Advances in Radio Are Largely Due to Boys, Says Expert," *Washington Post*, June 15, 1924; "Boy Scouts: The Museum in the Woods. Boy Scout Camps in New England. Scout Totem Pole. Photography Lessons. Camps with Museums. Dan Beard's Outdoor School. Electrically Lighted Camp. How It's Done in Texas. Good Turns at

Notes to Chapter 5   379

Lynn. Scout Radio Work. Learn by Doing," *New York Times*, July 24, 1921; Uthai Wilcox, "Making Home Interesting to the Boy," *Better Homes and Gardens*, November 1926, 11; "Boy Scouts," *New York Times*, May 11, 1924; "Scout Membership Grows: Youth Presses National Champion for Archery Honors—Jury of Boys Sits in Wyoming Court. Scouts to Run Own Hospital," *Los Angeles Times*, September 2, 1923; Howard Weeks, "Bedridden Lads Form Boy Scout Troop," *Detroit Free Press*, May 29, 1927; Ward Seeley, "The Boy Scouts Recruit Radio," *Wireless Age* 2 (1923): 277.

63. "Girl Scouts' Cookies Will Be Sold Today," *Boston Daily Globe*, November 3, 1923; "Cambridge Scouts to Have Cookie Day," *Boston Daily Globe*, October 22, 1926; "Girl Scout Cookies," *Boston Daily Globe*, November 4, 1923; Susan A. Miller, *Growing Girls: The Natural Origins of Girls' Organizations in America* (New Brunswick, NJ: Rutgers University Press, 2007); "Cambridge Girl Scouts to Have 'Cookie Day' for Camp Fund," *Boston Daily Globe*, February 6, 1926; "Girl Scouts of Hamilton: Cookie Sale Next Saturday," *Hamilton* [Ohio] *Evening Journal*, December 27, 1930; "Girl Scouts to Sell Cookies Today," *Detroit Free Press*, May 7, 1927; "Announce Plans for Cookie Sale by Girl Scouts," *Wisconsin State Journal*, February 10, 1929; "Girl Scout News," *Amarillo Sunday News and Globe*, April 7, 1929, 7; Stella Klopp, "A Critical Analysis of Current Newspapers and Magazines to Determine the Amount, Nature and Character of Home Economics Offerings to the Home and Community" (PhD diss., University of Southern California, 1928); *Scouting for Girls: Official Handbook of the Girl Scouts* (New York: Girl Scouts of America, 1920), 17. A few troops initially operated with vestiges of these concerns; in their first year of cookie sales Boston girls were permitted to bake and accompany chaperones to sell cookies but, adults took over when the money changed hands. Cookie sales were not always linked to cooking merit badges. In Cambridge, Massachusetts, only those who passed the cooking merit badge exam were drafted for baking service.

64. "Traffic to Be Bossed by Pupils," *Los Angeles Times*, September 13, 1926; "Scouts to Get Help in Radio Contest," *New York Times*, September 5, 1927; Ellsworth Collings and M. O. Wilson, *Psychology for Teachers: Purposive Behavior, the Foundation of Learning* (New York: Scribner's, 1930); "School Pupils Have Own Court for Violators of Safety Rules," *Boston Daily Globe*, December 8, 1926; "Asks Government Ban on Son's Radio Outfit: E. H. Palmer Says the Boy's Devotion to Station Ruins His Health and Schooling," *New York Times*, October 14, 1927; "Radio Department: Radio Grips Boys of School Ages. School Boys Have Been Among First in Experimentation in Wireless. Have Clubs," *Atlanta Constitution*, May 25, 1922; "Youth Deprived of Radio License," *Atlanta Constitution*, October 15, 1927.

65. Joseph Kett, *Rites of Passage: Adolescence in America, 1790 to the Present* (New York: Basic Books, 1977); Walter Stone, *The Development of Boys' Work in the United States* (Nashville: Vanderbilt University, 1933), 2, 66. Stone does in fact cover George's contributions in his book.

66. Erving Goffman, *Frame Analysis* (New York: Harper and Row, 1974), 560–561; Miles Orvell, *The Real Thing: Imitation and Authenticity in American Culture, 1880–1940* (Chapel Hill: University of North Carolina Press, 1989); Michael Taussig, *Mimesis and Alterity: A Particular History of the Senses* (New York: Routledge, 1993).

67. George Herbert Mead, *The Philosophy of the Present* (London: Open Court, 1932),169; George Herbert Mead, *Mind, Self and Society* (Chicago: University of Chicago Press, 1934), 151, 154; George Herbert Mead, *The Individual and the Social Self* (Chicago: University of Chicago Press, 1982).

68. William Graebner, *The Engineering of Consent: Democracy and Authority in Twentieth-Century America* (Madison: University of Wisconsin Press, 1987); A. Paul Hare, "The History and Present State of Small Group Research," in *Handbook of Small Group Research* (Glencoe, IL: Free Press, 1966); George Herbert Mead, *Mind, Self and Society* (Chicago: University of Chicago Press, 1934), 157.

69. L. L. Bernard, *An Introduction to Social Psychology* (New York: Holt, 1926), 21, 335; L. L. Thurstone, "Attitudes Can Be Measured,' *American Journal of Sociology* 33 (1928), 529–554; L. L. Thurstone, "The Measurement of Opinion," *Journal of Abnormal and Social Psychology* (1928): 415–430; L. L. Thurstone, "The Method of Paired Comparisons for Social Values," *Journal of Abnormal and Social Psychology* 21, 4 (1927): 384–400; L. L. Thurstone, "The Measurement of Psychological Value," in *Essays in Philosophy by Seventeen Doctors of Philosophy of the University of Chicago*, ed. Thomas Vernor Smith and William Kelley Wright (Chicago: Open Court, 1929): 157–174; L. L. Thurstone, "The Experimental Study of Nationality Preferences," *Journal of General Psychology* 1 (1928): 405–425; L. L. Thurstone, "Theory of Attitude Measurement," *Psychological Review* 36, no. 3 (1928): 222–241; L. L. Thurstone and E. J. Chave, *The Measurement of Attitude* (Chicago: University of Chicago Press, 1929); L. L. Thurstone, "A Scale for Measuring Attitude toward the Movies," *Journal of Educational Research* 22 (1930): 89–94; Jean Converse, "Attitude Measurement in Psychology and Sociology: The Early Years," in *Surveying Subjective Phenomena*, vol. 2, ed. Charles Turner and Elizabeth Martin (New York: Russell Sage Foundation, 1984), 3–40. L. L. Bernard, *An Introduction to Social Psychology* (New York: Holt, 1926), has a comprehensive bibliography of research in this area. Bernard more clearly illustrates his grounding in sociology in "A Classification of Environments," *American Journal of Sociology* 31, no. 3 (1925): 318–325.

70. Martin Bulmer, *The Chicago School of Sociology* (Chicago: University of Chicago Press, 1984); Robert Park, "The Natural History of the Newspaper," *American Journal of Sociology* 29 (1923), 277; Robert Park, "Urbanization as Measured by Newspaper Circulation," *American Journal of Sociology* 35 (1929), 60–79; Frederick Detweiler, *The Negro Press in the United States* (Chicago: University of Chicago Press, 1922); Robert Park, *The Immigrant Press and Its Control* (New York: Harper, 1922); Robert Ezra Park "Foreign Language Press and Social Process," *Proceedings of the National Conference of Social Work* (1920): 493–500; Robert E. Park, "Social Attitudes," in Robert E. Park and Ernest W. Burgess, *Introduction to the Science of Sociology* (Chicago: University of Chicago Press, 1921), 467–478, originally published in Robert E. Park, *Principles of Human Behavior* (Chicago: Zalaz, 1915), 18–34; Jennifer Light, *The Nature of Cities* (Baltimore: Johns Hopkins University Press, 2009); Charles Merriam, *New Aspects of Politics* (Chicago: University of Chicago, 1925); Charles Merriam, "Recent Advances in Political Methods," *American Political Science Review* 17 (1923): 275–295; Charles E. Merriam, *The Making of Citizens* (Chicago: University of Chicago Press, 1931); Harold Gosnell, *Getting Out the Vote: An Experiment in the Stimulation of Voting* (Chicago: University of Chicago, 1927); Harold Gosnell, "An Experiment in the Stimulation of Voting," *American Political Science Review* 20, no. 4 (1926): 869–874; Michael T. Heaney and John Mark Hansen, "Building the Chicago School," *American Political Science Review* 100, no. 4 (November 2006): 589–596; Charles Merriam, "The Significance of Psychology for the Study of Politics," *American Political Science Review* 18, no. 3 (August 1924): 469–488; Robert D. Leigh, "Public Opinion," *American Political Science Review* 20, no. 2 (May 1926): 404–407; Harold Lasswell, *Propaganda Technique in the War* (New York: Peter Smith, 1928), 8–9; Harold Lasswell, "The Measurement of Public Opinion," *American*

Political Science Review 25, no. 2 (May 1931): 311–326; Harold Lasswell, "Prussian Schoolbooks and International Amity," *Journal of Social Forces* 3 (1925): 718–722; Walter Lippmann, *Public Opinion* (New York: Harcourt, Brace, 1922).

71. E. S. Jones, "Opinions of College Students," *Journal of Applied Psychology* 10 (1926): 427–436; Eliot Porter, "Student Opinion on War: An Investigation" (PhD diss., University of Chicago, 1926); Harry Moor, "The Comparative Influence of Majority and Expert Opinion," *American Journal of Psychology* 32 (1921): 16–20; David Wheeler and Harry Jordan, "Change of Individual Opinion to Accord with Group Opinion," *Journal of Abnormal and Social Psychology* 24 (1929): 203–206; Walter Reckless, "The Natural History of Vice Areas in Chicago" (PhD diss., University of Chicago, 1925); Frederic M. Thrasher, "The Boys' Club Study," *Journal of Educational Sociology* 6, no. 1 (September 1932): 4–16; Frederic M. Thrasher, "Ecological Aspects of the Boys' Club Study," *Journal of Educational Sociology* 6, no. 1 (September 1932): 52–58; William I. Thomas and Dorothy Swaine Thomas, *The Child in America* (New York: Knopf, 1928); Jennifer Light, *The Nature of Cities* (Baltimore: Johns Hopkins University Press, 2009); Paul Cressey, "The Motion Picture Experience as Modified by Social Background and Personality," *American Sociological Review* 3 (August 1938): 516–525; Dana Polan, *Scenes of Instruction: The Beginnings of the U.S. Study of Film* (Berkeley: University of California Press, 2007); Mark Lynn Anderson, "Taking Liberties: The Payne Fund Studies and the Creation of the Media Expert," in *Inventing Film Studies*, ed. Lee Grieveson and Haidee Wasson (Durham, NC: Duke University Press, 2008); Paul Cressey, "The Motion Picture as Informal Education," *Journal of Educational Sociology* 7, no. 8 (1934): 504–515; Frederic Thrasher, "A Study of the Total Situation," *Journal of Educational Sociology* 1 (April 1928): 477–491, 599–613; Walter Stone, *The Development of Boys' Work in the United States* (Nashville: Vanderbilt University, 1933), 136; Charles E. Merriam, *The Making of Citizens* (Chicago: University of Chicago Press, 1931); Bessie Pierce, *Civic Attitudes in American School Textbooks* (Chicago: University of Chicago Press, 1930). On developmental psychology in the period, see Olive A. Wheeler, *Youth: The Psychology of Adolescence and Its Bearing on the Reorganization of Adolescent Education* (London: University of London Press, 1929; Leta Hollingsworth, *The Psychology of the Adolescent* (New York: Appleton, 1930).

72. Frederic Thrasher, *The Gang* (Chicago: University of Chicago Press, 1927), 291.

73. Frederic Thrasher, *The Gang* (Chicago: University of Chicago Press, 1927). Notably, there were some other scholars who questioned the value of Scouting and other organizations in this period as delinquency reduction tools. See Harold Levy, *Building a Popular Movement* (New York: Russell Sage Foundation, 1944), 88.

74. Frederic Thrasher, *The Gang* (Chicago: University of Chicago Press, 1927), 251, 355, 363; "Governing Themselves," *Youth's Companion* 79, no. 37 (September 14, 1905): 426; F. Allison Adams, "Police and Boy Groups Combine to Stop Crime," *New York Times*, March 8, 1925; Orange McMeans, "Boy Scouts Form Boy Gangs," *Survey* (March 1929): 54–59. Other work on public opinion and crime in this period included E. H. Sutherland, "Public Opinion as a Cause of Crime," *Journal of Applied Sociology* 9 (1924): 51–56. Notably, Thrasher was one of several Chicago sociologists to touch on the junior republic movement. See, for example, William I. Thomas and Dorothy Swaine Thomas, *The Child in America* (New York: Knopf, 1928), 121, 123, and an unpublished paper by Ernest Burgess referenced in Courtland Van Vechten's dissertation. Robert

Park had written about it during his earlier career as a journalist. See Robert Park, "Experiments in Child Human Nature," *New-York Tribune,* September 15, 1907.

75. Frederic Thrasher, *The Gang* (Chicago: University of Chicago Press, 1927), 251; Emory S. Bogardus, "Mirrored Nature," in *Fundamentals of Social Psychology* (New York: Century, 1924), 65–74.

76. "Miniature City Government Conducted by Public School Pupils in New York," *Washington Post Sunday Magazine,* March 25, 1906; Frederick Elmer Bolton, *Principles of Education* (New York: Scribner's, 1910); L. B. Stowe to Mr. G. A. Lightner, June 14, 1912, box 12, folder 10, WG Papers; "Ithacans Want to Join the Militia," *Syracuse Journal,* August 29, 1914; "National Guard Talk Revived," *Syracuse Post-Standard*, August 22, 1914; "'Daddy' George has brand new scheme; would form junior municipal government in all cities allowing boys and girls to vote for their own officers at the age of 16," *Ithaca Daily News* April 7, 1913; "Boys Form Two Political Parties," *Indianapolis Star,* July 28, 1907; James Rogers, *The State of Columbia, a Junior Republic* (San Francisco: Recorder Press, 1903); "Progress of the Schools," *Omaha Daily Bee,* November 26, 1899; "New York Boys Elect Playground City Mayor," *Los Angeles Herald,* August 17, 1905; Homer Lane to L. B. Stowe, June 11, 1912, box 12, folder 9, WG Papers; Speech, "Progress City: An Answer to the Demand for a Civic Education," folder 3, Progress City, ca. 1906–1920, HH Records MS 3319; Ludwig Bernstein, "Modern Tendencies in Jewish Orphan Asylum Work," *Annual Report of the Hebrew Sheltering Guardian Society,* 1907/1909, box 1, folder 4, Annual Reports (bound) 1905–1909, Records of the Hebrew Sheltering Guardian Society of New York, Center for Jewish History.

77. George Alonzo Mirick, *Progressive Education* (Boston: Houghton Mifflin, 1923), 158; Harry McKown, *The Student Council* (New York: McGraw-Hill, 1944; "Boy Scouts Must Be Like Daring Men," *New York Times,* October 9, 1910; *Handbook for Scoutmasters, A Manual of Troop Leadership* (New York: Boy Scouts of America, 1947), 11. On the continuation of dramatic methods in teaching, see Edgar Dale, *Audio-Visual Methods in Teaching* (New York: Dryden, 1946); Edward Olsen, *School and Community: The Philosophy, Procedures, and Problems of Community Study and Service through Schools and Colleges* (New York: Prentice Hall, 1945). I have written elsewhere about midcentury simulation-gaming, one example of this work. See Jennifer Light, "Taking Games Seriously," *Technology and Culture* 49 (2008), 347–375. Contemporary examples include Steven Hoffman, "Simulation as a Social Process in Organizations," *Sociology Compass* 1, no. 2 (2007): 613–636; and Catherine Lutz, *Homefront: A Military City and the American Twentieth Century* (Boston: Beacon, 2001). Other examples could include token economies, reality practice, and psychodrama. See Teodoro Ayllon and Nathan Azrin, *The Token Economy: A Motivational System for Therapy and Rehabilitation* (New York: Appleton-Century-Crofts, 1968); Eberhard Scheiffle, "The Theater of Truth: Psychodrama, Spontaneity and Improvisation; The Theatrical Theories and Influences of Jacob Levy Moreno," (PhD diss., University of California, Berkeley, 1995). Alvin Zander and Ronald Lippitt, "Reality Practice as Educational Method," *Sociometry* 7, no. 2 (May 1944): 129–151.

78. Frederic Thrasher, *The Gang* (Chicago: University of Chicago Press, 1927), 230–231. Others who took this view included William Healy and Augusta F. Bronner, *Delinquents and Criminals: Their Making and Unmaking, Studies in Two American Cities,* Judge Baker Foundation Publication no. 3 (New York: Macmillan, 1926), viii, 317; and Ben Lindsey, "The Movies Pro & Con," in *The Movies on Trial,* ed. William Perlman (New York: Macmillan, 1936). "Classification of Educational

Radio Research," issued by Federal Radio Education Committee with the cooperation of the US Office of Education, Federal Security Agency, Washington, DC, 1941, by HM Belleville, Research Manager, National Broadcasting Company; Cuthbert Daniel, Office of Radio Research, Columbia University, record group 119, Records of the National Youth Administration, Records of the Radio Projects Section, Fragment File of Robert B. Burton, Radio Engineer and Section Chief, Concerning NYA Amateur Radio Stations and Licenses, 1940–1942, box 1, National Archives and Records Administration (hereafter NARA).

79. Walter Stone, *The Development of Boys' Work in the United States* (Nashville: Vanderbilt University, 1933); George A. Coe, "The Children's Republic: A Christmas Story for Grown-Ups," *Association Monthly*, December 1921, 474–475; George A. Coe, *What Ails Our Youth* (New York: Scribner's, 1924); George A. Coe, "A Study in Civic Training," *Pedagogical Seminary* 29, no. 3 (1922): 205–231; David MacLeod, *Building Character in the American Boy* (Madison: University of Wisconsin Press, 2004); Harold D. Meyer, *A Handbook of Extra-Curricular Activities in the High School* (New York: Barnes, 1926); Louise Jerrel, "A Club Experiment in the Amos Hiatt Junior High School," *Elementary School Journal* 27, no. 7 (1927): 511–527; Ronald Wolters, *The New Negro on Campus: Black College Rebellions of the 1920s* (Princeton, NJ: Princeton University Press, 1975); Jasper Palmer, "The Democratizing Influences of the Schools of Today," *Elementary School Journal* 4, no. 6 (1924): 464–467; Frederic Thrasher, "The Sociological Approach to Educational Problems," *Journal of Educational Sociology* 9, no. 8 (1936): 476; R. D. Shouse, "High-School Clubs," *School Review* 36, no. 2 (1928): 141–146; "227,201 Enrolled in 296 Boys' Clubs," *New York Times*, January 15, 1928; Elbert K. Fretwell, *Extra-Curricular Activities in Secondary Schools* (Boston: Houghton, Mifflin, 1931); Jennifer Light, "Putting Our Conversation in Context," in *From Voice to Influence*, ed. D. Allen and J. Light (Chicago: University of Chicago Press, 2015). College enrollments also increased, but the numbers were comparatively few; see Paula Fass, *The Damned and the Beautiful: American Youth in the 1920's* (Oxford: Oxford University Press, 1977).

80. "Prisons and Criminals," *Austin Statesman*, January 11, 1922; "Jennings Uses War Experience in Rilling Prison," *New York Herald Tribune*, December 12, 1929; "Prison Reform at Portsmouth Killed," *Boston Daily Globe*, July 22, 1921; "A Prison Reformer," *New York Times*, October 22, 1926; Stephanie E. Przybylek, *Around Auburn* (Mount Pleasant, SC: Arcadia, 1998), 44; L. Demuth, "Communications: Industrial Democracy," *Survey* 43 (November 15, 1919): 130; Norman Thomas, *What is Industrial Democracy* (League for Industrial Democracy, 1925); Norval Morris, *The Oxford History of the Prison: The Practice of Punishment in Western Society* (New York: Oxford, 1997); "The Prison Revolts," *New York Herald Tribune*, July 30, 1929; "1,700 Auburn Convicts Mutiny, 2 Slain, 16 Shot in 5-Hour Fight," *New York Herald Tribune*, July 28, 1929; Herbert Carpenter, "Thomas Mott Osborne," *New York Times*, October 22, 1926; "Prison Problems Bring 1000 delegates here," *Boston Daily Globe*, September 9, 1923; John Walker Harrington, "Demands for State Prison Reforms Revived by the Riots at Auburn and More," *New York Herald Tribune*, August 4, 1929; James Hepbron, "The Waning of the Prison Club: Recent Penitentiary Riots in Light of the Osborne System," *Sun*, February 9, 1930; "Sing Sing Ready for Emergency, Lawes Asserts," *New York Herald Tribune*, July 30, 1929; "Prisons and Criminals," *Austin Statesman*, January 11, 1922; Laura Edge, *Locked Up: A History of the US Prison System* (Minneapolis: Twenty-First Century Books, 2009), 41; A. H. Wyman, "Recreation in Industrial Communities," *American Physical Education*

Review 24, no. 9 (1919): 477; A.H. Wyman, "Community Recreation as Part of Americanization Work," *Annual Proceedings of the National Association of Corporation Training* (1921), 888–892; "Any American Boy May Be President One of These Days and These Promising Young Officials of the Playground City of the Mingo Steel Works of the Carnegie Steel Company, Mingo, Ohio, Are Getting Good Training for Citizenship Either in Office or Out," photograph in *Playground* (December 1922), 394; "Boy Scouts News and Notes: Northern States," *Boys' Life*, October 1911, 30; "Manufacturers to Instruct Workmen," *Pittsburgh Gazette Times*, May 29, 1916; F. C. Henderschott, "The National Association of Corporation Schools," *Transactions of the American Institute of Electrical Engineers*, 1913; "Metropolitan Encourages Scout Movement," *Standard*, November 29, 1913; Mary Parker Follett, *The New State: Group Organization the Solution of Popular Government* (New York: Longman, Green, 1918); *Welfare Work for Policy-Holders* (New York: Metropolitan Life Insurance, 1915), 15; R. W. Corwin, "Our New Work," *Proceedings of the Annual Meeting of the National Civic Federation New York, November 22 and 23, 1909* (1910); "Group Organization," *Playground* 11 (1917): 170–171; Arthur James Todd, *Theories of Social Progress: A Critical Study of the Attempts to Formulate the Conditions of Human Advance* (New York: Macmillan, 1918), 530; Andrea Tone, *The Business of Benevolence* (Ithaca, NY: Cornell University Press, 1997); William Graebner, *The Engineering of Consent: Democracy and Authority in Twentieth-Century America* (Madison: University of Wisconsin Press, 1987); Dexter Simpson Kimball, *Plant Management*, Alexander Hamilton Institute, 1922, 309; "Gulf, Mobile & Northern Interests Boys in Safety," *Railway Age* 88, no. 23 (June 7, 1930): 1370; Harriet Jane Comstock, *A Study of Girls Work in Chicago, Prepared Under the Direction of the Committee on Girls Work of the Chicago Council of Social Agencies*, 1924; Louis Lyons, "New State Prison to Be Unlike Anything in the World," *Boston Daily Globe*, January 5, 1930; L. H. Robbins, "Where Prisoners Help to Run a Prison," *New York Times*, March 2, 1930; "Stone Walls Do Not Make this Maryland Test Prison," *Christian Science Monitor*, July 28, 1932; "Jail Within a Jail One of Features that Make Norfolk Prison Different," *Christian Science Monitor*, January 11, 1932; William Bilevitz, "Higher Education in the Prison," *Sun*, August 30, 1931; Louis Lyons, "Job and Hobby for Each Prisoner," *Boston Daily Globe*, July 3, 1932; "Teaching Convicts Community Life," *Boston Daily Globe*, January 11, 1932; "Reduced Terms Urged as Pay for Prisoners," *New York Herald Tribune*, January 5, 1931. Notably, although evidence showed many productive outcomes from the Mutual Welfare League at Portsmouth's highly conservative naval base, Osborne's intolerance of naval protocols and customs—and the growing sense that prisoners led freer lives than many sailors on shipboard—ultimately led to his departure, and the league disbanded soon after. Rodney Watterson, *Whips to Walls: Naval Discipline from Flogging to Progressive Era Reform at Portsmouth Prison* (Annapolis, MD: Naval Institute Press, 2014).

81. Frederic Thrasher, *The Gang* (Chicago: University of Chicago Press, 1927), 35, 37; Jasper Palmer, "The Democratizing Influences of the Schools of Today," *Elementary School Journal* 24, no. 6 (1924): 464–467; Frederic Thrasher, "The Sociological Approach to Educational Problems," *Journal of Educational Sociology* 9, no. 8 (1936): 476; Paula Fass, *The Damned and the Beautiful: American Youth in the 1920's* (Oxford: Oxford University Press, 1977); Ronald Wolters, *The New Negro on Campus: Black College Rebellions of the 1920s* (Princeton, NJ: Princeton University Press, 1975); Jennifer Light, "Putting Our Conversation in Context," in *From Voice to Influence*, ed. D. Allen and J. Light (Chicago: University of Chicago Press, 2015).

82. *Life of the Boys Brotherhood Republic* (Chicago: BBR, 1938); "Boy Republic's First Citizens Recall When Living Was Fighting," *Chicago Daily Tribune,* February 21, 1927; Stanley High and Herbert Paus, "Young Men in America," *Los Angeles Times,* August 20, 1939; "Young Reds Fight Police at Rally," *New York Times,* March 23, 1930; Jennifer Light, "Putting Our Conversation in Context," in *From Voice to Influence,* ed. D. Allen and J. Light (Chicago: University of Chicago Press, 2015); Robert Cohen, *When the Old Left Was Young: Student Radicals and America's First Mass Student Movement, 1929–1941* (New York: Oxford University Press, 1993); Robert G. Spivack, "The Growth of an American Youth Movement 1905–1941," *American Scholar* 10 (1941): 352–361; Arthur Clifford, *The Truth About the American Youth Congress,* Hotel Stattler, Detroit, Michigan: Committee of 76, American Youth Congress, 1935; William Hinckley, *Youth Seeks Peace, Freedom and Progress* (New York: National Council American Youth Congress, 1936); *Program of American Youth Congress* (New York: Continuations Committee, American Youth Congress, 1934); William Hinckley, *American Youth Acts: The Story of the American Youth Congress* (New York: National Council, American Youth Congress, 1936). There were earlier, small-scale stories. For example, "Boy City Defied Police to Help Fugitive; Wins" (*Chicago Daily Tribune,* August 10, 1920, 17) tells the story of how Arthur Shaffer played hooky from school and was sentenced to Parental School. He escaped and went to "the Northwest Boy City at 1208 Hoyne Avenue" where "the mayor of the boys' city, Dave Breitbart, 17 years old, and his investigating committee, consisting of Saul Goldman, 14, and Milton Jaffee, 14, delivered an ultimatum to the probation officers which provided that Arthur would be sent back to the Parental School on condition that his hair would not be clipped, that he would not be sent to St. Charles reformatory for the usual two year term given runaways, and that he would be paroled to the republic on Sept 14." They agreed to the terms. The following directory listed BBR as one of Chicago's "civic agencies." *Chicago Civic Agencies: A Directory of Associations of Citizens of Chicago* (Chicago: Union League Club Public Affairs Committee and University of Chicago Local Community Research Committee, 1927).

83. Louise Arnold Menefee, *American Youth: An Annotated Bibliography* (Washington, DC: American Council on Education, 1938); Merritt Madison Chambers, *Youth-Serving Organizations* (Washington, DC: American Council on Education, American Youth Commission, 1937); E. Franklin Frazier, *Negro Youth at the Crossways, Their Personality Development in the Middle States* (Washington, DC: American Youth Commission, 1940); H. P. Rainey, *The Plans of the American Youth Commission* (Washington, DC: American Council on Education, 1936); Richard Reiman, *The New Deal and American Youth: Ideas and Ideals in a Depression Decade* (Athens: University of Georgia Press, 2010); Robert G. Spivack, "The Growth of an American Youth Movement 1905–1941," *American Scholar* 10 (1941); Philip Altbach and Patti Peterson, "Before Berkeley: Historical Perspectives on American Student Activism," *Annals of the American Association of Political and Social Science* 395 (1971): 1–14; M. M. Chambers, "Organized Youth in America," *Journal of Educational Sociology* 11 (February 1938): 351–359; W. H. Cowley, "Student Unrest in Perspective," in *Conflict and Change on the Campus,* ed. William Brickman (New York: School and Society Books, 1973); Frank Ellsworth and Martha Burns, *Student Activism in American Higher Education* (Washington, DC: American College Personnel Association, 1970); John E. Kelly, "Little Red Schoolboys," *America* 60 (January 14, 1939): 344–345; Lombard Lee, "Imitative Youth," *Educational Forum* 3 (November 1938): 13–37; *Congressional Record,* Model Congress of Youth, Fourth Annual Session, Milwaukee,

July 2–5, 1937; Erik Gelman, *Death Blow to Jim Crow: The National Negro Congress and the Rise of Militant Civil Rights* (Chapel Hill: University of North Carolina Press, 2012); *Official Proceedings: Second All-Southern Negro Youth Conference, Chattanooga, Tenn., April 1–3, 1938* (Richmond, VA: Southern Negro Youth Congress, 1938); William Hinckley, *Youth Speaks for Itself* (New York: American Youth Congress, 1935, 1936) Johnetta Richard, "The Southern Negro Youth Congress: A History" (PhD thesis, University of Cincinnati, 1987); Britt Haas, "As They Saw the Thirties" (PhD diss., State University of New York, Albany, 2011); Thomas F. Neblett, "Youth Movements in the United States," *Annals of the American Association of Political and Social Science* 194 (1937): 141–151; Philip G. Altbach, *Student Politics in America* (New York: McGraw-Hill, 1974); Robert Cohen, *When the Old Left Was Young: Student Radicals and America's First Mass Student Movement, 1929–1941* (New York: Oxford University Press, 1993); Hal Draper, "The Student Movement of the Thirties: A Political History," in *As We Saw the Thirties*, ed. Rita Simon (Urbana: University of Illinois Press, 1969); Eileen Pagen, *Class, Culture and the Classroom: The Student Peace Movement of the 1930s* (Philadelphia: Temple University Press, 1982); Patti Peterson, "The Young Socialist Movement in America from 1905 to 1940: A Study of the Young People's Socialist League" (PhD diss., University of Wisconsin, 1974); Rebecca de Schweinitz, *If We Could Change the World* (Chapel Hill: University of North Carolina Press, 2009); *Youth: Journal of the Model Congress of the United States, Milwaukee* (New York: American Youth Congress, 1937); Lael Moon, "Youth Section Participates in Model Congress," *Proceedings of the American Country Life Association Conference* 20 (1938); Edith Ellen Ware and James Thomson Shotwell, American National Committee on International Intellectual Cooperation, *The Study of International Relations in the United States* (New York: Columbia University Press, 1938).

84. Walter Stone, *The Development of Boys' Work in the United States* (Nashville: Vanderbilt University, 1933), 136; Lombard Lee, "Imitative Youth," *Educational Forum* 3 (November 1938): 13–37; William George, *The Adult Minor* (New York: Appleton, 1937); Harold D. Lasswell and Dorothy Blumenstock, *World Revolutionary Propaganda: A Chicago Study* (New York: Alfred A. Knopf, 1939); Kathleen Jones, *Taming the Troublesome Child: American Families, Child Guidance, and the Limits of Psychiatric Authority* (Cambridge, MA: Harvard University Press, 1999); Richard Reiman, *The New Deal and American Youth: Ideas and Ideals in a Depression Decade* (Athens: University of Georgia Press, 2010); Stanley High, *The Revolt of Youth* (Nashville: Abingdon Press, 1923); Dave Nelson, "Camp Roosevelt: A Case Study of the NYA in Florida," *Florida Historical Quarterly* 86, no. 2 (Fall 2007): 162–185; A. D. Brown, *Youth Movements in the United States and Foreign Countries: Including a Section on the National Youth Administration*, US Library of Congress Division of Bibliography, June 12, 1936; Harvey Zorbaugh "Which Way America's Youth?" *Journal of Educational Sociology* 11, no. 6 (February 1938): 322–334. On young people's disproportionate unemployment, overseas youth movements, and fears of youth revolts in the US, see *Final Report of the National Youth Administration, Fiscal Years 1936–1943*, 83. However, it should be noted, the crime wave was a "state of mind" in Chicago and many other communities where delinquency was actually on the decline. Frederic Thrasher, *The Gang* (Chicago: University of Chicago Press, 1927), 230–231; William Healy and Augusta F. Bronner, *Delinquents and Criminals: Their Making and Unmaking, Studies in Two American Cities,* Judge Baker Foundation Publication No. 3 (New York: Macmillan, 1926), viii, 317; Ben Lindsey, "*The Movies Pro & Con*," in *The Movies on Trial*, ed. William Perlman (New York: Macmillan, 1936).

85. George Herbert Mead, *Mind, Self and Society* (Chicago: University of Chicago Press, 1934), 309.

86. Historians have observed the expanding conceptions of youth in the period. See Leta Hollingsworth, *The Psychology of the Adolescent* (New York: Appleton, 1930); William George, *The Adult Minor* (New York: Appleton, 1937); "Educators Forecast Lines of Progress in 1938," *New York Times*, January 2, 1938; Peter Blos, *The Adolescent Personality* (New York: D. Appleton Century, 1941); "Progressive Cities Stimulate Recreation for Negroes," *New Journal and Guide* (May 24, 1924): 9; Thomas Earl Sullenger, *Social Determinants in Juvenile Delinquency* (New York: Wiley, 1936); Patricia Clement, *Growing Pains: Children in the Industrial Age* (New York: Twayne, 1997); Rebecca de Schweinitz, *If We Could Change the World* (Chapel Hill: University of North Carolina Press. 2009), 162; Katharine DuPre Lumpkin and Dorothy Wolff Douglas, *Child Workers in America* (Freeport, NY: Books for Libraries Press, 1937); Charles H. Judd, "Federal Youth Services and the Schools," *NASSP Bulletin* 24 (1940): 15; Floyd W. Reeves and Howard M. Bell, "The Needs of Youth in Modern America," *NASSP Bulletin* 24 (1940): 7.

87. Lists of citizens over/under 16, box 4, folder 6, WG Papers; Memo from Spencer Miller "Confidential Memorandum," 1921, box 23, folder 21, WG Papers; "A 'Junior Republic' for Negro Boys Established Near Washington, DC: It is an improvement on other schools of the same kind and is doing as great a work as Booker T. Washington's School at Tuskegee, Alabama," *St. Louis Post-Dispatch*, September 2, 1900; "Out of the Gutter," *Los Angeles Times*, August 26, 1900; "Another Junior Republic," *New York Evangelist*, November 2, 1899, 19; "Junior Republic at Playground," *Los Angeles Times*, November 12, 1911; W. S. Scarborough, "The Negro Criminal Class—How Best Reached," *Voice of the Negro*, December 1, 1905, 867.

Chapter 6

1. The following are from WG Papers: Albert Howson to Edo Freeborn, December 19, 1932, box 33, folder 25; Untitled, September 26, 1932, box 33, folder 18; William George to George Christiancy, July 16, 1921, box 23, folder 2; *New York Times*, November 27, 1932, clipping reporting a new Warner Brothers picture, box 33, folder 22; Correspondence between William George and Warner Brothers, for example, William George to Warner Brothers, December 10, 1932, box 33, folder 24; Albert Howson to John Strain, December 16, 1932, box 33, folder 25; Correspondence between ex-citizens and Warner Brothers, box 33, folder 25; William George to Isador Witmark, box 33, folder 29; Correspondence with Warner Brothers, box 33, folder 30. Studio executives told George they would retitle the film *Reform School* and not refer to Freeville. The picture they ultimately released, *Mayor of Hell* (1933) starring James Cagney, portrayed the introduction of self-government at a state reformatory—loosely but unmistakably based on the George Junior Republic. As George put it, "No motorists would have stopped in front of any institution or boarding school...even one with a cottage system and mistake it for an American village." Untitled, August 21, 1935, box 35, folder 31, WG Papers.

2. Joseph M. Hawes, *Children Between the Wars: American Childhood, 1920–1940* (New York: Twayne, 1997); Paula Fass, *The Damned and the Beautiful: American Youth in the 1920's* (Oxford: Oxford University Press, 1977); H. M. Donovan, "The Age Factor," in *Advertising Response* (Philadelphia: Lippincott, 1924); Lisa Jacobsen, *Raising Consumers* (New York: Columbia University

Press, 2005); Rebecca de Schweinitz, *If We Could Change the World* (Chapel Hill: University of North Carolina Press, 2009); Viviana Zelizer, *Pricing the Priceless Child* (Princeton, NJ: Princeton University Press, 1994); David MacLeod, *The Age of the Child: Children in America 1890–1920* (New York: Twayne, 1998); Joseph Kett, *Rites of Passage: Adolescence in America, 1790 to the Present* (New York: Basic, 1977).

3. Walter Lippmann, *Public Opinion* (New York: Harcourt, Brace, 1922).

4. "Daddy George Gravely Ill After Operation," *Auburn Citizen*, March 20, 1929. The following are from WG Papers: William George to the board of trustees of the George Junior Republic Association, July 10, 1935, box 35, folder 27; William George, "Reason," August 16, 1935, box 35, folder 31; William George, untitled, August 19, 1935, box 35, folder 31; William George, untitled, August 20, 1935, box 35, folder 31; Mrs. Daddy to ex-citizens, July 25, 1932, box 33, folder 13; "Junior Citizens League," box 22, folder 4; William George to Paul Bolliger, October 19, 1934, box 35, folder 8; S. J. Phillips (judge) to Jacob Smith, September 8, 1930, box 32, folder 8; Judge Ann Kashmer to Jacob Smith, March 15, 1932, box 33, folder 4; John E. Rawley to Jacob Smith, March 15, 1932, box 33, folder 4; William George, "A Righteous Cause Founded on Justice Must Live," August 31, 1935, box 35, folder 31.

5. The following are from WG Papers: William George to Agnes Stebbins, March 28, 1932, box 33, folder 5; William George to Thomas Dixey, February 23, 1933, box 33, folder 35; Untitled, July 10, 1934, box 35, folder 2; Edo Freeborn to Honorable Clayton Lusk, August 6, 1934, box 35, folder 4; William George to the Editor, *Syracuse Journal American*, box 35, folder 10; Edith Freeborn to *National Republic*, December 2, 1934, box 35, folder 10; A. P. Fenderson to William George, February 21, 1935, box 35, folder 19. See also William George, *The Adult Minor* (New York: Appleton, 1937), 133, 137, 184; Vera Rockwell, *The New Pioneers* (Boston: Wilde, 1940); Jeanne Goldstein, "When Do Boys Become Men?" *Brooklyn Daily Eagle*, November 21, 1926; "Junior Republic's Methods Outlined," *Christian Science Monitor*, March 5, 1924; "Letter to the Editor," *Syracuse Post Standard*, October 24, 1933; "Junior Republic Founder Speaks," *Boston Daily Globe*, March 6, 1924, 3; Jack Holl, *Juvenile Reform in the Progressive Era: William R. George and the Junior Republic Movement* (Ithaca, NY: Cornell University Press, 1971). The following are from WG Papers: Horace Burkholder to William George, April 7, 1932, box 33, folder 6; Untitled dictation, August 10, 1932, box 33, folder 17; William George to Samuel Tatnall, July 21, 1921, box 23, folder 2; William George, "A Righteous Cause Founded on Justice Must Live," August 31, 1935, box 35, folder 31; William George to Sterling Edwards, January 29, 1935, box 35, folder 17; William George to Noel Sargent, February 3, 1935, box 35, folder 18; William George to Vera Rockwell, July 17, 1935, box 35, folder 28.

6. The following are from WG Papers: William George to Willard Hotchkiss, February 16, 1933, box 33, folder 35; "Dictated by Daddy George February 13, 1935, 'Things I want left behind me,'" box 35, folder 33; William George, "A Righteous Cause Founded on Justice Must Live," August 31, 1935, box 35, folder 31; William George to Guy Thompson re: League of Adult Minors, October 27, 1934, box 35, folder 8; William George to Noel Sargent, July 20, 1934, box 35, folder 3; William George to Aaron Levy, November 1, 1932, box 33, folder 21; William George to John Kinane, December 3, 1932, box 33, folder 24; Correspondence about Johnny Kinane and League of Adult Minors, box 35, folder 3; John Kinane to Dear Friend, c. 1934, box 35, folder 11; William

George to Leon Goldstine, January 3, 1935, box 35, folder 16; William George to Arthur Woods, February 12, 1932, box 33, folder 2; William Cox to William George, April 4, 1932, box 33, folder 6; Jesse Gordon to William George, May 27, 1932, box 33, folder 9; "The revelation of a social laboratory," October 13, 1931, box 33, folder 22 or 23; Meeting minutes of Phalanx, May 24, 1932, box 59, folder 4; "Extra," January 12, 1932, appended to minutes of the meeting called to consider Phalanx, December 18, 1931, box 59, folder 4; "Wanted: Active Participation for All Youth in Economic and Civic Life as Well as in the Spiritual, Social and Recreative," c. 1932, box 59, folder 5; Untitled document on the ten projects of Phalanx, January 20, 1933, box 33, folder 31; Untitled document, December 15, 1932, box 33, folder 29; Meeting minutes of March 8, 1932, meeting of Phalanx, box 59, folder 4. See also William R. George, *The Revelation of a Social Laboratory* (Freeville, NY: n.p., 1931). In the 1920s, George had called for a more right-wing approach to child welfare, one that acknowledged the value of some varieties of work for older youth. See "Right Wing Uplifters: There Is Need for Among Social Welfare Workers, W. R. George Declares," *Wall Street Journal*, June 18, 1928.

7. *First American Youth Congress: Held August 15, 16 and 17, 1934, at New York University in the city of New York* (program) (New York: AYC, 1934); World Youth Congress, *Youth Plans a New World: Being the Official Record of the First World Youth Congress, Geneva, 31.VIII.-6.IX.1936; Organised by the International Federation of League of Nations Societies* (Geneva: World Youth Congress, 1936). The following are from WG Papers: William George to Victor Tarrant, September 5, 1934, box 35, folder 7; William George to Noel Sargent, August 23, 1934, box 35, folder 4; Untitled document from Mrs. George about the first American Youth Congress, box 35, folder 11; Edo Freeborn to Frank Palm, February 12, 1935, box 35, folder 19; Edo Freeborn to Mr. and Mrs. George, June 20, 1935, box 35, folder 24; Edo Freeborn, "Dear Folks," June 17, 1935, box 35, folder 25.

8. The following are from WG Papers: William George to John Parker, January 15, 1935, box 35, folder 17; Untitled, September 22, 1932, box 33, folder 18; Malcolm Freeborn, "The Junior Governmental Plan: An Outline Study of the Junior Municipality Since the Founding of the Program in Cortland, New York, February 1933," box 33, folder 36; William George to Vera Rockwell, August 15, 1935, box 35, folder 30; Malcolm Freeborn, "The Adult Minor Governmental Program," Tompkins County Advisory Council Meeting, August 13, 1934, box 35, folder 4; *Youth Outlook: The Voice of America's Adult Minor* [stationery that shows the league published a paper with help from the *Homer Post* in Homer, NY], box 35, folder 8; E. C. Davis to William George, September 22, 1930, box 32, folder 8; "Adult-Minor Citizenship," box 35, folder 11; William George to Father Patrick Cleary, January 3, 1935, box 35, folder 16; Correspondence illuminates details of financial crisis, box 35, folder 31; William George to Jack Weeks, October 14, 1932, box 33, folder 19; "7:45 pm Daddy, Mrs. Daddy, Mal, Edo, Don, Esther present in our sitting room," August 29, 1935, box 35, folder 34. See also William George, *The Adult Minor* (New York: Appleton, 1937) 51; James Rogers, *The Child and Play: Based on the Reports of the White House Conference on Child Health and Protection* (New York: Century, 1932); Robert Clark, "Two Successful Attempts at Rudimentary Society," *Journal of Educational Sociology* 8, no. 1 (1934): 47.

9. The following are from WG Papers: Frank Searles to Edo Freeborn, February 12, 1932, box 33, folder 2; Malcolm Freeborn, "The Community and Youth Problems," box 35, folder 11; "Adult minor citizenship: participation in government by the adult minor: a fundamental need of

democracy," February 4, 1935, box 35, folder 18; William Gute to William George, June 30, 1913, box 14, folder 28; Letter from Syria [Harris LeRoy] to William George, July 19, 1914, box 16, folder 9. See also William George, *The Adult Minor* (New York: Appleton, 1937), 104.

10. William George, *The Adult Minor* (New York: Appleton, 1937). The following are in WG Papers: William George, "To the Executive Committee of the George Junior Republic Association, Inc.," February 4, 1935, box 35, folder 18; "Adult minor citizenship: participation in government by the adult minor: a fundamental need of democracy," February 4, 1935, box 35, folder 18; Malcolm Freeborn, "The Community and Youth Problems," n.d., box 35, folder 11; Correspondence between Malcolm Freeborn and adult minor officials, box 35, folder 20; Robert Alvort to Mal Freeborn, May 4, 1935, box 35, folder 22; "7:45 pm Daddy, Mrs. Daddy, Mal, Edo, Don, Esther present in our sitting room," August 29, 1935, box 35, folder 34; William George or Malcolm Freeborn to junior mayor of Cortland, February 19, 1935, box 35, folder 19; William George, "The Junior Municipality," 1921, box 23, folder 21; Malcolm Freeborn, "What Is the Junior Municipality?" February 16, 1934, box 35, folder 11; Malcolm Freeborn, "Adult-Minor Citizenship," n.d., box 35, folder 12; Malcolm Freeborn, "Adult minor citizenship: an outline study of the Junior Municipality since the founding of the program in Cortland, New York, February 1933," box 35, folder 18.

11. Dorothea Kahn, "Student Government Offers Training Class in Democracy," *Christian Science Monitor*, October 29, 1937; *Ford Republic: A Boys' Self-Governing Community*, Farmington, MI: n.p., 1936; "Learning by Doing," *New York Times*, January 30, 1933; "Citizenship Schooling Not New," *New York Times*, February 1, 1933; "Makes Plea for Democracy," *New York Times*, June 29, 1938; "Plans Better Way to Train Citizens," *New York Times*, January 27, 1933; "Self-Government Training Should Be Chief Concern of Schools, Leader Asserts," *New York Times*, November 6, 1932; "Teaching of Civics Held Inadequate," *New York Times*, June 8, 1936; Richard Welling, "Education in Citizenship," *New York Times*, May 6, 1936; Eunice Barnard, "The Task of Building Better Citizens," *New York Times*, July 3, 1932; A. O. Bowden and Ida Clyde Clarke, *Tomorrow's Americans: A Practical Study in Student Self-Government* (New York: Putnam's, 1930); Andrew Donson, "The Teenagers' Revolution: Schülerräte in the Democratization and Right-Wing Radicalization of Germany, 1918–1923," *Central European History* 44, no. 3 (September 2011): 420–446; Andreas Gayk, *The Red Child Republic Seekamp: Documentation of the First Socialist Child Camp, 1927* (Berlin: Worker Youth, 1928); Paul Felix Lazarsfeld and Ludwig Wagner, *Community Education by Educating Communities: Report on a Contribution of the Youth Movement to the Sozialpädagogik* (Vienna: Anzengruber o.J., 1924); Susan J. Berger, "The Children's Advocate: Janusz Korczak," *American Educational History Journal* 33, no. 2 (2006): 137–142; Lida Engel, "Experiments in Democratic Education: Dewey's Lab School and Korczak's Children's Republic," *Social Studies* 99, no. 3 (2008): 117–121; Richard Welling, "A Self-Governing German Camp," *New York Times*, December 10, 1915; Johannes Martin Kemp, *Kinderrepubliken: Geschichte, Praxis und Theorie radikaler Selbstregierung in Kinder- und Jugendheimen* (Berlin: Springer, 1995); Regina Lago de Comas, *Las repúblicas juveniles* (Madrid: Revista de Pedagogía, 1931); J. Piaget and J. Heller, *La autonomía en la escuela* (Buenos Aires: Losada, 1968); Albert Petrovich Pinkevich, Nucia Perlmutter Lodge, and George Sylvester Counts, *The New Education in the Soviet Republic* (New York: Columbia University, 1929); Betty Jean Lifton, *The King of Children: A Biography of Janusz Korczak* (New York: St. Martin's Griffin, 1988); "Editorial: Russia's Orphan Cities," *Pathfinder*, December 28, 1928, 9; Oliver Cornman,

"Principles and Methods of Pupil Government, School Cities," *Journal of Proceedings and Addresses of the National Education Association Annual Meeting* 47 (1908): 290; Otto Mowrer, "Authoritarianism versus Self Government," *Journal of Social Psychology* 10 (1939): 121–126; Edward Randall Maguire, *The Group-Study Plan: A Teaching Technic Based on Pupil Participation* (New York: Scribner's, 1928); Walter Robinson Smith, *Constructive School Discipline* (Chicago: American Book Series, 1936); Courtlandt Van Vechten, Jr., "A Study of Success and Failure of One Thousand Delinquents Committed to a Boys' Republic" (PhD diss., University of Chicago, 1935); "Prison Colony Successfully Governs Itself," *Christian Science Monitor*, October 10, 1928, 1; Alexander Forbes, The George Junior Republic: A Community Vital to the United States (Freeville, George Junior Republic, 1925); "Prison Ideals: An Ex-Governor on Value of Self-Government Education," *Manchester Guardian*, September 13, 1922; "German Prisons Like Schools with Promotions for Good Behavior," *Boston Daily Globe*, March 27, 1932; Charles Judd, "Education," *Recent Social Trends in the United States: Report of the President's Research Committee on Social Trends* (1933), 357; "Investigation of Communist Propaganda: Hearings," pt. 1, vols. 1–4, U.S. Congress, House Special Committee on Communist Activities in the United States, 1930, 12, 19; Lawrence Kohlberg, *Essays on Moral Development* (New York: Harper and Row, 1981), 403; *Life of the Boys Brotherhood Republic* (Chicago: BBR, 1938); "Boy Republic's First Citizens Recall When Living Was Fighting," *Chicago Daily Tribune*, February 21, 1927. BBR boys also participated in World War I. See "'Bad Boys' Helping to Defeat Germany," *Kalamazoo Gazette*, August 31, 1918.

12. Meeting minutes of Phalanx. May 24, 1932, box 59, folder 4, WG Papers: "Mulrooney Is Shown How Boys Run 'City,'" *New York Times*, January 7, 1933; "'Boys' Republic' Planned," *New York Times*, December 18, 1931; "LaGuardia Envious of a Boy Mayor, 16," *New York Times*, January 20, 1934; "Boys' Brotherhood Opens First Colored Republic on Tuesday," *Chicago Daily Tribune*, October 5, 1939; "Chicago Mayor Greets Big Brothers at Mass Meeting," *Chicago Defender*, February 11, 1939; "First Boys Republic Is Founded," *Chicago Defender*, October 14, 1939; "Donates Home for Boys Town," *New York Amsterdam News*, October 14, 1939; William George to Jack Robbins, July 19, 1935, box 35, folder 34; Manuall Brenner to William George, October 5, 1932, and William George to Manuall Brenner, October 8, 1932, box 33, folder 19, WG Papers; "Boys' Republic Deals Out Stock for Own Store," *Chicago Daily Tribune*, February 23, 1935; "B.B.R. of, by, and for Boys," *Rotarian* 48, no. 4 (April 1936): 21–23, 47; Webb Waldron, *Americans* (New York: Greystone, 1941); Richard Welling, *As the Twig Is Bent* (New York: Putnam's, 1942); *Proceedings of the Continental Congress of the Daughters of the American Revolution* (1938), 143; Writers' Program of the Work Projects Administration in the State of Illinois, *Illinois: A Descriptive and Historical Guide*, 1940, 271; *Life of the Boys Brotherhood Republic* (Chicago: BBR, 1938); William Welling, *East Side Story: The Boys Brotherhood Republic's First Fifty Years on New York's Lower East Side* (New York: BBR, 1982); "Boys' Republic Active," *New York Times*, January 16, 1939; "3140 Indiana Ave. Boys' Brotherhood Opens First Colored Republic on Tuesday," *Chicago Daily Tribune*, October 5, 1939.

13. "Boys' Republic Is Crime Cure: Enviable Record Achieved by Chicago Youths," *Spokesman-Review*, January 24, 1944; "Lyman Beecher Stowe Dead; Author and a Civic Leader, 82," *New York Times*, September 26, 1963; "William Harmon Made New Head of St. Charles," *Chicago Daily Tribune*, July 17, 1934; William Welling, *East Side Story: The Boys Brotherhood Republic's First Fifty Years on New York's Lower East Side* (New York: BBR, 1982); *Life of the Boys Brotherhood Republic*

(Chicago: BBR, 1938); Webb Waldron, "No Adults Allowed," *Reader's Digest*, April 1936, 79–82; "Boys Republic Governs Self," *Tuscaloosa News*, January 24, 1944; Charles J. Chapman, "An Experiment in Democracy," *Recreation* (January 1950): 470–472.

14. Webb Waldron, "B.B.R—of, by, and for Boys," *Rotarian* (April 1936), reprinted in *Life of the Boys Brotherhood Republic* (Chicago: BBR, 1938); "Boys' Republic Elects Mayor," *Chicago Daily Tribune*, October 15, 1939; "Rule Chicago an Hour," *Chicago Daily Tribune*, April 21, 1937; *Proceedings of the Attorney General's Conference on Crime Held December 10–13, 1934, in Memorial Continental Hall, Washington, D.C.* (Washington, DC: Bureau of Prisons, 1936); "Prosecutor Points to Folly of Crime in Address to Boys Tribune," *Chicago Daily Tribune*, October 13, 1934; Clyde Reed, "Self-Government for Problem Boys," *Delinquency News Letter*, 1936; S. Bayard Colgate, "Help the Boy to Help Himself," *American Journal of Correction* (1943): 9; Dorothy Louise Campbell Culver Tompkins, *Bibliography of Crime and Criminal Justice, 1932–1937* (Berkeley: University of California, Institute of Governmental Studies, 1939); *Life of the Boys Brotherhood Republic* (Chicago: BBR, 1938), 38; Clyde Reed, "Boys Brotherhood Republic: A Complete City Administration by Juveniles," *Police Journal* 19 (March 1933): 12; Sheldon Millman, "A Boy's View of Crime Prevention," *Police Yearbook 1938–1939*; Boys Brotherhood Republic, "Youth Investigates and Recommends," *Marriage and Family Living* 5, no. 2 (1943): 29–32; Jack Drucker, "Boys Brotherhood Protests: Its Mayor Holds Publication of Report of Teacher Survey Premature," *New York Times*, January 12, 1943; Molly Gordy, "A Nation within a City: A Boys Program About Law, Order and Leadership," *Newsday*, January 9, 1992, 25; "Boys Prepare Survey of Teachers," *New York Times*, December 30, 1942; "Boys' Republic to Honor Its Original 16 Members," *Chicago Daily Tribune*, January 27, 1935.

15. Sarah Stures, "Self Government in a Correctional School," *School and Society* 43, no. 4 (1936): 470–473; "Two Good Reasons Why There Is No Crime Wave in Milwaukee," *Christian Science Monitor*, January 31, 1931, 10; Margaret Root Zahler, "Study Groups Take Up Almost Any Recreational Interest," *Christian Science Monitor*, May 9, 1939, 13; Elizabeth Pendry and Hugh Hartshorne, *Organizations for Youth* (New York: McGraw-Hill, 1935); "Uncle Ray's Corner," *Atlanta Constitution*, December 1, 1934; Jerry Marcotte and Patrick McMahon, *The Formation of a New Republic: A Photographic History of Boys Republic* (Virginia Beach, VA: Donning, 2007); "Mayor Views Job as Housekeeping," *New York Times*, June 16, 1937; Peter Villa, "Junior City Mayor Decides Not to Quit," *New York Times*, August 23, 1937; "Boy Mayor at City Hall Today," *New York Times*, May 21, 1937; "They're Big Shots," *New York Amsterdam News*, August 28, 1937; Irvin Linn, "A Study of the American Boys' Commonwealth as a Youth Serving Agency in a Critically Changing Community"(MS thesis, George Williams College, 1950); "Junior Municipality Planned at Homer," *Binghamton Press*, August 7, 1934; "Marathon Is Interested in Junior Municipality," *Binghamton Press*, July 13, 1934; "Junior City Government," *Scholastic* 34 (February 11, 1939): 34; "Boy Mayor Resigns; Job Costs Too Much," *New York Times*, August 15, 1937; Lenore Bartlett, "7-Year-Olds from Green Acres Observe How a City Operates," *Washington Post*, February 16, 1938; Marion Paine Stevens, *The Activities Curriculum in the Primary Grades* (Boston: Heath, 1931); Harry Charles McKown, *Character Education* (New York: McGraw-Hill, 1935); Avah Willyn Hughes, *Carrying the Mail: A Second Grader's Experiences* (New York: Teachers College, 1933); Alice Elizabeth Carey, Paul Robert Hanna, and Junius Lathrop Meriam, *Catalog: Units of Work, Activities, Projects, etc., to 1932* (Berkeley: University of California Press, 1932); Wilson Gill, *The Civic Life*

of Children (Philadelphia: Patriotic League 1930); James Bartlett Edmonson, Joseph Roemer, and Francis Leonard Bacon, *Secondary School Administration* (New York: Macmillan, 1931), 119; "A 'School-City' Plan of Pupil Participation in School Control," *School Review* 44 (January 1936): 4–6; "W. L. Gill, Teacher and Engineer, Dies," *New York Times,* September 14, 1941; A. B. Caldwell, "North Junior City," *Junior-Senior High School Publications,* 1931; Wilson L. Gill, *Manual of the School Republic* (Philadelphia: Patriotic League, 1931); Wilson Gill, *The Gill Method of Moral and Civic Training* (Philadelphia: Patriotic League, 1933); "Newsboys Here Protest 17 Age Limit Proposal," *Boston Daily Globe,* April 24, 1934; "Dictatorship Rejected by Newsboyville Mayor," *Christian Science Monitor,* April 6, 1933, 2; "Boston Newsboys Learn While They Earn," *Christian Science Monitor,* July 17, 1930, 10; "'Mayor' Kramer Honored at Newsboyville Dinner," *Boston Daily Globe,* November 23, 1934; "Silverman Tells Newsies About City Government," *Boston Daily Globe,* January 3, 1931; "Boston's Newsboyville Elects Mayor After Two Weeks of Political Debate," *Christian Science Monitor,* January 21, 1930, 17; "Newsboy Officials Guests at City Hall," *Boston Daily Globe,* July 29, 1934; "Newsboys' Group Gets Experience in Conducting Boston City Affairs," *Boston Daily Globe,* December 11, 1932; "Newsboyville Former Mayors, Officials Meet," *Boston Daily Globe,* June 23, 1935; "Newsboys' Group Expects Increase," *Boston Daily Globe,* October 4, 1936; "'Mayor' Campo of Newsboyville Takes Tobin's Chair Briefly," *Boston Daily Globe,* April 19, 1939; "35 Boston Newsboys Capture City Hall; Get Official Autos for Their Sightseeing," *New York Times,* March 20, 1938; "Agassiz Village Reunion Attended by 300 Newsboys at Burroughs Foundation," *Boston Daily Globe,* April 1, 1938; "Newsboys' Reunion Is Noisy One," *Christian Science Monitor,* April 1, 1938; "Jury of Boys to Judge Young Traffic Offender," *Chicago Daily Tribune,* May 19, 1939; "Pedestrian Hit by Youth's Auto Dies in Hospital," *Chicago Daily Tribune,* June 2, 1939; *Ford Republic: A Boys' Self-Governing Community* (Farmington, MI: n.p., 1936); Courtlandt Churchill Van Vechten, *A Study of Success and Failure of One Thousand Delinquents Committed to a Boys' Republic* (Chicago: University of Chicago Press, 1935); Mildred Wilds, "Top Rank High School Seniors Tell Ambitions," *Chicago Daily Tribune,* June 16, 1940; "'Flower City' at Flower Technical High School for Girls: Chicago Girls School 'Mayor' Organizes a Cleanup Campaign," *Christian Science Monitor,* May 11, 1938; Elbert Fretwell, *Extra-curricular Activities in Secondary Schools* (Boston: Houghton Mifflin, 1931); Virginia Eldridge, *Play Cities* (Raleigh, NC, Raleigh Public Schools, 1931); "'Model' Youth Is Bandit," *New York Times,* June 2, 1935; Harold Diedrich Meyer, *The School Club Program: Organization, Administration, Activities* (New York: Barnes, 1931); Rollo La Verne Lyman and Philip Wescott Lawrence Cox, *Junior High School Practices* (Chicago: Laidlaw, 1935); A. O. Bowden and Ida Clyde Clarke, *Tomorrow's Americans* (New York: Putnam's, 1930; Paul Washington Terry, *Supervising Extra-curricular Activities in the American Secondary School* (New York: McGraw-Hill, 1930); George Butler, *Playgrounds: Their Administration and Operation* (New York: Ronald Press, 1936); "Junior City's Mayor Inducts Two Aides" *New York Times,* September 12, 1937. Related organizations such as the Model League of Nations and Junior League of Nations also continued. See *New Outline for Model Assemblies* (New York: League of Nations Association Educational Department, 1930); John Eugene Harley, *International Understanding: Agencies Educating for a New World* (Stanford, CA: Stanford University Press, 1931); Elizabeth Erwin (Miller) Lobingier and John Leslie Lobingier, *Educating for Peace* (Cleveland: Pilgrim Press, 1930); James Thomson Shotwell, American National Committee on International Intellectual Cooperation, *The Study of International Relations in the United States: Survey for 1937* (New York: Columbia University

Press, 1938); *Text for a Model Council and a Model Assembly of the League of Nations*, League of Nations Association (U.S.), Educational, 1930; Lyman Spicer Judson, *The Student Congress Movement: With Discussion on American Neutrality* (New York: Wilson, 1940); *High Points in the Work of the High Schools of New York City* (New York: Board of Education, 1940). To be clear, not every setting moved toward revitalized democracy. After its relocation to the countryside in the 1910s, the Hebrew Sheltering Guardian Society Orphan Asylum restructured its self-government system. The "Lewisohn Democracy," as it was called after Adolph Lewisohn, was a prominent feature of asylum life in the 1910s but subsequently declined and ultimately disappeared after Lewisohn's death in the 1938. See varied annual reports in Board of Directors Annual Reports 1922, 1924, 1926, 1928, 1930, 1932, 1934, 1936, Center for Jewish History, Records of the Hebrew Sheltering Guardian Society of New York, 1879–1970, I-43, box 2, folder 6.

16. Richard Reiman, *The New Deal and American Youth: Ideas and Ideals in a Depression Decade* (Athens: University of Georgia Press, 1992); Richard Reiman, "Planning the National Youth Administration" (PhD diss., University of Cincinnati, 1984); Calvin Beckett, "A Study of the National Youth Administration Work Projects for Negroes in Fulton County, Georgia" (MSW thesis, Atlanta University, 1940); "NYA Plans Part-Time Jobs for 94,000 Youths: Program Not to Conflict with Private Industry; National Resources Committee Issues Report Predicting Population Change Favoring Rule of Country by Older People," *Commercial & Financial Chronicle* 141 (October 26, 1935): 2675–2676; "New Deal Underwrites Youth Movement: National Youth Administration Will Broaden Policy Devised to Prepare Youth for Broad Service," *Sphere* (August 1935): 25–26; M. H. S. Hayes, "Present-Day Youth and the NYA," *Occupations* 15 (January 1937): 301–305; W. K. Layton, "The Junior Placement Service and the NYA," *Occupations: The Vocational Guidance Magazine*, May 1937, 729–731; Rosalie Borus and Gilbert Harris, "A Study of 26 Young People Employed on a National Youth Administration Project," *Jewish Social Service Quarterly* 13 (December 1936): 276–279; "Youth, One-Sixth of the Nation, in Distress: What the New Deal's National Youth Administration Is Doing for Young America," *Advance* (September 1938): 8–9; Federal Security Agency, War Manpower Commission, *Final Report of the National Youth Administration: Fiscal Years 1936–1943* (Washington, DC: Government Printing Office, 1944); Betty G. Lindley and Ernest K. Lindley, *A New Deal for Youth: The Story of the National Youth Administration* (New York: Viking, 1938); Palmer O. Johnson and Oswald L. Harvey, *The National Youth Administration* (Washington, DC: Government Printing Office, 1938); "Colored People Urged to Enter Youth Projects," *Negro Star*, January 24, 1936; "Mrs. Bethune Explains NYA Program to Entire Nation," *Plaindealer* (Kansas City), September 4, 1936; "Opportunity for Negro Youth," *Negro Star*, October 30, 1936; "NYA Gives Employment to Many Negro Youths," *Kansas Whip*, November 10, 1939; "National Youth Administration Statement Submitted to the Subcommittee of the Committee on Appropriations, House of Representatives, Seventy-Sixth Congress," folder National Youth Administration, record group 119, Records of the National Youth Administration, National Archives and Records Administration (hereafter NARA); Records of the Resident Center Section, subject file 1939–1943, Ninth Corps Area—Quoddy Clippings, box 4, NARA; NYA Bulletin Y-18: "Suggested Methods for Community Organization and for Recreation Employment Opportunities for Youth 1936," record group 119, Records of the National Youth Administration, Records of the Division of Community Organization, Correspondence of the Director with Youth Organizations, 1935–1937, box 1, NARA; Deborah Lynn Self, "The National Youth Administration in

Texas, 1935–1939" (master's thesis, Texas Tech University, 1974). According to the NYA's final report on the program from 1943, there were 595 resident training centers, although this figure is contradicted by a report in 1941 of 622 resident projects in 46 states. See "Questions on NYA Resident Centers for Report to the American Youth Commission," folder Resident Centers and Youth, record group 119, Records of the National Youth Administration, Records of the Resident Center Section, subject file 1939–1943, Research—Resident Centers 1940, box 6, NARA.

17. "File of Molly Yard, Assistant Information Specialist on Youth-Interested Organizations 1940–1941. Reference and Information," record group 119, Records of the National Youth Administration, Records of the Office of the Director, box 4, NARA; "Agencies, List of," folder Com. Org., record group 119, Records of the National Youth Administration, Records of the Division of Community Organization, Correspondence of the Director with Youth Organizations, 1935–1937, box 1, NARA; "Youth Congress Condemns the NYA Program," folder American Youth Congress, record group 119, Records of the National Youth Administration, Records of the Division of Community Organization, Correspondence of the Director with Youth Organizations, 1935–1937, box 1, NARA; "Report Division of Community Organization National Youth Administration, February 7, 1936," folder Community Organization, record group 119, Records of the National Youth Administration, Records of the Division of Community Organization, Correspondence of the Director with Youth Organizations, 1935–1937, box 2, NARA; "Community Organization: Private Agency Cooperation," folder Suggestions for Brochures, record group 119, Records of the National Youth Administration, Records of the Division of Community Organization, Correspondence of the Director with Youth Organizations, 1935–1937, box 1; "American Youth Congress, Report of Cabinet Meeting, January 18, 1941, by Molly Yard," folder Town Meeting of Youth, contains information on American Youth Congress and its local affiliates, record group 119, Records of the National Youth Administration, Records of the Office of the Director, box 1, NARA; "File of Molly Yard, Assistant Information Specialist on Youth-Interested Organizations 1940–1941," American Friends Service Committee-International Student Service, box 1, NARA; folder Local Councils, contains information on AYC local councils, including their newspapers/newsletters and bulletins, record group 119, Records of the National Youth Administration, Records of the Office of the Director; "A program of recreation and community activities for youth," folder Recreation, record group 119, Records of the National Youth Administration, Records of the Division of Community Organization, Correspondence of the Director with Youth Organizations, 1935–1937, box 3, NARA; "A suggested recreation service of the National Youth Administration, folder Recreation, record group 119, Records of the National Youth Administration, Records of the Division of Community Organization, Correspondence of the Director with Youth Organizations, 1935–1937, box 3, NARA; "To all supervisors of full-time and part-time resident projects. From Mr. A. B. Walker, Director of Recreation. Subject: Aims and Objectives of the Oklahoma State-wide recreation program," folder South Charleston Regional Project, record group 119, Records of the National Youth Administration, Records of the Resident Center Section, subject file 1939–1943 NYA-US Army Station Relations, box 7, NARA. The academic orientation of the agency is apparent in the numerous bibliographies on recreation, group work, leadership, community organization, and related topics in agency files. See "To Mr. Harry V. Gilson from Emmett R. Ruskin, June 19, 1941. Subject: NYA Conference to be Held in Chicago for Selected Administrative Employees in Regions II and IV," folder Dead Inter-Office Correspondence

1939–1940, Incoming, record group 119, Records of the National Youth Administration, Records of the Resident Center Section, subject file 1939–1943; "Army File–Food Cost Control, Agencies, List of," folder Com. Org., record group 119, Records of the National Youth Administration, Records of the Division of Community Organization, Correspondence of the Director with Youth Organizations, 1935–1937, box 1, NARA; "Ernestine Grigsby, director of division of community organization, to Gerald Barnes 1938," folder Suggestions for Brochures, record group 119, Records of the National Youth Administration. Records of the Division of Community Organization, Correspondence of the Director with Youth Organizations, 1935–1937, box 1, NARA; "Brief bibliography in community organization" and "Organizing the community for sound planning and intelligent action," December 23, 1935, folder Community Organization, record group 119, Records of the National Youth Administration, Records of the Division of Community Organization. Correspondence of the Director with Youth Organizations, 1935–1937, box 2, NARA; folder leadership training, record group 119, Records of the National Youth Administration, Records of the Division of Community Organization, Correspondence of the Director with Youth Organizations, 1935–1937, box 2, NARA; "Outline of discussion group of the National Youth Administration staff members, led by Dr. EC Lindeman, NYA headquarters, September 16, 1935," folder NYA seminars, record group 119, Records of the National Youth Administration, Records of the Division of Community Organization, Correspondence of the Director with Youth Organizations, 1935–1937, box 3, NARA; "A brief recreation bibliography," attached to "Some suggested recreation employment opportunities for youth, December 23, 1935," folder Recreation, record group 119, Records of the National Youth Administration, Records of the Division of Community Organization, Correspondence of the Director with Youth Organizations, 1935–1937, box 3, NARA; Bureau of Public Administration, University of California, "Suggested reading list in personnel administration," folder Public Administration, record group 119, Records of the National Youth Administration, Records of the Division of Community Organization, Correspondence of the Director with Youth Organizations, 1935–1937, box 3, NARA; "Some suggested recreation employment opportunities for youth, December 23, 1935," attached is "a brief recreation bibliography," which includes literature on group processes as well as Thrasher's gang study, folder Recreation, record group 119, Records of the National Youth Administration, Records of the Division of Community Organization, Correspondence of the Director with Youth Organizations, 1935–1937, box 3, NARA; William J. Campbell, cover note, with National Youth Administration for Oklahoma, Houston A. Wright, director, untitled bulletin on guidance and training, no folder, record group 119, Records of the National Youth Administration, Records of the Division of Community Organization, Correspondence of the Director with Youth Organizations, 1935–1937, box 1, NARA; "Community planning for the out-of-school youth engaged in work projects of the national youth administration for Oklahoma," record group 119, Records of the National Youth Administration, Records of the Division of Community Organization, Correspondence of the Director with Youth Organizations, 1935–1937, box 1, NARA; "Community organization," folder Community Organization, record group 119, Records of the National Youth Administration, Records of the Division of Community Organization, Correspondence of the Director with Youth Organizations, 1935–1937, box 2, NARA; "Letter to Aubrey Williams from Richard Brown, Subject: Youth Conference, November 21, 1935," record group 119, Records of the National Youth Administration, Records of the Division of Community Organization, Correspondence of the Director with Youth Organizations, 1935–1937, box 2, NARA; "Youth employee planning boards and their employment in the State of Illinois," folder Youth Participation, folder marked "Inactive," record group 119, Records of the National Youth Administration, Records of the Office of the Director, File of Molly Yard, Assistant Information Specialist on Youth-Interested Organizations 1940–1941, Reference and Information, box 4, NARA; "To Molly Yard from Pauline Redmond, Subject: Cleveland Youth Council, May 6, 1941," folder Youth Participation, folder marked "Inactive," record group 119, Records of the National Youth Administration, Records of the Office of the Director, File of Molly Yard, Assistant Information Specialist on Youth-Interested Organizations 1940–1941, Reference and Information, box 4, NARA; folder Youth Councils, folder marked "Inactive," record group 119, Records of the National Youth Administration, Records of the Office of the Director, File of Molly Yard, Assistant Information Specialist on Youth-Interested Organizations 1940–1941, Reference and Information, box 4, NARA; "Finds Idle Youth Are Led into Crime," *New York Times,* April 6, 1936; George Bellamy, "Meeting the Recreational Needs in a Rapidly Growing City," *Ohio Bulletin of Charities and Correction* 23, no. 1 (February 1917); George Butler, *Playgrounds: Their Administration and Operation* (New York: Barnes, 1936); Jesse Steiner, *Americans at Play* (New York: Arno, 1933); Jesse Steiner, "Research Memorandum on Recreation in the Depression," *Social Forces* 17, no. 3 (1937); David B, Wolcott, *Cops and Kids: Policing Juvenile Delinquency in Urban America, 1890–1940* (Columbus: Ohio State University Press, 2005); James Rogers, *The Child and Play: Based on the Reports of the White House Conference on Child Health and Protection* (New York: Century, 1932); Jesse Steiner, "Recreation and Leisure," *Report of the President's Research Committee on Recent Social Trends* (1933); Charles Wheeler, "A Boy Scout Program as an Aid in the Police Juvenile Problem," *Yearbook of the International Association of Chiefs of Police,* 1938–1939, 209–212; M. L. Pettit, "An Experiment in the Use of Recreation in Treating Delinquency," *National Probation Association Yearbook* 25 (1931); Karl Johanboeke, "Waging War on Juvenile Delinquency," *Recreation* 27 (1933); Glen O. Grant, "Recreation as Crime Prevention," in *The Offender in the Community: Yearbook, NPA,* 1938; Ernest W. Burgess, "Delinquency or Recreation," in *Delinquency and the Community in Wartime,* ed. Marjorie Bell (New York: National Probation Association, 1944); James Hepbron, "Athletics as an Ounce of Prevention," *Sun,* June 11, 1933. Notably, a number of social scientists used the NYA itself as a subject for study or employed NYA (and WPA) workers to assist in information gathering. See, for example, Frank Espe Brown, "The Program and Policies of the National Youth Administration, 1935–1938, with Special Reference to the Program of the National Youth Administration in Chicago" (master's thesis, University of Chicago, School of Social Service, 1939); Arthur J. Todd, with William F. Byron and Howard L. Vierow, *The Chicago Recreation Survey, 1937*, sponsored jointly by the Chicago Recreation Commission and Northwestern University, conducted under the auspices of the Works Progress Administration, National Youth Administration, and Illinois Emergency Relief Commission (Chicago: Chicago Recreation Commission, 1937); Louis Wirth, Margaret Furez, and Edward L. Burchard, *Local Community Fact Book, 1938* (Chicago: Chicago Recreation Commission, 1938).

18. "N. Y. A. Teaches 45 Boys to Do Chores of Farm," *New York Herald Tribune,* March 31, 1940; "Camp on Patapsco Is Planned by NYA," *Sun,* May 14, 1938; Betty and Ernest Lindley, *A New Deal for Youth* (New York: Viking, 1938); Rose Peld, "Out of School, They Find No Employment," *New York Herald Tribune,* July 17, 1938; "604 Youths Enrolled at Slossfield NYA Project," *Chicago*

Defender, June 28, 1941; "Junior Workers' First Two Weeks in Resident Centers," folder Counseling, record group 119, Records of the National Youth Administration, Records of the Resident Center Section, subject file 1939–1943, Army File–Food Cost Control, NARA; Theodore L. Heller, "Report on Resident Centers," n.d., folder L. H. Dickinson, record group 119, Records of the National Youth Administration, Records of the Resident Center Section, subject file 1939–1943, Army File–Food Cost Control, NARA; Richard Reiman, "Planning the National Youth Administration" (PhD diss., University of Cincinnati, 1984), 473; Deborah Lynn Self, "The National Youth Administration in Texas, 1935–1939" (master's thesis, Texas Tech University, 1974); "NYA Work Center Will Be Operated in City," *Hartford Courant,* May 19, 1939; "NYA Projects Available to City Departments," *Hartford Courant,* September 27, 1939; "NYA to Establish City Clerical Pool," *Hartford Courant,* September 9, 1939; Richard Reiman, *The New Deal and American Youth: Ideas and Ideals in a Depression Decade* (Athens: University of Georgia Press, 1992), 156; National Youth Administration, *Quoddy Regional Project: An Experiment in Youth Rehabilitation,* 1940; "Citizenship," folder Leisure Time—Self-government, record group 119, Records of the National Youth Administration, Records of the Resident Center Section, subject file 1939–1943, Food Service-Library, NARA. Regardless of gender integration, much training followed federal relief programs' gendered precedents: both boys and girls learned industrial, commercial, and business occupations, but only programs for girls included homemaking. In Batesville, Arkansas, for example, groups of four lived for one month in a model cottage, keeping house and caring for Dorothy, a baby onsite since she was two weeks old. See National Youth Administration, *Quoddy Regional Project, an Experiment in Youth Rehabilitation,* 1940; J. W. Hull, "Batesville Resident Training Center, Batesville, Arkansas," *NASSP Bulletin* 24 (1940): 120.

19. Deborah Lynn Self, "The National Youth Administration in Texas, 1935–1939" (master's thesis, Texas Tech University, 1974); Federal Security Agency, War Manpower Commission, *Final Report of the National Youth Administration: Fiscal Years 1936–1943* (Washington, DC: Government Printing Office, 1944); National Youth Administration, *Quoddy Regional Project: An Experiment in Youth Rehabilitation,* 1940; C. R. Bradshaw, "Youth Offers Its Services to You in the NYA Program," *Michigan Municipal Review* 9 (January 1936): 3; Karr Shannon, *A History of Izard County, Arkansas* (self-published, 1947); Bruce Lee Melvin and Carle Clark Zimmerman, *Rural Poor in the Great Depression: Three Studies* (New York: Arno, 1938); J. F. Sullivan, "Berlin Resident Center," *NASSP Bulletin* 24 (1940): 137; Dave Nelson, "Camp Roosevelt: A Case Study of the NYA," *Florida Historical Quarterly* 86, no. 2 (2007): 162–185; Dorothy Canfield Fisher, *Our Young Folks* (New York: Harcourt, 1943); Robert H. Bremner, ed., *Children and Youth in America: A Documentary History,* vols. 1–3 (Cambridge, MA: Harvard University Press, 1974); I. G. Munro, "Salem Girls' Resident Center, Salem, Oregon," *NASSP Bulletin* 24 (1940); D. B. Lasseter, "Resident Training Program in Georgia," *NASSP Bulletin* 24 (1940); R. B. Mchenry, "North Carolina Vocational Training Program, *NASSP Bulletin* 24 (1940); J. J. Cory, "Colorado-Wyoming Vocational Training Program," *NASSP Bulletin* 24 (1940); "A Coöperative Program of Vocational Training," *NASSP Bulletin* 24 (1940); National Youth Administration, *Quoddy Regional Project: An Experiment in Youth Rehabilitation,* 1940; J. W. Hull, "Batesville Resident Training Center, Batesville, Arkansas," *NASSP Bulletin* 24 (1940); Susan Wladaver-Morgan, "Young Women and the New Deal: Camps and Resident Centers, 1933–1943" (PhD diss., Indiana University, 1982). Testing info, rating scales, and forms, including "Activities Department Report" with activities including Village Council, sports, Radio

Club, as well as another document, "Citizenship Report," can be found in folder Counseling, record group 119, Records of the National Youth Administration, Records of the Resident Center Section, subject file 1939–1943, Army File–Food Cost Control, NARA.

20. *Ye Village Crier*, June 8, 1937, folder Quoddy, record group 119, Records of the National Youth Association, Records of the Resident Center Section, Records Concerning Quoddy Village Resident Project at Eastport, Maine, 1936–1939, box 2, NARA; "Weekly Wash," *Quoddy Eagle*, August 20, 1938, folder Quoddy—Karl Borders, record group 119, Records of the National Youth Administration, Records of the Resident Center Section, subject file 1939–1943, Quoddy, June 1937-December 1939, box 5, NARA; "Quoddy (Passamaquoddy) Regional Center, Quoddy Village, Maine," *NASSP Bulletin* 24 (1940): 115; National Youth Administration, *Quoddy Regional Project: An Experiment in Youth Rehabilitation*, 1940; "NYA Builds Fine Police Radio in Maine," *Radio and Television* (March 1941), folder Amateur Licenses and Radio, record group 119, Records of the National Youth Administration, Records of the Radio Projects Section, Fragment File of Robert B. Burton, Radio Engineer and Section Chief, Concerning NYA Amateur Radio Stations and Licenses, 1940–1942, box 1, NARA; "Report of Radio Progress," May 18, 1940, memo to Aubrey Williams, administrator, from Robert R. Burton, radio engineer, record group 119, Records of the National Youth Administration, Records of the Radio Projects Section, Fragment File of Robert B. Burton, Radio Engineer and Section Chief, Concerning NYA Amateur Radio Stations and Licenses, 1940–1942, box 1, NARA; Karl D. Hesley, Administrator, New York State, by William L. King, Director, Division of Work Projects, to Mr. John H. Lasher, Division of Work Projects, National Office, Attention: Mr. Robert B. Burton, Chief Radio Projects Section, September 6, 1941, Subject: Report on NYA Amateur Radio Stations, record group 119, Records of the National Youth Administration, Records of the Radio Projects Section, Fragment File of Robert B. Burton, Radio Engineer and Section Chief, Concerning NYA Amateur Radio Stations and Licenses, 1940–1942, box 1, NARA; Bernard S. Miller, State Youth Administrator for New Jersey, to Mr. John H. Lasher, Director, Division of Work Projects, National Office, Subject: Report on NYA Amateur Radio Stations in the State of New Jersey (there were multiple reports for other states), record group 119, Records of the National Youth Administration, Records of the Radio Projects Section, Fragment File of Robert B. Burton, Radio Engineer and Section Chief, Concerning NYA Amateur Radio Stations and Licenses, 1940–1942, box 1, NARA. The 1930s were an era of excitement about amateur broadcasting, and NYA youth were no exception. Some arrived with radio licenses; others acquired them while participating in onsite radio clubs.

21. Lewis Lorwin, *Youth Work Programs, Prepared for the American Youth Commission* (Washington, DC: American Council on Education, 1941); Rodney Watterson, *Naval Discipline from Flogging to Progressive Era Reform at Portsmouth Prison* (Annapolis, MD: Naval Institute Press, 2014); C. W. Taussig, "Youth and Democracy," *School Review* 44 (April 1936): 244–246; C. W. Taussig, "The Demands of the Present Crisis upon the High School," *Education Digest* 2, no. 7 (March 1937): 52; Richard Reiman, *The New Deal and American Youth: Ideas and Ideals in a Depression Decade* (Athens: University of Georgia Press, 1992), 156; Britt Haas, "As They Saw the Thirties" (PhD diss., State University of New York, Albany, 2011); Bryan Nicholson, "Apprentices to Power: The Cultivation of American Youth Nationalism, 1935–1970" (PhD diss., University of Illinois, 2012); William Graebner, *The Engineering of Consent: Democracy and Authority in Twentieth-Century America*

(Madison: University of Wisconsin Press, 1987); Susan Wladaver-Morgan, "Young Women and the New Deal: Camps and Resident Centers, 1933–1943" (PhD diss., Indiana University, 1982); "CCC Held Failing to Prepare Boys for Self-Government," *Washington Post,* December 13, 1940; Samuel Farkas Harby, *A Study of Education in the Civilian Conservation Corps Camps of the Second Corps Area, April 1933 to March 1937* (Ann Arbor: Edwards, 1938); Kenneth Holland and Frank Ernest Hill, *Youth in the CCC* (Washington, DC: American Council on Education, American Youth Commission, 1942); "Camp Mayor," *Times,* July 6, 1937; "Camp Cross Boys Elect Own Council," *Hartford Courant,* June 19, 1934; Frank Hull, *The School in the Camps: The Educational Program of the Civilian Conservation Corps* (New York: American Association for Adult Education, 1935); "Whiskered Youths Back from Camps," *New York Times,* September 24, 1933; Neil Maher, *Nature's New Deal: The Civilian Conservation Corps and the Roots of the American Environmental Movement* (New York: Oxford University Press, 2008); Dave Nelson, "Camp Roosevelt: A Case Study of the NYA," *Florida Historical Quarterly* 86, no. 2 (Fall 2007): 162–185; Kenneth Holland, "Work Camps for Youth," in *American Youth: An Enforced Reconnaissance*, ed. Thacher Winslow and Frank Davidson (Cambridge, MA: Harvard University Press, 1940); *Report of Resident Schools and Educational Camps for Unemployed Women, 1934 and 1935* (Washington, DC, Federal Emergency Relief Administration, 1936); William George to Vera Rockwell, August 15, 1935, box 35, folder 30, WG Papers; Eunice Barnard, "Urges Laboratory on Public Affairs," *New York Times,* December 28, 1933.

22. Quoddy Regional Project, *The Quoddy Village Youth Government*, 1941; Untitled article, *Springfield Republican*, June 12, 1938, 4; Kevin P. Bower, "Out of School, Out of Work: Youth, Community, and the National Youth Administration in Ohio, 1935–1943," *Ohio Valley History* 4, no. 2 (Summer 2004); "Citizenship," folder Leisure Time—Self-government, record group 119, Records of the National Youth Administration, Records of the Resident Center Section, subject file 1939–1943, Food Service-Library, NARA; "Boston Boy Chosen 'Mayor' at Quoddy," *Boston Daily Globe,* June 20, 1937; "Quoddy Village Is Governed by NYA Youth Group," *Christian Science Monitor,* September 15, 1937; Gordon Halstead, *Work-Study-Live: The Resident Youth Centers of the NYA* (Lima, NY: NYA Resident Work Center, n.d.), available at New Deal Network, accessed June 9, 2016, http://newdeal.feri.org/wsl (site discontinued). "South Charleston Regional Resident Work Experience Center, Youth Government," folder South Charleston Regional Project, record group 119, Records of the National Youth Administration, Records of the Resident Center Section, subject file 1939–1943, NYA-US Army Station Relations, box 7, NARA; NYA Quoddy Regional Project, "Constitution of the Quoddy Village Youth Government," 1941; NYA Quoddy Regional Project, "The Quoddy Village Youth government," 1941; "The Civicism Program," folder South Charleston Regional Project, record group 119, Records of the National Youth Administration, Records of the Resident Center Section, subject file 1939–1943, NYA-US Army Station Relations, box 7, NARA; Dave Nelson, "Camp Roosevelt: A Case Study of the NYA," *Florida Historical Quarterly* 86, no. 2 (Fall 2007): 162–185; NYA, *Final Report of the National Youth Administration, Fiscal Years 1936–1943* (Washington, DC: War Manpower Commission, 1944), 98; Richard A. Reiman, "Planning the National Youth Administration: Citizenship and Community in New Deal Thought" (PhD diss., University of Cincinnati, 1984), 6–9; "State Conference, NYA Resident Centers Here," *Otsego Farmer and Republican*, November 7, 1941, 2; Memorandum from Karl Borders to Aubrey Williams and Orren H. Lull, September 1, 1938, Subject: Recommendations on Passamaquoddy Work experience project, folder Quoddy—Karl Borders, record group 119, Records of the National

Youth Administration. Records of the Resident Center Section, subject file 1939–1943, Quoddy, June 1937-December 1939, box 5, NARA.

23. Andrea Tone and William Graebner, *The Engineering of Consent: Democracy and Authority in Twentieth-Century America* (Madison: University of Wisconsin Press, 1987); Alice F. Liverright to Hilda Smith, Subject: Camps for youth 16 to 24 years of age, record group 119, Records of the National Youth Administration, Records of the Division of Community Organization, Correspondence of the Director with Youth Organizations, 1935–1937, box 2, NARA; Hilda Smith, "Workers Education as Determining Social Control," *Annals of the American Academy of Political and Social Science* 182 (November 1935); Richard Reiman, *The New Deal and American Youth: Ideas and Ideals in a Depression Decade* (Athens: University of Georgia Press, 1992); Unknown writer [likely Mrs. Daddy] to Alexander Forbes, July 2, 1935, folder 34, box 35, WG Papers; William George to Vera Rockwell, July 17, 1935, folder 28, box 35, WG Papers; Alexander Urbiel, "The Making of Citizens: A History of Civic Education in Indianapolis, 1900–1950" (PhD diss., Indiana University, 1996); Bryan Nicholson, "Apprentices to Power: The Cultivation of American Youth Nationalism, 1935–1970" (PhD diss., University of Illinois, 2012); William George to C. Spencer Miller, November 20, 1920, box 22, folder 13, WG Papers; William George to John M. Weeks, March 18, 1921, box 22, folder 21, WG Papers; *Bulletin* 20, March 1921, box 22, folder 22, WG Papers; *Bulletin* 28, "Self-Government, Inc.," June 1921, box 22, folder 29, WG Papers; William George to John Calder, July 21, 1921, box 23, folder 2, WG Papers; Harold Yetman to William George, October 6, 1921, box 23, folder 7 or 8, WG Papers; William George to Alexander Woollcott, October 12, 1921, box 23, folder 12, WG Papers; William George to Jerome Barnum, June 23, 1934, box 35, folder 2, WG Papers. "American Legion to Teach Appreciation of Democracy," *Christian Science Monitor,* January 9, 1939; "Coolidge Praises Junior Citizens; Gov. Allen Also Commends Glen Ridge Idea," *New York Evening Post,* July 13, 1921; "Speaker Made Life Member of Boys Republic," *Washington Post,* February 21, 1939; "Judge Gives Legion Flag to Boys' Republic here," *Chicago Daily Tribune,* March 16, 1929; *The Ohio Government in Brief, Prepared for Buckeye Boys' State* (Delaware, OH: American Legion Department of Ohio, 1935); Cortez Ewing, *An Introduction to the Government of Oklahoma* (Oklahoma City: [Shawnee] Americanism committee, American Legion Department of Oklahoma, 1939); "Legion to Hold Boys' Civic Camp for 1,200 Youths," *Chicago Daily Tribune,* June 9, 1935; "1st Model State Government Is Conducted by Boys of W. Va.," *New Journal and Guide,* July 16, 1938, 15; "Mountaineers Set Up First Boys' State," *Chicago Defender,* July 9, 1938; "Rotary Hears Legion Heads," *Oregonian,* March 13, 1940; Tom Lewis, "News of the Week in Veterans' Posts," *Los Angeles Times,* March 10, 1940; "Juniors in Glen Ridge in Government Move," *Newark Evening News,* March 4, 1921. Some Legion posts sponsored related programs. See "Alliance Veterans Post Conducts Balloting for Junior Police Staff," *Cleveland Call and Post,* August 23, 1941. There were a few direct connections between the republic movement and the NYA, however. For example, Harold Strong, who headed Litchfield's George Junior Republic, joined the advisory committee to nearby Nepaug Village Resident Training Center. Former Newsboy Republic official William Haber, by then a University of Michigan economist, joined Michigan's National Youth Administration. See Allan Lindstrom, "Boys' Village Has Making-Good Habit: Nepaug Village Is One Town Where Only Youths Govern, While Learning How to Earn Livelihoods," *Hartford Courant,* August 13, 1939; William Haber to Richard Brown, February 18, 1936, record group 119, Records of the National Youth Administration,

Records of the Division of Community Organization, Correspondence of the Director with Youth Organizations, 1935–1937, folder Local Studies in Michigan, box 2, NARA; "NYA Advisory Committee Is Announced by Dodd," *Hartford Courant,* May 28, 1938; Hilda Smith, "A College Summer School for Women in Industry," *Christian Science Monitor,* April 19, 1923.

24. File of Molly Yard, assistant information specialist on youth-interested organizations, United Christian Youth—Various Organizations, Records of the National Youth Administration. Records of the Office of the Director, box 3, NARA; Monmouth County YMCA, "A Handbook for City-Borough and Township Sponsors of the Monmouth County Boy-Good Government Programs," folder Youth Government, "Work-Book for 'Boy-Legislators' and Hi-Y Clubs, Model Legislature State Capitol, Trenton, NJ, April 26–7, 1940," Rutherford YMCA, "Youth in Rutherford Government" [expansion of Monmouth government], folder Youth Government, NARA; William George to David Lawrence, January 8, 1932, box 33, folder 1, WG Papers; "Merriam [California governor] Swears in Boys' Governor," *Los Angeles Times,* June 30, 1938; "A 'Forty-Ninth State'—Made Up of Boy Citizens," *Christian Science Monitor,* July 19, 1938; "Camp for Boys: Self-Government Fostered in New Program," *Oregonian,* April 24, 1937; "Lads to Create a 'Boys' State' at Springfield," *Chicago Daily Tribune,* June 2, 1935; "50 Chicagoans Will Go Today to 'Boys' State,'" *Chicago Daily Tribune,* June 23, 1935; "Maine Township Boys to Attend Citizens' Camp," *Chicago Daily Tribune,* June 14, 1936; "Kathleen McLaughlin, "Schoolboy Stirs Auxiliary with an Address Calling on Americans to Uphold Democracy," *New York Times,* September 21, 1937; "Mrs. FDR Dedicates W. Va. High School," *Afro-American,* June 18, 1938; "Forest Park Lad Is Elected Boys' State Governor," *Chicago Daily Tribune,* June 24, 1938; "Girls' State Governor Candidates Announced," *Chicago Daily Tribune,* June 27, 1940; "Youths Take Firm Anti-Liquor Stand in American Legion Camp in Iowa," *Christian Science Monitor,* June 30, 1938; "Plans Reunion for Citizens of Boys' State," *Chicago Daily Tribune,* November 20, 1938; "Old Dominion Boys' State Ends Sessions at Virginia Tech," *Washington Post,* June 25, 1939; "Politics to Boil as 220 Launch Boys' State Today," *Washington Post,* June 18, 1939; "W. Va. Boys to See How State Is Run," *Chicago Defender,* May 27, 1939; "American Legion to Teach Appreciation of Democracy," *Christian Science Monitor,* January 9, 1939; "Moving Forward: Forty-Ninth State," *Chicago Daily Tribune,* June 26, 1938; "300 Youths to Participate in Little Rhody Boys' State: The Week in Rhode Island Cost to Be Modest," *Christian Science Monitor,* June 7, 1940; "High School Girls Check Up on Governmental Affairs," *Los Angeles Times,* April 23, 1940; "Legion Welcomes State Youth to Model Summer Encampment," *Los Angeles Times,* June 23, 1940; Betty Browning, "Auxiliary of Legion to Have Girls' State," *Chicago Daily Tribune,* June 23, 1940; Betty Browning, "Girls Set Up a State, Learn How to Run It," *Chicago Daily Tribune,* June 29, 1940; A. Gardiner, "Patriotic Societies," *Journal of Educational Sociology* 10, no. 6 (1937): 365–368; Charles Dwight McDonald, "A Study of the Educational Values of the Buckeye Boys' State" (master's thesis, Ohio State University, 1938); F. J. Brorsen, "A Survey of the Boys' State Program" (master's thesis, Stanford University, 1941); "Negro Boys' State: School Officials Backbone of Negro Boys' State," *West Virginia Educational Bulletin* 8, no. 11 (June 1941); "Burleigh Wins Presidency of Boys Republic," *Washington Post,* February 6, 1939; "Regional HQ for Boys Republic and Girls Republic to be Est. at 2460 Sixteenth Street, Youth Organizations to Establish Quarters," *Washington Post,* April 2, 1939; "Youth Republics to Start Campaign," *Washington Post,* February 12, 1939; "Speaker Made Life Member of Boys Republic," *Washington Post,* February 21, 1939; "Judge Gives Legion Flag to Boys' Republic Here," *Chicago Daily Tribune,* March 16, 1929;

First Sunflower Girls' State, Washburn College, Topeka, Kansas: June 11 to 18, Inclusive, 1939: A Project in Practical Americanism and Citizenship Training (Topeka: Kansas State Printing Plant, 1939); "Europe's War Ours Too Says Youth Leader," *Seattle Daily Times*, June 20, 1940; "Youth Leader, Here, Tells of Junior Statesmen," *Seattle Daily Times*, December 5, 1937; Nate White, "'Junior Statesmen of America': Its Program for Awakening Civic Responsibility," *Christian Science Monitor*, December 13, 1941; "Junior Statesmen Reject 'Isms' but Urge Unity," *Christian Science Monitor*, June 29, 1940; Lewis Rex Miller, "'Junior Statesmen of America,'" *Christian Science Monitor*, November 23, 1937; "Model Politics: Junior Statesmen Hold Real Convention," *Washington Post*, August 16, 1936; "Junior Statesmen in 5th Anniversary," *Seattle Daily Times*, November 9, 1939; "Badly Advised," *Seattle Daily Times*, June 29, 1940; Sabra Holbrook, *Children Object* (New York: Viking, 1943); "2 Youth Groups Plan Campaign of Patriotism," *Washington Post,* January 30, 1939; F. Kenneth Harder to William George, regarding vision of a youth's village board, youth's police force and similar ideas for Hempstead, box 33, folder 4, WG Papers; "Boy Governments in 34 States Show Value of American Way: They're All for America," *Christian Science Monitor*, July 10, 1940; "1,000 at Meeting as Legion Opens Anti-red Fight," *Chicago Daily Tribune*, January 5, 1935; "Vermont Boys Conduct 'State' in Course About Government," *Christian Science Monitor*, June 21, 1938; "'Boy's State' to Teach How Government's Run," *Washington Post*, April 12, 1936; "Hiatt Reports on Boys State," *Palm Beach Post*, June 18, 1941; "A 'Forty-Ninth State'—Made Up of Boy Citizens," *Christian Science Monitor*, July 19, 1938. The era's enthusiasm for democratic group processes wasn't limited to youth organizations. For example, Hilda Smith Worthington, who supervised worker democracy efforts early in her career, modeled FERA camps on resident workers schools. The CCC, which contacted the National Self-Government Committee for advice on self-government, sent its supervisors to foremen's training camps to learn nondirective leadership principles.

25. Cover note, William J. Campbell with document "National Youth Administration for Oklahoma, Houston A. Wright, director," untitled bulletin on guidance and training, no folder, record group 119, Records of the National Youth Administration, Records of the Division of Community Organization, Correspondence of the Director with Youth Organizations, 1935–1937, box 1, NARA; "Community planning for the out-of-school youth engaged in work projects of the National Youth Administration for Oklahoma," record group 119, Records of the National Youth Administration. Records of the Division of Community Organization. Correspondence of the Director with Youth Organizations, 1935–1937, box 1, NARA; "South Charleston Regional Resident Work Experience Center, Youth Government," folder South Charleston Regional Project, record group 119, Records of the National Youth Administration, Records of the Resident Center Section, subject file 1939–1943, NYA-US Army Station Relations, box 7, NARA; Federal Security Agency, War Manpower Commission, *Final Report of the National Youth Administration: Fiscal Years 1936–1943* (Washington, DC: Government Printing Office, 1944), viii.

26. E. Campbell, "Gauging Group Work: An Evaluation of a Settlement Boys Work Program," National Youth Administration, Detroit, Michigan, 1938; N. Cantor, "Group Work and Social Science," *Group Work, 1939* (New York: American Association for the Study of Group Work, 1939); Susan Wladaver-Morgan, "Young Women and the New Deal: Camps and Resident Centers, 1933–1943" (PhD diss., Indiana University, 1982); Harry Gilson, Regional Resident Project Director, West Virginia, to William G. Carnahan, Regional Representative NYA, Lock Six, NYA Project,

South Charleston, April 22, 1940, "To all supervisors, coordinators, foremen," Subject: The training institute for National Youth Administration, September 29, 1938, folder Quoddy—Karl Borders, record group 119, Records of the National Youth Administration, Records of the Resident Center Section, subject file 1939–1943, Quoddy, June 1937–December 1939, box 5, NARA; folder Quoddy Regional Project—general correspondence, record group 119, Records of the National Youth Administration, Records of the Resident Center Section, subject file 1939–1943, Quoddy, June 1937-December 1939, box 5, NARA; National Youth Administration, *Quoddy Regional Project: An Experiment in Youth Rehabilitation*, 1940; "Citizenship," folder Leisure Time—Self-government, record group 119, Records of the National Youth Administration, Records of the Resident Center Section, subject file 1939–1943, Food Service-Library, NARA; "South Charleston Regional Resident Work Experience Center, Youth Government," folder South Charleston Regional Project, record group 119, Records of the National Youth Administration, Records of the Resident Center Section, subject file 1939–1943, NYA-US Army Station Relations, box 7, NARA; Federal Security Agency, War Manpower Commission, *Final Report of the National Youth Administration: Fiscal Years 1936–1943* (Washington, DC: Government Printing Office, 1944), viii; William Graebner, *The Engineering of Consent: Democracy and Authority in Twentieth-Century America* (Madison: University of Wisconsin Press, 1987); Britt Haas, "As They Saw the Thirties" (PhD diss., State University of New York, Albany, 2011).

27. Federal Security Agency, War Manpower Commission, *Final Report of the National Youth Administration: Fiscal Years 1936–1943* (Washington, DC: Government Printing Office, 1944), vii, viii, 194; "Quoddy 'Grads' Landing Good Jobs," *Eastport Sentinel*, August 21, 1940, folder Quoddy Clippings. record group 119, Records of the National Youth Administration, Records of the Resident Center Section, subject file 1939–1943, Quoddy, June 1937-December 1939, box 5, NARA; Memo from Anthony Zill to Mr. Gilson, November 9, 1939, Subject: Preliminary Consideration on Follow-up of Quoddy Enrollees, folder Research—NYA Projects, record group 119, Records of the National Youth Administration, Records of the Resident Center Section, subject file 1939–1943, Research—Resident Centers 1940, box 6, NARA; "Quoddy Village Youth Government," folder Leisure Time—Self-government, record group 119, Records of the National Youth Administration, Records of the Resident Center Section, subject file 1939–1943, Food Service-Library, NARA; Gordon Halstead, *Work-Study-Live: The Resident Youth Centers of the NYA* (Lima, NY: NYA Resident Work Center, n.d.), available at New Deal Network, accessed June 9, 2016, http://newdeal.feri.org/wsl (site discontinued); Folder Quoddy Regional Project—general correspondence, record group 119, Records of the National Youth Administration, Records of the Resident Center Section, subject file 1939–1943, Quoddy, June 1937-December 1939 box 5, NARA; Susan Wladaver-Morgan, "Young Women and the New Deal: Camps and Resident Centers, 1933–1943" (PhD diss., Indiana University, 1982); "South Charleston Regional Resident Work Experience Center, Youth Government," folder South Charleston Regional Project, record group 119, Records of the National Youth Administration, Records of the Resident Center Section, subject file 1939–1943, NYA-US Army Station Relations, box 7, NARA.

28. Gordon Halstead, *Work-Study-Live: The Resident Youth Centers of the NYA* (Lima, NY: NYA Resident Work Center, n.d.), available at New Deal Network, accessed June 9, 2016, http://newdeal.feri.org/wsl (site discontinued); Federal Security Agency, War Manpower Commission, *Final Report*

of the National Youth Administration: Fiscal Years 1936–1943 (Washington, DC: Government Printing Office, 1944); Harry Haller, "Youth Administration, in New Headquarters, Pushes Task of Preparing Young for Life," *Sun,* May 14, 1939; Harvey Zorbaugh, "Which Way America's Youth?" *Journal of Educational Sociology* 11, no. 6 (February 1938): 322–334; "NYA Really Doing Something About Youth Problem," *Austin American,* January 15, 1939, 3; "The NYA Resident Training Center," *Christian Science Monitor,* October 18, 1938; National Youth Administration, *Quoddy Regional Project, an Experiment in Youth Rehabilitation,* 1940, 2; Eunice Barnard, "Youth Cries Out for a Salvaging Hand," *New York Times,* July 1, 1934; Nancy E. Rose finds similar distinctions in relief programs for adults. See Rose, "Production-for-Use or Production-for-Profit? The Contradictions of Consumer Goods Production in 1930s Work Relief," *Review of Radical Political Economics* 20, no. 1 (1988): 46–61.

29. National Youth Administration, *Quoddy Regional Project, an Experiment in Youth Rehabilitation,* 1940; Karl Borders to Mr. Aubrey Williams and Mr. Orren H. Lull, September 1, 1938, Subject: Recommendations on Passamaquoddy work experience project, folder Quoddy, record group 119, Records of the National Youth Association, Records of the Resident Center Section, Records Concerning Quoddy Village Resident Project at Eastport, Maine, 1936–1939, box 2, NARA; "To the prospective enrollee," rev 2/10/1941 in [Miscellaneous Publications] Quoddy Regional Project (Quoddy Village, Maine: 1941) online at Hathi Trust; "The Quoddy Village Youth government," [Miscellaneous Publications] Quoddy Regional Project (Quoddy Village, Maine: 1941), 2 online at Hathi Trust.

30. Eunice Barnard, "Youth Cries Out for a Salvaging Hand," *New York Times,* July 1, 1934; "NYA Really Doing Something About Youth Problem," *Austin American,* January 15, 1939; "The NYA Resident Training Center," *Christian Science Monitor,* October 18, 1938; Federal Security Agency, War Manpower Commission, *Final Report of the National Youth Administration: Fiscal Years 1936–1943* (Washington, DC: Government Printing Office, 1944); Gordon Halstead, *Work-Study-Live: The Resident Youth Centers of the NYA* (Lima, NY: NYA Resident Work Center, n.d.), available at New Deal Network, accessed June 9, 2016, http://newdeal.feri.org/wsl (site discontinued); W. L. Rhyne, "Work Camps as Education," *High School Journal* 30, no. 4 (1947): 212–216.

31. Gordon Halstead, *Work-Study-Live: The Resident Youth Centers of the NYA* (Lima, NY: NYA Resident Work Center, n.d.), available at New Deal Network, accessed June 9, 2016, http://newdeal.feri.org/wsl (site discontinued); "Prepared Men and Patriotism Themes of NYA Meeting," *Eastport Sentinel,* July 24, 1940, folder Quoddy Clippings, record group 119, Records of the National Youth Administration, Records of the Resident Center Section, subject file 1939–1943, Quoddy, June 1937-December 1939, box 5, NARA; "Quoddy 'Grads' Landing Good Jobs," *Eastport Sentinel,* August 21, 1940, folder Quoddy Clippings, record group 119, Records of the National Youth Administration, Records of the Resident Center Section, subject file 1939–1943, Quoddy, June 1937-December 1939, box 5, NARA; "Showed Pictures of Village at Capitol," *Eastport Sentinel,* January 22, 1941, folder Quoddy Clippings, record group 119, Records of the National Youth Administration, Records of the Resident Center Section, subject file 1939–1943, Quoddy, June 1937-December 1939, box 5, NARA; "Citizenship," folder Leisure Time—Self-government, record group 119, Records of the National Youth Administration, Records of the Resident Center Section, subject file 1939–1943, Food Service-Library, NARA; "The Regional (South Charleston) Resident Work Experience Project," folder Counseling, record group 119, Records of the National Youth

Administration, Records of the Resident Center Section, subject file 1939–1943, Army File-Food Cost Control, NARA; O. W. Kaye, "Cassidy Lake Resident Center, Chelsea, Michigan," *NASSP Bulletin* 24 (1940): 131; Fred van Defender, "Bread and Butter Is Chief Concern for This College," *Springfield Republican*, May 13, 1940; "500 Young Men Off for Quoddy Study Tomorrow," *Boston Daily Globe*, July 13, 1940; Federal Security Agency, War Manpower Commission, *Final Report of the National Youth Administration: Fiscal Years 1936–1943* (Washington, DC: Government Printing Office, 1944); Harry Haller, "Youth Administration, in New Headquarters, Pushes Task of Preparing Young for Life," *Sun*, May 14, 1939. After the 1938 publication of Dewey's *Education and Experience*, such language resonated still further with his ideas. Even the observers who called the RTCs "work camps" emphasized their educational ambitions; see, for example, W. L. Rhyne, "Work Camps as Education," *High School Journal* 30, no. 4 (1947): 212–216. This educational frame was consistent with interpretations of Freeville as an educational institution; many educators cited George in their textbooks. R. H. Jordan, *Extra-Classroom Activities in Elementary and Secondary Schools* (New York: Cowell, 1928), 978; Roscoe Pulliam, *Extra-Instructional Activities of the Teacher* (New York: Doubleday, 1930), 73, 76, 82; R. Emerson Langfill, Frank Cyr, and N. William Newson, *The Small High School at Work* (New York: American, 1936), 158; Paul Terry, *Supervising Extracurricular Activities* (New York: McGraw Hill, 1930), 116; Lillian Kennedy Wyman, *Character and Citizenship through Student Government* (Philadelphia: Winston, 1935), 2.

32. William George to Charles Powlison of National Child Welfare Association, February 16, 1932, box 33, folder 2, WG Papers; "Activities of National Youth Administration, 1935–40," *Monthly Labor Review* (May 1941): 1189; Table 8, "Selected Major Accomplishments of NYA Work Projects in the Field of Public Building and Public Improvement, Fiscal Year, 1939–40," in Lewis Lorwin, *Youth Work Programs: Problems and Policies* (Washington, DC: American Council on Education 1941), 66; Deborah Lynn Self, "The National Youth Administration in Texas, 1935–1939" (master's thesis, Texas Tech University, 1974); Work Progress Administration, "Suggested Projects in State and Local Government: Public Service Projects," November 25, 1935, folder Public Service Projects, record group 119, Records of the National Youth Administration, Records of the Division of Community Organization, Correspondence of the Director with Youth Organizations, 1935–1937, box 3, NARA; "A Program of Recreation and Community Activities for Youth," folder Recreation, record group 119, Records of the National Youth Administration, Records of the Division of Community Organization, Correspondence of the Director with Youth Organizations, 1935–1937, box 3, NARA; National Youth Administration, "Statement Submitted to the Subcommittee of the Committee on Appropriations, House of Representatives, Seventy-Sixth Congress," folder National Youth Administration, record group 119, Records of the National Youth Administration, Records of the Resident Center Section, subject file 1939–1943, Ninth Corps Area—Quoddy Clippings, box 4, NARA; NYA Bulletin Y-18, "Suggested Methods for Community Organization and for Recreation Employment Opportunities for Youth, 1936," record group 119, Records of the National Youth Administration, Records of the Division of Community Organization, Correspondence of the Director with Youth Organizations, 1935–1937, box 1, NARA; "Some Suggested Recreation Employment Opportunities for Youth, December 23, 1935," folder Recreation, record group 119, Records of the National Youth Administration, Records of the Division of Community Organization, Correspondence of the Director with Youth Organizations, 1935–1937, box 3, NARA.

33. Press release, "Williams Announces Four Federal Projects for Employment under National Youth Administration," October 21, 1935, folder Public Service Projects, record group 119, Records of the National Youth Administration, Records of the Division of Community Organization, Correspondence of the Director with Youth Organizations, 1935–1937, box 3, NARA; "In Classroom and on Campus: California School of Government Has a Broad Curriculum for Training of Public Officials," August 11, 1935, folder Public Service Projects, record group 119, Records of the National Youth Administration, Records of the Division of Community Organization, Correspondence of the Director with Youth Organizations, 1935–1937, box 3, NARA; Bureau of Public Administration, University of California, "Suggested reading list in personnel administration," folder Public Administration, record group 119, Records of the National Youth Administration, Records of the Division of Community Organization, Correspondence of the Director with Youth Organizations, 1935–1937, box 3, NARA; Otis Wingo, National Institution of Public Affairs, to Dean Friend, August 6, 1935, folder Public Administration, record group 119, Records of the National Youth Administration, Records of the Division of Community Organization, Correspondence of the Director with Youth Organizations, 1935–1937, box 3, NARA; Otis Wingo, National Institution of Public Affairs, to Ivan Asay (NYA), August 10, 1935, included copy of memo "Memorandum of government apprenticeship training program of the National Youth Administration: A summary," folder Public Service Projects, record group 119, Records of the National Youth Administration, Records of the Division of Community Organization, Correspondence of the Director with Youth Organizations, 1935–1937, box 3, NARA; National Youth Administration, "Statement Submitted to the Subcommittee of the Committee on Appropriations, House of Representatives, Seventy-Sixth Congress," folder National Youth Administration, record group 119, Records of the National Youth Administration, Records of the Resident Center Section, subject file 1939–1943, Ninth Corps Area—Quoddy Clippings, box 4, NARA; Karl Borders to Mr. Aubrey Williams and Mr. Orren H. Lull, August 2, 1938, Subject: Some observations on the NYA work experience project at Quoddy Village, folder Quoddy, record group 119, Records of the National Youth Association, Records of the Resident Center Section, Records Concerning Quoddy Village Resident Project at Eastport, Maine, 1936–1939, box 2, NARA. Washington, D.C., headquarters recruited young adults to work in the NYA's central offices in cooperation with the National Institution of Public Administration.

34. Richard Reiman, *The New Deal and American Youth: Ideas and Ideals in a Depression Decade* (Athens: University of Georgia Press, 1992); Federal Security Agency, War Manpower Commission, *Final Report of the National Youth Administration: Fiscal Years 1936–1943* (Washington, DC: Government Printing Office, 1944); Britt Haas and J. W. Studebaker, "Definition of the Respective Functions of the United States Office of Education and the National Youth Administration," Statement issued as mimeograph by the United States Office of Education; W. A. MacDonald, "Viewpoint on Education," *New York Times,* October 12, 1941. On efforts to organize NYA workers unions in different settings, see Britt Haas, "As They Saw the Thirties" (PhD diss., State University of New York, Albany, 2011), 194; Kevin Bower, "Relief, Reform, and Youth: The National Youth Administration in Ohio, 1935–1943" (PhD diss., University of Cincinnati, 2003), 60. As Haas explains, "Adult labor union leaders came to support the NYA because it was seen as a way to keep young workers out of regular wage work in the short term. And, if they joined the NYA Workers Union, then they were introduced to the labor union at an early age, which, union leaders hoped, would make them

more loyal to the future success of the labor movement as a whole" (195n84). Substantial coverage of the NYA in the *National Association of Secondary School Principals Journal* (for example, in April 1940) reflects concerns about a takeover of the US educational system.

35. Jeffrey Pilz, "The Beginnings of Organized Play for Black America," *Journal of Negro History* 70, no. 3/4 (1985): 59–72; E. B. Henderson, "The Participation of Negro Youth in Community and Educational Programs," *Journal of Negro Education* 9, no. 3 (1940): 416–424. There were some exceptions, see, for example, "Social News," *Topeka Plaindealer*, October 7, 1927; "Cut This Out Quick," *Topeka Plaindealer*, November 18, 1927; "Hope Presbyterian Church: The Church with a Community Program," *Broad Ax*, January 24, 1925; "Springfield Colored Girl Scouts Win Contest with Negro National Anthem," *People's Elevator*, April 16, 1925; "Girl Scouts Increasing," *Savannah Tribune*, September 6, 1919. On the exclusion of African Americans from rural programming, see Gabriel Rosenberg, *The 4-H Harvest* (Philadelphia: University of Pennsylvania Press, 2015).

36. Jennifer Light, *The Nature of Cities* (Baltimore: Johns Hopkins University Press, 2009); Jennifer Light, "Building Virtual Cities, 1895–1945," *Journal of Urban History* 38, no. 2 (2012): 336–371; Mary Dudziak, *Cold War Civil Rights* (Princeton, NJ: Princeton University Press, 2000); Thomas Jackson Woofter et al., *Negro Problems in Cities* (New York: Institute of Social and Religious Research, 1928); Gardner Murphy and Rensis Likert, *Public Opinion and the Individual: A Psychological Study of Student Attitudes on Public Questions, with a Retest Five Years Later*, prepared under the auspices of the Columbia University Council for Research in the Social Sciences, 1938; "Slum Peril Deemed National Emergency," *New York Times*, June 23, 1935; Ira De A. Reid, "General Characteristics of the Negro Youth Population," *Journal of Negro Education* 9, no. 3 (1940): 278–289; Mapheus Smith, "A Comparison of White and Indian Student Attitudes toward the Negro," *Journal of Negro Education* 6, no. 4 (October 1937): 592–595; H. Meltzer, "Group Differences in Nationality and Race Preferences of Children," *Sociometry* 2, no. 1 (January 1939): 86–105; Goodwin Watson, "Social Attitudes," *Review of Educational Research* 5, no. 3 (June 1935), 259–272; Mapheus Smith, "A Study of Change of Attitudes Toward the Negro," *Journal of Negro Education* 8, no. 1 (January 1939): 64–70; "Social Welfare Work for Police," *Christian Science Monitor*, February 27, 1918; August Vollmer, "The Policeman as a Social Worker," *Proceedings of the International Association of Chiefs of Police* (1919), 32–38; Arthur Woods, "Woods Urges Police to Advise Children and Not Chase Them," *New-York Tribune*, February 19, 1919; William Quinn, "The San Francisco Police Department Big Brother Bureau," *Yearbook of the International Association of Chiefs of Police, 43rd 1936–7*; Raymond Blaine Fosdick, *American Police Systems* (New York: Century, 1920); Frank White, "A Man Who Has Achieved the Impossible," *Outlook*, September 26, 1917, 124; "The Police as Social Workers," *Outlook*, December 18, 1914, 861–862; Floyd Allport and Daniel Katz, *Students' Attitudes: A Report of the Syracuse University Reaction Study* (Syracuse, NY: Craftsman, 1931).

37. "A 'Junior Republic' for Negro Boys Established Near Washington, DC: It Is an Improvement on Other Schools of the Same Kind and Is Doing as Great a Work as Booker T. Washington's School at Tuskegee, Alabama," *St. Louis Post-Dispatch*, September 2, 1900; "Out of the Gutter," *Los Angeles Times*, August 26, 1900; "Another Junior Republic," *New York Evangelist*, November 2, 1899, 19; "Junior Republic at Playground," *Los Angeles Times*, November 12, 1911; W. S. Scarborough, "The Negro Criminal Class—How Best Reached," *Voice of the Negro*, December 1, 1905, 867; "Youth City Gets Started; Evans Lauded: North Philly Center Answers Great Need, Say Speakers,"

Philadelphia Tribune, December 19, 1940; "Youth Town's First Mayor Takes Office," *Philadelphia Tribune,* July 4, 1940; "Youth City to Help Stop Purse Thefts," *Philadelphia Tribune,* April 10, 1941; "Father Flanagan's Boys' Home Is Mecca of Homeless Boys of All Religions and Colors," *New Journal and Guide,* April 18, 1931; "Boys' Home Houses Homeless of All Colors," *Afro-American,* April 18, 1931; William J. McKiernan, "The Intelligent Operation of Playgrounds," *Proceedings of the Playground Association of America Proceedings of the Second Annual Playground Congress New York City, September 8–12, 1908* (New York: Playground Association of America, 1908), 109; M. P. Rogers, "Junior Republic for Colored Boys," *Our Day* 19 (January 1900); "Negro boys' junior republic—within the Hart Farm School—a most valuable institution of Washington, DC, founded by Professor Hart, of Howard University, a worthy fellow of Booker T. Washington," *Springfield Republican* August 26, 1900; "Training in thrift: A novel manner of teaching orphans to be frugal and industrious. Form of Junior Republic. Reward paid for service and good conduct. The idea was worked out and put into effect by Miss White at the Johns Hopkins Colored Orphan Asylum, Remington Avenue and Thirtieth Street," *Sun,* June 3, 1899; Jennie Campbell, "Children in the Capital," *New York Observer and Chronicle,* February 14, 1901; "DC Rescue of the Waifs," *Washington Post,* October 21, 1902; Kelly Miller, "The Hart Farm School," *Southern Workman,* October 1902; "Penalty Fits the Crime: Code Adopted by the Newest Juvenile Republic. Young Nation Rules Itself," *Sun,* February 27, 1903; "A Visit to the 'George Junior Republic,'" *Friends' Intelligencer* 57, no. 23 (June 9, 1900): 457; "Our Graduates," *Crisis,* July 1, 1916, 119; Naomi Cooper, "Educational Notes," *Chicago Defender,* March 19, 1927, 11; Thelma Berlack, "Irma Minott Elected Mayor of School City of Girls' Junior High," *New York Amsterdam News,* January 26, 1927; "Chicago Girls School 'Mayor' Organizes a Cleanup Campaign," *Christian Science Monitor,* May 11, 1938; "Billiken Was School Mayor: Robert Crawford Was Mayor of His School," *Chicago Defender,* July 2, 1938, 12; "League's Clean-Up Drive Shows Visible Results Here," *Afro-American,* July 13, 1929, 16; "The Junior Page: Clean Block Clubs Now Being Organized," *Afro-American,* July 20, 1935, 19; "Youth Appointed Assistant Junior Chief of Police," *Chicago Defender,* May 25, 1940, 3; Charlotte Crump, "Hill City Needs NYA's Broad Program to Make Golden Opportunity for Trained Girls," *Pittsburgh Courier,* September 30, 1939; "State's N. Y. A. Work Outlined Here by Donovan," *Boston Daily Globe,* February 19, 1940; Lyman Amsden, "Report of State of Junior Civic Leagues," *Atlanta Constitution,* December 12, 1915; "Second and Third Ward Junior Civic Leagues," *Atlanta Constitution,* May 20, 1917; Naomi Cooper, "Educational Notes," *Chicago Defender,* March 19, 1927; "Junior Republic at Playground: Violet Street Center Elects Mayor and Council; Most of the Officials Are of Age and Honors Are Divided Between White Persons and Negroes—Another Election Next Saturday for Two Offices," *Los Angeles Times,* November 12, 1911; "NYA Funds Will Pay Workers on Hill City Project, Not Pay for Equipment," *Pittsburgh Courier,* November 18, 1939. NYA workers also helped programs in white communities. "Boston Police Stations List Youths for Part-Time Jobs," *Christian Science Monitor,* January 3, 1940.

38. "Boys' Republic Pushes $25,000 Fund Campaign," *Chicago Daily Tribune,* April 17, 1943; Barbara Lonnborg, *Boys Town: A Photographic History* (Boys Town, NE: Donning, 1992); "Council Hears of Hill City's Splendid Work," *Pittsburgh Courier,* February 8, 1941; "Youths Get Jobs, Learn Faming, at Boys' Town Near Clarksville," *Dallas Morning News,* September 9, 1940; Fred Kelly, "'Boystowns' for Cleveland Youth," in *Public Recreation in the City of Cleveland* (Cleveland: Department of Public Properties, 1939); Writers Program of the Works Projects Administration in

the State of Ohio, *Cleveland's Boystowns*, 1940; "Boys Town Group to Broadcast Junior Republic's Story," *Hartford Courant*, March 20, 1949; Hugh Reilly and Kevin Werneke, *Father Flanagan of Boys Town: A Man of Vision* (Boys Town, NE: Boys Town Press, 2008); "17 Year Old Mayor Tells Kelly of Jailless Village," *Chicago Daily Tribune*, November 19, 1936; "Boys' Home Houses Homeless of All Colors," *Afro-American*, April 18, 1931, 12; "Boys Town, Nebr., Is Run by and for the Boys," *Washington Post*, February 23, 1936; "'Boys Town' Real Life," *Los Angeles Times*, September 12, 1938; "Father Flanagan's Home Is Mecca of Orphan Boys," *Chicago Defender*, April 11, 1931; "La Guardia's Job Stuns Mayor of 17," *New York Times*, November 20, 1936; "Boys Govern This Nebraska Town," *Lake Benton Valley News*, July 10, 1936; "Move Underway to Establish Permanent 'Boys Town' in Philly," *Pittsburgh Courier*, May 4, 1940; "Youth City Gets Started; Evans Lauded," *Philadelphia Tribune*, December 19, 1940; Fred Kelly, "Boystowns for Cleveland Youth," *Recreation* 33 (November 1939): 437–440; Robert W. Chamberlin, Department of Public Safety, Robert A. Burri, Department of Public Health and Welfare, J. Noble Richards, Division of Recreation, *Cleveland's Boystowns: A Report Prepared by the Executive Committee for Cleveland's Boystowns*, 1940; "Father Flanagan Portrays Himself," *Washington Post*, August 17, 1938. Plans were afoot to create other Boys Towns, including by Louis Mayer, but many never happened. See LeRoy Ashby, *Saving the Waifs: Reformers and Dependent Children, 1890–1917* (Philadelphia: Temple University Press, 1984), 130; Abe Hill, "Boystown Benefit Greatest in History," *New York Amsterdam News*, December 25, 1943; "Negroes Set Up Boys' Town; Bar No Race or Creed," *Chicago Daily Tribune*, June 21, 1941;"New Boys Town to Be Promoted by Negro Group," *Chicago Daily Tribune*, October 5, 1941; "Backs 'Boystown,'" *New York Amsterdam News*, December 18, 1943; "Provincetown Boys' Town Mayor, Chief, Come to Boston to Learn About Junior Police," *Boston Daily Globe*, January 29, 1939; "Louis B. Mayer Offers Fortune to Aid Youth," *Atlanta Constitution*, September 15, 1938. Note that Cottage Row had long been referred to as the "Boys Town" on Thompsons Island. "A Vocational School a Hundred Years Old," *Outlook*, July 28, 1915, 734.

39. Myron E. Moorehead, "An Evaluation of the Friendly Service Bureau in Its Crime Prevention among Negroes in the City of Columbus, Ohio, 1921–1930" (master's thesis, Ohio State University, 1935); "Model City! Boys of Junior Crime Prevention Bureau to Set Up 'Hill City' with Own Officers at New Granada Saturday Morning," *Pittsburgh Courier*, March 25, 1939; "Hill City Receives Gymnasium Grant," *Pittsburgh Courier*, January 13, 1940; "Hill City," *Time*, September 11, 1939, 62; "These Youngsters Govern 'Hill City,'" *Pittsburgh Courier*, March 8, 1941; David B. Wolcott, *Cops and Kids: Policing Juvenile Delinquency in Urban America, 1890–1940* (Columbus: Ohio State University Press, 2005); Robert Hughey, "Spanning Time," *Pittsburgh Courier*, August 19, 1939; Webb Waldron, "Gang Goes Uphill: Story of Hill City Municipality of Negro Youth in Pittsburgh's Harlem," *Survey Graphic* 29 (March 1940): 182–185.

40. "Boys Organize as Police: South Portland Lads Get Ideas from City Official," *Oregonian*, April 12, 1913; "Columbus 'Youth City' Gets Ready for Annual Elections," *Cleveland Call and Post*, November 1, 1941; Myron E. Moorehead, "An Evaluation of the Friendly Service Bureau in Its Crime Prevention among Negroes in the City of Columbus, Ohio, 1921–1930" (master's thesis, Ohio State University, 1935).

41. Jennifer Light, "Building Virtual Cities, 1895–1945," *Journal of Urban History* 38, no. 2 (2012): 336–371; LeRoy Ashby, *Saving the Waifs: Reformers and Dependent Children, 1890–1917*

(Philadelphia: Temple University Press, 1984). From HH Records, container 54, Hiram House Publications, Newsletters and Promotional Pamphlets, folder 1 Publications: [Most likely George Bellamy], Progress City Speech of July 13, 1925, container 26, folder 8 Progress City 1925; *Hiram House Life, Progress City Edition,* July 9, 1936, and August 23, 1937; and "Police Women," *Hiram House Life, Progress City Edition,* August 13, 1936. "Young Men in America" *Los Angeles Times,* August 13, 1939; Alex Zirin, "Bradley Spurs Sandlot Drive," *Plain Dealer,* July 3, 1940; Boystown Executive Committee and Writers' Program, *Boystowns* (Cleveland: Special Committee on Boystowns, 1939); "Community's 'Boys' Town' Elects City Officials," *Cleveland Call and Post,* February 23, 1939; Fred Kelly, "Boystowns for Cleveland Youth," *Recreation* 33 (November 1939): 437–438; "Huck Finn Boystown Receives Flag from Boydston Post Officials," *Cleveland Call and Post,* March 21, 1940; Eliot Ness, "Juvenile Delinquency and the School," *Phi Delta Kappan* 22, no. 7 (March 1940): 337–339, 344; Fred Kelly, "'Boystowns' for Cleveland Youth," in *Public Recreation in the City of Cleveland* (Cleveland: Department of Public Properties, 1939); Writers Program of the Works Projects Administration, *Cleveland's Boystowns* (1940); "Cleveland's 'Boystown' in Old Police Stations," *Sun,* October 1, 1939.

42. "Youth City Gets Started; Evans Lauded: North Philly Center Answers Great Need, Say Speakers," *Philadelphia Tribune,* December 19, 1940; "Youth Town's First Mayor Takes Office," *Philadelphia Tribune,* July 4, 1940; "Youth City to Help Stop Purse Thefts," *Philadelphia Tribune,* April 10, 1941; "Youth City Officers to Be Installed," *Pittsburgh Courier,* June 8, 1940; "Speakers Commend 'Youth City' at Inaugural Program," *Pittsburgh Courier,* July 6, 1940; John Perdue, "Civic League Head Commends Youth City," *Philadelphia Tribune,* July 11, 1940; "Youth City Finds Favor with the Public," *Philadelphia Tribune,* February 20, 1941; "Youth City Courtmen Hold First Practice," *Philadelphia Tribune,* November 14, 1940; "To Elect Officers for Youth City," *Philadelphia Tribune,* May 16, 1940; Jennifer Light, *The Nature of Cities* (Baltimore: Johns Hopkins University Press, 2009); Hattie Todd, "My Thoughts About Progress City," *Progress City News,* August 3, 1925, container 26, folder 8 Progress City 1925, HH Records; "Extra," *Merryburgh Journal,* n.d. (most likely 1928), container 54, folder 2, Progress City ca. 1906–1920, HH Records; P. D. Graham, "The Cleveland Study of Community Centers from the Standpoint of the Schools and Private Effort," *Proceedings of the National Conference of Social Work* (Chicago: University of Chicago Press, 1931), 372. Organized by a youth worker rather than the police department, Youth City nonetheless garnered advocates and assistance from Philadelphia's department of public safety. They were hopeful the youth, who established their headquarters at a former nightclub, would help prevent further neighborhood deterioration.

43. "Council Hears of Hill City's Splendid Work," *Pittsburgh Courier,* February 8, 1941; Elbert Kennedy, "News of Hill City," *Pittsburgh Courier,* January 4, 1941; "Hill City to Try New Plan," *Pittsburgh Courier,* September 6, 1941; Elbert Kennedy, "News of Hill City," *Pittsburgh Courier,* August 30, 1941; "Youth City to Help Stop Purse Thefts," *Philadelphia Tribune,* April 10, 1941; Webb Waldron, "A Gang Goes Uphill: Story of Hill City Municipality Negro Youth in Pittsburgh's Harlem," *Survey Graphic* 29 (March 1940): 184; Bessie Holloway, "'Let Children Feel They Are Important,' Father Flanagan Advises at Hill City," *Pittsburgh Courier,* November 4, 1939; "Hill City," *Time,* September 11, 1939, 62; "Hill City Reduces Juvenile Crime in Pittsburgh," *Afro-American,* March 23, 1940, 12. Ness quoted in *Hiram House Life, Progress City Edition,* July 9, 1936, container 54

Hiram House Publications, Newsletters and Promotional Pamphlets, folder 1 Publications, HH Records; Fred Kelly, "Boystowns for Cleveland Youth," *Recreation* 33 (November 1939): 437–440; "These Youngsters Govern 'Hill City,'" *Pittsburgh Courier*, March 8, 1941; James M. Reid, "Positive Bad Turns to Positive Good in Youth's Model Project," *Pittsburgh Courier*, March 22, 1941; United States Senate Committee on the Judiciary, *Juvenile Delinquency, Pittsburgh, Pa. Hearing Before the Subcommittee to Investigate Juvenile Delinquency of the Committee on the Judiciary, United States Senate, Eighty-fourth Congress, First Session, Pursuant to S. Res. 62, Investigation of Juvenile Delinquency in the United States. December 7, 1955* (Washington, DC: GPO, 1956), 80; Elbert Kennedy, "News of Hill City," *Pittsburgh Courier*, January 25, 1941; James Reid, "Youth Builds a Model City: 'Bad Boys' Make Good Leaders in Their Own Town, Hill City," *Pittsburgh Courier*, March 1, 1941; "Boys Rescued from Crime by Pittsburgh's 'Hill City': 2,000 Enrolled Y.M.C.A. Secretary Funds Donated," *Christian Science Monitor*, August 22, 1939; Cecil Clare North, *The Community and Social Welfare: A Study in Community Organization* (New York: McGraw-Hill, 1931), 268; P. D. Graham, "The Cleveland Study of Community Centers from the Standpoint of the Schools and Private Effort," *Proceedings of the National Conference of Social Work* (Chicago: University of Chicago Press, 1931), 372.

44. Container 52 Hiram House records 1893–1968, Hiram House publications, employees' guides, Camp-Progress, folder 4 "Progress City" 1936 (Macey), HH Papers; Container 52 Hiram House records 1893–1968 Hiram House publications, employees' guides, HH Papers; "These Youngsters Govern 'Hill City,'" *Pittsburgh Courier*, March 8, 1941; James Reid, "How Youth Runs Model City: Young Officials Have Keen Sense of Responsibility," *Pittsburgh Courier*, March 8, 1941: 13; Eliot Ness, "The Participation of Boys," *Phi Delta Kappan* 22, no. 7 (March 1940): 338, 344; Webb Waldron, "A Gang Goes Uphill: Story of Hill City Municipality Negro Youth in Pittsburgh's Harlem," *Survey Graphic* 29 (March 1940): 184; James Reid, "Hill City's Criminal Court Breaks Up 'Red Ace' Gang," *Pittsburgh Courier*, March 15, 1941; James Reid, "Positive Bad Turns to Positive Good in Youth's Model Project," *Pittsburgh Courier*, March 22, 1941.

45. Rebecca de Schweinitz, *If We Could Change the World* (Chapel Hill: University of North Carolina Press, 2009); Webb Waldron, "The Story of Hill City, Condensed from *Survey Graphic*," *The Negro*, March 1, 1946, 49; "Youth City Honors Mrs. Mary Bethune," *Afro-American*, October 4, 1941, 15; "These Youngsters Govern 'Hill City,'" *Pittsburgh Courier*, March 8, 1941; James Reid, "How Youth Runs Model City: Young Officials Have Keen Sense of Responsibility," *Pittsburgh Courier*, March 8, 1941.

46. Howard McKinney, "Function of Junior Crime Prevention Bureau and Hill City Municipal Court," *Pittsburgh Courier*, August 5, 1939; Turner Catledges, "Ohio Groups Seek Race Tension Cure," *New York Times*, July 15, 1943; James Reid, "Positive Bad Turns to Positive Good in Youth's Model Project," *Pittsburgh Courier*, March 22, 1941; Webb Waldron, "A Gang Goes Uphill: Story of Hill City Municipality Negro Youth in Pittsburgh's Harlem," *Survey Graphic* 29 (March 1940): 182–83, 185; "These Youngsters Govern 'Hill City,'" *Pittsburgh Courier*, March 8, 1941; "Hill City Reduces Juvenile Crime in Pittsburgh," *Afro-American*, March 23, 1940, 12; "Hold Birthday Fete for McKinney, Hill City Head," *Pittsburgh Courier*, October 7, 1939; "Distinguished Visitors Grace Hill City Court," *Pittsburgh Courier*, August 12, 1939; "Judge Lecher Will Speak at Hill City Meet," *Pittsburgh Courier*, November 18, 1939; "Hill City Officials at John Wesley Church," *Pittsburgh Courier*, December 2, 1939; "Elected and Appointed Officials of the Municipality of Hill City,"

Pittsburgh Courier, April 15, 1939; Robert Hughey, "Spanning Time," *Pittsburgh Courier,* August 19, 1939; Jessie Mae Jones, "'Tom, Dick and Harry' Given Trial in Hill City's Court," *Pittsburgh Courier,* September 9, 1939; "Youthful Officials of Hill City to Open Spirited Drive Against Crime," *Pittsburgh Courier,* May 27, 1939; Bessie Holloway, "'Let Children Feel They Are Important,' Father Flanagan Advises at Hill City," *Pittsburgh Courier,* November 4, 1939; "'Hill City' Mayor Receives Benefit Check," *Pittsburgh Courier,* May 13, 1939; Webb Waldron, *Americans* (New York: Greystone, 1941); Webb Waldron, "The Story of Hill City, Condensed from *Survey Graphic*," *The Negro,* March 1, 1946.

47. James Reid, "Hill City's Criminal Court Breaks Up 'Red Ace Gang,'" *Pittsburgh Courier,* March 15, 1941; Robert W. Chamberlin, Department of Public Safety, Robert A. Burri, Department of Public Health and Welfare, J. Noble Richards, Division of Recreation, *Cleveland's Boystowns: A Report Prepared by the Executive Committee for Cleveland's Boystowns* (Cleveland: Boystown Executive Committee Writers' Program, 1940); "Jimmie Buys 'Hill City' Bonds," *Pittsburgh Courier,* October 14, 1939; "Erskine Hawkins Plays for Hill City Benefit," *Pittsburgh Courier,* June 24, 1939; "Columbus 'Youth City' Gets Ready for Annual Elections," *Cleveland Call and Post,* November 1, 1941; "Community's 'Boys' Town' Elects City Officials," *Cleveland Call and Post,* February 23, 1939; "Boystown Mayor Makes Appeal to Citizens," *Cleveland Call and Post,* February 29, 1940; "Erskine Hawking Coming for Hill City Picnic at Olympia Park June 27," *Pittsburgh Courier,* June 17, 1939; Elbert Kennedy, "News of Hill City," *Pittsburgh Courier,* August 16, 1941; Elbert Kennedy, "News of Hill City," *Pittsburgh Courier,* July 26, 1941; "Hill City Council Issues Bonds to Establish Budget: Public to Be Asked to Purchase Bonds to Help Provide Equipment and Facilities for Model City—Has No Regular Support," *Pittsburgh Courier,* September 9, 1939; "Boys Rescued from Crime by Pittsburgh's 'Hill City,'" *Christian Science Monitor,* August 22, 1939; "Youth City Gets Started; Evans Lauded: North Philly Center Answers Great Need, Say Speakers," *Philadelphia Tribune,* December 19, 1940; "A Real S.O.S.," *Philadelphia Tribune,* March 7, 1942; "Youth City Officers to Be Installed," *Pittsburgh Courier,* June 8, 1940; "Speakers Commend 'Youth City' at Inaugural Program," *Pittsburgh Courier,* July 6, 1940; "Youth Town's First Mayor Takes Office," *Philadelphia Tribune,* July 4, 1940; "Youth City to Help Stop Purse Thefts," *Philadelphia Tribune,* April 10, 1941; "'Youth City' to Dedicate Headquarters," *Philadelphia Tribune,* December 12, 1940; John Perdue, "Civic League Head Commends Youth City," *Philadelphia Tribune,* July 11, 1940; "Youth City Finds Favor with the Public," *Philadelphia Tribune,* February 20, 1941; "Youth City Courtmen Hold First Practice," *Philadelphia Tribune,* November 14, 1940; "To Elect Officers for Youth City," *Philadelphia Tribune,* May 16, 1940.

48. James Reid, "Positive Bad Turns to Positive Good in Youth's Model Project," *Pittsburgh Courier,* March 22, 1941; "Hill City," *Time,* September 11, 1939; Webb Waldron, "Gang Goes Uphill," *Survey Graphic* 29 (March 1940): 182–185; "Hill City Council Issues Bonds to Establish Budget," *Pittsburgh Courier,* September 9, 1939; Elbert Kennedy, "News of Hill City," *Pittsburgh Courier,* January 25, 1941; "Council Hears of Hill City's Splendid Work," *Pittsburgh Courier,* February 8, 1941; James Reid, "Hill City's Criminal Court Breaks up 'Red Ace Gang,'" *Pittsburgh Courier,* March 15, 1941; "These Youngsters Govern 'Hill City,'" *Pittsburgh Courier,* March 8, 1941; Robert W. Chamberlin, Department of Public Safety, Robert A. Burri, Department of Public Health and Welfare, J. Noble Richards, Division of Recreation, *Cleveland's Boystowns: A Report Prepared by the*

Executive Committee for Cleveland's Boystowns (Cleveland: Boystown Executive Committee Writers' Program, 1940), 13; Howard McKinney, "Function of Junior Crime Prevention Bureau and Hill City Municipal Court," *Pittsburgh Courier,* August 5, 1939; Turner Catledges, "Ohio groups Seek Race Tension Cure," *New York Times,* July 15, 1943; "These Youngsters Govern 'Hill City,'" *Pittsburgh Courier,* March 8, 1941; "Hill City Reduces Juvenile Crime in Pittsburgh," *Afro-American,* March 23, 1940; "Hold Birthday Fete for McKinney, Hill City Head," *Pittsburgh Courier,* October 7, 1939; "Distinguished Visitors Grace Hill City Court," *Pittsburgh Courier,* August 12, 1939; "Elected and Appointed Officials of the Municipality of Hill City," *Pittsburgh Courier,* April 15, 1939; Robert Hughey, "Spanning Time," *Pittsburgh Courier,* August 19, 1939; Jessie Mae Jones, "'Tom, Dick and Harry' Given Trial in Hill City's Court," *Pittsburgh Courier,* September 9, 1939; "Youthful Officials of Hill City to Open Spirited Drive Against Crime," *Pittsburgh Courier,* May 27, 1939; Bessie Holloway, "'Let Children Feel They Are Important,' Father Flanagan Advises at Hill City," *Pittsburgh Courier,* November 4, 1939; "'Hill City' Mayor Receives Benefit Check," *Pittsburgh Courier,* May 13, 1939; Webb Waldron, *Americans* (New York: Greystone, 1941); Webb Waldron, "The Story of Hill City, Condensed from *Survey Graphic,*" *The Negro,* March 1, 1946.

49. The following are in WG Papers: William Gute, "Letter to the Trustees, parents of citizens and all interested in the George Junior Republic," August 1908, box 4, folder 25; postcard invitation to the Berkeley Lyceum, 1897, box 2, folder 6; Samuel Tatnall to William George, January 24, 1921, box 22, folder 16. William Osborne Dapping, *The Muckers: A Narrative of the Crapshooters Club* (Syracuse, NY: Syracuse University Press, 2016); John Balderston, "My Opinion of the G. R.," *Junior Citizen* 1, no. 1 (1898), 2; "Junior Republic Meeting," *Buffalo Courier,* March 8, 1901; "Junior's President Talks," *New York Times,* March 29, 1897; "Latest News from Boy City: Political, Circus, Sunday-School and Other Items in the Daily Paper of 'Kidville,'" *Salt Lake Telegram,* August 10, 1907; Harriet Hickox Heller, "The Playground as a Phase of Social Reform," *Proceedings of the Second Annual Playground Conference* (1909), 182; "Where a City Is Run by Children," *Cleveland Plain Dealer,* July 29, 1906; "The Pictures," *Wairarapa Daily Times* [New Zealand], 4 Haratua [May] 1918, 3; Juvenile Court at Winona, "'Citizens of Boys' City Will Pose as the 'Culprits,'" *Indianapolis Star,* July 14, 1907; Junior Town Reporter, "Junior Towners Program Planned: Second Meeting Held; Welfare Commissioners Named," April 29, 1930, 8; "Picks Ideal Boy for World Tour," *Chicago Daily Tribune,* April 13, 1913; *Life of the Boys Brotherhood Republic* (Chicago: BBR, 1938). *Progress City News* was published continuously throughout that program's run. In some cases, local commercial media supported these efforts. For example, *Progress City News*'s first issue in July 1906 was an insert in the *Cleveland Plain Dealer*, local newspapers in Omaha gave "generous space" to news from the playground-based Juvenile City, and "Junior Town reporters" were invited to publish in rural community papers. Administrators of these programs also turned to junior citizens to assist publicizing their work. At Winona's Boy City, for example, mock trials at the summer Chautauqua demonstrated the workings of the juvenile court, and some of Brown's boys went on tour to describe life in the miniature municipality to audiences across the globe. BBR youth road-tripped to cities around the United States to share their experiences and encourage the start-up of new republics.

50. Ludwig Bernstein, "Modern Tendencies in Jewish Orphan Asylum work," in *Annual Report of the Hebrew Sheltering Guardian Society*, box 1, folder 4 Annual Reports (bound) 1905–1909, Records

of the Hebrew Sheltering Guardian Society of New York, Center for Jewish History, 33; L. C. Day, "A Small Boy's Newspapers and the Evolution of a Social Conscience," *Pedagogical Seminary* 24 (1917): 180–203; Erkki Huhtamo, *Illusions in Motion: Media Archaeology of the Moving Panorama and Related Spectacles* (Cambridge, MA: MIT Press, 2013); Paula Petrik, "Desk-Top Publishing: The Making of the American Dream," *History Today* 39 (1989): 12–19; Paula Petrik, "The Youngest Fourth Estate: The Novelty Printing Press and Adolescence, 1870–1876," in *Small Worlds: Children and Adolescence, 1850–1950*, ed. Elliott West and Paula Petrik (Lawrence: University of Kansas Press, 1992); Susan Douglas, "Amateur Operators and American Broadcasting: Shaping the Future of Radio," in *Imagining Tomorrow. History, Technology, and the American Future*, ed. Joseph Corn (Cambridge, MA: MIT Press, 1986), 35–57; William Boorman, *Developing Personality in Boys: The Social Psychology of Adolescence* (New York: Macmillan, 1929); Meredith Anne Bak, "Perception and Playthings: Optical Toys as Instruments of Science and Culture" (PhD diss., University of California, Santa Barbara, 2012).

51. William George, *The Adult Minor* (New York: Appleton, 1937), 77; "Text of Junior Municipality Broadcast on Homer," *Homer Post*, March 22, 1935, 6. The following are in WG Papers: William George to L. Freedman, January 19, 1933, box 33, folder 31; William George to Jack Weeks, October 14, 1932, box 33, folder 19; William George to Bernard Shapero, October 14, 1932, box 33, folder 19; William George to Johnny Kinane, October 14, 1932, box 33, folder 19; "To the Executive Committee of the George Junior Republic Association, Inc.," February 4, 1935, box 35, folder 18; Charles Taylor to M. J. Freeborn, May 13, 1935, box 35, folder 33; *Youth Outlook: The Voice of America's Adult Minors* [stationery that shows the League published a paper with help from the *Homer Post* in Homer, NY], box 35, folder 8. "Father Flanagan's Boys' Home Is Mecca of Homeless Boys of All Religions and Colors," *Philadelphia Tribune*, April 9, 1931; Boys Brotherhood Republic, *Life of the BBR* (Chicago: BBR, 1938), 23; "Boys' Club News Culled from Many Sources," *Boys Workers Round Table* (Midsummer 1923), 30; Alfred E. Cornebise, *The CCC Chronicles: Camp Newspapers of the Civilian Conservation Corps* (Jefferson, NC: McFarland, 2004); William Burroughs, *Boys in Mens' Shoes* (New York: Macmillan, 1944); "Boston Newsboy Is Eagerly Awaited," *Boston Daily Globe*, March 31, 1935; Pearl Strachan, "The Wide Horizon," *Christian Science Monitor*, May 27, 1938; Lewis Rex Miller, "Junior Statesmen of America," *Christian Science Monitor*, November 23, 1937; Arthur Richard Choppin, *Yearbook, Louisiana Boys' State* (Baton Rouge, LA: American Legion, 1939); "Boys Learn Citizenship in Own 'State': California Boys Run State," *Christian Science Monitor*, July 8, 1939; Norman Radder, *Newspapers in Community Service* (New York: McGraw-Hill, 1926); Harold Lasswell et al., *Propaganda and Promotional Activities: An Annotated Bibliography* (Minneapolis: University of Minnesota Press, 1935). The Chicago BBR publication was *Boys World*.

52. *Ye Village Crier*, June 8, 1937, folder Quoddy, record group 119, Records of the National Youth Association, Records of the Resident Center Section, Records Concerning Quoddy Village Resident Project at Eastport, Maine, 1936–1939, box 2, NARA; "Weekly Wash," *Quoddy Eagle*, August 20, 1938, folder Quoddy—Karl Borders, record group 119, Records of the National Youth Administration, Records of the Resident Center Section, subject file 1939–1943, Quoddy, June 1937-December 1939, box 5, NARA; "Quoddy (Passamaquoddy) Regional Center, Quoddy Village, Maine," *NASSP Bulletin* 24 (1940): 119; National Youth Administration, *Quoddy Regional Project: An Experiment in Youth Rehabilitation*, 1940, record group 119, Records of the National

Youth Administration, Records of the Resident Center Section, subject file 1939–1943, Quoddy, June 1937-December 1939, box 5, NARA; "Quoddy on the Air" [from Bangor's WLBZ], *Eastport Sentinel,* September 25, 1940, reprinted from *Quoddy Eagle,* folder Quoddy Clippings. record group 119, Records of the National Youth Administration, Records of the Resident Center Section, subject file 1939–1943, Quoddy, June 1937–December 1939, box 5, NARA; Ivan Asay, "The National Youth Administration Faces the Problem of Community Relations," August 20, 1935, folder Community organization, record group 119, Records of the National Youth Administration, Records of the Division of Community Organization, Correspondence of the Director with Youth Organizations, 1935–1937. box 2, NARA; Federal Security Agency, War Manpower Commission, *Final Report of the National Youth Administration: Fiscal Years 1936–1943* (Washington, DC: Government Printing Office, 1944); Susan Wladaver-Morgan, "Young Women and the New Deal: Camps and Resident Centers, 1933–1943" (PhD diss., Indiana University, 1982); "Radio," folder Radio, record group 119, Records of the National Youth Administration, Records of the Radio Projects Section, fragment file of Robert B. Burton, Radio Engineer and Section Chief, Concerning NYA Amateur Radio Stations and Licenses, 1940–1942, box 1, NARA; Public Information on the Student-Aid Program, Cabel Phillips, Division of Public Relations, folder Student Aid Publications, record group 119, Records of the National Youth Administration, Records of the Public Relations Section, Part of a Personal or Desk File of Cabel Phillips, Publications Expert in the Former Publications Division, 1935–1937, box 1, NARA; "To All NYA students June 1938," folder Student Aid Publications, record group 119, Records of the National Youth Administration, Records of the Public Relations Section, Part of a Personal or Desk File of Cabel Phillips, Publications Expert in the Former Publications Division, 1935–1937, box 1, NARA; Cabel Phillips to staff members, Subject: Digest of current magazine articles, folder Miscellaneous, record group 119, Records of the National Youth Administration, Records of the Public Relations Section, Part of a Personal or Desk File of Cabel Phillips, Publications Expert in the Former Publications Division, 1935–1937, box 1, NARA; Howard Bell, "The Conservation of American Youth through Community Youth Programs," *Phi Delta Kappan* 21, no. 8 (1939): 383–384, 391; "Active Program Being Launched at the Village," *Eastport Sentinel,* July 24, 1940, folder Quoddy Clippings, record group 119, Records of the National Youth Administration, Records of the Resident Center Section, subject file 1939–1943, Quoddy, June 1937-December 1939, box 5, NARA. Other NYA newspapers included *The Armonian* from the South Charleston Regional Project in West Virginia, and *Youth,* a weekly from Residential Center of Williamsport, PA. "Recreational Activities, South Charleston West Virginia Regional Project, National Youth Administration" folder South Charleston Regional Project, record group 119, Records of the National Youth Administration, Records of the Resident Center Section, subject file 1939–1943, NYA-US Army Station Relations, box 7, NARA.

53. "Court of Youths Judges Own Cases in 'Hill City,'" *Pittsburgh Courier,* July 8, 1939; "Hill City Officials Plead for Cooperation of Parents," *Pittsburgh Courier,* July 22, 1939; "Publicity Focus on Crime Prevention," *Pittsburgh Courier,* October 7, 1939; "Huck Finn Boystown News," *Cleveland Call and Post,* July 20, 1940; Elbert Kennedy, "News of Hill City," *Pittsburgh Courier,* August 2, 1941; Elbert Kennedy, "News of Hill City," *Pittsburgh Courier,* January 18, 1941; Elbert Kennedy, "News of Hill City," *Pittsburgh Courier,* March 1, 1941; Elbert Kennedy, "News of Hill City," *Pittsburgh Courier,* July 12, 1941; Elbert Kennedy, "News of Hill City," *Pittsburgh Courier,* July 19, 1941; Elbert Kennedy, "News of Hill City," *Pittsburgh Courier,* April 19, 1941; Elbert Kennedy, "News

of Hill City," *Pittsburgh Courier,* March 8, 1941; Elbert Kennedy, "News of Hill City," *Pittsburgh Courier,* August 16, 1941; Elbert Kennedy, "News of Hill City," *Pittsburgh Courier,* July 26, 1941; Elbert Kennedy, "News of Hill City," *Pittsburgh Courier,* July 19, 1941; *Merryburgh Journal* (multiple issues, HH Records); "Father Flanagan's Boys' Home Is Mecca of Homeless Boys of All Religions and Colors," *New Journal and Guide,* April 18, 1931, 7; Robert W. Chamberlin, Department of Public Safety, Robert A. Burri, Department of Public Health and Welfare, J. Noble Richards, Division of Recreation, *Cleveland's Boystowns: A Report Prepared by the Executive Committee for Cleveland's Boystowns* (Cleveland: Boystown Executive Committee Writers' Program, 1940); "Hill City Court Is Held in Sewickly," *Pittsburgh Courier,* November 11, 1939; "Youth Town's First Mayor Takes Office," *Philadelphia Tribune,* July 4, 1940; Jessie Mae Jones, "'Tom, Dick and Harry' Given Trial in Hill City's Court," *Pittsburgh Courier,* September 9, 1939; "Huck Finn Boystown to Hold Open House," *Cleveland Call and Post,* May 25, 1940.

54. James Stevens, "Activities for Unemployed Teachers," *Junior-Senior High School Clearing House* 8, no. 6 (1934): 376–378; John Loftus, "Changes in Elementary Schools During 1929," *Journal of Educational Sociology* (1930): 473–480; Glenn Kendall, "Experience in Developing a Community Program of Education," *Social Forces* 19, no. 1 (October 1940): 48–51; Milosh Muntyan, "Community School Concepts," *Journal of Educational Research* 41, no. 8 (April 1948): 597–609; Nathan Peyser, "The School as the Center of the Community," *Journal of Educational Sociology* 9, no. 6 (February 1936): 354–358; Lloyd Allen Cook, *Community Backgrounds of Education* (New York: McGraw-Hill, 1938); Samuel Everett, ed., *The Community School* (New York: Appleton-Century, 1938); Edward Olsen, *School and Community: The Philosophy, Procedures, and Problems of Community Study and Service through Schools and Colleges* (New York: Prentice Hall, 1945), 272; Morris Mitchell, *Youth Has a Part to Play* (New York: Progressive Education Association, 1942); Elizabeth C. Morriss and Howard W. Odum, "Citizens Reference Book: A Textbook for Adult Beginners in Community Schools," *Journal of Education* 107, no. 1 (January 2, 1928): 24; H. B. Alberty and Boyd H. Bode, *Educational Freedom and Democracy* (New York: Appleton-Century, 1938); N. L. Engelhardt and N. L. Engelhardt Jr., *Planning the Community School* (New York: American Book, 1940); C. C. Minty, "How Minneapolis Schools Conduct Field Trips," *Business Education World* 18 (June 1938): 810–814; Theodore Reller, "Procedures in Identifying and Appraising Community Resources Having Educational Values," in *Twenty-sixth Annual Schoolmen's Week Proceedings* (Philadelphia: University of Pennsylvania, School of Education, 1931), 220–228; Teachers College Community Service Center, *Community News and Education* (New York: Teachers College, Columbia University); D. Harley Fite, "Making the School a Community Center," *Education* 60 (February 1940): 362–372; H. W. Hurt, "Relation of the School to Other Educative Forces in the Community," *Clearing House* 8 (May 1934): 526–531; *Journal of Educational Sociology* special issues: "Schools that Serve the Community" (February 1936), "Education and the Community" (April 1936), "Community Coordination and Social Programs" (September 1936), "Community Agencies and Character Growth" (March 1937), "Proceedings: National Educational Conference on Community Coordination" (October 1937), "The Yonkers Plan of Community Coordination" (January 1938), "Cooperation of Schools and Community Agencies" (April 1938); Jane Mayer and Miriam Sutherland, "The Community a Laboratory," Progressive Education Association Service Center Pamphlet, 1941; Herschel W. Nisonger, *The Role of the School in Community Education* (Columbus: Ohio State University, 1940); Morris Randolph Mitchell, "Youth Has a Part to Play," *Progressive Education* 19

(February 1942): 87–109; Julian E. Butterworth, "The Interaction of School and Community in a Democratic Society," *Journal of Educational Sociology* 14, no. 4 (December 1940): 230–249; Educational Policies Commission, *Social Services and the Schools* (Washington, DC: Educational Policies Commission, 1939), 10; Elsie Clapp, *Community Schools in Action* (New York: Viking, 1939); James A. Michener, "Participation in Community Surveys as Social Education," in "Utilization of Community Resources in the Social Studies," ed. Ruth West, 144–163, at 153, *Ninth Yearbook, National Council for the Social Studies*, 1938; M. M. Chambers and Howard M. Bell, "How to Make a Community Youth Survey," *American Council on Education Studies*, series 4, vol. 3, no. 2 (Washington, DC: American Council on Education Studies, 1938); L. C. Davis, "Field Work in Geography," *Educational Method* 17 (March 1938): 293–296; Mildred P. Ellis, "Framingham Facts: Our Pupils Investigate Local Standards of Living," *Clearing House* 16 (November 1941): 140–142; Paul R. Grim, "Housing Study: Our Pupils Investigate," *Clearing House* 16 (March 1942): 402–404; Wilbur C. Hallenbeck, "Surveying the Community," in *Community Life in a Democracy*, ed. Florence E. Bingham (Chicago: National Congress of Parents and Teachers, 1942); J. Fred Murphy, "A Student Survey of Local Occupations," *Social Studies* 27 (November 1936): 474–476; Bernice Newell, "Trends in Community Surveys," *Educational Method* 18 (October 1938): 7–13; Arthur Repke, "Society Is Our Laboratory," *Social Education* 3 (December 1939): 620–622; J. B. Sears, "School and Community Surveys," *Review of Educational Research* 9 (December 1939): 508–513; Lloyd Allen Cook, "Methods of Community Study," in *The School and the Urban Community*, Proceedings of the Eleventh Annual Conference of Administrative Officers of Public and Private Schools, vol. 5, ed. William C. Reavis (Chicago: University of Chicago Press, 1942), 201–214; Paul R. Hanna and Research Staff, *Youth Serves the Community* (New York: Appleton-Century, 1936); Walter W. Herkness Jr., "Philadelphia's Student Volunteer Service Corps," *School Executive* 62 (December 1942): 15, 38.

55. Sonja Dümpelmann, *Seeing Trees* (New Haven, CT: Yale University Press, 2019); R. J. Bretnall, "Welfare Workers: Millburn High Serves Community as Legal Administrative Unit of Department of Welfare," *Clearing House* 16, no. 6 (February 1942): 329–331; Kermit Blank, "The Weather Club," *School Science and Mathematics* 37 (February 1937): 147–150; "Pennsylvania Federation Aids U. S. and State in Elm Survey: Conservation Unit and School Officials Enlist Children's Services to Get Reports on Condition of Trees, Club Marks Newtown's 250th Anniversary," *New York Herald Tribune*, May 6, 1934; Florence S. Harper, "Students Make a Recreational Survey," *Educational Method* 18 (March 1939): 279–283; Clement T. Malan, "Social Survey of a School District," *Social Education* 3 (September 1939): 409–412; A. P. Gossard, "High-School Pupils Study Their Community," *School Review* 43 (April 1935): 268–272; Miriam Sutherland, "The Children Survey the Community," *Curriculum Journal* 10 (November 1939): 317–319; Douglas S. Ward, "Community Surveys for Junior High Schools?" *Social Education* 4 (December 1940): 553–556; *Community Surveys by Rural High Schools* (Madison, WI: Agricultural Experiment Station and Department of Public Instruction, 1941); National Child Welfare Association, *Adventures in the Knighthood of Youth* (New York: National Child Welfare Association, 1931); Elizabeth Pendry and Hugh Hartshorne, *Organizations for Youth* (New York: McGraw-Hill, 1935); Orrin Evans, "Mayor Wilson Offers $300 in Prizes to Clean Block Campaign," *Philadelphia Tribune*, July 22, 1937; Ray Butts MacLean, *Minnesota and the Junior Citizen* (St. Paul, MN: Webb, 1936); *Junior American Citizens Handbook, 1937–1938* (Washington, DC: Daughters of the American Revolution, 1937).

56. John P. Sullivan, "Present Status of Safety Education in Some Representative School Systems," *American Journal of Public Health* 28 (October 1938): 1183; Commonwealth of Pennsylvania, Department of Public Instruction, *Safety Education in the Public Schools: A Manual of Organization and Administration, Curriculum Studies Bulletin* 94 (1935); "Bill in State Legislature Threatened Junior Police System," and Verne Homman, "Racine Officials Defend School Safety Patrols," *Racine Journal Times Sunday Bulletin,* May 7, 1939; A. R. Lauer, "Problems of the School Patrol," *Phi Delta Kappan* 23, no. 6 (February 1941): 230–235; "Kiwanis Told of New Traffic Aid," *Austin Statesman,* February 11, 1935; "Junior Traffic Patrols in Schools Save Lives of Many Children," *China Press,* May 22, 1932; Roy C. Bryan, "Should Pupils Take Part in Maintaining Good Discipline?" *School Review* 43, no. 6 (June 1935): 451–455; "Entitled to Protection," *Christian Science Monitor,* October 11, 1932; Robert E. LeAnderson, "The Utilization of Community Agencies and Resources," *Phi Delta Kappan* 21, no. 5 (January 1939): 181–184, 193; "Safety Club," *Junior Republic Citizen* (1936), 81; "Tackling Traffic Problems," *New York Times,* October 24, 1937; Reginald Cleveland, "Training of Driver Held Safety Need," *New York Times,* April 1938; "World at Play," *Recreation* 34 (1940): 385; "Safety Patrol Inaugurated," *Austin Statesman,* April 26, 1937; "Warring on the Speeders," *Atlanta Constitution,* November 25, 1935; Grace Hendrick Eustis, "Safety Campaign Begun by Women: National Organizations Join in New Drive to Decrease Traffic Accidents, Schools Urged to Help, Instruction in Regulations to Guide Children Advocated as Means to Save Lives," *New York Times,* October 25, 1936.

57. William Graebner, *The Engineering of Consent: Democracy and Authority in Twentieth-Century America* (Madison: University of Wisconsin Press, 1987) and Walter Stone, *The Development of Boys' Work in the United States* (Nashville: Cullom and Ghertner, 1935) document the influence of group work on youth work.

58. "Boy Scouts of America," *New International Year Book* (New York: Dodd and Mead, 1921), 96; Boy Scouts of America, "Commission Report on Scout Work among Negroes," in *Official Report of the Sixth National Training Conference of Scout Executives* (French Lick, IN: BSA, 1936), 518–525; Boy Scouts of America, "Commission Report on White Nationality Groups," in *Official Report of the Sixth National Training Conference of Scout Executives* (French Lick, IN: BSA, 1936), 840–848; Margaret Campbell Tillery, "The Boy Scout Movement in East Harlem, New York" (PhD diss., New York University, 1935); "Council Organizes to Spread Boy Scout Ideal to All Areas: Leaders of American Boy Scouts," *Christian Science Monitor,* May 16, 1938; "Giving the Dramatic Instinct a Chance," *Municipal Record* [San Francisco], vol. 17, 1924; Boy Scouts of America, *Handbook for Boys,* 1911; "Practical Citizenship, as Set Forth in a Letter from Colonel Theodore Roosevelt, Honorary Vice-president, Boy Scouts of America," *Outlook,* July 20, 1911; Boy Scouts of America, *Handbook for Scoutmasters,* 1913; "Boy Scouts Must Be Like Daring Men," *New York Times,* October 9, 1910; Boy Scouts of America, *Handbook for Scoutmasters, A Manual of Troop Leadership* 1947, 11; M. D. Taylor, "A Selected List of Government Publications for Boy Scouts," *Wilson Bulletin,* June 1931; F. A. Silcox, "Seven Millions Unite to Rescue America's Wildlife from Decimation," *Washington Post,* February 9, 1936; "Scouts Lend Aid to Wild Life," *New York Times,* December 29, 1935; "5 Scouts Work 5 Months, Save Thousands of Birds," *New York Herald Tribune,* June 9, 1935; "Tree Planting Is New Scout Work: Reforestation Project Is Inaugurated by New Jersey Troop," *Washington Post,* July 7, 1935; "Boy Scouts at Camp Wilson Will End Season on September 15:

Sea Scout Divisions Planned by Many Capital Troops, Nation-Wide Program in Nut-Tree Planting Arranged," *Washington Post,* September 1, 1933; "Hungry Birds Fed by Boy Scout Army," *Christian Science Monitor,* December 30, 1933; "Scouts Plant Trees Tomorrow, Honoring Nation's Famous Men: Hundreds of Boys Take Part in Arbor Day at Anacostia," *Washington Post,* April 20, 1934; "Boy Scout Patrol Finds 6,394 Park Violations," *New York Times,* December 31, 1934; "Scouts Are Planting Trees," *New York Times,* May 3, 1936; "Scouts to Plant Trees: Boys to Set Out 4,000 Pines at Camp Roosevelt, N.J.," *New York Times,* March 27, 1939; "A Day with the Boy Scouts," *New York Times,* August 13, 1939; "Boy Scouts Report on 10-Year Patrol," *New York Times,* January 16, 1938; "Trees Set Out by Scout Troop: Six Hundred Planted by 'Adventurers' on Burned-Over Hillside," *Los Angeles Times,* May 15, 1938; "Boy Scouts Are Cited: Osborne Praises Albany County Troop for Conservation Work," *New York Times,* June 9, 1935; "Scouts Aid in Conservation," *New York Times,* February 2, 1936; "Valentine Lauds Scouts: Commends Their Conservation Work in Palisades Park," *New York Times,* October 1936; "Boy Scouts Aid the Wild Birds," *New York Times,* February 23, 1936. Certainly, Scouts never lost their connection to nature. Already in the 1920s they were planting numerous trees, and a conservation badge had existed since 1925.

59. "G-man Here to Study Junior Police Corps," *Boston Daily Globe,* March 24, 1939; Richard Wilson, "Fears Grip Hoodlums," *Los Angeles Times,* March 29, 1934; "Boy Detective Tries to Find a Murderer," *New York Times,* February 9, 1933; Boy Scouts of America, *Fingerprinting* (New York: Boy Scouts of America, 1938); "Youth Leader, Here, Tells of Junior Statesmen: Founder of Nonprofit California School to Confer with J. Edgar Hoover on Juvenile Crime in US," *Seattle Daily Times,* December 5, 1937; "Boy Scout Troop Fingerprinted for U.S. Files," *Atlanta Constitution,* April 24, 1935; J. Edgar Hoover, chapter on fingerprinting in Franklin Mathiews, *Boy Scouts' Book of Indoor Hobby Trails* (New York: Appleton-Century, 1939); "Success of Youth Plan Depends on Execution," *Christian Science Monitor,* July 12, 1935; "Fingerprinting of U.S. Boy Scouts Voted by Council," *Christian Science Monitor,* May 23, 1936; "Children Fingerprinted In Leesburg, Fla., Schools," *Christian Science Monitor,* October 17, 1940; "He Fingerprints Both Races," *Afro-American,* February 10, 1940, 6; "Fingerprint Enrollees in 1600 CCC Camps," *Philadelphia Tribune,* November 11, 1937; "Fingerprint Bridge California's Latest," *Sun,* June 9, 1936; "To Fingerprint Scouts," *Hartford Courant,* March 3, 1939; "N.Y.A. Halts Fingerprinting," *New York Herald Tribune,* February 1, 1940. The NYA halted its involvement after 1940.

60. "Junior Inspectors Elect: Boys and Girls Name Leaders in Cleaner Streets Drive," *New York Times,* March 30, 1936; "Girl Again Is Elected City Junior 'Mayor,' Boys Are Swept into Political Obscurity," *New York Times,* June 15, 1941; "Junior Inspectors Have Busy Summer," *New York Times,* August 1, 1937.

61. "Junior Police Unit Is to Aid El Centro," *New York Times,* August 30, 1936; "Spokane Junior Police Formed," *Christian Science Monitor,* December 23, 1939; "Youth Appointed Made Chief of Junior Police," *New Journal and Guide,* May 25, 1940; "Boys to Help Police at Huntington Beach," *Los Angeles Times,* June 30, 1933; "250 City Boys Swoop Down on 'Jupoco,'" *Christian Science Monitor,* August 17, 1942; "Junior Police Arrange Jubilee," *Christian Science Monitor,* May 15, 1940; "Boston Junior Police Show Friends New Skill," *Christian Science Monitor,* April 27, 1939; "Inglewood Unit in Demand for Public Appearances," *Los Angeles Times,* November 28, 1938; "Junior Police Prove Aid to Citizenship," *Christian Science Monitor,* January 5, 1940; "Babe Ruth Aids Police

Baseball Plan for Boys," *New York Herald Tribune,* April 25, 1932; James Hepbron, "Athletics as an Ounce of Prevention," *Sun,* June 11, 1933; "Junior Police Aid Delinquency Drive," *New York Amsterdam Star-News,* December 6, 1941; "Timilty to Organize 'Police Force' of Boys," *Christian Science Monitor,* April 25, 1938; B. E. Bigelow, "Boston Junior Police Corps Finds Camp Better than Streets," *Christian Science Monitor,* August 19, 1939; "Spooks Quieted on Boston's Most Orderly Halloween," *Boston Daily Globe,* November 1, 1938; "Police Guardrooms to Be Play Halls," *Boston Daily Globe,* April 26, 1938; I. H. Grace, "Tough Kids Make Good Cops," *New York Herald Tribune,* April 6, 1941; "'Junior Police' Taught How to Trail Suspects," *New York Herald Tribune,* November 29, 1936; "Junior Police Crack Down on Light Breakers, Bikemen," *Hartford Courant,* September 20, 1936; "Track and Field Meets, Municipal Fireworks, Provide Safe Celebrations of Fourth," *New York Herald Tribune,* July 5, 1936; "Police Allow Boys to Act as City Cops," *Hartford Courant,* July 9, 1939; "Junior Police Work Goes on Even in the Vacation Period: Here Are Good Citizens in the Making," *Christian Science Monitor,* January 4, 1940; *Annual Report of the Police Commissioner for the City of Boston,* 1938 and 1939; "Jobs as Crime Prevention," *Christian Science Monitor,* January 4, 1940; "Pennsylvania Junior Police Put Brakes on Youth Crime: Poor Home Conditions Expansion Planned," *Christian Science Monitor,* September 27, 1941; "'Junior Police' Aid Juvenile Law Keeping," *Christian Science Monitor,* November 9, 1939; Mabel Travis Wood, "Playground Work Activities Just 'Fun' for Boys and Girls," *Christian Science Monitor,* July 17, 1930; "Boston Junior Police Present Show in Roxbury, Attended by More than 1200," *Boston Daily Globe,* April 21, 1939; "Application Blank for Junior Police," *Boston Daily Globe,* August 22, 1938; "Vacant Lots Urged as Play Spots for Younger Children," *Boston Daily Globe,* December 8, 1940.

62. Philip Cox, *Creative School Control* (Philadelphia: Lippincott, 1927), 18, 246. Harold Diedrich Meyer, *A Handbook of Extra-curricular Activities in the High School* (New York: Barnes, 1926) used the language of "morale" to make a similar argument. Of course, there had been some earlier studies of student media, such as Thomas Gatsischeck, "A Statistical Study of the Content of Newspapers," *School and Society* 3 (1918): 140–144. But there was rapid growth in this period. See Harry McKown, *School Clubs* (New York: Macmillan, 1929); Lloyd Allen Cook, "Democracy as an Agency of Social Control," *Elementary School Journal* 40, no. 1 (September 1939): 15–27; B. M. Huff, *Laboratory Manual for Journalism* (Chicago: Mentzer, Bush).

63. Pierce Fleming, "Moving Pictures as a Factor in Education," *Pedagogical Seminary* 18 (1911): 336–352; Agnes Benson, "Uses of the Victor and Player-Pianos in Schools and Social Centers," *NEA Journal on Proceedings and Addresses of the Fiftieth Annual Meeting,* 1912, 1230–1237; A. L. Benson, "Substitute for Schoolbooks" *World Today* 21 (March 1912): 1923–1927; Earl Kirkpatrick, "Motion Pictures in the School," *Oregon Teachers Monthly* 21 (1917): 363–367; "Moving Pictures as an Aid to Teaching Trades," *Scientific American Supplement,* January 30, 1909, 76; F. W. Sanderson, "The Kinematograph as an Aid in Education," *School World* 15 (May 1913): 166–170; B. H. Darrow, *Radio: The Assistant Teacher* (Columbus, OH: Adams, 1932); US Bureau of Education, Library Division, *List of References on Moving Pictures in Education,* 1914; Louise Dean, "Pryor Children Enjoy Imaginary Trip to Rocky Mts.," *Atlanta Constitution,* March 15, 1914; Phyllis Blanchard, "The Motion Picture as an Educational Asset," *Pedagogical Seminary* 26 (1919): 284–287; G. Stanley Hall, "Gesture Mimesis, Types of Temperament, and Movie Pedagogy," *Pedagogical Seminary* 28 (1921): 171–201; James N. Emery, "The Slide Route to Africa," *Educational Screen*

5 (1926): 170; Anna Verona Dorris, "Educating the Twentieth-Century Youth" *Clearing House* 69, no. 2 (1995): 77–79; A. Vermont, "The Teacher of French and His Opportunity," *High School Journal* 5, no. 6 (October 1, 1922): 153–156; Gordon Allport and Hadley Cantril, *The Psychology of Radio* (New York: Harper, 1935), 4; Alberta Wolgamott, "Moving Pictures in Industrial Education," *Manual Training and Vocational Education* 17 (June 1916); J. Wallace Wallin, "The Moving Picture in Relation to Education, Health, Delinquency, and Crime," *Pedagogical Seminary* 17 (1910): 129–142; Paula Fass, *The Damned and the Beautiful: American Youth in the 1920's* (New York: Oxford University Press, 1977); Jennifer Light, "Putting Our Conversation in Context," in *From Voice to Influence*, ed. D. Allen and J. Light (Chicago: University of Chicago Press, 2015); Paula Petrik, "Desk-Top Publishing: The Making of the American Dream," *History Today* 39 (1989): 12–19; Paula Petrik, "The Youngest Fourth Estate: The Novelty Printing Press and Adolescence, 1870–1876," in *Small Worlds: Children and Adolescence, 1850–1950*, ed. Elliott West and Paula Petrik (Lawrence: University of Kansas Press, 1992); Elbert Fretwell, *Extra-curricular Activities in Secondary Schools* (Boston: Houghton Mifflin, 1931); Howard Jones, "Tech High Boys Take Pride in Newspaper All Their Own," *Atlanta Constitution*, November 7, 1920; Lewis Todd, *Wartime Relations of the Federal Government and the Public Schools, 1917–1918* (New York: Teachers College Press, 1945); "Printing in California Schools," *Industrial-arts Magazine* 8 (1919); Elmer Chank, "Boys, Ten, Make Profit on Their Own Newspaper," *China Press*, August 16, 1927, 14; *C.B.C. Star*, Chicago Boys' Club, Valentine Branch, 1939; James Rogers, *The Child at Play* (New York: Century, 1932), 164; "Boys and Girls Issue Playground Newspaper for Sullivan Park," *Dallas Morning News*, March 12, 1940; "Bay Ridge Editors Win in Park Contest: *Eiriksson Park Weekly* Named Best of 39 in Youngsters' Newspaper Contest," *New York Times*, November 15, 1935; "A Playground Newspaper," *Playground* (February 1918): 520; George Butler, *Playgrounds: Their Administration and Operation* (New York: Barnes, 1936); "Stadium Grounds Season Near End," *Trenton Evening Times*, August 29, 1935; "Stunt Day Planned; Social Events to Be Held at Tapley Playground Today," *Springfield Republican*, July 13, 1932; Phoebe Valentine, *The Village: An experiment in educational play conducted by the Smith Memorial Playgrounds*, unknown binding, 1925; *Madison: An Interpretation by the Youth of the City* (Madison, WI: Junior Civic League, 1927); "Pioneer Radio Man Says Radio Will Help Form International Boy Scout Order," *Harrison Times* [Arkansas], January 26, 1915; Arthur Lynch, "A Complete Wireless Telephone Transmitting and Receiving Station Which May Be Carried by a Single Boy Scout" *Radio Broadcast* 1 (1922); 54; "Scout Activity Threatened," *Centralia Evening Standard*, April 16, 1919; "Boys' Club Exhibit of Home-made Radios Opens," *Chicago Daily Tribune*, April 17, 1924; "Nearly Every Boy Scout Has Radio Receiver," *Chicago Daily Tribune*, August 17, 1924; "Radio Raid on Maj. Dillon," *Los Angeles Times*, June 18, 1922; Robert Heinl, "Youth Predominant in Developing Radio Activities of World," *Washington Post*, July 24, 1927; W. E. Downey, "Amateurs' Work Promotes Radio," *New York Times*, September 9, 1928; "US Has 14,902 Hams as Radio Reserve Force," *Chicago Daily Tribune*, October 31, 1926; "Amateurs in Radio Are Experimenting with Short Waves," *Washington Post*, April 15, 1928; US Department of Commerce, *Amateur Radio Stations of the US* (Washington, DC: GPO, multiple dates). Related to this new tradition was the view, updating earlier proposals to replace teachers with technology, that film might replace universities. See Edward Van Zile, *That Marvel the Movie* (New York: Putnam, 1923).

64. Philip Cox, *Creative School Control* (Philadelphia: Lippincott, 1927), 199; Earl Kirkpatrick, "Motion Pictures in the School," *Oregon Teachers Monthly* 21 (February 1917): 363–367; William

Byron Forbush, *Dramatics in the Home* (Philadelphia: American Institute of Child Life, 1914); Harry Alan Potamkin, *The Compound Cinema* (New York: Teachers College Press, 1977); Harry McKown, *Audio-Visual Aids to Instruction* (New York: McGraw-Hill, 1949). Minnie Herts Heninger, "The Spoken Drama versus the 'Movies' for Children," *Journal of Genetic Psychology* 31 (1924): 388–398.

65. *Radio Amateur News,* March 1920, 492 (also listed as *Electronics World* vol. 1) lists multiple high school radio clubs. "School Runs Radio Station," *New York Times,* March 22, 1937; James Downey, "Radio in the Schools," *Journal of Education* 103, no. 24 (June 17, 1926): 665–666; Willis Sutton, "Daily Radio in the Schools," *Journal of Education* 105, no. 22 (May 30, 1927): 596; "Radio in the Schools," *Science News-Letter* 15, no. 418 (April 13, 1929): 236; Frank Carr, "Radio in the Schools," *Journal of Education* 111, no. 23 (June 9, 1930): 643–644, 646; I. Keith Tyler, "Radio in the High School," *Educational Research Bulletin* 14, no. 8 (November 13, 1935): 208–212; J. J. Tigert, "Radio in the American School System," *Annals of the American Academy of Political and Social Science* 142, Supplement: Radio (March, 1929): 71–77; "Expansion of 'Schools of Air,'" *Journal of Education* 112, no. 3 (July 21, 1930): 70; Margaret Anne Egan, "Study of the Use of Radio in Education" (master's thesis, University of Southern California, 1933); William C. Bagley, "Radio in the Schools," *Elementary School Journal* 31, no. 4 (December 1930): 256–258; "School Radio Station Sought," *Christian Science Monitor,* August 7, 1915; "Radio Club to Host Parents," *Washington Post,* April 7, 1922; "Technical High Has Oldest School Radio Club in City," *Washington Post,* April 9, 1922, 7; "High School Radio Club Plans Concerts," *Los Angeles Times,* April 25, 1922; "Among the Radio Clubs," *Washington Post,* June 11, 1922; "School Radio Development Asked by Teachers' League," *Christian Science Monitor,* July 6, 1925; Margaret Harrison, "Modern Trends in Education and School News of Interest to Teacher and Layman," *New York Herald Tribune,* March 22, 1931; "Pioneering in School Radio Begun by Cleveland Schools," *Christian Science Monitor,* April 6, 1938; Bernice Stevens, "How School Radio Programs Can Make the Class Work Vivid Through Dramatization," *Christian Science Monitor,* May 25, 1940; "Two Schools with Radio Broadcasts," *School Review* 45 (June 1937): 412; Carroll Atkinson, *Development of Radio Education Policies in American Public School Systems* (Edinboro, PA: Edinboro Educational Press, 1939), 186, 230; "Education on the Air," *Ohio State University Yearbook,* 1936; National University Extension Association, *Proceedings* 25, no. 7 (1940); Armstrong Perry, *Radio in Education: The Ohio School of the Air* (New York: Payne Fund, 1929); Amanda Lynn Bruce, "Creating Consumers and Protecting Children: Radio, Early Television and the American Child, 1930–1960" (PhD diss., Stony Brook University, 2008); Leonard Power, *Local Cooperative Broadcasting: A Summary and Appraisal,* Federal Radio Education Committee, with US Office of Education, Federal Security Agency, 1940; Ronald Lowdermilk, *Radio in Informal Education: A Conference Report* (Columbus: Ohio State University, 1942); "Student Radio to Report the Game," *Detroit Free Press,* November 6, 1920; "Radio Workshop on the Air," *Washington Post,* February 17, 1939; "Text of Talks on 'Student Radio Workshop,'" *Washington Post,* March 10, 1939; "172 Cardozo Pupils Heard in Broadcast," *Washington Post,* April 9, 1939; "The Radio Workshop: McKinley Pupils to Broadcast a Program of Young America," *Washington Post,* November 11, 1939; "Roosevelt High Students Help Chest Campaign with Program," *Washington Post,* November 19, 1939; "Eastern High Hears Itself Go on the Air," *Washington Post,* February 18, 1940; *Radio and the Classroom* (Washington, DC: National Education Association, Department of Elementary School Principals, 1940); Lola Berry, *Radio Development in a Small City School System* (Boston: Meador, 1943); "McKinley High Pupils on Radio Workshop:

53-Piece Orchestra, Two Glee Clubs on Post-WJSV Program," *Washington Post,* March 10, 1939; "Texts of Student Radio Workshop Speeches," *Washington Post,* February 24, 1939; "Armstrong High Pupils to Be in Radio Workshop," *Washington Post,* November 25, 1939; Carroll Atkinson, *Education by Radio in American Schools* (Nashville: George Peabody College, 1938); Boyd Baldwin, "Broadcasting as a High School Activity," *Bulletin of the Department of Secondary School Principals of the National Education Association* 21 (November 1937): 27–29.

66. Lillian McNulty, "The Problem of School Film Production," in *The Motion Picture Goes to School,* ed. Hardy Finch.

67. Hardy Finch, ed., *The Motion Picture Goes to School: A Collection of Discussions on Paper, on School Film Production and Allied Subjects* (National Council of Teachers of English, Committee on Standards for Motion Pictures and Newspapers, 1940); Edgar Dale et al., *Proceedings of a Conference on the Educational Production of Motion Pictures* (Columbus: Ohio State University, 1939); Floyd Brooker and Eugene Herrington, *Students Make Motion Pictures: A Report on Film Production in the Denver Schools,* American Council on Education, 1941; William Lewin, *Photoplay Appreciation in American High Schools* (New York: Appleton, 1934); Paul Saettler, *The Evolution of American Educational Technology,* 2nd ed. (Charlotte, NC: Information Age, 2004); Eleanor Child and Hardy Finch, *Producing School Movies: A Manual for Teachers and Students Interested in Producing Amateur Films* (National Council of Teachers of English, 1941); "The Motion Picture in Education: Its Status and Its Needs," American Council on Education Pamphlet Series (April 1937); Edward Olsen, *School and Community: The Philosophy, Procedures, and Problems of Community Study and Service through Schools and Colleges* (New York: Prentice Hall, 1945).

68. "Four New Tests Offered Scouts," *Louisville Courier-Journal,* April 3, 1927; "Boy Scout Writes on Movement," *Pittsburgh Courier,* May 21, 1927; "Scouts and Campfire Girls Working for Woman's Edition," *Atlanta Constitution,* March 30, 1913; "Boys' Amateur Newspaper," *Sun,* March 14, 1920; "Boy Scout Press Association Makes Plans for the Year," *New York Times,* November 11, 1928; "Boy Scouts to Hold Annual Press Association Meeting," *New York Times,* February 24, 1929; "Two Boy Scouts to Receive Journalistic Work Awards," *New York Times,* March 17, 1929; "Boy Scout Press Body Re-elects Officers," *New York Times,* May 29, 1932; "Boy Scout Press Club Elects," *New York Times,* February 24, 1929; "To Award Black Bequests," *New York Times,* May 26, 1932; "Silver Jubilee to Be Observed by City Scouts," *Washington Post,* January 11, 1935; "Scouts Devote Coming Year to Jamboree," *Washington Post,* August 24, 1934; "The Way It Was: The Golden Age of Scout Journalism," *Scouting,* March/April 1992; "Scouts Arrange Wider Activity for Press Club: Program to Be Pushed Until Silver Jubilee Begins Next Year," *Washington Post,* December 21, 1934; "Boys Urged to Study Great Editors' Lives," *New York Times,* February 13, 1934; "Boy Scout Editors Meet," *New York Times,* May 21, 1932; "Scout Editor Is Youngest in Country," *Washington Post,* December 1, 1935; "Scouts Publish First Issue of Jubilee Journal," *Washington Post,* October 26, 1934; "Boy Scout Press Club Revamped as News Staff," *Chicago Daily Tribune,* January 3, 1932; "Troop 21, Boy Scouts to Edit Newspaper," *Hartford Courant,* April 30, 1933; "Boy Scouts May Win Four New Merit Badges: Journalism, Canoeing, Salesmanship, Weather Have Now Been Added to the List," *New York Times,* January 30, 1927; "Scouts Active as Journalists," *New York Times,* January 10, 1937; "Boy Scout Daily Newspaper Reported Jamboree Affairs," *New York Times,* September 22, 1929.

69. Arthur Lynch, "A Complete Wireless Telephone Transmitting and Receiving Station Which May be Carried by a Single Boy Scout," *Radio Broadcast* 1 (1922): 54–57; James West, "The Scout World," *Boys' Life*, November 1921, 21; "Colorado Boy Scouts Run Their Own Radio Station," *New York Times*, February 13, 1927; Armstrong Perry, "Boy Scout's Place in the Radio Game," *Radio Broadcast*, February 1923, 275–281; A. H. Lynch, "What Radio Holds for Boy Scouts," *Radio Broadcast*, July 1923, 251–254; "Big Radio Chance for the Scouts," *Literary Digest* 76 (1923): 27; Samuel Kaufman, "New York Boy Scouts to Study Radio Work at Bear Mt. Camps," *New York Herald Tribune*, July 17, 1927; Samuel Kaufman, "Boy Scouts Plan to Broadcast from New Up-State Camp Site," *New York Herald Tribune*, December 11, 1927; James Cartier, "Boy Scouts Greatly Interested in Radio: Seventy-five Per Cent Own Receivers; Many Thousands Are Licensed Amateur Operators; Radio Instructors at Summer Scout Camps," *New York Herald Tribune*, September 14, 1924; "Boy Scout Radio Head Lauds Navy's Aid for Amateurs," *New-York Tribune*, December 25, 1922; "Boy Scouts Asked to Help Enforce Radio Laws," *New York Herald Tribune*, May 11, 1924; "Boy Scout Notes," *Washington Post*, June 8, 1924; "Membership Blank for Radio Network," in several issues of the 1928 run of *Boys' Life*; Samuel Kaufman, "Boy Scouts Plan to Broadcast from New Up-State Camp Site: Huge Camp Near Monticello May Be Equipped with Station to Broadcast Woodland Programs; Radio an Important Part of Scout Work Throughout U.S.," *New York Herald Tribune*, December 11, 1927; "17th Birthday of Boy Scouts Falls Tuesday: 7-Day Program Celebrating Anniversary of Movement Will Include Nation-Wide Radio Broadcast," *New York Herald Tribune*, February 6, 1927; "Newark Council Broadcasts Weekly—Civic Work Assisted in Tennessee and Missouri," *New York Times*, February 13, 1927; "Scouts Broadcast over Own Station," *Washington Post*, July 1, 1937; "Eagle Scouts Enact on Radio Exploits of Town and Camp," *Christian Science Monitor*, December 14, 1935; "Boy Scouts Test New Signal System," *Hartford Courant*, May 8, 1938; "Troops in American Territory Number 25,000—Merit Badge Talks to Be Broadcast," *New York Times*, March 6, 1927.

70. "Youngsters' Work Aired," *New York Amsterdam News*, March 13, 1937; "Boy, 12, to Sing Bit Role at the Opera Saturday," *New York Times*, January 22, 1939; "Matthew Napear, Laguardia Aide: Insurance Broker, 72, Dies," *New York Times*, April 16, 1968; "Inspector's Club Protects Youths," *New York Amsterdam News*, February 11, 1939; "Pittsburgh Pupils to Learn Lessons of Civic Government," *Christian Science Monitor*, August 17, 1940; Betty Driscoll, "Hub Sanitation 'Juniors' Plan to Get Study Women's Activities: Thursday Programs," *Christian Science Monitor*, January 9, 1946; Harry Granick, *Underneath New York* (New York: Fordham University Press, 1991); "Topics of the Times," *New York Times*, September 6, 1940; "Youngsters Eager to Spend City Cash," *New York Times*, September 5, 1940; "Girls Win Offices in Child Congress," *New York Times*, May 26, 1940; "To See How City Is Run," *New York Times*, July 14, 1940; "Girl Again Is Elected City Junior 'Mayor,'" *New York Times*, June 15, 1941; "Junior City-County Federation," *Pittsburgh Courier*, September 30, 1939; "Junior Inspectors Aid Anti-litter Fight: Junior Inspectors' Club of Greater New York," *American City* 53 (January 1938): 55–56; "Young Clean-Up Aides Forming Local Units," *New York Times*, March 15, 1936; "Junior Inspectors' Club," *Atlanta Constitution*, August 28, 1940; "Clean Street Club Is 100,000 Strong," *New York Times*, May 27, 1935; "Christmas Spirit Enlivens the City," *New York Times*, December 24, 1934; "2 NY Children Win Courtesy Medals," *Afro-American*, February 19, 1938, 13; "Find Courtesy Counts," *New York Amsterdam News*, February 19, 1938; "Young America Rebels Against 'Yes Sir' or 'Ma'am': They Won for Their Manners,"

Christian Science Monitor, February 15, 1938; "Ten Polite Children Get Medals," *New York Times*, February 12, 1938; "Courtesy Classes Begin in Schools Tomorrow," *New York Times*, January 16, 1938; "The Feminist Viewpoint: Junior Inspectors' Club," *New York Amsterdam News*, October 23, 1937; "500 Children at 'Jamboree,'" *New York Times*, December 20, 1938; American Public Works Association, *Public Works Engineers' Yearbook*, 1939, 310; "Junior Inspectors to Elect," *New York Times*, May 19, 1940; "Children to Run City for Day," *New York Times*, August 20, 1940; "To See How City Is Run: School Children Will Sit in Executives' Chairs for Day," *New York Times*, July 14, 1940; "City Junior Leaders Pledge Wide 'Reform,'" *New York Times*, June 21, 1941; "Refugee Girl, 11, and Bronx Boy, 14, Selected from Among 100,000 as the City's Brightest," *New York Times*, November 15, 1940; Hayes Richardson, "The Children Get a Chance," *National Municipal Review*, 1946; Ronald Lowdermilk, *Radio in Informal Education: A Conference Report* (Columbus: Ohio State University, 1942).

71. Floyd Brooker and Eugene Herrington, *Students Make Motion Pictures: A Report on Film Production in the Denver Schools* (Washington, DC: American Council on Education, 1941); Eleanor Child and Hardy Finch, *Producing School Movies: A Manual for Teachers and Students Interested in Producing Amateur Films* (National Council of Teachers of English, 1941); Paul Terry, "Democratic Principles of Supervision for Extra-curriculum Activities," *School Review* 45 (November 1937): 655–661; Carroll Atkinson, *Development of Radio Education Policies in American Public Schools* (Edinboro, PA: Edinboro Educational Press, 1939); Ruth Livermon, "An Elementary School Makes a Utilization Film," *Educational Screen*, October 1939, 280–281. Atkinson reviews numerous safety clubs on the air produced by school districts; many also published safety papers. See "Children Get Copies of New Safety Paper," *Boston Daily Globe*, June 25, 1926.

72. "Junior Police Patrol to Be Aired on W-G-N," *Chicago Daily Tribune, October 27, 1935*; "Bartholomew Becomes Junior Police Captain," *Hartford Courant*, December 3, 1937; I. Keith Tyler, "Radio and Youth," in Ronald Lowdermilk, *Radio in Informal Education: A Conference Report* (Columbus: Ohio State University, 1942), 4; Sherman P. Lawton, "Youth Organizations and Radio Workshops," in Ronald Lowdermilk, *Radio in Informal Education: A Conference Report* (Columbus: Ohio State University, 1942), 24. Lawton follows Robert Hiestand, "Radio Production as a Resource for the Group Leader," in this volume. Notably, despite years of radio clubs replacing actual clubs, the reverse also occurred. One former agent, observing kids playing FBI, started the children's radio program *Junior G-Men*, a "club of the air" so popular that young listeners clamored for actual clubs, which were soon organized across the US.

73. Fred van Defender, "Bread and Butter Is Chief Concern for This College," *Springfield Republican*, May 12, 1940; "Youth City Gets Started; Evans Lauded: North Philly Center Answers Great Need, Say Speakers," *Philadelphia Tribune*, December 19, 1940; "20 Years Ago in the *Modesto Bee*," *Modesto Bee*, August 7, 1957; Webb Waldron, "No Adults Allowed," *Readers Digest*, April 1936, 79–82; *Life of the Boys Brotherhood Republic* (Chicago: BBR, 1938); "Boys' Republic to Expand: Job of Supervisors," *Christian Science Monitor*, May 18, 1937; "Boys in 34 States to Guide Mythical Governments," *Austin American*, July 7, 1940; "Legion Sets Up 'Boys' State' at Fulton Camp," *Atlanta Constitution*, June 1, 1941; "Boys to Set Up a 'State'" *New York Times*, April 17, 1938; Harold Smith, "Boys Try Hand at Running Own State This Week," *Chicago Daily Tribune*, June 19, 1938; "Two Boys' States for New England: Rhode Island and Vermont Join Growing Union," *New York Times*, June 19, 1938; Jack Drucker, "Boys Brotherhood Protests: Its Mayor Holds Publication

of Report of Teacher Survey Premature," *New York Times*, January 12, 1943; "Boys State Starts," *Oxnard Press-Courier*, June 23, 1941; "170 'Girls State' Delegates Depart," *Berkeley Daily Gazette*, June 18, 1941; "Boys State Sees 'Hot Campaign,'" *Palm Beach Post*, June 23, 1940; "Americanism Commission's Report Urges Alien Curb," *Los Angeles Times*, September 18, 1938; "Greeting Time at Boys State," *Milwaukee Journal*, June 22, 1941; "Legion to Sponsor Government Study," *New York Times*, June 23, 1938; "Dubuque Boys State Delegates Reach Camp," *Telegraph-Herald*, June 3, 1940; "Boy Governments in 34 States Show Value of American Way: They're All for America," *Christian Science Monitor*, July 10, 1940; Charles Chapman, "An Experiment in Democracy," *Recreation* (January 1950): 471; "The American Legion Youth Program," *Phi Delta Kappan* 25 (1943): 165; G. H. Hallett Jr, "Proportional Representation Advancing," *National Municipal Review*, 1939; "Boys to Set Up a 'State,'" *New York Times*, April 17, 1938. James Emery and James Kinder make clear how the new focus on "representational and experiential materials and technics" that affected learners' mental images was increasingly narrowed. See Emery, "Sources of Visual Aids at Moderate Cost," *Educational Screen* 3, no. 6 (1924): 211–213; and Kinder, "Visual Aids in Education," *Review of Educational Research* 12, no. 3 (1942): 336–344.

74. "Scouts Are Planting Trees," *New York Times*, May 3, 1936; "Boy Scout Press Association Makes Plans for the Year," *New York Times*, November 11, 1928, 165; Edward Olsen, *School and Community: The Philosophy, Procedures, and Problems of Community Study and Service through Schools and Colleges* (New York: Prentice Hall, 1945), 271; "Junior Police Save $25,000 for Berkeley," *Christian Science Monitor*, April 6, 1933; "Berkeley Proud of Service of the Junior Traffic Police," *Christian Science Monitor*, December 23, 1940; "Boy Scouts Protect Forests," *New York Times*, December 1, 1935; "Boy Scouts Are Cited: Osborne Praises Albany County Troop for Conservation Work," *New York Times*, June 9, 1935; "Track and Field Meets, Municipal Fireworks, Provide Safe Celebrations of Fourth," *New York Herald Tribune*, July 5, 1936; "Schools Issue Licenses for Pupils' Cycles," *New York Herald Tribune*, November 23, 1937; "Accidents to Children in Streets Cut 75 Per Cent by Play-Yard Campaign in Flint, City of Cars," *New York Herald Tribune*, December 29, 1935; "Realtor Recommends Junior Police Force," *New York Amsterdam News*, February 8, 1936; "Pennsylvania Junior Police Put Brakes on Youth Crime," *Christian Science Monitor*, September 27, 1941; "Describes Reduction in Boston Crime by Junior Police Force," *Chicago Daily Tribune*, November 12, 1938. Although settlements were disappearing from the American landscape, some that persisted pursued similar programs. For example, in *Making a Better Neighborhood* (Boston: Beacon Press, 1935), Thelma Burdick and Josephine Gifford described the vacation program at a settlement in which kids studied their neighborhood as a prelude to improvement.

75. Carroll Atkinson, *Development of Radio Education Policies in American Public Schools* (Edinboro, PA: Edinboro Educational Press, 1939), 15; Eleanor Child and Hardy Finch, *Producing School Movies: A Manual for Teachers and Students Interested in Producing Amateur Films* (National Council of Teachers of English, 1941); Norval Martin, "Interpreting the Public Schools through Motion Pictures," *Educational Screen* (May 1939): 151–152; W. D. Trautmen, "Student Production of a Newsreel, Movie Record, or Propaganda Film," *School and Society* (April 9, 1938): 484–485; Hardy Finch and Eleanor Child, "The Production of School Public Relations Films," *School Management* (March 1941): 195, 202, 203; Mary Ruth Hodge, "Making a Motion Picture of 'The Lady of the Lake,'" *English Journal* 27, no. 5 (May 1938): 388–396; Hardy Finch, ed., *The Motion Picture Goes to*

School: A Collection of Discussions on Paper, on School Film Production and Allied Subjects (National Council of Teachers of English, Committee on Standards for Motion Pictures and Newspapers, 1940); William Wagner, "School-Made Motion Pictures for Public Relations in Ohio," *Educational Screen* 19 (January-February-March 1940): 8–10, 50–52, 99–100; Ruth Livermon, "An Elementary School Makes a Utilization Film," *Educational Screen* (October 1939): 280–281; William Hard and Roy Wenger, *Making School Movies* (Columbus: Ohio State University, Bureau of Educational Research, 1941); George V. Denny Jr., "Radio Builds Democracy," *Journal of Educational Sociology* 14, no. 6 (February 1941): 370–377; *Education on the Air*, Ohio State University Yearbook 7 (1936), 194; William Allison Yeager, *Home-School-Community Relations: A Textbook in the Theory and Practice of Public Schools Relations* (Pittsburgh: University of Pittsburgh, 1939); Jessie M. Starkey, "Student Publications as an Aspect of a Public School Relations Program" (master's thesis, University of Pittsburgh, 1936); John Erle Grinnell, *Interpreting the Public Schools* (New York: McGraw-Hill, 1937); Arthur B. Moehlman, *Social Interpretation: Principles and Practices of Community and Public-School Interpretation* (New York: Appleton, 1938); E. L. Callihan, "Publicizing the School," *Phi Delta Kappan* 23 (April 1941), 285–286; B. M. Kohler, "Tell It to the Community—One Board Found It Worth While," *Nation's Schools* 27 (June 1941): 31–32; Hadley Cantril and Gordon Allport, *The Psychology of Radio* (New York: Harper, 1935).

76. Eleanor Child and Hardy Finch, *Producing School Movies: A Manual for Teachers and Students Interested in Producing Amateur Films* (National Council of Teachers of English, 1941), 8.

77. Kenneth Holland, "The Implications of Work Camps for Secondary Education," *NASSP Bulletin* 24 (1940): 29; William Lewin, "The Business of Running a High School Movie Club," *English Journal* 23, no. 1 (1934): 37–47; Eleanor Child, "Making Motion Pictures in the School," *English Journal* 28, no. 9 (1939): 706–712; Curriculum Section, Los Angeles City School System, *Radio Bulletin* 1 (September 1937); Edwin P. Adkins, "A Student Council Takes to the Community," *Clearing House* 15, no. 3 (November 1940): 138–140; "A Journalism Club Supplies School News for the Local Paper," *School Review* 45 (May 1937): 328; Floyd Brooker and Eugene Herrington, *Students Make Motion Pictures: A Report on Film Production in the Denver Schools* (Washington, DC: American Council on Education, 1941); Norval Martin, "Concrete Suggestions as to How a School May Visualize Itself Before the Eyes of the Community," *Educational Screen* 18 (1939): 151–152; W. G. Hart, "The School-Made Film in a Public Relations Program," *American School Board Journal* 101 (September 1940): 26; William Hart, "A Clearing-House for School-Made Public Relations Films," *Educational Screen* (February 1940), 65; John E. Grinnell, "Newspaper Publicity for the Public Schools of Minnesota" (master's thesis, University of Minnesota, 1925); Belmont Mercer Farley, *What to Tell the People About the Public Schools: A Study of the Content of the Public School Publicity Program*, Teachers College Contributions to Education, no. 355 (New York: Teachers College, Columbia University, 1929); Stan Atkin, "Radio Broadcasting as an Agent to Furthering Public Relations in Our Schools" (master's thesis, University of Southern California, 1941); W. G. Reeder, *An Introduction to Public School Relations* (New York: Macmillan, 1937); Ruth Livermon, "A Elementary School Makes a Utilization Film," *Educational Screen 18* (October 1939): 280–281; Ronald Lowdermilk, *The School Radio-Sound System* (Washington, DC: Federal Radio Education Committee with the cooperation of the US Office of Education Federal Security Agency, 1941);

Reid Seerley, *Radio in the Schools of Ohio* (Washington, DC: Federal Radio Education Committee with the cooperation of the US Office of Education, 1942); "The School Newsreel," *School Review* 45 (November 1937): 641–642; W. D. Trautmen, "Student Production of a Newsreel, Movie Record, or Propaganda Film," *School and Society* (April 9, 1938): 484–485; Hardy Finch and Eleanor Child, "The Production of School Public Relations Films," *School Management* (March 1941): 195, 202, 203; William Wagner, "School-Made Motion Pictures for Public Relations in Ohio," *Educational Screen* 19 (January-February-March 1940): 8–10, 50–52, 99–100; William Hardt and Roy Wenger, Making School Movies (Columbus: Bureau of Educational Research, Ohio State University, 1941); George V. Denny Jr., "Radio Builds Democracy," *Journal of Educational Sociology* 14, no. 6 (February 1941): 370–377; *Education on the Air*, Ohio State University Yearbook, vol. 7 (1936), 194; William Allison Yeager, *Home-School-Community Relations: A Textbook in the Theory and Practice of Public Schools Relations* (Pittsburgh: University of Pittsburgh, 1939); Jessie M. Starkey, "Student Publications as an Aspect of a Public School Relations Program" (master's thesis, University of Pittsburgh, 1936); John Erle Grinnell, *Interpreting the Public Schools* (New York: McGraw-Hill, 1937); Arthur B. Moehlman, *Social Interpretation: Principles and Practices of Community and Public-School Interpretation* (New York: Appleton-Century, 1938); E. L. Callihan, "Publicizing the School," *Phi Delta Kappan* 23 (April 1941): 285–286; B. M. Kohler, "Tell It to the Community—One Board Found It Worth While," *Nation's Schools* 27 (June 1941): 31–32. A few districts did have directors of school publicity. Working without large staffs, however, they were much aided by student media projects. Paul A. Hedlund, "School Publicity in the Press," *Elementary School Journal* 31, no. 8 (April 1931): 585–591.

78. R. J. Bretnall, "Welfare Workers: Millburn High Serves Community as Legal Administrative Unit of Department of Welfare," *Clearing House* 16, no. 6 (February 1942): 329–331; George Kimball, "Junior Safety Patrol: A Project in Democracy" (Seattle: Washington Education Association, 1940), also appeared in *Washington Education Journal* (March 1940): 126; Morris Mitchell, *Youth Has a Part to Play* (New York: Progressive Education Association, 1942), 1; Edward Olsen, *School and Community: The Philosophy, Procedures, and Problems of Community Study and Service through Schools and Colleges* (New York: Prentice Hall, 1945); Morris R. Mitchell, "Taking Dewey Seriously," *Progressive Education* 15 (February 1938): 110–117; "Approves Lynn Auto Driving Plan," *Boston Daily Globe*, April 3, 1938; Wilbur G. Lewis, "Low Crime Record Held in Rochester," *New York Times*, January 17, 1932; "Timilty Reports Drop in Crime; Junior Police Work Reviewed," *Christian Science Monitor*, January 24, 1940; "Stephen Harrigan Dies, Leader in Junior Police Corps, Brighton," *Boston Daily Globe*, January 8, 1941; "San Francisco's Traffic Needs," *New York Times*, January 7, 1934; "Boys March Toward Better Citizenship; Junior Patrol Halts Deaths," *Los Angeles Times*, March 22, 1940; "Junior Traffic Patrol Boasts Safety Record," *Los Angeles Times*, February 5, 1946; Florence W. Barton, "Youth on the Job," *Parents Magazine*, January 1939, 23, 65–66; Harl R. Douglass, "Youth, School, Work and Community," *School and Society* 50 (July 15, 1939): 65–71; Horace B. English, "Education through Work in a Time of Social Change," *Educational Method* 15 (November 1935): 67–71; William S. Girault and Stewart T. Walton, "We Gave Them Experience," *Educational Method* 18 (March 1939): 262–265; M. P. Moe and L. O. Brockman, *Utilizing Community Resources for Vocational Guidance and Training* (Helena, MT: The Authors, 1937); Philip Cox, *Creative School Control* (Philadelphia: Lippincott, 1927), 199; Edward Olsen, *School and*

Community: The Philosophy, Procedures, and Problems of Community Study and Service through Schools and Colleges (New York: Prentice Hall, 1945) has a chapter on school public relations and media production with an extensive bibliography. See also William C. Reavis, ed., The *School and the Urban Community* (Chicago: University of Chicago Press, 1942), 76–78.

79. Edward Olsen, *School and Community: The Philosophy, Procedures, and Problems of Community Study and Service through Schools and Colleges* (New York: Prentice Hall, 1945); Mildred P. Ellis, "Framingham Facts: Our Pupils Investigate Local Standards of Living," *Clearing House* 16 (November 1941): 140–142; Morris Mitchell, *Youth Has a Part to Play* (New York: Progressive Education Association, 1942); "Berkeley Proud of Service of the Junior Traffic Police," *Christian Science Monitor*, December 23, 1940; "Traffic to Be Bossed by Pupils," *Los Angeles Times*, September 13, 1926; Paul R. Hanna and Research Staff, *Youth Serves the Community* (New York: Appleton-Century, 1936).

80. "Fin Com Asks Reforms Before Police Quota Rise," *Boston Daily Globe*, January 8, 1941; "Scouting Chief Calls Service Help to Nation: Boy Scouts Continue Work Toward Useful and Patriotic Deeds," *Christian Science Monitor*, February 9, 1933; Bert Edgar, "A Study of the Educational Value of the Boy Scout Program" (master's thesis, Colorado State College, 1935); Stanton Leggett, "Community Educational Organizations and Youth Groups External to the School," *Review of Educational Research* 10, no. 4, Organization and Administration of Education (October 1940): 362–369; Edward Olsen, *School and Community: The Philosophy, Procedures, and Problems of Community Study and Service through Schools and Colleges* (New York: Prentice Hall, 1945); "Boy Scouts Aid the Wild Birds," *New York Times*, February 23, 1936; "Boy Scouts Protect Forests," *New York Times*, December 1, 1935; "Police Juvenile Aid Bureau Head Tells of Crime Prevention Effort," *New York Herald Tribune*, March 12, 1936; "Junior Traffic 'Cop,' 5, Halts Police Cruiser in Brighton to Allow Little Girls to Pass," *Boston Daily Globe*, May 28, 1938; "Junior Police Cuts Accidents at LaGrange," *Atlanta Constitution*, November 22, 1941; "Boys Are Real Cops in This Town," *Hartford Courant*, November 6, 1938; "Crippled Boy 'Sleuth' Aids in Lindbergh Case," *Los Angeles Times*, March 24, 1932; "Boy Sleuth Praised," *Chicago Daily Tribune*, December 2, 1937; "Boy Detectives Break Up Juvenile Gang," *Los Angeles Times*, July 17, 1936; "Boy Detectives to Help Police Run Down Boy Thieves," August 11, 1934; "Trail of Bandits Traced by Work of Boy Detectives," *Christian Science Monitor*, February 10, 1934; "Juvenile Brockton Firebugs Nabbed by Boy Detectives," *Boston Daily Globe*, October 9, 1933; "Boy Detectives Trap Paper Theft Suspect," *Los Angeles Times*, September 9, 1929; "Boy Detective Avenges Sister," *Chicago Daily Tribune*, March 18, 1935; "Boy 'Detective' Nabs Man," *Chicago Defender*, April 2, 1938; "Boy Detective Secures Arrest of Suspect Trio," *Boston Daily Globe*, February 1, 1940; Josephine Ripley, "Finding Rowdyism Not Funny Made Hartford Boy Detective: Boy Detectives Know There's No Fun in Crime," *Christian Science Monitor*, December 21, 1940; "Boy Police Force," *Sun*, June 13, 1926; "St. Louis Plans Junior Police," *Detroit Free Press*, July 8, 1921. "Boy Scouts on the Air Waves," *New York Times*, January 16, 1938, includes a side note pointing readers to pages with "additional hobby news."

81. "Tree Planting Is New Scout Work," *Washington Post*, July 7, 1935; "Junior Police Work Goes On Even in the Vacation Period," *Christian Science Monitor*, January 4, 1940; "Junior Police Crack Down on Light Breakers, Bikemen," *Hartford Courant*, September 20, 1936; "Timilty Reports Drop

in Crime; Junior Police Work Reviewed," *Christian Science Monitor,* January 24, 1940; "Plan for Junior Police Dropped," *Sun,* January 5, 1937; "Mirror of the World's Opinion: What Criminals Cost, Saving Trees and Boys, Wanted—Men," *Christian Science Monitor,* November 10, 1933; "Newark Junior Policeman Put in Jail for Zeal," *New York Herald Tribune,* April 12, 1931; "Boy Scouts Protect Forests," *New York Times,* December 1, 1935; "Police Allow Boys to Act as City Cops," *Hartford Courant,* July 9, 1939; "Increased Boy Delinquency," *Hartford Courant,* May 9, 1933; "Roosevelt Likens Scouting Service to NRA Ideals: Roosevelt and Boy Scouts Exchange Greetings," *Christian Science Monitor,* August 24, 1933; August Vollmer, "Police Study Environment of Childhood," *Christian Science Monitor,* March 17, 1930; "Scout Survey to Check Role of Each Youth," *New York Herald Tribune,* October 15, 1939; Harold P. Levy, *Building a Popular Movement: A Case Study of the Public Relations of the Boy Scouts of America* (New York: Russell Sage Foundation, 1944). Levy's analysis of the Boy Scouts' public relations work mentioned newspaper and radio activities from Washington headquarters while ignoring similar activities in local troops—even the journalism merit badge had been expanded to include radio, public speaking, and salesmanship. And he identified the public relations function of "symbols," including the uniform and daily good turn, while overlooking the agency of the boys who wore these outfits and did these daily good deeds.

82. Neil Maher, "'A Confluence of Desire and Need': Trees, Boys Scouts, and the Roots of Franklin Roosevelt's Civilian Conservation Corps," in *FDR and the Environment,* ed. David Wolner and Henry Henderson (New York: Palgrave Macmillan, 2005), 49–83; Neil Maher, *Nature's New Deal: The Civilian Conservation Corps and the Roots of the American Environmental Movement* (Oxford: Oxford University Press, 2008); Howard Bell, "The Conservation of American Youth through Community Youth Programs," *Phi Delta Kappan* 21, no. 8 (1939): 383–384, 391; "Soil Service May Aid CCC on State Project," *Sun,* November 12, 1939; "CCC's Capacity to Train Youths for Jobs Proved," *Christian Science Monitor,* July 10, 1937; "Death Valley's Terrors Converted into Scenic Charms by Boys of C.C.C. Camps: Work Army Conquers Last Desert Frontier, Poison Sink Loses Menace as Wells Sunk, Roads and Trails Built, New Scenic Beauty Opened to Tourists," *Los Angeles Times,* January 21, 1934; "Roosevelt Interest in Trees Comes from Long Association," *Christian Science Monitor,* April 25, 1933. There were a few direct links between the programs; for example, the CCC built facilities for Scouts and lent them equipment, and participants from both organizations occasionally collaborated as well. "CCC and Boy Scouts Called Bars to Crime: Director of United States Bureau of Prisons Talks to New England Scout Group," *Christian Science Monitor,* April 25, 1935; "CCC and Boy Scouts Hunt Lost Man, 86," *Hartford Courant,* December 27, 1934; Chester Washington, "'Ches' Washington Rows Around Flooded Districts and Tells of Pitiable Scenes Witnessed—Colored CCC Workers and Boy Scouts Active," *Pittsburgh Courier,* March 28, 1936; "Meriden Fire Rages over Forest Area: Large Group Fights to Check Flames on West Mountain Before Five Houses Are Reached," *Hartford Courant,* October 27, 1935; "Boy Scouts Aid Coast Guard at Wreck of Lake Steamer: Troop of Kenosha, Wis., Lads Patrol Beach and Take Over Duties of the Station Tree Planting by Scouts," *New York Times,* November 24, 1929; "Mirror of the World's Opinion: What Criminals Cost, Saving Trees and Boys, Wanted—Men," *Christian Science Monitor,* November 10, 1933.

83. "An Ounce of Prevention," *Christian Science Monitor,* January 25, 1940; "Why Not Join Hands?" *Christian Science Monitor,* January 23, 1941; "To Train Teachers for Junior Police," *Boston*

Daily Globe, September 3, 1938; "Walpole Residents Call Junior Police Mere Tale Bearers," *Christian Science Monitor,* June 3, 1938; "Truck Ignores Junior Police: 1 Dead, 2 Hurt: Plunges onto Walk into Children," *Chicago Daily Tribune,* March 11, 1926; A. Stein, "Voice of the People: Annoyed by the Junior Police," *Chicago Daily Tribune,* February 1, 1928; "School Traffic Cop Loses Case: Dorchester Judge Says He Has No Authority," *Boston Daily Globe,* November 4, 1926; George S. Goodell, "Inquiry," *Journal of Educational Sociology* 1, no. 8 (April 1928): 505; "Juvenile Court Is Failure: St. Louis Tribunal Had Boys for the Police Officers," *Spokesman-Review,* January 8, 1915; "Junior Juvenile Court Is Abolished by Judge," *St. Louis Post-Dispatch,* January 6, 1915, 5; "An Ounce of Prevention," *Christian Science Monitor,* January 25, 1940; "Junior Police Given First-Aid Certificates," *Boston Daily Globe,* December 1, 1940; "This Junior Traffic Patrol of Emerson School, East Boston, Gave a Drill Before the Massachusetts Safety Council," *Boston Daily Globe,* April 30, 1929.

84. "Cooperation Gets Results," *New York Times,* November 8, 1936; "Juvenile Court Is Failure: St. Louis Tribunal Had Boys for the Police Officers," *Spokesman-Review,* January 8, 1915; "Junior Traffic Police Opposed at San Diego," *Los Angeles Times,* September 5, 1931; "School Guard Meeting Set," *Los Angeles Times,* September 22, 1941; "Child Police Issue Raised: School Board Liability Under Debate in Junior Patrol Plan at Santa Barbara," *Los Angeles Times,* December 1, 1935; "San Diego Junior Traffic Patrol Compiles Enviable Safety Record," *Christian Science Monitor,* October 5, 1940; "Junior Traffic Police Proposal Meets Rebuff," *Los Angeles Times,* December 1, 1935.

85. "School Guard Meeting Set," *Los Angeles Times,* September 22, 1941.

86. Ruth Peterson and L. L. Thurstone, "The Effects of a Motion Picture Film on Children's Attitudes towards Germany," *Journal of Educational Psychology* 25 (1932): 241–246; L. L. Thurstone, "Influence of Motion Pictures on Children's Attitudes," *Journal of Social Psychology* 2 (August 1931): 291–305; A. D. Annis and N. C. Meier, "Induction of Opinion through Suggestion by Means of Planted Content," *Journal of Social Psychology* 5 (February 1934): 68–81; William Biddle, *Propaganda and Education* (New York: Teachers College, 1932); William Keh-Ching Chen, "The Influence of Oral Propaganda Material on Students' Attitudes," *Archives of Psychology* 23, no. 150 (1933); William Carr, "School Child and Propaganda: The Conundrum of the Educator," in *Proceedings of the National Conference of Social Work* (1931), 597–605; Arthur Kellogg, "Minds Made by the Movies," *Survey* 22 (May 1933): 245–250; Ruth Peterson and L. L. Thurstone, *Motion Pictures and the Social Attitudes of Children: A Payne Fund Study* (New York: Macmillan, 1933); "Invasion of Schoolrooms by Propaganda Worries Educators," *Boston Daily Globe,* June 17, 1928; "Dan Beard Predicts U.S. Boys Will Overcome Propaganda," *Washington Post,* June 17, 1940; Benjamin Fine, "Fight Propaganda by School Course," *Times Wide World,* 1939, 57; "Screen Ills Diagnosed," *Los Angeles Times,* June 3, 1934; William Biddle, "Pupils See Tactics of Propagandists," *New York Times,* March 27, 1932; Clive Morgan Koon, *Motion Pictures in Education in the United States* (Chicago: University of Chicago, 1934); Philip Rulon, *The Sound Motion Picture in Science Teaching* (Cambridge, MA: Harvard University, 1933); Robert Lingel, *Educational Broadcasting: A Bibliography* (Chicago: University of Chicago, 1932); Werrett Wallace Charters, *Research Problems in Radio Education,* National Advisory Council on Radio, Education Information Series 4, 1931, 1–17; Clive Morgan Koon, *The Art of Teaching by Radio,* US Office of Education Bulletin 4 (Washington, DC: GPO, 1931); Helen Muller, *Education by Radio* (New York: Wilson, 1932); Geddes Rutherford, "Radio as a Means of Instruction in Government," *American Political Science Review* 27

(1933): 264–274; F. E. Taylor, "Civic Education by Radio," *National Municipal Review* 16 (November 1927): 683–684; Lee Grieveson and Haidee Wasson, eds., *Inventing Film Studies* (Durham, NC: Duke University Press, 2008); Dana Polan, *Scenes of Instruction: The Beginnings of the U.S. Study of Film* (Berkeley: University of California Press, 2007); Amanda Lynn Bruce, "Creating Consumers and Protecting Children: Radio, Early Television and the American Child, 1930–1960" (PhD diss., Stony Brook University, 2008); Garth Jowett, Ian Jarvie, and Katherine H. Fuller, *Children and the Movies: Media Influence and the Payne Fund Controversy* (New York: Cambridge University Press, 1996); Anna McCarthy, *The Citizen Machine: Governing by Television in 1950s America* (New York: New Press, 2010); Lea Jacobs, "Reformers and Spectators: The Film Education Movement in the Thirties," *Camera Obscura* 8, no. 1 (1990); Eric Smoodin, "What a Power for Education: The Cinema and Sites of Learning in the 1930s," in *Useful Cinema*, ed. Charles Acland and Haidee Wasson (Chapel Hill, NC: Duke University Press, 2011); Mary Townes, *Teaching with Motion Pictures: A Guide to Sources of Information and Materials* (New York: Columbia University Teachers College, 1938); Frederic Thrasher, "The Sociological Approach to Educational Problems," *Journal of Educational Sociology* 9, no. 8 (1936): 479; Edgar Dale et al., *Proceedings of a Conference on the Educational Production of Motion Pictures* (Columbus: Ohio State University, 1939); "Urge Teaching on Propaganda," *Boston Daily Globe*, November 19, 1938; "Motion Pictures in the School," *Oregon Teacher Monthly*, February 1917; Eleanor Child, "Making Motion Pictures in the School," *English Journal* 28, no. 9 (1939): 706–712; "Educators Differ on School Radio," *New York Times*, March 9, 1941; S. A. Courtis, "The Fascist Menace in Education," *Education Digest* 4, no. 7 (1939): 35.

87. Richard Steele, *Propaganda in an Open Society: The Roosevelt Administration and the Media, 1933–1941* (Westport, CT: Greenwood Press, 1985); Carroll Atkinson, *Development of Radio Education Policies in American Public Schools* (Edinboro, PA: Edinboro Educational Press, 1939); I. Keith Tyler, "Radio and Youth," in Ronald Lowdermilk, *Radio in Informal Education: A Conference Report* (Columbus: Ohio State University, 1942), 6; Floyd Brooker and Eugene Herrington, *Students Make Motion Pictures: A Report on Film Production in the Denver Schools*, American Council on Education, 1941; Eleanor Child and Hardy Finch, *Producing School Movies: A Manual for Teachers and Students Interested in Producing Amateur Films* (National Council of Teachers of English, 1941); "A Town Within a Town," *Municipal Record*, San Francisco Board of Supervisors, 1920, 50; Deborah Lynn Self, "The National Youth Administration in Texas, 1935–1939" (master's thesis, Texas Tech University, 1974); Anna Siomonpoulos, "Entertaining Ethics: Mass Culture and American Intellectuals of the 1930s," *Film History* 11, no. 1 (1999): 45–54; Jonathan Auerbach, *Weapons of Democracy* (Baltimore: Johns Hopkins, 2015); Mary Swain Routzahn, foreword to *Building a Popular Movement: A Case Study of the Public Relations of the Boy Scouts of America*, by Harold P. Levy (New York: Russell Sage Foundation, 1944), 13; Mary Swain Routzahn, "Publicizing Human Needs," *Public Opinion Quarterly* 1, no. 4 (1937): 126–131. Helen MacGill Hughes, "Human Interest Stories and Democracy," *Public Opinion Quarterly* 1, no. 2 (1937): 73–83 described publicity as a substitute for direct encounters. On publicity for government, education, and social service, see Evart Routzahn, *Elements of a Social Publicity Program* (New York: Russell Sage Foundation, 1920); Marshall Dimock, "Selling Public Enterprise to the Public," *National Municipal Review* 23 (December 1934): 660–666; Carter Alexander, "Research in Educational Publicity," *Teachers College Record* 29 (March 1928): 479–487; Better Schools League, *Publicity Materials for School Bond Campaigns*, 1928; L. Morris et al, "Annotated Bibliography of Researches in Educational Publicity to June,

1927," *Teachers College Record* 30 (October 1928); C. M. Bolser, "Have You a Director of Publicity in Your School?" *School and Society* 12 (November 27, 1920): 513–517; "City Government's Advertising Opportunity," *Printers' Ink* 3 (May 6, 1920): 41–44; Wylie Kirkpatrick, "The Preparation of Public Reports: Telling Citizens How the Public Job Is Done," *American City* 44 (April–May 1931): 113–115, 125–127; Mary Swain Routzahn and Evart Routzahn, *Publicity for Social Work* (New York: Russell Sage Foundation, 1928).

Conclusion

1. William Byron Forbush, *Dramatics in the Home* (Philadelphia: American Institute of Child Life, 1914), 15 [Also in his *Manual of Play* (Philadelphia: George W. Jacobs, 1914), 141–142 on Plays of Impersonation]; Elnora Whitman Curtis, *The Dramatic Instinct in Education* (Boston: Houghton Mifflin, 1914), 94; B. H. Darrow, *Radio: The Assistant Teacher*, (Columbus, OH: R. G. Adams, 1932); John Dougall and Nora Alice Way, "How the Social Forces of a Community Are Coordinated to Serve Children," *Journal of Educational Sociology* 11, no. 8 (1938): 483–496; Charles E. Merriam, *The Making of Citizens* (Chicago: University of Chicago Press, 1931); Harold D. Lasswell, Ralph D. Casey, and Bruce Lannes Smith, *Propaganda and Promotional Activities, An Annotated Bibliography* (Minneapolis: University of Minnesota Press, 1935); Edgar Dale, *Audiovisual Methods in Teaching* (New York: Dryden Press, 1969).

2. On this sheltering, see, for example, Richard Tompkins, "Schools' Report War Tool," *Sun*, August 13, 1944; Etna M. Kelly, "Children at School," *Popular Photography*, March 1947, 52. A report called "All the Children," depicting students in US schools, was airdropped overseas by the Office of War Information.

3. "Youth Republic Aids War with Work Program: Upstate Community Enrolls More 'Citizens,' Expands Buildings and Courses," *New York Herald Tribune*, July 12, 1942; "Junior Republic Geared for War: Self-Governing Children Have Increased 'State' Output," *New York Times*, January 10, 1943; Mary Kelly, "Young Citizens of the George Junior Republic Know What It Is to Make a Town Successful," *Christian Science Monitor*, February 13, 1943.

4. "Boystowns," *Encyclopedia of Cleveland History*, https://case.edu/ech/articles/b/boystowns/; "Cleveland's Boystown Centers," *Industrial Arts & Vocational Education* 35 (1946): 207; William Ganson Rose, *Cleveland: The Making of a City* (Cleveland: World, 1950), 1011; "James Robinson Dies at 86," *New Pittsburgh Courier*, July 19, 1997; "James S. Robinson Jr., Teacher, Pioneer on Civil Rights Scene," *Pittsburgh Post-Gazette*, July 17, 1997; "Hill City Helped Inner City Youth," *Pittsburgh Post-Gazette*, February 13, 2001; Hill City Youth Municipality, Friendly Service Bureau, Department of Public Safety, Activities Report for January 1946 from Black Buzz News Service, the James S. Robinson Jr. Project, Robinson Family Archives, Pittsburgh, PA; "Youth City Opens Canteen for Visiting Servicemen," *Philadelphia Tribune*, August 21, 1943; "Youth City Plans Soldiers Party," *Philadelphia Tribune*, July 4, 1942; W. Rollo Wilson, "War Hero Gets Youth City," *Philadelphia Tribune*, October 2, 1943; "A Real SOS," *Philadelphia Tribune*, March 7, 1942; "Free Course in Commerce at Youth City," *Philadelphia Tribune*, August 14, 1941 "Youth Groups in City to Sponsor Conference on Defense and Negro," *Philadelphia Tribune*, February 20, 1941; "NY

Pastor Speaks at Youth Meeting," *Philadelphia Tribune,* June 19, 1941; "New Mayor: His First Act Is to Hire Ex-Youth City Aides," *Philadelphia Tribune,* August 21, 1941; "Youth City Buyer Defends Purchase," *Philadelphia Tribune,* October 30, 1943; "Nearly $100 Received 2nd Week of Youth City Membership Drive," *Philadelphia Tribune,* April 10, 1943; Sherry Stone, "Sam Evans, at 88, Continues to Speak Out on the Issues," *Philadelphia Tribune,* August 2, 1991; "Acorn to Oak," *Philadelphia Tribune,* March 7, 1942; "Youth City Bears Down in Drive as Big Checks Come Rolling In," *Philadelphia Tribune,* September 6, 1941; "Musicians to Aid Youth City Dance," *Philadelphia Tribune,* April 10, 1941; "Youth City Head Aids Hale America Campaign," *Philadelphia Tribune,* October 25, 1941, 2; Arthur Fauset, "I Write as I See," *Philadelphia Tribune,* April 17, 1941; "Youth Plan Conference on Defense Jobs," *Philadelphia Tribune,* February 6, 1941; "Youth City Not Affiliated with Any Body," *Philadelphia Tribune,* January 23, 1941; "Marian Anderson Makes Youth City Present of $100," *Philadelphia Tribune,* January 30, 1943; "Leading Democrats Meet at Youth City; Nix to Run in Council Race," *Philadelphia Tribune,* February 20, 1943; "Youth City Class Gets R. C. Certificates," *Philadelphia Tribune,* August 1, 1942; "Youth City to Solicit Funds Sun.," *Philadelphia Tribune,* April 18, 1942; "Seek End of J.C. in Fire, Police Depts.," *Afro-American* March 27, 1943; "Youth City Founder Award," *Philadelphia Tribune,* March 14, 1942; "Youth City May Renew Study Classes," *Philadelphia Tribune,* August 8, 1942; "Sponsors Give Youth City $2,111," *Philadelphia Tribune,* April 3, 1943; "Citizens Back Youth City Drive," *Philadelphia Tribune,* March 27, 1943; "Mrs. Roosevelt Receives Plaque from Race Youth," *Atlanta Daily World,* September 23, 1942; "99th Leader Wins Youth City Award," *Chicago Defender,* October 2, 1943; "Middle Atlantic AAU Sponsors Boxing Show for Youth City," *Philadelphia Tribune,* September 18, 1943; "Youth City Center Faces Closing," *Philadelphia Tribune,* August 21, 1943; "Evans Named Head of Youth Confab Group Philadelphia," *Philadelphia Tribune,* November 8, 1941; "Youth City, Nationally Known as 'Capital' Faces Closing as Debts Pile Up," *Philadelphia Tribune,* March 7, 1942; "Choral Ensemble Recital to Help Save Youth City," *Afro American,* March 17, 1942; Rusty Pray, Dwight Ott, and Tom Infield, "Samuel L. Evans, 1902–2008: A leader of Phila. leaders," *Philadelphia Inquirer,* June 15, 2008; Samuel Evans, "Having Your Say," *Philadelphia Tribune,* May 25, 1993; "Youth City Canteen Host to Service Men," *Philadelphia Tribune,* September 11, 1943. Similar civil defense activities, including first aid training, communications, and canteen corps, were part of NYA resident training center programs to give youth "training in good organization." Document: "To regional directors. Attention resident center and service projects supervisors," from Albert H. Huntington Junior and Mrs. Winthrop D. Lane, National Office, Subject, Youth Participation in Civilian Defense Programs, April 10, 1942, Record Group 119, Records of the National Youth Administration. Records of the Resident Center Section, Subject File 1939–1943, Food Service-Library, Folder Leisure Time—Self-government, NARA.

5. "Lieut. Murphy Tells of New Program to Save Delinquents," *Washington Post,* March 23, 1944; "Atlanta Studies Plan Which Transformed Slum Youth," *New Journal and Guide* August 4, 1945; Cecile Davis, "Young Negro Patrolman in Capital Works Amazing Reform with Kids," *Atlanta Constitution,* July 18, 1945; Adele Bernstein, "Junior Police Regional Plan to Have Trial," *Washington Post,* July 7, 1944; "D.C. Drops Charge Against Founder of Junior Police," *Washington Post,* March 23, 1949; "Cowan's Youth Program Draws Senator's Praise," *New Journal and Guide,* June 25, 1949; Alfred Smith, "D.C. Junior Police Corps Breaking Up Boys Gangs," *Chicago Defender,*

November 27, 1943; Adele Bernstein, "700 Juvenile Gang Members Achieve Self-Reformation," *Washington Post,* December 2, 1943; Adele Bernstein, "Negro Named to School Patrol for Reducing Juvenile Crime," *Washington Post,* December 3, 1943; "Virginians Study D.C. Junior Police," *Washington Post,* March 26, 1948; Adele Bernstein, "Murphy Heads New Police Juvenile Unit," *Washington Post,* March 12, 1944; "Example of D.C. Policeman Pictured in Vandalism Drive," *Atlanta Daily World,* July 19, 1945; "Cleveland to Copy Capitol's Junior Police-Citizen Corps: Cleveland Police Officers Fly to Capitol for Study 'Robbers' Become Cops Under Unique Plan to Harness Gangs," *Cleveland Call and Post,* February 9, 1946; "To Try Out a New Approach to Kid Gangs," *New York Amsterdam News,* May 25, 1946; "Cleveland to Copy D.C. Junior Police as Crime Check," *Washington Post,* February 3, 1946; "Atlanta Studies Washington's Plan in Curbing Delinquency," *Philadelphia Tribune,* August 4, 1945; Earl Conrad, "Yesterday and Today," *Chicago Defender,* November 16, 1946; "They Fought with Rocks Once," *Washington Post,* August 1, 1947; "Officer Tells of Curbing Boy Crimes," *Washington Post,* January 8, 1944; "In Place of Crime," *Washington Post,* March 13, 1944; Senate Committee on the Judiciary, *Recommendations for Action by the Panels of the National Conference on Prevention and Control of Juvenile Delinquency* (Washington, DC: US GPO, 1947), 134; "Fighting Delinquency," *American Journal of Corrections* (1945): 18; "Film on FBI Work Will Entertain Jr. Police Corps," *Washington Post,* December 9, 1943; Republics planned but never fully operational included Milwaukee and Los Angeles branches of the BBR. Following two other failed attempts by BBR alums to organize a California outpost, Harry Slonaker (who had established the NYC branch) finally succeeded with a Boy City Boys Club in San Jose. "LA Meeting Called on Boy Aid," *Los Angeles Times,* October 3, 1943; "Social Center Held Dire Need in Fifth Ward," *Milwaukee Sentinel,* May 29, 1941; "A Boys' Town Goes Up Here," *Milwaukee Journal,* April 29, 1940; "Flophouse Dressed Up to House Boy Republic," *Milwaukee Journal,* July 10, 1940; "Old Flophouse to Shine Forth as Boys' Club," *Milwaukee Journal,* June 23, 1940; "Advance Order Given in Festival Fund Drive," *Milwaukee Sentinel,* March 13, 1941; "Seek Worst Boy in US to Make Him 100% Good," *Chicago Daily Tribune,* January 4, 1918; "Nuf Said," *Newsboys' World,* May/June 1918, 10; "New Boys Town to Be Promoted by Negro Group," *Chicago Daily Tribune,* October 5, 1941; "Negroes Set Up Boys Town: Bar no Race or Creed," *Chicago Daily Tribune,* June 21, 1941; "D. O. Cohan Dies on Train," *Los Angeles Times,* October 3, 1943; "Memorial Play Center to Be Opened Feb. 22," *Los Angeles Times,* January 30, 1947, 5; "Meeting Called on Boy Aid," *Los Angeles Times,* October 3, 1943; "Negro Policeman Points Way to End Delinquency," *Atlanta Daily World,* December 14, 1943; On civil rights and national security, see Mary Dudziak, *Cold War Civil Rights* (Princeton, NJ: Princeton University Press, 2000). Many African Americans embraced the "Double V" campaign initiated by the *Pittsburgh Courier* for victory over Nazism abroad and racism at home—and this included the population of Hill City and Youth City as well. See "NY Pastor Speaks at Youth Meeting," *Philadelphia Tribune,* June 19, 1941.

6. Philip Kent, "Lathrop Junior City," *National Association of Housing Officials Notes on Management Practice* (February 1944); "Race Relations, White Kids Rebuff Hate Elect Negro Boy 'Mayor,'" *Chicago Defender,* March 20, 1943; "Youthful Lad of Wellstown Is Re-elected," *Chicago Daily Tribune,* August 13, 1944; "Children Elect City Officials," *Chicago Daily Tribune,* February 22, 1942; "Star in Football Is Named Mayor for Junior City," *Chicago Daily Tribune,* December 13, 1942; "Our Town," *Chicago Daily Tribune,* August 31, 1941; "Colored Boy Is Chi 'Official,'" *Atlanta Daily*

World, May 9, 1945; "The Junior State of Altgeld Gardens," *Monthly Report of the Executive Secretary of the Chicago Housing Authority* (1944), 16; "Lathrop Junior to Elect Mayor, City Officials," *Chicago Daily Tribune*, November 29, 1942; "Lathrop Homes Children Elect City Officials: Youths to Have Own Court to Keep Order," *Chicago Daily Tribune*, February 22, 1942; Katherine Stroud, "Recreation Goes Political, Altgeld Junior State Chicago," *Recreation* 39 (January 1946): 554; "Boy 'Mayor' of Wellstown," *Chicago Defender*, August 14, 1943; "Girl Becomes Mayor of 'Wellstown,'" *Chicago Defender*, September 6, 1941; "Ida B. Wells Homes Mark Second Year by Jubilee," *Chicago Daily Tribune*, August 3, 1942; "Club Meetings to Emphasize Civic Themes," *Chicago Daily Tribune*, January 21, 1945; "4th Wellstown Jubilee to Open Tuesday Night," *Chicago Daily Tribune*, July 30, 1944; Chicago Housing Authority, *Children's Cities* (Chicago: Housing Authority, 1946); "Youth Made Wellstown Mayor," *Chicago Daily Tribune*, August 7, 1943; "Receives Congratulations," *Chicago Defender*, August 15, 1942; "12-Year-Old Girl Elected Mayor," *Atlanta Constitution*, October 26, 1941. In a testament to some continued links between republic experience and later life, however, Slaughter notably went on to become a public relations spokesperson for the nation's federal housing agency and one of the few African American members of the National Press Club. In a related move, other housing agencies started junior police programs; see "Junior Police Get Their Rewards," *Philadelphia Tribune*, August 14, 1941; Juttee T. Garth Sr. "Juvenile Delinquency and Suggested Treatment," *Pennsylvania Probation and Parole Quarterly* (October 1945).

7. Helen Cody Baker and Mary Brayton Swain Routzahn, *How to Interpret Social Welfare: A Study Course in Public Relations* (New York: Russell Sage, 1947); Leonard Koos, "Educational News and Editorial Comment," *School Review* 54, no. 1 (1946): 5–6; *Journal of Proceedings, Board of Supervisors, City and County of San Francisco* (1945 and 1946); "Junior City Regime Starts with Pep," *San Francisco Examiner*, November 16, 1945; Edvina Cahill, "Keep the Kids Busy," *Crisis* (March 1947): 74; Burt Morley Kebric, *Selected Bibliography on Junior Cities and Similar Projects* (Chicago: Management Division, National Association of Housing Officials, 1945); Ruth Lee Harrington, "How Young Citizens Gain Firsthand Experience in Governing a City: San Francisco's Youth-Governed Junior City Builds Citizens Tested for Responsibility," *Christian Science Monitor*, August 31, 1943; "'Junior City' Plan Approved; To Aid War Workers' Children," *San Francisco Examiner*, July 19, 1944; "Junior Self Rule Approved," *San Francisco Examiner*, July 26, 1944; "Eastern Woman Appointed Head of S.F. Junior City" *San Francisco Examiner*, December 22, 1944; "New Plans for 'Junior City,'" *San Francisco Examiner*, Morgue SF Examiner Clippings File (undated).

8. NYA, *Final Report of the National Youth Administration, Fiscal Years 1936–1943*, 83; A. H. Raskins, "NYA Will Abolish All Non-war Jobs," *New York Times*, February 28, 1942; "NYA Jobs-for-Youth Program Now Needs Youths for Jobs," *Christian Science Monitor*, September 1, 1942; "Amsterdam Girls Study Aviation Mechanics," *Schenectady Gazette*, October 1, 1942; "NYA Finding Workers to Aid Defense," *Hartford Courant*, June 9, 1941; Allan Lindstrom, "Boys' Village Has Making-Good Habit," *Hartford Courant*, August 13, 1939; "Lots of Work and Some Play Make Boys Good Citizens: NYA Answer to Nazi Youth," *Austin American*, May 25, 1941; "Victory Program Adopted by NYA," *Sun*, January 9, 1942; "Boys and Girls Trained for Defense Work in 600 Federally Financed Resident Centers," *Washington Post*, May 4, 1941; "NYA Youth War Worker to Be Feted," *Hartford Courant*, February 27, 1942; "Plainville Man Elected Mayor of Quoddy Village," *Daily Boston*

Globe, August 24, 1941; "Quoddy Youths in U. S. Posts in California," *New York Amsterdam Star-News,* November 15, 1941; "First Negro Mayor at Quoddy," *Pittsburgh Courier,* August 1, 1942; Eleanor Roosevelt, "My Day: Boy's NYA Project Is Self-Governing," *Atlanta Constitution,* June 24, 1941; "Quoddy Village Is Governed by NYA Youth Group," *Christian Science Monitor,* September 15, 1937; Evelyn Morris, "Try-out Experience at N.Y.A. Work Center," *Occupations: The Vocational Guidance Journal* 19, no. 6 (March 1941): 436–440; "NYA Work Center to Train Youths," *Evansville Argus,* July 11, 1941; Kenneth Holland, "The Implications of Work Camps for Secondary Education," *NASSP Bulletin* 24 (April 1940): 29–42; "Like College Is Ranger's War School," *Dallas Morning News,* April 25, 1943; "NYA Mayor Visits Campbella, NB," *Pittsburgh Courier,* August 15, 1942; Foster Hailey, "480,000 in NYA Aid in Defense Work," *New York Times,* March 3, 1941; "Wilberforce Youth 'Most Valuable for War Production' in NYA Center," *Cleveland Call and Post,* February 28, 1942; Jay Franklin, "An Industrial C. C. C.," *Daily Boston Globe,* June 1, 1940; "First Resident NYA Center to Open Soon," *Sun,* December 7, 1941; India Moffett, "Women in War Work," *Chicago Daily Tribune,* May 6, 1942; "By Teaching and Experience, N.Y.A. Shows Girls How to Make Their Own Living," *Austin American,* March 5, 1939; Arthur Wimer, "NYA Plans on Training Will Expand," *Hartford Courant,* October 10, 1940; George Britt, "War Workers in the Making: In New York one NYA center has poured a stream of 'shop-broken' workers into the war industries and, in doing so, itself filled important orders for the navy; how the National Youth Administration is helping break the bottleneck in labor supply," *Survey Graphic* 31 (May 1942): 235–240; Foster Hailey, "Keeping Up Morale Is Half NYA's Task," *New York Times,* March 4, 1941; "NYA Preparing Youngsters for Defense Roles: Skilled Labor in State Greatly Increased by Training," *Atlanta Constitution,* March 23, 1941; "Maine NYA Projects Train Eager Boys for Defense Jobs: NYA Project that Leads to Jobs," *Christian Science Monitor,* February 14, 1941; Edward Moore, "Youth Training Needed: Proposal to Abolish NYA Viewed as Erroneous Step," May 2, 1943; "Army Depends on Its Industrial Backing, So NYA Trains Young Men to Operate Machinery for Sinews of War," *Austin American,* February 22, 1942; "NYA Trained Students Are Finding Jobs in Ohio," *Cleveland Call and Post,* January 24, 1942; "NYA Aims to Train 600,000 Workers," *New York Times,* April 9, 1942; "1,450 Ohio Race Youths Serve NYA," *Chicago Defender,* October 5, 1940; "Race Youth Shares Largely in State NYA Program: Number Has Doubled Since September 3,072 Race Youth Employed in Month of March," *New Journal and Guide* May 10 1941; "NYA Tax Exemption Request Refused," *Sun,* June 11, 1941; Richard Reiman, *The New Deal and American Youth: Ideas and Ideals in a Depression Decade* (Athens: University of Georgia Press, 1992); Dewey Fleming, "Supporters Urge Permanent NYA," *Sun,* March 28, 1942; Dewey Fleming, "NYA Costs Taxpayer 12 Times as Much as All U. S. Courts," *Sun,* February 17, 1942; "Merging of C. C. C. and N. Y. A. Is Urged by Youth Commission," *New York Herald Tribune,* January 18, 1942. Document: Report of Verona, NJ, NYA youth conference. February 12, 1941, Folder: New Jersey, record group 119, Records of the National Youth Administration, Correspondence, report, and informational file of Harry Dreiser, administrative assistant and editor of *Youth and the Community,* 1941–1942, box 1, NARA; Document: To all junior personnel (attention all senior personnel) from Louis Varrichione, Project Director, September 16, 1942, Subject: junior project foremen, record group 119, Records of the National Youth Administration, Records of the Resident Center Section, Subject File 1939–1943, Food Service-Library, Folder Leisure Time—Self-government. To S. Burns Weston (assistant to chair of national advisory committee) from Wesley S. Thurstin, Assistant Director, Division of

Reports, Columbus (Ohio), Subject: Youth-Democracy program: Regional, November 24, 1940, Folder Bulletin—procedure, record group 119, Records of the National Youth Administration, Correspondence, report, and informational file of Harry Dreiser, administrative assistant and editor of *Youth and the Community*, 1941–1942, box 1, NARA. Document: "Summary of youth participation in advisory activities exclusive of actual youth membership on state and local committees," Folder Youth Participation, Note on top of folder said "Inactive," record group 119, Records of the National Youth Administration, Box Records of the Office of the Director, File of Molly Yard, Assistant Information Specialist on Youth-Interested Organizations 1940–1941, Reference and Information, box 4, NARA. Document: "Youth participation in NYA advisory Committee Work," 8-14-41, Folder Youth Participation, note on top of folder said "Inactive," record group 119, Records of the National Youth Administration, Box Records of the Office of the Director, File of Molly Yard, Assistant Information Specialist on Youth-Interested Organizations 1940–1941, Reference and Information, box 4, NARA. Document: Proposal for the National Youth Administration Program, Folder National Youth Administration, record group 119, Records of the National Youth Administration, Records of the Resident Center Section, Subject File 1939–1943. Ninth Corps Area—Quoddy Clippings, box 4, NARA. *No Slave Labor: Exposing Plans to Regiment Youth in Forced Labor Battalions: Proposing a Real Program for Jobs and Training for American Youth* (New York: New York Youth Congress, 1940); Edward Angly, "A. F. L. Assured Defense Plans Won't Cut Pay: Aubrey Williams Declares Vocational Training Work Will Respect Labor Policy," *New York Herald Tribune,* February 1, 1939; "California League [of municipalities] and NYA Institute Statewide Survey of City Facts," *Western City* (May 1941): 30–31; B. G. Graham, "Pittsburgh Vocational Training Program," *NASSP Bulletin* 24 (1940): 149; D. G. Johnson and T. R. Sarbin, "Work Performance of N.Y.A. Students: That Student N.Y.A. Workers Can with Proper Placement Show Remarkably Satisfactory Work Performance Is the Conclusion Reached by the Authors in Reporting the Results of a University of Minnesota Survey; How the Supervisors Rated the Students and How the Work Ratings Were Distributed over the Four-Year Period," *Occupations* 9 (October 1940): 36–38; M. H. Proctor, "The Opinions of a Group of Negro Boys About National Youth Administration Employment and Related Subjects," *Smith College Studies in Social Work* 11 (September 1940): 61–87; "Quoddy Village spreads democracy under VV," *Pittsburgh Courier,* July 4, 1942, 15. There were also a few youth democracies in this period that looked to older models of mirroring actual places, for example, Hobbytown at Pittsburgh's Irene Kaufman Settlement and Cleveland's Village at the University Settlement. See "Hobbytown: A Miniature Community Which Is Governed by Its Youthful Citizens on Democratic Lines," *Recreation* 34 (November 1940): 486–506; William Susumu Oshima, "The Village: A Play Group for Young Children of Elementary School Age in University Settlement, Cleveland, Ohio," (master's thesis, Ohio State University, 1956). The Kaufman settlement was funded by Henry Kaufman in memory of his daughter; initially he had contemplated financing the Pennsylvania George Junior Republic. See Mrs. Enoch Rauh to William George, January 25, 1908, box 4, folder 14, WG Papers.

9. "Scout Wins Acclaim for Aiding FBI," *Hartford Courant,* January 4, 1945; Charley Cherokee, "National GRAPEVINE," *Chicago Defender,* October 20, 1945; "Hoover Spurs Youth Program," *Atlanta Constitution,* November 23, 1943; "200 Police Hear FBI Specialist at Bristol Meet," *Hartford Courant,* August 29, 1944; "G-man Here to Study Junior Police Corps.," *Daily Boston Globe,* March 24, 1939; J. Edgar Hoover, *Juvenile Delinquency* (New York: Catholic Information Society, 1945);

Luis Alvarez, *The Power of the Zoot: Youth Culture and Resistance during World War II* (Berkeley: University of California Press, 2009); Mary Kelly, "Teen-Agers in Overprivileged Communities Need Youth Centers, Too," *Christian Science Monitor,* July 29, 1944; "Early Training Urged to Curb Delinquency," *Washington Post,* August 8, 1947; "Guidance of Youth Put on Community," *New York Times,* October 31, 1944; "Hoover Hails YMCA in Delinquency Fight," *New York Times,* October 13, 1943; J. Edgar Hoover, "How Good a Parent Are You?" *Los Angeles Times,* April 20, 1947; "JE Hoover Elected Boys Clubs Director," *New York Times,* October 14, 1943; Richard Wilson, "Fears Grip Hoodlums," *Los Angeles Times,* March 29, 1934; "These Boys Are Operating a Real Detective Agency," *Daily Boston Globe,* July 5, 1942; John Floherty and Mike McGrady, *Youth and the FBI* (Philadelphia: Lippincott, 1960); "Children's Pranks Held a War Danger," *New York Times,* June 14, 1943; Christopher W. Wiley, "Teacher, Pioneer on Civil Rights Scene" [James S. Robinson obituary], *Pittsburgh Post-Gazette,* July 16, 1997; "Boy Governments in 34 States Show Value of American Way: They're All for America," *Christian Science Monitor,* July 10, 1940; J. Edgar Hoover, "The Challenge to Youth" [commencement address to Boystown], Washington, DC, Federal Bureau of Investigation, 1941; "Film on FBI Work Will Entertain Jr. Police Corps," *Washington Post,* December 9, 1943; "FBI Chief Lauds D.C. Cop's Plan to Hit Delinquency," *Chicago Defender,* February 26, 1944; Ruth Lee Harrington, "How Young Citizens Gain Firsthand Experience in Governing a City: San Francisco's Youth-Governed Junior City Builds Citizens Tested for Responsibility," *Christian Science Monitor,* August 31, 1943; Edvina Cahill, "Keep the Kids Busy," *Crisis* (March 1947): 74; "Cop Praised by FBI in Child Delinquency Drive," *Chicago Defender,* April 22, 1944; J. Edgar Hoover, *Juvenile Delinquency* (New York: Catholic Information Society 1945); "These Boys Are Operating a Real Detective," *Daily Boston Globe,* July 5, 1942; Richard Powers, *G-Men: Hoover's FBI in American Popular Culture* (Carbondale, IL: Southern Illinois University Press, 1983); John Floherty and Mike McGrady, *Youth and the FBI* (Philadelphia: Lippincott, 1960).

10. William Graebner, *The Engineering of Consent: Democracy and Authority in Twentieth-Century America* (Madison: University of Wisconsin Press, 1987); Harry Elmer Barnes and Negly Teeter, *New Horizons in Criminology* (New York: Prentice Hall, 1943). Urquart encouraged this line of thinking with his own published work. Donald T. Urquhart, "Crime Prevention through Citizenship Training at the George Junior Republic," in Sheldon Glueck and Eleanor Glueck, *Preventing Crime* (New York, McGraw-Hill, 1936), 305–330; *Report of the Committee on Crime Prevention of the American Prison Association,* 1942; Sheldon Glueck and Eleanor Glueck, *500 Delinquent Women* (New York: Knopf, 1934); Karen Lee Riley, *Schools Behind Barbed Wire* (Lanham, MD: Rowman & Littlefield, 2002); Alexander Leighton, *The Governing of Men* (Princeton, NJ: Princeton University Press, 1945), 49; Brian Hayashi, *Democratizing the Enemy* (Princeton, NJ: Princeton University Press, 2004), 106; Sarah Sturges, "Self-Government in a Correctional School," *School and Society* 43 (April 1936): 470–473.

11. Alexander Leighton, *The Governing of Men* (Princeton, NJ: Princeton University Press, 1945), 49; US Department of the Interior, War Relocation Authority, *Community Government in War Relocation Centers* (Washington, DC: US GPO, 1943), 3–4; Takeya Mizuno, "The Creation of the 'Free' Press in Japanese American Camps," *Journalism and Mass Communication Quarterly* 78, no. 3 (2001): 506–513; Lauren Kessler, "Fettered Freedoms: The Journalism of WW2 Japanese Internment Camps," *Journalism History* 15, no. 2 (1988): 60–69; "Japanese Evacuees Publish Own Paper,"

New York Times, July 30, 1942; Alice Myers, "Smashing Racial Prejudices Aim of Girl Reserve Leaders," *Christian Science Monitor,* November 9, 1942.

12. *Community Government in War Relocation Centers* (Washington, DC: GPO, 1943); Alexander Leighton, *The Governing of Men* (Princeton, NJ: Princeton University Press, 1945); Brian Hiyashi, *Democratizing the Enemy* (Princeton, NJ: Princeton University Press, 2004); Rosalie Wax, "The Destruction of a Democratic Impulse: An Exemplification of Certain Problems of a Benevolent Dictatorship," *Human Organization* 12, no. 1 (Spring 1953): 11–21. Sol Tax, a former Milwaukee newsboy, was among the social scientists who studied the camps. For an example of a camp constitution, see *Constitution and By-Laws: Self Government Assembly of the Santa Anita Assembly Center* (Arcadia, CA: Santa Anita Assembly Center: n.d.), http://cdm15831.contentdm.oclc.org/cdm/ref/collection/p15831coll18/id/20

13. Jennifer Light, "When Computers Were Women," *Technology and Culture* (1999): 455–483; Ruth Milkman, *Gender at Work* (Urbana: University of Illinois Press, 1987).

14. Edward Olsen, *School and Community: The Philosophy, Procedures, and Problems of Community Study and Service through Schools and Colleges* (New York: Prentice Hall, 1945); L. W. Anderson, "Conservation Fair: A Wartime School-Community Project," *Clearing House* 18 (1944): 329–331; Natsuki Aruga, "An' Finish School: Child Labor During World War Two," *Labor History* 29 (1988): 498–530; Dorothy Baruch, *You, Your Children and War* (New York: Appleton, 1943); Robert Kirk, *Earning Their Stripes: The Mobilization of American Children in the Second World War* (New York: Peter Lang, 1994); Angelo Patri, *Your Children in Wartime* (Garden City, NY: Doubleday, 1943); Barbara Tucker, "Agricultural Workers in World War Two: The Reserve Army of Children, Black Americans, and Jamaicans," *Agricultural History* 68 (1994): 54–73; Lisa Ossian, *The Forgotten Generation: American Children and World War Two* (Columbia: University of Missouri Press, 2011); Ronald Cohen, "Schooling Uncle Sam's Children: Education in the USA, 1941–1945," in *Education and the Second World War,* ed. Roy Lowe (New York: Routledge, 1992); Richard Ugland, "'Education for Victory': The High School Victory Corps and Curricular Adaptation During World War Two," *History of Education Quarterly* 19, no. 4 (1979): 435–451; "Schools Put Total War on Curricula," *Washington Post,* August 31, 1942; Benjamin Fines, "Private Schools Stress War Role," *New York Times,* December 20, 1941; "High Schools to Let Boys Skip Non-War Courses," *New York Herald Tribune,* October 28, 1942; "Wade's Report Shows Effect of War in Schools," *New York Herald Tribune,* December 14, 1942; "Educators Urge Schools Adjust Curricula with War Program," *Daily Boston Globe,* September 1, 1942; Frank Henry, "Changes in City's Schools Brought About by the War: Classrooms Geared to the War Exertion," *Sun,* October 18, 1942; "War in Classroom as Schools Open," *New York Times,* September 14, 1942; "Negro Schools Take Part in War Conservation Program," *Washington Post,* March 5, 1943; "Schools Shift Classes to Aid War Industry," *Atlanta Constitution,* September 1, 1943; "Schools' War Job Outlined: Superintendents Tell of Gearing Training to Meet Conditions," *Los Angeles Times,* October 13, 1942; "Schools to Open Tomorrow on War-Time Note," *New York Herald Tribune,* September 13, 1942; John Studebaker, "Education for Self-Government," *School Life* 25 (February 1940): 129; Millicent Taylor, "Importance of Teaching Democracy Also Stressed Role of Schools in War Effort Told to N.E.A," *Christian Science Monitor,* June 30, 1943; Samuel Everett, "Adapting the School to the Changing Social Scene," *Review of Educational Research* 13, no. 1 (February 1943): 38–47; Lloyd Allen Cook,

"Education for Community Unity and Action," *Review of Educational Research* 13, no. 1 (February 1943): 48–59; "High School Posters to Aid in Campaign for War Chest," *Los Angeles Times*, October 26, 1943; "'Schools-at-War' Launch Vigorous Bond Campaign," *Los Angeles Times*, November 22, 1944; "City's Schools Open Drive for War Bond Sale," *Christian Science Monitor*, December 12, 1944; "Public Schools Playing Important War Effort Role, Woods Advises Stevenson," *Austin Statesman*, May 4, 1942; "2nd District Schools Are 'All-Out' in War Effort," *Newsday*, October 23, 1942, 5; "War Bond Sales of 10 Schools May Pay for 3 Ambulances," *Washington Post*, May 20, 1943; Benjamin Fine, "High Schools Meeting War Test," *New York Times*, June 20, 1943; W. R. McConnell, "War Gives Zest to Geography in the Schools," *New York Times*, April 27, 1941; "Approve 51 More Schools for Use in War Training," *Chicago Daily Tribune*, February 14, 1943; "12 Month Term in High Schools Urged for War," *Chicago Daily Tribune*, May 2, 1942; "Schools Chart Broad Plans to Aid War Effort," *New York Herald Tribune*, January 10, 1942; "War Work Taught 246,000 in Schools," *New York Times*, July 20, 1944; "War Challenges Private Schools," *New York Times*, December 12, 1942; R. D. Kellogg, "Self-Government in Schools," *New York Times*, January 8, 1943.

15. Richard Tompkins, "Schools' Report War Tool," *Sun*, August 13, 1944; "Schools in the War Efforts," *Phi Delta Kappan* 25, no. 1 (1942): 21–22; Richard Ugland, "'Education for Victory': The High School Victory Corps and Curricular Adaptation During World War Two," *History of Education Quarterly* 19, no. 4 (1979): 435–451; Richard Ugland, "The Adolescent Experience During World War II: Indianapolis as a Case Study" (PhD diss., Indiana University, 1977); "Schools Gear for War," *New York Times*, September 13, 1942; "Schools Send 3,000 a Month into War Jobs," *Chicago Daily Tribune*, May 29, 1943; "Urge High School Youth to Join Victory Corps," *Cleveland Call and Post*, October 10, 1942; Scott Hart, "High Schools Go to War: A Victory Corps," *Washington Post*, September 26, 1942; Emily Towe, "'Army' of High School Students Being Trained for War Roles," *New York Herald Tribune*, April 11, 1943; John Studebaker, "Educating Youth to Meet National Problems: The Vision of a Democratic Society," delivered at the 78th Annual Convention of the National Education Association, July 3, 1940, Milwaukee, Wisconsin, *Vital Speeches of the Day*, vol. 6, 655–659; William Avirett, "Flood of War Activities Viewed as Handicap to Schools' Work," *New York Herald Tribune*, December 26, 1943; "Pease Pupils Take Spending Money and Turn It Over to Junior Red Cross," *Austin Statesman*, November 21, 1941; "Art Classes Helping Army," *Austin Statesman*, January 9, 1942; Julietta Arthur, "A Stitch in Wartime," *New York Herald Tribune*, March 15, 1942; American National Red Cross, *Chapter Organization for the Development of the American Junior Red Cross* (Washington, DC: American National Red Cross, 1942); Margaret K. Bolanz, "A Survey of the Junior Red Cross as an Integrating Element in the Elementary School Curriculum" (master's thesis, University of Akron College of Education, 1944); Vivian Sowers Rankin, "The Place of the Junior Red Cross in Today's Crisis," *Pi Lambda Theta Journal* 9, no. 3: 74–76; Calanthe M. Brazelton, "Tucson High Goes to Town on the Junior Red Cross," *Clearing House* 17, no. 3: 156–160; "Foreign Aid Emphasized by Junior Red Cross," *Hartford Courant*, November 11, 1945; Ronald Bauer, "The Utilization of the Junior Red Cross as an Enrichment Program in the Schools" (master's thesis, University of North Dakota, 1943); American Junior Red Cross, *List of Articles for Production* [for the Armed Forces] (Washington, DC: Red Cross, multiple dates); Margaret Schmid, "The Organization and Activities of the Junior Red Cross in the Elementary Schools," (master's thesis, Southwest Texas State Teachers College, 1944); Edward Olsen, *School and Community: The Philosophy, Procedures, and Problems of Community Study and Service through Schools*

and Colleges (New York: Prentice Hall, 1945); Harvey Zorbaugh, "The Morale Needs of Youth," *Journal of Educational Sociology* 16, no. 4, Children at War (December 1942): 241–248; Margery Rae, "The NSPA and High School Newspapers," *Christian Science Monitor*, June 27, 1942; "Press Convention Attended by 2,300," *New York Times*, March 24, 1944; "High School Press Helps Sell $536,718 in Bonds in Five Days," *New York Herald Tribune*, March 13, 1943; "News Specialists Will Address High School Journalists at G.W.," *Washington Post*, November 29, 1942; "High School Paper 'Must Justify Itself,'" *Austin Statesman*, November 5, 1942; "Duties of Newspapers in War Told Writers," *Los Angeles Times*, April 22, 1942; "School Editors, Staffs Attend Journalism Clinic," *Atlanta Constitution*, November 4, 1944; "School Editors Urged to Heed Code of Censor," *New York Herald Tribune*, March 12, 1943; "School Press Rated Vital by Baldwin," *Hartford Courant*, October 7, 1945; "Queens Pupils Turn Actors in Patriotic Film," *New York Herald Tribune*, May 10, 1942; "Thousands of High School Students Throughout U.S. View World Problems," *Christian Science Monitor*, September 26, 1944; "High School Pupils in Radio Debate Today," *Hartford Courant*, December 8, 1944; "St. Thomas High School Next on 'Citizens' Show," *Chicago Daily Tribune*, February 8, 1942; "High School Group to Interpret News," *Los Angeles Times*, May 3, 1945; "Radio Newscasts for Schools," *Christian Science Monitor*, March 29, 1944, 1;"Educators Discuss Youth Role in War," *Washington Post,* January 31, 1942; "Youngsters of Junior Red Cross Interpret Their Homelands to One Another in Albums," *Christian Science Monitor*, February 7, 1942; "Junior Red Cross to Make Splints," *Sun*, February 9, 1942; "NYA Operating 7 Radio Units: Approval Awaited on 14 More Clubs," *Austin Statesman*, August 28, 1940; *Radio Service and Related Occupations: Prepared on NYA Guidance Project, Louisville, Kentucky, Under Supervision of W. Edmund Baxter, Administrative Assistant* (Louisville, KY, 1938), record group 119, Records of the National Youth Administration, Records of the Radio Projects Section, Fragment File of Robert B Burton, Radio Engineer and Section Chief, Concerning NYA Amateur Radio Stations and Licenses, 1940–1942, box 1, NARA; "NYA Builds Fine Police Radio in Maine," *Radio and Television*, March 1941, folder Quoddy Clippings, record group 119, Records of the National Youth Administration, Records of the Resident Center Section, subject file 1939–1943, Quoddy, June 1937-December 1939, box 5, NARA; Robert E. Asher to Mr. Roswell, September 13, 1941, Subject: Proposed Amateur Radio Station Directory, folder NYA Amateur Radio Station Directory, Disapproved. See also document in this folder titled "Amateur Radio Station Directory," National Youth Administration, Federal Security Agency, September 1941; Folder Radio, record group 119, Records of the National Youth Administration, Records of the Radio Projects Section, fragment file of Robert B. Burton, Radio Engineer and Section Chief, Concerning NYA Amateur Radio Stations and Licenses, 1940–1942, box 1, NARA. Although the nationwide amateur communication system, operated by NYA youth, provided emergency communications when a blizzard on the East Coast knocked out power to other local stations, Washington headquarters scrapped its planned NYA station directory the following year. This decision did not end amateur broadcasting, but rather backed away from using the stations for official business.

16. "National Board Outlines War Duties of Boy Scouts," *New York Herald Tribune*, December 26, 1941; "Cookies for the Army from the Girl Scouts," *New York Times*, October 28, 1942; Marcia Davenport, "The Girl Scouts—Our Home Front Reserve," *New York Times*, November 15, 1942; "Defense Parley for Girl Scouts Is Slated Feb. 9: One-Day Institute to Chart War-Time Activities Is Announced by Leader Officers of Girl Scouts at Headquarters Here," *New York Herald Tribune*,

January 24, 1942; Mary Spargo, "Boy and Girl Scouts Serve Community in Many Ways: Scouts Render Needed Services," *Washington Post*, November 2, 1942; "Nassau Girl Scouts Launch War on Rats," *Newsday*, July 2, 1942; "Girl Scouts Tackle Odd Jobs in Victory Fund Stamp Drive: Girl Scouts Save Odd Pennies to Tip Odds Against Axis," *Christian Science Monitor*, October 27, 1942; Frederick Lewis, "Blueprint for Junior Citizenship," *Recreation* (November 1943); "Girls Now Junior Police," *New York Times*, March 16, 1943; "Schoolgirl Police Release Boypower," *Globe and Mail*, March 17, 1943; "Junior Police on Job," *New York Times*, January 1, 1942; "First Depositor at National Shawmut 'Drive In' Is Junior Police Corps," *Daily Boston Globe*, January 11, 1942; "Boys Collect Decrepit Jallopy and 'Ride' Free into Theater," *Christian Science Monitor*, October 26, 1942; "Junior Traffic Patrol Sets Perfect Record," *Los Angeles Times*, June 13, 1944; Joseph Dineen, "The Record Parade," *Daily Boston Globe*, May 31, 1942; "Youngsters Help Civilian Defense Work," *Austin American*, April 12, 1942; "'Youth Army' Being Enlisted," *Los Angeles Times*, March 8, 1943; "School News Digest," *Clearing House* 17, no. 2 (October 1942): 112; J. J. Buliverio, "Police Force," *Hartford Courant*, November 20, 1940; "Enlarged Junior Police Force Planned," *Los Angeles Times*, November 11, 1943; "Students Solve Police Problem of Man Power at Norwood, N. J.," *New York Herald Tribune*, December 16, 1942; "Turning the Soil [photo]," *Boston Globe*, April 29, 1943; Adelaide Handy, "War Tasks Done by Girl Reserves," *New York Times*, July 19, 1942; "Junior Army," *Atlanta Constitution*, October 4, 1942; "Jangos on the Home Front," *Washington Post*, November 7, 1943; "Junior Army of 85,000 Opens Waste Paper Drive," *Christian Science Monitor*, March 30, 1944; "The Boy Scouts," *Newsday*, February 10, 1941, 11; "President Praises Girl Scouts for Both Peace and War Work," *Christian Science Monitor*, March 12, 1941; "Boy Scouts Helping to Fight the War," *New York Times*, January 1, 1942; "Boy Scouts to Get Posts for Victory," *Washington Post*, January 11, 1942; "Boy Scouts Get First Defense Job," *Chicago Daily Tribune*, January 12, 1942; "Y.W.C.A. Girl Reserves Share War Effort as Aides in Hospitals and Domestic Work," *New York Times*, January 18, 1942; "Boy Scouts Serve Nation at War for Second Time," *Philadelphia Tribune*, February 7, 1942; "10,000 Girl Scouts to Aid in War Here," *New York Times*, March 26, 1942; "Cookie Sales of Girl Scouts to End Today: Many Servicemen Receiving Delicacies from Parents," *Atlanta Constitution*, March 31, 1942; "Senior Service Girl Scouts Set to Help in War," *Hartford Courant*, May 31, 1942; "42,000 Boy Scouts Give Out Circulars," *New York Times*, July 14, 1942; Adelaide Handy, "War Tasks Done by Girl Reserves: Already 347,000 in Country Fill Places of Older Workers," *New York Times*, July 19, 1942; "Girl Scouts Tackle Odd Jobs in Victory Fund Stamp Drive," *Christian Science Monitor*, October 27, 1942; Alice Myers, "Smashing Racial Prejudices Aim of Girl Reserve Leaders," *Christian Science Monitor*, November 9, 1942; "Girl Scouts," *New York Times*, November 20, 1942; "South Side Girl Reserves Help Hospital Staffs," *Chicago Daily Tribune*, December 13, 1942; "Girl Scouts Will Stress War Service," *Hartford Courant*, January 12, 1943; "45,000 Boy Scouts Here to Sign War-Aid Pledges," *New York Herald Tribune*, April 16, 1943; "Girl Scouts Here to Work on Farms," *New York Times*, April 30, 1943; "Mayor Swears 500 Boy Scouts as O. W. I. Aids," *New York Herald Tribune*, June 13, 1943; "100 Girl Scouts as Farmerettes Help Relieve Shortage Up-State," *New York Times*, July 10, 1943; "Boy Scouts to Serve as Dispatch Bearers," *Christian Science Monitor*, March 22, 1943; "2,000 Boy Scouts Aid in Potato Harvest," *New York Times*, September 15, 1943; "1800 Boy Scouts Help Save Crops in Three States," *Daily Boston Globe*, September 26, 1943; "D.C. Girl Scouts Make Fag Bags for U.S. Forests," *Washington Post*, October 10, 1943; "Hour-Check Presented by Girl

Scouts," *Washington Post,* March 14, 1944; "Redondo Girl Scouts Make Hospital Toys," *Los Angeles Times,* May 29, 1944; "Girl Scouts Served 224 Agencies in 1944," *New York Times,* April 11, 1945; "Local Boy Scouts Get Instructions for Traffic Count," *Atlanta Daily World,* May 10, 1945; "Girl Scouts Aid Cherry Harvest," *Los Angeles Times,* June 22, 1943; "Clark-Diversey Youth Reserves Planning Dance," *Chicago Daily Tribune,* February 14, 1943; Earl Banner, "Boston's Junior Police Join Victory Gardeners," *Daily Boston Globe,* April 14, 1943; "Boys Plan a Garden Despite Big Hazards," *New York Times,* May 12, 1942; "Children Helping Cleanup Drive in South Boston," *Daily Boston Globe,* April 2, 1944; "Junior Police on Job," *New York Times,* January 1, 1942; Joseph Dineen, "The Record Parade: South Boston Junior Police Lads Ring Doorbells, Get 2447 Disks," *Daily Boston Globe,* May 31, 1942; "Young Auxiliary Police Groups Roll in Paper," *Los Angeles Times,* February 16, 1944; "Junior Police to Aid Drive for Salvage," *Los Angeles Times,* November 23, 1944;" Junior Naval Militia Fights Change of Title: Private Group for Boys Challenges Authority of Adjutant General to Ban Use of 'Naval' and 'Militia,'" *New York Herald Tribune,* April 14, 1938; "Junior Naval Reserve to Add Army Training," *New York Herald Tribune,* July 4, 1938; "Use of 'Militia' by Boys Barred," *New York Times,* April 14, 1938; "Big Gain Noted in Membership of Boy Scouts," *Atlanta Constitution,* January 8, 1943; "Girl Scouts Open Drive for Leaders," *New York Times,* March 10, 1943; William Strand, "Call 1 1/2 Million Boy Scouts for Defense Tasks: Will Give First Aid and Act as Fire Guards," *Chicago Daily Tribune,* January 11, 1942; "Vast Wartime Achievements Crown 35th Anniversary of Boy Scouts: Democratic Youth-Service Answer to Nazi Philosophy, Aid War Effort, Nazi Agents Caught, Boy Scouts Saluted by Military Chiefs," *Christian Science Monitor,* February 7, 1945; "Boy Scouts Sell War Bonds," *Atlanta Daily World,* January 19, 1944; "Scouts as Aid to War Lauded by Roosevelt," *Christian Science Monitor,* February 8, 1943; "Former Scouts Back from War Will Organize," *Chicago Daily Tribune,* March 3, 1946; "Scouts Will Distribute 'Nassau at War' Posters," *Newsday,* April 10, 1943, 6; "American Boy Scouts Deep in the War Effort," *Hartford Courant,* September 5, 1943; "National Board Outlines War Duties of Boy Scouts," *New York Herald Tribune,* December 26, 1941; "Hour-Check Presented by Girl Scouts," *Washington Post,* March 14, 1944.

17. "Junior Police Air Raid Messengers," *Christian Science Monitor,* October 24, 1941; "Girl Scouts to the Rescue!" *Hartford Courant,* March 12, 1944; "Boy Scouts Stress Emergency Theme for Year: At Their Country's Service," *Hartford Courant,* February 8, 1942; "Boy Scouts Try to Serve U.S. in Emergencies," *Austin American,* February 22, 1942; "Board Not for Junior Police Plan," *Hartford Courant,* April 29, 1943; "High School Girls and Hospital Service: Pros and Cons of Part-Time Hospital Service," *American Journal of Nursing* 44, no. 1 (1944): 47–52; Barbara Pfeiffer, "Girl Reserves in Training: Defense Work Includes Tri-Y 'Victory Games,' Y.W.C.A. Instruction," *Los Angeles Times,* April 29, 1942; "Girl Scouts Put in Extra Work on War Duties," *Chicago Daily Tribune,* December 19, 1941; "National Board Outlines War Duties of Boy Scouts," *New York Herald Tribune,* December 26, 1941; "Defense Work Given Support of Girl Scouts," *Chicago Daily Tribune,* December 28, 1941; William Strand, "Call 1 1/2 Million Boy Scouts for Defense Tasks," *Chicago Daily Tribune,* January 11, 1942; "Defense Parley for Girl Scouts Is Slated Feb. 9," *New York Herald Tribune,* January 24, 1942; Mary Spargo, "Boy and Girl Scouts Serve Community in Many Ways," *Washington Post,* November 2, 1942; "Boy Scouts Emphasize Fitness," *Austin Statesman,* June 15, 1942; Marcia Davenport, "The Girl Scouts—Our Home Front Reserve," *New York Times,* November 15, 1942; "25% of Our Soldiers Former Boy Scouts, Says Dr. West, New Chief of Organization,"

New York Times, April 1, 1943; "American Boy Scouts Deep in the War Effort," *Hartford Courant*, September 5, 1943; Ambrose Calive, "Schools in the War Effort," *Chicago Defender*, December 19, 1942; Cecile Hallingby, "Girl Scouts' Place in Defense Outlined," *Los Angeles Times*, May 21, 1941; "Boy Scouts Called to New Services," *Christian Science Monitor*, January 22, 1942; "President Praises Girl Scouts for Both Peace and War Work," *Christian Science Monitor*, March 12, 1941; "Girl Scouts Aid War Effort," *Philadelphia Tribune*, November 7, 1942; Juanita Morris, "Girl Scouts Discuss Prejudices; Find Differences 'Just Don't Exist,'" *Cleveland Call and Post*, February 12, 1944; "$30,000 Donated to Aid Race Boy Scouts," *Atlanta Daily World*, June 14, 1945; "War Has Turned N. Y. Girl Scouts to World Topics, *New York Herald Tribune*, December 3, 1945; "Girl Scouts Plan Defense Services," *New York Times*, October 21, 1941; "Boy Scouts Hailed for 1943 Services," *New York Times*, February 25, 1944; "Girl Scouts to Get Simple War Tasks: National Head Says Little Girls Won't Be Sent Out to Do a Big Girl's Job," *New York Times*, January 24, 1942; "War Place Urged for Younger Girls," *New York Times*, June 12, 1943; "Junior Civic League Formed," *New Journal and Guide*, February 22, 1941; "War Has Turned N. Y. Girl Scouts to World Topics: G. I. Brother's Visit to Far Lands Helps Incentive for International Badge, American Girl Scouts Learn the Ways of Other Lands," *New York Herald Tribune*, December 3, 1945; "Scouts Drive for World Citizenship," *Newsday*, September 5, 1946, 42; "Brownies Are Helping in War Work," *Christian Science Monitor*, October 13, 1942; "Senior Service Girl Scouts Set to Help in War," *Hartford Courant*, May 31, 1942. In some cases, "junior" activities increasingly referred to older young adults.

18. "Junior Police in Plea to Roosevelt," *New York Amsterdam Star-News*, February 7, 1942; "Junior Traffic Patrol Sets Perfect Record," *Los Angeles Times*, June 13, 1944; Edward Olsen, *School and Community: The Philosophy, Procedures, and Problems of Community Study and Service through Schools and Colleges* (New York: Prentice Hall, 1945); William Avirett, "Flood of War Activities Viewed as Handicap to Schools' Work," *New York Herald Tribune*, December 26, 1943; Benjamin Fine, "High Schools Meeting War Test," *New York Times*, June 20, 1943; Margaret Schmid, "The Organization and Activities of the Junior Red Cross in the Elementary Schools," (master's thesis, Southwest Texas State Teachers College, 1944); *Opportunities for Service in the American Junior Red Cross* (Washington DC: Red Cross, 1943); Ronald Bauer, "The Utilization of the Junior Red Cross as an Enrichment Program in the Schools" (master's thesis, University of North Dakota, 1943); Margaret K. Bolanz, "A Survey of the Junior Red Cross as an Integrating Element in the Elementary School Curriculum" (master's thesis, University of Akron College of Education, 1944); "Defense Participation to Be Topic at Southern Junior Red Cross Rally: Session to Be Held at Tuskegee," *Atlanta Daily World*, March 23, 1941; "Local Girls Work for Junior Red Cross," *Hartford Courant*, April 13, 1941; "Red Cross Junior Body Is Organized," *Hartford Courant*, May 27, 1941; "Like Veterans Girls Purl One Knit Two," *Hartford Courant*, July 27, 1941; "Children to Aid in Defense Work," *Sun*, September 8, 1941; "Junior Red Cross Body Plans for School Year," *Hartford Courant*, October 9, 1941; "Parish Schools Join in Junior Red Cross Drive," *Hartford Courant*, November 12, 1941; "Pease Pupils Take Spending Money and Turn It Over to Junior Red Cross," *Austin Statesman*, November 21, 1941; "Leading Schools Indorse Red Cross War Drive," *Washington Post*, December 28, 1941; "Beverly Hills Y Forming Junior Red Cross Unit," *Chicago Daily Tribune*, January 4, 1942; Willis Sutton, "The Junior Red Cross Teaches Service to Mankind," *Atlanta Constitution*, January 18, 1942; "Red Cross Gets Aid of City's Students," *New York Times*, January 31, 1942; "10 Schools Pick Sponsors of Red Cross," *Austin Statesman*, March 6, 1942; Julietta Arthur, "A Stitch

in Wartime," *New York Herald Tribune,* March 15, 1942; "Junior Red Cross of Lexington Salvages Paper," *Christian Science Monitor,* March 21, 1942; "Will Aid Men Overseas," *New York Times,* April 6, 1942; "Red Cross Juniors Stress Fit Living," *Washington Post,* April 8, 1942; "War Jobs Keep Jr. Red Cross from Recess," *Washington Post,* July 12, 1942; "Camp Fire Girls Hold Day Camp," *Atlanta Constitution,* July 27, 1942; Genevieve Reynolds, "Junior Red Cross to Keep Youths Busy," *Washington Post,* August 6, 1942; "Children's Work Aids Soldiers," *Los Angeles Times,* August 14, 1942; "President Praises Junior Red Cross," *New York Times,* September 15, 1942; "Negro Schools Have 7,958 on Junior Red Cross Roster," *New Journal and Guide,* September 19, 1942; "1,300 Articles Promised for Red Cross," *Austin Statesman,* October 16, 1942; "Junior Red Cross Unit Making Surgical Dressings," *Washington Post,* October 31, 1942; "Red Cross Juniors Vote Quota Boosts," *Washington Post,* February 3, 1943; "Rockville Has Clubs for Junior Red Cross," *Hartford Courant,* February 28, 1943; Calanthe M. Brazelton, "Tucson High Goes to Town on the Junior Red Cross," *Clearing House* 17, no. 3 (1942): 156–160; Vivian Rankin, "The Place of the Junior Red Cross in Today's Crisis," *Pi Lambda Theta Journal* 19, no. 3: 74–76; Ronald C. Bauer, "The Utilization of the Junior Red Cross as an Enrichment Program in the Schools" (master's thesis, University of North Dakota, 1943); American Junior Red Cross, *Program for Service* (Washington, DC: American National Red Cross, 1943); "A Leisure Time Map of Denver, for Members of the Armed Services by Junior Red Cross of the Denver Public Schools" (Denver: Denver Public Schools, 1945); Dulce Parker, "Club Activities," *Los Angeles Times,* February 28, 1943; "Education in Citizenship," *New York Times,* March 11, 1943; "Nursing Classes for Young People," *Atlanta Constitution,* April 7, 1943; "Hinsdale Junior Red Cross Girls Help Hospital," *Chicago Daily Tribune,* September 19, 1943; "Westlake Girls Pledge War Work," *Los Angeles Times,* October 14, 1943; "Junior Red Cross Mobilizes," *Hartford Courant,* October 31, 1943; "Junior Red Cross Takes Active War Work Role," *Los Angeles Times,* October 31, 1943; "Pupils of Kindergarten Join Junior Red Cross," *Sun,* November 21, 1943; "Elizabeth Curran Reports on Junior Red Cross Work," *Hartford Courant,* June 19, 1944; "Red Cross Juniors to Aid Drive," *Hartford Courant,* February 24, 1945; "Junior Red Cross Opens Workroom," *Atlanta Constitution,* June 18, 1945; Richard Ugland, "The Adolescent Experience During World War II: Indianapolis as a Case Study" (PhD diss., Indiana University, 1977); "Junior Army Still a Bit Young for Service Despite Offer by Its Rapidly Advanced 'Capt.,'" *New York Times,* December 19, 1941; Gustave Feingold, "War Impact on Public Schools," *Hartford Courant,* August 29, 1943; "Schools Seen Victim of War," *Sun,* June 11, 1944; "Young War Workers Keep Schools Closed," *New York Times,* August 12, 1943; "War-Time Jobs Cut Enrollment in High Schools," *New York Herald Tribune,* April 23, 1943; "Boys' Republic Will Require Military Drill," *New York Times,* August 4, 1940; Sabra Holbrook, *Children Object* (New York: Viking, 1943); Walter Herkness Jr., "Philadelphia's Student Volunteer Service Corps," *School Executive* 62, no. 15 (1942): 38; L. W. Anderson, "Biology Class Led Fight Against Mosquitoes," *Clearing House* 17 (January 1943): 267–270; Stuart Chase, "Bring Our Youngsters into the Community!" *Reader's Digest* 40 (January 1942): 7–10; Leone Davidson, "Consumers' Cooperative of Centerville," *Progressive Education* 19 (April 1942): 203–206; Lowry Nelson, "Planning and Organizing Cooperative Community Projects," *Social Education* 7 (February 1943): 68–70; Verner M. Sims, "Education through Community Improvement," *Progressive Education* 19:332–35 (October 1942); Estelle S. Smith, "Community Living Isn't Extracurricular," *School Executive* 62 (March 1943): 38–41, 46; Lucile Spence, "Block Beautiful: Pupil Club Changes a Community," *Clearing House* 16 (September 1941): 3–7; Maurice

E. Troyer, "Educating Through Community Service," in *Toward a New Curriculum: 1944 Yearbook, Department of Supervision and Curriculum, National Education Association* (Washington, DC: National Education Association, 1944; United States Office of Education, "Together We Serve," *Education and National Defense Series Pamphlet 24* (Washington, DC: Government Printing Office, 1942); Morris R. Mitchell, *Youth Has a Part to Play*, Progressive Education Association Service Center Pamphlet 6; Helen Lynch, "City Planners from Little Children Grow," *School Executive* 63 (October 1943): 35–36; *Community Surveys by Rural High Schools*, University of Wisconsin–Madison Agricultural Experimentation Station, 1941; Howard E. Wilson, "School and Community Life in the Social Studies Program," *Review of Educational Research* 11, no. 4, pt. 2, *Social Studies* (October 1941): 459–464; Ralph W. Tyler, "The Responsibility of the School for the Improvement of American Life," *School Review* 52, no. 7 (September 1944): 400–405.

19. Jeanne Boydston, *Home and Work* (New York: Oxford University Press, 1990); Nancy Folbre, "The Unproductive Housewife: Her Evolution in Nineteenth-Century Economic Thought," *Signs: Journal of Women in Culture and Society* 16, no. 3 (Spring 1991): 463–484. Notably, there have been some recent efforts to call attention to similar circumstances in US prisons. See Noah Zatz, "Prison Labor and the Paradox of Paid Non-Market Work," in *Economic Sociology of Work* (Research in the Sociology of Work, vol. 18), ed. Nina Bandelj (Bingley, UK: Emerald, 2009); Noah Zatz, "Working at the Boundaries of Markets: Prison Labor and the Economic Dimensions of Employment Relationships," *Vanderbilt Law Review* 61 (2008): 857–958.

20. Personal communication, Alison Arieff, September 27, 2016; Harl Douglass, "Youth and the Schools," *High School Journal* 1, no. 6 (1938): 201–210, 232; US Scouting Service, http://usscouts.org/servicetoamerica.asp; Gabriel Sherman, "Joe Nocera on Why College Athletes Should Be Paid, How the NCAA Is Like Enron, and What It Was Like Being Pushed Out at the *Times* Op-ed Desk," *New York Magazine*, March 18, 2016; Leah Yared, "Harvard Files Amicus Brief Against Graduate Student Unionization," *Harvard Crimson*, March 1, 2016; Glenda MacNaughton et al., *Young Children as Active Citizens* (Newcastle upon Tyne: Cambridge Scholars Publishing, 2008); Martin Alan Greenberg, "A Short History of Junior Police," *Police Chief* 75, no. 4 (2008): 172–180; R. Schmidt, "Emergency Services Explorers," *Law and Order* 42, no. 12 (1994): 37–39; M. Gray, "Junior Cops on the City's Blocks: Law Enforcement Explorers Gain Leadership, Policing Skills," *Detroit News*, March 19, 1997; Allan Jaklich, "Teens Form Youth Council in West Chicago," *Chicago Tribune*, October 29, 1967; "Youth Courts: The Power of Positive Peer Pressure," *New York State Bar Association Journal* 83, no. 1 (2011): 1–68; Scott Peterson and Michael Elmendorf, "Youth Courts: A National Youth Justice Movement," *Corrections Today* 63, no. 7 (December 2001): 54–56, 58, 112–113.

Epilogue

1. *Juvenile Delinquency: Utilization of Surplus Military Installations for Boys Town Type Projects, Hearings Before the Subcommittee to Investigate Juvenile Delinquency of the Committee on the Judiciary, United States Senate, Eighty-Fourth Congress, second session, pursuant to S. Res. 62 and S. Res. 173, Eighty-Fourth Congress, Investigation of Juvenile Delinquency in the United States, July 10 and 11, 1956*, published 1956, pp. 1, 3, 20, 25, 51. A related hearing was held in Pittsburgh, which included discussion of Hill City. See United States Senate Committee on the Judiciary, *Juvenile Delinquency*,

Pittsburgh, Pa. Hearing Before the Subcommittee to Investigate Juvenile Delinquency of the Committee on the Judiciary, United States Senate, Eighty-Fourth Congress, First Session, Pursuant to S. Res. 62, Investigation of Juvenile Delinquency in the United States. December 7, 1955 (Washington, DC: GPO, 1956), 80.

2. "'Junior Republic' Launches Drive to Augment Facilities," *Christian Science Monitor,* May 8, 1947; Elsie Parker, "Citizen Action," *National Municipal Review* 35, no. 8 (September 1946): 426–431; Elizabeth Rotten, *Children's Communities: A Way of Life for War's Victims* (Paris: UNESCO, 1949); "Villages of Peace," *Elementary School Journal* 65, no. 4 (1965): 184–189; Ludwig Liegle, "Children's Republics—Documentation and Analysis of a 'Modern' Educational Setting," *Zeitschrift fur Pedagogik* 35, no. 3 (May 1989): 399–416; Therese Brosse, *Homeless Children: Report of the Proceedings of the Conference of Directors of Children's Communities* (Trogen, CH: UNESCO 1950); Samuel Boussion, Mathias Gardet, and Martine Ruchat, "Rebuilding a World Devastated by War," in *A History of UNESCO: Global Actions and Impacts,* ed. Poul Duedahl (London: Palgrave Macmillan, 2016); Mary Buchanan, "The Children's Village," *Christian Science Monitor,* August 12, 1950; "A Children's Village," *Manchester Guardian,* December 11, 1951; Margaret Whittemore, "International Children's Village," *Christian Science Monitor,* September 25, 1950; Elisabeth Rotten, *Children's Communities: A Way of Life for War's Victims* (Paris: UNESCO, 1949); M. Fritz Wezel, "Meeting of Directors of Children's Villages," Paris, October 1, 1948, UNESCO, https://unesdoc.unesco.org/ark:/48223/pf0000144223; Eberhard Mobius, *The Children's Republic: Bemposta and the Muchachos. Tr. by Stacy C. Schmidt* (New York: Avon, 1976); Martin Kemp, *Kinderrepubliken: Geschichte, Praxis und Theorie radikaler Selbstregierung in Kinder- und Jugendheimen* (Berlin: Springer, 1995). On Germany, see Amanda Grozbean, "Teaching Democracy: Re-educating German Youth After World War II," *Sextant* 9 (2012–2013); "Youth Self-Help," *Information Bulletin* (August 1950): 19–20. See also: "2-A-41 Self government programs in German schools, letter from Maj. Gen. Edward Witsell to Richard Welling," October 3, 1945; "2-A-32 Plan for Self-government in German schools, correspondence with Richard Welling," September 17, 1945; "2-A-79 Reference material for State Department from national Self Government Committee, correspondence and bibliography," April 30, 1946, to May 24, 1946; "2-A-155 Textbook and pamphlets for German and Japanese schools, letter from Richard Welling to Brig. Gen. George F. Schulgen with bibliography," December 12, 1946; "2-A-169 Services offered to experts sent to Germany on student self-government, letter, cable, and clipping," February 14, 1947; all referenced in Gary Tsuchimochi, ed., *The US Occupation of Germany: Educational Reform, 1945–1949* (Washington, DC: Congressional Information Service, 1991). This was part of a larger program of youth activities organized by the US armed forces. See *The US Armed Forces German Youth Activities Program, 1945–1955* (Historical Division Headquarters, US Army Europe, 1956).

3. As early as the 1930s, even youth organizations like the Boy Scouts, which previously had rallied public attention to George's work (for example, by publishing stories about self-government at Freeville in the Scouting magazine or expressing interest in starting a junior municipality), seemed to forget his central role in spreading the youth self-government they admired. "We have just been receiving literature from the National Self Government Committee," wrote H. W. Hunt, national director of the Boy Scouts of America to George in 1932. Hearing talk of George's ambition "to organize a national committee on self-government" he wondered if George was aware of the organization with "comparable purpose" and encouraged him to get in touch. In fact,

George was "well acquainted with the purposes of the National Self Government Committee," he replied, for it had been established in 1904 as the School Citizens Committee to bring junior republics into the nation's schools—and he and other republic board members had participated in its activities ever since. "Some of the members of the directorate of that organization are on the board of trustees of the George Junior Republic Association as well as the National Association of Junior Republics," George explained to Hunt. James West to L. B. Stowe, box 12, folder 18, WG Papers; H. W. Hunt, national director of Boy Scouts of America, to William George, November 2, 1932, box 33, folder 21, WG Papers; William George to H. W. Hunt, November 5, 1932, box 33, folder 21, WG Papers. Of course he was not entirely forgotten. See, for example, Quentin Reynolds, "Long Shadow of William George," *Reader's Digest* 67 (July 1955), 153–156.

4. Jacob Smith, preface to William George, *The Adult Minor* (New York: Appleton, 1937). One exception was Boys Republic in Italy. "Boys Honored by the Smallest Republic in the World," *New York Times*, July 10, 1950; "Boys Republic Leaders of Italy Explain Gains," *Los Angeles Times*, August 1, 1950; "U.S. Union Hails Woman Founder at Boy's State," *Chicago Daily Tribune*, July 15, 1951; Johannes Martin Kemp, *Kinderrepubliken: Geschichte, Praxis und Theorie radikaler Selbstregierung in Kinder- und Jugendheimen* (Berlin: Springer, 1995). Ruth Lloyd to Mrs. Daddy, June 15, 1953, box 46, folder 9, WG Papers, noted that USIA was distributing a story and pictures of the Freeville republic to eighty-eight countries.

5. Bernard Mergen, "The Discovery of Children's Play," *American Quarterly* 27, no. 4 (1975): 399–420; Gary Cross, *Kids' Stuff: Toys and the Changing World of American Childhood* (Cambridge, MA: Harvard University Press, 1999); Alexandra Rutherford, *Beyond the Box* (Toronto: University of Toronto Press, 2009); Ariel Eisenberg, *Children and Radio Programs* (New York: Columbia University Press, 1936); Lucas Waltzer, "An Uneasy Idealism: The Reconstruction of American Adolescence from World War II to the War on Poverty," (PhD diss., City University of New York, 2009); Amanda Lynn Bruce, "Creating Consumers and Protecting Children: Radio, Early Television and the American Child, 1930–1960" (PhD diss., Stony Brook University, 2008); Lizabeth Cohen, *A Consumers' Republic* (New York: Vintage, 2003): Lisa Jacobsen, *Raising Consumers* (New York: Columbia University Press, 2005); James Gilbert, *A Cycle of Outrage* (New York: Oxford University Press, 1986); Theodore Belzner, "Junior Republics Advocated," *New York Times*, letter to the editor, July 25, 1944; A. S. Rosenthal, letter to editor, "Junior Republic Praised," *Los Angeles Times*, December 26, 1942; "George Junior Republic," *New York Times*, July 10, 1948. James Coleman, *Youth: Transition to Adulthood* (Chicago: University of Chicago Press, 1974). *Wyatt v. Stickney*, 325 F.Supp. 781 (M.D. Ala. 1971) is among the cases prohibiting inmates from doing institutional maintenance.

6. *Chicago Youth Centers: The First 50 Years* (Chicago: Chicago Youth Centers, 2006); "Form New Group to Aid Three City Boys' Clubs," *Daily Defender*, September 18, 1956. One of the three groups was the American Boys' Commonwealth, originally founded as a splinter group from the BBR.

7. Morgan Barnes, letter to the editor, *Christian Science Monitor*, July 29, 1949; William Ganson Rose, *Cleveland: The Making of a City* (Cleveland: World Publishing, 1950), 1011; Richard Harris, "Juveniles of All Types Go into Boystown; Emerge Wiser," *Cleveland Call and Post*, June 18, 1949; Ralph Matthews, "Politicians of Tomorrow Learn Ropes at Boystown," *Cleveland Call and Post*, April 30, 1955; "Mayor Gives Oath to Boystown Mayors," *Cleveland Call and Post*, November 30,

1968; "Bogan, Johnson Are Boystown Mayors," *Cleveland Call and Post*, December 26, 1970. The subject of sporadic news coverage, the Boystowns were not mentioned in local media after that date, with the exception of a photograph depicting the teardown of the E. 55th and Perkins Boystown City Hall. Cindy Cooper, "Photo Standalone 3," *Cleveland Call and Post*, June 16, 1973; Isolde Weinberg, "He Polishes Rough Diamonds," *Washington Post and Times-Herald*, May 3, 1964; Mabs Kemp, "A Time to Celebrate," *Afro American*, May 23, 1987; Porter Shreve, "Seniors Needed," *Washington Post*, November 25, 1993; William Welling, *East Side Story* (New York: Boys Brotherhood Republic, 1982); Richard Shepard, "About New York," *New York Times*, December 22, 1979; Phyl Garland and Julia Moore, "Break Ground for New Hill City Municipality," *Pittsburgh Courier*, July 9, 1960; "Hill City Speaking," *Pittsburgh Courier*, December 5, 1959; Lawrence Werner, "City Applauds as Pittsburgh Slum Kids Battle for Decency," *Chicago Defender*, January 18, 1964; Ann Frank, "Boys Republic Marks 50th Anniversary," *Los Angeles Times*, August 11, 1957; "The Junior Republic's First Fifty Years," *Hartford Courant*, October 24, 1954; Betty Bond, "Gilbert Students Enjoy Conference at Junior Republic," *Hartford Courant*, December 2, 1951; "150 Students Expected at State Parley: 50 Adult Advisers of Councils Also to Attend Litchfield Conference," *Hartford Courant*, November 11, 1951; Paul Concannon, "Junior Republic Citizens Hold Officer Elections," *Hartford Courant*, June 24, 1951; Harry Batz, "Youth Comments," *Hartford Courant*, January 17, 1954; Robert Bulkley Jr., "Junior Republic Citizens in Connecticut School Run a 'State,' Earn and Learn," *Washington Post*, September 24, 1939; E. Roy Ray, "Junior Sleuths of Litchfield: Here's How Boys at the Republic Take Law into Their Own Hands," *Hartford Courant*, January 17, 1954; "Study Grassroots Democracy," *Hartford Courant*, November 18, 1951; Statement by Lindsay H. Welling, chairman of the BBR expansion committee, September 22, 1958, on document "The Boys Brotherhood Republic of New York Inc: A Unique Pilot Project in Juvenile Democracy," box 100, folder 13, WG Papers; "The Boys Brotherhood Republic of New York Inc." c. 1958, box 100, folder 13, WG Papers; "Boys Republic Report" (Chino, CA: Boys Republic, 1999). Boys City Boys Club, which became an affiliate of the Boys Clubs of America in 1956 and later one of the Boys and Girls Club of Silicon Valley, gradually removed self-government from its roster of activities. See George LaJeunesse, "Years without a Generation Gap," *San Jose Mercury News*, May 5, 1974; "New Boys Club Is Dream Realized for 'Uncle Harry,'" *San Jose Mercury News*, January 5, 1969; Clubs—Boys City, *San Jose Mercury News* Clippings Files, California Room, Martin Luther King Jr. Library, San Jose, CA. The NYC BBR merged with the Henry Street Settlement and opened programming to girls. To be sure, some youth workers held on to the older view, for example, Hill City hired Harold Griffin, a former American Boys' Commonwealth staff member as its executive director in the 1950s. Photo Standalone 17—No Title, *Chicago Defender* April 7, 1956. Junior Statesmen also continued, now as Junior States of America.

8. William George, untitled document, seems to be directed to Mrs. Daddy [c. 1935], box 35, folder 32, WG Papers; Daniel North, "Rebuilding a Pocket-Size Republic: Connecticut's Most Extraordinary School Progresses with Its 10-Year, $700,000 Renewal Program," *Hartford Courant*, June 24, 1956; "11 Houses Open in Litchfield to Benefit School," *New York Herald Tribune*, July 25, 1949; "Social Workers Elect Junior Republic Head," *Hartford Courant*, June 29, 1957; "Junior Republic Added Several Facilities in '57," *Hartford Courant*, December 14, 1957; "Junior Republic Plans to Help 60 Young Boys," *Hartford Courant*, March 3, 1960; Gene Welsh, "How Juvenile Care Came of Age: Modern psychiatry and wisdom of old combine in advanced concepts of aid to

disturbed boys at junior republic," *Hartford Courant,* January 31, 1960; Interdisciplinary conference, October 10–11, 1953, box 46, folder 11, WG Papers; Donald Urquart to all staff, September 23, 1958, box 46, folder 34, WG Papers; New Citizens Test, September 9, 1958, box 46, folder 34, WG Papers; Robert Pittenger and Paul Martineau, "Some Notes on the Authority Structure and the Responsibility of Adolescents in the George Junior Republic," *Journal of Nervous & Mental Disease* 133, no. 4 (1961): 339–345; Tom Henshaw, "Boys Junior Republic," *Sun,* June 22, 1958, F3; *Annual Report* (Connecticut junior republic, 2011); Susan Pearsall, "A Reform School in Litchfield Where Bad Boys Find Good," *New York Times,* May 5, 1992; James Coleman, "Schools Look to Society as a Resource," *New York Times,* January 12, 1970; "Heads Junior Republic," *New York Times,* January 11, 197; "President, 16, Exchanges Views with UN Leaders," *New York Times,* December 5, 1954; Tom Henshaw, "Boys Junior Republic," *Baltimore Sun,* June 22, 1958; "Eisenhower Greetings Go to Head of Boy Republic," *New York Times,* November 16, 1952; "George Junior Republic Elects," *New York Times,* November 4, 1953; "Visiting Day Aids [Litchfield] Junior Republic," *New York Times,* July 7, 1950; "Fear Delinquency Rise," *New York Times,* January 25, 1951; "Girls Rule 'Junior Republic,'" *New York Times,* November 18, 1951; "Upstate 'Republic' for Troubled Youth," *New York Times,* December 20, 1978; "Boys Honored by the Smallest Republic in the World," *New York Times,* July 10, 1950; Katherine Young, "Architect Heads Drive for Teen-Ager Project," *New York Times,* November 3, 1957; "Social School Helps Youths Get Adjusted," *Hartford Courant,* August 2, 1953. Other institutions dropped self-government more gradually. Articles in professional psychiatric publications reflect the growing presence of these medical professionals. See R. E. Pittenger, Observation of a Comprehensive Legal System in Microcosm at the George Junior Republic," *Canadian Psychiatric Association Journal* 9 (1964): 493–501.

9. "Fund Drive Is Begun by Junior Republic," *New York Times,* October 30, 1958; "For Junior Citizens," *New York Times,* October 15, 1953; "George Junior Republic," *New York Times,* November 11, 1950; "Work Plays Vital Role at George 'Republic,'" *Christian Science Monitor,* September 17, 1949; "NY School Expands Youth Self-Rule," *Christian Science Monitor,* February 3, 1951; Ann Frank, "Boys Republic Marks 50th Anniversary," *Los Angeles Times,* August 11, 1957; Kimmis Hendrick, "Boys Fashion Wreaths of Art to Help Pay for Their Keep," *Christian Science Monitor,* December 15, 1951; "Farmers of Tomorrow," *Los Angeles Times,* February 17, 1949; "Boys Republic Makes Dairy Paying Feature," *Los Angeles Times,* October 18, 1953; "Auxiliary's Board Gathers at Junior Republic School," *Los Angeles Times,* June 13, 1948; "Junior Republic Gives Well-Rounded Training," *Los Angeles Times,* November 27, 1950; Ed Ainsworth, "Renaissance Art Aids Boys School," *Los Angeles Times,* August 13, 1951; James Coleman, "Schools Look to Society as a Resource," *New York Times,* January 12, 1970; Timothy Smith, "Community Governed by Youth," *Christian Science Monitor,* May 31, 1961; Reynolds Dodson, "A Nation Run by Kids," *Boston Globe,* September 2, 1979; Jonah Steinberger, "Teens Judge Peers in Own Community," *Boston Globe,* October 15, 1972; Robert Pittenger, "Observation of a Comprehensive Legal System in Microcosm at the George Junior Republic," *Canadian Journal of Psychiatry* 9, no. 6 (1964): 493–501.

Index

Abbott, Lyman, 31
activism, youth, 15, 151, 197–198, 201, 211, 217
Addams, Jane, 2, 91, 124
adult minors, 15, 200–204, 206–207
advertising and public relations:
  for community-based youth programs, 16, 181, 187, 202, 221–223, 236, 238, 241, 251
  for George Junior Republics, 46, 53, 221
  for government programs, 7, 16, 161, 202, 221–222, 233, 238, 241, 249
  and imitative instinct, 66
  for republics, 16, 81, 99, 131–132, 183, 201–202, 221–223, 238, 245
  for schools, 16, 202, 229, 233–234, 237–238, 241
  for youth-serving institutions, 16, 95, 202, 221–222, 238
African Americans, 67, 213–214, 250, 255
  and conceptions of youth, 15, 199, 214, 226–227
  and republics, 150, 200–202, 205–206, 214, 216–223, 242–243, 247
  schools for, 51, 75, 112, 124
Alabama Child Labor Committee, 158
Allendale, 2, 53–54, 56, 62–64, 90, 99, 102, 112, 123
Allin, Arthur, 68, 70, 76
Almy, Frederick, 34, 43
Altgeld Junior State, 243, 255

alumni associations, 6, 48, 123, 148, 151, 156, 209
American Boys Commonwealth, 222
American Institute of Child Life, 2, 153
American Institute of Social Service, 121
American Junior Naval and Marine Scouts, 179
American Legion, 2, 182, 209–209. *See also* Boys State; Girls State
American Municipal Association, 81
American Political Science Association, 81
American Public Health Association, 158
American Social Science Association, 21
American Women's Republic, 184
American Youth Commission, 198
American Youth Congress, 197, 203, 207, 217, 246
American Youth Reserves, 249
Anderson Boyville, 101
Andrews, William, 182
Anti-Cigarette League, 97
Army Amateur Radio System, 187
Association of Practical Housekeeping Centers, 96
Atkins, T. Benjamin, 70
Atlantic Woolen Mills, 167, 180, 242
Atwater School (Wisconsin), 224, 232
Auburn Prison, 121–122, 197, 221
augmented reality, 8, 134

Babcock, Lester, 180, 184
Bading, Gerhard, 134

Baker, S. Josephine, 183
Balderston, John, 221
Baldwin, James Mark, 66, 69
Banjo, 24
banks, children's, 1, 63, 74, 91–92, 128–129, 151, 170
  Allendale, 53–54
  Anderson Boyville, 101
  Boy City, 100
  Boyville (Gary), 106–107, 128
  Freeville, 25–26, 29
  prisons, 121
  Progress City, 93
  Worcester Garden City, 113
Barrows, Samuel, 98
Bedford, Nat, 101
Beebe, Alfred, 59
Beebe, Katherine, 75
Beeks, Gertrude, 105, 111, 115
Bellamy, George, 92, 94, 145
Benson, O. H., 174, 183, 230
Berkeley Traffic Safety Commission, 233
Bernard, L. L., 92
Bernays, Edward, 234
Bernstein, Ludwig, 91–92, 94, 119, 221
Beyer, J. F., 99
Blackman, William, 43
Blow, Susan, 69, 75
Boston Farm School, 55, 73, 155, 184
Boston Newsboys Republic, 133–135, 156, 183
Boston Normal School, 117
Boy Cities, 9, 104, 107, 153, 183, 214, 239, 253
  Charlevoix, 100
  as competitor organization to George Junior Republics, 12, 97–98, 100–101
  Gary, 12, 106–107
  International Boy City, 129
  National Boy City, 129, 183
  Winona, 99–102, 112–113, 116, 128, 195, 221. *See also* Anderson Boyville; Boytown (Gary); Boyville (Gary); Canyon Crest Ranch

Boy City Film Co., 183
Boy Scout Press Association, 230
Boy Scout Radio Network, 230
Boy Scouts. *See* scouting
Boyd, Elmer James, 218
Boys and Girls Republics, 209
Boys Brigades, 53, 100, 166
Boys Brotherhood Republic (BBR), 2, 13, 147–148, 151, 158, 197–198, 204–206, 221–223, 232, 255
Boys City Boys Club (San Jose), 255
Boys City, Hebrew Sheltering Guardian Society, 91, 195, 222
Boys Club Federation of America, 122, 202, 243
boys clubs, 5, 90, 193
  and community-based activities, 13, 82, 88, 157, 174
  and republic movement, 12, 24, 97, 100, 103, 128, 135, 148, 180
  and republics' component activities, 3, 48, 85, 228. *See also* Boys Brotherhood Republic; Boys City Boys Club; Boys Club Federation of America; Boys Industrial Association; Bunker Hill Boys Club; Chicago Boys Club; Columbia Park Boys Club
Boys Industrial Association (Scranton), 130
Boys Republic (Italy), 254
Boys State, 209, 232, 246, 255
Boys Town (film), 214–215
Boys Town (Omaha), 214, 221–222, 246, 248, 253–256
Boys Towns, 9, 15, 195, 202, 206, 214, 239, 244, 253, 255
boys work, 82, 97, 101
Boystowns (Cleveland), 202, 206, 214, 216–217, 220–221, 224, 227, 239, 242, 255
Boytown (California), 83, 99
Boytown (Gary), 106–107, 124–125, 128
Boyville (Gary), 106–107, 116, 125, 128, 133, 146
Brace, Charles Loring, 46
Bradley, Charles, 56, 184
Bradley, Edward, 53–54, 56

Brewer, John, 83
Brewster, Esther (Mrs. Daddy), 30, 46, 112, 181, 202
Brotherhood of David, 141
Brown, Willis, 12, 97, 102, 117, 120, 129, 146, 183, 214, 239
  in Gary, 104, 106–107, 128
  in Salt Lake City, 97–100
  in Winona, 99–101
Bryan, William Jennings, 116
Bunker Hill Boys Club, 204
Bureau of Labor and Charities (New York), 44
Burgess, Ernest, 192
Burroughs, Harry, 183
Burroughs Newsboys Club, 183
Burton, Harold, 216
Butler, Judith, 6

Cabrini Junior City, 243, 255
California Juvenile Court Association, 99
California State Reformatory at Ione, 122
Camp Fire Girls, 14, 141, 143, 146, 151–152, 160, 174, 184
Campbell, William, 207
Canyon Crest Ranch, 98–99, 106
Carlisle Indian School, 51, 103
Carnegie, Andrew, 2, 46
Carnegie Steel, 214
Chadsey, Mildred, 116, 145
Charity Organization Society of Buffalo, 43
Charity Organization Society of New York, 7
Chautauqua, 10, 97, 99–100, 128–129. *See also* Junior Towns
Chemawa Indian School, 128
Chicago Area Project, 220
Chicago Boys Club, 128, 130, 190
Chicago Crime Commission, 205
Chicago Youth Centers, 255
child-centered curriculum, 52, 76, 78, 91, 157
child development, theories of:
  and mediated experience, 6–7, 11, 49, 52, 65–72, 79–80, 102, 114, 116, 118, 127, 143, 146, 159, 222, 239–241

  ties to education, 7, 51–52, 73–75, 97, 104, 114, 153, 158, 166, 170, 172, 190, 222, 241
  ties to parenting, 57, 75
  ties to youth work, 7, 82, 85, 89–90, 93, 98, 104, 113–114, 124, 129, 140, 142, 153, 166, 183, 187, 190, 222, 241. *See also* group processes; imitation; playworlds; recapitulation; social sciences
Children's Aid Society, 46, 203
Children's Congress, 227
Christamore Settlement, 155
Christian Endeavor, 22, 55
Christian Templars, 101
City of Telhi, 83, 90, 115
City of Tuxis, 119
civil service exams, 1, 23, 25, 33, 35, 54, 60
Civilian Conservation Corps (CCC), 208, 213, 236
Clark, William, 78
Clark University, 51, 93, 170
Clayton, Constance, 2
Cleveland, Alfred, 2
Clopper, Edward, 156
Coe, George, 196
Collegeville, 80
Columbia Park Boys Club, 83–84, 129
Columbia University, 12, 97, 129, 158, 168, 171, 177, 182–183, 196
Commons, John, 24, 43, 48, 80–81, 122, 134, 156
communism, 204, 210, 214
community education, 224, 248
community organization, 15, 192–194, 200–201, 204, 213, 216–217, 220–221, 227–228, 230
cone of experience, 240
Congress of Industrial Organizations, 237
Constitutional League of America, 182
Cooley, Charles Horton, 191
Cooley, E. G., 173
Cornell University, 21, 43, 45, 102, 123, 129, 131, 202
Cornman, Oliver, 117, 205

Cottage Row, 55, 64, 73, 124, 129, 243
Cowan, Oliver, 243
Cox, Phillip, 227–228, 234
Creel Committee on Public Information, 170, 182, 196, 254
Cressey, Paul, 192–193
Cronson, Bernard, 57, 62–63
Cresson Medal, 84, 103
Cumberland County Board of Agriculture, 235
Curtis, Elnora, 157–158
Cutting, R. Fulton, 57–58

Dale, Edgar, 237, 240
Dapping, William, 2, 45, 180, 221
Daughters of the American Revolution, 46, 56, 81, 182
Davis, Philip, 134, 183
Dean, Arthur, 168–169, 171, 177
Depew, Chauncy, 41
Derrick, Calvin, 122
deskilling, 7, 111, 123, 241, 255
developmental psychology. *See* child development
Devine, Edward, 7, 111
Dewey, John, 94, 103, 105, 177, 191, 206, 234, 239
  and Laboratory School, 51–52, 76–79, 96, 112
  on mediated experience, 7, 11–12, 51–52, 76–79, 108–109, 116, 146, 212, 224, 227, 235, 241
  and republic movement, 11, 81, 205
Dickey, Sol D., 99–100
Dimmick, Benjamin, 116
discipline, 6, 74, 120, 122–123, 182, 188, 190
  democratic, 34, 111, 120, 147, 149, 182, 247
  friendly, 98, 118–120, 149–150, 217, 234
  militaristic, 23–24, 34, 91, 102, 118, 120, 122, 150, 177
  peer, 15, 57, 61, 107, 190, 240, 251. *See also* Foucault, Michel; Friendly Service Bureau; Mutual Welfare Leagues; social sanitarium
Dodge, Grace, 96
double consciousness, 52, 67
double life, 4, 9, 11, 49, 65, 75, 79, 83, 143, 159
  disappearance of, 15–16, 161, 166, 191
  versus sheltered childhood, 7, 16, 69, 115–116, 124, 239. *See also* Forbush, William Byron
Drum, Charles, 81
Du Bois, W. E. B., 67
Dutton, Samuel, 119

East Side Protective Association (New York), 136
educational theory. *See* child-centered curriculum; community education; experiential education; learn by doing; learning and earning; new education; social efficiency
Einstein, Albert, 67
Eliot, Charles, 31, 94
Ellwood, Charles, 66, 75
Elmira Reformatory, 120, 122
Elsom, J. C., 100, 158
Emerson School, 106–107, 128
Ethical Culture School (New York), 182
everyday performance, 4–6, 12–13, 85, 241
Exeter Academy, 124
experiential education, 74, 77, 234, 239
extracurricular activities, 91, 179, 184–185, 198, 228–229, 235, 249

Fairbanks, Charles, 116
family economy, 5, 7, 52, 89–90, 104, 128, 167, 231, 241
farming, children and, 5, 90, 114, 177, 187
  farm schools and school farms, 55, 74, 91, 106, 169, 177, 179, 232, 249
  at George Junior Republic, 25–26, 89, 242
  and NYA, 206, 211, 238
  playing, 68, 70
  at republics, 53, 55, 64, 98–99, 106, 112, 129. *See also* Boston Farm School; Industrial Colony Association; Long Island Food Reserve Battalion; McDunough Farm School; New York Farm Cadets; US Department of Agriculture; US Working Reserve

Index

fascism, 199, 204
Federal Bureau of Investigation (FBI), 199, 226, 246–247
Federal Emergency Relief Administration, 208
female suffrage, 26–27, 32, 44, 46, 58, 149, 152, 184, 195
financial aid. *See* learning and earning
Fiske, George Walter, 117
Flanagan, Father Edward, 221, 254
Fleming, Pierce, 227
Floody, Reverend R. J., 93–94, 113, 170, 176
Forbush, William Byron, 13, 55, 64, 141–143, 146, 152–153, 158, 196, 228
  and double life, 2, 16
Ford, Pronty, 217
Ford Republic, 99, 102, 123, 132, 150, 183, 205, 256
forestry, 141, 225, 232–233, 236
Foucault, Michel, 6, 120, 123–124
4-H Clubs, 174, 226, 230, 232
4-Star Clubs, 237
Foxy, 35
Franklin Institute, 84
Fraxter, W. D., 99
Freeborn, Malcolm, 202–204, 208
Fretwell, Elbert, 158, 182–183
Freud, Sigmund, 67
Friendly Service Bureau, Pittsburgh Police Department, 214
Froebel, Friedrich, 69–70, 73–75, 79, 108, 254

Galpin, F. T., 100
gamification, 8, 64–65, 74, 96–97, 117, 119, 128, 134, 146, 152
  and erasure of economic productivity, 14, 107, 114, 153, 158, 213, 235
gangs, 72, 82–83, 98, 118, 130, 153, 193–196, 216
  in Chicago, 149, 205
  in Denver, 154
  in New York City, 22–24, 45, 135, 216, 230
  in Washington, DC, 243. *See also* instincts

garden cities, 9
  Berkeley, CA, 170
  Cambridge, MA, 94
  Worcester, MA, 93–94, 112–113, 170
gardening, children and, 48, 239, 249
  at George Junior Republic, 25–26
  at republics, 1, 54, 93–94, 112–113
  at schools, 74–76, 103, 106, 110, 172, 179. *See also* US School Garden Army; garden cities
Garfield, James, 116
Gary Plan, 108–111, 173, 224. *See also* Emerson School
Gaudiopolis, 253
George Junior Republic Association, 31–32, 46, 81, 102, 104, 151, 153, 181
George Junior Republics:
  California Junior Republic (Chino, CA), 101, 129, 170, 255
  Carter (Redington, PA), 56
  Flemington Junction (NJ), 102, 118, 128
  Freeville (NY), 1–4, 6, 10–11, 14–15, 21–40, 42–49, 51–59, 61, 64, 73–76, 79–80, 83–84, 89–90, 94, 97, 99, 101–102, 104, 107, 111–112, 116–125, 127–132, 134–135, 138, 147–150, 153, 165–168, 170, 179–180, 182, 184, 188, 195, 200–204, 206, 212, 214, 216, 221, 241–242, 248, 253–256
  Grove City (PA), 102, 127, 180, 214, 255
  Litchfield (CT), 84, 180, 214, 255–256
  National Republic (Annapolis, MD), 56, 64, 120, 167
  Strawbridge (NJ), 102. *See also* George Junior Republic Association
Georgia Juvenile State, 99, 102, 183
Gill, Wilson, 11–12, 78, 80–82, 92, 114, 117–119, 143, 182, 206, 239
  and Children's International State, 129
  and collaborations with local governments, 58–61, 133, 138, 140, 183
  and Cuba, 80–81, 138

Gill (cont.)
  and Good Government movement, 10, 56–58, 60–61, 64, 84, 103, 112, 134
  and Indian schools, 103–104
  and New York City schools, 57–60
  relationship with William George, 51, 56, 80, 99, 102
  views on how republics worked, 10, 56, 58, 61, 65, 72, 79, 154. *See also* School Citizens Committee
Gillette, Harry, 76
Gilman, N. P., 104–105
Gilson, Harry, 207–208, 210–211, 222
Girl Reserves, 249
Girl Scouts. *See* scouting
Girls City, Hebrew Sheltering Guardian Society, 91, 93, 195, 222
Girls State, 209, 255
girls work, 96
Gladden, Washington, 31, 35, 44
Goffman, Erving, 6, 122, 191, 232
Good Government Movement (Goo Goos), 22–23, 25, 38, 76, 104, 108, 135, 149–150, 157–160, 199
  support for junior republics, 2, 9–10, 31, 46, 102, 195. *See also* Gill, Wilson; Milwaukee Bureau of Economy and Efficiency
Gordon, Mrs. Frank, 148
Gosnell, Harold, 193
Grammar School No. 1 (New York City), 63
Gratz, Simon, 60
Griffenhagen, Max, 99
group processes, theories of, 15, 191–199, 216
  media production and, 226–228, 232, 243
  in NYA programming, 207–208, 211
  republics as applications of, 202, 204–205, 217, 221, 243, 253. *See also* gangs
Gulick, Luther, 146, 151–152
Gunckel, John, 153
Gute, William, 118, 204

Haber, William, 2
Hahn, Charles, 101, 129

Hall, G. Stanley, 2, 93, 143, 157, 191, 199, 241
  contributions to child development theory, 11, 65, 67–72, 77–78, 116, 147, 191, 194, 239
  contributions to education, 11, 51–52, 65, 74–76, 79, 118, 124, 172, 177
  contributions to youth work, 82, 102, 141, 153, 158
Hall, Windy, 235
Halstead, Gordon, 209, 211–212
Hamilton Fish Park (New York City), 116, 136, 195
Hampton Institute, 51
Harris, F. W., 94
Harris, William T., 34, 66, 73, 82
Hart Farm, 214
Harvard University, 51, 76, 94, 123–124, 129
Haynes, S. W., 100–101
health, sanitation and street cleaning departments, municipal:
  and community based youth activities, 135, 138–139, 141, 147, 150, 155, 157, 160, 227, 231, 241
  cooperation with republics, 58–59, 116, 145, 150, 216, 227, 241
Health and Happiness League, 144
Hearst, William Randolph, 46
Hebrew Sheltering Guardian Society Orphan Asylum, 91, 93–94, 99, 112, 116, 118, 121, 129, 148, 195
Heiniger, Minnie Herts, 12
Heller, Harriet Hicox, 99
Henderson, Harry, 218
Hepner, Walter, 237
Herbart, Johann Friedrich, 108
Hiestan, Robert, 232
High School Victory Corps, 249
Hill City Youth Municipality, 2, 214, 216–221, 223–224, 226, 242, 247, 255
Hiram House Settlement, 92, 94–95, 112–113, 145, 216. *See also* Progress City
Hocking, Agnes Boyle O'Reilly, 118
Holbrook, Sabra, 250
Hollingsworth School (Philadelphia), 60

home economics, 3, 16, 90, 95, 97, 151, 191
  in schools, 14, 51, 106, 169, 172, 196, 225. *See also* Camp Fire Girls; Girl Scouts; Kitchen Garden Associations
Hoover, Herbert, 199
Hoover, J. Edgar, 2, 185, 226, 246
Horne, Harold, 158, 175
Hotchkiss, Willard "Uncle Hotchie," 31, 203
housing projects, 217, 243–244, 255
Howard, Ebeneezer, 93
Hulburt, E. D., 151
Hull, William, 28, 30, 34–35
Hull House, 53
Huntington, Emily, 96
hypnosis, 66–68, 72–73, 75, 78, 118, 132, 205

imitation, 15, 192–193
  in cultural transmission, 11, 52, 65–66, 71, 74–76, 78–79, 118, 191, 239
  in human development, 6, 11, 51, 64–67, 69–76, 77–79, 81–82, 110, 113, 118–119, 135, 140–141, 143, 152, 157, 172, 191, 195, 228, 239
immigrants, 22–23, 73, 98, 169, 183, 192, 199, 213
  at George Junior Republic (Freeville), 1, 10, 23, 31, 35, 45
  at other republics, 2, 54, 56, 58, 61, 80, 83, 182, 200, 247
industrial betterment, 105, 114, 120, 159
Industrial Colony Association, 55
industrial democracy, 59, 121, 152, 197
instincts, 82, 98, 115, 118, 135–136, 192, 204
  dramatic, 6, 13, 69–69, 156–158, 161, 194
  imitative, 11, 51, 65–66, 68–69, 72–73, 75, 89, 96, 107, 110, 194
  migratory, 6, 49, 129, 135
  play, 11, 52, 65, 72, 78–79, 89, 166, 222
International Penal and Prison Commission, 98
International Prison Conference, 122
internment camps, 6, 247–248
Iwahig Penal Colony, 123

James, William, 67, 69, 76, 191
Jenks, Jeremiah, 21, 43–44
Judson, Harmon, 116
Junior Achievement Bureau, 183
Junior American Republic, 76
Junior American Statesmen, 209
Junior Army-Navy League, 166
Junior Citizens, 209–210
Junior Citizens Service Corps, 249
junior civic leagues, 125, 127, 144, 147, 155, 157, 160, 225, 228, 233
  African Americans in, 214
  during wartime, 14, 169, 172, 174
Junior Employment Service, 206
junior juvenile courts, 16, 135, 139, 145, 236
junior municipalities, 1, 9, 13, 130–132, 143, 148, 151, 157, 184, 191, 203–204, 206, 210, 239
  and American Legion, 209
  Cortland, 127, 131, 147, 182, 202, 222
  interest from other local governments, 131, 147, 182
  Ithaca, 127, 131, 149, 156, 182, 195
  as models for other programs, 213–214
  and Self Government, Inc., 181, 200
  in war, 167
Junior Municipality of Wellstown, 243, 255
Junior Naval Reserve, 166
junior police, 13, 15–16, 85, 116, 148, 151, 184, 193–195, 226, 236, 251
  and African Americans, 216–218, 221, 223, 227, 247
  as basis for republics, 216
  at Boy Cities, 106
  as community-based programs, 125, 127, 135–138, 147, 149, 151–155, 157–158, 160, 233, 235–236
  at garden cities, 93
  at George Junior Republic, 25–26, 29, 31, 33, 35, 38, 132, 182
  at playground republics, 91, 112
  at Progress City, 146

junior police (cont.)
  at school cities and republics, 58–59, 61, 64–65, 81, 103
  and traffic duties, 230, 233
  in wartime, 174, 244, 247, 249–250. *See also* Junior Police and Citizens Corps
Junior Police and Citizens Corps, 243, 255
Junior Police Athletic League, 227
Junior Red Cross, 170–174, 249–250
Junior Reserve Officer Training Corps, 166
junior sanitary inspectors and street cleaners, 3, 7, 13, 17, 184, 235, 239
  as community-based youth programs, 138–139, 152–153, 155, 157–158
  at the George Junior Republic, 25
  at school cities and republics, 57–60, 112, 196
  at other republics, 83, 91, 135, 145, 148. *See also* New York City Junior Inspectors Club
Junior Towns, 9, 129, 183, 188, 214, 253
junior traffic patrols, 8, 14, 166, 190, 239, 250
  scope of activities, 185, 188–189, 226, 232–234, 236–237. *See also* Berkeley Traffic Safety Commission
junior truant officers, 7, 17, 57–58, 61, 112, 127, 132, 235, 241
Juvenile City League, 138, 233
juvenile court:
  diverting cases to youth for adjudication, 12, 135, 148, 155–156, 158, 160, 221, 236
  and sheltered childhood, 5, 62, 149, 239
  support for republic movement, 2, 81, 84, 97–102, 116, 134, 146–147, 150, 226. *See also* Brown, Willis; Griffenhagen, Max; junior juvenile courts; Lindsey, Ben; Wilbur, Curtis; youth courts
juvenile delinquency, 98, 165, 181, 183, 189, 199, 204, 243
  causes of, 53, 130, 143, 182, 193, 197, 202, 226, 235–236
  children adjudicating, 7, 13, 107, 145
  children arresting, 23, 153, 239

and George Junior Republic, 121
and republic movement, 128, 205–206, 216, 220–221, 243–244, 253, 255

Kane, Thomas, 99
Kellom School (Omaha), 60, 195
Kelly, Fred, 216
Kelsey, Carl, 127
Kilpatrick, William, 234
Kinane, John, 203, 212
Kindergarten movement, 69, 74–75, 79, 96, 105, 159
Kinderspielstadt, 256
Kirkland, J. B., 180, 202
Kirkland Settlement, 54
Kitchen Garden Associations, 96–97
Kittredge, Mabel, 96
Knighthood of Youth, 189, 225
Knights of King Arthur, 14, 127, 140–143, 152–153, 155, 174, 228
Koos, Frank, 92, 94

La Guardia, Fiorello, 205
labor unions, 13, 51, 105, 109, 111, 114, 121–122, 124, 251
  absence at republics, 44, 151–152
  and US National Youth Administration, 211, 213
Laboratory School, University of Chicago, 7, 11, 51, 76–79, 98, 112
Lane, Homer, 102, 132
Lasswell, Harold, 192–193
Lathrop Junior City, 243, 255
Lawton, Sherman, 232
League of Adult Minors, 203
League of Good Citizenship, 144
learn by doing, 97, 165, 175, 187, 189, 229, 242, 245
  and John Dewey, 11, 51, 76–77, 94, 105
  and republics, 82, 102, 107, 112, 124, 165, 207–208, 212, 242, 255
learning and earning, 31, 35, 78, 107, 114–115, 203, 212

Lee, Joseph, 121
Leland, Arthur, 91–92, 94, 112
LeRoy, Harris, 204
Lewis, Oscar, 122
Lewisohn, Adolf, 121
Liberty Loans, 170, 174, 178, 189, 233, 249
Lindsey, Ben, 2, 98–101, 104, 132, 144, 149, 153–154
Ling, Ping, 170, 172
Lippmann, Walter, 192, 199, 202, 227
Little Citizens League, 144
Little Commonwealth, 132
living villages, 17, 22, 40–45, 48, 57, 84, 116, 129, 152, 239
Lone Scouts. *See* scouting
Long Island Food Reserve Battalion, 177
Longfellow School (Alameda), 132
Los Angeles Parental School, 99
Lovejoy, Owen, 183
Lyman School, 118
Lynch, Arthur, 186

MacCracken, Henry, 173, 176, 205, 221
Maine Highway Patrol, 208
Marbourg, Nina Carter, 89
Marovitz, Sidney, 2
Marshal, Eileen, 94
Mason, Gregory, 157
Massachusetts Boys Town, Inc., 253
Massachusetts Department of Education, 185
Masscky, Frank, 142, 146
McCormick, Cyrus, 2, 54
McDunough Farm School, 55, 147
McGovern, Francis, 134
McIntire, Ross, 247
McKay, Henry, 193
McKiernan, William, 113, 118–119, 214
McKinley, William, 84
McKinney, Howard, 216, 218–219, 247
McKown, Harry, 228
McLaughlin, May, 184
McNulty, Lillian, 229
McQueen, Steve, 2

Mead, George Herbert, 191–192, 199
media, youth-produced, 1, 16, 48, 202, 232–235, 237
 film, 8, 221, 229–231, 249–250
 newspapers, 29, 56, 91, 100–101, 106, 112, 116, 134, 141, 205, 207, 209, 214, 221–224, 227–228, 230, 243–244
 radio, 8, 185–190, 208, 214, 216, 221–224, 226, 228, 230–231, 244, 249–250. *See also* advertising and public relations; Boy Scout Press Association; Boy Scout Radio Network
media betterment, 237
Merriam, Charles, 192–193
Merryburgh, 217, 223
Metro-Goldwyn-Mayer, 214
Michigan Supreme Court, 150
military drills, 14, 24, 26, 74, 91, 166–168, 210
Millburn High School (New Jersey), 225
Miller Jr., Spencer, 151, 180, 182, 204–206
Millman, Barney, 190
Milwaukee Boys Republic, 134, 150
Milwaukee Bureau of Economy and Efficiency, 134
Milwaukee Newsboys Republic, 134–135, 143, 147, 149, 154, 156, 160, 174, 183, 195
 graduates, 2
 media production, 134, 221
 strike prevention, 206
 in wartime, 170
Milwaukee Street Trades Department, 134–135, 154, 156, 170. *See also* Milwaukee Newsboys Republic; Powell, P.O.
Mitchell, Morris, 235
model environments, 6, 10, 22, 40–41, 52, 65, 79, 112, 212
 model cottages, 95–96, 112, 132, 145, 239
 model kitchens, 11, 48, 91, 112, 114, 196, 229
 practice studios, 228. *See also* Association of Practical Housekeeping Centers; living villages; Palestine Park; panoramas; sham battles; wax museums; worlds fairs
Model League of Nations, 184, 196

Model United Nations, 196
modern subjectivity, 40, 49, 52, 57, 67, 90, 152, 191, 193, 196
Montessori, Maria, 79
Montgomery School (New York), 81
municipal housekeeping, 13, 128, 159–160, 175
Murdoch, Mrs. W. L., 158
Mutual Welfare Leagues, 121–122, 181, 197, 208

National Association for the Advancement of Colored People (NAACP), 199, 217, 220
National Association of Housing Officials, 243–244
National Association of Junior Republics, 12, 102, 130–132, 148, 157, 181
National Child Labor Committee, 111, 156, 183
National Child Welfare Association, 189
National Civic Federation, 105, 121
National Conference on Charities and Corrections, 100
National Municipal League, 64, 157
National Safety Council, 189
National Self Government Committee, 204–205, 208. *See also* School Citizens Committee; Self Government Committee; Self Government Inc.
Native Americans, 80, 140, 200, 247–248
  playing Indian, 68, 83, 143, 146
  schools for, 51, 75, 103, 112, 120, 124
  at worlds fairs, 41, 43–44. *See also* Carlisle Indian School; Chemawa Indian School; Woodcraft Indians
Neilsen, John, 116
Nesbitt, Algie, 220
Ness, Eliot, 2, 216–217
New Castle Workhouse, 181
new education, 11–12, 14, 52, 72–74, 76, 82, 107, 109
New Paltz Normal School, 80
new penology, 98, 104, 120, 122

New York Association for Improving Conditions of the Poor, 57
New York Child Labor Commission, 177
New York City Bureau of Child Hygiene, 183
New York City Junior Inspectors Club, 226, 230–231
New York City Merchant's Anti-Litter Bureau, 203
New York Farm Cadets, 177
New York Police Department Crime Prevention Bureau, 205
New York Public Service Commission, 109
New York School of Philanthropy, 7
New York State Board of Charities, 43
New York State Department of Conservation, 233
New York State Military Training Commission Bureau of Vocational Education, 168
New York State Prison Commission, 122
New York University, 102, 237, 243
newsboys, 13, 130, 133, 152–153, 158, 177, 189. *See also* Boston Newsboys Republic; Burroughs Newsboys Club; Milwaukee Newsboys Republic
Norfolk Street Vacation School (New York City), 58

O'Hanlan, R. J., 62
orphanages, 3, 12–13, 46, 82, 103, 148, 214, 222, 253. *See also* Hebrew Sheltering Guardian Society Orphan Asylum
Osborne, Thomas, 31–32, 35, 39, 43, 53, 84, 102, 112, 122, 221
  and prisons, 120, 122, 180–182, 208
Osgood, Kenneth, 208

Palestine Park, 10, 40
panoramas, 10, 21, 40, 45, 48, 67, 147, 222
Park, Robert, 192
Parkhurst, Charles, 23, 31
parks, 13, 23, 141
  Georgia, 147
  New York City, 116, 135, 154–155, 195

Pittsburgh, 221
St. Paul, 112
Wisconsin, 224
parks departments, municipal, 112, 136, 154, 157, 225
Parola, Marie, 63
Parsons, Frank, 64
Patriotic League, 56–58, 80, 99, 103
Paul Revere Neighborhood Project, 217
Payne Fund, 237
Peixotto, Sidney, 129
Peppers, Horace, 244–245
Pestalozzi, Johann, 79, 108, 254
Pestalozzi Children's Village, 253
Phalanx, 203, 205, 212
play cities, 170, 225
Playground Association of America, 121
playground republics, 2, 9, 12–13, 124, 132–133, 135, 156, 183, 195, 214
  Cleveland, 145
  Louisville, 91–92, 94
  Newark, 112
  New York, 57, 116, 136
  Omaha, 99. See also Cottage Row; Smith Memorial Playground Villages
playgrounds, 80, 98, 129, 136, 197, 228, 239, 241, 256
  and sheltered childhood, 5, 12, 90
  kids building and maintaining, 7, 12, 85, 103, 106, 112–113, 131, 148–149, 157, 205, 221, 236
playworlds, 11, 13, 52, 69–72, 75–76, 103, 128, 130, 133
police, 23, 57, 107, 144, 154–155, 185, 208, 211, 214, 239, 241
  and George Junior Republic, 31, 33, 83
  support for republics, 2, 15, 58, 60, 134–135, 149–150, 202–203, 238
  support for youth activities, 14, 130, 135–136, 141, 146–148, 160, 203, 226, 233, 235, 237. See also Boystowns (Cleveland); Hill City Youth Municipality; junior police; Junior Police Athletic League;

Junior Police and Citizens Corps; New York Police Department Crime Prevention Bureau; Youth City Columbus; Youth City Philadelphia
Portsmouth Naval Prison, 182, 188
Potamkin, Harry, 228
Powell, Perry "Pop", 134, 154, 156, 170
preparedness, 14, 166–167, 173, 174, 245, 250
Prison Association of New York, 122
prisons, 41, 114, 159
  at republics, 1, 25–26, 35–38, 43, 64, 102, 150, 220
  ties to republic movement, 90, 119–124, 148, 180–182, 195, 197, 247–248, 254. See also Auburn Prison; Iwahig Penal Colony; New Castle Workhouse; new penology; Portsmouth Naval Prison; Sing Sing Prison
Progress City, 92–94, 112–114, 125, 138, 195, 214, 221, 243
  community-based activities, 112, 145–146, 217
  influences on other republics, 99, 145, 183, 216
project method, 225
propaganda, 170, 193, 198, 209, 222, 233–234, 237, 240, 242
PS 125 (New York City), 132
public opinion, 15, 192–194, 200, 202, 204, 213, 227–228, 234, 249
Puffer, J. Adams, 118, 136, 194

Queens of Avalon, 141, 143, 152–153, 184, 228
Quoddy Resident Training Center, 207–208, 210–211

Ray Plan, 80
Reamer, John, 131
Rebecca McClennan, 122
recapitulation, 11, 32, 52, 69–71, 74, 79, 82, 146, 194, 204, 239
Reckless, Walter, 193
Reeves, Floyd, 198

Reid, James, 217–218
resident training centers, 15–16, 202, 206–214, 221–222, 238, 244–247, 249
Richardson, F. W., 43
Richmond, Julius, 2
Riis, Jacob, 2, 9, 31, 45, 104, 149, 151
Robbins, Jack, 147–148, 151, 205
Robert, Jeanne, 129
Robinson, Edgar, 119
Robinson, James, 247
Rockefeller, John, 46
Rogers, E. A., 226
Rogers, Ethel, 114
Rogers, James, 83–84, 102, 115, 204, 228
Rooney, Mickey, 214–215
Roosevelt, Franklin Delano, 199, 206, 208, 213, 238, 249
Roosevelt, Theodore, 23, 31, 58, 80, 116, 120, 135
Rosser, David, 227
Routzahn, Mary Swain, 238, 245
Royce, Josiah, 69, 118, 191
Russell Sage Foundation, 236, 238

Saddle and Cycle Club, 149
safety education, 15, 185, 189, 228–230
Safety Villages, 256
San Francisco Junior City, 243, 245–247, 255
Sawyer, Wiliam, 116
Schell, Montgomery, 31
scholarships. *See* learning and earning
school boards, 60, 115, 237
school cities and school republics, 9, 64, 75, 82, 112, 117, 119, 135, 143, 148, 153
 African Americans and, 214
 Alameda, 64, 132
 Alaska, 103
 collaborations with local officials, 58–61, 138, 140, 156–157
 Cuba, 80–81, 133
 fun, 80, 123
 Milwaukee, 62–63, 90, 134
 Native American Schools, 103
 Newark, 132
 New Paltz, 80
 New York City, 56–63, 81, 132–133
 Omaha, 60, 195
 Philadelphia, 60, 117, 205
 versus George's republics, 15, 80, 84, 204, 239, 253. *See also* Constitutional League of America; Patriotic League; School Citizens Committee; School Republic Federation of the USA
School Citizens Committee, 81, 121, 181. *See also* National Self Government Committee; Self Government Committee; Self Government Inc.
School Republic Federation of the USA, 182
scientific management, 2, 104–105, 108, 114–115, 128, 211. *See also* Good Government Movement; industrial betterment; social efficiency
Scott, Colin, 117
scouting, 5, 151, 153, 181, 183, 214
 Boy Scouts, 13–14, 16, 125, 127, 140–143, 145–147, 152–153, 155, 157–158, 172, 174–175, 177, 185–190, 195, 226, 228, 230–231, 236, 240, 249, 251
 changing interpretations of, 15–16, 166, 191, 193–197, 226, 240
 and community service, 153, 155, 233, 235–238, 250
 Girl Scouts, 14, 172, 174, 177–179, 185, 187–190, 226, 230–231, 233, 24–251
 Lone Scouts, 143, 230
 and self-government, 143
 and theories of child development, 146, 153, 232
 in wartime, 14, 174, 247. *See also* Boy Scout Press Association; Boy Scout Radio Network
Searles, Frank, 203
Seidel, Emil, 150
Self Government Committee, 121. *See also* National Self Government Committee; School Citizens Committee; Self Government Inc.

Self Government Inc., 181–182, 204. *See also* National Self Government Committee; School Citizens Committee; Self Government Committee
self-government, 73, 102, 116–117, 119–120, 130, 134, 152, 181, 183, 190, 200, 253
  at Allendale, 90
  at Boys Brotherhood Republic (BBR), 181, 198
  at businesses, 121, 123, 152
  at City of Tuxis, 119
  in community-based youth organizations, 140, 143, 150, 154, 187, 195, 214, 216, 220, 226–227
  at George Junior Republic (Freeville), 25, 27, 31, 132, 150, 180, 256
  at Hebrew Sheltering Guardian Society Orphan Asylum, 91, 129, 222
  at housing projects, 243, 245, 255
  at internment camps, 247–248
  at playgrounds, 92, 118, 183
  at prisons, 120–123, 181, 197
  at resident training centers, 207–208, 211–212
  at school cities and republics, 60, 62, 64, 80, 81, 119, 182
  at schools, 99, 169, 172, 185. *See also* Mutual Welfare Leagues; National Self Government Committee; School Citizens Committee; Self Government Committee; Self Government, Inc.
separate spheres, 7, 17, 115–116, 159, 175
settlements, 88, 90, 105
  and republics, 12–13, 24, 82, 85, 98, 103, 135
  and republics' component activities, 3, 12–13, 48, 82, 96, 112, 144, 231. *See also* Christamore Settlement; Hiram House Settlement; Hull House; Kirkland Settlement; South Park Settlement; Worcester Social Settlement
Shady Hill School, 118
sham battles, 17, 32, 40, 83–84, 166
Shaw, Albert, 31, 60, 63–64

Shaw, Clifford, 193
Shaw, Lesley, 216
Simons, R. H., 139
Sing Sing Prison, 121–122, 151, 181
Sisson, Everett, 99
Slaughter, Adolf, 243
Slicer, Thomas, 64
Smith, Jacob "Jakey," 28, 30–31, 45, 150, 180, 202
Smith Memorial Playground Villages, 183
Snedden, David, 12, 110, 114, 119–120, 124, 182
social efficiency, 12, 105, 107–110, 112
social gospel, 23, 46, 56
social sanitarium, 150, 181, 203
social sciences, 15, 191–193, 196, 198, 202, 204, 213, 220, 222, 240
  interest in republics, 21, 46, 80. *See also* American Social Science Association
Society for the Prevention of Cruelty to Children, 37, 44
Sons of Boone, 141, 143, 146
South Park Settlement, 83–84
Southern Negro Youth Congress, 197, 199, 217
Spain, Daphne, 159–160
Spaulding, Theodore, 220
Spokane Parental School, 118, 204
St. Paul's School (New Hampshire), 180
State of Columbia, 83, 114, 129, 195
Stebbins, Cyril, 170
steropticon, 31, 53, 84
steroscope, 6, 40–41, 48, 74, 141, 196, 240
Stiller, Jerry, 2
Stivers, Camilla, 159
Stone, Walter, 130, 190, 198
Stowe, Lyman Beecher, 102, 104, 151, 194, 204, 242
Stralem, Donald, 253–254
Strong, Josiah, 31, 104, 121
Strong, William, 58
Studebaker, John, 99, 171, 249
suggestion (as a technique), 73–76, 78, 81, 110, 118–123, 191–193, 207, 210

Sullivan, Tim, 154
surveys and censuses, 7, 29, 106, 139, 144, 155, 174–175, 206, 225, 235
Sweeney, John, 154
Swift, Edgar James, 83, 119

Taft, William, 116
Talbot, Anna Hedges, 174
Tarde, Gabriel, 66, 68, 75–76
Taussig, Charles, 208
Taxes, 1, 26, 184
Taylor, Frederick Winslow, 105
Telegraph Hill Neighborhood Association, 83–84
Texas Agricultural Extension Agency, 238
13th Avenue School (Newark), 132
Thrasher, Frederic, 192–194, 196–197, 237
Thrasher, Max Bennett, 55, 73
Thurstone, L. L., 192
Todd, Arthur, 83, 99, 121
token economies, 53–55, 62, 93, 100, 120–122, 150, 216–217
　at George Junior Republic (Freeville), 1, 25–26, 28–29, 30–31, 35–37, 44, 48, 84, 89, 242, 256
Tolman, William Howe, 31, 104
Tracy, Spencer, 214–215
Tree, Thomas, 131
Turner, Victor, 6
Tyler, I. Keith, 231

Underwood, 141
UNESCO, 253
United States Society, 209
University of Chicago, 78, 191–192, 198. *See also* Laboratory School
University of Pennsylvania, 127, 129
Urquart, Donald, 202, 256
US Army, 120, 166, 187–188, 204
US Army Cadet Corps, 166
US Bureau of Education, 111
US Bureau of Indian Affairs, 2
US Children's Bureau, 12, 161, 168, 176–177

US Department of Agriculture (USDA), 169, 174, 187, 204
US Department of Labor, 161, 173, 177, 197. *See also* Junior Employment Service; US Children's Bureau; US Working Reserve
US Department of the Interior, 169, 238
US Farm Security Adminitration, 232
US Federal Security Administration, 244–246
US Film Service, 238
US Food Administration, 170
US Fuel Administration, 170
US Information Agency, 254
US National Park Service, 251
US National Recreation Service, 204
US National Youth Administration (NYA), 2, 206–207, 210–213, 224, 226, 234, 238, 246, 249. *See also* resident training centers; US Federal Security Administration
US Navy, 120, 166, 186–188, 204, 208, 247, 250, 253. *See also* Portsmouth Naval Prison
US School Garden Army, 169–170, 176
US Senate, 253, 255
US Soil Conservation Service, 232–233
US State Department, 253
US Steel, 105
US Treasury Department, 170
US War Assets Administration, 255
US War Relocation Authority, 247
US Weather Bureau, 155
US Working Reserve, 177
US Works Progress Administration, 206, 211, 214, 227
USA camp, 55, 64, 141

Vidor, King, 183
virtual worlds, 8
vocational, industrial, and manual education, 3, 5, 74, 114, 151, 198–199, 232
　at Allendale, 54
　at Boston Farm School, 55
　at Boy Cities, 100–101
　at Canyon Crest Ranch, 98–99

conceptual links to junior republic movement, 10, 16, 75, 90, 97, 166, 191, 196, 239, 256
during war, 14, 170, 172–173, 242, 245, 248
in Gary schools, 106, 108–111
at George Junior Republic, 26–28, 48, 101, 168, 180, 242
at Norfolk Street Vacation School, 58
at Hebrew Sheltering Guardian Society, 129
media making as, 8, 228–229
NYA and, 206–207
at prisons, 120, 122–123
at Progress City, 92–93
at World's Columbian Exposition Children's Building, 57
at youth-serving institutions, 83, 91

war, 185, 193, 202
 Civil War, 166
 Spanish-American War, 80, 166
 World War I, 14, 121, 161, 165–179, 181–182, 184, 188, 192, 196–197, 199, 214, 228, 233, 248
 World War II, 4, 6, 16, 241–251, 253–255
Waring, George, 58–60, 80, 135, 138, 153, 157
Warner Brothers, 201, 214, 242
Washington Irving High School, 129
wax museums, 6, 10, 22, 40, 48, 67, 116, 147
Wayne County Probate Court, 150
Welfare League Association, 180
Welling, Richard, 157, 165–166, 180, 242, 253–254
 networks, 31, 81, 92, 102, 148, 204–205. *See also* National Self Government Committee; School Citizens Committee; Self Government Committee; Self Government Inc.
West, James, 152
West Farms School, 57, 63
Weston Electrical Instrument Co., 121
Wheeler, Benjamin Ide, 43
White, Theodore, 2
whites, 10, 22, 35, 41, 45, 150, 199, 240

and civic education, 23, 61, 206
and sheltered childhood, 201, 214, 220
Whitman, Charles, 149
Wilbur, Curtis, 99
Wilcox, Delos, 60, 64, 103
William Demuth and Co., 197
William George Agency for Children's Services, 256
Wilson, August, 216
Wilson, J. Bert, 131
Wilson, Woodrow, 170
Wilson Industrial School for Girls, 96
Winona Assembly and Summer School, 99–100
Wirt, William, 104–106, 108, 111, 128
women, 5, 7, 13, 115, 152, 159–160, 175–176, 236, 248, 251
 and republic movement, 82, 124, 184. *See also* Daughters of the American Revolution; female suffrage; municipal housekeeping; separate spheres; women's clubs; Women's Municipal League of New York
women's clubs, 46, 54, 57, 144, 147, 159–161, 184
Women's Municipal League of New York, 138
Wood, Leonard, 80
Woodcraft Indians, 141, 143
Woods, Arthur, 152–153
Worcester Social Settlement, 93
World Youth Congress, 197
worlds fairs and industrial expositions, 10, 40, 44–45, 57, 70, 121, 132, 183
 Chicago, 41–42, 57, 65, 97
 Paris, 41, 84
 San Francisco, 129, 183
 St. Louis, 84
Wright, Clarence, 233

Yeager, William, 234
YMCA Model Legislatures, 209
YMCAs, 82, 105, 193, 226, 231
 and republics, 12–13, 97, 99–100, 128, 131
 and republics' component activities, 3, 12–13. *See also* City of Tuxis; Collegeville;

Milwaukee Boys Republic; YMCA Model Legislatures
Young Reviewers Clubs, 237
Youth Builders, 210, 250
Youth City Columbus, 214, 216, 220
Youth City Philadelphia, 2, 214, 216–217, 220, 224, 232, 242–243
youth courts, 48, 74, 129, 227, 251
  at Boy Cities, 12, 106–107
  at Boys Brotherhood Republic (BBR), 205
  at Ford Republic, 102, 150
  at George Junior Republics, 1, 10, 25–26, 31–33, 45
  at Hill City, 217, 224
  at junior municipalities, 131
  at Milwaukee Newsboys Republic, 134–135, 154
  at playground republics, 91
  at resident training centers, 208–209
  at San Francisco Junior City, 244
  at school cities and school republics, 58, 62, 65, 81
  traffic courts, 185
  at Wellstown, 243
  at William George's fresh air camp, 24.
  See also junior juvenile courts
youth militia, 24, 26, 48, 99–100, 166, 172

Zavenski, Billy, 53
Zeidler, Carl, 2
Zelizer, Viviana, 188

Press
et Rossi
Main Street, 9th floor
02142

.edu
tt@mit.edu
253-2882

authorized representative in the EU for product safety and compliance is

y Access System Europe Oü, 16879218
tamäe tee 50,
, 10621

r.requests@easproject.com
2 56 968 939

N: 9780262539012
ase ID: 153493941

www.ingramcontent.com/pod-product-compliance
Lightning Source LLC
Chambersburg PA
CBHW080752300426
44114CB00020B/2713